P9-CEL-900

CONCORD PUBLIC LIBRARY
45 GREEN STREET
CONCORD, NEW HAMPSHIRE 03301

DISCARDED

LIBERACE

Liberace

AN AMERICAN BOY

Darden Asbury Pyron

THE UNIVERSITY OF CHICAGO PRESS

CHICAGO AND LONDON

780.07
LIB

DARDEN ASBURY PYRON is professor of history at Florida International University. He is the editor of *Recasting:* Gone with the Wind *in American Culture* and the author of *Southern Daughter: The Life of Margaret Mitchell.*

The University of Chicago Press, Chicago 60637
The University of Chicago Press, Ltd., London
© 2000 by Darden Asbury Pyron
All rights reserved. Published 2000
Printed in the United States of America

09 08 07 06 05 04 03 02 01 00   1 2 3 4 5

ISBN: 0-226-68667-1 (cloth)

Frontispiece courtesy of the Liberace Foundation, Las Vegas, NV. The Liberace Foundation, founded by Liberace in 1976, is a nonprofit organization providing scholarships for students in the performing and creative arts. For a list of funded schools or grant guidelines, please write to the Liberace Foundation at 1775 East Tropicana Avenue, Las Vegas, NV 89119.

Library of Congress Cataloging-in-Publication Data

Pyron, Darden Asbury.
    Liberace : an American boy / Darden Asbury Pyron.
        p. cm.
    Includes bibliographical references (p.) and index.
    ISBN 0-226-68667-1 (acid-free paper)
    1. Liberace, 1919–   2. Pianists—United States—
Biography.   I. Title.

ML417.L67 P97 2000
786.2'092—dc21
    [B]   99-08931

This book is printed on acid-free paper.

This book is dedicated to my mother, Jo Scott Pyron,
and to the memory of my grandmother,
Marian Asbury Pyron (1892–1972).

CONTENTS

Contents

PREFACE

This is not the book I first imagined writing.

In mid-November 1991, I was stranded in Washington, D.C., for a day. Rummaging around the remainder section of a local bookstore, I encountered Scott Thorson's memoir of his years as Liberace's lover. I remembered a little of Liberace from his television days when I was a boy, and I recalled only the headlines of Thorson's "palimony" suit against the entertainer. The book's revelations intrigued me. I flipped to the photographs. They included images of Thorson before and after he underwent plastic surgery to make him resemble his patron. The longer I stared, the more bizarre the episode seemed. I wondered what Liberace could have been thinking; I also reflected on the plastic surgeon who had performed the operation, and on the society that encouraged such transformations. These questions inspired the first idea of a Liberace biography in my mind. I composed some more questions and determined that I could put together a quick, hard little study before I went on to more serious subjects. It didn't work out that way.

The more I reflected on the subject, and the deeper I dug into the data, the more complicated the Liberace problem seemed to become. While the peculiarities, even anomalies, of Liberace's private life had first piqued my interest, other issues soon competed for my attention. Increasingly, Liberace seemed to me a kind of emblem of modern America, overflowing with both the virtues and the vices of the contemporary national character. I began imagining him as the American Boy. Even so, his sexual peculiarities became more glaring as I continued my research. Paradoxically, as he became more and more representative, he grew increasingly less typical. I made my own resolution to the conundrum. It seemed that his homosexuality encouraged his campy artificiality; the campiness, in turn, encouraged the caricature, in life and art, of the American dream. The anomalies, then, became the very sources of his representativeness.

The simple little book I had imagined was no longer so simple. What I envisioned as a three-year commitment, from beginning to end, stretched on and on. But other difficulties complicated the work. Few fellow academics and, more critically, fewer presses shared my enthusiasm for the project. With a small number of notable exceptions, like my old book-reviewing friend from the *Miami Herald,* Bill Robertson, folks were mostly incredulous that I—or anyone, for that matter—would devote serious attention to such a character. My faithful agent, Jonathan Dolger, was hard pressed to find a publisher willing to consider even the prospectus. He offered his own take on publishers' skepticism: he suspected the prejudice of even gay editors. What does a dead, closeted queen performer, adored by "Midwestern grannies" (as the actor Tony Perkins called Liberace's audiences) have to say to contemporary gay men? Not much, came the answer. That his life might speak to others seemed incomprehensible.

Other problems arose in the writing that had nothing to do with publishers' skepticism. Sometimes the project seemed as incredible to me as it appeared to editors. Reading Liberace's memoirs regularly prompted this response. Their syrupy tone, coyness, and evasions grated, sometimes furiously, on my nerves. Formal criticisms of the showman exacerbated my own misgivings. The harshest depict the pianist as nothing less than a cultural demon and a sexual monstrosity. He undermined the highest standards of taste, even while he broke down traditional sexual or gender boundaries, ran the complaints. The criticisms, even the most violent, like Howard Taubman's scathing 1954 critique in the *New York Times* or William Conner's 1956 broadside in the London *Daily Mirror,* contain truth. Criticism of the showman continues over a decade after his death. The cudgels are wielded now, paradoxically perhaps, by gay writers instead of by his old enemies among the sexually orthodox.

I was not unsympathetic to the biases. Insofar as the criticisms identified the entertainer as a womanish, lower-class, consumer sissy who corrupted art (and maybe the youth of America), I was not eager to justify, much less identify with such a figure. If the queer stuff doesn't get you, the class and cultural angle will—although as the academic critic Kevin Kopelson has noted, the two can be inextricably combined. I dealt with the difficulty in part by trying to objectify the critics, much as I sought to objectify Liberace himself. This led, however, to other complications in the conceptualization of the project, as I began reflecting on the nature of twentieth-century American culture. A short book was developing into a mighty long manuscript.

Other problems complicated the original plan. From beginning to end, confirming sources, facts, and data proved particularly difficult. Unlike Margaret Mitchell, the subject of my previous project, for which I could consult extraordinarily rich literary documentation, Liberace's life has been extremely difficult to pin down. In some cases, confirming the most basic information—when he was living where, for example—was hard or impossible. The question of where he was living with whom is, obviously, more problematical still. He confessed his own weakness regarding dates, and his chronologies sometimes make no sense. He also dated various episodes in his life differently at different times. Beyond this, Liberace was notoriously secretive, and he revealed little that he did not want revealed. His memoirs leave out much. At least as much as any memoirist, perhaps more, he shaped events both consciously and unconsciously to fit his own image or sense of things. He left almost no private literary sources to check against the public imagery.

Liberace manipulated journalists and newsmen no less assiduously than he did his fans and readers. Insofar as newspapers provide major sources of data about his life, this material is, then, suspect, too. Journalistic sources produced other problems. If the data from standard, establishment newspapers like the Milwaukee *Journal-Sentinel* and the *Washington Post* come with a spin, making sense of the tabloids' stories poses yet more difficulties. But papers like the *Globe,* the *Star,* and the *National Enquirer*—not to mention the sensational scandal rags like *Hollywood Confidential, Rave,* and *Hush-Hush*—provide significant chunks of information about the performer. The lines between fact and fancy blur constantly. Dealing with gossip, rumor, and hearsay proved a persistent challenge. Oral history has been a doubly problematical source of information, too. Besides the normal liabilities of such recollections, old friends and associates have been reluctant to speak or reluctant to speak for the record.

The same problems apply to other sources of data. Liberace was constantly suing or being sued, and court records provide a potential check against the rumor. They have a downside: depositions are fragmentary, rulings are obscure, and not least, statements are contradictory. Then, too, the showman lied, even under oath, while his antagonists hardly refrained from self-interested testimony, either. The same problems and more apply to the most important outside testimony, Scott Thorson's *Behind the Candelabra.* It is the only extended, insider's account of the showman's life not governed by Liberace's image making. But Thorson had his own agenda. Even if one takes his facts as essentially true, his voice in the text differs significantly from how he sounded elsewhere, as, for example, in the surviving depositions from his five-year lawsuit against his old lover. His literary co-author rounded out his prose, to say the least. Then, too, his judgments contain many of the old problems of gossip and rumor.

Secondary sources don't always help. Liberace's 1987 biographer, Bob Thomas, a popular journalist, has produced a journalistic account that compounds the Liberace problem almost as much as it contributes to a solution. Something of a Hollywood insider, he draws on fresh sources, especially on interviews with old Liberace associates. At the same time, he relies uncritically on newspaper reports; he spins fictional dialogue from these and fails to cite sources or evidence anywhere. The question of what of his account is fact and what is fiction obscures the record one more time. Just so, empirical evidence sometimes confounded Thomas's judgments, speculations, and even factual evidence, otherwise defined.

Jocelyn Faris's *Bio-Bibliography* is different. Lacking much interest in biographical conjecture, Faris catalogues published sources of Liberace's career. Her work offers an extraordinary wealth of raw information, and this biography would hardly have been possible without her awe-inspiring labor. Even so, her compilation is not complete. The absence of data, particularly at critical junctures in Liberace's career, skews her generalizations. Confusion characterizes even the most empirically based sources, then.

In short, unambiguous evidence is not very apparent anywhere in Liberace's record. If the historian's ideal of three facts for every generalization were to be applied, we would be able to say very little about Liberace's life. The gaps are vast. Contradictions muddle even what should be obvious. This book resolves the difficulties variously. I have taken a shard of reality—like Liberace's reference to an early engagement at Spivy's Roof in Manhattan—and played it out against verified bits of historical truth—like the historian George Chauncey's connection of "the enormous lesbian Spivy" and the whole gay scene in New York in the early forties. I try a similar test with gossip and rumor: I attempt to determine how closely they conform or fail to conform to other patterns. The method works better on some occasions than it does on others. Research has turned up some of my own errors as the result of such speculating. In all the early drafts of this book, for example, I rejected Scott Thorson's judgment about how Liberace got new boys. Thorson asserted that Liberace's friends effectively procured them for him. Though Thorson himself entered the showman's life this way, more or less, to make such a judgment would appear to have been outside the range of what Thorson could actually have known. That Liberace got new lovers this way seemed unlikely to me as well, in light of Rock Hudson's situation, for example. Late in the production of this book, however, I was able to make sense of the novelist John Rechy's references to "the star" in the late fifties—actually Liberace—that confirm the pattern Thorson described. I had looked to the wrong model: George Cukor, not Hudson, provided the appropriate prototype. I changed my interpretation.

I have dealt with the ambiguity of the data in other ways as well. Thus, I have approached lacunas—most notably, Liberace's homosexuality itself, which he publicly ignored throughout his whole life—not as the absence of something, but as material things themselves. Liberace was a gay man; he never admitted it in public. The lies and failures to deal with his own sexual appetites and affectional longings I take as critically as his actual sexual values. They help define who he was, where he came from, and how homosexuality worked or failed to work for him. I take his lies and public denial further, using them as guideposts in the larger wilderness of gender and sexual identities in twentieth-century American history.

I have tried to turn the liabilities of the data into virtues in other ways. There is a mythic Liberace, in part self-constructed; it bears a sometimes tenuous relationship with the otherwise obscure real man. Thus, he once referred to himself as a "one-man Disneyland" who had no existence outside the performance. Instead of deconstructing the myth, I have set out to analyze the mythologizing—how it worked, how it worked so long, so successfully, and what its author might have had in mind. The process of analyzing Liberace's own mythic ambitions also introduced the importance of the idea of mythic reality in general in understanding his life. He constructed his own myths, but these also resonated with other mythic truths, such as those of the Oedipal family, the American dream, and the human comedy in general as performed for three thousand years in the Western tradition.

Henry James insisted that we only have three or four stories to tell. Genius lies in telling them as if they had never been told before. In this regard, Liberace was a special kind of genius—that, at least, is one thing I discovered in re-creating his life. Specifically, he applied the same formulas to his act for fifty years, pleasing audiences all along. When accused of unoriginality, he retorted that he would change when the crowds stopped coming and the audiences stopped laughing. Except for one brief period, they never did. His formulas worked. Beyond this, they intrigued me. Liberace himself discussed the nature of art and how aesthetics spoke—or failed to speak—to the human condition. His success argues that he got the big formulas as well as the little ones right. That is another thesis that I advance here; once again, it goes far, far beyond what I first imagined on that blustery Washington day in 1991.

I began this book as a kind of exercise. I intended to take Liberace seriously, but I had no burning affection for the subject. As I worked, my attitudes changed; so did the book. If Liberace never charmed me the way he did innumerable audiences, still, I came to respect him, in some ways even to admire him. And, from the beginning to the end, he never bored me. His life taught me things. The research—touring the Liberace Museum in Las Vegas, tromping along the gilded avenues of West Hollywood, and poring over scandal sheets—was special fun. With all its complications, writing was equally engaging. In its own way, settling on this topic was as fortuitous and gratifying as my discovery of Margaret Mitchell as a subject of biography twenty years ago.

In the process of both researching and writing this book, I have run up numerous debts. Florida International University has supported me with travel funds, research money, and a sabbatical. I could hardly have finished without this aid. Research assistants Tim Van Scoy, George Schmidt, and Franni Ramos labored above and beyond their obligations. So did Kevin Taracido, who researched Liberace's 1956 Cuba trip for me. Linda Salup was no less energetic but labored for devotion alone. Joy Reitman of the Milwaukee *Journal-Sentinel* made my research easier; so did the staffs at the Milwaukee Public Library, the Milwaukee Family Center of the Church of Jesus Christ Latter-day Saints, the Milwaukee County Historical Society, and the Las Vegas Public Library. I appreciate all the assistance from the folks at the Liberace Museum in Las Vegas, but the archivist Pauline Lachance made my work there easier than I ever imagined.

I regret having been able to arrange so few interviews with Liberace's friends and associates, but this makes me appreciate all the more those who did speak. Beyond formal interviews, I have delighted in the numbers of people who have shared Liberace stories with me. I mention my subject, and everybody seems to be off and running with tales of their own about their Aunt Mae or their grandmother or some other family member's devotion to the showman. Folks offer evidence of their own affection, too, under the most peculiar circumstances. By Discovery Bay in Jamaica, my friend Marina Ituarte described an intimate concert in Mexico City; over pasta in Florence, Victor and Ana Marie Carrabino recounted their encounter with the performer in Tallahassee; sharing office doughnuts in Miami, Maezel Brown described a charity concert for poor kids in Kansas City she had attended over four decades before.

From 1951 to 1986, the responses were all the same: he put on a hell of a show. Everyone had stories. Remembering Liberace's television days, my aging bank teller still waxed wistful about Lee's beautiful things—she always wanted a candelabrum, she told me; my neighbor across the canal described how the pianist was the only gay public figure to admire on television when he was a little boy. Some, like the Cuban telephone repairman—inventor, in his own testimony, of "the educational piñata"—volunteered theories as well as stories about the showman's attraction. I got story after story from antique traders: the silver dealer who sold Lee a diamond ring remembered the beefy bodyguards; the shopkeeper in Connecticut joked about Scott Thorson's jewelry, but not about Liberace's largess. At a friend's wedding in Coral Gables, I was quizzed intelligently about my research, and I discovered that Richard and Ruth Shack had socialized with the showman for years through common associations with MCA. The narratives sometimes got much more personal. On three or four occasions, to my astonishment, they included sexual experiences with the gaudy performer. I have included only a tiny fraction of all these tales in the text. I did not even get the names of all the storytellers. All of them enriched my understanding of Liberace the man and Liberace the performer.

I owe still more direct debts. Two of my seminars on twentieth-century American history read and criticized two earlier versions of this book. I have profited from my students' observations about contemporary culture as well as from their comments on the book itself. Friends, academic and otherwise, have deepened my understanding of the subject, not to mention the peculiarities of modern American civilization, homosexual culture, and aesthetics in general. We argued furiously about these matters, but Dan Childers, John Bailly, Barry Sparkman, Alfredo Cruz, and Natalia Garcia helped me refocus the whole text after one particular discussion.

Another category of folk have kept me primed with more discrete material: a cartoon here, a television reference there, a magazine citation somewhere else, or useful books or bibliographies. Among these I mention Butler Waugh, Mike Ebner, Joyce Peterson, Sarah Awan, David Lavin, David Lee, and Fernando Quiroga.

More often than not, especially early on, friends encouraged me with their skepticism, but the project has never been without supporters. I have mentioned Bill Robertson already. Jean Trebbi was great. Tony and Sylvia Vera-Leon have cheered *An American Boy* for five years in New York, Miami, and the mountains of North Carolina. The historian John

D'Emilio encouraged it in terms that still inspire me. More critically, the novelist-essayist-biographer Edmund White earned my gratitude by suggesting in the fall of 1997 that I contact his friends at St. Martin's and at the University of Chicago Press. As a result of his kindness, my heirs will have one less bulky, unpublished manuscript to deal with.

A number of readers, professional and lay, have plowed through various drafts of this manuscript. No one has followed this project more closely than Howard Kaminsky. I owe no one deeper thanks, especially considering that he still finds Liberace a horror. He has criticized two or three drafts line by line, but he reads for structure and ideas as well as for spelling, usage, grammar, and syntax. Flaws and shortcoming remain, but *An American Boy* is better for his bracing criticism. I could ask for no more intelligent readers than my old teacher Bill Harbaugh, my colleague Nicol Rae, and my friend Miguel Costa, who doubled as a research assistant, too. Mike Novak's enthusiasm cheered me when I needed it especially. Ruth Barzel, who provided fastidious copyediting, also offered praise that kept up my spirits. I owe different sort of thanks to the two anonymous readers for the University of Chicago Press. Their criticisms sharpened my revisions. Press production editor Jenni Fry has made this a better book, while Doug Mitchell has been as encouraging an editor and advocate as any writer or scholar could wish for. Finally, in the very last stages of editing, my friend André McKennon has been my strong right arm. For the assistance and support of all these folks, I am deeply appreciative.

Liberace

Don't be misled by this flamboyant exterior.
Underneath I remain the same—a simple boy
from Milwaukee.

LIBERACE

WISCONSIN RHYTHM AND BLUES

Frances Zuchowski and her husband Salvatore Liberace were ill prepared for the prodigies of her accouchement in the village of West Allis, Wisconsin, on May 16, 1919. She gave birth to twins that day. While one baby was, mysteriously, born dead, the survivor weighed a phenomenal thirteen pounds. More notable, this infant entered the world still enveloped in the delicate, transparent membrane of the birth sac. He was born with a caul. In many primitive or traditional societies, to be born "under the veil" portends wonders and marvels. It marks out genius, supernatural powers, mysterious gifts, sixth sense, cosmic insight—and just plain good luck. It was the perfect entrance into the world for one who would later make a reputation for spectacular entrances, but, more than that, the magic of the caul illuminated his whole biography. Years after his own death, even, his family continued to explain his career and personality in the context of the genius of his birth.[1]

Wladziu Valentino Liberace, otherwise known as Walter, Wally, Lee, and, eventually, just plain Liberace, fulfilled the promises of his entrance into the world. As a toddler, he was a prodigy, a musical marvel. He was otherwise singular as a child, a boy, an adolescent, and a man. His peculiarity, however, gains the most extraordinary meaning from the antithetical circumstances of his rearing. All his life, his eccentricities played against the most conservative and traditional patterns of his community, his family, and his faith. These, no less than his personal genius, constituted a part of who he was. The contours of his career, his audience appeal, and the shape of his act itself do not make sense except in the context of his social background.

He grew up in the working class, blue-collar, farmer-tan heartland of the American Midwest. He carried its fuzzy, nasal way of talking to his grave. His beginnings marked his character indelibly. Just so, for all the bickering and hostility of his immigrant parents, an American ideal of domesticity governed his whole life, while his religious faith, inculcated at both hearth and altar, shaped that life no less critically from beginning to end.

The community of his birth and nurture, the twin villages of West Allis and West Milwaukee, Wisconsin, might have been a movie set for an American community in the three decades before World War II. They lay an easy trolley ride of about five miles from the great urban center of Milwaukee to the east. Locals could take advantage of the wonders of Milwaukee if and when they chose. For those like the Liberace family, with pretensions to art, the elegant Pabst Theater, built with donations from one of the city's great fortunes, provided a regular venue for musical and theatrical events. With its large, diverse population, its monumental stone office buildings, and its deep roots in high Germanic civilization, Milwaukee provided a sophisticated cultural center in the early decades of the century for everyone north of Chicago—including people in the rural hinterland as far west as Madison.

While the metropolis to the east exemplified urban culture, the famously rich Wisconsin farmland began at the very western edge of West Allis. If anything, country life impinged even more directly on these communities than did the urban civilization of Milwaukee. The presence of the Wisconsin State Fairgrounds almost in the heart of West Allis formalized the role of the country in the town. Then, too, plenty of orchard and dairy farmers' sons actually attended West Milwaukee High School with the children of West Allis's shopkeepers, craftsmen, and industrial workers.

West Allis and West Milwaukee melded something then of metropolis and country. They epitomized small-town America. But, more American still, the two towns represented a melting-pot diversity that came with industrialization in the region. The two communities, indeed, were bracketed and defined geographically by two of the great manufacturing enterprises of the state, even of the Midwest. The huge Harnischfeger metalworks sat on the eastern border, while toward the farmlands rose the still more impressive and important industrial plant of the Allis-Chalmers Corporation. Both were producers of heavy machinery. Of the two, Allis-

Chalmers was particularly important. In its second and third decade of operation, it employed as many as five thousand workers and could produce gargantuan castings of up to 120 tons. Not inappropriately, journalists referred to it as "America's Krupp," after the great German machineworks of the same period.[2] The life of the community was inseparable from the local plants. "They'd say that opportunity waits at Harnischfeger's gate," observed a local historian, "and it was Harnischfeger and Rex Chainbelt and all the other industries that were here, and that's what really caused West Milwaukee to develop." As a journalist reported, "West Milwaukee was a lunch bucket town when Lee was growing up."[3]

All these once-bustling factories—Rex Chainbelt, Allis-Chalmers, Harnischfeger—are closed and abandoned now, their ruins Rust Belt monuments. All fell victim to foreign competition, shifting patterns of labor, and alterations in American foreign policy—and, indeed, to the epochal shifts in domestic and cultural life in the United States in the decades after World War II. These changes are a part of Liberace's history, too; they are cause as well as effect. But in 1919, the year of his birth, few could have prophesied such upheavals in these quiet, hardworking communities.

Although legally separate, the twin villages of West Allis and West Milwaukee blended imperceptibly one into the other and formed a coherent community. Roads defined them. Running due east-west, Greenfield Avenue marked the northern limit; it cut directly from the heart of downtown Milwaukee to the Milwaukee County line. On a southeastern diagonal below, Beloit Road outlined the southern boundary. These two arteries formed two sides of a triangle of roughly three and a half miles on the north and four and a half on the south; the third side extended a mile or so to the west along 108th Street running north-south. The most important street, National Avenue, split this triangle down the center. Lying parallel to Beloit just to its north, it linked the villages and served as their main street.

It was a walking neighborhood. Indeed, enough of the old ways persist that one could still live there without a car at the end of the twentieth century. Shopping, greengrocers, and bakeries were nearby; so were diners and family restaurants. The neighborhood boasted numerous churches that described the community's demographic and religious diversity. If the dome of the grand Catholic basilica jutted above the skyline in the west, most of the houses of worship were more modest. The Liberaces' parish church in the east, St. Florian's, with its connected Carmelite cloister, had some claims to style, but the Polish Catholic and Lutheran churches were no more than functional places of devotion for their working-class parishioners. The community supported its own schools. Four Liberace children attended Pershing Elementary. West Milwaukee High School provided special cause for local boasting. Besides its claims to academic excellence, it was also one of the few distinguished examples of architecture here. After over a half century, its present users take as much obvious pride in its grounds and its elegant Spanish Baroque architectural style as did its first students and teachers when Walter Liberace graduated in 1937.

Like the mostly humble public buildings, the blocks and blocks of West Allis's and West Milwaukee's residences confirmed the nature of the community's life and aspirations. Here, its working-class conservatism showed clearest yet. There were virtually no apartments or tenements; instead there was street after tree-shaded street of freestanding houses. Some few might have boasted two or two and a half stories, and more than three bedrooms; most were considerably smaller. Even the most modest, however, reflected their owners' pride in tidy lawns and neat hedges. Almost everyone had a garden. Lilacs scented the air in May, roses later; hollyhocks re-seeded themselves year after year in garden after garden, while devoted residents replanted annuals every spring and set out small vegetable plots with the last frost. People liked it here. They stayed put. People resided in the same community year after year; they maintained the same residences for decade after decade. The pattern persisted even into the second generation. Folks who grew up here even in the twenties still remain, three quarters of a century later. Exaggerating the tradition of stability, local households provided each other sweethearts and spouses: young men and women who had grown up together in the same neighborhood wound up wedding each other and living close to their parents.[4]

The streets of quiet homes have not changed very much in seventy-five years. The trees might have grown, and the dwellings in the district might have acquired additions and brighter paint, but the great majority of the houses built during the first three decades of this century still survive. Almost all are still recognizable in ground plan from insurance maps drawn in the 1920s; indeed, one can even travel the whole triangle of streets using 1930s maps.

While the lawns and shade trees of private homes account for the suburban tranquillity of the district, city maps—then and now—reveal parks and public greens that further the impression. Mostly of standard, smallish size, they were all dwarfed by one of the great public spaces of

Milwaukee County, the nearly half-mile square of rolling grounds and ancient trees of the veterans retirement home on National Avenue just north and east of its diagonal intersection with Greenfield. Generations of Milwaukeeans knew this simply as "the Home." The national government developed the site soon after Appomattox as a benefit for Civil War veterans, and it soon sprouted its Second Empire-style buildings that housed these veterans' diminishing numbers down into the 1930s. When the last of these ancients were gone to their rewards with Generals Grant and Sherman—and maybe even with Lee, Jackson, and Beauregard—the federal government used the grounds for new veterans affairs offices that now line National Avenue between Forty-fourth and Fifty-seventh Streets. But on the gentle rise in the middle of the tract, the original, 120-year-old buildings appear undisturbed—as do the enormous conifers, ginkgoes, and other trees that shade the park.

The Home—encompassing stately buildings, aged veterans, lofty trees, and rolling grounds—was a part of the heritage of West Milwaukee, West Allis, and their citizens. The American past bumped as unobtrusively onto the present as did the two villages into each other. As a boy, Wally Liberace, son of an Italian-born father and a Polish-speaking mother, regularly walked across the street from his home on National Avenue to play among the gnarled relics of Gettysburg, Shiloh, and Antietam.

American history lurked in the shadows of the Home's great firs and oaks; the American present blossomed elsewhere in the village streets. West Allis and West Milwaukee offered models of twentieth-century American ethnic diversity. If now—as in 1920—the city directories reveal little or nothing of Jewish or Black culture, the great industrial plants attracted all manner of other folks. Meanwhile, the agricultural hinterland offered a population almost as varied. Southern Italians shared coffee with German Protestants, German Catholics went off to the plants with Czechs and Poles, men with Swiss ancestors and roots among Southern Baptists led unions of them all, while everyone drank the milk from the dairy farms of native-born Scots-Irish Americans.

For all the variety of the people, however, no evidence exists of ethnic or religious animosities. Something of the same holds for class antagonisms. If, five miles away, visitors could see the great Victorian mansions of the fabulously rich, Milwaukee had less to boast of in its crowded tenements. In contrast, in West Allis and West Milwaukee there was little architectural distinction between the dwellings of the rich and those of the poor. In the exigencies of the Great Depression, union radicalism thrived and spawned communism and communist sympathizers, yet even class antagonism seem to have been projected outside the community itself. Even so, the existence of a powerful left influence within the union at Allis-Chalmers, for example, seems a particular function of odd, local circumstances.[5]

By and large, these classical immigrant communities devoted themselves to the ideals of family, hard work, education, self-actualization, and geniality. If the residents flirted with communism in the thirties, they mainly played their music, drank their beer, and danced their polkas in the evenings. Most of them attended their various churches on Sunday, but no one seemed particularly troubled by those who stayed home. In the forties, their young men fought the fascist East and West without political reservations. The return of prosperity after the war rekindled the old expectations of the promise of American life, even as the establishment's crusade against communism during the strike of 1946–47 penalized the dissidents. Radicalism did not survive here after 1950.

On the eve of the Great Depression, West Milwaukee and West Allis provided a microcosm of Midwestern American values. With their diversity of farmers and industrial workers, shopkeepers and craftsmen, natives and immigrants, ancient veterans and hustling foreigners, these two villages bred in their heyday a kind of natural community based on values of progress, economic advancement, and tolerance under the general aegis of American institutions. These are, in any event, the very values that their most native son, born here in those most peculiar circumstances on May 16, 1919, and christened Wladziu Valentino Liberace, reflected and echoed to the tips of his twinkling toes and glittering fingers all his life.

The influence of this small-town, Midwestern world on the life of the pianist known to the world after 1963 as "the Showman" is incalculable. For the first years of his life, he hardly even visited any other place. He considered West Allis his legal residence until he was in his early twenties. Well after his relocation to New York and then California, his mother continued to live in the family house on National Avenue until she moved to California with her son. Liberace's sister, Angie, remained in the house where she had grown up for many years after her brother had left. Even after he had lost all family connections with the area, Liberace returned often to play the local theaters with special enthusiasm. It remained his hometown, full of old friends and rich associations. It affected him permanently. He never lost his Midwestern twang, but the influences of his West Milwaukee upbringing lurked in his heart as well as on his tongue.

The trajectory of his career, and his ambition, energy, perseverance, and good nature all represent elements of his baptism in Midwestern American values. He was the working-class son of immigrants who seized the brass ring of American promise to make his own way through hard work to fabulous wealth and fame. He is a paradigm for his generation. Even the contents of his biography—with all its eccentricities and perversions—mirror elements of his West Milwaukee heritage. They do so doubly. On the one hand, his excesses represent no more than every working-class family's dreams of profligate wealth pushed to caricatured extreme; on the other hand—and perhaps more critically—his life represents, literally, a reverse image of the most conservative values of his upbringing. His eccentricities confirmed rather than repudiated the conservatism of his origins. He did not approach his life, dress, and style as normal. He calculated his eccentricity or even outrage within the most conservative frame of politics and social order. Conservative in his own politics and faith, he sought neither to overthrow standards nor to impose new ones by his outrages against convention. He was a cultural eccentric, not a rebel, much less a revolutionary. Indeed, he did not like rebels and revolutionaries. Eschewing politics in general, he had no tolerance in particular for dissidence and dissidents. Harry Truman, Dwight Eisenhower, and Ronald Reagan invited him to the White House, and the three represent a kind of centrist ideal he himself approved of. Along the same lines, he cared nothing for "alternative lifestyles." He never liked hippies, and they gave no evidence of liking him. The same holds for alternative sexual lifestyles. Despite his own homosexuality, he evidenced little sympathy for gay liberation, and in the post-Stonewall world of politicized homosexuality, gays tended to return the sentiment.

Liberace's audience appeal supports the conservative biases of his West Milwaukee heritage. He did not play to crowds that dressed as flamboyantly as he. Indeed, the core of the faithful sprang from roots close to his own: conventional, traditional, lower-middle-class small towners. The people with whom he grew up or people very much like them—ordinary middle-of-the-road Americans, conservatives, blue-collar folk, some of them with extra money in their pockets—remained the heart of his enduring audiences. These were the people he played to. He did it naturally; he was one of them. He confirmed their values even as he inverted and transgressed them. This indeed was a part of his genius of playing borders and margins against the center, of performing the outsider in the middle of things. While other elements also contribute to his peculiar circumstances, a critical source of his character lies along National Avenue and Beloit Road.

Despite his double dip of Midwestern and American values, Liberace's actual roots did not run very deep in the rich Wisconsin soil. Like the families of most of his neighbors in Milwaukee County, his family had appeared here late in the high tide of immigration around the turn of the century. His family, and, in turn, the immediate environment of his domestic circle, offers the second great source of his character and of an understanding of his career. Family and culture played against each other and played themselves out in his biography to the end. If he never really abandoned West Allis, neither did he ever escape his parents and their formidable impact on his life. The perpetual discord at the Liberace hearth affected him, as did the sources of that conflict: two powerful parents with antithetical values from conflicting cultures. At the same time, despite the dissonance, the power of family and family attachments he knew as a child influenced almost everything he did: it governed his relations with his actual family long after he had outgrown its circle. Family values also shaped his attitude toward friends, audiences, and homosexual liaisons. Understanding his family illuminates his shadowy interior life as well. Beyond this, Salvatore Liberace, son of Naples, and Frances Zuchowski, child of Krakow, were colorful and even emblematic characters in their own right.

Born in 1886 in the Italian village of Formia near Naples, Salvatore L. Liberace should not have been anywhere near the dairy farms of Wisconsin after emigrating to the United States around the first decade of the new century. If not in Italy, he belonged in Philadelphia with the rest of his family. All his American connections lay there, where his older brother, Benjamin, had settled before him. The Pennsylvania branch of the family was already taking its own route of Americanization: they anglicized the pronunciation of their surname—dropping the emphasized final "e"—and moved into medicine and other middle- and upper-middle-class professions as the century progressed.[6] Sal, or Sam as friends knew him, had another destiny. He never anglicized his name. Unlike his brother, he evidenced no interest in middle-class professionalism either for himself or for his brood. He lacked that sort of ambition. Indeed, he lacked ambition—traditionally defined, at least—altogether. Economically, he never made it to fully self-sustaining middle-class prosperity. Most of his life, he hung near the ragged upper fringe of the proletariat. The fate seemed a function of choice, however perverse the decision and disastrous the consequences. He was a musician in Italy, and he would be a musician in the United States. If his adopted country scorned artists, that was Americans' problem, not his. It was, in any case, music that brought him to the upper Midwest by the close of the century's first decade, although the specific date of his arrival is not clear.

Salvatore Liberace was a professional French horn player who toured with John Philip Sousa's prestigious concert band, according to his son. The year 1910 found him performing in Wisconsin. When the Sousa troupe moved on, Sal Liberace stayed.[7] He had found a woman. Eros confounded his life. If love did not thwart his musical career, it gave him more than excuse enough for the peculiar course of his ambitions over the next thirty years, and had every manner of direct and indirect influence on his children and family.

As he emerges from the fragmentary records, Sam Liberace was a curious character. He demonstrated nearly equal parts Latin machismo, artistic devotion, and bohemian self-indulgence. Domineering, demanding, and even tyrannical, he was an exacting taskmaster and a relentless perfectionist. He lacked all patience for others' opinions. His character allowed no room for either compromise or affection. He possessed a fierce temper, and physical violence was a normal part of his domestic life. While these aspects of his character helped shape the personalities of all his children, they affected his family more directly and immediately in the early years of his marriage. His unwavering commitment to art and music in an environment that was seldom congenial meant many things; not least, it meant that he was a notoriously poor provider. His economic inadequacy was the flip side of his devotion to the muse. Both these elements reverberate through the children's judgment of the father.

Issues about working, employment, and money dominated the Liberace household and accounted for a host of difficulties in the family circle as the boy grown rich and famous remembered them.[8] The problem emerged at the beginning; it assumed almost legendary proportions in family lore. Thus, Lee Liberace launched his own recollections of his parent with a discussion of the difficulties of making a living as a musician in Wisconsin in the decades after 1900, long before his own birth. Soon after Sam's marriage in 1910, then, the paucity of jobs in Milwaukee prompted him to return to Philadelphia with his young wife. The couple remained in Pennsylvania for the birth of their first child in 1911, according to their son, but the relocation gave rise to the first great dispute between husband and wife, and, jobs or no, the couple soon returned to West Allis.[9]

After his return to Milwaukee County, Sam was working, if not always on his instrument of choice. Photographs capture him playing not French horn but trumpet in 1911; another image memorializes him with his old instrument performing with the Harvester Band of Milwaukee in September 1912.[10] Other evidence, however, poignantly confirms the son's description of the difficulty his father had in finding employment as a musician. Sam's earliest notices in the West Allis City Directory in 1911 and

1912, for example, list him as a laborer, a "machine hand," or a "tinner." As late as 1918, the listings retain this identification. In 1921, he identified himself as "musician," but in 1925 his tag is "grocer." A man did what he could to keep body and soul together and provide for his dependents. In this regard, Sam Liberace only repeated the pattern of innumerable others in comparable circumstances. The Casadontes, a family closely related to the Liberaces, were in a similar situation. Alexander Casadonte, who lived around the corner from the musician's family and who was later to wed Sam's ex-wife, listed himself in the directory at various times as a laborer and a confectioner as well as a musician.[11] If it was perhaps necessary for men to abandon their passion in order to eat, such decisions had ramifications. For a man like Salvatore Liberace, who defined himself as an artist, manual labor must have proved especially galling. His son recalled that it was just that when, later, his father "had to get himself some kind of factory work. It was a terrible blow to his aesthetic sense," he related. "His once immaculate hands turned calloused and grimy from handling tools and machinery, and he rarely played his beautiful brass French horn. He did, however, get it out occasionally and polish it with loving care."[12]

There were other problems associated with Salvatore Liberace's commitment to making his livelihood through music. Not least, of course, he proved incapable of sustaining a regular income except in the flushest times, and flush times were not the norm for most of his married years. If the circumstances might have created tensions in the most loving of homes, in the Liberace household the problem was all the more severe. The woman Sam Liberace had married numbered neither grace, tolerance, nor affection among her virtues. The two of them, Salvatore L. Liberace and Frances Zuchowski, made an odd couple from the outset. Not an easy man himself, Salvatore had courted a harridan, whether or not he knew it. He wed Frances on September 9, 1910, in Milwaukee.[13] She was why he was living in Wisconsin and perhaps why he was working as a machinist in West Allis when he wanted to be playing the horn in Philadelphia.

Salvatore Liberace was twenty-five and his bride eighteen when they married. Although he stood only five feet three inches tall, Sam Liberace was a handsome man with his dark complexion, thick black hair, and obsidian eyes. He had a squarish face and close-set eyes, but his generous mouth and full, naturally red lips exaggerated the sensuousness of his exotic swarthiness. His bride was perhaps a couple of inches taller than her diminutive mate. Although her hair was dark, too, she was otherwise fair. A buxom girl, she loved to cook and eat, and added weight with years. A photograph at the time of her marriage reveals a busty young woman with a peculiarly heart-shaped visage. She had a high brow and a prominent chin, and, in spite of her wide-set eyes, her features seem to crowd the center of her face. It was a look underlined by her thin lips and small mouth that appear almost to recede into her face because of her long, sharp nose and pointed chin. Altogether, the photograph gives the young woman a somewhat pinched look.[14] The image certainly suited her character.

Frances Zuchowski's ethnic and personal background contrasted sharply with her groom's. Her young husband was a loner, who seemed to have lived in America parentless, having immigrated here when he was around twenty. She, in contrast, was American born of Polish parents and maintained close familial ties. The Zuchowski clan was large, too. Frances came from a brood of seven—six girls, one son. Her parents seem to have left Europe in the 1880s, and they staked their American claims near the town of Menasha, Wisconsin, soon after. On the outskirts of the larger city of Appleton, Menasha lay on the northeast shore of Lake Winnebago about 100 miles north-northeast of Milwaukee and about the same distance from the state capital, Madison. The family supplemented its income by working in the local paper mills in Menasha and Neenah, just across the river, but they identified themselves chiefly as farmers and country folk.

If family and farming focused Zuchowski values for two generations, so did religion and the church. Indeed, piety, family, and farming all tended to reinforce one another. The Zuchowskis were traditional, conservative, and religious in the manner of Polish immigrants to America, and of Poles in the Old Country, for that matter. They gave one of their daughters to the church, for example, and she took the name of Sister Mary de Sales in the Order of St. Joseph at Stevens Point, Wisconsin, where she spent her whole life.[15] While Frances Zuchowski failed to take orders, she was hardly less devoted than her sister. As one of her son's friends wrote, she had two passions even in old age: the church and her children.[16] The friend might have added money, too, for she was as tight and materialistic as she was conservative and traditional.

The Zuchowskis of Menasha were hardworking and poor, and had few luxuries, but they lived well after the manner of farmers and country people. Their grandson recalled them as being not without culture. He remembered them as "a family of amateur musicians who gave lessons and were very popular in concerts on the local church and charity circuit."[17] According to one family story, his grandmother Zuchowski had lived in Berlin, and while working in a music studio, had met the very young Ignacy Paderewski, for whom she had acted as translator.[18]

While Liberace might have linked his mother's people generally with music, he never related them, as he did his father, with the arts or culture in any other way. Then, too, if the Zuchowski clan enjoyed music, Frances herself did not share their affection. On the contrary, her son described her even as positively discouraging it. Still further, in his memory (in particular contrast with his father), she lacked aesthetic sense altogether. While the son conceded that the mother had "a flair for interior decoration," he returned much more often to terms like "shabby" and "drab" to describe her attitude to life; "mean" fits, too. Even after her son became rich, for example, Frances Liberace took little pleasure in his efforts to beautify her life or her person. "I sometimes find it hard to believe how long it took me to convince Mom that she should have her hair done by a professional. She considered it the height of luxury and an unforgivable extravagance," he wrote.[19]

As here, Liberace's autobiographical references to his mother generally reflect the values of a narrow, immigrant country girl who never transcended her rural Wisconsin upbringing—who, conservative to the core, never even seemed to have imagined such transcendence. Rejecting innovation out of hand, she preferred the old, the tested, the tried. She kept her coal stove and her icebox into the late forties, for example, and when freezers came into use, "Mother wouldn't have one in the house. She stuck to her idea that it was unhealthy to eat food that had been frozen," her son remembered.[20] She lived as if value began and ended with farm life in the Midwest. "She grew up with simple things," her son wrote, "and those were the things she understood and preferred."[21] Frances Zuchowski honored her Polish provincial country legacy in other ways. Her son also described her as hardworking, determined, and unpretentious, but also as materialistic, headstrong, and quarrelsome. Although respectful and not really invidious, his remarks also leave the impression that his parent was cheap and graceless. Thus, he memorialized the way she resented both the time and money that her husband devoted to the children's musical training. He recorded, too, the way she sought sympathy from neighbors by complaining about her two youngest "practicing the piano and George taking violin lessons—all that money being spent on music lessons" while she slaved away at work.[22]

The union of the conservative Polish farm girl and the worldly Neapolitan musician was not made in heaven; it was, however, fruitful. Within a year of their marriage, the couple produced their first child, George, born in 1911 in Philadelphia, according to his brother.[23] Two years later, on December 11, 1913, Frances gave birth to a girl, Angelina Anna, named for her maternal grandmother; she was christened at St. Florian's Church in West Milwaukee a few months later. On May 16, 1919, five and a half years after Angie's appearance, came the omen-laden birth of the third surviving child. For the survivor of this double birth, his parents chose a polyglot name that echoed the divergent ethnicities of his heritage. He was Wladziu Valentino. Wladziu was the Polish Walter that his family favored, either that or Wally. The performer himself, in fame, circulated the story that his mother chose his second name after the Italian heartthrob, silent-movie star Rudolph Valentino. This is perhaps true, but as the actor did not soar to international fame with his film *The Sheik* until two years later in 1921, it is unlikely. The source of the name remains otherwise ambiguous, too, because Valentino Liberace had been Salvatore's father back in Naples, and his paternal grandfather seems a more likely source of the boy's appellation than his mother's fancy does.[24] In any case, the division of his name between his Polish and his Italian roots serves as a nice device for understanding his own sharply divided debts to his mother and his father.

When the third Liberace child was twelve and the senior sibling twenty, their parents gave them a final brother, Rudolph Valentino, born in 1931. He was always Rudy. Perhaps the mother really had intended to identify her third child with her movie-star hero, but her husband's father's name diluted her purpose. In her third son's name, she allowed no ambiguity. By this time, in any case, she no longer compromised on much of anything. Indeed, even earlier, both Frances and Salvatore Liberace found little basis for compromising on issues large or small. Their house echoed with conflict. Almost from the beginning of their marriage, fighting dominated the family circle.

The couple exchanged real blows, and they swapped verbal brickbats, too. Indeed, their fighting assumed almost mythic status, at least in the recollections of their second son. He placed their first confrontation a decade before his own birth in the 1910–11 fight about moving to Philadelphia. Sam persuaded Frances to go. He wanted to remain there; she did not. "The City of Brotherly Love didn't instill any sisterly love in her heart. She didn't like the metropolitan place. . . . She longed for the simple life in a small friendly community where everyone knew and loved his neighbors."[25] Frances won, but Sam would have his day.

On returning to Milwaukee County, the Liberace family found a place to live on Fifty-first Street, one of West Allis's main north-south thorough-fares. The first city directories list them at 709 Fifty-first. This is where Walter Valentine and his dead twin were born. The house stood on the west side of the street, almost exactly halfway between National Avenue and Beloit Road, the major, diagonal cross streets in West Allis. The dwelling survives. In a row of nearly identical homes, the house sits about twenty-five feet back from the road. With gabled short side to the street, its front door—directly beneath the central window in the eaves—opened onto a small living room, with other rooms stacked up behind.

Poverty dominates almost every reference Liberace made to child-hood, but, despite his memories, the old house on Fifty-first Street was a modest but adequate dwelling for a small family in humble circumstances. So too was the dwelling a block or so up, at 635 Fifty-first (now 1649 Six-tieth Street), where the family had relocated by 1925. It resembled the other house in general form. This is the place that Liberace recalled best from these years, although he seems to have conflated the two houses. His memories of this second house and the move there also relate to new difficulties between his parents. Frances turned the house into a grocery store as well as a residence.[26] She concocted the arrangement ostensibly for economic reasons, but other forces seem to have been at work, as well.

The general economic prosperity of the mid-twenties buoyed up even the musician corks of West Allis, like Sam Liberace. After 1925, he never again listed himself as anything but "musician" in the city directory. His son remembered his playing at the great movie theaters of the era, for example, the Alhambra, where live orchestras accompanied the silent films. He was providing for his family in a way he had not done before. He was even saving money, his boy remembered, cash that soon after 1925 permitted them to purchase a new house of their own in a nicer neighbor-hood. In spite of their increased prosperity, however, Sam's wife deter-mined to enter business on her own. When the family moved up the street around 1924, she opened the grocery store. The enterprise pleased no one in the family but Frances herself. The house was not large, and now they had still less space. "When you walked through a door in the rear of our store," the pianist recalled, "you were in our living room." Nor did the store provide much income. Later, Liberace compared the store to a farm: "You may not make a lot of money, but you can always find something to eat. I can remember running from our little kitchen out into the store to get a couple of potatoes, or something for dinner." While at age five or six, the youngest family member was spared any real chores having to do with the business, his mother dragooned both George and Angie into helping out. They tended the counter and made deliveries. Both disliked it. Nothing in their father's history suggests any affinity at all for the grocery scheme.[27] While the store was Frances's brainstorm entirely, she managed to identify her husband with the business, too. Thus, in the city directory of 1925, "grocer" follows his name.[28] If having a store in his front room offended Sam Liberace, perhaps this accounts for another anomaly in the public records of this time. The 1925 West Allis Directory names Salvatore as a resident-grocer at 709 Fifty-first Street, but the Milwaukee City Directory lists him as an inhabitant of that city, registering him at a different address—424 Layton Avenue, a couple of miles east of the other house. It also records his profession, once more, as "musician."

The grocery-store scheme lasted only a couple of years at most, at least according to official records, from when Wally Liberace was around six until he was about seven. He made it a central part of his memoir, however, where it plays a kind of iconographic role, standing for everything he hated. While he never criticizes his mother outright, he leaves little room for doubt about his skepticism of her judgment. Theirs was not, he determined, "a proper house." Canned goods and oranges in the front room constricted the family's living and thereby limited privacy twice over, once with customers and again with each other. It exaggerated controversy within the household. Did his father actually move out in these years? Did Wally want to flee with him? He remained with his mother, his siblings, and the potato bins in the front room. He was not a happy six-year-old. Liberace as an adult almost never complained or criticized and had little patience for those who "kvetched," as he put it. He avoided making disapproving or invidious remarks. When he did so, he often followed the observation with some aside to disguise or mute his discontent. After a half century, however, the memory of the grocery store in the front parlor still unsettled him. It suggests his larger, only semiconscious dissatisfaction with his childhood; it stood as an emblem for other conflicts at his hearth in these years. They were numerous.

The houses on Fifty-first Street echoed regularly with the Liberaces' squabbles. Dissension revolved around money, but disagreements over finances revealed deeper differences between the parents. Salvatore had his own way of doing things and his own commitments, and he refused to bend for any exigencies. In a single image, one of Salvatore's old friends left a nice record not only of the father but of the sources and potential sources of conflicts in the family as well. "The artiste, he called himself," John Hlaban recalled. "At home Ma (Liberace) would be on the front porch, hammering or sawing or doing something, and the old man would say, 'Not my line.' Sam, the artiste," Hlaban chuckled.[29]

Sam Liberace did not consider himself subject to ordinary rules. He scorned repairs and household chores as being beneath his dignity and left such drudgery to his simmering wife; he also manifested his arrogant singularity in other ways. He held no regular job. The stock market crash in '29 and the Depression played havoc with his career. He was a professional musician, however—the "artiste"—and when he couldn't play his horn, he did not work. Although he played in the Milwaukee Symphony, according to his daughter, and took occasional industrial jobs, according to his son, he was basically unemployed after 1929.

Salvatore Liberace's identity as "artiste" manifested itself in still other ways; these, in turn, possessed their own repercussions for his relations with his wife and children. Music, which was the key to his superiority, had to be perpetually present in his home. Along with the melodies of his horn, his Victrola, his record collection, and his piano dominated his household. In keeping with his aesthetic arrogance, he wanted only the best of each. Was the family scraping by for lack of money? No matter. He owned the best record player available, a "very special Orthophonic Victrola." He demanded the splendid machine also because of his equally high-caliber collection of recordings. "We had Caruso, of course, and Galli Curci, Giovanni Martinelli, Geraldine Farrar . . . all the great opera and concert stars of the early twentieth century," Sal's son recalled. "The classical Victor records were called Red Seal Records, and people took pride in owning a large collection of them. We did, too," Liberace continued. "But the difference between our collection of Red Seal records and most people's collections was that we really played ours . . . all the time. . . . My Dad and his fine record collection . . . introduced me to the great names of music." [30]

No record survives of the kind of piano in the household, but Liberace later identified the upright as "a little tired and worn." He compared it invidiously to the grands he played when he began formal instruction. [31] His complaint not withstanding, the piano, like the "very special Orthophonic Victrola," was most certainly the best Salvatore could afford—more likely, it was better than he could afford. His second son often testified to his father's selectivity and discrimination. The senior Liberace regularly proclaimed that, "a musician is only as good as his instrument." The son never challenged the pronouncement directly, but he periodically probed his parent's assertion. "I didn't dare talk back to my father, but occasionally I'd throw in something that bothered him. Like when I asked him if he wouldn't rather hear a good musician on a bad instrument than a poor musician on a great instrument," he related. "To this day I don't know what I would answer to that question, but my father's answer was simply, 'A poor musician desecrates a great instrument.'" [32] Regardless of the brand of the piano, however, Liberace made it clear that, thanks to his father, it occupied a prominent place in his home. The entertainer correctly described the piano as a central element in most households at the time. "In ours it was more than a big piece of furniture to gather around for a little casual singing," he testified. "To the Liberaces the piano was a way of life." [33]

So here, then, was the Neapolitan immigrant, marginally employable, with a only a small, unsteady income, spending money on instruments and music that a rich man might covet. But there was more. He demanded all this not merely for himself but also for his children. As a superior being, he would impose his standards on his children. They would be superior beings, too. The element that separated Salvatore Liberace from the herd would also distinguish his offspring. His son's recollection captures a hint of that ambition: "My dad's love and respect for music created in him a deep determination to give as his legacy to the world, a family of musicians dedicated to the advancement of the art." [34] Once he had set upon this or any other course, Sam became as implacable as the tides: "Just as soon as the sun rose in the east every morning each of us began taking piano lessons at the age of four. That was Dad's plan. Get them early and keep them at it. He followed this routine just as carefully and as perfectly as he followed the beat of whatever conductor he was playing under." [35]

Both ends and means of Salvatore's ambitions generated sharp tension within his family. It irritated his wife increasingly over the years. She steamed over the record player, for example. "It was a tremendous luxury," her son remembered.

> I remember my mother and father having the most noisy
> argument over it. We needed many other things, my mother
> argued, but my father always spent his money on the phono-
> graph because it reproduced the sound of music so beauti-
> fully. My father said it was more important to have music in
> the house than even food. . . . My mother was more practical.
> She worried about whether we had clothes, whether we had
> coal for the fire and food on the table. My dad was more aes-
> thetic. He'd save up his money and take me to concerts which
> we could not really afford. [36]

Along with precious victrolas, costly pianos, and high priced concert tickets, the expenses of the children's music training aggravated the mother's discontent. Frances groused bitterly about spending money on luxurious music lessons while she sweated at her grocery business or slaved in the factory. "But their father insists they are all going to be professional musicians like he is," she grumbled. "Personally, I think they'd be better off learning the grocery business, but I have nothing to say. He's the boss."[37] The boss? Sam Liberace was closer to a tyrant. "I remember hearing many arguments and loud words when things didn't go just the way he wanted them to go," the middle boy remembered. "His Italian temper was something we grew to fear and Mother had only to say 'Wait til your Dad comes home,' to turn rebellious hellions into little angels."[38]

The father brooked no opposition to either the form or content of his ambitions for his offspring. If his circumstances in Milwaukee left him little opportunity to shape his own musical destiny, Sal Liberace never questioned his aesthetic values, and he determined that all his children would share his commitments. His rigor and perfectionism left no room for his wife's reservations, nor for childish foibles. His eldest, then, George, was banging away at the piano by 1916, and Angie was playing well before her little brother was born. Both, however, rebelled in their own way. George compromised. He hated piano lessons, but his switch to the violin by 1923 or so satisfied his father. Angie was less fortunate. She loathed musical discipline, but she offered no substitute to satisfy her parent. Despite skipped practices and disastrous recitals, her father did not bend. Because "Dad was such a hard taskmaster," the younger brother determined, "he turned her off to music."[39]

Sal Liberace left no evidence of giving easy praise; approval stuck in his craw. A perfectionist, as his son described him, he drove all relentlessly before him. His children responded variously to his demanding nature. The circumstance embittered his daughter, but his ambition created still other violent eddies in the household. It generated bad blood between Angie and her younger brother. Wally turned out to be a musical prodigy, and the race between them was over before it began. "Angie had a rough time not only with the piano lessons but also with me. It wasn't that she didn't like music or that she didn't like me," the pianist wrote. "I guess I made her self conscious because music that was a problem for her came easily to me."[40] The brother became the measure of her inadequacies by the father's standards.

As if in a predictable effort to win his parent's praise, Wally pressed his advantage. The artist told of one incident that suggests the degree of competition between brother and sister at recitals. Angie had played poorly, and, "when it was all over I'd . . . rush up to her and say 'Angie, did you play that *bad!* You hit a clinker. It was awful! Let me show you how it should go,'" he recounted. "Then I'd play it right there in front of all the people." The episode ended with his sister's tears, his mother's anger, and his own complete identification with his father. He had, indeed, become Salvatore Liberace. "I couldn't help it," he concluded coolly. "Like my Dad I'm a perfectionist. I want to see that everything is done properly."[41]

The great showman as an adult left other even more compelling evidence of his close, if warped identity with his parent. His earliest memory revolved around his father. He remembered his age as two; Salvatore had taken the toddler to work with him. In the early twenties, the era of vaudeville and silent films, the transplanted Neapolitan musician played in the orchestra that accompanied the movies in one of the great old theaters of Milwaukee, the Alhambra. The little boy was there so often "that it almost became a second home to me," he related. "I spent many hours each day sitting in the first row engrossed in the happenings on the stage, while Dad watched me out of the corner of his eye from the pit, which he called 'the hole.' Between shows he'd come and get me and take me with him to the orchestra room where his fellow musicians, who were not involved in the continual card game that is always going on in an orchestra room, would take a little time to play with 'Boo-Loo.' That was Dad's nickname for me. Why he called me that even he couldn't remember."

The memory is significant because it establishes Liberace's father as central in his life, making Salvatore the primary—if distracted—nurse or caregiver, imagining a "second home," and configuring that home as a world of theater, men, and music. The memory becomes more significant, however, in the particular context in which Liberace related it, for this general recollection prologued a second, much more explicit memory. It involved Liberace's discovery of both himself and the world simultaneously, and only his very late acknowledgment of the presence of females in his otherwise all-male cosmos.

The memoirist launched into the other episode immediately after recounting the scene in the orchestra pit at the Alhambra Theater. "But there were times when conditions were such that Dad couldn't take 'Boo-Loo' with him," he began the second narrative. Unable to care for the child, the father turned over his responsibilities not to his wife but to his daughter. Only six years older than the baby, however, at one point Angie became so engrossed in her play that she forgot about her brother, and he wandered off, walking twenty blocks to the Wisconsin State Fairgrounds that lay in the north part of West Allis. "The music and happy noises that rise from any fair attracted me," he related, and "for a little while I lived in the beautiful world of sights, sounds and smells that make a wonderful place of any fair or amusement park."

When the park security discovered him, the officers interrogated the two-year-old, and he reconstructed his baby answers in a way that related

back to his earlier experience with his father at the theater. He identified himself specifically as his father's child: "What's your name, sonny?"
the officer asked. The child repeated his father's name for him—"Boo-
Loo"—and the dialogue continued:

> "What is your Daddy's name?"
> "I don't know."
> "What does your Momma call you?"
> "My Mama calls me kid."
> "What does your Daddy do?"
> "He plays a toot-toot."
> "Where does he play the toot-toot?"
> "In the hole."

After describing his parents' anxiety, Liberace concluded the memory by
relating a triumphant episode before his return home: "The reunion was
preceded by one of the happiest times of my life. What two-year-old kid
wouldn't find sheer, unadulterated joy, riding through the streets of his
home town sitting in the sidecar of a police motorcycle?"

If Liberace's association with his father were not apparent enough
from the body of the memory itself, the tale's coda, which juxtaposes the
two stories against his own discovery of music, emphasizes it even more.
"It was not long after my unscheduled visit to the Wisconsin State Fair
that I discovered the upright piano in our living quarters," he concluded,
and the rest, he implied, was history.[42]

That the episode might not have happened exactly as he remembered
it is beside the point. As he structures it, the memory amplifies the intimate relationship—in his own sense of things—between his father, the
"beautiful world of sights, sounds and smells," and his own career. It contrasts the shadowy images of his mother and the irresponsibility of his
sister with a colorful, sensuous, public world of men, art, adventure, and
performance. In one respect, the story turns the toddler into his father.
Wally became Salvatore, the performer in the policeman's sidecar. And
Wally as Salvatore, not to mention Salvatore as Salvatore, was not an ordinary being.

But Wally Liberace had a mother, too. This Polish peasant woman
was altogether as demanding as her husband. She had her own ambitions
and her own ambitions for her children. She wanted material security
first, and with it practicality—in contrast to her husband's financial insol-
vency and high-flown notions about artiste-ery. Her admonitions about
business and selling groceries gave verbal form to her goals. Her daily life
confirmed the same sentiments as she sawed and hammered on the front

porch, organized the grocery goods in what otherwise would have been her living room, and, during the Great Depression, trudged off to work in a cookie factory while her husband listened to Geraldine Farrar on his Victrola or played penny-ante poker with fellow musicians in the orchestra pit of the Alhambra. If her activities offered a countermodel, they implied reproach as well, but Frances Zuchowski was not one to suffer in silence and do her duty. Lacking subtlety and generosity, she vented her resentments freely. Hence the rancorous arguments her children remembered. Locked in battle with her husband, she looked for allies in her offspring. Her behavior gave rise to other tensions in the family.

While her husband's deportment generated angry rivalries among the siblings, so did hers. Narrow and manipulative, she did not merely compete with her husband for her children's allegiance; she spawned more rivalries among the four, playing favorites, and endlessly controlling them. She did so even as she entered her dotage. The showman's most famous lover, Scott Thorson, witnessed the performance even when Frances was in her eighties. He marveled at her performance with her superstar child. "She knew exactly how to manipulate him," he wrote. After one sojourn with her and her son, he mused that "She played him even better than he played the piano." "She dominated them as youngsters," Thorson believed, "and she continued to dominate them as adults. On occasion, I actually saw her poke them with her cane to get their attention. . . . Frances could be a sweet old lady one minute and a merciless nag the next." Quoting her celebration of Lee as a baby, he confirmed that her caul-born child was always her favorite; Lee himself concurred and considered the favoritism and inequity the source of his sister's and brothers' resentment.[43]

All this wrangling seemed to affect Angie—and later, Rudy—the most, while George escaped the worst consequences of both sibling and parental rivalries. Indeed, George's younger brother memorialized him as "the great arbitrator, the great keeper of the peace among us children," "a force for good in the musical feuds over the piano." For whatever reason, the eldest son also played the same role with both Frances and Salvatore. He managed to please each without antagonizing the other. Perhaps his birth and babyhood at the beginning of their marriage represented an easier time for his parents, while the couple's hostility grew yearly when his siblings were growing up. "His music lessons always met Dad's approval and, what's more, he pleased Mom by pretending to be interested in the grocery business," his brother wrote. Suggesting the riptides of their domestic life, however, (and perhaps something of his own jealousy at his brother's ease, too) the memoirist added immediately, "I say 'pretending to be interested' because if he really had been he'd have gone into it instead of becoming a musician." [44]

Long after the world-famous entertainer had abandoned his Walter/ Wally identity, family, to a large degree, continued to play an important role in his life and in shaping his public self. He provided his siblings jobs and support; he showered them with gifts and benefices; he employed them in his entourage; he made them a part of his act—indeed, during the height of his career, he integrated his mother and elder brother so thoroughly into his performance that they became a part of his persona. Familial duty played the most active role in his character, but the crosscurrents and paradoxes of Fifty-first Street in West Allis persisted in the glory days of Hollywood and Las Vegas. The tensions and ambiguities about his mother and father permeated his life.

In public, he identified himself so closely with his mother that the association became inseparable from his public life. His critics, especially in the fifties, regularly used the relationship as prima facie evidence of the performer's decadence. While his critics identified has as a "Mama's Boy," a euphemism for queer and sissy, he harbored the most conflicted passions toward his mother. If he loved and respected her, he left evidence of equally potent resentment of this yokel dowager whom he himself had helped invent. He confided to Scott Thorson that he considered his mother's attitude as "completely suffocating and damn near incestuous." He was past sixty when Frances died in 1980 at almost ninety. Only with her death did he profess to escape her influence. "I'm finally free," he confessed in his only reference to her passing. [45]

His relationship with Salvatore, if anything, was more complicated still. His autobiography hints at its labyrinthine qualities, which he himself seemed to understand only partially. He memorialized over and over his debts to his father, his identity with his parent, his psychological kinship. Despite these testimonies, however, he broke with his father in 1940 and never reestablished cordial relations. For over a decade, he failed even to speak to Sam Liberace. A reunion arranged by a mutual friend, Steve Swedish, in 1953 left no evidence of altering the performer's public or private attitudes. [46] Even then, their reunion was engineered in secret, with arrangements being made for Sam to perform in the orchestra at one of his son's concerts. The son was not at all pleased with the surprise. [47] Twenty years had failed to soften the force of his rejection.

Reflecting on the psychological interpretation of homosexuality that ascribes the condition to a boy's obsession with his mother and hatred of his father, Scott Thorson related how Liberace believed those circumstances described his own life perfectly: "Lee said he had the perfect parents to blame."[48] If the circumstances of his life were more complicated than Liberace might have known, they were infinitely more complicated than his still-adolescent boyfriend could recognize, and the performer's attitude toward his father played a direct role in his affairs with a string of young lovers, not least Scott Thorson himself.

But all this—fame, wealth, lovers, and a gay world—lay impossibly far from the smiling American village of West Allis in 1926.

In those days we had a long, open porch across the front of the house. The kids would pass by and hear him practicing. They'd yell all kinds of names at him. They called him a sissy because he preferred the piano to baseball and football.

ANGIE LIBERACE

THE GREAT ESCAPE

The undated newspaper photograph captures a child dressed for a play. He is wearing caveman garb, a fur-like garment worn toga style across one shoulder. Barefoot, he kneels, holding a spearlike section of bamboo. Behind him, a little girl rests her hand on his right shoulder while directing his attention to some object out of the frame. Caught in full profile, he shows a sharp nose and a more sharply pointed chin. With his slender, well-shaped arms and legs, he is very thin, but even pretty, for a boy.

The pointed chin and nose came from the Zuchowskis, but the snap fails to show the full, naturally dark lips his father had passed on to him. Serious and unsmiling in his outlandish getup, the image also reveals nothing of the deep dimples that creased his cheeks with every grin. The exact circumstances of the photograph are not clear, but in it, Wally Liberace looks to be around nine.[1] The year was probably 1928, perhaps early 1929, although it may have been a year earlier. Whether it was 1927, '28, or early '29, however, this was a notable time for the boy in the picture. These years were hardly free of problems of one kind or another for Sam and Frances Liberace's family, but the eve of the Great Crash was as close as the Liberaces ever got to bliss. It began with the move from West Allis to West Milwaukee, less than a mile away on National Avenue. In 1926, his mother had abandoned the living-room grocery business, and the family had left its fifteen-year residence on Fifty-first Street, and bought a house on National Avenue across from the National Soldiers Home. They were moving up in the world.

The move to 4301 National Avenue resolved some of tensions of the Liberaces' domestic life, even as it represented other improvements already taking place. Fifteen-year-old George, thirteen-year-old Angie, and Wally, their seven-year-old brother, now had much more space than they'd had in the original house; the new place must have seemed a mansion in comparison. Though not grand, the house was far from small. Occupying a corner lot, the house, with its half second floor and basement, contained probably two thousand square feet of living space. It even boasted modest luxuries, like the small stained-glass window that still graces the living room.

Not only was the house more spacious, but the quality of the space was much improved, too. Everyone was glad to be free of the groceries. "I guess the most wonderful thing about our new home was that you didn't have to walk through a grocery store to get into it," the youngest child remembered. "It was, as my friends in England would say, 'a proper house.'" It was a good house. His mother demonstrated her culinary skills in not one but two kitchens. While she cooked for company on the main floor, for every day, Frances preferred the basement kitchen, where she "cooked on a great big coal stove and kept things fresh in an old-fashioned icebox, which hadn't as yet become old fashioned." Between 1926 and the Great Crash, Sal worked more steadily than before or after, and Frances played proper housewife in her proper house. Extremely neat and tidy, she made the house sparkle, according to her son. In her one concession to the arts, she "made sure there were real lace curtains in the windows and kept old-fashioned lace antimacassars on the arms and the backs of all the chairs so that people's hands and the oil from their hair wouldn't soil the upholstery." Sal loved gardening, and the yard delighted him. His son remembered his lilac bushes in particular, the house being filled with their fragrance in May, around his birthday. "I don't want anybody to think that we didn't have nice neighbors, but our house stood out from all the others," the entertainer boasted long afterwards.[2]

The house was new, too. All the houses in the triangle area between National Avenue and Beloit Road, running east-west, and Fifty-sixth Street, which ran north-south, had been constructed within the preceding two or three years before 1926. Some were larger than others, but all boasted amenities like sun porches or small gardens colorful with summer flowers. Although National Avenue was even busier than Fifty-first Street, it had advantages the other thoroughfare lacked. All these houses looked out on the beautiful, rolling grounds of the National Soldiers Home with its huge trees, old even when Wally Liberace saw them through his window across the street.

The Liberaces had moved to a thoroughly middle-class neighborhood of the upwardly mobile, and the mere fact that they could afford such a place indicates a major shift in their fortunes. The house was a step up in two ways. First, the family now owned a comfortable house in a nice neighborhood, in contrast to the cottage they had previously shared with potatoes and canned goods; second, they could now number themselves among a minority of Americans anywhere in the country who owned any real property at all. In 1926, probably less than 40 percent of U.S. residents were property owners. The new neighborhood shared many characteristics of the old, however. No less than the community at large, the quiet streets that gridded the area between National and Beloit were peopled by a diversity of inhabitants. The names spoke volumes: Lymans, Dodges, Pritchards, and Hanleys passed Grabeks, Skacels, and Dobrotinseks on the way to work, school, or church; these in turn lived no farther away from Arseneuses, Nelesens, Kissingers, Haerles, and Hipschmanns. This part of the community was as self-contained as Fifty-first Street. The stretch of National Avenue near the Home offered everything from gasoline stations and barbershops to grocery stores and tailors. Then, as now, it boasted plenty of taverns and eateries, although no one was buying legal beer in the twenties.[3] George and Angie could walk to high school, while Pershing Elementary School, where their little brother enrolled in the first grade, was only two blocks from the Liberaces' back door. St. Florian's Church, where Angie had been christened, was only a couple of blocks beyond the primary school.

In his memory, the world-famous pianist always associated his childhood with material deprivation, but the record does not sustain this judgment, or not completely. The early years on National Avenue were even bountiful. Visits to his maternal grandparents, Frank and Anna Zuchowski, in the country added to the pleasure of these times. Menasha lay 100 miles away on hard country roads, and the trip in the family Ford provided an occasion for adventure in itself. "And that it survived the roads of rural Wisconsin should stand as testimony to the greatness of American automotive engineering," the memoirist added. While his father had rustled up the vehicle in some unknown way, Liberace also noted pointedly that his mother did all the driving.[4]

Frank and Anna Zuchowski lived in a tidy gabled house with a large summer porch off the rear wing on land adequate for gardens and livestock.[5] All was not completely well on their farm; much later, the entertainer made passing reference to his grandparents "having difficulty and facing divorce."[6] As his memoir scants his grandfather, failing even to offer his name, the other remark suggests that Frank Zuchowski might have been as difficult as Liberace's own father. He was, in any case, as revealed in photographs, gangling and lanky, with a huge, 1880s-type drooping mustache.[7] Liberace's grandmother was quite different. A tiny woman with hair pulled back in a tight little bun, she was the focus of the boy's devotion on those visits in the country. Beyond the troubling grandfather, farm life delighted him. He recalled it with unalloyed pleasure. "Grandmother raised chickens and cared for a marvelous kitchen garden. Grandfather took care of the pigs, a couple of cows and an old horse that was in about the same class as our Ford. There were fragrant fruit trees everywhere. From there and the harvest from her garden, Grandmother used to put up 'goodies' for the winter. But, looking back, I can't imagine how she had any left by the time winter arrived." While a considerable portion of the Zuchowskis' preserves bounced and jounced back to West Milwaukee in the Liberaces' Ford, Mrs. Zuchowski also used her larder to fatten up her city-bred grandchildren. "I was a very skinny little kid, and Mom found that our visits to Grandmother's house were not only fun for me but healthful as well. In this Grandmother concurred and collaborated," the musician reflected. "I always managed to gain a few important pounds at her urging. Her favorite expression, at least the one I heard her use most, was 'Yitz, yitz, liebchen' . . . 'Eat, eat, dear child.' And eat I did! I loved my grandmother and I couldn't refuse her anything."[8]

The absence of electricity, running water, and other modern conveniences might have posed a hardship for the family, but their very lack added to the "fascination, the glamour of the place" for the city grandchildren. "We loved the scent of oil lamps and the aroma that came from the stove . . . ," the grandson wrote much later. A cistern of fresh rainwater for washing hair intrigued him, while the mysteries of the barn galvanized his imagination. Also, unlike the strictures that surrounded his life in West Milwaukee, Menasha had "no restrictions on what we could or could not do or where we might go on the farm and we got into all kinds of scrapes, falling out of hay mows, being kicked by cows, learning about life. . . ."[9]

The halcyon days lasted three years. They vanished with the stock market crash in October 1929. By the time prosperity returned after the war, the economic insecurities of over a decade and a half had changed the Liberace family completely and had insinuated themselves irrevocably into the American psyche.

It is not possible to overemphasize the impact of the Great Depression on a whole generation of Americans. Sam's and Frances's family is representative. The Liberace children's age group bore its brunt: born in 1911, George was eighteen when it hit, Angie was sixteen, Wally, ten, and as a child the youngest, Rudy, born in 1931, knew nothing but its deprivation. This was Richard Nixon's generation, Lyndon Johnson's, Ronald Reagan's. It was John Kennedy's, too, only his father's immense wealth spared him its scars. Almost no one escaped unscathed. As chronicled most graphically in *Let Us Now Praise Famous Men* by Walker Evans and James Agee, few suffered as much as did the Southern poor, who were at the mudsill even before the crash. Southerners, however, had been bred on social and religious fatalism at least since the Civil War, and they had planted pessimism with their first crops of tobacco, corn, and cotton. Among industrial workers, craftsmen, and new immigrants of the North, the circumstance was different. Having partaken of an American promise denied Southern sharecroppers, the exigencies of the thirties seemed unjust, anomalous, and even un-American. It prompted not the sharecroppers' fatal acceptance but increased energy and labor, commitment and belief. This circumstance also helps account for the kind of home-brewed radicalism and corn-fed communism the era witnessed in the United States—and in which West Allis and Allis-Chalmers labor unions developed a remarkable share. Thus ran the logic: if prosperity and progress were American benefits, their denial was therefore un-American, so immigrant communists could be more American, as it were, than native-born capitalists. The identification of progress, prosperity, and the American way also contributed significantly to the collapse of socialism with the economic recovery after the war, and the ease with which even arch-radicals—not to mention the rank and file—slipped into the suburbs and suburban life in the fifties and after.

The effects of the Depression, however, lasted long, long after economic recovery. The catastrophe still echoes in the lives of the men and women who endured it over half a century after the panic closed its last bank. Deprivation produced various effects. It made some mean, mercenary, and guarded; in others it nurtured profligacy. Postwar cultural phenomena even combined the two. Liberace, it goes without saying, represented the tendency toward prodigality. While his excesses can be read, then, as a function of his deprivations as a boy, his profound audience appeal reflects aspects of this generational influence as well. Actually, his appeal suggests a coming together of the opposing tendencies of the Depression: millions in his age cohort found his extremes gratifying even when they could not or would not go to his limits of consumption. Different combinations of these diverse responses to the Depression echoed through the fifties and sixties in still other ways. They help account for peculiarities of the Baby Boomer generation, for example. If the parents were deprived, they would sacrifice for their sons and daughters, who would not know want. The self-indulgence of young men and women of the sixties and seventies was one result. Even the Baby Boomers' rejection of standards, style, and convention coursed through Liberace's later career and underlined a generational split in his appeal. In any event, the Great Depression was the watershed for America—and for the Liberace family on National Avenue, West Milwaukee, Wisconsin.

In 1929, no one could have foreseen the hard times that would set in during the winter of 1929–30. At the time, the focus was on immediate problems. In the Liberace household, Sam's work was the first to go. In the twenties, his employment, however unsteady, had enabled the family to buy the house on National Avenue. His income secured their status and guaranteed their material well being. The panic threatened it all. Coinciding with the depression, changing social customs redoubled his economic woes. The son explained: "Radio, which supplied free entertainment to people without the means to go to theater, cut down box office grosses all across the nation. This combined with sound pictures, a great novelty, began to cut the heart out of vaudeville." In the absence of concert work, Sam Liberace had lived off of this sort of theater performance. It ended. "Theaters didn't need musicians anymore. Live talent simply ceased to exist as far as cities like Milwaukee were concerned." [10] In an interview decades later, Angie related that her father was out of work for ten years after the Great Crash—except for a stint with the WPA Symphony in Milwaukee. [11] The senior Liberace never surrendered his title of "musician" in the city directory, but, according to his son, he returned to the temporary employment of the factories, with terrible consequences to his pride. [12] In factories or playing in WPA orchestras, however, he failed to pull his share of the family load. Even so, his unemployment did not prevent his macho antagonism toward others taking up the slack. "He began to do a lots of crazy little things, like hiding the alarm clock so my mother would be late for work and maybe lose her job," the entertainer wrote. "He didn't mean anything evil. It was just that he was such a proud man." [13]

It was bad for Frances, too. She had to leave the luxury of her two kitchens for factory work. She took a job at a local cookie company. Her life—and her family's—became still more complicated when, soon after the crash, she became pregnant, at nearly forty, with her fourth and last child. By the time of Rudy's birth in 1931, the movie idol Valentino was long gone from the scene, but naming her final child after the star suggests the harried mother's efforts to re-fire the ashes of a happier time. If that was her aim, it didn't work. On the contrary, the baby became something of a symbol of the family's financial and social disorder as the thirties wore on. [14] Long afterwards, Scott Thorson listened to the surviving Liberace siblings discuss these days, and he repeated their sentiments about the new child, Rudy: "In a happier household he would have been the baby and his mother's favorite. But Frances used to look at her youngest and say, 'You should never have been born. You're an accident!'"[15] On top of all this, her husband was trying to get her fired from her factory job.

If Rudy ultimately bore the brunt of the burdens, at the time, misfortune fell heavily on all the Liberace children. Want shoved each into the workplace. "All of us kids, except Rudy who was younger than I am and so was still too young to contribute to the family coffers, chipped in whatever we were able to earn," reported the pianist. George, entering his twenties, waited tables, taught violin, and played clubs before he left home in 1933 or '34. Angie, at eighteen, worked as a stenographer and by twenty earned a portion of the family income as a nurse's assistant in a local doctor's office. Besides turning his own musical interests to financial account, the second son also did a disastrous tour washing dishes. "We took whatever we could get," he said.[16] None of it sufficed, and they resorted to the dole. "I used to pick up the groceries from the relief station in a coaster wagon," the entertainer recalled, adding, "I hated it with a bitter passion."[17]

When he became famous, the showman joked about their poverty. In those days, he wore George's old clothes, which, he explained was not a joke, "because they weren't really hand-me-downs. He was also wearing them. We took turns." He also explained his adult love of luxury and finery in terms of his "humble beginnings," "the poverty I knew when I was a child," and in "psychological" compensation for "those drab surrounds of my youth and the dull clothing that was all we had."[18]

Other circumstances complicated the family's arrangements. By 1934, George had married and moved out with his bride, a singer at a spot where both he and his brother played, Sam Pick's Club Madrid on the outskirts of Milwaukee. Three years later, however, by 1937, the City Directory lists him again as a resident at the National Avenue house.[19] He returned minus the wife—the first of five spouses. If Rudy absorbed and refracted family tensions one way, George's serial monogamy suggests other evidence of the family's distress. The ins and outs of Frances's children, however, were nothing compared to her own new ins and outs with her husband. To add further fuel to her ancient dissatisfaction with Sam as breadwinner, spouse, and father, and to increase the burden of her Depression-era poverty, Frances now discovered that her husband was philandering.

Sometime in the mid- to late thirties, probably by the time Rudy had enrolled in the second grade in the fall of 1937, which was about the same time George returned home, their father, entering his fifties, began seeing another woman. A widow and musician, Zona Gale Smrz lived a couple of miles northeast of the Liberaces near the Marquette University campus. She played the cello and taught at the old Milwaukee-Downer College. If Sal had played around previously, this time he was serious. After the courts dissolved his union with Frances in 1941, he and Smrz wed in 1943, and they remained together until her death, twenty-seven years later.[20]

Reflecting on the affair long after, Liberace, the celebrity, added another dimension to his father's faithlessness and to the disruption of his parents' marriage. As a devout Catholic, he told Scott Thorson, his mother disapproved of divorce. "According to Lee," Thorson related, "she couldn't face the potential scandal, the disgrace that would follow the dissolution of her marriage. Frances didn't want the world to know that her husband had left her for another woman. She told her four children to keep the secret from everyone: playmates, neighbors, and friends."[21] Even if Frances might have drawn back from divorce initially, her husband's behavior—and her own bile—tipped her in the other direction by 1940.

Like Sal, she, too, would remarry, in 1943, but she neither forgot nor forgave her first husband. In the sixties, she scorned his efforts at peacemaking.[22] Her later resentment, however, paled beside her attitude in the years just preceding the divorce in 1940. A family friend related one version of her wrath. "Ma," as the neighbors called her, stopped by regularly to share coffee and spleen with John Hlaban and his wife. "One day Ma comes in," the neighbor reminisced, "says she's been to the lawyer about a divorce, says she tells the lawyer this, she tells the lawyer that, and finally the lawyer says, 'Doesn't your husband have any other name than that old bastard?'"[23] The formal complaints, even in legalese, capture some of Sal's offense against her—her lawyer noting that Salvatore "has thrown objects at her, failed to show any love or affection for her, stayed away from home for long periods of time, and failed to contribute any support for plaintiff and the minor child."[24]

After the early thirties, little relieved the bleakness of the Liberace household. The escape to the Zuchowskis' farm in Menasha had offered reprieve earlier, but this trip became increasingly difficult, especially after Rudy's birth. This left Christmases as almost the only leavening of the sodden lump of the Liberaces' lives in the dismal decade. When wealthy and famous later, Liberace made the holiday grand indeed and explained his "extra special love" as stemming "from my childhood in the lean years when we always managed to pull ourselves up by our financial bootstraps and enjoy some of the things we had deprived ourselves of all year. . . . I don't know how they did it, but somehow my Mother and Father managed to provide us kids with everything we had to do without," he reminisced.[25]

They invested pleasure in the smallest amenities. When his mother worked at the cookie factory, she brought home bags of rejects for her children. Angie and Wally spent the holiday "decorating them and disguising the imperfections, and icing them in various ways to make them look festive." Just so, enchantment surrounded even mundane gifts. "I remember," he reflected, "being absolutely elated over getting a new pair of shoes or a pair of sox without any darns in them."[26] It was not an uncommon story for a Depression Era child.

As a man, Liberace also made it clear that the season ameliorated more than material deprivations. The Liberace children's poverty was emotional as much as physical; Christmas provided respite. Betraying the normal absence of affection in the household, he insisted that he cherished the season "because of the love that was lavished on us children at Christmas." He credited his parents' efforts: "During my childhood in the Depression years, when both Mom and Dad were working, it took a lot of getting together, of loving and sharing to make Christmas the memorable occasion it always turned out to be," he wrote. Indeed, "the giving and receiving of loving thoughtfulness" dominated his early recollections of the season. "Our family forgot all the little quarrels every family has during a lifetime and we were happy together."[27]

Yet even this blessed season brought its troubles for Wally Liberace. Poverty prohibited elaborate playthings, but some few toys found their way beneath the tree each year. And the family maximized its minimums by carrying these treasures over from one Christmas to the next to be hauled out again and used as decorations. From year to year, the collection grew slowly but steadily. The second son treasured these luxuries. The plan disintegrated with the birth of his younger brother. "You can imagine how I felt when my toys, that had come down to me from George and Angie, were finally given to Rudy," he wrote. "It wasn't that I didn't want Rudy to have them. It was that little Rudy seemed to have a built-in destruction mechanism when it came to playthings. Things we had enjoyed for years lasted only a few minutes when Rudy went to work on them," he grieved. "I remember being in my late teens and actually shedding tears at seeing some of my most cherished childhood possessions disintegrate before my very eyes." His complaints brought no relief; they even precipitated rebuke. He was too old to play with them anyway, his parents scolded. "Nevertheless, when my parents weren't looking, I tried to glue some of the broken pieces together."[28]

At best, then, even the season's gifts and his parents' cessation of hostilities for the holidays did not redress the liabilities at 4301 National Avenue. The Liberaces' second son had a peculiar need for compensation. He was different from the others from the very beginning.

With his dead brother and his caul, Wally Liberace had begun life different. The anomalies increased with time. While surviving photographs from the early twenties reveal a hearty, round-faced toddler of three or four, by the time he was ready to enter school, he had endured major sicknesses. "He was always a tiny sickly kid and he missed a lot of school," his sister remembered. "He had one siege of pneumonia after another. There were many times when my folks despaired of his life." He himself also referred to his illnesses, repeating that he was undersized as a boy as a result of a severe case of pneumonia when he was young.[29] The illnesses and reputation of illnesses served to exaggerate his uniqueness in the family circle. They help account, too, for other family stories of his mother's and grandmother's special affection and favoritism toward him. The worst was past by the time he reached the third or fourth grade, when his "cave boy" picture appeared in the Milwaukee *Sentinel*. He does not look unhealthy, but he was reed thin—certainly not the chubby toddler of his earliest photographs.

Still other elements distinguished the child. From the time he uttered his first words up through his adolescence, he had his own most peculiar way of speaking. Later, he compared his speech with the way Lawrence Welk spoke. While he attributed the peculiarity to the curious inflections of his father's Italian-influenced English and his mother's Polish accent, none of his siblings shared the pattern. His speech was so unusual that his recitations always evoked his schoolmates' derision, even though most shared comparably mixed ethnic backgrounds. He also revealed, in his autobiography, that he could not pronounce his own name until he was thirteen years old. By the time he started school, the idiosyncrasy was so severe that his father looked for professional help. "Lee was about 7 or 8 when Sam came up to me after a rehearsal and told me he was worried about his boy," the family friend Steve Swedish told a reporter. "Lee couldn't talk well." Swedish suggested that the child might be "tongue-tied," and Salvatore visited a physician to have the skin beneath the boy's tongue clipped. It didn't help. Swedish, who had recommended the physician, also thought that the problem lay in the boy speaking so fast "that the words would get jumbled up." So he also recommended a speech therapist, Fr. Raphael Hamilton at Marquette University. Hamilton worked with the boy for seven years, according to the family friend, "giving him exercises to slow his speech and make it clearer." In an interview in 1987, after the pianist's death, Swedish explained to the reporter, "'What he did was make Lee concentrate on his vowels,' Swedish said, performing a creditable imitation of the Liberace speech pattern. 'You see? It was Father Hamilton who gave Liberace his personality.'"[30] The performer's mincing, nasal Midwestern-Wisconsin accent became a hallmark, but by the time he reached the age of fifteen, around 1934, the most notable eccentricities of his speaking had disappeared. He recorded that at this time, one of his favorite teachers, Sylvia Becker, suggested that he enroll in a special summer course, which finally seemed to solve the worst of his speech problems.[31]

Besides his speech, his manners and habits marked him. As a boy, he disliked sports and the rough-and-tumble games his peers played. "It wasn't that I had anything against the games," he wrote in his autobiography. "It was just that you got dirty playing them. I didn't like that." Preferring the indoors, he made a virtue of more domestic pastimes. His father as well as his mother cooked, and from a very early age, he also took to the kitchen. He not only cooked, he cooked festively. As an adult, he related how his father, even at the height of the Depression, prepared food pleasant to see as well as satisfying to consume. The son followed the model. Decorating the defective baked goods from Johnston's Cookie Factory at Christmas served the same purpose. He sewed, too. "While the boys I played with made model cars and model airplanes, I liked to make things out of fabrics I found lying around. For example, if a nice piece of cloth came to hand, I'd figure out how I could fit it to one of our chairs that needed recovering." On another occasion, he taught his mother to execute one of his millinery designs, which won high praise from her friends.[32]

Queer in speech and habit as a boy, Wally Liberace soon enough discovered other meanings of queer. "He said he'd always known he wasn't like other boys, but he'd never been able to label the difference," reported Scott Thorson.[33] The neighborhood knew the label. Pershing Elementary School lay just around the corner from the Liberaces', and the children on their way to school shouted their epithets, his sister recalled. "They'd yell all kinds of names at him. They called him a sissy."[34] By age ten, he began having crushes on his male teachers, he later told his friend, and the classic phenomena of boyhood homosexuality began kicking in. Terror wrestled with guilt in the prepubescent boy. The social stigma of being queer/homosexual or merely different horrified him, even as he more or less innocently continued his cooking, decorating, music, and lisping. Not only was he alienated from his peers, he feared he might be insane, as well: "He had to be crazy, sick, out of his mind, he thought, to be attracted to men," Thorson later recollected.[35] Religion offered consolation even as it exaggerated his miseries. Indeed, the church influenced the boy in the profoundest and most various ways. It affected his attitudes about sexuality, but, more grandly, it provided a general focus for his life both as a boy and as a man. Along with Midwestern working-class culture, the peculiar circumstances of his home life, and the Great Depression, Catholicism was the fourth important social element that shaped his character and his values.

He got double doses of the faith—one at the hearth and one at the altar. The brand of religion that he inherited from his parents was a peculiar one. Beyond the specific manifestations of their faith, Salvatore Liberace and Frances Zuchowski represented singular forms of Catholicism that contrasted with the Irish-dominated American Church. Italian Catholicism tended toward a passionate and aesthetic expression of faith, while the Polish variety emphasized conservative personal devotion. If the two branches stressed different varieties of mysticism, both contrasted with the doctrinal purity and prophetic dogmatism of the Irish clerics. The conservative, even superstitious piety of the Poles stayed with Liberace to the end of his life, and the festive faith of Naples influenced him as powerfully.

The Liberace children might have absorbed such values around their dinner table, but their actual churchgoing focused and institutionalized their faith. St. Florian's was their parish church. Angie had been christened there on February 15, 1914, when the family had lived a mile away in West Allis.[36] The church was only three blocks away from the new house on National Avenue. It was almost as new as the neighborhood itself. With its attached Carmelite cloister, the church had been built in 1912. Executed in a stripped-down Romanesque style, it sprouted twin towers at the front and a long, simple east-west nave. Like the fancy high school, it lent a touch of elegance to the neighborhood. The structure lacked the grandeur and richness of the great churches in downtown Milwaukee, but the marble columns flanking the altar and, most of all, the brilliant windows that lined the nave, suggested the mystery of the Eucharist, the majesty of Rome, and the power and nobility of ancient Catholic tradition. The subjects of the windows, like St. Florian, the patron of the parish, were an unusual and mixed lot. Besides St. Florian himself, depicted in the first fenestration to the right as one left the altar, the windows honored St. Theresa, St. John of the Cross, St. Mary Magdalene, and St. Albert; the north side of the church depicted St. Joseph, St. Teresa, St. Simon Stock, St. Anne, and St. Richard.

The spectacle of the mass as celebrated in this sensuous environment left a permanent impression on Wally Liberace. With an eye already turned to color and design, he admired the brilliant vestments, which changed with the seasons, that the servers of the mass wore each Sunday. In normal seasons, the priests' gowns and chasubles were celebratory enough, but at Easter or Christmas and on other high holy days the clerics blossomed into a vested splendor that Walter remembered forever. The candelabrum, one of the first objects he used to add glamour to his image, was a silent tribute to the votive lights at St. Florian's altar, even as his exuberant costumes paid tribute to the priests of his childhood. Wally Liberace grew up with all this—literally—spectacular evidence of faith.

Later in life, the showman played fast and loose with doctrinal purity, but early on he derived critical lessons from the church. Beyond his mother's simple piety, which he never lost, his appreciation of the church was more aesthetic than theological. The showiness and spectacle of the mass, and Catholicism's traditional appeal to the senses, he considered a fundamental source of the religion's power. "The Catholic Church has never lost sight of this," he insisted: Catholics "value the mystery of flickering candles, the glory of statuary and art. They know a ceiling by Michelangelo surpasses any other ceiling there is. They know that people want to escape into another kind of world." [37]

Did he theorize as an adult about people's need to escape the mundane? During his childhood, throughout the Great Depression, Catholicism was the one thing that never failed Wally in its ability to transcend the grind of the everyday. The glory and serenity of the mass compensated to some degree for the strictures and deprivations in his home. But the church exerted other sources of appeal, as well. It offered other consolations; it even held a resolution of his sexual nightmares. "I once thought I ought to become a priest," he related in his memoir. [38] Wally Liberace was neither the first nor last gay boy to consider this track. One scholar has summarized the attraction:

> Catholicism in particular is famous for giving countless gay
> and proto-gay children the shock of the possibility of adults
> who don't marry, of men in dresses, of passionate theatre, of
> introspective investment, of lives filled with what could, ide-
> ally without diminution, be called the work of the fetish. . . .
> And presiding over all are the images of Jesus. These have,
> indeed, a unique position in modern culture as images of the
> unclothed or unclothable male body, often in extremis and/or
> in ecstasy, prescriptively meant to be gazed at and adored. [39]

If no one questioned priests' rejection of marriage and women, the church served as more than an elaborate beard; indeed, the total prohibitions against clerical sexuality offered special comfort and support for boys fighting a sexuality deemed deviant. Giving up sex meant giving up a form of sex especially abhorred in Rome: it was a solution that offered a double benefit.

Catholicism might have provided one way out of his homosexual dilemma, but it exaggerated the problem in other ways. Catholic doctrine, with its strictures against same-sex coupling, in particular, afflicted this youth as it has innumerable Catholic gay boys. The novelist John Rechy captured the torment in his *Sexual Outlaw:*

> You had to tell your "trespasses" to a faceless, whispering
> voice that kept insisting, "How many times did you commit
> that sin? How many times?" Locked in guilt even when you
> had no cause to feel guilty. After confession and fasting, came
> the Sunday morning purification. Communion! You knelt to
> receive the wafer that was the precious body of Christ. It was
> all over so quickly, especially since there had been so much
> agony in confession and fasting! And you knew that soon, too
> soon, you'd be huddled kneeling guiltily in the darkness
> again before that mysterious little screen window of the con-
> fessional and addressing the faceless presence: "Bless me fa-
> ther, Father, for I have sinned." [40]

Like the boy John Rechy, Wally Liberace prayed. He pleaded for divine intervention. "Lee told me he prayed for a miracle, something to alter him so that he could look at girls with the same lust they inspired in other boys," Thorson wrote. St. Jude was deaf; the ivory-skinned figure on the cross was another naked man. Intensely religious, the boy hated the idea of avoiding mass, communion, and confession. Rejecting the faith never seemed to cross his mind, but his homosexual longings were as obdurate as church doctrine itself. "No matter how hard he tried, curiosity about the mysteries of sex, and his own sexuality, obsessed him." He could not confess, yet he sinned, he felt, in failing to do so. "He was damned if he did and damned if he didn't," Thorson said Liberace had told him. [41]

Here he was then, skinny little Wally Liberace, his family surviving on public charity, the National Avenue house an armed camp. Yelling broke the nights' silence, his parents hurled objects at one another, and the siblings were at war with each other for crumbs of affection. His speech impediment generated snickers from his classmates, and his habits invited their taunts. On top of this, he discovered himself lusting after other males. What of the caul-born child's good fortune? Curses seemed his fate, instead.

Music offered a singular kind of solace amid this chaos that, unlike the joys of Christmas, was neither seasonal nor temporary. It offered none of Catholicism's censorship, either. The piano became a way of life, a refuge from the shabbiness of his existence, the disorder of family conflict, and his inner demons. It pulled him to another world, even as his difficulties encouraged him to flee. His music was the great escape, but in the context of genius and talent, it became something else, as well. It had possessed a transforming power long before he began fretting over his parents' squabbles or his lust for other males. He was a prodigy; he possessed prodigious talent, prodigious will, prodigious ambition to make a musical career.

Wladziu Valentino Liberace had been born to music. By 1919, his elder brother had been playing the piano for five years, and his sister Angie for three, and the tones of his father's horn reached the baby's cradle, too. He took his first steps to the rhythms of Caruso, Galli Curci, Giovanni Martinelli, Geraldine Farrar, and Paderewski in the background. He was programmed with music, scheduled, like his siblings, to begin lessons at age four. He didn't wait.

The first manifestation of his genius is legendary. The main story, repeated over and over with some variation, changed little in essence over time. In an early interview with his sister, a journalist recorded Angie's recollection that "at 3, little Walter was playing the battered family upright by ear. His sister will never forget that first tune: 'Yes, We Have No Bananas.'" "You could never keep him off that piano bench," she reflected. "He'd just brush you aside."[42] In his autobiography, Liberace cited the recollections of Angie and his mother to confirm that he was playing while still in diapers. "As soon as I could reach the keyboard, I played whatever I heard her practice . . . and accurately!" Long before he was able to read music, he could play anything perfectly by ear. He was so gifted, the story ran, that Angelina fooled her parents by letting her toddler brother play her lessons in her stead, when they weren't looking. With Frances listening to make sure her daughter was practicing, Angie would "skip out to play baseball or something with the kids and I'd carry on with her practicing."[43]

Wally possessed an extraordinary, natural gift of being able to replicate the sounds he heard. Taking over Angie's practicing offered only one evidence of his talent. Angelina described another when she recounted an incident that took place during the same period, around 1926. "I remember when I was 13 I spent a whole year memorizing 17 pages of

'Midsummer Night's Dream.' One day Lee . . . climbed up on the piano bench and asked me what I was doing. I told him," she related. " 'Here, give that to me,' he said. 'I'll show you how it's done.' It took him a day to look over that music — then he sat down and played it through perfectly. Imagine how I felt! A little 7 year old kid showing me up! I think he has a photographic mind." [44]

He was a prodigy. His father knew it, and he treated him accordingly.

The exact date varies depending on the source, but around the age of three or four, Wally began formal piano instruction. Here is Angie's version, with a special twist: "He was 4 when my dad decided to break him of playing by ear and started giving him piano lessons. Dad taught all of us to play the piano." [45] After less than a year or so, Sam Liberace determined that the child needed more professional direction, and he enrolled him with a local teacher, a Mrs. Martin, with whom the boy studied for four years. [46]

By around 1926, when he was seven or so, he played better than his own teacher. He learned a long Mendelssohn piece by memory after only a couple of days study. By the time he was in first or second grade, he had also developed very clear ideas about proper playing. This was a critical juncture in his musical career; it was also the point at which a major series of events transformed his life. For one thing, the family bought the new house and moved.

In his memoir, Liberace described the relocation to National Avenue as an epochal event. Leaving the grocery-store house on Fifty-first for the new place on National Avenue was "an overwhelming experience," he wrote. He identified the move as the watershed of his boyhood. "It's a traumatic experience to a child, the first time he has to say good-bye to everything he's learned to associate with his security," he related. "But while it is difficult saying farewell to old friends and familiar things it's full of the adventure of finding new friends and exploring new surroundings. All this is an example of how deeply I was affected by our first move." [47] The recollection is curious. In the first place, it was not the first time the family had moved, but the second in the space of a couple of years. In addition, Liberace gave every indication of how happy otherwise he and his clan were to relocate. As for leaving old friends, he left no other record of having had any; on the contrary, all the evidence affirms that he was a solitary child from the beginning: he played indoors and did not go out. Finally, however, if it seems an exaggeration to describe the relocation to a much better place only a mile away as a "trauma," other unsettling things were going on in the boy's life, and he might have focused on the move as troubling him instead of on those other difficulties. He does not make the association, but the family moved around the time he entered school, which was also the period during which he endured his sieges with pneumonia. The move and his bout of illness together seem to have cost him the grade he lost in school. Meanwhile, his father had become so concerned about the little boy's speech impediment that he was taking his son to doctors, therapists, and even surgeons. While none of these details are included in his memoir, he describes other milestones of this period explicitly.

For one thing, he experienced an aesthetic revelation at this age. It centered on the Polish patriot-pianist, Ignacy Paderewski. The great patriot-performer had played a seminal part in the boy's life from very early in Liberace's musical career. Paderewski figured centrally in family lore; Wally's grandmother told stories of knowing the young pianist in Berlin, for example. By the time he was six or so, he recounted, he was playing his father's Paderewski recordings, listening to the notes, the musical line, and the intonation. "I'd spend hours listening to his recordings, playing them over and over again. Then I'd try to imitate his interpretations." [48]

Paderewski had all manner of effect on the child's ambitions. Here was a Polish national, for one thing, who had turned his talent into worldwide fame. Born in 1860, he had won international celebrity by the age of thirty. In Vienna, Paris, London, and New York he had impressed audiences and critics alike as the leading pianist of his time. His musical renown launched him into the realm of high international politics, and he had helped influence the formation of an independent Poland after World War I. His prestige also led to his appointment as premier of the new Warsaw government in 1919. His energy and ambition matched or even exceeded his talent. Legends circulated about his performing with broken, bloodied fingers. His discipline became legendary too. "If I don't practice for one day," he said, "I know it; if I don't practice for two days, the critics know it; if I don't practice for three days, the audience knows it." He also helped create the modern model of the musical celebrity. According to his biographer, he inspired advertising campaigns for popular products and insinuated himself into popular lore all over Europe, and, after extraordinary American tours in the early 1890s, in the United States, as well. He grew very rich in the process. Paderewski offered a model for the poor but aggressively ambitious "little Polish boy" from Southside Milwaukee, as he was known. [49]

Paderewski influenced the child in other ways, as well. The boy's devotion to the legendary musician helped shape his style, and his peculiar approach to the literature. Paderewski cut across popular audiences and

classical forms. He attracted concertgoers who otherwise never set foot in
a concert hall. He did so, in part, through dramatic and, literally, spectacular playing. Like Liszt—whose tradition he continued and elaborated
on—Paderewski created a unique personality for the concert platform;
just so, he generated, also like Liszt, a mystical devotion in his audiences,
especially among women.[50] The boy absorbed it all.

All this provided a background for Walter Liberace's epiphany when
he actually met the great man around 1927. The encounter, he always insisted, altered his life.

The experience assumed legendary proportions in family lore, but, as
for all legends, several versions of the tale exist. Frances Liberace identified the famous pianist as an associate of her family who actually visited
their home in Milwaukee.[51] In stark contrast, Liberace himself identified
the event not with his mother but with his father. In his autobiography, he
begins the Paderewski story with reference to how his "dad and his fine
record collection . . . introduced me to the great names of music," including Paderewski, specifically. He followed this assertion with one about
how his father then actually managed to arrange for his family to be introduced to the great man: "You can imagine what a thrill it was to all of us,
but particularly to me, when Dad came home one day and announced that
Paderewski was going to give a recital at the Pabst theater in Milwaukee,
and we were all going."[52]

Meeting with his idol was a turning point in the boy's musical career.
For days, he wrote, "I was intoxicated by the joy I got from the great
virtuoso's playing. My dreams were filled with fantasies of following his
footsteps . . . or finger prints." He continued: "These dreams were encouraged by the fact that the great man had graciously received our family
after his performance. He talked to us and gave sincere words of encouragement to my parents and to me when he heard that I could play some
of the famous selections he played that evening, selections from Liszt,
Bach, Mozart and Beethoven. The scope of this repertoire impressed him
so that he put his hand on my head and said, 'Someday this boy may take
my place.' I was eight years old." The music and the challenge, he related,
affected everything about his life. "Inspired and fired with ambition, I began to practice with a fervor that made my previous interest in the piano
look like neglect." Perhaps this was one source of the trauma he identified
with moving: if he had had friends before, he did not play with them now.
He became the butt of neighborhood children's jokes, the sickly mama's
boy who played the piano all the time. His obsessions became public.[53]

In any case, his post-Paderewski obsession worried his parents, who
fretted about his health. His mother simply instructed him to quit. "'Stop!'

Mom used to say." She was concerned that he looked too pale and that other people would think he was sick, he related. His father took a different tack. Salvatore told him to consider his music. "You need the exercise. To be a great pianist you must have great physical stamina. Run around. Build yourself up physically." The admonitions had no affect. "I tried to obey my parents, but my heart really wasn't in it, and I don't think exercise that you don't enjoy really does you any good. So I continued to plug away at the old masters."[54]

The trials of 1926–27—sickness, school, speech impediment, moving, and musical revelations—found some resolution in another great event of this time, his discovery of a new music teacher who became the most important person in his life outside his family for the next two decades.

He had started piano lessons with his father at around the age of three. By 1923, Salvatore had turned him over to Mrs. Martin. After four more years of lessons with this teacher, he related, "there was no question that I knew more great music and could play it a great deal better than she could." It took no effort on Mrs. Martin's part, he wrote, "to convince my father that I required more advanced training than she was equipped to give me." Salvatore, then, began the search for an instructor worthy of his child's talent. Thus Florence Bettray-Kelly appeared on the scene.[55]

Florence Kelly had earned a bachelor's and a master's degree at the Chicago Musical College. She had studied with Paul Stoye, Rudolph Reuter, Moritz Rosenthal, and Glenn Dilliard Gunn. Even as a mature musician, she continued her instruction with the latter. She studied composition and composed, too, her work "winning the approval of music critics and the public as well." As a young woman she had placed well in both national and regional music competitions, and she continued successfully on the concert circuit in the thirties. "As a professional pianist, she has successfully appeared throughout the northwest where her press comments have been uniformly flattering," her biographical notice in the Wisconsin College of Music Bulletin noted. She taught a few seasons at the College of Music in Milwaukee in the early thirties, where, according to its bulletin, her "natural gifts combined with brilliant playing have made her remarkably successful in the development of pupils."[56] The Depression played havoc with her career, just as it did with Sal Liberace's and with those of so many other musicians of the era. To provide her daily bread, she taught privately and found work where she could, for example, at the house orchestra of local radio station WTMJ, where she heard the Liberace boy's name for the first time in the mid-twenties.[57]

One associate of long standing described Florence Kelly as "an elegant lady."[58] She combined femininity, however, with elements normally associated with masculinity: she was furiously uncompromising, willful, and outspoken. As demanding as Sam Liberace ever thought of being, her perfectionism came without the Oedipal, competitive, or resentful edge that affected the boy's relation with his father. Just so, her womanliness possessed none of the suffocating attentiveness and aesthetic ignorance of his mother. Coupled with her musical talent, the combination was particularly attractive for her student, Walter Liberace.[59]

Florence Kelly left her own record of taking on the fledgling musician from West Milwaukee. A guitar player in the house orchestra at the radio station where she played brought the boy to her attention. "'There's a little Polish piano player on the South Side who has lots of talent,' the guitarist said. "'He comes from a poor family but if someone would just take him in hand. . . .'"[60] The teacher did indeed take in "the little Polish boy." She instructed him for over a decade and a half, secured him scholarships, and guided his career to notable heights before he was twenty.

Kelly also "took the boy in hand" in the rougher sense of the expression. Even as a seven- or eight-year-old, he had developed an intractable spirit, which was perhaps obscured by his eccentricities. It did not show in every aspect of his life, as the smile, dimples, and pleasing ways often masked the trait, nor was he hard the way his parents were, but determination, ambition, and willfulness already permeated his character. As his sister observed later of her brother in his childhood, "He always had a goal, but he'd never tell anyone about it until he reached it. He always had a driving ambition. No obstacle was too great for him."[61] His single-minded determination manifested itself mostly relative to music and the piano—as his sister's references to his pushing others off the piano bench or playing things the way they must be played suggests. Liberace acknowledged the trait himself in recollections of similar episodes. The teacher was devoted to Walter and his talent, but she was no less indomitable. She was, indeed, every bit as stubborn as her student, even as she acknowledged and nurtured his genius. If fiercely loyal and affectionate to each other, the two nevertheless battled furiously. In an interview long after their first lessons, a newspaper reporter captured the relationship of two intensely stubborn wills at war. She conceded his talent from the first, but she launched immediately into the difficulties of his character. "He had talent all right, but he certainly was set in his ways—even then," she added without pause. "He would do just so much—and no more. We had lots of tussles. When he worked, he slaved, but it was the hardest job in the world to get him to work. That was the cause of all our squabbles."[62]

She described one of the most notable of these "squabbles" to the same reporter. It was 1934. Walter was fifteen. He was supposed to play the composition "Forest Murmurs" on the air at Radio Station WTMJ, where she was the house pianist. "What a fight we had over that number!" Kelly recalled twenty years later. "He brought it back to me after learning only two pages. He flatly refused to finish it." In Kelly's rendition of the story, she drove him out of the studio, throwing the sheets after him in the presence of other studio employees. " 'I won't have anything to do with you until you learn this number,' I yelled as he slammed the door," she recalled. She then brought her big guns to bear by calling Salvatore in on the fight. "Then I telephoned his father—something I rarely had to do— and told him that Walter wasn't working. His dad said he'd fix him. He did, too: he locked up the family piano for one week. Walter pleaded, but his dad wouldn't let him go near it. By the end of the week Walter was begging to practice. It didn't take him long to learn 'Forest Murmurs' after that." [63]

Wally offered his own version of the story in which the fight occurred after an on-air performance he had botched.

> When the program was over I walked out of the studio into
> a sort of lounge area where other performers waited between
> rehearsals or to get into a studio to do a show. Mrs. Kelly
> was waiting for me with fire in her eyes. She had a terrible
> Kelly-type temper and she was so angry she grabbed my mu-
> sic from me and flung it in my face, sheet by sheet. She re-
> minded me that she'd told me that I wasn't prepared to play
> that song and I'd proved it to the whole world. She really let
> me have it, and I was more embarrassed than I'd normally be
> because all the musicians sitting around in the lounge were
> friends of my father's. They taunted me with lines like,
> "Shame! Shame! Wally didn't do his lesson."

When I got home the news had already reached my father and, of course, perfectionist that he was, he agreed totally with Mrs. Kelly. . . . So he called the station and told them that he'd prefer it if his son didn't appear on the air anymore until he was more thoroughly prepared for it. [64]

Stubborn and exacting, Florence Kelly pushed her student to excel. If he resisted and bridled, he also responded to her challenge. "I entered him in everything that came along and he won 'em all," a reporter quoted the teacher as saying. [65] Thus, when he was eleven, in 1930, she encouraged him to enter a National Federation of Music Clubs piano competition, which he won handily, defeating twelve female rivals for the prize. [66]

Kelly's version of Walter's victory underlines the boy's stubborn perfectionism even as it introduces the intimacy and comradeship the student and teacher shared. He was Walter, but she was also now "Florence," in her memory, at least. "I can still see him sitting on my davenport that night after the concert and saying, 'Why, I wouldn't think of playing the way some of those girls did, Florence! You wouldn't allow me to play that way! They were terrible . . . just terrible!' " [67] Here was the same arrogance that had made him push his sister off the piano bench and humiliate her in public; it was Salvatore Liberace's arrogance played out in a second generation.

In 1933, two years after the National Federation of Music Clubs competition, Kelly arranged for Walter's first formal recital at the Wisconsin College of Music. Four years later, she was still pushing him. She entered him in a still more prestigious competition, less to demonstrate his talent, she recalled later, than to check his ego; she intended "to pin his ears back," she said. It did not work out exactly as she planned. Playing a program of Beethoven, Liszt, and Chopin, he performed at the Athenaeum in Milwaukee under the auspices of the Society of Musical Arts. He won. Late that night, the elated young man borrowed a nickel for the pay phone to share his victory with his teacher.[68] It was a double triumph. Besides the laurels of the Society of Musical Arts, his playing also won the seventeen-year-old boy his first public notice and first press accolades. Roy L. Foley, music critic for the Milwaukee *Sentinel,* was very impressed. He played, Foley wrote on January 8, 1937, "with a vigor that indicates much youthful physical power. His desire to 'go,' with the toning of years and deeper experience, should win him a considerable place in music." The Liszt, most notably, prompted a special note. That piece, the critic observed, elicited "Mr. Liberace's talents for flair and showmanship." [69]

Late the following year, the young pianist won additional plaudits and public notice in a still more significant performance. "A crowd of 500 acclaimed Walter Liberace . . . at the Elks Club auditorium for a fine performance of the Liszt A Major Concerto with the Wisconsin Symphony orchestra," wrote the *Sentinel* critic, Edward P. Halline, on November 18, 1938. "The young Milwaukeean made the piano's voice resound eloquently. He kept his grip on the music," he also noted, "even in the composer's most elaborate flights." [70]

Such praise was not enough. The boy wanted more. The break came in 1938. "After being recommended, and auditioning, I had the opportunity to give a concert at Kimball Hall in Chicago," he later wrote. This performance met with more laudatory reviews. "One of the Chicago critics wrote that I had every quality a virtuoso should possess," he remembered fondly. The concert led, in any case, to greater honor, when, with Florence Kelly's assistance, he won an audition with Frederick Stock, the conductor of the Chicago Symphony Orchestra, to perform with one of the great ensembles of the United States.[71]

The audition itself was memorable. The boy and his teacher took the train to Chicago, but a Milwaukee snowstorm that hit the day before the audition was scheduled delayed their trip. They found the huge, cold, barnlike orchestra hall empty except for Stock himself and another young auditioner. The conductor "was tearing him to pieces, making him start over again and again. I can still see Stock down in the orchestra pit, his elbows resting on the footlights," Florence Kelly recalled. "He would hum the orchestra parts out loud, then conduct the piano parts with a baton, rapping it loudly on the stage when something displeased him." Much did. Although terrified by this carnage, Walter, according to his teacher, "played so well that Stock let him go through the entire Liszt A major concerto without interruption."[72]

At the same audition, Stock had nodded approval to another young pianist from Milwaukee who won her audition with Chopin's Concerto in F Minor, and Shirley Sax played with the Chicago Symphony the following spring. Florence Kelly had to wait another year, but on the wintry night of January 16, 1940, her twenty-year-old prize pupil soloed the Liszt A Major Concerto with the Chicago Symphony at the brilliant Pabst Theater in downtown Milwaukee. His performance won praise in two reviews in Milwaukee papers. The *Journal's* music critic, Richard S. Davis, observed that "Liberace played with great credit to himself and his teacher." His playing, he concluded "disclosed a considerable gift for brilliant pianism."[73] The *Sentinel's* critic, if anything, was more generous. Edward Halline observed how the pianist had kept Liszt's "bombastic passages within reason and he did not miss some of the piano's most liquid conversations with the woodwinds. . . . One always felt the sure hand of the craftsman, and sometimes there came the transfigured moments which only genius can create."[74] It was a triumph of the first order for the twenty-year-old, especially because it took place in the very spot where, less than fifteen years before, the great Paderewski had anointed the child of poor immigrant parents. It was a dream fulfilled—a goal accomplished thanks to considerable talent, but also as the result of quite as much Trojan effort and Olympian ambition. It was not to be Liberace's last such achievement, by any means. Already, his brain was working on other schemes beyond the Chicago Symphony and beyond Chicago. He longed to escape, but he was also turning his will toward creating a new world free of the strictures of the Liberace household. He created a new self in the process.

He'd be home by three, get in a few hours at the piano, have a hurried dinner, and rush back to school, where he played piano for silent movies shown in the auditorium. He had already started to make a local name for himself as a musical prodigy. If he couldn't be "normal," he decided to make a virtue of being "different."

SCOTT THORSON

 *Three*

Sows' Ears/Silk Purses

By age ten, he was an accomplished pianist. He was a prodigy, but he also devoted himself to his art with the energy of an adult. He worked all the time: his parents could not tear him away from the upright in their parlor, where he practiced. He knew the great performers of his craft, and he could distinguish their styles. He knew the literature, too. The devotion was paying off in the form of increasingly impressive victories. Some things his victories did not help.

For all his knowledge, ambition, energy, and art, Walter Liberace's boyhood was a disaster. Along with his speech impediment, peculiar ways, and antisocial behavior, his interest in music alienated him. His peers equated musical ability with being a mama's boy and a sissy. About the time he entered high school, however, or a little before, he discovered new music, new uses of music, and, indeed, a new self. With music, he invented a new personality.

The process of reinvention was critical; it related, not coincidentally, to his homosexuality, which it helps illuminate. As important, it inaugurated a process of self-creation that characterized the performer's entire life. While music was integral to his own transformation, the young man also transformed his music in the process of transforming himself; he discovered a different mode of musical expression that encouraged his personal reinvention. Finally, his new music and his new persona resonated through his inner life. His turning to popular music amplified difficulties with his father even as it provided a weirdly Oedipal resolution of that critical relation. Not least, of course, the new music and the new persona also put bread on the Liberace table, not a minor concern in the hungry times after 1929 that never seemed to end. The Depression was not going away, but people still liked to laugh and sing. Wally Liberace discovered his capacity to delight the folks. They responded enthusiastically to his talents. His turning to popular music, then, represented a unique mix of social, economic, personal, and domestic motives, which combined to produce something altogether new in the Liberace household and in its shrinking violet of a second son.

Wally Liberace's interest in popular music preceded his fascination with the classics. The turn to popular music, however, was neither a necessary nor a natural development of his musical career; indeed, it ran counter to some of the most profound biases of his childhood.

Later in life, Liberace argued that Ignacy Paderewski, the great idol of his life, had approved of popular music. He made the connection in 1951 during the first real interview he did for his hometown newspaper, The Milwaukee *Sentinel*. In a conversation with the great pianist that took place when her son was only seven, according to Liberace, his mother had demanded that the master tell her if her boy should be "wasting his time" on light works. "Yes, if he wants to play that," Paderewski supposedly replied. "The other will come later, if it comes. I do the same. I found that Americans prefer lighter music and I give it to them. At the same time I can play the serious music I want to."[1]

If Wally might have been attracted to popular music from the first, and if he later found even classical justification for the form, he received no support at home for the inclination. Did he like popular songs, show tunes, and jazzy melodies? Frances Liberace, according to the Paderewski story, was skeptical. Her opposition paled beside her husband's. Sam Liberace was not an easy man when it came to any issue he made his own. On this one, perhaps even more than on others, he was intransigent. He insisted over and over upon classical training and performance. Even much later, when his son was gaining wealth and celebrity by performing popular music, he muttered to friends about Walter "playing that BS."[2] Earlier, it was worse. In the twenties, neighbors had recommended capitalizing on the boy's genius. "'You should let him work in some kind of child prodigy act and tour the country with it. He'd make big money,'" one visitor insisted. Sam's response never varied: "Wally's going to study music and finish his schooling in the proper manner. I won't let him prostitute his Talent.'"[3]

Combined with personal motives, economic necessity pushed the boy to violate his father's will. The two causes played off each other. The economic motives took precedence, at least initially. About the time he won the Wisconsin Federation of Music Clubs prize, he played commercially for the first time. He did not play Liszt. Chopin was absent from the program, and so was Mozart.

He remembered himself as being ten years old; he was likely a little older, by which time the country was deep in the Great Depression. He remembered the old Alhambra, where his father played in the house orchestra, as the site of his achievement. The theater was sponsoring a promotional program, "Milwaukee on Parade," and the boy attended the audition. The show was intended for adult performers, and the auditioners ignored the little boy in his coveralls until members of the house dance troupe interceded. He won a spot in the production. Without telling his family, he got the dancers to obtain a costume for him. He needed a special platform and a bench so he could reach the keys. The stagehands pitched in, and the dancers helped, too. He needed music, as well. "They had to give me something to play because they couldn't see Liszt's 'Hungarian Rhapsody' as the ideal number for a vaudeville show. . . . So they had a man play a number for me, and I learned how to play it from listening to him." After the show, one of the Fanchon & Marco dancers celebrated his talent. "She said that the man who had played the number for me said to her when I was on, 'Why can't I play like that?'" He and I wondered the same thing. I, too, wondered how I played like that."[4]

Angie Liberace remembered the story a little differently. She placed the "talent review" at the Wisconsin Theater instead of at the Alhambra, and she dated the episode during the Depression, when her brother was around eleven or twelve. According to her, he badgered the manager for days before he relented and allowed Wally to perform. "After a week of chasing him away they finally decided to let him play," she said. She confirmed that her brother had done it all in secrecy without telling anyone in his family, however. "The first thing we knew about it was when Florence called my father, 'Do you know what Walter's doing?' she asked. 'He's playing at the Wisconsin theater. He's pretty good, too!' I'll never forget," Angie concluded; "he got $75 for appearing in that show for a week. It seemed like a million at the time!"[5]

Liberace himself added a significant trailer to his retelling. If the gig had surprised the whole Liberace household, it infuriated the father. "Instead of that appearance being a triumph for me at home, it was a disaster. Dad got awfully mad," he recalled. "I wasn't playing the kind of music he wanted me to learn or to perform, and he told me so with a lot of emphasis and muscle." His father loathed the music, disliked the venue. Had Salvatore Liberace, artiste, wasted his life in the hole at the Alhambra accompanying silent movies? He took out his indignities on his son. Masculine pride exaggerated his loathing. He despised the idea of living off his children's income. " 'No kid of mine's going to take over the responsibility for my family,' " he said, even when his own financial contributions to the household were nonexistent or pitifully small.[6]

Even over the father's objections—and perhaps because of them—the boy seized other opportunities for gaining fame and fortune by performing popular music. By the time he was in his early teens, he was performing every Saturday afternoon on the local radio station WTMJ. His father did not protest. After all, Sam played for the same radio station, as did Florence Kelly. Not least, of course, the boy was playing classical music, although, given the brouhaha that arose over Liszt's "Forest Murmurs," he was perhaps not devoting all he could to this sort of public performance. He played for anybody who would pay him. "He was so busy. He was trying to make a buck all the time," one friend laughed.[7] He played for dancing classes and Polish weddings. He himself recalled so many performances for Hadassah, the Jewish women's organization, that people began assuming he was Jewish, he joked.[8] A fellow musician remembered that the Wauwatosa Women's Club extended regular invitations to his friend to play for teas and fashion shows.[9]

About the time the radio regularized his performances, he found a more lucrative and exciting way of making money, creating, in the process, more difficulties at home. When Wally was fourteen, three older boys, Del Krause, Carl Lorenz, and Joe Zingsheim, tapped him for the pianist of their group, the Mixers. Although Krause lived nearby, he had never met Wally until around 1931 or 1932, when Wally was twelve or thirteen. "He was a mama's boy, never out much in the neighborhood," Krause reminisced sixty years later.[10] Krause knew the boy's reputation as a piano player, however. Hearing him play regularly increased Krause's respect. He had an infallible ear, Krause testified. "He never had to use spots (sheet music). All you had to do was hum a few bars and Walter could play it." He was a natural musician. He "could make an out of tune piano sound good," he declared.[11]

It was not a bad time to be able to play jazz and honky-tonk. In 1932, the country had rejected the Republicans and elected Franklin Roosevelt president. The repeal of prohibition quickly followed his inauguration. Suddenly, the famous beer-hall tradition of the sturdy folk of Milwaukee

County flourished again—and legally. Bars, saloons, and gin mills soaked up entertainment. "The first job we ever played together was at Little Nick's on Muskego and Mitchell Sts in 1933," recalled Krause. "The place had been an ice cream parlor during Prohibition, but it became a gin mill when beer came back in 1933." The group pulled in no more than two dollars a night, but in the heart of the Depression, none of the members groused about the money or anything else.[12] Frances, conversely, raged.

Sam hated popular music for aesthetic reasons, but his wife had other objections. According to Krause, Ma Liberace kept a crucifix on the household piano.[13] The image suggests her limits and her ideals. The Mixers played few spots where crosses and pictures of Jesus hung on the walls. With her conservative, Polish, religious background, Frances Liberace associated the kinds of venues where the Mixers performed with sin and corruption. Meanwhile, her son's new job undermined her control of her adored third child. Frances was not happy. The passage of half a century did not dull her offense, according to Scott Thorson, who, much later, heard about Lee playing with the Mixers. "Frances," he recounted, "recalled being furious when Lee told her about the opportunity. She didn't want her baby hanging around older men, playing in speakeasies or even worse places. There was no telling what went on in dives like that, she warned Lee."[14] On one occasion she prohibited her son from leaving the house altogether. Krause had to find a ladder and sneak Walter to their gig through an open window.[15] The Mixers seldom saw Sam around, but Wally's "domineering" mother filled the breach. When she relaxed her guard and let her son out at all, she persistently waved them off her porch with the admonition, "Del, you take care of him!" as they mounted the streetcar that ran down National Avenue to Milwaukee. "She groomed him," Krause related, saying that she warned Walter over and over again as they departed, "Behave! Behave!"[16]

The Mixers played together for about seven months, until the three founders graduated from high school in 1934. Afterwards, Wally played with other groups, including the Rhythm Makers, which made around the same amount of money and played in similar venues as the Mixers had, according to one of the new band's members, Wallis Schaetzke, who grew up a couple of blocks away from the Liberaces. They took home about a dollar sixty a night, he remembered, "after knocking out songs until midnight."[17]

Wally also played with his brother, George. Together, they performed fairly regularly in various spots around Milwaukee, including Sam Pick's

Club Madrid, a fancy watering spot for those who still had money. This was where George had met his first wife, a cabaret singer. "This was one of our classier jobs," Liberace said later. "The big nightclubs of the day all had an orchestra plus a floor show featuring a soubrette or pop singer, a prima donna who did the light opera numbers, and a blues singer who sang songs like "Body and Soul" and "Love for Sale." My job was to accompany the singers as they went around the room between shows, singing requests from the audience. People would tip them five or ten dollars for each number, and they would split whatever they got with me." [18] In his autobiography, he describes one particularly memorable performance at the Club Madrid. He got roaring drunk, he remembers, fell off the piano bench in the middle of playing "The Carioca," and threw up all over his brother's borrowed dress clothes on the way home. "The next thing I remember was being delivered to my outraged parents, very much the worse for wear in George's very messed-up tuxedo." [19] Neither then nor later, he protested, was he fond of alcohol. Generally, he was in greater danger from drunk patrons than from getting drunk himself, as his friend Joe Zingsheim from the Mixers recalled. "I remember one night he was playing piano in my brother's gin mill and someone poured beer over his hands. He never missed a beat, he just kept on playing." [20]

Not all his gigs were as classy as the ones he played at Sam Pick's, nor as prim as the women's club teas. Some engagements were even rowdier than those that took place at the gin mills. He played stag parties, for one thing. His parents disapproved, so he lied to get out of the house. Sometimes he accompanied pornographic films, and he provided music for live strippers. "I loved to punctuate their movements with special chords and riffs as I accompanied their weird gyrations." He was sixteen, he remembered, when in the midst of naked women and cheering men, the police broke in. The authorities turned him over to his parents, who raged and attempted to restrict him to performing at more genteel locations. But the cash called, and he was off again to the freedom and ready money of Milwaukee's fleshpots.[21]

With money in his pockets, his confidence soared. He was transforming himself. Photographs of his various bands reveal the change. They show a smiling and self-possessed teenager, a sanguine young man. By the age of seventeen, playing on his own and earning his own income, Wally Liberace had come a long way from where he'd been when he had entered high school. In 1932, he had been a skinny seventh-grader with an embarrassing speech impediment; he had little life outside practicing the piano. By 1934, the boy who, two years earlier, couldn't pronounce his own name was speaking as clearly as his peers, even if—as one family friend remembered—in "a voice that you don't often hear at football games."[22]

Classical music had provided an escape from some of the horrors of his childhood; popular performance did the same thing even better. Had his classmates ignored or mocked his burgeoning career as a classical prodigy? His vocation as popular entertainer had diametrical effects. Instead of separating him from his peers, popular music became a source of community with them. One of his old friends, Joe Zingsheim, told a journalist how the schoolboy musician "hurried home for lunch and back to school each day so that he could play dance music for his classmates on an old piano in the West Milwaukee High School gym. 'He could play anything they asked him to play,' said Zingsheim. 'If he didn't know the song, he'd asked them to sing a little and then he would know how to play it.'"[23] Schoolmates, especially girls, always thronged around the banged-up instrument in the gymnasium.[24] Sometimes he invited his classmates back home with him during his lunch break, where he would entertain them at the family piano. They accepted.[25] He played anything. A friend could hum a bar or two of some current song, and he was off. Through popular music—and his great gift—he turned his sissy liability into an asset.

So it was with much of his life at West Milwaukee High between 1933 and 1937. Was he making "a virtue of being 'different,'" as Scott Thorson put it?[26] If he made his "differences" charming, it was an extraordinary feat, for his eccentricities remained as numerous as they were flagrant. Indeed, formal music and classical piano playing were only minor details among his social liabilities.

For better or for worse, Walter Liberace was not a normal boy. Steve Swedish, an old family friend, insisted that "anyone who knew Liberace in high school and just afterwards had no doubts about his sexual orientation. 'I don't know what might have happened in later life,'" he told a newspaper reporter, "'but when he was here, he was—what do you call it?—heterosexual.'" Steve Swedish was either blind or ignorant. Wally Liberace was a mama's boy, a sissy, and faggy ways distinguished almost everything he did long after 1932.[27]

Unlike most boys, Walter had no "girl problems." "He was very popular with the girls; they always crowded around him at the piano," but theirs was a pal, confidante kind of relationship, nothing romantic, Del Krause noted.[28] Wally enjoyed female company, but he never expressed any interest in dating girls, recalled another old high school friend.[29] This was not the most peculiar of his eccentricities.

As a little boy, he had disliked the outdoors and sports. The prejudice persisted into high school. "He didn't go out for sports. He was always in dramatics and classes pertaining to theatrics," said his friend William Schmidt, who had performed with him in the Rhythm Makers.[30] Walter pursued other classes and competed in still other areas normally considered the domain of girls. "He was a great typist," a female classmate recalled. "In competitions he'd beat everybody, women included." He liked home economics and boasted of his culinary skills. His teacher offered her own opinions: "His cooking was very artistic. He took a lot of pride in his work. Everything had to be just so."[31] He himself had persuaded the staff to inaugurate the cooking course for boys, and the males followed his lead with enthusiasm. "It was a new thing," recalled a member of that first class. "We had a heck of a time."[32]

Did his father consider himself an "artiste"? His second son outpaced him, both in degree and in type. He was so gifted a draftsman and painter that some teachers debated about whether he should give up music for the other art form. He turned anything into art. "He used to carve animals and figures out of soap," his principal related. "Other kids would make snowmen in the winter. Not Walter—he'd turn out a fantastic snow sculpture of a deer or a horse. He'd have all the kids in the neighborhood icing it for him."[33]

Age increased his love of fabrics and design. He played with cloth; he re-upholstered his parents' furniture; he designed clothes; he tried his hand at millinery.[34] Like *La Bohème*'s Mimi, he made silk flowers. He won local fame for this skill. Thus, he came to make silk corsages for his classmates. "When we'd have dances—the June prom, the Silhouette Dance, where all the girls asked out the boys—he'd make up different corsages,'" a high school friend remembered. "All the fellows would buy them from him to give to the girls."[35]

He loved pretty things and dressed accordingly. His home ec teacher offered one view: "He used to come to me with his clothes problems. 'What color do you think I should wear with this tie?' he'd ask me. He loved gay clothes." Examining an old high school annual fifteen years later, Joseph Schwei, his assistant principal, pointed out the boy's graduation photo. "Look. That's a purple boutonniere. . . . That was Walter for you. And see that double breasted vest with lapels. Nobody but Liberace would have dared to dress like that in those days—and the kids liked him for it."[36] "He was a real showman," the principal observed on another occasion. "He could get by with anything. The fellows liked him."[37] Henry Mahr, a violinist with the Rhythm Makers, remembered the fancy boy in spats. "He always wore a vest and suit to school. The rest of us were wearing sweaters," recalled another old bandmate.[38] Del Krause recalled him in cutaways and evening dress at school. Strange? Confirming their principal's judgment, his old friend asserted, "He was accepted, whatever he did or wore."[39] He was making a virtue of being different.

If he favored costume on a daily basis, formal dress-up occasions— character days—at school elicited the most imaginative efforts. Steve Denkinger had known the boy since they were in the seventh grade. "He'd always dress up," Denkinger said. "One year, he dressed up like Greta Garbo. Wally, he always won first prize."[40]

He made his interest in fashion design a matter of public consumption, and it won his school chums' affectionate regard. When the emcee of his high school fashion show fell sick, Walter substituted for her. "That night he came out on the stage in a beret, smock and flowing artist's tie. He had a long pointer and an easel. He did a perfect job of describing the clothes. It brought down the house—and I don't know one boy who resented it; everybody thought it was a big joke."[41]

On his own, a million miles from the nearest homo, light years away from any gay subculture, a lone invert, Wally Liberace rediscovered a standard sissy boy's response to his own peculiarities. The good citizens of West Milwaukee had no word for it. Others did: camp. A survival technique, it mocked and objectified itself, even as it objectified and mocked the world. It celebrated style over content, appearance over substance— including, of course, substantial differences and conflict; exaggeration, caricature, and artifice dominated the style. The artiste in flowing smock and jaunty beret was already a caricature when the high school student swished into the role; parodying such parody represented the perfect expression of the form. More critically, Walter Liberace, like many before and after, parodied himself or what he might have been: Spats? Tails. Purple boutonnieres! GRETA GARBO!! The Marquess of Queensbury condemned Oscar Wilde for "posing" as a sodomite. The artifice of posing and posturing—for Wilde no less than for the West Milwaukee adolescent—dulled the social threat of sexual deviance, by, paradoxically, making it more obvious, more artificial, more fake, less real. Caricature suggests humor, too, almost by definition, while smiles and laughter, by extension, defuse antipathy.[42] The antipathy was always there, in any event. It lurked in the nearest dark corner, including the dark corners of the gay boy's psyche: hostility, real or imagined, informed the camp strategy.[43] While his peers tolerated—even loved—the eccentric, West

Milwaukee also considered this circumstance anomalous. The natural social default for gender deviation was hostility, rejection, ill will; tolerance, popularity, and affection always required explanation and justification. "The fellows liked him," the principal added, not ungratuitously, after cataloging Wally's deviations; "I don't know one boy who resented it; . . . everybody thought it was a big joke." The authorities apologized, effectively, for the absence of queer bashing.[44]

If Walter Liberace never got bashed, if he, on the contrary, won the plaudits of his schoolmates, he nevertheless led a highly conflicted life. Taking a cue from the feminist philosopher Judith Butler, modern academic critics refer to all gender distinctions as performance rather than as natural activity. Performativity rather than being becomes the watchword. This generalization rather diminishes the particular difficulties of the campy production that Walter Liberace felt it necessary to maintain in high school. His perpetual staginess required extraordinary energy, even as it conflicted with a different self that he defined as real. With his new persona, the mama's boy fought more demons inside than outside. Scott Thorson later recounted Liberace's dilemma this way: "Adolescence can be agony for anyone, but it was a special hell for Lee. Still struggling to deal with his own sexual identity, he had to live through the torture of hearing his classmates making crude jokes about 'homos.' Every time it happened he recalled dying a little inside." He told Thorson he made "an all-out effort to transform himself into a heterosexual. . . . He would look at a shapely bosom or a round female rear and will himself to feel desire. But then his eyes would stray to a pair of broad shoulders or well-muscled arms and the battle would be lost. He couldn't help being attracted to men."[45]

The circumstance was actually more complicated than Thorson's rendering—or perhaps Liberace's memory—suggests. His dilemma rotated not merely on the axis of erotic longing for other men but on his other affections, affectations, and passions—the sissy ways that characterized his life long, long before he indulged in sex with fellows. He was who he was—the admirer of men and boys, but, no less, he was the devotee of art and music, a slave of beauty, a hierophant in life's show. If men filled his fantasies, so did silk corsages, flowing smocks, dandy dress, artwork and sculpted animals, the well-turned musical phrase—or even the decorative bit of parsley dashed across a plate of spaghetti. He could resist having sex with other men; the other sources of his queerness, however, were beyond his power of transformation, almost beyond his awareness. Thorson summed it up. "He had to face the truth. He couldn't change, no matter how hard he tried. Being gay was as much a part of him as the color of his eyes or his hair."[46]

All of this, not merely his longing for other men, set him at odds with almost every conventional value in the world of West Milwaukee. Indeed, it set him at odds with virtually every accepted value in the world at large. Here was the problem. He could not, would not change his own nature, but the world was equally intractable. Even so, he hated conflict, despised contention, and longed to please and to belong. His art bridged that gap. It blunted enmity; it soothed the savage passions of his classmates and community. And perhaps his greatest artistic achievement was that of creating and re-creating himself. As he remade his speech, he reworked his life. In this regard, his life mirrors the fundamental issues and dilemmas homosexual boys and men perpetually encounter.

As long as children are conceived by standard methods and raised by ordinary men and women, homosexual boys will have one model for their lives—a model that fails to apply to their adult lives and affections and that sometimes fails to kick in at all. By six or so, when they discover the world beyond the hearth, they will already be off center from the model, eccentric, first queer, and only then, gay. They will be odd, in effect, before they have much sense of sex, per se, of any sort. Wally Liberace's sense of trauma, which he associated with his family's move in 1926, might represent a first, presexual manifestation of difference and peculiarity. As his sexual consciousness grew, so did his sense of estrangement, so that as a sixty-year-old he recalled adolescence as his time of alienation, guilt, and outlawry—despite his not having violated any social norm of sexual activity.

What does all this mean for a life? What does it mean for one life in particular? It suggests, for one thing, that every gay boy has to create and recreate his own model. If the father model doesn't work exactly, and the mother model doesn't work exactly, and the family coupling model doesn't work exactly, the boy experiments and plays with various models and combinations of models, or creates new models. The experimentation might be sexual—hence the regular inclusion in Gay ISO ads of headings like "Bi-Curious" or the justification of homosexual activity as "experimenting around." It involves sexual inventiveness. The experimentation, play, and curiosity, however, is more than physical: it involves the spirit as well as the body. In one regard, this is the very stuff of art, insofar as the experimenting involves not merely creating models, but the idea of creation itself. In the absence of fixity, the making of things, making things new, remaking things, becomes the focus of existence. By the same token, insofar as one's own being is the most immediate thing that one can have or make, creating a persona, experimenting with personae, performance and acting—and with it dress and illusion—come close to the heart of the homosexual male experience.[47]

Regardless of the theoretical bases or implications of homosexuality, these elements appeared early in the life of the high school student, Walter Valentino Liberace. His adolescent flair for drama and theatrics, his fascination with dress and clothing, and his concern with the shape, form, and presentation of all things speak to this characteristic in his life—the centrality of art: homo faber, man maker with a twist. He was a self-conscious actor in a play. He wrote his own part. He rendered a classic performance. He projected a very clear self-image—confident, insouciant, daring. He gave evidence, even at the time, however, that this was an act and that he was not always on. People remembered a disparity between the gay blade and another boy. "For all his energy and involvement in school activities, classmates said Liberace maintained a calculated detachment from other students," a reporter wrote in summary after interviewing his chums. "He wasn't the type of fellow to fool around in classes with the other kids," one boy said. "It didn't seem like the same relationship I had with other fellows. It wasn't that kind of tomfoolery. He'd talk to you, but he was reserved. I don't think he palled around with anybody outside school." Another friend from the Rhythm Makers concurred: "He wasn't the mingling type. He went his own way."[48] If this recollection suggests isolation, detachment, and even loneliness, his revelations about his high school years to Scott Thorson long after confirms it. "Alienated from his family and his peers," according to Thorson, "he experienced terrible guilt, as if he'd committed an unspeakable crime that must forever be hidden. It was, he recalled unhappily, the worst period of his life."[49]

If Wally Liberace was not happy, and if he created his charming persona the way he created animals out of soap and snow, he possessed social gifts, too, quite as remarkable as his musical and artistic ones. Perhaps he worked at it, perhaps it was cultivated, but the basis of his appeal was indubitably sincere: he really did enjoy other people, he delighted in pleasing them, he loved making folks happy. His old friends and associates never differed on this question. One summed it up: "He was very considerate of others, too. He didn't do just what he had to do—he was always thinking of helping out the other fellow. We all liked Walter very much."[50]

Was Frances's boy grim in the privacy of his own room? He confessed decades later that Pagliaccio's spirit of the clown masked his pain. The circumstances take another turn here, too, for people and performing also elevated his spirits and lifted him outside himself. His show was not all tragedy disguised. In the smock, substituting for the lady emcee, pointing out the high points of high school high fashion, he was surely playing the clown, but he was not always weeping on the inside. If he transformed an audience with laugher, the laugher transfigured him as well. The stage, the dramatic rendering, possessed a transformative power that blunted the analogy with *Pagliacci*. Not only could he transform audiences with his humor, he could transform his own humors. "Vesti la guibba"? He sang it in a major key.

It took some doing to carry all this off. A half century later, he still shuddered at the terror of being caught out. As a teenager, he threw courage up against his fears. As an adult, he often referred to bravery. "When you are doing something you believe in, you've always got to stick to it. It isn't always easy."[51] If facing a line of determined football players on a playing field requires one form of courage, for a mincing high school boy to face the enemy every day in every school corridor—not merely in an athletic contest once a week during the athletic season—requires another. There is gallantry, even nobility, in both performances. In later years, at least as he relived these times for his teenage boyfriend Scott Thorson, the horror might have blotted out the joys and benefits of West Milwaukee High, but his classmates celebrated his accomplishments. They celebrated him. If he forgot it, his classmates held him in the highest affection and regard, and they captioned his yearbook photo with a notable tribute:

> Our Wally has already made his claim
> With Paderewski, Gershwin and others of fame.

He finished West Milwaukee High in the spring of 1937. He had just turned eighteen, making him a year older than most of his classmates. He now faced the problem of what to do next. He left no evidence of ever having questioned his plans to devote his life to music, but he had not resolved the wheres and hows of this commitment. Indeed, the high school annual's tribute captures one of the problems he faced that summer he graduated: the choice of Gershwin and popular music versus Paderewski and the classics.

Throughout the thirties, the young man had bifurcated his life along these lines, without much overlap between the two. He continued to do so for the next few years as well. His Paderewski discipline dominated one part of his life. He tried to capitalize on classical music, too. No later than 1938, perhaps earlier, Florence Kelly had negotiated her prize student a contract with a booking agency, and he began a community concert series, touring "all over the Midwest playing large towns and small cities in Wisconsin, Minnesota, Illinois and Michigan."[52] He ventured as far west on the circuit as Omaha, Nebraska, where a dated photograph from 1939 depicts him.[53] As an outgrowth of these early tours, he had played Kimball Hall in Chicago in 1938, won his audition with Frederick Stock soon after, and performed with the Chicago Symphony in January 1940. He was twenty. He was still touring perhaps even into 1941. The concert circuit provided both cash, however pitiful in amount, and even a modicum of fame. "Brilliant Young Pianist Appearing in Concert" proclaims the poster, and names the venue as "Congregational Church Auditorium." The city remains anonymous, but it could have been one of scores of New England-like towns and villages in the upper Midwest, where hardpressed citizens tried to scratch out a little culture as the Depression stretched on and on. Touring had its glamour, too, however limited. The publicity stills reveal a part of it: the serious young artist, barely out of his teens, dressed in the elegant tails and white tie, or a little less formal, in a tuxedo and black tie.[54]

This was Walter's Paderewski career. Meanwhile the "Gershwin" impulses pulled him relentlessly in another direction.

On the surface, at least, he performed popular music chiefly for the cash. As his friends recalled, he chased the dollar relentlessly. About the time he graduated from high school in 1937—and as late as 1939, according to one source—he toured with a local dance band, the Jay Mills Orchestra, even when he was playing the community concert circuit, too.[55] He was the youngest member of the group until the vocalist Vivian Stapleton, later known as Vivian Blaine, joined it. When not working, the two of them hung out at skating rinks and other benign spots, while the rest of the band was boozing and carousing.[56] The orchestra played out of town with more professional musicians for better audiences, but otherwise their engagements differed little from those of the Mixers and the Rhythm Makers. One report has it that Frederick Stock disapproved of such activity before Walter's performance with the Chicago Orchestra. Just as likely, it conflicted too sharply with playing serious concerts, which still took precedence, according to Liberace's own judgment at this time.

He continued to pick up other popular-music gigs. As the thirties wore on, the saloons and "gin mills" he'd played as a hustling teenager gave way to slightly fancier watering holes. A couple of these stand out. He got his first out-of-town engagement playing on his own probably in 1938 or early 1939. He was around nineteen at the time. He described the gig as a six- or seven-month engagement at a saloon called the Wunderbar in Wausau, Wisconsin, the major city in central Wisconsin, about ninety miles inland from Green Bay. In addition to being his first independent performance, the Wunderbar job provided the occasion for his experimentation with names that would match his new, popular-music persona. His autobiography memorializes the effort. "Walter Valentino Liberace sounded too high class," he determined. "W. V. Liberace sounded a like a sign on the desk of a vice-president of something. I couldn't use Walter Valentino because it sounded too Latin for that part of the world." The management of the place then came up with "Walter Buster Keys." He kept Walter so that the boy would listen when anyone addressed him, Liberace explained. "Buster was an acknowledgment of my youth and seemed to describe my 'joi de vivre' as well as my piano playing technique." The name lasted no longer than his run in Wausau.[57] In *The Things I Love,* he offered a different story: he adopted the name to hide his identity as a popular performer from the manager of the Chicago Symphony, who objected.[58]

Although the young piano player had been on the road a good bit before this with the community concert tours and the Jay Mills Orchestra, he had never spent so much time away from home at one stretch, and certainly not in one place. He fell into a pattern that was to characterize much of his life thereafter. He took up with people. In Wausau, he moved in with "a lovely Irish family" and became, in effect, a part of their domestic circle. He continued his religious life in Wausau, too. As he tells it in his autobiography, a local church choir lunched at his saloon, and the director invited him to sing with them. He picked out Gounod's "Ave Maria" (based on a Bach theme) and sang the solo in the very large church, where, he judged, "I made a very small, unresonant sound. They never asked me to sing another solo," he concluded, but he continued to participate in services by playing the organ occasionally.[59]

Offers from other cities started coming in during this period. In 1939, "Ice Vanities of 1940" offered him an eight-week contract at eighty dollars a week to accompany the skaters on a tour of major cities in the northwest. Alverdes restaurant, a swanky dining room in St. Paul, offered him sixty-five dollars a week for an unlimited engagement. He turned both down in favor of a long and notable run at the posh Red Room at the old Plankton Arcade in downtown Milwaukee in 1939. He played from five o'clock to midnight, earning thirty-five dollars a week, plus all the food he could eat.[60] The pay was good, but the gig was also particularly attractive in that it enabled him to live at home. Moreover, and perhaps more important, it allowed him to continue his musical studies with his piano teacher. The explanation he made to his new employer, Max Pollack, that he was turning down other job offers and working in the Red Room because it was more convenient for his "future concert engagements,"[61] is suggestive of the tension present in his musical life. Liszt and Paderewski still held the upper hand, if tenuously.

If it offered decent and convenient work, the Red Room still posed problems for the twenty-year-old performer. For one thing, Pollack's piano, like most saloon instruments, was awful. Some of these pianos achieved legendary status within the fraternity Walter Liberace was in the process of joining. One member left a classic account. "Ivories were discolored and chipped or missing altogether; the felts looked like they had been chewed by crazed rodents; the strings were coated with a whitish substance that could only be salt . . . , and the casting was studded with drink rings and cigarette burns." The broken ivory actually gashed this performer's finger, and his blood joined other performers' salty sweat on the strings. "Here's what you should do with this aberration," the pianist's bandleader instructed the saloon owner: " 'Tune it, clean it thoroughly, refurbish the felts and hammers, polish the casing. Then hire a handyman to chop it up for firewood. And you know what you'd have?' the owner shook his head. 'A bad fire.' "[62]

The bane of any pianist, such instruments drove the perfectionist Walter Liberace to distraction. It is fitting, then, that one of the few surviving letters in his hand chronicles his efforts to get a new piano for his show in the Plankton Arcade. The note is vintage Liberace, too: it is at once diffident and deferential, yet he remains very clear about his own needs and desires. The letter had two purposes, one direct, one implied. Most obviously, he wanted a new piano, and his request emphasizes first his concern with quality, but hardly less his attention to style, presentation, and appearance. "You realize, Max, that in order to do my best work, I must have a good piano and the piano now in use is on its last legs," he wrote his boss at the Red Room. "I tried it when I was in Milwaukee last, and know that it would be a hindrance to my playing to work on that instrument. . . . A small grand of good make would not only lend distinction to the room but sound well." And he concluded with his little curl of modesty: "Just a suggestion, of course." Beyond the explicit desire for a new instrument, he also suggested implicitly that he deserved a raise. By stating that he had received offer of jobs that paid sixty-five and eighty dollars a week, he implied, however modestly, that Max Pollack should be paying him more. This was not the last time that his ambivalence between modesty and avarice would appear.[63]

Did he get a good piano? The record does not say. Whether with a high-quality instrument or a poor one, however, the young performer had made his mark. His boss knew he had a prize, and by 1942, Max Pollack was paying him a phenomenal ninety dollars a week. Walter Liberace earned his keep. He may have longed for wealth and fame, but he was just as bent on giving folks their money's worth. He did, and audiences responded. One of his bosses from these days, Walter Ludwig, marveled over the performer. "He's the only musician I ever had in a commercial restaurant in Milwaukee that people applauded after he finished a set of numbers. There were lots of times when we had customers waiting in line for tables." Liberace was honing his style, too. His pressing for a good— and beautiful—piano represented only one manifestation of his concern about presentation. One friend remembers that he was already costuming himself by then, as well.[64]

His old boss, Ludwig, remembered other peculiarities from these days at the Plankton Arcade. The young musician repeated the pattern he had established in Wausau of taking up with folks. "He practically lived with us," Ludwig insisted. "When my wife and I went on vacations, Walter went along. And you know what he'd do? He'd take along a practice keyboard—a cardboard affair. No matter where we were he'd practice on that thing at least three hours a day."[65] As this recollection affirms, the young piano player maintained a rigorous routine and schedule for himself. Neither his ambition nor his energy flagged. Joe Zingsheim, one of the original Mixers, still played occasionally while doing stints on the family farm, and he recalled his friend's will and energy from the Red Room days. He "would get off work at 1 A.M. and he would come and play for us at parties. I remember one party that Wally came to after work. He was still playing at 5 A.M. when I went home to New Berlin to milk the cows."[66] His friends recalled his musicianship and his show-business sense; they also recalled him as a "go-getter and a very hard worker." "He was a worker," his friend Zingsheim repeated. "You'd have to ask him to stop playing sometimes."[67]

These furiously capitalistic, Gershwin elements of his life were completely out of synch with the Paderewski side. In 1939, however, the young pianist experienced an epiphany that suggested a way to combine the divergent halves of his musical life. He repeated the story over and over. It figured significantly in his memoirs and in newspaper interviews. Four decades later, according to Scott Thorson, even while he shied from other tales of his youth, he still delighted in describing the episode.

Between runs at the Plankton Arcade, Liberace had continued his formal concert tours of the upper Midwest. Indeed, that was one reason he accepted employment in the Red Room—to allow him freedom to continue playing traditional concerts. It was probably in the spring of 1939, then, that his agency had booked him in La Crosse, the Mississippi port city on the Wisconsin border with Minnesota. He played a successful, standard, all-classical program. The applause prompted encores. During this informal part of the performance, he began chatting with the audience. Someone shouted "Play 'Three Little Fishies'!" a nonsense song, made the most popular radio tune in the country by the bandmaster Kay Kyser. After offering a standard rendition, he played it after the manner of Bach, which delighted the concertgoers. "It not only got me a big hand," he told an early interviewer, "it got me this head on the review in the La Crosse newspaper the next day: 'Three Little Fishies Swim in a Sea of Classics.' Right then, I knew what people wanted.'" Later, he theorized about the affair. "I showed I understood the humor behind the request," he wrote in his autobiography. "I was trying to tell the people that you could have fun at a concert without sacrificing the greatness of the music. I was trying to show that music is not all heavy-handed culture, that it has its humorous side, just as great literature does." [68]

The triumph extended beyond the Mississippi River port city. Liberace told of how the wire services picked up the story, with its jazzy headline, and gave him completely unexpected publicity. He had hit pay dirt, he told his friend long afterwards. "He finally had the schtick that would set him apart from every other piano player on the circuit. From then on he closed every performance by asking for requests, which he'd interpret in the style of one or more of the classical composers. Audiences loved his new gimmick. The idea proved to be so popular that he later wished he could have patented it." [69]

Walter Liberace had hit on something, but his hit was not quite as novel as he made it out to be. The blind pianist, Alec Templeton, had built his impressive radio reputation by doing the same thing. Famous for his rendition of "Boogie Woogie Washerwoman," he played classics as well and combined the two forms exactly as the young Liberace was doing, translating them into popular tunes and doing the opposite with popular songs. Through the thirties, Templeton remained an important referent within the musical world. Indeed, the blind pianist provided a standard comparison with the up-and-coming pianist from Milwaukee before the latter completely eclipsed him in the 1950s. Walt Disney's 1940 feature-length cartoon, *Fantasia,* was based on much the same idea, with Mickey Mouse acting out "The Sorcerer's Apprentice," and magic mushrooms and elephants cavorting to Tchaikovsky, Ponchielli, and the like.

Disney made Bach and Borodin immediately accessible to the folks. Templeton and Liberace were doing the same.

Though his ensuing act may not have been entirely unique, Liberace still considered his La Crosse experience the most important episode in his professional life. Still, it took considerable time for the implications to sink in. If the young classical pianist now closed his concerts with parodies, this had no affect on his musical career at first. It would take another two years or more before it began to make a difference. The La Crosse affair is significant in another way, though. It possessed more immediate implications for the young man's life, at least in his imagination. Just as the trauma with which he freighted the move to National Avenue in 1926, when he was seven, shed light on the difficulties in his life at that time, so the La Crosse concert illuminated another metamorphosis when he was twenty. The incident provided him with the excuse or opportunity to redefine his relations with his father.

The psychological subtext of Walter's revolution with respect to his relationship with Sam Liberace is hardly subtle. The younger Liberace described it clearly in his autobiography, shifting immediately from the public and professional meaning of La Crosse to its personal and domestic implications. He associated the two, making no transition between them. La Crosse was his big breakthrough, but it is inseparable from his breaking his father's will, breaking his father, and, ultimately, breaking with his father entirely. Thus, he continued, the episode "made my Dad swallow his pride and allow me to contribute to the support of the family which was still very badly off financially." It marked another kind of turning point with his father, too: "Dad also relented and let me follow my musical career in any direction it led me or that I chose to direct it." After a brief reference to his father's failures, he returns to the theme of his own musical liberation from his father's design—or tyranny. "At last I felt free to play and interpret any kind of music without fear of raising any parental wrath, restrictions and restraints. And I think that was when I began to develop the style of performing that in the not too distant future was to earn me the sobriquet, 'Mr. Showmanship.' . . . It tells people who don't already know it that they are going to get more than just a piano recital when they come to see me."[70] At this point, Sam vanished from his son's aesthetic world.

A messier story roils beneath the surface of this narrative of independence. If his memoir does not describe them clearly, other sources betray more obscure motives that came into play in the rebellion of the son against the father. The subtext itself possesses subtexts. These emerge in an interview he did for a book called *The First Time,* which was published late in 1975. A classic artifact of sexually revolutionized America, this collection of interviews by Karl Fleming and Anne Taylor Fleming offers the personal recollection of a variety of famous and then famous characters about their earliest sexual encounters.[71] After its publication, Liberace protested that he had been misled. He never repudiated the interview; he just insisted that the authors had wanted only the earliest recollections of the famous.[72] If this is so, his revelations are even more illuminating. He began his story with a general discussion of sex and changing sexual mores, including gratuitous references to homosexuality—even if not his own. The tale then detours through the Liberace family's sexual conservatism as the context for his teenage years, and across the rowdy days playing the gin mills and roadhouses in the thirties, which included his first lay, the ostensible object of the interview. With hardly a bridge, however, he jumped backwards again, willy-nilly, to family sex: his brother, masturbation, and most arbitrarily of all, his father. Pausing to describe his father's personal insensitivity and inflexibility, he launched immediately into a discussion of Sam's sex life and its traumatic impact on Walter himself. His father had a mistress, whom his son found out about around the time of the La Crosse concert—"I was about 19," he said. He discovered Sam's philandering in a peculiar way that exaggerated his own sense of betrayal. Leopold Stokowski was coming to Milwaukee. As a surprise, Walter bought concert tickets for his father and himself. Sam refused to go with him. Wally attended, anyway. "So I went to the concert, and there sitting two rows in front of me was my father with another woman. That's how I found out he'd had a mistress for years. . . . It was a terrible shock to me. To think that my father was living with two women! I couldn't conceive of that. It made a tremendous mark on me at the time, because I really took it very emotionally."[73]

As told, this narrative underlines the father's rejection of the son, rather than the other way around. Liberace concluded this interview with even stronger evidence of the anxieties his father generated in the younger Liberace even in his dotage, over a quarter century after the Stokowski concert. In the seventies, Liberace's brother had installed their father in a California nursing home, he continued. "He's next to being a vegetable," Liberace said. "The last time I went to see him he didn't recognize me, and that hurt me. He told my brother George, 'That's not him. I know my boy, and that's not him,'" He concluded: "I made my brother promise not to ever force me to go again."[74]

The old man possessed, it seems, unutterable power to reject and wound his boy, even then. Liberace's memoir hints at the same thing. "He's very old as I write this and has finally come around to admitting that he's proud of the fact that George and I have made the name Liberace internationally famous," Liberace wrote about his almost ninety-year-old parent.[75] The reference does not convince the reader that the old man really is proud—or that the son is truly convinced he has finally won his father's praise. Another interview confirms the suspicion that, even at this late stage, Liberace did not have his father's approval. The Liberaces' old friend John Hlaban repeated a snatch of a conversation between the father and son that underlined Sal's skepticism about his son's career, even when the younger Liberace had become famous: "The old man, the artiste, asked the kid, Lee, 'Why do you play that BS? Why don't you play Rachmaninoff?' But Liberace just wanted to make people happy."[76]

If Salvatore Liberace had repudiated his son, his son played the same game and beat his father with his own brand of punishment. The Stokowski concert coupled with the revelation at La Crosse provided an excuse for vengeance worthy of Neapolitan *mafiosi*. He never made up with Sam. Still, Salvatore survived like some ghostly palimpsest in his son's psyche. According to Scott Thorson, Liberace "seethed with helpless rage every time he thought about the old man."[77] The antagonism suggests his ongoing—and futile—hope for Sam's acceptance. "Liberace never stopped trying to get his father's approval," judged Michael Segell, a writer who worked with the showman earlier.[78]

There were other manifestations of Sam's power. The old man had been demanding, tyrannical, and even physically violent with his children. He was a perfectionist, according to his boy; he was impossible to please. Yet the desire to satisfy him, emulate him, and replicate his standards dominates his middle son's career. Dealing with that influence was a critical issue within his interior life as well. His shift to a new—and profitable—musical form after La Crosse was a means, in this regard, of asserting his own identity in the face of his parent's influence. Conversely, and paradoxically, perhaps, with the real, flesh-and-blood father exiled, the son simply internalized the elements of his father's authority. If he had driven himself (fruitlessly, as it turned out) previously to meet his father's exacting standards of excellence, Liberace's ambition and drive now existed completely for themselves. His own aspirations were as insatiable as his father's demands had been. He had liberated himself from his father and his father's musical standards, but he now became that stricturing parent himself.

In short? Walter Liberace's deep and complicated relationship with his father governed much of what he did, and how he did it. It cast its long shadow even over his sexual preferences and attractions. If in his public career—and even in aspects of his private life—his mother seemed dominant, Frances provided a kind of smoke screen for her son's still-more-problematic relationship with Salvatore. Insofar as the La Crosse concert represented a major realignment of Liberace's inner life, it would be a heavy weight on the young performer's future, heavier indeed than he himself knew.

Appropriately enough in this season of Oedipal realignment with his father, he also discovered sex, both hetero- and homosex, according to different renderings.

The memoirist left a literary record of how his popular music led to his first sexual encounter with a woman. He offered various versions of the experience. In his memoir, he claimed to have been sixteen or a little younger when the cops raided the place where he had been playing for stag parties and strippers. "Needless to say," he wrote, "before the joint I was playing in was hit by the police, I had ceased to be a virgin and found out exactly the meaning of the word, 'prostitute.'"[79] He filled in some of the details of the story for the Flemings in *The First Time*. His age had dropped to thirteen in this account. When he was playing Pick's Club Madrid, one of the singers had volunteered to take him home after they knocked off. "She was a big, chesty broad who sang blues songs. She was a very good-looking woman, and kind of wild, but she was old enough to be my mother—in her thirties." It was summer. The night was warm. She pulled over and began groping the boy. She went down on him. "I didn't quite know what was happening, but I liked it, I liked it," he wrote. "I was all ready in a few minutes for a repeat. Then she crawled over on my lap and screwed me. It was very fast, like would you believe about five strokes?" He returned to her apartment for more, but what dominated his memory as much as anything was getting her lipstick off his white trousers.[80] In his last memoir, *The Wonderful, Private World of Liberace*, the venue is the same, but the chesty broad gets a name. Otherwise, the particulars hardly change. The blues singer, "Miss Bea Haven," gave him a lift home from work and "took 'advantage' of me," he wrote. "She was twice my age and very experienced but she made me feel grown up and manly at last. After that, being around girls my own age didn't excite me at all," he concluded. "Compared to Miss Bea Haven, they all seemed so adolescent."[81]

The episode is not unconvincing. Walter was fifteen or sixteen years old when George married his first wife, the Club Madrid singer. His youth and the nature of the club environment lends plausibility to the tale, as do its classic Liberacean details, like the color of his trousers and his concern with removing the lipstick stains. But he told Scott Thorson a very different deflowering story. He didn't like girls at all, he said to Thorson. But to avoid being designated as a "fag," he insisted, he would have done anything. "If it meant dating he'd do that too, even though the thought of getting physically close to a girl made him nauseated," Thorson related. "Fortunately, he never had to carry his pretense that far." [82]

His saloon engagements, he told Thorson, showed him another world. He discovered gay men. He was performing at the Wunderbar in Wausau, Wisconsin. It was the last half of 1939. As he played, he looked around and saw "men coming in together who weren't the usual after-work blue-collar crowd." He was naïve, he told Thorson, but he finally recognized that they were fellow queers. And true to a classic pattern among homosexual men, the discovery lifted a burden of isolation and alienation from his shoulders, even if he felt too modest and insecure to risk conversation with any of them. "Knowing he wasn't alone, seeing that other men like him were capable of enjoying their lives helped to relieve his sense of isolation." The community remained spiritual only briefly, according to Thorson's account. " 'I could hardly miss the guy,' Lee told me, reminiscing about his first lover. 'He was the size of a door, the most intimidating man I'd ever seen. Every time I looked out in the audience there he was, smiling at me. From then on, he showed up wherever I worked. He'd buy me drinks during our break and tell me how much he liked listening to my music. One night he asked to drive me home. That's the night I lost my virginity,' Lee told me privately." He had hit pay dirt again. He was being courted by "a football hero from the Green Bay Packers." [83]

In one regard, the story is as fantastic as the prostitute version. If the friendly prostitute—the tart with heart—is a sexual fantasy of one order, making it with a door-sized football player is a comparable one from the other side of the fence. Perhaps the entertainer, who, as always, was eager to give his audience what he thought they longed for, then, was telling his readers—chiefly women—what they wanted to hear, while to his boyfriend, he simply inverted the sexual identity of the person to whom he lost his virginity. But other components of the story, as Thorson retold it, make it seem quite as plausible as the Bea Haven narrative. Liberace was playing the Wunderbar in Wausau during this period around 1938 or '39, which was far enough away from Green Bay to make it seem reasonable that an athlete from there would risk a gay encounter without too much fear of being discovered by his teammates or anyone else who knew him.

Even if Liberace's lover had been an insurance salesman, rather than a football player, however, what followed the encounter, according to Thorson's retelling, also smacks of reality.

> According to Lee, sex was a part of the relationship, but not the most important part. He'd never been able to share his deepest feelings with his family and he felt he couldn't trust anyone in the straight world. The football player became Lee's first confidante. He also introduced Lee to other gay men. Many of them came from other cities and they told Lee to look them up if he ever visited their hometowns. Although Lee did not realize it at the time, he was laying the foundation for his own gay network, a group he remembered turning to for companionship, understanding, and sexual gratification in the years to come when so much of his life would be spent on the road. . . .
>
> The year 1940 found him playing two or three gigs a week, making a circuit from Green Bay to Sheboygan to La Crosse and then back to Milwaukee. On the road, Lee said, he made use of the telephone numbers he'd been accumulating. His knowledge of the gay world expanded with each new contact and sexual encounter.

If he did indeed have his first homosexual experience when he was around the age of twenty, the episode occurred within months of the La Crosse concert and the discovery of his father's love affair with Zona Gale Smrz, the very time when he was discovering his own voice in still other ways. This was a critical period for him. Then, too, his own career was coinciding with momentous events in world and national history. In January 1940, his adolescent concert career peaked with his performance at the Pabst Theater with the Chicago Symphony. Four months earlier, the German invasion of Poland had provoked the onset of World War II. The year 1940 saw inexorable forces pulling the United States toward that conflict. Long before Pearl Harbor, the war was already transforming the United States. The economic stagnation that had debilitated the country—and wracked individual households, not least the Liberaces'—was giving way to jobs and prosperity. The country was on a cusp. So was Walter Liberace. By 1940, he was earning a salary that made him look like a millionaire against the deprivations of the mid-thirties. He had found a niche doing what he loved—pleasing people by playing the piano. He had liberated himself, both socially and aesthetically, from his father's grip. He had discovered he not only lusted after men and males' company, but that he could satisfy those desires. He was, however, not at all content. He craved more. He wanted more than Milwaukee—not to mention Sheboygan, La Crosse, and Green Bay—could give him. Wisconsin could not contain his energies and ambition as he entered adulthood. Wartime America was the perfect place for him to experiment and stretch his wings.

Three cheers and a boola-boola for that Gotham haunt of the Westchester aristocracy, the Plaza Persian Room. Its new show is so good, the cigaret gal, who's seen 'em come and go, with jaded eye, said it's the best she's watched here. I agree. The star is a young pianist-entertainer, Liberace.

LEE MORTIMER

CHICO AND CHOPIN

The period from 1941 to 1947 is the most obscure of Liberace's life. His memoir scants it, and he spoke of it seldom to others. What enigmatic references exist muddle dates and data. Fragmentary data suggest only outlines of his wartime history and raise almost as many questions as they answer. Even his place of residence in these years cannot be definitively determined. City directories confirm that he had abandoned Milwaukee by 1942: that year marked the last time his name appeared officially as a part of the Liberace household on National Avenue. While he would relocate to Southern California around 1947, his whereabouts in the interval are uncertain. The murkiness of this period is not irrelevant to his biography in itself, but some things are indisputable. What is clearest of all is that between 1941 and 1944, Walter Liberace changed his entire approach to music. He changed the music he played, he changed the style, he changed the venue, he changed the audience. These adjustments, in turn, established him as one of the up-and-coming entertainers of his generation, which is also clear from otherwise obscure evidence. He abandoned the formal concert stage entirely and remade his career around popular audiences and popular music. Although their nature is more uncertain still, changes in his personal life paralleled the metamorphosis of his career.

Walter Liberace's hometown newspapers shed the first light on the native son's career during this otherwise dark period. Although the pianist departed his hometown more or less permanently in 1941, he returned to

Milwaukee to play important concerts, one in 1942, another two and a half years later in 1944. Newspaper reviews of these programs offer a measure for evaluating transitions in his aesthetic, and they hint at the larger changes in his life that were occurring simultaneously.

On January 16, 1940, Liberace had performed the Liszt A Major with the Chicago Symphony at the Pabst Theater in Milwaukee. No jazzy encores followed the applause. Nine months later, in October, he played another major concert at another Milwaukee concert hall, the Athenaeum. The program for that performance does not exist, but one review indicates his shifting focus. The La Crosse experience was taking root. While laudatory, the notice also suggests some skepticism about the alteration. "A few whose experience had been voluntarily confined to classical music expressed dismay when the young pianist ventured into modern composition," wrote newspaper critic William H. Radloff on October 18, "but on the whole his effort to present a versatile program was well received." [1]

After this concert, Liberace disappeared from Milwaukee for a year and a half. He returned in March 1942, when he took to the stage again. The program he played included a new act in which he played along with phonograph recordings of great pianists.[2] He was still experimenting. Two and half years later, he played the Pabst Theater again. This final wartime engagement revealed his full evolution. Everything about the performance of November 19, 1944, differed completely from his first engagement in the hall, not quite five years before. The programs bore no resemblance to one another. Nor did the form or the presentation of the concerts. Also entirely different was their appeal, the audiences too. As remarkable as these other changes were, however, the publicity surrounding the concert differed in both degree and in kind from the publicity that preceded the earlier one. The new style of marketing portended these other changes.

Posters tacked up around town and quiet notices in the local papers were now things of the past. Hoopla became the order of the day. Actually, Liberace's '42 performance had presaged the publicity campaign two years later. The entertainment writer Buck Herzog, not the classical-music reviewer, reported that performance. After referring to an "extensive concert tour of the East," Herzog noted that the hometown boy had "received salvos of press praises for his unique piano renditions synchronized with phonograph records of the masters." [3]

Who was supposed to review Liberace's performances? The fine-art critics or the popular-entertainment writers? Liberace's new performance tangled the categories. Buck Herzog wrote up the '42 engagement, but the 1944 performance ricocheted back to the music critic Edward P. Halline (who had praised the pianist's traditional concerts of 1938 and 1940). In the mood of the moment, however, the classical reviewer employed the exaggerated language more closely associated with sports and entertainment journalism. Not least, the day before the actual concert, on November 18, he previewed the program with the most untraditional hyperbole. "Long hairs and bobby-soxers may not lie down together like the lion and the lamb at the Pabst tomorrow afternoon," he enthused, "but young Walter Liberace, whose home town is Milwaukee, hopes to have them rolling in the aisle with his explosive pianistic mixture of the classics and boogie woogie. For he is spreading both gospels, hoping to soften the Bach-hardened hearts of one group and to open the jazz jangled ears of the other."[4]

The program itself confirmed the promo. The pianist opened with Beethoven's D Minor Sonata, opus 31, number 2, and Chopin's Nocturne in F Sharp Major. He played these straight, proving, according to one critic, that "he could handle both masters adequately." It was the audience's last glimpse of tradition that evening. The critic described what happened next. "With the aid of a phonograph sitting sedately beside his piano, Mr. Liberace summoned full symphony orchestras to accompany him in excerpts from several famous concertos. He went along in perfect unison with Egon Petri in Liszt's concerto in A major; with an unnamed soloist in the same composer's "Hungarian Fantasy"; and with Vladimir Horowitz in an excerpt from Tchaikovsky's B minor ("Tonight We Love") classic." Liberace did not wait for encores to demonstrate the Templeton-La Crosse trick, either. Thus, as a part of the regular program, he transformed "Home on the Range" and "Deep in the Heart of Texas" into Strauss-style waltzes, "while 'Mairzy Doats,' not a concert standby," sniffed the critic, "was offered in the style of Bach, Brahms, Chopin and Paderewski." After the intermission, he performed Gershwin's "Rhapsody in Blue," Cole Porter's "Begin the Beguine," selections from Duke Ellington, and some boogie-woogie.[5]

The performance received mixed reviews. It amused, even delighted Edward Halline of the *Sentinel,* who had effectively shilled for the pianist the day before. The performer, he noted, "scrambled the masters, dressed up popular airs in classic garments and superimposed his nimble performance on those of major orchestras, as reproduced by a phonograph. . . . The program was mainly a series of stunts, expertly done, and Mr. Liberace had his good-sized audience applauding enthusiastically most of the time."[6] Over at the *Journal,* however, the music critic looked askance. Without invidiousness, he called the performance "a jukebox piano recital," but he reported the phonograph trick with raised eyebrows. The gambit was "novel and well-performed," he conceded, but he observed in passing, too, that the performer could play adequately enough without needing "the aid of another pianist on a machine." He praised more reluctantly still Liberace's classicizing of popular tunes. "In both these sections of the program," he wrote, "Mr. Liberace showed versatility and wit reminiscent of Alex Templeton. But there was left the impression that a little of such gamboling goes a long way." As for the Gershwin, Porter, and Ellington? "He played this idiom with skill, and did not need the runs and other embellishments which he frequently employed."[7]

With the development of his act from 1940 to 1944, Walter Liberace was obviously trying to make sense of his epiphany in La Crosse. What exactly did he have in mind? He himself offered various explanations about what he was doing and his reasons for doing it. These differ significantly, yet, taken together, they reveal facets of a whole life.

His most standard explanation of his change revolved around his dissatisfaction with the limits of traditional concerts. He disdained the sharp distinctions, for example, between classical and contemporary music. Music was music, he insisted. He rejected the distinctions, too, between highbrow and lowbrow audiences, the "long hairs" versus the "bobby-soxers." Halline wrote that Liberace "hoped to soften the Bach-hardened hearts of one group and to open the jazz jangled ears of the other," but the words could have been the pianist's own.

He disliked even more the isolation of the performer from the audience, he insisted, and what he considered the tendency of classical concerts to isolate and fragment the audience itself. "I felt being a concert pianist was a very lonely business," he wrote in his memoir. "I felt as if I were up there playing alone and each of the people in the audience was alone in his own little world listening to me. The audience never came together as it did when I played the 'Three Little Fishies.'" If he wanted to break down the isolation between the performer and the audience, then, he also wanted to unify, in effect, the audience itself, by reemphasizing the power and delight of all melody and rhythmic line. He wanted to present music to new audiences in a new way. He wanted to give folks "something new and different, . . . to introduce people, who had never been to a piano recital or a symphony concert because they thought it would bore them, to the wonderful works they'd been denying themselves." About the same time, he confessed later, he realized "that my heart was not in concertizing but in entertaining."[8]

1 (above) The "artiste"—as Salvatore Liberace called himself—cut a darkly handsome figure despite his diminutive height of five foot three. Violent, irascible, and relentlessly devoted to music, he was nearly equal parts Latin machismo and bohemian self-indulgence. *Courtesy of the Liberace Foundation, Las Vegas, NV.*

2 (left) Materialistic and possessive, headstrong and outspoken, Frances Zuchowski Liberace never transcended her rural Wisconsin, Polish immigrant roots. From her marriage in 1910 until her death, she had two passions in her life, the church and her children. *Courtesy of the Liberace Foundation, Las Vegas, NV.*

3 (right) The union of the conservative Polish farm girl and the worldly Neapolitan musician was not made in heaven; it was, however, fruitful. Taken around 1925, this photo shows the three eldest Liberace children: Wally on the left, wearing the cap; George, holding his brother's dog; their cousin Esther; and, on the right, sister Angelina. Aged six or seven, the youngest child had already established his reputation as a musical prodigy. *Courtesy of the Liberace Foundation, Las Vegas, NV.*

4 (below) As an adult, Liberace called the move from West Allis to West Milwaukee a traumatic experience. The new house on National Avenue, however, was a step up in every way for his family. Indeed, from 1926 to 1929, before the Depression, was the best time the Liberaces ever experienced as a family. *Courtesy of the Liberace Foundation, Las Vegas, NV.*

5 Around the time of the move to National Avenue in 1926, a series
of events changed Wally Liberace's life. Besides weathering the
"trauma" of the move itself, he began studying with a new piano
teacher. Florence Kelly was more than his teacher, however; for
almost two decades, she remained the most important person in his
life outside his family. A disciplined pianist herself, she was also "an
elegant lady" who was at the same time furiously uncompromising,
willful, and demanding. She was the perfect mentor for the distracted
prodigy. *Courtesy of the Liberace Foundation, Las Vegas, NV.*

6 As a small child, Wally Liberace knew the Polish virtuoso Ignacy Paderewski from his father's collection of famous Victor Red Seal recordings. Around 1926 or 1927, he actually met the great man. From then on, the brilliant, eccentric Paderewski acted as a goad and model for the young pianist. Liberace identified himself publicly with his idol, especially early in his career, as demonstrated in this photo of the twenty-four-year-old musician placing a wreath at Paderewski's tomb. *Photo: Chase Statler, Washington, D.C. Courtesy of the Liberace Foundation, Las Vegas, NV.*

7 Performing in Chicago's Kimball Hall, winning auditions with Frederick Stock of the Chicago Symphony, and even soloing with that august ensemble in 1940, Walter Liberace had established a musical reputation that provided the basis for numerous concert tours of the upper Midwest, from Sheboygan to Omaha, in the late thirties. Already keen to public relations, he was still a teenager when he circulated attractive publicity stills like this one prior to his engagements. *Photo: Maurice Seymour. Courtesy of the Liberace Foundation, Las Vegas, NV.*

8 (left) Despite his passion for classical music, popular performance attracted him, too. The cash appealed, but playing pop music also resolved some of the deepest tensions of his interior life. In any case, 1937 was not a bad time for playing jazz and boogie-woogie. The teenaged Wally Liberace—hands on the piano on the right—profited twice over, then, by performing with various local bands in the mid-thirties. *Courtesy of the Liberace Foundation, Las Vegas, NV.*

9 (opposite, bottom) Around his twenty-first birthday, his life changed. He began jazzing up his formal concerts even as he dressed up his supper-club show, as here at an unnamed club, appearing in the most elegant eveningwear. The watershed year of 1939–40 also saw his break with his father, and his discovery of homosex when he was playing a six-month gig in Wausau, Wisconsin, just inland from Greenbay. *Courtesy of the Liberace Foundation, Las Vegas, NV.*

10 (above) In 1941, he decamped for New York to make his "big splash." "I had gone as far as I could in my home town," he said. "I was still only a big frog in a little pond. I felt I wasn't getting the recognition I deserved." Glory followed only after four years of relentless effort and deprivation, but his poverty during those first few years did not diminish the pleasure he took in Christmas in Manhattan, which he celebrated with his elder brother just after Pearl Harbor. *Courtesy of the Liberace Foundation, Las Vegas, NV.*

LIBERACE
(Liber'AH'Chee)
At The World's Most Priceless Piano

MANAGEMENT
MCA
Artists Ltd.
Music Corporation of America

11 (opposite) Homosexuality remained his secret in those years, but while he may have resisted having sex with other men, the other manifestations of his queerness were beyond his power of transformation, almost beyond his power of awareness. If men filled his fantasies, so did silk corsages, dandy dress, and pretty pictures. *Courtesy of AP/Wide World Photos.*

12 (above) Under the aegis of his West Coast patron, Clarence Goodwin, Walter Liberace's career changed radically around 1946 or '47. He launched a recording career and gave up his "finger-synching" act. Not least, he bought and traveled with the very grand Blüthner piano. Besides being a brilliant-looking, brilliant-sounding instrument, the "priceless" $25,000 grand became a major ploy in his new publicity offensive after the war. *Courtesy of the Liberace Foundation, Las Vegas, NV.*

13 (above) Among other innovations of his postwar public relations campaign, he adopted the gimmick of going only by his last name. He used its phonetic spelling as an added trick. His move to California, around the time of his Long Beach Municipal Auditorium performance of February 1947, also put him at the center of the American entertainment industry. *Courtesy of the Liberace Foundation, Las Vegas, NV.*

14 (opposite) A journalist from the Milwaukee years had referred to the pianist as a public relations genius. His self-promotion campaign of 1947 characterized this talent as nothing had before. He flooded the entertainment market with his advertising postcards, and he never missed an opportunity for feeding journalists with "story ideas." While he filled his 1947 press kit with such leads, it did not exhaust his repertoire. Thus, he introduced in a press release the notion, illustrated here, of "warming his hands with the vapor from hot water to relax his fingers" before every performance. Newsmen ate it up. *Courtesy of AP/Wide World Photos.*

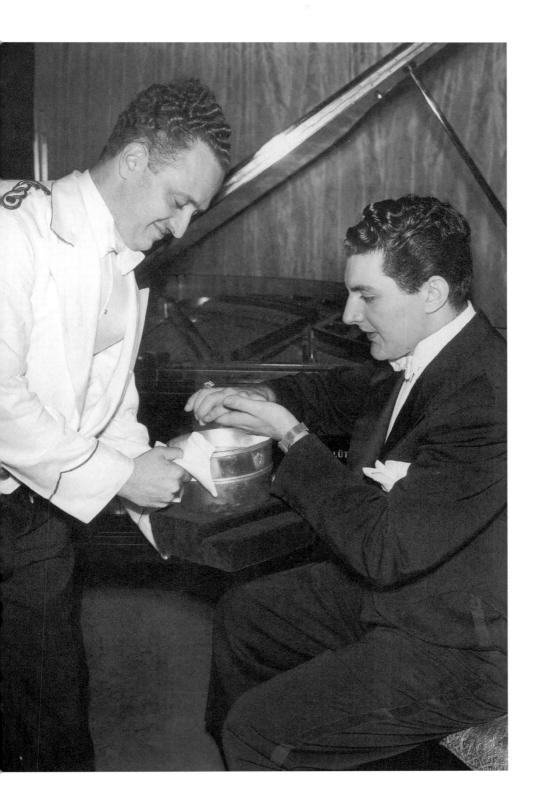

15 The publicity campaign coupled with the shift to Hollywood paid off.
By 1949, Liberace was playing the hottest clubs in the United States.
He broke into movies and won an invitation to play the White House
the same year. On the evening of February 25, 1950, he performed in
the East Room for the Washington Press Photographers Ball with
such other notables as Dorothy Lamour, Wally Cox, Marge and Gower
Champion, Jo Stafford, and Jack Benny. In the audience, of course,
was President Harry S Truman. Still, the showman's ambition remained
unsated. *Courtesy of the Liberace Foundation, Las Vegas, NV.*

He was formulating a new aesthetic and a new sort of sociology of performing, in effect. Both, however, corresponded to more interior motives that had manifested themselves even in his high school years. As a teenager, he had felt personal alienation, which was comparable, of course, to the isolation he identified with the concert stage. Unable, in effect, to deal with the real world on a day-to-day basis, the teenage Wally Liberace had conjured a new one that he could manage and control. It was the gang in the high school gym hanging around the battered old piano he was playing. It was the crowd in the school auditorium who joined his conspiracy of making fun of himself in his flowing smock and beret. He had broken down their hostility even as he resolved his own alienation; in the process, he created a new community around his own new persona. He redefined social relations and social order through art, entertainment, and performance. As he acknowledged, this characteristic itself arose out of his need to redress his sense of personal isolation, which was rooted, in part, in sexual alienation. From his mid-teen years, he nurtured his ability to please people, to get them out of themselves, to make them laugh: to create a new world for them, and, of course, for himself. After 1941, such personal motives coincided perfectly with his new professional ones.

While aesthetics as well as psychology inspired the alteration of Liberace's career toward boogie-woogie and away from the classics, he later admitted that still other considerations came into play in his decision to change tacks. Forty years later, he told Scott Thorson that he had abandoned the concert stage because he considered himself inadequate as a classical pianist. According to Thorson's account, the Pabst Theater performance with the Chicago Symphony marked the watershed in Liberace's life. "By the evening of the concert Lee told me he knew the Liszt concerto so well he could have played it backward," Thorson reported. "His performance was received exactly as he had anticipated. He didn't set the concert hall on fire—but he didn't disgrace himself either. A warm wave of applause greeted the end of his performance. The critics were kind, in view of his obvious youth, but Lee hadn't indelibly impressed any of them with his brilliance. He felt a mild depression that quickly passed. And then, without looking back, he returned to the world he loved—the world of saloons and night clubs."[9]

Events did not actually transpire like this. The Pabst concert was no failure by any means. On the contrary, the reviews lauded the performance. "A gift for brilliant pianism" is not merely "kind"; and while "the sure hand of the craftsman" might be damning praise, "transfigured moments which only genius can create" is not.[10] Indeed, the reviews of the first Pabst engagement were far more uniformly laudatory than were those greeting his aesthetic experiments in '42 and '44. If his Pabst performance cannot objectively be called a failure, the possibility that the pianist believed it so subjectively bears closer examination.

Liberace knew how he played. He was smart as well as talented. He had studied all the great piano literature. Even so, he had always leaned toward certain forms and expressions of classical music. The romantics, especially the late ones, dominated his repertoire. He loved Chopin, but he venerated Liszt, Tchaikovsky, and Paderewski. He adopted the style of late romantics, too, with their tendency toward bombast, extravagance, flamboyance, and drama in interpretation. Whatever the demands of his audience, he testified later, "in the depths of my soul, I am still a romantic."[11] When he was seventeen, his first newspaper review noted his "youthful vigor," "physicality," and "talents for flair and showmanship"—the hallmarks of late-romantic performance; even so, the same reviewer suggested the need for "toning of years and deeper experience"—more subtlety and nuance, in effect. "The runs and other embellishments" condemned by another reviewer were a part of this whole dramatic approach. Perhaps the performer's sense of inadequacy, then, arose from his inability or refusal to adapt or change the style to fit different forms, or perhaps even to alter his repertoire. By the time of the first performance at the Pabst, after all, he had already offered the Liszt A Major Concerto twice publicly in Milwaukee. Perhaps, then, he believed that he had gone as far as he could go doing what he did the way he did it. By the same token, he could turn this liability, otherwise defined, to better account by doing something different for a different audience.

Beyond this, other notions of inadequacy also came into play in his decision to abandon the traditional concert stage. Thus, if the end was not merely excellent concert playing—which Walter Liberace might have achieved—but a more grandly conceived notion of Musical Success, his concert career in general, and his first Pabst performance in particular, could well have seemed inadequate. Liberace's perfectionism and ambition goaded him constantly. Over and over, in various contexts, the performer discussed his father's intractable perfectionism; he had inherited the characteristic, he insisted. According to Florence Kelly, from the time he was eleven, he had condemned other children for their failure to measure up not only to his own standards but also to a formal, abstract standard of virtue and excellence. He demanded that of himself, and the sense of his own limits hung over him always and compelled him to make major alterations to his life and career. He was driven. He did not want anything ordinary, not even ordinary success.

Measured against his own ambitions, then, the plaudits of Milwaukee critics might have seemed faint praise, and the applause of audiences in Sheboygan, Decorah, and Dubuque more anemic still. He was at least as determined, willful, and ambitious as he was talented, and so his shift to a new form of musical expression around 1940 arose in a certain measure out of his search for a field or venue worthy of his best, most ferocious energies. He envisioned his program shift as the way to attracting larger audiences. Larger audiences, in turn, pointed the way to Fame. Almost as important, he calculated that his decision to change his course could lead to glory and cash. He had calculated the main chance all his life. Popular entertainment offered the possibility of larger and more imme-diate monetary rewards than did plodding through the cornfield concert circuit of the Middle West. Who were the great pianists, beyond Horo-witz, Rubinstein, and Iturbi? In comparison, popular entertainment was a much broader field. He determined that he could capitalize, literally, on audience enthusiasm. Describing people's reaction to his fun and whimsy in La Crosse, he said, "they relaxed and enjoyed themselves and . . . they smiled. That was the big thing, for me. They smiled a way that they hadn't for the straight classical repertoire, no matter how well I performed." The house lights rose; a light bulb glowed above his head: "And suddenly I had an idea of how to make piano playing pay more than the $35 a week I had been getting." [12]

Last, if not least, Liberace also professed to prefer a different audi-ence. "I was happy playing classical music. I love it," he testified. "But the people for whom I played the classical music were not the people I wanted to please. Early in my career I had traveled as a concert pianist and had often played to a handful of musical purists. But I longed to please the man on the street, the people who had relatively little appreciation of music." [13] It was his neighbors in West Allis he wanted to please, his par-ents' friends in West Milwaukee he longed to delight. His career change honored them.

The desire to alter the relationship between audience and performer, his personal imperatives to charm and delight, his furious ambition, his desire for wealth and fame, and, finally, his identity with the common folk all drove the evolution of Liberace's career, but it took some time for him to pull it all together between 1940 and 1944. Neither the process, the chronology, nor even site of that development is clear. When did the young pianist give up the traditional concert stage? He might have continued his community concert series into the new decade, but he left no record of playing those upper Midwest towns after 1940. The Athen-aeum concert in the fall of 1940—he was twenty-one—was the last verifiable classical concert that he performed in the more-or-less traditional manner. The transformation did not occur exclusively in Milwaukee, either; indeed, the major line of development took place outside his hometown. As his ambition drew him away from the classical stage, so his ambition also outgrew Milwaukee and the Midwest. In the weeks or months after his fall Athenaeum concert in 1940, he left his native turf for what the journalist Buck Herzog had described—obviously with assistance from the performer—as "an extensive concert tour of the East."[14] He abandoned National Avenue for Fifth Avenue.

In *The Things I Love,* Liberace described his shift to New York City: "I left Milwaukee in 1941 and went East to make my big splash. I was already twenty-one years old and figured I had gone as far as I could in my home town. I had the best jobs, the best work, and was the most sought-after pianist in town. Indeed, I had more work than I could handle, but I was still only a big frog in a little pond. I felt I wasn't getting the recognition I deserved."[15]

The duration of his tenure in Manhattan is obscure. Also in *The Things I Love,* he jests that he never even made it there, as he got hung up in New Jersey. The same book, however, describes his first home away from Milwaukee, "a one-room apartment in New York."[16] He was certainly in residence in the city by Christmas, when a dated photograph captures him in Times Square and a second shows him in what is obviously his "one-room apartment" with his older brother before a decorated tree.[17]

He returned to Milwaukee in the spring of 1942 but disappeared again almost immediately, apparently going to New York again. Although he traveled extensively between 1942 and 1947, he was certainly back in New York regularly during this period, and his experiences in the metropolis are important to understanding his development, both musical and personal.

Liberace liked challenges, and New York was a challenge of the first order. His first sojourn in the city in 1940–41 was especially hard. "An extensive concert tour of the East" was hyperbole or an inside joke. He revealed some of the tribulations he experienced to Scott Thorson forty years later. If he had been a big frog in Milwaukee's small pond, as he told Thorson, he was hardly a tadpole in Manhattan's lake. "For a while he actually went hungry," Thorson wrote. He hit the Horn and Hardart cafeterias, making tomato soup out of ketchup and hot water. "It took guts to stay on—but stay on he did, Lee told me proudly."[18] Indeed, his determination—his ambition—never flagged. "People who know him best say Walter Valentino Liberace always has a goal," an interviewer noted in

1953. This first stint in Manhattan offered proof of that assertion: "When he was an unknown musician in New York—washing dishes while pounding the pavements in search of concert assignments, his goal was Carnegie Hall. 'I used to sit in Radio City all day with a dollar in my pocket,' says Liberace. 'I'd walk past Carnegie Hall and say to myself: 'Someday I'm going to give a concert there.'"[19] Sometimes he made it into the halls, Carnegie and others. With no money for tickets, he appeared at intermission dressed in his dinner jacket and drifted back into the auditorium when the bells sounded. He caught concerts and Broadway plays this way. "This system worked equally well at the Metropolitan Opera, and I must say," he added, "that half an opera is better than no opera at all."[20]

While scrabbling for food, scavenging culture, and calculating his career, he did what he could to hold body and soul together. He repeated how he had worked as a rehearsal pianist in these times. "Those experiences in cold, drafty halls gave him a healthy respect for the dancers and singers, the 'gypsies' of Broadway," he told Thorson. "As he played he watched, judging the individual performers, developing an eye for talent that would serve him well in the years to come when he would choose acts for his own shows."[21] During this first residency in Gotham in 1941, or perhaps during the second in 1942, he made some cash playing as an accompanist. He recalled a stint with the famous vocalist Helen Morgan, which likely fell within this period. "I was a good foil for her. I was an emotional kid, and when she sang 'Bill,' the tears would roll down my cheeks," he laughed long after. "But when I'd heard it a lot, one night I didn't cry. Helen got furious with me. 'What are you trying to do,' she said, 'ruin my act?'"[22] He made reference to playing clubs and private parties in these years, too, but it seems more likely that these engagements took place in the later New York period rather than during the tough year and a half after he first abandoned Milwaukee.[23]

He got some reasonable gigs. He had one job that lasted for about six months in West Orange, New Jersey, across the Hudson River from New York City.[24] He told a newspaper reporter that he had played a concert with the New Jersey Philharmonic Orchestra, as well, "and was offered the opportunity to appear with Martin Gould to present 'Rhapsody in Blue'"[25] These jobs allowed him to feast on something more than watery ketchup soup, but they did not satisfy his ambition. In 1941, he signed for a multiperformance engagement to play the Normandie Roof, the fancy dining room at the swank Mont Royal Hotel in Montreal, Canada.[26] World events undercut his pleasure. As 1942 dawned, America's entry into World War II cast a pall over the futures of all young men his age.

With the declaration of hostilities in December 1941, draft boards around the country began calling up American men to service. As a strapping, single, twenty-two-year-old man, Walter Liberace was a prime candidate. It was perhaps to answer a draft-board notice that the pianist returned home in the spring of 1942. George joined the Seabees and served honorably in the Pacific, entertaining troops and winning some small fame in the process. His younger brother did not go off to war. He told Thorson that a "cyst on his spine" exempted him.[27] He returned to New York, where he continued to innovate and to experiment with performance.

In spite of the draft and military service, scores of musicians and performers still trooped about Tin Pan Alley and the country looking for their break, something to distinguish themselves from the others. The gimmick of playing with the phonograph provided just the trick for Walter Liberace. It was, as an early reviewer had noted, "an innovation entirely his own."[28] It remains so. The scheme required a quirky imagination coupled with enormous technical skill and awesome audacity—not to mention hokey sincerity tinged with camp. He described the innovation and how it came about in his autobiography.

> I'd seen vaudeville acts where men who couldn't sing a note,
> mouthed their impressions of Rudy Vallee, Bing Crosby,
> Morton Downey, Jimmy Durante and other big recording
> stars. It always got a big hand. . . . But it set me to thinking
> about how the gimmick might be adapted to music.
>
> Ever since I was a very little boy I'd been able to play,
> almost immediately, anything I heard. So with that for a
> starter I began to experiment on doing an act with me at the
> piano, "sitting in" as it were, with some of the big popular
> bands of the day or substituting for one of the great concert
> pianists playing with one of the big symphony orchestras. I
> figured if people with no voice at all could get big hands
> mouthing along with a singer, I, who really could play the
> piano, could make it big with the same basic idea. . . .
>
> I spent many hours rehearsing with recordings of Arthur
> Rubinstein, Vladimir Horowitz, Paderewski, Jose Iturbi,
> playing as solo artists with the greatest symphony orchestras
> like the New York Philharmonic under Toscanini, the Phila-
> delphia Symphony under Stokowski, the Boston Pops un-
> der Fiedler, the London Philharmonic under Sir John Barbi-
> rolli. . . . I was brazenly placing myself in the same league

with these great names of music. But I realized that in doing
so I had to be very good.

What emerged was the music of two pianos, mine and
the great artist with whom I was playing. These blended into
one as if I, alone, were being accompanied by a great concert
orchestra.[29]

Afterwards, he tended to gloss over the innovation, obscuring it even as
he muddled this whole period of his life. Thus, his memoirs insist that the
act lasted only for a brief time: union opposition cut it short. "They said
by doing what I was doing I was using records to take the place of live
musicians and keeping them out of work." So, he concluded, "my gimmick, like most gimmicks, was short lived."[30] In fact, it was not short lived
by any means. He practiced it for five or six years. More critically, it provided the heart of his act and the basis of his waxing fame in the early
forties. After 1942, his "finger synching" propelled him to fame and glory.
He had worked out an act that differentiated him from other performers.
Indeed, he had worked out a distinguished performance on its own terms.
He had an act and a half. He was becoming a hot commodity.

Abel Green, one of the most important men at *Variety,* offered a
thumbnail sketch of what the showman did in reviewing Liberace's intermission act in the Persian Room of Manhattan's Plaza Hotel around 1945.
By this time, Liberace had honed his act to perfection. "Liberace brings a
nice style to the big league nitery circuit with his legit and synchronized
piano recital. It runs the gamut from synchronizing with the Boston Pops
recording of Gershwin's 'Rhapsody in Blue' (playing the Jesus Sanroma
part) to a legit Chopin recital of the 'Polonaise,' Grieg, '12th Street Rag,'
boogie-woogie, Beethoven and a novelty piano duet with a femme customer (who gets a token gift for her collaboration)."[31]

The flawless accompaniment to the phonographs astonished audiences, but, as Abel Green suggested, the act went beyond the skill of
nimble fingers. The pianist also played classical music, or classic themes
and excerpts unaccompanied by recordings. He mixed in popular music
or ballads just as easily. "Running the gamut of concert timbre, hot music,
and Alec Templeton operatic travesties," the variety delighted audiences
as much as his pianistic skills did. He played Jerome Kern off against
Helen Morgan, "The Warsaw Concerto" against boogie-woogie, Chopin
against Gershwin, and back again. Indeed, the unpredictability of the mix
provided an extra fillip of audiences' pleasure. Thus, one critic celebrated
"that touch of whimsy that makes him give out with a bit of boogie just at
the point when you expect the classics."[32]

Pianistic virtuosity and musical variety constituted only one part of his act. True, he could play the piano, but he played the house as well—or better. He created an extraordinary rapport with his audiences. He loved integrating the patrons into his act; they loved participating. Taking popular requests provided only one source of the fun. He also gave piano lessons. It was his best trick, observed one reviewer, "getting some patron who doesn't know one note from a hole in the head, to make his debut in a duet with Liberace. They all laugh when he sits down at the piano and they are still laughing when he gets up which is a neat job unless one evening Iturbi shows up and fools Liberace." [33] In his interchanges with the audience, he made dialogue as central to his act as playing the piano. Dialogue was important to the request part of his performance, and to his lessons, too. Beyond this he ad-libbed easily and worked his patter to a fine art. "Likability," "personableness," and similar terms permeate almost every discussion of his act from these early years.

He made it all look easy, but he was working very hard. His act was a whole little cosmos in which he was a divinity of the parts. More than one reviewer noted the skill with which the performer managed and mastered everything, however small—lighting, props, entrances, exits, and other particulars. Presentation was as critical to him as what he did and how he interacted with the audience. "Not to underestimate the virtuosity of Liberace," apologized one critic, but the pianist's control over the minutia of the act demanded equal respect. "Incidental as these details are to a performance, we admire the attention that has gone into making the visual picture and mood as well-groomed as the star and his training.[34] Echoing this praise of Liberace's command of details, another reviewer gave, in the process, a nice word picture of what it was like, sitting in a darkened room anticipating the performance: "Bob Grant and his smooth dance crew 'roll the drums,' the lights go out, and you hear exquisite piano playing of the Chopin score from 'Song to Remember.' Then on the climax and crescendo, the lights gradually brighten to full, and seated at a magnificent Concert Grand, in white tie and tails, is a dark, handsome young man of some 27 years whose resemblance to Cornel Wilde, who played the title role in the picture, is startling." [35]

He mastered other details, too. If he apprehended a critical source of audience delight in the mix and match of classical and popular, other elements of the act built this same juxtaposition into the very structure of the performance. The grand piano, the classical music, the formal eveningwear, and later the inevitable candelabra, all bespoke formality, elegance, and traditional culture. The patter, the folksy asides, his friendliness, sympathy, and "just folks" attitude toward performance played off another set of values entirely. His extraordinary audience appeal suggests the power of his insights—or instincts—in structuring this duality into his performance.

Whatever the source of his magic, however, he was bowling people over. The impression was perfect. It was all too splendid! "Just imagine one so youthful, handsome, and personable being so great a virtuoso as LIBERACE!" sang the critics.[36]

By 1943 or '44, Walter Liberace had perfected his act, but he had also found the perfect vehicle for its delivery. Had he scorned the physical limits of the traditional concert stage? It was not a medium that lent itself to his act, anyway. Thus, the reviewer for the Milwaukee *Journal* had complained that the piano had overpowered the phonograph in 1944. The innovation called for a more intimate environment. It was made to order for fancy nightclubs and elegant dining establishments. Indeed, Liberace's whole act complemented this setting, just as his supper-club performances help illuminate an institution and an era.

Squeezed between the eras of big bands on the one side and television on the other, the supper club has attracted little attention as a cultural phenomenon. In its heyday in the forties, it mirrored peculiar social and economic circumstances of the decade. It drew on the tradition of European café society after World War I, but, more strictly American, it lacked the flapper generation's avant-garde daring and recklessness. The Depression had tempered and moderated café-society cynicism. The supper club reflected, in part, the era's wartime prosperity after the exigencies of the Great Depression. Although big bands, swing, and even movies dominated popular, democratic entertainment from the thirties, the fancy dining rooms, supper clubs, and exclusive nightspots filled a breach for the middle and upper classes. Their associations lay not only with the elites, but with old-line Protestant elites, in particular. Thus it was that one reviewer referred to one of the most notable of the Manhattan clubs as "the Gotham haunt of the Westchester aristocracy." Indeed, a kind of WASPy tone permeated "the big league nitery circuit," as one non-WASP critic called it. Slightly understated Anglo elegance dominated the form, and terms like "svelte," "swank," "posh," "smart," and "sophisticated" permeated the standards of the institution. It was a world of tuxedos and dinner jackets, of long gowns and corsages, of tinkling crystal and muted conversation.

Catering to a unique audience, the clubs were founded in notions of sophistication and wealth, good manners and refinement. The club was an urban phenomenon, too, when WASPy elites had no fears about strolling downtown streets all night. More often than not, the clubs were attached to the grandest old downtown hotels, which were themselves in their fullest pre-interstate highway bloom of elegance. Every great city had its great hotels—the sources of local pride: the Peabody in Memphis, the Fairmont in San Francisco, the Plaza and Waldorf-Astoria in New York, the Bellerive in Kansas City, the Copley Plaza in Boston, Baker's in Dallas, the Monteleone and Roosevelt in New Orleans, the William Penn in Pittsburgh, Chicago's Palmer House. And all the great hotels had their elegant dining rooms and supper clubs with the names that make a kind of subtle litany: the Embassy Room, the Terrace Room, the Vanity Fair Room, the Empire Room, the Wedgwood Room, the Flame Room, the Persian Room, the Normandie Roof. They all became Walter Liberace's turf. Although swank hotel dining rooms defined the norm, some cities, especially the greatest metropolises, spawned even more sophisticated clubs independent of the hotels. In New York, there was Le Ruban Bleu, Spivy's Roof, and the Rainbow Room in a penthouse at Rockefeller Center, all of which Liberace played in these years. Manhattan also boasted the Stork Club and the Latin Quarter. Hollywood offered Ciro's and Mocambo; he performed there, too. All formed a variation on the theme. Their clientele tended to be more urbane, stylish, and liberated than the patrons of the standard supper club. All, however, also sprang from the same or similar circumstances.

Club patrons had a certain amount of both cash and free time. Servants might have kept the children, for example, while parents were out enjoying a night on the town that might have included a romantic evening in the hotel attached to the club. But, especially in heat of wartime and just after, the institution suggested romance in the absence of children and servants, too. Military uniforms competed with tuxedoes and dinner jackets over martinis, and the circumstance of soldiers added urgency to the romance of the supper-club scene as young men prepared to enlist, packed for the front, or celebrated their leave from war. With elegant young women in eveningwear hanging on their arms, they offer a snapshot of a passing moment in American history.

This was the venue; this was the audience upon which Walter Liberace built his fame. Truly, in the decade after 1942, few entertainers knew this circuit so completely. And few turned it so completely to personal and professional advantage.

He had inaugurated his supper-club act in 1941 at the Normandie Roof at Montreal's Hotel Mont Royal. He scored high and won a return engagement the next year, at which he claimed the salary of $350 a week, ten times what he had earned in Milwaukee's Red Room three years before. That year, he also added the Flame Room at the Radisson Hotel in Minneapolis. Two years later, he was doing better still. In 1943, he signed on for a whole series of engagements at the Statler chain of hotels. He played the Terrace Room in Detroit, the Terrace Room in St. Louis, and the Oval Room at the Copley Plaza, Boston. He had found his niche.

His career expanded even more significantly in 1944. While still playing in Montreal, he added the Embassy Room in the national capital, the Cleveland Statler's Terrace Room, and the Vanity Fair Room in Toronto. He had returned to his hometown in the fall to play what reviewers called the "jukebox recital," but by this time, such programs had become anomalous. He was not one to turn down a lucrative gig, however, especially in his hometown. In any case, he quit Milwaukee for Las Vegas, Nevada, almost immediately after the November 19 engagement. His month-long run between Thanksgiving and Christmas, 1944, at the Ramona Room of the Last Frontier Hotel, was the first in what would be literally hundreds of performances in the gambling center over the next forty-three years. While his association with Las Vegas forms a separate chapter in his life, still, his initial performance in Nevada affirms all the other patterns in Liberace's wartime career.[37]

While Las Vegas—and Liberace, too, for that matter—would became synonymous with vulgarity and democratic taste from the mid-fifties or early sixties, a different standard prevailed in the forties. The Last Frontier and El Rancho Vegas, the first two hotels on what would be later be called the Strip, were at that time more rural, Western versions of the great inner-city hotels and clubs where Liberace had been playing since 1941. Elegance reigned. The main dining and entertainment facility—the Ramona Room—was done up in Western style with flagstones, exposed beams, and wagon-wheel chandeliers. It was only pseudo-rough, however. It could seat six hundred guests at one time and boasted an excellent stage with perfect sightlines. The Western elegance came with a great deal of cash. Maxine Lewis, the entertainment director, offered him an initial salary of seven hundred dollars a week. After his first performance, she doubled it for his six-week run, which would have grossed him a whopping nine thousand dollars.[38] He was on a roll.

In 1945, the performer added another monument to his career—a very significant twelve-week run at the Empire Room at Chicago's most prestigious hotel, the Palmer House, where he played with another performer fated for a national reputation, Mike Douglas. He worked with pre-fame Marge and Gower Champion at this time, too.[39] This was also the year that he performed at the Buffalo Statler's Terrace Room and the

William Penn Hotel in Pittsburgh. Most important, however, he was making an impression back in New York City, apparently his base of operations all along. He entertained the tuxedo- and gown-clad guests at the ultra-sophisticated Rainbow Room opened by the Rockefellers in a penthouse high above Rockefeller Center. He had still more notable engagements in Manhattan. His greatest break came with his stint at the swankest of the swank supper clubs, the Persian Room, at the plushest of hotels, the Plaza.

It was 1945. He was still only the intermission act, performing for a scant twelve minutes, but he was playing the most famous room in New York and seconding one of the biggest draws of the era, the pianist Hildegard, who also, by a fluke, happened to be a Wisconsin native. He drew considerably on the other star's technique. Thirteen years older than her fellow Milwaukeean, Hildegard had won her spurs on the supper-club circuit in the thirties but really came into her own with the war. While, in later years, she forgot that her fellow pianist from the Midwest had performed while she took her break at the Plaza, she did recall him studying her performance at Chicago's Palmer House. "Of course I knew him, and he would sit there and just watch me over and over and over again, so he got a lot of ideas from me," she told a reporter long after. Practicing classy elegance and very high style, she maintained a certain aloofness from the audience and went by only one name. She insisted that she always left her fans wanting more. She played in elbow-length gloves that became her signature. She practiced other techniques that audiences loved—and that Liberace copied. "I gave away roses to VIPs and other people," she said, "and also he noticed that I had a handkerchief and that I had characteristics—roses and the hanky and the glove—that were a part of my image." "I wore elaborate clothes, too," she added. If the young man from West Allis had watched her closely in Chicago, he admired her in New York, too, long before they shared billing. In 1941, he had practiced his artistic skills for her, hand painting a white satin blouse with her portrait and her trademarks—roses, a glove, and a keyboard—which she treasured for forty-five years.[40]

Besides the fact that he was sharing a billing with a celebrity pianist at one of the great spots in Manhattan, Liberace had still other reasons to boast about his performance at the Persian Room. The Bible of the entertainment world, *Variety,* reviewed the act, which is notable in itself. It did not merely note the performer, however; its editor, Abel Green, wrote the glowing notice that appeared on July 18, 1945. "Liberace looks like a cross between Cary Grant and Robert Alda (who plays Gershwin in the Warner Picture). He has an effective manner, attractive hands which he spotlights properly and, withal, rings the bell in a dramatically lighted, well-presented, showmanly routine. He should snowball into box office, which at the moment he's not, but he's definitely a boff cafe act." [41] "A boff cafe act." "Snowball into box office." The pianist had just turned twenty-six. He was arriving, or at least the big guns were signaling his arrival. Coming from *Variety,* coming from "Abel," as the editor signed himself, this was both gold and goad.

New York was noticing Liberace. Manhattan was remembering his name. And, with unflagging energy, he did everything to keep that name before the public. Thus, in addition to his paying work, he played a benefit concert in Madison Square Garden to a crowd of twenty-five thousand in the first year after VJ Day.[42] It was a comparable performance, it seems, to the one he played in October 1946 at Carnegie Hall.[43] Other gigs were coming in, too.

He played the ultra-smart club Le Ruban Bleu in 1945.[44] In his auto-biography, he linked this engagement with his performance at another club, Spivy's Roof, which he characterized as "a favorite hangout of very sophisticated East Side clientele." He was rubbing shoulders with other comers. At Le Ruban Bleu, he appeared on the same bill with Ella Fitz-gerald, "a jazz singer who really rocked the hip crowd that first got acquainted with her type of singing when she worked the spots on 52nd Street in New York." He shared billing with other rising stars, too. He raved about the Revuers at Spivy's, who "sang original comedy songs and did sketches which they made up themselves." All the members of the quartet went on to fame and celebrity. Liberace gave them their due: "The four people in The Revuers were Judy Holliday, one of Broadway's and Hollywood's finest comediennes; Betty Comden and Adolph Green, who have written some of our greatest musical shows for both the stage and pictures; and Imogene Coca, who also went on from The Revuers to enormous success as a comedienne." [45]

The Rainbow Room, Spivy's, and Le Ruban Bleu contacts led, in turn, to other engagements. The oilman Paul Getty numbered among those who frequented Spivy's, and such sophisticates provided more opportunities for the entertainer. In his memoir, Liberace remembered Getty with special affection. The millionaire, recalled the pianist,

> used to invite us to his swank Park Avenue town house after
> hours to entertain his friends and guests until the wee hours.
> He never failed to slip a folded bill (usually $100) into my
> palm when he shook hands as I left the party. Or the time he
> slipped something into my handkerchief pocket of my tux

when I wasn't aware of it. I later discovered accidentally when
I pulled out the handkerchief to mop my brow that the something was five $100 bills which came in very handy during
those low-salaried days ($175 a week salary was the going
rate in those 'chic' East Side places if you were lucky).[46]

If his memoir recalls such affairs with affection, Scott Thorson remembered a more rancorous tone. "When he wasn't booked at clubs he supported himself by playing at private parties in the greater New York area.
Lee had uncomfortably vivid memories of those parties: the luxurious
homes and the self-assurance of the people who lived in them," Thorson
related. "He'd take a bus or commuter train to his destination and be
admitted through the servants' entrance. The handsome tip he received
at the end of the evening merely fueled Lee's resentment. 'Most of those
people treated me like a waiter or a cab-driver,' he later complained, still
smarting from injured pride."[47] Whether the slights were real or imaginary, his vaulting ambition needed few goads. He was, in any event, making a name for himself. New contracts rolled in every year; he consistently
renewed the old ones. Audiences were eating him alive. Critics loved him.

If the old hand "Abel" could nod approval in *Variety* and anticipate
Liberace's coming fame, other critics confirmed his arrival when he went
from intermission act in 1945 to headliner in the Plaza's Persian Room
only two years later. Along with Walter Winchell, one of the important
gossip columns of the time, Lee Mortimer of the *New York Sunday Mirror*
agreed with the jaded cigarette girl that it was one of the best acts he had
ever seen. The star "has a better left hand for boogie-woogie than anything in Harlem, 52nd St., or the Village," Mortimer told his readers.[48]
Other critics shared Mortimer's excitement over the act. "With all due
respects to the many talented performers who have worked at the Persian
Room at some time or another, we feel their current presentation of
LIBERACE . . . is their finest to date—not only their finest," the critic ef-
fused, "but one of the most differently outstanding artists to ever appear
in a nite club." This reviewer went on to praise the performer's "showmanship, magnetic charm, and personality." "We were thrilled as were all
who attended the packed premiere last Thursday nite," he concluded.
"There were shouts of bravo and encores galore. Liberace finally had to
beg off graciously with the hope all would return for more and there is no
doubt—all will!"[49]

Was he knocking 'em dead in Gotham? Entertainment editors and
reporters in the hinterland waxed as rapturous as the New York critics.

By 1947, Liberace was stealing the show at the Empire Room in Chicago. "There is the excitement of showmanship shined to a blinding sheen, a positive musicianship and expressive versatility that is pianist LIBERACE.... 'Summertime Review' deserves the word 'exciting,' and we urge you to see what we mean in person at the Palmer House," wrote Gene Morgan of the Chicago *Daily News*. "Solidly talented as a pianist, he performed his serious numbers with distinction, his humorous ones with an understated satire that was delicious. A thoroughly good entertainer," crowed the *Tribune* after the same performance. The Chicago *Times* was equally laudatory. Liberace was supplanting Chicagoans' old favorite, Hildegard, Ray Hunt observed. "Half the time he's spoofing," remarked another Chicago reviewer, "But he's not kidding when he lights into those ivories in a 'Tea for Two' that breaks the track record or a 'Warsaw Concerto' with all the stops pulled right out by the roots." "He's all lit up like Hildegard, only he can play the piano and he doesn't insult the audience," the *Times* reviewer continued. He wowed 'em in Detroit, too, where he "made like Chopin one minute and then turns on a Chico Marx bit the next."[50]

And so it went everywhere. He "mowed 'em down" in February 1947 at the Detroit Statler's Terrace Room, but he returned in September to even more enthusiastic praise. He's "smoother and suaver," observed the *News* on May 7, 1947. "But there is also his piano lesson you've seen of course, but he has learned how to make it even more easy and laugh-getting but always in good taste. He does two hot numbers with Joe Sudy's Orchestra and especially we like his Helen Morgan-Jerome Kern bit, in which we heard him sing for the first time. He was called back again and again."[51]

He was wowing audiences, and none of his success was luck. If his first boss from the old days at the Plankton Arcade had remembered how the adolescent piano player had practiced for hours a day on a cardboard keyboard in the absence of a real piano, if teacher and family recalled his willfulness and determination, these elements contributed to his success in the mid-forties. With an extraordinary energy level, he practiced relentlessly, up to six hours a day, but he worked on his act and publicity no less diligently. He was making himself.

His attention to the details of his act matched his attention to promotion. He had signed on with Music Corporation of America in 1941, and MCA, apparently, had negotiated his contract in Montreal. He wanted more. He figured the largest music agency in the United States was not working hard enough in his behalf. He would do it himself. He determined, he wrote later, "that I would have to do something dramatic in order to make a name for myself. I would have to do *something* to take myself off the bottom of [MCA's] list. So I went on a campaign, as it were, of self-publicity." [52] He publicized himself primitively, but effectively. He mailed penny postcards to "entertainment buyers" all over the country. "Have you heard of Liberace?" read the cards, which also listed where he was appearing and how he could be reached. [53] A slightly later variation of these cards survives in the Liberace Museum. With the name "LIBERACE" written artfully on the diagonal beside a sketch of a concert grand, the card also carries the following information along the bottom edge:

> LIBER-AH-CHEE
> NEW ON SIGNATURE RECORDS!
> ORDER FROM YOUR LOCAL DISTRIBUTOR

He made up hundreds of these and mailed them almost indiscriminately. He professed to never having heard of Las Vegas, much less of Maxine Lewis or of the brand-new Last Frontier where she worked. But off a card went to Nevada, for example, and a record-breaking run resulted. And so it went.

Taking Gypsy Rose Lee's admonition to heart—"You Gotta Have a Gimmick"—he worked relentlessly on his own image and his own performing tricks in these years. The classical-to-popular shtik was only the first. Performing to records distinguished him more thoroughly. In 1945, he came up with his candelabra as a prop. Candelabra of course became, literally, his trademark. He repeated the story of the candles countless times. He had seen the film *A Song to Remember,* starring Cornel Wilde, Paul Muni, and Merle Oberon, about the life of Chopin. "It interested me to see that in the film, whenever the great composer played, he had a candelabra on the piano," he noted. It seemed natural for Liberace to follow suit. The classical imagery, the general association with wealth, luxury, and class, and the specific association with Chopin (not to mention the free ride on the film's coattails) all fascinated the pianist. Not least, he already had a working theory about the importance of lighting to his act's success; he was working on particular notions about candlelight, half-light, and other partial illumination as a source of mystery, excitement, and romance that went back to his earliest experiences at St. Florian's Church in West Milwaukee. "So I went out to a little antique shop and bought a brass candelabra for $15 and a quarter's worth of candles and put it up on the piano that evening when I did my act. After that whenever I opened somewhere, reviewers commented on the candelabra." [54]

He had his phonograph that played his symphonic accompaniments. He had his white tie and tails. He had his candelabrum. He had his witty patter and repartee. He had created an image for himself. He was also inventing a new name for the image.

He circulated a score of stories about renaming himself. Most consistently, he associated his rebirth with his idol Paderewski. He told the simplest version of the story in his autobiography. In 1939 or '40, he returned to Wausau's Wunderbar after his stint as "Walter Buster Keys" and came up with the idea of using only his last name. "With the greatest conceit in the world, I reasoned that if my idol, Paderewski, could become world famous using only his last name, Liberace couldn't be so bad," he wrote.[55] He embellished the Liberace-Paderewski story on other occasions. In his press kit of 1947, he offered this response to the question of "why Liberace uses the last name only": "It was at the suggestion of the late Paderewski, Poland's most distinguished pianist, who did not achieve world-wide recognition until after he dropped his first name."[56] The story grew more elaborate over the next few years. In 1951, a journalist interviewed him and reported that the great concert pianist had visited the Liberaces' home around 1927 and had "suggested eliminating the first two names."[57] In still another variation on the theme, *The Things I Love* credits the naming innovation to Paderewski's tour manager, who was also public relations director of the Statler Hilton in Washington.[58]

In the late 1970s, Liberace told another story about how he chose his stage name that had nothing to do with his aesthetic idol. He told Scott Thorson that he simply did not like his first name. "Maybe Walter sounded all right with Pidgeon, but it sounded awful with Liberace," he complained.[59] His fellow Milwaukeean, Hildegard, had made her reputation with one name and gloves, but, without the impossibly Polish Wladziu and the dowdy Walter, Liberace's unusual Italian surname had a dash that was lacking in the other pianist's solid German identity. In this regard, Scott Thorson recalled something of homosexual panache in his old lover's decision to adopt only his last name. "In his opinion, 'Liberace' sounded important, unique, *fabulous!*" Thorson quoted.[60] Along the same lines, the showman was working out a whole theory about hierarchies, society, and entertaining, and the new name fit his theory in that it evoked a certain sense of royal prerogative, like Charles, Elizabeth, or Nicholas did. No other identity was needed. The name might have served other purposes, too. Ever so subtly, it affirmed his identity with his Italian father over and against his Polish mother.

By 1945, the showman had, in any event, identified himself with his new name and his new name with his new performing persona. He had played Las Vegas as "Walter Liberace" in 1944; with his return to the Ramona Room in September 1946, however, he was officially "Liberace." When, as late as 1947, a reviewer referred to him as "Walter Liberace," for example, the entertainer discreetly blacked out the Walter in his photocopied press release.[61]

The name change fit into a much larger pattern of his efforts at self-promotion and reinvention in the mid-forties. Thus, the name became an end in itself, a point of distinction, just as spelling it phonetically—"Liber-AH-chee"—became a standard element in his publicity, for example, on the postcards promoting his records. Soon enough, the name became an important part of his press releases, and—soon enough again—a standard item in news stories about him. By 1947, for instance, even Milwaukeeans who had known Sam, Frances, George, Angie, Wally, and Rudy for decades were now treated to journalistic direction on pronouncing the single patronymic. "LIBER-AH-CHEE," instructed the writers at the *Sentinel*.[62]

The entertainer was manipulating his own image, and this exercise in public relations was an important part of his career; at the same time, he was delighting audiences and giving them what they wanted. Their pleasure delighted him as well, and he was only returning their favor. Reviewers noted such peculiar aspects of his performance as his "respect for his audiences." He made people relax and laugh. He played every sort of music, including requests he had never heard of before. He wisecracked. He ad-libbed. By 1945, he had become a consummate showman, and people could hardly get enough of him. He was doing what had he always wanted to do.

After 1940, especially after 1942, he was doing what he always wanted to do sexually, too. As he settled into his act, he was also settling into a new world of urbane, homosexual culture. Scott Thorson related how his companion's work as a New York rehearsal pianist "contributed to his knowledge of the entertainment industry's extensive gay community. Many of the dancers and singers he met were homosexual. He said that his earlier loneliness evaporated as he found new friends, new lovers."[63] Beyond such generalities, what was happening in the entertainer's private life? If his autobiography is silent on the topic, even his memoir alludes, at least for cognoscenti, to this sexual underground: "Spivy" of Spivy's Roof offers the initial key to the young pianist's queer closet.

In *Gay New York,* his examination of changing patterns of homosexual culture in the twentieth-century metropolis, George Chauncey examines the smart clubs on the Upper East Side that catered to "a sophisticated clientele," to use Liberace's language. "Sophisticated"? It meant patrons who failed to blink at the urbane male couples scattered about the room or lounging at the bar. "Sophisticated"? It meant these very gay couples who shared jokes over martinis. "Sophisticated"? It meant appreciation for the eccentric Spivy herself, and for the clubs that allowed her space and glory. She needed room. Chauncey chronicles how this "enormous lesbian" held court in various Upper East Side night spots. She made her reputation first at Tony's on Fifty-second Street, where she sang raunchy songs in the back room for the gay patrons who frequented the place.[64] Tony's figured significantly in the elegant, understated, underground homosexual culture of the era. Otis Bigelow, "the best looking man in Manhattan" in 1942, recalled it fondly. "Gay bars, no, I didn't go to those until later. But there were elegant bars like Tony's on Swing Alley on West 52d Street where Mabel Mercer sat and sang," he related. Rich, youngish bachelors maintained elegant apartments nearby, and almost every afternoon one or more of them held open cocktail hour. "More often than not someone would say, 'Well, I have tickets to the ballet and we can drop in on Tony's later.'"[65]

Tony's, where Spivy sang, had competition. Indeed, Spivy offered it herself in 1940, when she opened her own club, the Roof—Spivy's Roof—in the penthouse at Fifty-seventh and Lexington Avenue. Liberace knew the place intimately. Like Tony's and like Spivy herself, it was more or less openly gay—"sophisticated," as Lee put it. "According to a jazz pianist who worked for Spivy in the 1940s," Chauncey writes, "her club welcomed small numbers of gay people, so long as they were 'discreet.' The policy encountered little opposition, for, as successful business people, many of Spivy's patrons had every reason to hide their sexual identities. Lesbians and gay men sometimes went to the club together as "couples." Nonetheless, Spivy still instructed her doorman to exclude homosexuals whenever their numbers or overtness began to threaten the club's reputation."[66]

Chauncey chronicles other such sophisticated venues that appear in Liberace's record. The Plaza Hotel itself, where he had played intermission in 1945 and headlined two years later, was another notable gay rendezvous. The performer could hardly have missed its Oak Room, where well-dressed men subtly scoped out other gentlemen. The hotel was a hot spot in general. "'The Plaza Hotel, of course,'" one of Chauncey's interviewees observed, "'was a choice place to conduct yourself with decorum and make a pretty good pickup.'"[67]

There were plenty of opportunities everywhere for homosexual liaisons in Gotham. "In New York one can live as Nature demands without setting every one's tongue wagging," wrote one provincial invert who had moved to the city in 1882. What was true in the Gilded Age also applied, perhaps to an even greater degree, sixty years later in wartime New York.[68]

If, as Chauncey argues, sexual lines were changing and hardening in the period between 1920 and 1940, the war and the period just after it witnessed the most phenomenal liberation in the city's homoerotic culture. It was an excellent time and a splendid place for men who loved men.

New York had always maintained two general homosexual subcultures. On the one hand, there were what the writer Arthur Laurents derided as "the silver and china queens."[69] They were WASPy, rich, discrete, and sealed off from the hurly-burly. One member of this group described it long afterward: "Gay society at that point was so hermetic and so safe and so wonderful. Everybody was very classy in those days. There was no trade. There were no bums. Everybody that you met had a style of elegance. It was not T-shirts and muscles and so on. It was wit and class. You had to have tails and be polite. Homosexuality was an upscale thing to be. It was defined by class. There wasn't dark cruising."[70] Obedient to rules of public order, this community met and mingled easily with the gentry of the standard sexual persuasion, sophisticates who accepted or overlooked the homosexuality of their associates and friends. Objections? It was not homosexuality per se that offended but rather outré behavior. Thus, flaming fags and roaring dykes were not welcome. Otherwise, order reigned. A famous maxim summarized the spirit of the day: " 'My dear, I don't care what people do as long as they don't do it in the street and frighten the horses.' "[71]

Beyond these enclaves of aristocratic hauteur, another world of male-male sexuality thrived in New York. It was gutsier, sweatier, and more proletarian, ethnic, and diverse; it revolved around sex, not around class. Subtle it was not. It happened in the streets; no one cared if it scared the horses. The war increased it exponentially. Arthur Laurents, who mocked the Upper East Side gay gentry, delighted in this other homosexual cosmos. "New York in wartime was the sexiest city in the world," he enthused. "*Everybody* did it—in numbers." He continued, "There were two great bars in Manhattan, the Oak Bar at the Plaza and the bar at the Savoy Plaza. Oh, the cream of the crop," he enthused. "All you had to do was just go. You wouldn't get in if you didn't have a uniform on. I felt guilty, I wanted to change—and I loved it. I never had so much sex in my life. It was incessant."[72] The future composer Ned Rorem echoed this reaction: "During the war, when I think of my own sleeping around, my hair stands on end. The *thousands* of people I went to bed with! Much of that had to do with being a teenager, but it had to do with the war too. Although I was not in the army, I'm sure that had a lot to do with the military.[73]

Gore Vidal delineates the same picture in his memoir, *Palimpsest*. He writes that he and maybe thousands of other young American men

were enjoying perhaps the freest sexuality that Americans
would ever know. Most of the boys knew that they would
soon be home for good, and married, and that this was a
last chance to do what they were designed to do with each
other. . . . It was my experience in the war that just about everyone, either actively or passively, was available under the
right circumstances. . . . Although the traditional hysteria
about same-sexuality ran its usual course in the well-policed
army camps Stateside, bars like the one on the ground floor
of the Astor Hotel throve. At any time of day or night, hundreds of men would be packed six-deep around the long oval
black bar within whose center bartenders presided.[74]

Indeed, the old Astor Hotel at Seventh Avenue and Forty-fifth Street was
a gay Kaaba Stone in homosexual Mecca. The Astor had been a notorious
rendezvous from early in the century, but "it reached the zenith of its
popularity during World War II, when it developed a genuinely national
reputation among gay servicemen as a place to meet civilians when passing through New York," according to Chauncey.[75]

It was not a gay bar, strictly speaking. Plenty of patrons who had no
interest in homosex drank there, too. The one group congregated know-
ingly on one side of the great horseshoe-shaped bar, while the others,
mostly without a clue, wound up on the other. In the recollections of some
gay patrons, the staff worked at propriety, as George Chauncey summarized relations at this famous watering spot in quoting one of his
informants.

"The management would cut us down a little bit when it felt
we were getting a little obvious. If you got a little too buddy,
or too cruisy . . . too aggressive, they'd say cut it out, men,
why don't you go somewhere else? You had to be much more
subtle." Men on the other side of the bar, however, were allowed to "do anything they wanted," the man added. . . .
"they could touch because it was obvious they were butch."
Gay men had to be "subtle" so that the straight men among
them—including the occasional strangers who unknowingly
sat down on the gay side of the bar—would not realize they
were surrounded by queers. They used the same clues they
had developed in other contexts to alert each other to their
identities: wearing certain clothes fashionable among gay
men but not stereotypically associated with them, introducing
certain topics of conversation, or casually using code words

well known within the gay world but unremarkable to those outside it (such as "gay"). Using such codes men could carry on extensive and highly informative conversations whose significance would be unnoticeable to the people around them.[76]

Despite such precautions, sometimes innocents who wound up on the other side of the bar did realize. A patron from those years—a gruff, resolutely straight, former baseball player who wore his uniform well—recounted his experience long after. In the summer of 1942, just before he shipped out on the Queen Elizabeth for the European front, 2nd Lt. W. H. Harbaugh wandered into the Astor Bar for a drink. "I had always sat at the other side. Now I wondered why the fellow next to me was so friendly. I looked around, realized what I had got into, drank my beer fast and left."[77]

The special gift of telling comradery from lust was no particular skill of ordinary gents who eschewed this sort of sex. If the innocent second lieutenant misread his barmate's friendliness, perhaps the other fellow did so as well, and then perhaps this randy fellow determined to follow another model entirely—simply to run the flag up the pole and see what happened. It was standard operating procedure in these years, when lines defining straight and queer gave at various pressure points. The freewheeling atmosphere of the Astor bar encouraged such experiments, even if all did not partake.

Sexual experimentation at the Astor even caught the eye of scientists. The hotel became so famous, according to Gore Vidal, that Dr. Alfred Kinsey, of *Sexual Behavior in the Human Male,* "used the mezzanine of the Astor as a sort of office, where he would interview 'human males' about their sex lives." The place changed Kinsey's way of seeing the world, the novelist insisted. "It was by observing the easy trafficking at the Astor that he figured out what was obvious to most of us, though as yet undreamed of by American society at large: Perfectly 'normal' young men, placed outside the usual round of family and work, will run riot with each other."[78]

For any man who lusted after other men, sex was easy in New York. It was a splendid time for any fellow who relished the occasional stand up, lie about, or roll over with another man, after which he would return to spouse or fiancée or girlfriend or his completely hetero messmates with a conscience no more troubled, perhaps, than it would have been had he visited a female prostitute.

How did it actually work? What did the fellows do? The homosexual world was in sharp change in this period, as George Chauncey describes it, but all manner of sex was readily available almost anywhere.

"Sophisticated" clubs and bars—the Astor bar, the Plaza's Oak Room, Tony's, Spivy's Roof—offered one kind of opportunity for sexual liaisons. One man chatted up another. A typical sequence of events followed. The most beautiful boy in New York during World War II left one version of the turn. He would meet a likely fellow at the Astor or the Oak Room, perhaps, an out-of-towner who was staying at the St. Regis, say. "I would walk him home, and he would say, 'Why don't you come up for a drink?' And he would say, 'Well, why don't you stay over? We'll have breakfast and it'll be nice. Don't walk all that way home: you can sleep on my sofa,'" Otis Bigelow reminisced. "Then there would be a little bit of this and that. It was friendly prep-school sex." [79]

Gore Vidal grew nostalgic over a different kind of sex in a different sort of bed in a very different environment. There were no prep-school dalliances at the Baths. "I also discovered, that magical winter, the Everard Baths," he wrote, recalling the season of 1945–46, "where military men often spent the night, unable to find any other cheap place to stay. This was sex at its rawest and most exciting, and a revelation to me." [80] Located in a former church building, the Everard had been in operation since 1888 at 28 West Twenty-eighth Street, immediately west of Broadway, "in the heart of the Tenderloin entertainment district, where it was surrounded by famous theaters and restaurants and by infamous resorts such as the Haymarket and the French Madam's, as well as some of the city's largest brothels," according to Chauncey. It was only one of numerous such places where one could pick up willing men. [81]

Sliding down the scale of politesse, a horny male could find still other outlets for his passions, often in the briefest encounters. Broadway offered a large selection of "nightclubs run by immigrants, gangsters, and other 'lower class' impresarios," Chauncey argues. No silver and china queens here. Male prostitutes were everywhere in this section. But soldiers and civilians alike also loitered and cruised, not for money, but for instant, anonymous gratification. According to Chauncey, "the highly flamboyant working class 'painted queens' who gathered at Bryant Park" near the New York Public Library represented a similar extreme of homosexual style. Public lavatories offered another outlet. [82] Wherever it took place, the process hardly varied. One looked out for a single loitering male. When one caught the eye, glances passed, and sometimes short vacuous sentences. Some other words might follow. Beyond, conversation generally ceased as couples swung into a vacant stall, ducked behind the bushes, or fled around a dead corner alley where they would unzip their trousers, pull out their penises, and masturbate. A variation on the theme might involve one or both of the men performing fellatio in the shadows. If the weather was pleasant, a shirt might rise, and one man would fondle a chest or nipples. Trousers and underpants might fall at the desire or request of one party or the other for a hand's caress or for even just a look. Sometimes, hard, fast kisses might be exchanged. In other circumstances, not always rare, even in the most public places—police, passersby, and horses notwithstanding—one man might perform anal sex with another. On other occasions, perhaps rarer still, one party might take the other back to a flat or hotel room for a hit of men on men.[83] In that circumstance, any variety of couplings might occur. This was New York's stranger sex available around Broadway and in the parks. It was easy, quick, and almost risk free.

Risks were there, however. Although, as Vidal notes, "newly invented penicillin had removed fears of venereal disease,"[84] the men in Bryant Park, the boy hookers on Broadway, "trade"—straight men looking for homosex, or "rough trade"—straight men of the working classes wanting male gratification, all offered some potential threat and danger. Some thrived on the excitement. At the same time, other dangers were real indeed, whether or not they provided a sexual rush. If they were disdainful of "dark cruising," the gentlemen from the Upper East Side were home free. Others were not. The vice squads might descend at any time, in any place. Although gay clubs and baths were raided regularly, putting the fear of God into many visitors, even nonhomosexual clubs with a heavy gay patronage were monitored by the vice patrols, and most, like the Astor bar or Spivy's Roof—even though the latter was run by a lesbian—practiced self-censorship.

Did Walter Valentino Liberace indulge in any of these activities in that first year or so in New York in 1941, which he spent walking the city's streets? And what about when his rocket was soaring three years later? He spoke little of these days and left no record other than what Thorson recollected. One might expect the good-looking twenty-one-year-old Midwestern musician to have had access to any variety of this sex that he chose. Street sex was there to be had for a glance. He certainly indulged his appetites freely later, but what he did in his younger years is uncertain. Scott Thorson's memoir suggests one possible pattern. Thorson recalled Lee telling him how he had preferred older men in his younger days, and his club dates—not merely those at Spivy's Roof, but certainly the ones at the Plaza with its cruisy Oak Room, and even the parties at the Gettys'— provided ample opportunity for the handsome young performer to be passed notes or offered drinks by graying gentlemen in good suits. His attendance at the Metropolitan Opera, one of the most notable of all the classy pickup spots, would have cast him in the same company. If the tradey life pleased him in middle age, his preferences in the forties would have lain much more with the gentlemen on the Upper East Side.

What he did and how he did it and with whom he indulged himself is lost to the record. Still, homosexual New York was his turf after 1940, and he would have known all these venues, whether or not he utilized the facilities. This became his scene. And if he told Thorson the truth, he established connections in all the cities he played—Detroit, Washington, Boston, Minneapolis, Chicago, Montreal. These large metropolises spawned a same-sex underground, even if it remains as shadowy in history as it did in life. Sex that was unsanctioned by religious or secular law could only exist here. The sex life of the young Walter Liberace, in the process of becoming Liber-AH-chee, is as shadowy as that underground world. Whatever he was doing privately, however, he never relaxed the furious focus of his professional life.

Well before the end of World War II, the musician had found his social or sexual niche. He had won a considerable reputation as an entertainer and was making extraordinary money. If he delighted New York audiences, he maintained an aggressive following in the hinterland. He continued to renew his old hotel engagements while expanding his new contracts. His Las Vegas performances introduced him to a still-wider audience, and by 1947, at the latest, he began playing the same sort of high-class hotels and supper clubs in the West that he had in the East. He had fulfilled Abel Green's prediction that he would be "box office boff." For all the triumphs, however, he was not content. As the war ran down and peace followed, he remained dissatisfied. Indeed, right about at the war's end, when he was around twenty-seven or so, he underwent a major crisis. He was still dreaming of bigger and better. By 1947 he had changed direction one more time.

He was an unknown in the movie capital in those days. When it came time for her to leave, he turned to her and said: "Florence, some day I'm going to crack this town wide open!"

FLORENCE BETTRAY-KELLY

THE SUCCESSFUL UNKNOWN

World War II changed the United States forever. The transformation of American life in the wake of that conflict is incalculable. Demographics hint at the revolution. If always on the move, Americans were moving now like they never had before. They abandoned one region for another; they left the countryside for the cities and the cities for the suburbs. All manner of Americans swarmed West: California boomed. Blacks thronged from the rural and village South to every great metropolis in the country, and, by the sixties, for the first time since slavers commenced their trade to Anglo-America in the seventeenth century, more blacks lived outside Dixie than in it. A parallel shift occurred among urban whites. With money in their pockets and babies crowding their apartments, they began to look to suburban housing developments as the answer to long-deferred dreams. Cheap, mass suburban housing was, simultaneously, putting home ownership within the range of almost all but the poorest of citizens.

These primary demographic patterns produced still more secondary effects. Increasingly abandoned to a black underclass, urban cores began collapsing onto themselves; the old urban infrastructure disintegrated, too. With suburbs, of course, came suburban commerce, like malls, and a still more critical alteration in transportation: the shift to automobiles and multi-laned roadways, the abandonment of public transportation, especially trains, and the rise of air traffic. Always fascinated by cars,

Americans sealed their affection in these years when a car came within almost everybody's reach and when increasing numbers of families had two. These trends played off one another, so that the destruction of urban centers, for example, now increasingly black, poor, and powerless, became a purposeful matter of policy in the urban-renewal campaigns of the sixties. The development of massive highway systems—as wide as a football field is long—through the heart of American metropolises indicated one aspect of the shifting power structures and demographic patterns in the decades after the war. Indeed, little captures so completely both cause and effect of the massive changes in American life as does the inauguration of the federal interstate highway system in 1956.

Americans were on the move, moving faster and faster, farther and farther. They were moving up as well as out. As with the accelerating patterns of home and property ownership, prosperity and wealth was filtering down and across the social scale. The poor were moving into the middle class. Federal guaranteed housing loans accelerated the trend. The GI Bill opened up higher education to the masses, and the imprimatur of bourgeois culture followed—even as traditional education, like the traditional city, was being radically redefined in the process.

While such changes affected every aspect of American life, one of their critical implications was to undermine localism and parochial or provincial values with a more homogeneous national culture. Interstates were the same everywhere; malls became interchangeable. Suburban development imposed common standards from California to Long Island, Chicago to Dallas, Seattle to Miami. A new social-economic system developed, and with it a new American type emerged. It centered on the buying and production of consumer items and the shift away from capital goods and production. Indeed, the term "consumer" came to supplant the older political concept of citizen. "Consumerism" became the great, if anxiety-producing purpose of the American republic. If automobile-crowded interstates and goods-filled suburban shopping malls came to symbolize national culture, television tied it all together in an even neater package. While television both encouraged and embodied translocal democratic or mass culture, the development of such huge public but private entertainment centers as Disneyland, Disney World, and Las Vegas did exactly the same thing, and did so simultaneously.

Some parts of the country denied these changes. The bred-in-bone conservative South resisted after a fashion, if often in a rear-guard and only half-articulate manner. From the opposite end of the political spectrum, leftist, highbrow opinion in the East challenged the changes as well. The latter would play an important part in the Liberace story. It not only impugned the suburban commercialism of the new era but spearheaded a campaign against Liberace himself. New York intellectuals and intransigent Confederates notwithstanding, however, most Americans considered the alterations in national life natural and good, excellence itself. No part of the country welcomed them more enthusiastically than California did. Nowhere did they have a greater and more immediate impact. Indeed, Southern California represented a model and a test case of the demographic, economic, social, and cultural revolutions in the decades after World War II. It is altogether appropriate, then, that Walter Liberace, the successful supper-club entertainer, abandoned both West Milwaukee and now Manhattan for the suburban life of Southern California, just as he determined to launch a new career as well. The American boy was mid-passage in the American postwar dream.

It took him a little time to wind up there in sunny California. The entertainer had never played the West before his first engagement at the Last Frontier in 1944. He returned to the Last Frontier in September of 1946, when he led the bill, and again in March of 1947, when he won even grander billing for his two-week run there. The interval between these last two engagements found him in Los Angeles. In February 1947, he gave a concert at the Long Beach Municipal Auditorium—where, one more time, he won the concertgoers' cheers. This was the first of a series of engagements on the West Coast. He made a long-run performance that spring and into summer, for example, at the Continental Room of the Hotel San Diego.[1] Soon after, he moved to the West Coast permanently. He arrived there, most circuitously, by way of Boston.

In 1943, the performer had played the Oval Room at the Copley Plaza Hotel in Boston for the first time. He repeated the bill regularly over the next few years. At one of the later dates, probably in '46, he found a particularly attentive patron in Clarence Goodwin, a wealthy California businessman in Boston for a shoe manufacturers' convention. Goodwin liked Liberace's act; he liked the performer, too. He offered inspiration and good will: "He'd frequently stop and talk to me and give me encouragement which is a great help to a young performer," the pianist recalled. Goodwin gave him his card and invited him to call if he hit the West Coast. It was probably late 1946 or early 1947 when the pianist, fresh from his Las Vegas run, arrived in Los Angeles. Ensconced at a hotel in Santa Monica, the entertainer pulled out Goodwin's card. He called him. The telephone conversation resulted in a dinner invitation—and much more.[2]

Clarence Goodwin had a big car and a driver and lived in "an exquisite house in Hollywood, . . . a place that was exactly like what I'd expect a Hollywood star to have, swimming pool and everything," the pianist recalled long after. More than the wealth and material comforts, however, the family itself delighted Liberace. He found "a good home-cooked meal in a nice comfortable happy home . . . surrounded by love. . . . What impressed me most about the Goodwins," he continued, "was that they were such a closely knit family, a beautiful mother, handsome father and two grown sons who, with their fiancées, had dinner with us." After eating, the family asked him to play. He obliged readily, "because such a warm feeling had grown up between us. I even fell in love with their piano," he related. At this point, the Goodwins inquired about his present lodgings. Discovering that he was staying at a hotel, they insisted that he live with them during his stay in California. After initial protests, the pianist agreed to give up his hotel room and move in. The very next morning he was unpacking at the Goodwins, and he "became a part of their happy family."[3] He lived with them for a year, he said.

The Goodwin stay acclimatized him to living in California, but it has other significance, too. This was at least the third time he had taken up with strangers and joined their family circle. When he was playing the Wunderbar in Wausau, he told of the "lovely Irish people who had taken me in." Walter Ludwig, his old boss at the Plankton Arcade, wrote of having a similar relationship with the young musician.

Liberace's ability to establish familial relations with strangers illuminates various aspects of his character. On the one hand, his personality invited such intimacies. As a person, he projected much the same quality he did as a performer—he had the attributes of a loyal son, a devoted brother, an endearing friend. His personality was "nonthreatening" in the most positive, engaging ways; he charmed and delighted people, made them feel good or better, and encouraged them to want more of him—hence the invitations to "join the family." On the other hand, taking up with families, as he did with the Goodwins, answered some of the oldest needs in his own life. He dreaded loneliness. This very anxiety had driven him to abandon the concert stage for more intimate and friendly supper-club settings. The sources of this anxiety illuminate the showman's personality.

On the simplest, most obvious level, his sense of alienation grew out of his peculiar childhood. While it has been said that "dysfunctional family" is redundant, Frances and Salvatore Liberace's domestic relations—exacerbated by the insecurities of the Great Depression—fell especially wide of a Norman Rockwell paradigm. With a nagging, possessive mother, a demanding, authoritarian father, and relentless competition among the siblings, the pianist grew up amid domestic tensions that included physical as well as verbal violence. If this circumstance might have prompted Diogenes-type cynicism about family life, in Frances's and Sal's boy it produced the opposite effect. The stress exaggerated Liberace's celebration of the ideal. He was a fiercely driven and furiously willful man, and his search for the perfect family paralleled his relentless quest for fame and fortune. With all innocence, sincerity, and honesty, Liberace defended the most traditional and conservative definition of family values. He extolled the ideal without cant or hypocrisy. He loved the warm family circle; he idealized it in its very absence in his own life.

His search for family and community, however, redressed another imbalance in his life. It remedied his loneliness as a function of his sexual exceptionalism. In intimate conversations with Scott Thorson, he dwelt upon his oppressive loneliness and alienation as the West Milwaukee Queer Boy. While he played the terrific sport—and played it well, winning the affection and even the admiration of his high school mates—the most astute of his chums remembered his isolation and distance from the others. Much about the dynamics of his social life—and even aspects of his career—are readable as manifestations of the effort to transcend sexual exile. He remolded his audiences, for example, as the perfect family that accepted him as he was, that, indeed, demanded him as he was.

All his life, he repeated this pattern represented by the Goodwins, although for shorter periods of time. Family after family took him in, cooked for him, and put him up. He did the same, turning his hotel rooms into cozy chambers where he fed, entertained, and cozied up with friends, coworkers, and fellow performers. He did so memorably in Chicago, for example, where he played the Palmer House in major engagements right after the war. "Because of the long booking," he explained, the hotel had designed a suite for him, complete with kitchen facilities. He used it to entertain the entire troupe that was performing in the Empire Room. This included the young Mike Douglas, who was singing with Kay Kyser's orchestra, and a whole crew of young women from the Merrill Abbott Dancers.[4] His press kit made special references to cooking for guests in his hotel rooms between performances. He put his domestic talents to work as a publicity gimmick, but they went beyond that. He reveled in making his environment inviting. He prided himself on carrying "personal effects with him to make each suite seem like home," he wrote. Besides "rows and rows of shoes, boxes of records, a full-size gas station-type soft drink dispenser, miniature piano collection," and a myriad of even more diverse items, he also boasted that "a steady stream of visitors" kept him company at every one of his homey apartments.[5]

He did not have to invent domesticity with the Goodwins. It came ready-made. If the Goodwin family met his test of domestic perfection, Liberace's vision of an ideal man was mirrored even more exactly in its patriarch. Handsome, self-possessed, a bountiful provider, and master of his estate, Clarence Goodwin represented a conservative icon of masculinity in Liberace's extended treatment. The Liberace memoir suggests how Goodwin fulfilled the showman's fundamental needs—needs that grew out of imperatives in his own character. For all Liberace's furious willfulness and stubborn ambition, he hated conflict almost pathologically. The two tendencies in his character—willfulness and the desire to avoid conflict—often clashed. He needed a stiff right arm. As a consequence, he was attracted to characters who could shield him from discord and contention, even as they did battle with his foes. Goodwin represented one—and not the last—model of the type. He volunteered to front for him; besides his disinterested concern with the pianist's career, however, he was also kind, solicitous, nurturing, and generous. These characteristics came with no apparent strings. He protected without suffocating; he was encouraging but not demanding, devoted yet respectful. He was, in Liberace's treatment, the perfect man, and he represents the ideal parent and father in the memoir. Neither Sam nor Frances could have played this role. If Frances's protectiveness suffocated her son, this cross-gendered American version of maleness was alien to Sam's Italian brand of masculinity. Its male ends/female means worked perfectly for this new son.

With Clarence Goodwin, the Good Father assumed his proper role in Liberace's memoir. The Loyal Son put himself into the older man's hands. "Mr. Goodwin . . . was, of course, a very good businessman. He was also very kind and generous," Liberace began. He continued, "He began to sort of take a fatherly interest in me and appointed himself, unofficially, as my business manager. He asked me how I was doing and I told him I thought I was doing rather well, but no doubt, I could do better. He asked me how much I was getting and when I told him he said, 'I don't think they're paying you enough. The next time your agent calls with an offer just tell him it's not enough, that you think you deserve more. Better still, if you want me to, I'll speak to him. You're an artist. You shouldn't have to talk business.'"[6]

Beyond his discovery of the ideal patriarch in Clarence Goodwin, his year-long stay with the Goodwin family otherwise changed his life. After he moved out of the Goodwins' home, he never lived in the East or Midwest again. Indeed, he seems to have gone directly from living with the Goodwins in Hollywood to buying his own California home around 1948. He chose a prototypical suburb, North Hollywood in the San Fernando Valley.

In his egregiously charming press kit of 1947, created the year before he got his first housing loan, he included, along with recipes and other trappings of domesticity, a description of his "dream home"—"a ranch-type house (with a swimming pool) in southern California—plus cocker spaniels."[7] He realized something like his dream when he bought a house on Camellia Street in North Hollywood. Even if his home lacked a pool and was a bungalow rather than a rambling ranch house, it was a model house in a perfect suburban community.

North Hollywood lay at the northern base of the Santa Monica Mountain Range across from Los Angeles and Hollywood proper. From exotic Sunset Boulevard, one could cut across the mountains on Laurel Canyon Drive or Cahuenga Boulevard to the perfect grids of the suburbanizing San Fernando Valley just north of the Los Angeles River that cut through the valley. While the great housing boom took off after the war, the development on Camellia Street had begun earlier, in the late thirties. This had been farmland, but by the time Liberace moved here, trees were growing, adding a touch of permanence and a sense of settled life to the street. Its dwellings were all built simultaneously, and, after the fashion of the time, represented two alternating models. They possess a charm lacking in much postwar development. Set back about twenty-five feet from the quiet street, they came with small front lawns and back gardens, although between the houses there was almost no space. Additions have enlarged some of them, but in their original form, they would averaged about fifteen hundred square feet of space, with three tight bedrooms.

Liberace had bought his house on the street from the character actress Lurene Tuttle, who later appeared with him in his 1955 film, *Sincerely Yours*. Twenty-five years after the purchase, he still romanticized the place. "It was not only the first house I owned in California, it was the first one I ever owned anywhere. And like the homes of so many ambitious young newcomers to Los Angeles, it was in San Fernando Valley. But that was before 'the Valley' became, as it is today, mountain-to-mountain houses. Then it was still kind of country and western, still sage-brushy enough to inspire the hit song that told the story of a man who was going to 'settle down and make the San Fernando Valley my home.'"[8]

The young performer loved the valley and fit into suburban life with hardly a hitch. To go with his nice house, in 1949, he learned to drive and purchased a fancy Oldsmobile Delta 88 convertible.[9] The American boy was home free.

The American boy was also an American gay boy, and as a homosexual man, he had other reasons to celebrate his new home. While no public evidence whatsoever survives about his sex life between 1947 and 1953, the showman had relocated to a homosexual center almost as freewheeling as New York. Southern California had a dish for any palate. In the course of hitching up with the Goodwins, for example, he made passing reference to his hotel in Santa Monica. With its snowy white beaches and beautiful sunbathers, Santa Monica was a kind of homosexual heaven after the war.

John Rechy left one notable, if somewhat morbid, version of "living the life" in Santa Monica in his autobiographical novel, *City of Night*. Crystal Beach focused the action. Every variety of men who wanted men was here, he began:

> the queens in extravagant bathing suits, often candy-striped, molded to the thin bodies—tongued sandals somehow worn like slippers; the masculine-acting, -looking homosexuals with tapered bodies and brown skins exhibiting themselves lying on the sand, trunks rolled down as far as possible—or going near the ocean as if undecided whether to dive in, posing there bikini-ed, flexing their bodies, walking the long stretch of beach, aware of the eyes which may be focused on them; the older men who sit usually self-consciously covered as much as the beach weather allows, hoping perhaps for that evasive union, more difficult to find now—ironically now, when the hunger is more powerful, the shrieking loneliness more demanding; the male-hustlers, usually not in trunks, usually shirtless, barefooted, levis-ed, the rest of their clothes wrapped beside them, awaiting whatever Opportunity may come at any moment, clothes, therefore easily accessible for moving quickly for whatever reason.

"Sally's Bar," located a block from this scene, offered both assignation spot and watering hole for more or less off-duty gays.[10]

Gay life in Los Angeles and Hollywood was even easier than in Santa Monica. Although writing slightly after Liberace first moved in among the palms and bougainvillea, Rechy, again, offers a fitting memorial to the California dream for the gay subculture. It beckoned gay men from everywhere. "You come here to find the wish fulfilled in 3-D among the flowers . . . and the invitations of The Last Frontier of Glorious Liberty (go barefoot and shirtless along the streets) have promised us longdistance for oh so long." [11] He chronicled the ease and ubiquity of homosex in Los Angeles, from the "youngmen" of Pershing Park and the cheap bars and hotels downtown, to the private parties of the bourgeoisie in Hollywood Hills and the elegant decadence of the famous parties of "the famous director," George Cukor. If Rechy and others chronicled the perpetual threat of police raids, arrest, and public censure, gay culture still thrived. Gay clubs, for example, came and went almost with the seasons, but some entrepreneur was always willing to take the risk and open another. The Waldorf, the Cellar, 326, the House of Ivy, the Open Door, the Cherokee House, the infamous Chee-Chee's, Maxwell's, the Crown Jewel. Individual gay bars might have sprouted like mushrooms in a summer field to vanish almost as quickly, but the city was never without its male-male saloons; others, Sally's in Santa Monica, for example, flourished in outlying towns. And with the bars, of course, came a whole culture. Southern California was gay for the asking.[12]

Even if he never confessed it publicly, this was Liberace's world after 1946. Beyond this, he settled comfortably into the whole California scene. As he adapted to his new environment, he also altered his career one more time, abandoning the phonograph part of his performance. He transformed his act around the time he moved into his new home. The phonograph was gone by 1947, when he explained to his hometown newspaper that "the phonograph contraption split my audience. Some of them liked it, some of them complained that they would rather hear me play alone. I had to conclude that the phonograph was too much of a gadget novelty. It was giving me the wrong buildup, as a mechanical performer." [13] Twenty-five years later, he offered another explanation in his autobiography. The unions, he sneered, protested that his recorded music was keeping live musicians from playing. "I am now glad," he concluded, "because it forced me to come up with my own individuality in playing rather than bask in the glory of other performers by imitating them." [14] While he tended to downplay the significance of the innovation, the shift represents a major break with his own past, for playing to the New York Philharmonic and the other great symphonic ensembles had kept alive something of the concert-stage discipline, however altered its presentation had become. Henceforth, the arrangements were his own; he was following his own genius, his "own individuality."

The recording gimmick had given his act a classy tone. When he dropped it, he hit on another device that would do the same thing. He continued to offer his own idiosyncratic versions of Liszt, Tchaikovsky, and Rachmaninoff to supper-club audiences, but he now did so on a spectacular piano that traveled with him on every engagement, no matter where he performed. It suited him perfectly.

Most practically, this spectacular new instrument resolved his constant dissatisfaction with pianos on the road. Beginning with the poor excuse for a piano he'd found at the Plankton Arcade in 1940 in Milwaukee, he'd been forced to play on one inadequate instrument after another. "I was fed up with finding bad pianos in the smaller cities. I wanted a piano that not only sounded but looked the best." Had he been on speaking terms with his father, Sam might have nodded approval at his purchase.[15] Haunting the piano exchanges in Los Angeles in the winter of 1947, he found the instrument of his dreams in Long Beach. It was a very rare, custom-made, double-strung, gold-leafed, oversized grand that had been made in Leipzig by Julius Blüthner and brought to the United States before the war. Its twin had been destroyed in the conflict. It cost twenty-five thousand dollars at a time when a family might have purchased a modest dwelling for a fifth of that amount. Typical of the showman's record, two very different versions of the piano's acquisition appear in the sources. The piano salesman himself left one account. He insisted that the young pianist had bought it on the monthly installment plan, not every payment of which he had made on time.[16] Lee himself left another version. He saw the piano and fell in love with it, he related, but lacked the money to buy it. He informed Mr. Goodwin. "The next day, the piano was in their living room. He had bought it. And he made arrangements for me to pay him back a little at a time as I was working. What could I say? I was overwhelmed by Mr. Goodwin's kindness. But it turned out to be a shrewd investment. With my new piano, Mr. Goodwin managed to get even bigger increases in my salary! I was able to pay him back in less than a year." [17]

The Blüthner grand filled various functions in Liberace's new career. Beyond its practical virtues, it provided a most dramatic publicity device. The piano, indeed, represented only one element of a new publicity campaign that the entertainer launched around 1947 as a part of his remade self.

Years after the showman first made himself famous, Walter Monfried, the longtime drama critic at the Milwaukee *Journal,* referred to the pianist "in his own way [as] a sort of public-relations genius." He related that as early as the Plankton Arcade days, "whenever Lee came into the office with an idea it was always a good one. It was a good idea for a story." [18] The showman's press kit of 1947, which survives at the Las Vegas Public Library, offers primary evidence of Monfried's assertion.

The kit contains predictable information, like professional accomplishments, reviews, a biography, and so forth, but it goes far beyond any of this standard data. It is made up of eighteen pages of story ideas, quirky themes, and distinctive elements that distinguished the entertainer. One page consisted of interview and picture ideas. There were three pages on Liberace as cook, complete with his recipes, including "LIBERACE HAMBURGER," "LIBERACE SALAD," and "DESSERT—LIBERACE FLAMBEAU." [19] The kit also demonstrates how completely—and effectively—he turned his great, grand piano into a trick for seizing public attention.

Walter Monfried of the Milwaukee *Journal*—the same man who referred to the pianist as a public-relations genius—revealed the way the piano worked as a gimmick for the entertainer soon after Liberace acquired the instrument. "You can generally expect something new from him, and he does not disappoint," Monfried described Liberace. "He has now taken on a partner," he concluded: the Blüthner. In the 1947 press kit, the grand piano dominates three of the six features the showman used to publicize himself—"THE STORY OF LIBERACE'S PRICELESS PIANO" is only one story provided for journalists. With its "gold-cushioned seat and its adjustable levels," even the bench—"as strikingly beautiful as the piano"—became news. The details of transporting it provided still more advertising copy. It moved "in a specially-designed shock resistant crate, cushioned with tailor-made paddings," read the press releases.

> Weighing 1,700 pounds, the grand piano's great length and width—four inches larger than any piano built—and heaviness makes the big difference in moving. That's where Liberace's piano moving talent comes in.
>
> Not even the Iturbis, nor any other pianists, attempt to take their piano with them from job to job. But Liberace's act is centered around the world's largest piano.
>
> So when moving times comes along, Liberace spits on his hands, rolls up his sleeves, takes out a special crate and padding, worth $3,000 and supervises the work on the impressive moving job. The average cost of a move from one city to another is $1,000—plus premiums on a special $150,000 insurance policy.

The biggest, the rarest, and—most important—the costliest: Liberace used all to masterful effect in his references to the piano, and ultimately to his career. The hype was, too, splendidly American, complete with the oxymoronic references to a priceless piano costing twenty-five thousand dollars. At worst, the entertainer's campaign represents the cheapening of art for a mass audience that Ortega y Gasset prophesied and analyzed in his work, *The Revolt of the Masses.* This is no inconsequential consideration. From another, more genial perspective, the showman falls in an old line from an ancient American tradition of adapting art and traditional culture—Liszt and custom grands—to provincial American democratic tastes and audiences. P. T. Barnum would have smiled, and Walt Whitman would have recognized a brother. The poet who wrote his own reviews, hoodwinked that staid Yankee Ralph Waldo Emerson, and composed odes to himself and the bumptious American Self would have been as happy as Barnum.

Like both Barnum's and Whitman's, Liberace's campaign was as effective as it was vulgar. The most cursory survey of press reviews underlines the critics' debts to Liberace's own projection of himself. Unlike Walter Monfried, who was aware and appreciative of being manipulated, most journalists quoted from the showman's press releases without irony or references to the source. Indeed, some journalists, under their own byline, reproduced the exact stories from the press kit.[20] Most others took their leads from the press kit section entitled "Interview And Picture Ideas." Liberace and his act, however, were more than public-relations manipulation. The recipe for "Liberace hamburger," for example, in the press kit hints at this other element: it is as honest as it is hokey. Great PR? It also suggests an underlying sincerity and simplicity. These elements, in turn, completely permeated Liberace's act, and even his personality. He effected a nearly unique combination of sincerity and artifice.

Reviewers almost invariably picked up on these elements of his act. While they relied heavily on his kit for their impressions, they also alluded regularly to other themes of his performance beyond the purview of the entertainer's publicity—his sincerity: how much he loved performing, how much he liked his audiences, and how his audiences responded in kind, calling him back for encore after encore. He gave them what they wanted and more, and with an energy that had not waned since the Red Room days in Milwaukee, when he played until dawn as his friends went off to chores on the farm.

With the old verve, a new act, and splendid publicity, Liberace's career advanced notably after '47. His mainstay remained fancy hotel dining rooms and supper clubs; he played from coast to coast now, however.

Thus, in the summer of 1948, he headlined the bill at the Fairmont Hotel in San Francisco and at the Wedgwood Room at the Waldorf-Astoria across the continent.[21] In between, he played all spring and early summer at the Pere Marquette Hotel in Peoria, Illinois.[22] Later the same season, he performed for ten weeks at the Palmer House Empire Room in Chicago.[23] He maintained a furious schedule. One account of his pre-celebrity bookings from the fall of 1951 exists; it differs little from his schedule of three years earlier. He departed on a Friday morning from a Lake Tahoe engagement for the Bellerive Hotel in Kansas City, where he played that same night and for the next month. From Missouri, he entrained for a run at New Orleans's Hotel Monteleone. He left New Orleans after another month-long engagement for a comparable run at Baker's Hotel in Dallas, Texas, before playing Las Vegas again.[24]

His Las Vegas gigs were growing increasingly important to him. He, likewise, became a mainstay at the Last Frontier. In 1948, he led the New Year's Eve show in the Ramona Room, for which there was a full-page ad in the *Las Vegas Review-Journal*. Two months later, he celebrated another milestone when the same paper ran an even grander notice, spreading his name (now no longer spelled phonetically) in huge block letters across the bottom of the page. "Hollywood Welcomes Las Vegas's Favorite Entertainer," it read, "LIBERACE" (in giant, flame-decorated letters) "Now starring at Mocambo, Sunset Strip, Hollywood." That September, the occasion of his seventh return engagement, the Last Frontier purchased even more advertising space in the newspaper to herald his return.[25] Mocambo was the hottest supper club in Hollywood, but soon Liberace was top billing at the equally famous Ciro's, and he was hobnobbing with celebrities like Rosalind Russell, Clark Gable, Van Heflin, Gloria Swanson, and Shirley Temple.[26] He was a very hot property by 1950.

The mid-century mark—he was thirty-one—brought another coup: an invitation to play the White House. On the evening of February 25, 1950, he performed in the East Room for the Washington Press Photographers Ball. The photographs memorializing the affair reveal him as particularly striking in the company of such celebrities as Dorothy Lamour, Wally Cox, Jack Benny, and, of course, the president of the United States, Harry S Truman.[27]

A command performance at the center of American political power indicated how far the West Allis piano player had advanced since his Plankton Arcade days or even since the Pabst Theater performances in 1940—or how far he had traveled since his twelve-minute intermission act at the Plaza Hotel in the summer of 1945. Still, he wasn't happy. He continued to measure himself against almost impossible standards, as if Sam were still prodding him invisibly from behind.

In 1985, he surveyed his postwar career for a *Washington Post* reporter. "Prior to t.v. I was what you might consider a successful unknown. I made a decent salary as a cafe society entertainer." He continued: "When I came to California in the 1940's, I played the Mocambo, which was a popular nightspot, where I actually got paid by the night, depending on how good the business was." [28]

Here is one more demonstration of the performer belittling his actual achievements in the context of his impossible ambitions. This reconstruction contains quite as much error as it does truth. On the one hand, the recollection underestimates his success in 1950. He was playing some of the most famous venues in the United States. By his own reckoning, he was making an enormous amount of money. His first two-month engagement in Las Vegas in 1944 alone grossed him over ten thousand dollars. An entertainer's entertainer, he delighted critics, reviewers, and other performers, too. Extremely popular with audiences, he won return engagements in virtually every club he played. He delighted presidents as well as proles. On the other hand, none of it satisfied him. Did he suggest tin cup or pro bono work at the Mocambo (or at Ciro's, he could have added)? These engagements at Hollywood's ultraprestigious Sunset Strip clubs put him in contact with some of the most powerful figures and most famous celebrities in the film industry and in American culture. Rubbing elbows with the rich and famous brought as much discontent as it did satisfaction, though. These people reminded him of his own shortcomings, and he measured himself constantly against the most exalted standards. When asked what labor wanted, Samuel Gompers supposedly cried, "More!" It was an American idiom. Liberace spoke it with his soul.

Measured against his vaulting ambition, the showman's dissatisfaction was just as real as his successes. Beyond this, he was disillusioned with his work. Perhaps he anticipated that even the solidest clubs—Ciro's, Mocambo, the Wedgwood Room, the Stork Club, and all the rest—institutionalized in the hearts of the greatest cities, were doomed, along with the old downtowns themselves. More likely, he simply craved a bigger audience, more money, and more fame than nightclubs provided. He could bring the house alive at the Ramona Room, but it only held six hundred people. "More," he chanted with Gompers. His memoirs, in any case, illustrate his discontent. While generally putting the happiest possible face on his own circumstances in his autobiography, he lingered uncharacteristically over the liabilities of his club dates. People want to drink, not listen, he muttered. "A salesman wants to relax a prospect. A guy wants to make a girl. A fellow's been jilted and he wants to forget." The liabilities mounted: "Everybody has his favorite song which he hums for you. An impromptu quartet is formed to serenade you. And, suddenly, you wish you were someplace else." He had little better to say about the supper-club circuit. As an intermission act—like the one he performed at the Plaza even in 1945—he could not dominate an audience, either. He wrote: "The girls are on their way to the powder room to touch up their makeup, and the guys are absorbed in speculating whether the cost of the evening has been worth it so far and whether it'll get any better. If the chances for the latter look good, it's likely that he'll call for his check and they'll leave . . . for his place or hers to be decided in the cab." The woes of a supper-club performer. He mused further: "Have you ever played 'Tea For Two' while listening to celery and olives, cold consume, tossed salad, beef Wellington with broccoli and lyonnaise potatoes, strawberry parfait and coffee for one hundred and thirty-two people?"[29]

Scott Thorson remembered even more extreme dissatisfaction that colored his companion's recollections of the supper-club years. If the lover's recollection can be trusted, the sense of failure and inadequacy haunted Liberace from very early on. He had won a notable reputation—and again, decent income—in the Midwest by his late adolescence. "But something was missing," he told his lover. "The way things were going he feared he'd be just another nameless, faceless piano player for the rest of his life, growing old and tired as he drove from one forgettable booking to another. He was just twenty-one but, Lee later remembered, he often felt like a fifty-year-old failure."[30]

The sense of inadequacy drove him to seek real fame and fortune in New York, but Thorson remembered his companion's criticism of his achievement there, too. The Persian Room? Socializing with the salacious Spivy, hanging out with the kingmaker Walter Winchell, meeting princes like Paul Getty? He bitterly resented his circumstances as they appeared in contrast with theirs. His experiences in Hollywood gave rise to the same anxiety. Playing with Spike Jones and palling around with Jack Benny was just as unfulfilling as hobnobbing with New York's upper crust had been. "From what Lee said," wrote his lover, "frustration and ambition played leapfrog as he schemed and slaved to create the career and the life of his dreams."[31]

Unhappy with the clubs, he was testing other water everywhere. Although he professed to dislike the medium, he broke into radio in these years. He performed with the likes of James Melton, and with his fellow

Midwesterner Hildegard, for example. Dick Jones of the Mutual Network praised his performance as possessing "the appeal of Sinatra, the showmanship of Brisson, the wit of Templeton, and the virtuosity of Horowitz." Perhaps under the guidance of Clarence Goodwin, he launched a recording career at this time as well. By mid-1947, he had signed with the Souvenir label and produced a couple of records. One featured "Begin the Beguine" and flipped to "Ritual Fire Dance," while the second mixed "Boogie Woogie" and "Warsaw Concerto."[32] Nothing much came of either disc. The same year he cut a disc for Sonora. Simultaneously, he was negotiating with two other companies. He cut two records with Daytone in 1947 and 1948. They repeated musical numbers from the earlier records, including "Ritual Fire Dance" and "Warsaw Concerto"; they added "Tea for Two" and "12th Street Rag."[33] In 1948, he shifted labels to Signature and produced a half dozen records that year. Among the numbers, he recorded "12th Street Rag," "Malaguena," "Tea for Two," "I Don't Care," "Tico Tico," "Temptation," and "Traumerei." Under this label, he also re-recorded the Manuel de Falla number and "Warsaw Concerto."[34] If little came of these initial ventures, he dismissed them once he'd achieved superfame as even more inconsequential than they actually were. Thus, he mentioned only one disc, which he called "a kind of specialty thing," and ignored everything else.[35] His recording career went nowhere for three years after this, and he explored still more curious avenues to fame in these years. Thus, in 1951, he appeared in a national beer-advertising campaign, with spreads in *Life* and *Collier's* magazines. "It's the break Liberace has waited for and we hope it's the last rung to the top of the ladder of success," one devoted newspaper writer enthused. "Here's one lad who really deserves any and all acclaim that he receives."[36]

He was not on the West Coast, however, to break into radio, records, and beer commercials. He was there for Hollywood. HOLLYWOOD. In Liberace's view, that remained the main highway to celebrity.

In his autobiography, and sometimes in interviews, he professed a lack of interest in the movie studios. While everybody supposedly thinks about stardom, he insisted, "that idea had never entered my head. I was still so wrapped up in being a good piano player that nothing else was on my mind except getting as much money as a good piano player could possibly earn."[37] He was certainly interested in making loads of money as a pianist, but he gave no evidence of seeing a movie career as being incompatible with his music. If Sonja Henie and Johnny Weissmuller could turn careers as ice skater and Olympic swimmer into Hollywood stardom, why couldn't he, as a musician and talented entertainer, do the same? he might have reasoned. Despite his protests, too, Hollywood exerted an inexorable pull not only on him as an individual but on his whole generation.

Hollywood reflected essential elements of American life in this period. In one regard, it represented a kind of radical American democracy: the idea that anyone could go to Hollywood, be "discovered," and be rewarded with wealth and fame. In its most extreme form, it was not even necessary to go to Hollywood: Hollywood would come to you. Thus, David Selznick's brilliant, myth-inspired—and myth-inspiring—search for his leading lady in *Gone with the Wind* led him all over the United States for his screening tests. That he settled on Vivien Leigh—a professional actress and an India-born Brit, at that—affected the dream not a whit.

If radically democratic in one regard, however, Hollywood fame represented antithetical ideas, as well, which were also indicative of the age. Once tapped by Fortune, Fame, Jack Warner, or David Selznick, "stars" became a different breed of folk: hierarchs of beauty, icons of elegance, and, most of all, the embodiment of charismatic glamour. Stars were no longer normal people but idols to be worshipped from afar. Realism had nothing to do with this world, and the more artificial the celebrities, the more compelling the appeal to the audience. Image and impression were everything. Makeup and fashion in the period reflected the tendency—Joan Crawford's eyebrows and shoes, for example; Cary Grant's patent-leather hair. Indeed, the glory bubbled over onto makeup artists, who approached celebrity status themselves. While female stars like Greta Garbo, Marlene Dietrich, Joan Crawford, and Mae West might have represented the very essence of this artificiality, art, and hierarchy, it also shaped, with equal force, if in a rather different way, the image of masculine icons such as Robert Taylor, Tyrone Power, Clark Gable, and, most of all, perhaps, Cary Grant. They represented polish, urbanity, clean profiles, and sophistication. They were artificial men—and gods to a generation or more. Hollywood, then, was not just fame, not just wealth; it represented a cult of glamour gods and goddesses. It was a fantasy world, and it was all the more compelling because of that.

The showman Liberace knew all this. Indeed, he articulated a regular theory about glamour, celebrity, and stardom in his autobiography, and his assertions about entertainment, stars, and their relationship to the folks focused on such cinematic icons as Marlene Dietrich and Joan Crawford. Greta Garbo (who, along with Dietrich and Crawford, was another icon of gay culture) had inspired his fantasies even as a teenager. As he duly noted in his memoirs as well, this sort of world had special appeal to common folk—people whose humdrum lives lacked art, beauty, or mystery. The cult of Hollywood, stars, and celebrity, then, proved an especially compelling creed among the mass of Americans nurtured in Anglo-Puritan values and raised up in the Great Depression.

Wally Liberace fit this mold himself. Over and over, his memoir notes the lack of beauty, excitement, or enchantment in his childhood. Hollywood was everything his life had not been; the world of movies redressed the lack for him even when he was in his boyhood. Movies had been his own mother's way of escaping from her dreary life, and she had named two of her sons after her Italian screen heartthrob, he insisted. He considered the Alhambra, Milwaukee's great old cinema, his second home. This world drew him as powerfully as a magnet attracts metal filings. There were, however, other sources of the Wisconsin piano player's almost cosmic attraction to this world of fantasy.

It is no accident that homosexual culture established a special relationship with Hollywood. If the common folk, their lives lacking grace, idolized Hollywood, the memoirs of young homosexual men, if for different reasons, brim with comparable descriptions of their attraction to the world of stars. To cite contemporary examples, Paul Monette and Andrew Sullivan, whose youths were radically different from one another, have both recounted their loving devotion to scrapbooks of their Hollywood idols when they were boys.[38] Insofar as Hollywood represents a world of illusion, of fantasy and unreality, it corresponds to many fundamental impulses within gay life. That was a world, too, of illusion and illusions. What is a drag queen? What do you see, a man or a woman? A man in a business suit? What do you see, a husband? A father? Or could it be a homosexual male? Two worlds of illusion coincided.[39]

Liberace's combination of class and homosexual biases made Hollywood's attraction all the more compelling. But, of course, the West Milwaukee boy was no ordinary sissy born into poverty and content to make secret scrapbooks of Hollywood stars. An engine of ambition, he set specific goals for himself and drove toward them as surely as a locomotive under full steam. In this regard, however much he discounted it, everything in his life propelled him toward the studios, Hollywood and Vine, and the star-studded world of Los Angeles.

Beyond such circumstantial evidence, however, the showman left actual information indicating that he wanted a studio career. Many years later he told Scott Thorson that "he dreamed of being a movie actor, of leaving his handprints in the cement of Graumann's Chinese Theater in

Hollywood, of winning an Oscar." [40] He revealed the same aspirations to journalists as early as 1944. That year, after his initial engagement at the Last Frontier, he told a reporter for the *Las Vegas Review-Journal* that he was soon to be headed for Culver City and an MGM screen test. In a full-bloom starlet fantasy, he continued: "The screen test will determine whether I go to Mexico City and South America or remain in California." [41] He seems actually to have done some shorts of one kind or another before the war's end, as he recorded that his brother, stationed overseas, had seen him unexpectedly in camp. There is no other record of the achievement. In 1946, back in Las Vegas, he continued to talk of his dreams of a movie career. "At the end of his engagement here," a journalist reported, "he expects to go to Hollywood, where he has a contract for motion picture work with Universal Studios." [42] In May 1949, under the auspices of L. B. Mayer, he auditioned for Metro-Goldwyn-Mayer, without any tangible results. [43]

The following year produced the results he craved. After three years of hanging around near the center of the movie capital, he was finally discovered.

If he got to Los Angeles by way of Boston's Copley Plaza Hotel, he got to the movies by way of the White House, at least according to the earliest published version of the adventure. At the White House Press Photographers Ball in 1950, he related, he had met Nate Blumberg, the head of Universal Pictures, who, by coincidence, also hailed from Milwaukee. The pianist's performance delighted Blumberg, and the studio head instructed his minions back in Hollywood to get in touch with the entertainer. [44] The showman's memoirs offer a variation on the story. They omit any reference to the White House, Nate Blumberg and all. Instead, the showman recounted how he had been performing at Ciro's when his agent, Bill White, called to tell him the Universal-International producer, Michael Kraike, was coming to his show for the specific purpose of sizing him up as a potential movie actor. Kraike was actually one of Blumberg's men. Liberace professed to have little interest. "The whole incident was so casual that I really didn't give it another thought," the showman wrote later. "Then about a week later, Bill called to tell me to meet him out at Universal in Mike Kraike's office. Mike wanted Louis Lipstone, who was in charge of music, to hear me play." Debating over what he should perform, he settled on a very abbreviated Liszt concerto—his magic music from the days of Frederick Stock and the Chicago Symphony performance. His agent fumed, and other studio people went bug-eyed over the possibility of an audience sitting still for six minutes of "Carnegie Hall stuff." The studio called him back again later, however, to read some lines.[45]

The studio was not exactly clear about what to do with the pianist. At the same time, however, Mike Kraike was producing a "potboiler," *East of Java,* for Shelley Winters. He created a role for the pianist in the film. Co-starring Winters, Macdonald Carey, and Frank Lovejoy, the film re-creates essentially the same plot as that of *Rain,* or the more contemporary Hedy Lamarr film, *White Cargo.* Liberace appears as a down-and-out concert pianist completely incidental to the plot. His character has abandoned his career and drifted off to the South Pacific. It was "a Hoagy Carmichael sort of character with long hair," as he described the part.[46] He played honky-tonk to Winters's cabaret singer, but in one episode, Kraike allowed him center stage to play his Liszt and mull over a lost career. When Liberace reflected on this cinematic moment of glory, the image of his father came to mind, not incidentally. "It's funny," he related in his memoir, "the character I played was what I started out to be in real life, the kind of musician Dad wanted me to be but which I never became."[47] What was that future his father wished for him? That he become a down-and-out failure of a concert pianist? The recollection both confirmed and denied Sam Liberace's influence.

The film, released as *South Seas Sinner,* went nowhere. Liberace's career continued to languish—by his own reckoning, at least—in the hottest clubs and nightspots in the country.

Almost twenty-five years later, Winters and Liberace reminisced about the movie. Invited to substitute for Johnny Carson on "The Tonight Show," Liberace asked his old co-star to appear with him. What remained clearest in their minds was less the production itself than the publicity tour they made around the country to promote the movie in 1950. The top-billed Macdonald Carey did not accompany them. It turned out to be a real show tour, complete with musicians, the Bobby True Trio, to cover, supposedly, for Winters's lack of musical ability. Touring by train, the troupe visited twenty cities, and afterwards the pianist used the trip as an excuse to hold forth upon a variety of issues: the nature of the American audience, changes in Hollywood promotion, and changes in attitudes among performers themselves. The studios no longer did this sort of populist tour, he grieved in 1973. "We didn't just show up somewhere and say hello in a sort of condescending way or say a few words on some local radio and TV show. We did an act! Shelley sang, I played for her." They didn't behave like movie stars, either. Winters confused the dining-room staff by demanding to toss her own salad, and when she ordered a chateaubriand apiece for everyone on the tour, Liberace asked to take home the leftovers. "This embarrassed everybody because we were supposed to be high-priced, high-living movie stars who didn't have to care about money. The maitre d' was embarrassed for us, and showed it, but he brought the doggy bag," the showman related. They were behaving like folks, not like celebrities. However sincere the folksiness, the would-be movie star was playing a part as well, even here. His skill at performing in two worlds simultaneously, of playing two roles—that of down-home boy and that of glittering star—at the same time, was not the least of his appeal.

Liberace also used his recollection of the tour as an excuse for discussing contemporary entertainers' lack of sympathy for American audiences. In the absence of such forays into the heartland, he reflected, young performers come to believe that "Los Angeles and New York are all there is to America. Travel, as I do and you'll find out that's not true," he added. "There's a whole, big, wonderful country between LA and NYC. It's full of lots of smart people with opinions and tastes of their own. You have to be prepared to please that whole country. You have to be prepared to entertain everyone. If you have something for everybody, they'll have something for you . . . their love and appreciation."[48]

The promotional tour went considerably further than *South Seas Sinner* itself. The pianist's studio career petered out just as thoroughly. He came as close to sour grapes as he ever did in discussing the failure in his autobiography. Winters wanted to become a real actress, he related, "and she made it. I thought I'd become an actor, but I guess I didn't go about it the right way. I practice playing the piano instead of making faces."[49] He had not given up hope of an acting career, however. In the early spring of 1951, he told a reporter in Milwaukee—where he was headlining the fancy Schroeder Hotel—that he would soon be heading back West to work in another movie.[50] Contracts were not forthcoming, but he kept applying pressure. He possessed, now, as professional and expert a manager as there was in the United States. Signing on with Seymour Heller after *South Seas Sinner* was an additional benefit he derived, he insisted, from the movie's promotional tour.

Management had been a problem for him. As early as 1943, he had signed on with the Music Corporation of America, and he had acquired the services of Mae Johnston, who won him initial bookings on the supper-club circuit, including his gig as intermission pianist at the Plaza in New York.[51] After the Navy had released his older brother, George, from active service, Liberace employed him, a talented musician in his own right, to assist him as a general manager of sorts. Lee admired and trusted George, and he liked the idea of keeping things in the family. Employing his brother represented one more manifestation of his familial conservatism. George helped run the musical end of things, and also made engagements, arranged finances, and publicized the act. George had moved to California about the same time his brother did, which facilitated their arrangement.

In his autobiographical treatment of Clarence Goodwin, Liberace makes reference to still another manager, who remains un-named. In any case, Clarence Goodwin, by 1947, pointed in the direction that the pianist wanted and needed to go. Goodwin had "appointed himself, unofficially, as my business manager," the pianist related. With Goodwin running interference for him, rejecting offers summarily when the pianist himself (then and later) said "no" only with difficulty, Liberace's reputation grew as his income soared. "Everybody thought that I'd been doing so well that they became embarrassed to offer me the salary I'd been getting. They'd call a second time and a third time until they really were offering more money than I could afford to turn down," he related. "So I graciously was persuaded to take certain jobs."[52]

After 1948, the showman made passing reference to another manager, identified only as Bill White, an agent who supposedly had a drinking problem and who, Liberace complained, lacked a clue as to how best to market him, as the entertainer revealed in his first brush with movie fame in 1950. Liberace suggested that he got his movie role in *South Seas Sinner* almost in spite of his agent. "I couldn't reach him when I needed him, and often when I did reach him it was a waste of time to talk to him. I was very unhappy."[53] If Liberace was distressed by this professional relationship, however, the promotional tour with Shelley Winters and the Bobby True Trio, according to his memoir, provided him with a new agent and gave his career after 1951 new professional footing.

With the exception of one interlude between 1958 and 1961 or so, Seymour Heller of Gabbe, Lutz, and Heller, an artistic-management firm, assumed responsibility for Liberace's career from 1951 until the entertainer's death in 1987. The group managed such notables as Lawrence Welk, Frankie Laine, Mel Torme, Al Martino, and the Andrews Sisters. In his autobiography, the entertainer maintained that he had heard of Heller through Bobby True, one of Heller's clients. After receiving rave reviews of Liberace from the other musicians, Heller agreed to catch the pianist's Circus Room show at the grand old San Diego hotel, the Del Coronado, where Liberace had a month-long engagement.

Heller liked what he saw, and agreed to enter into a contract with the entertainer.[54]

Sam Lutz, another partner in the management firm, recalled a slightly different version of the relationship's origins, according to Bob Thomas. The Liberace brothers had pestered the agents to take them on, but to no avail. Watching Liberace perform at a local Los Angeles theater, the Orpheum, did nothing to increase the pianist's credit; shortly afterwards, however, Lutz, who was staying at the Del Coronado, attended Liberace's show with his friend, the movie show-tune composer, Leo Robin, who is most famous for his melody "Thanks for the Memories." Robin agreed to render a professional opinion. He reacted just like Nate Blumberg; the show bowled him over. "Sign him, Sam," he instructed Lutz.[55] A decades-long professional relationship between Liberace and Heller followed.

Heller played a central role in Liberace's career and even in his life. "He is like a mother hen and a wet nurse, or whatever you want to call him," the entertainer described him. "But he is a very devoted man and great friend, and consequently, he feels that he has to check with me every day, if only to find out if I am well." He was the perfect manager, the showman insisted, "because he never really does anything without consulting the artist, and that's why it's such a good marriage." "When it comes to paying bills, I consult my accountant. When it comes to my career, it's Seymour Heller," he described their relationship after twenty years.[56]

Heller, as suggested by the entertainer himself, was not an ordinary artistic manager. He played a critical, even essential role for the pianist aside from the technical ones of arranging for bookings, publicity, and the like. He complemented Liberace's own character in a definitive way. Heller was comparable to Clarence Goodwin, as Liberace described the latter in his life: both were front man, aegis, shield. He also depicted Goodwin as a gentleman, however, who was motivated by kindness, generosity, and fatherly affection. Seymour Heller made no pretense to such virtues. He was more street fighter than patriarch. If Goodwin represented the strong right arm, Heller was the powerful left hook. He did not mind doing dirty work on his client's behalf. On the contrary, he seemed even to relish it. When Liberace himself shied from going to the mat, Heller stripped and oiled himself up for combat.

After their first meeting in 1977, Scott Thorson described Heller as "a small man in his mid-fifties, balding, with a permanent frown etched on his face." Heller was jealous of Thorson's position in the Liberace camp, according to Liberace's young companion, but he complemented his client completely. "Businesslike and pragmatic, Heller made the ideal foil for Lee. Heller played hardball when negotiating contracts, while Lee played the smiling, agreeable, 'anything goes' entertainer."[57]

In various critical episodes, especially those involving the showman's romantic life, Heller did Trojan service in defense of his client, and those affairs make best sense only if Heller's part in them is clarified. Over the years, Heller stationed himself on the front line to take—and give— the heat when his client himself proved almost congenitally incapable of saying no and leading charges. In this regard, as Thorson judged, Heller balanced perfectly aspects of Liberace's own personality, and their long-term relationship suggests how profoundly the showman lacked the killer/fighter qualities that appeared to come more naturally to his feisty agent.[58]

On occasion, Liberace mocked his manager. He jested about his gracelessness, which was so antithetical to the performer's own beguiling charm. Sometimes he directed jibes at Heller's Jewishness. Scott Thorson reported one incident: "'You can't come over tonight, Seymour,' Lee would say with ill-concealed glee. 'I'm cooking pork for dinner.'"[59] He evidenced some skepticism about Heller's ability to manage, much less see, the big picture, and he liked his manager on a short leash, taking his orders and carrying out instructions, he implied. Then, too, his appreciation of more genteel management ran very deep. Indeed, in one critical—and crisis—phase of his career in the late fifties, he jettisoned Heller and resorted to the more civil and courtly style he had appreciated in Clarence Goodwin. The disasters of that phase of his career, however, affirmed his own need for Heller's more bare-knuckles approach, and from then on he stuck with the feisty New Yorker almost to the end, when, on his deathbed, he changed his will, resorting one more time to another model for handling his career, this time posthumously. Nevertheless, Heller served him faithfully, and it was for good reason that Liberace considered signing with him as one of the most important events of his career.

So it was as the century broke in two. The pianist was playing important hotels and clubs all over the country, coast to coast, north to south. He had changed his act and was still knocking critics over; audiences adored him. The act had won him a loyal following from New York to San Diego, from Chicago to New Orleans and Dallas. By 1947, Chicago had actually spawned the first Liberace fan club. With his new piano, he was demonstrating his talent for self-publicity, but he had found himself a very well-placed, aggressive new agent who complemented his own energies. Beyond this, he was thirty-two years old and still craved more. His greatest claim to national celebrity was a small part in a bad movie that only loyal fans in Milwaukee paid much attention to. The issue remained of how to turn his ingratiating manner and killer act to real effect with a large audience. At this point, his life intersected with television. And television was just intersecting with national history, with what were to be awesome consequences. Liberace found his medium, but in the fancy Midwestern piano player, the medium found its own, as well.

So you see, television is not one huge audience.
It is a huge number of small audiences. . . . It's
a very personal thing. If you can produce
this kind of show on television you'll be holding
lightning in a bottle.

DON FEDDERSON

Six

Lucky Channel 13

In his publicity releases—collected in his press kit of 1947—Liberace describes himself as standing exactly six feet tall and weighing 175 pounds. The weight was a little low for what actually registered on the scales, and he stood much closer to five foot seven or eight, only a little taller than his mother. He sported a full head of very thick black hair. For the time being, it was his own. It usually shone with pomade; not plastered down, it mounted in great wavy masses above his forehead. With his sharp nose and pointed chin, he had a decent profile, while a distinctive widow's peak exaggerated the heart shape of his face. His wide-set brown eyes crinkled to an almost oriental look when he laughed, and he laughed often. The smiles and laughter also revealed the deep dimples in his cheeks. His thin upper and full lower lip set off a striking set of white teeth. Some time around 1950 or so he capped them all. Unlike his younger brother, Rudy, who could have doubled for Errol Flynn, Liberace was not a classic male beauty, but he was striking in his own way, especially when he dressed well, in black tie and tuxedo or still more formal white tie and tails, his standard performing garb. Under normal circumstances, the peculiarities of his speech—a combination of a nasal Milwaukee whine and his own patterns, best described as purring—would have been a liability, but he turned even his mincing tones to advantage using humor and self-parody.

He was not the comeliest man in the world, but his personality lit up a room—or a whole performance hall. He possessed an enormous capacity to delight people; it was as much of a talent as was his gift for music, and, in television, he found the vehicle for giving himself to multitudes. It took time, though.

As soon as he moved to Los Angeles, he had begun experimenting with the new medium. By the fall of 1947, he bragged about being "one of the first instrumentalists to be featured in full-color television (NBC)" and about having been called the "Chopin of Television." Well before his own breakthrough with the medium, he had performed on such programs as *This Is Show Business, The Morton Downy Show, The Kate Smith Show,* and *Cavalcade of Stars.* He had appeared on Jimmy Durante's program and had played with Frank Sinatra, Jack Smith, and Spike Jones. In October 1951, he appeared for the first time on the *Texaco Star Theatre* with the great comic Milton Berle, who would become a lifelong friend.[1]

He liked television; he did not like the way television used him. He intuited that a great portion of the problem lay in the medium itself: the camera's inability to tolerate a static scene. "When Liberace would report for a guest star stint in those days, the director would throw up his hands in despair and cry, 'What are we going to do with you?'" one journalist paraphrased the performer himself. "One director even told him it was too bad he didn't play a clarinet instead of a piano. 'With a clarinet,' he explained, 'at least there'd be a little action.'"[2] "On my guest shots," Liberace insisted, "they used so many gimmicks trying to make my part of the show interesting that they entirely overlooked the most interesting thing I had to offer—me and my playing."[3] He managed to find ways to compensate later, but he hated the camera's frenetic motion in his earliest performances: "they shot me from almost every angle and in almost every possible way," he remembered.

> On one show the camera was about 20 feet from me, and between it and me were all kinds of musical instruments on pedestals. I was doing a three minute number and by the time the camera moved in through all those instruments, I had finished my piece. On another show I was surrounded by a ballet and a chorus. I would play a couple of bars, then they'd switch the camera from me to the ballet. They'd come back to me for another few bars, then aim the lens at the chorus. There was so much to watch and so little of me, I wondered if anyone even saw me at all.[4]

He no longer considered himself an accompanist. Especially not an accompanist for dumb instruments on pedestals. He intended to be seen. He was not performing for national audiences in order to be invisible. His problem would be how he could turn his piano playing, himself, and his very static grand piano into objects worthy of the camera's attention.

As usual, the entertainer was aiming for the biggest game, network television. He disregarded local stations. He misjudged his circumstances. Network television was never his friend, but network television itself hardly dominated the television market in 1950. The play between local stations and network programming constitutes a critical element, even so, in understanding when and how the showman finally made it big in 1952.

Before 1952, television remained an essentially local phenomenon. The fall of 1951 inaugurated the shift toward national television—and network power—with the completion of a transcontinental coaxial cable. The most dramatic demonstration of the nationalization of the medium came on *See It Now* on November 18, 1951, when the distinguished newsman, Edward R. Murrow, simultaneously broadcast live images from CBS's Manhattan studios of the Golden Gate Bridge, Alcatraz, and the San Francisco skyline alongside views of the Brooklyn Bridge, Manhattan, and New York Bay. The implications of this innovation were far reaching. For one thing, it opened a very lucrative, national market to advertisers. The demand for television advertising soared. So did profits. At the end of 1951, for the first time in broadcast history, television profits exceeded those of network radio operations. Costs ballooned as well, especially costs of sponsoring network programs in prime time. All this affected programming. It confirmed the latent conservatism of the medium. With so much cash at stake, neither sponsors nor producers wanted to challenge the tried-and-true formulas of scheduling. If a performer had not made a reputation on radio, he had little chance of breaking into television, but the 1950–51 season had effectively exhausted radio's stable. Ambitious young performers, like Steve Allen—or Liberace, for that matter—had to do shows far off prime time, or take their chances with local stations. In any case, the '51–'52 network season offered little that was new.[5] Of the ten top shows in the Nielsen ratings, eight were either holdovers from the previous season—like Arthur Godfrey's *Talent Scouts, Texaco Star Theatre,* and *The Colgate Comedy Hour*—or they simply repeated the pattern of these programs, as with *The Red Skelton Show* or *Your Show of Shows*—vaudeville-like variety programs.[6] Of the two innovations, *I Love Lucy* and *The Jack Benny Show,* the former was doubly significant. It introduced a series of other critical changes in this Golden Age for television.

While *Lucy* introduced the domestic situation comedy to television, *The Jack Benny Show* had it two ways: on the other, it drew on the "sitcom" formula, and on the other, it confirmed the popularity of the tried-and-true variety show.[7] *Jack Benny* involved a play within a play: a domestic comedy about planning a variety show. A comic genius, Benny was able to play on either the variety aspect or on the domestic situation for laughs. *Lucy* provided a purer version of domestic comedy, and its popularity demonstrated viewers' affection for the intimate, domestic, and familial in the medium. Thus, for example, the episode in which Little Ricky was born, on January 19, 1953, attracted a phenomenal 70 percent of the television audience that night. The series in general, and this episode in particular, marks another kind of benchmark in understanding the nature of early television.

The day after Lucy delivered Little Ricky, the networks showed Dwight Eisenhower being inaugurated as president of the United States. If millions, from California to Maine, participated in that event in their own living rooms, the *Lucy* watchers outnumbered the Ike observers by millions that night and by millions more every week. The huge numerical differences in the two audiences affirmed the nature of the medium in another way. The contrast between the new president's inauguration and Lucy's "parturition" defined television's essential function as a vehicle for entertainment and amusement.[8]

I Love Lucy represented cause as well as effect for other elements critical to this period. *Lucy*'s rating in the 1952–53 season pushed CBS ahead of NBC for the first time in a decades-long competition. It prompted a rush to adopt the new sitcom formula. More important, however, it accelerated the transfer of programming authority from New York to Los Angeles. This shift was extraordinary in itself and had important implications for television in the mid-fifties.

The shift began before *Lucy*'s success. Indeed, according to one source, the chief impact of the coaxial cable's completion in 1951 had been to make Los Angeles available as a live origination point afterwards. "Performers who had moved East to host the top variety shows on NBC and CBS immediately transferred back to the West Coast, where their film and radio careers had long been centered."[9] *I Love Lucy* initiated a "stampede" to California, in one critic's view. It prompted another equally critical change: the turn to filmed instead of live performances. The 1952 season—the year after the Ricardos first appeared—witnessed almost a doubling of filmed series; they rose in number from twenty-five during the previous season to forty-six that year. While new shows were produced on celluloid, old programs, like *The George Burns and Gracie Allen Show,* which had previously been produced live, were now transferred to film. The shift to film responded to the economic imperatives of the medium. It increased profits. It lowered cost by encouraging stations to offer a thirteen-week summer rerun series during the time when stars were vacationing from their regular program, rather, for example, than producing new programs. The greater economic value lay in marketing the films over and over and over to local stations in reruns.[10]

The film/rerun policy had still other implications. It affected program content. Insofar as producers calculated film's rerun value in a national market, they tended to minimize or omit the topical, the political, and the controversial. What resulted was cheerful drama that emphasized the universality of personalities, characters, and, more explicitly, domestic situations. "Most of us are from the motion picture business, where we worked under a code for a long time so we automatically observe good taste in programs," said one of the early West Coast television producers, "We must also consider the rerun value of a film," he added, "which would be impaired if we injected controversial material."[11] The reruns played like Roman farce over Attic comedy, the one emphasizing general situations and folly, the other so self-consciously topical, political, and controversial that non-Athenians might not fully get the joke.

But still other elements were at work in the shift to Hollywood, to film, and to a rerun strategy, and all of these elements had potent implications for the career of the ambitious young piano player from Milwaukee. By the end of 1952, both of the two major networks had opened studios in Los Angeles, "so that for the first time," one authority insists, "New York and Los Angeles were competing on an equal footing." That the two were in competition is obvious; that they were on "equal footing" is more questionable. Los Angeles represented a different broadcast philosophy from New York. In drama, for example, the New York aesthetic celebrated experimentation and novelty, controversy and innovation. These grew organically from the nature of the New York theater— and through different sets of values that were percolating throughout the East. "The East Coast, Broadway-based live TV plays were, by their very nature, imperfect. Like any individual performance on Broadway, mistakes were bound to occur and often did. Even the best performances were usually gone after one broadcast, because few were kept on kines. Yet these limitations were a source of strength. Producers were more willing to experiment with new ideas and challenging themes because the plays were one-shot affairs. If they did not work, there was always next week."[12]

As summarized here, this approach to live New York television theater actually suggests the profounder biases in the East that contrasted with values spawned in Hollywood. With its roots in a deeper, darker philosophical approach to life, "New York," as represented in a peculiar and distinctive mind or mindset, drew on equal parts of a Judeo-Calvinist tradition that celebrated controversy, conflict, argument, righteousness, and theory; skeptical of capitalistic virtues, it also leaned toward the political left. Such values contrasted not only with a Hollywood world view but ran against the grain in large parts of the country as well.

The Heartland as well as Hollywood emphasized the comfortable and the familiar; it celebrated such alternative values as accommodation, common sense, practicality, and making one's own way. Commerce and money were just fine. In contrast, New York tended to "play to the problem" and appeal to particular (in both senses of the term) audiences; beyond this, it disdained, consciously, provincials and a provincial mentality. If the *New Yorker* magazine scorned "the little old lady in Dubuque," Hollywood loved her. In contrast to the New York aesthetic, Hollywood played to the common denominator and a general audience. Where the East Coast aesthetic looked askance at popularity and a cash nexus, Hollywood relished both. Where the one challenged American enthusiasm and innocence — and, indeed, doubted patriotism and American values — the other relished it all, even as movies represented the very embodiment of genial American vulgarity.[13]

The tension between Hollywood and New York suggests not merely a struggle over television programming but also an ideological cleavage in American culture that would have extraordinary meaning for post–World War II American history. Insofar as the Great Depression, World War II, and a host of other influences seemed to undermine traditional values, the first guns of a "culture war" were sounding, although from these early days it was not clear who was on what side.

The conflict between New York and Hollywood, the meaning of film, popular audiences versus particular ones — all of these elements lay quite beyond the control, or even the ken, of most Americans in 1953. These social forces, however, were the rising tide; they helped carry the West Allis piano player's bark farther than even he might have imagined. He was calculating; he was lucky, too. He had moved to Los Angeles at the perfect time. He was primed and seasoned when the coaxial cable and *Lucy* revolutionized television production. His supper-club act, honed night in and night out across the country, had prepared him to appeal to any audience. More directly, his gigs all over the United States reaffirmed his kinship with and affection for the folks, for popular taste and values. If movies failed to make his name a household word, and if network broadcasting failed to exploit his genius, he was still honing his act in preparation for the biggest break of all.

For at least two years prior to 1952, he made all the rounds and did everything he was supposed to do "in a vain attempt to interest the big networks in a Liberace show." But, as a reporter noted, "he failed to shake the widespread conviction among video show producers and network executives that the TV public would not respond to his type of entertainment."[14] Only then did he turn to local television and accept an outstanding offer from a new station, KLAC, in Los Angeles. The history of local broadcasting in Los Angeles fills out the picture of network television history even as it bears more direct relation to the showman's rise to fame in 1952.

Local television in Los Angeles began in 1947, when Klaus Lansberg, a brilliant Jewish German émigré, inaugurated the city's first commercial television station, KTLA. A programming genius, he initiated the first children's programs, the *Hopalong Cassidy* series, and the first science fiction show—*Space Patrol.* He launched a spate of musical variety shows, *Dixie Showboat, Frosty Frolics, Ina Ray Hutton and Her All Girl Orchestra* (that had also played Vegas with Liberace), and *Lawrence Welk.* He took his cameras to location at the Aragon Ballroom and the Santa Monica Pier, but the studio performances were just as important. *Dixie Showboat,* for example, which featured Country and Western, or, as it was known then, hillbilly music, catered to Okies and Arkies who had wound up in the area during the Great Depression and the wartime industry boom. Such programs followed a particular form, with a front door opening to a camera as if it were a guest, and the performers speaking affectionately to the lens-guest as a welcomed visitor in the hillbilly household.

Lansberg made other innovations in the medium. His cameramen appeared wherever something seemed to be happening. He turned human-interest stories into news, news into entertainment. Once, for example, he provided round-the-clock coverage of the ill-fated attempt to rescue a small child who had fallen into an abandoned well in 1949. The coverage galvanized the city, won national media treatment, and dominated the television ratings. Along the lines of the coverall-clad yokels welcoming the camera-guest-viewer into their "home," the affair of the girl in the well "intimized" a news or human-event story. Viewers lost the sense of being merely passive observers; they felt engaged in the rescue operations; they became a part of the broadcast; they gained membership in a family of television watchers. The unknown child's death, then, became a "personal" loss. Lansberg's camera "created" an event that then demanded a certain effect, popular grief, in this case, for a figure who would have been of no national consequence otherwise.

Lansberg employed comparable genius in experimenting with other kinds of programs and performers, too. He introduced the world to Korla Pandit, for example, an exotic-looking Indian who played the electric organ. Extremely popular, Pandit played over nine hundred programs, and he remembered Lansberg's instructions long after. They echoed to the Yokels' "Ya'll come on in!" and the technically engendered mass sympathy for the child in the well. "You are playing to one person when you perform on television," Lansberg admonished the organist. "Play to that one." The program had its own gimmicks, too, which heightened its appeal. The camera played up Pandit's very handsome, if delicate, or even feminine, good looks—his dark, long-lashed eyes, in particular. The show followed an invariable formula. With the tremulous tones of "Song of India" in the background, the camera always opened on the large, glittering jewel in Pandit's striking turban—the two unvarying props—before dollying back to reveal the musician's sexily downcast eyes, and only then pulling back farther to reveal the pretty face, now smiling and uplifted, and then the whole man at performance. Another gimmick: in nine hundred shows, Pandit never spoke a word, again on Lansberg's instructions, to increase the sense of exotic mystery associated with the turban, the jewel, and the inscrutable Orient.[15]

Lansberg's successes with KTLA established the norm for local broadcasting in Los Angeles, and soon other commercial stations were offering aggressive competition. Independent station KLAC—Lucky Channel 13—was an important challenger. Its innovative manager, Don Fedderson, was no slouch either, even when taking his cues from the boy genius over at KTLA. To become most famous later for the television series *The Millionaire,* Fedderson had acquired rights, for example, to the baseball and football games of the local college and professional teams.[16] He hired "the nation's first disc jockey," Al Jarvis, and initiated an afternoon program with Jarvis and Betty White, where famous recording figures stopped by to chat and advance their latest releases.[17] Signing up Liberace was another effort to innovate programming, seize a market, and fill air time.

Fedderson had first seen the pianist perform in the Circus Room of San Diego's great Victorian hotel, the Del Coronado, some time in 1950, or perhaps the year after. It was a particularly notable performance. In Liberace's dramatic retelling, a heavy fog had rolled in from the Pacific, and the rotten weather had virtually eliminated hotel guests. The performer played to a house of only seventeen people. It has been said that the mark of the best performers is an ability to work a scanty audience as energetically as a great one. Liberace himself theorized about the difficulties of a small crowd. "When the house is full a certain amount of excitement rubs off on the audience before you even get on the stage. Everyone in a packed theater says to himself, 'If all these other people came, I must have been right to come, too.'" Empty seats, vacant tables, he mused, have the opposite effect. Patrons feel that they've erred, "and this makes them more selective about what they see on the stage and harder to please. The fact that more people didn't come makes them feel that maybe the performer is slipping. The result is that you have a house full of critics." That evening, he pulled out the stops. "If those seventeen people are expecting a show—a show they will *get*," he determined.[18]

Among those empty tables and chairs sat Jack Hellman, a radio and television writer for *Variety*, and Fedderson, the new manager of Channel 13. As he had been doing for a decade, Liberace bowled his audience over. He didn't pay much attention to the two television men. Nor did his agent. "Seymour hadn't bothered to tell me," he related.[19] The station manager wanted a contract, but Liberace hesitated. He resisted for two years. Fedderson kept the pressure on. Circumstances finally dictated the deal with KLAC: "When the pianist found he could not break into the networks, he finally accepted this offer, largely, he said, to try out his ideas as to how he should be telecast."[20]

The Liberace Show aired for the first time at 7:30 P.M. on Wednesday, February 3, 1952, which was to be its standard slot for the next year. It lasted fifteen minutes. While, later, the pianist joked about competing with *Hopalong Cassidy*, he did not face much competition in the 7:00 to 8:00 P.M. slot. Of the six Los Angeles stations, five ran half-hour programs from 7:00 to 7:30, without much coherence. They ranged from *The Son of Monte Cristo*, the news, *Mr. Wizard*, and *Blue Ribbon Bouts*, to the *Invitation Playhouse* that preceded *The Liberace Show* on KLAC. Just before network programming kicked in at 8:00, the 7:30 and 7:45 slots were still more broken up. Liberace vied with five programs, among them *After Dinner Round-up with Jimmie Dolan* (Channel 9), *Jungle Adventure* (Channel 5), and the only other character who made it big, the playfully ambiguous Pinky Lee.[21] If the slot picked up audience carryover from the drama before, it offered the clearest alternative to hillbilly roundups and the juvenile high jinks of Pinky Lee. It worked.

It was artfully done, too. Directed by Jim Hobson, the show was broadcast live before a live audience in the Music Hall, an old movie theater in Beverly Hills. The performer wore a plain tuxedo and played a grand piano decorated, simply, with his now-trademark candelabrum. In a format he had perfected in his supper-club act, he played a mixture of condensed classics and pop tunes, intermixed with his supper-club patter. His brother George conducted the house orchestra, and the piano-playing brother conversed with the violinist brother, who did not speak. If he had not been able to win a network contract, he had not been happy with the networks' camerawork and his own inability to influence his presentation. Having his own show guaranteed that he would have authority over the production. An early reviewer summarized how the show worked: "Soft lights, sweet strings, brother George—smiling and silent, and plenty of closeups of Liberace and his candelabra."[22] He had worked out this format with Fedderson, an L.A. reporter noted. They had agreed that "he should be presented simply and intimately, much as he was used to working in night clubs. To his playing of hot and classical music he added considerable showmanship and a friendly 'homey' quality that quickly made him 'just folks' to his audience here. For some of the more erudite music critics, he dealt a little too much in 'schmaltz.' But, as he will tell you, he's never been a 'stern longhair' and his warm personal approach to his televiewers soon helped him to build up a large following in a surprisingly short time."[23]

This very early review is useful in that it captures Liberace's act when the performer was right on the cusp of national celebrity. It summarizes in a straightforward manner the sources of his appeal, even as it introduces the invidious references to "erudite critics" and "schmaltz" that would soon become almost inseparable from any press notice. That first year on KLAC, however, almost no one expressed anything but pleasure with *The Liberace Show*. Outrage and offense did not spill over the dikes of public delight for another year and a half.

Fedderson paid the star a thousand dollars per session, which Liberace then divvied up among himself, his brother, and the five-member band. Without a sponsor at first, KLAC met expenses out of the station's general revenues. Fedderson quickly found enterprises to support the show. By mid-February 1952, after a couple or three weeks of shows, he persuaded the Citizens National Trust and Savings Bank to pick up the show's tab. If reluctant at first, soon enough Liberace's first local sponsor was boasting about the pianist's multiplication of its revenues. Thus, for example, on one evening's show, the pianist announced that everyone who opened a new account with ten dollars or more would receive a free recording. The next day, according to newspaper reports, the bank opened to a huge line of people, which bankers mistook for the beginning of a banking panic. They had forgotten the television offer. "In two weeks the bank had 2,350 new depositors."[24] Three months after the offer had been announced, the bank had honored $600,000 in new deposits. After two years, they attributed a significant portion of $1,400,000 in new accounts to the Liberace sponsorship.[25]

Sponsorship was linked with popularity. The show made an almost immediate impact. While local newspapers failed to notice the program, viewer response compensated for print media's obliviousness. While entry to the production site at the Music Hall was free, soon patrons were reportedly scalping tickets for fifty dollars each. By spring, a million and a half Los Angelenos were watching Liberace every Wednesday night. According to another source, the show was winning the highest ratings ever registered by an independent television station in the city. The attraction rippled out beyond the television set. Liberace's on-air announcement that he would play the Pasadena Civic Auditorium prompted a run on the box office, and all seats were sold within forty-eight hours.[26] Three months after his initial show, the pianist filled the house at Los Angeles' Philharmonic Auditorium, his one-shot appearance netting him over four thousand dollars. His greatest prize still lay ahead. Within six months of his first television appearance, he also packed the Hollywood Bowl, an unprecedented achievement for the thirty-three-year-old pianist.[27] Indeed, his July 19 performance, which inaugurated the Hollywood Bowl Pops series, was the only concert to fill the famous amphitheater to capacity in 1952: twenty thousand people bought tickets. No one has matched the achievement since.[28] And again, he profited grandly, with a check for five thousand dollars.[29] It was much more than the money, though, and perhaps even more than the fame that sealed his accomplishment in the Bowl. It was his own driving ambition. The Bowl did it for him.

After a half century, this huge outdoor theater has lost much of its cachet. If later generations are inured to its appeal, it, like Carnegie Hall and Radio City Music Hall, focused the imagination of more than one generation of artists and performers. For the popular musician, it represented the height of achievement. In the winter of 1947, the twenty-seven-year-old Midwestern piano player had visited the site as a lowly tourist as soon as he had landed in Los Angeles. "I wandered onto the famous band shell and looked over the vast auditorium of empty seats. As I did so I promised myself that someday I'd be on that stage again, but playing the piano with all the seats occupied." "My main ambition," he wrote, "the one thing my life was pointed at, was to play the Hollywood Bowl."[30] About the same time, his faithful piano teacher, Florence Kelly, visited him in Los Angeles, and he revealed to her his broader ambition in moving to Movieland. "He was an unknown in the movie capital in those days," she recalled for a reporter. "When it came time for her to leave, he turned to her and said: 'Florence, some day I'm going to crack this town wide open!'"[31] In five years, he was doing it.

The Milwaukee piano player was hot stuff. Publicity fed on itself in a publicity-mad town. The talk of the city, he got his first shot at national fame in 1952, almost simultaneously with the Bowl performance, when NBC tapped him as the summer replacement for Dinah Shore's twice-a-week fifteen-minute program from July 1 to August 28.[32] These were pre-film, pre-rerun days, and he performed live, as he did on his own show. That fall, in a poll conducted by a local monthly magazine, *Televiews,* thirty thousand respondents voted him their favorite performer of everyone appearing on television.[33] In February 1953, the fifth annual meeting of the Television Association of Arts and Sciences awarded him two Emmies—one for outstanding local television show and the other for outstanding male television performer.[34]

Something was happening.

Partly responsible for the L.A. Liberace phenomenon was the performer's own personality, his ability to play to a television audience, and, not least, a producer who allowed and encouraged him to do just that. Besides the consummate "showmanship" that one of the earliest reviewers had remarked on, Liberace also conveyed a "warm personal touch," "a friendly 'homey' quality that quickly made him 'just folks' to his audience." From the earliest accounts of his oldest acquaintances, warmth, sincerity, and affection governed his character as much as they did his act. In his television show—as in his club performances—he aestheticized these impulses to make them a working part of his performing persona. In his imagination, mythical, invisible Goodwins clustered around the television set, in the same way that Clarence, his wife, his two sons, and their girlfriends had gathered around the piano in their Hollywood parlor in the spring of 1947. He used his own personality to re-create something that he adored. His later syndicator, Reuben Kaufman, summarized what he thought was going on when asked about Liberace's popularity: "I think it may be because he appeals to everybody who tried to learn to play the piano as a child and gave up. Also, I think he hit upon an old, half forgotten American home custom which was very pleasant. Remember how the family used to gather around the piano while mother or father banged out popular tunes."[35] It was just an act, but it wasn't just an act, and perhaps the audiences responded to the man behind the performance.

Whether or not the performer was actually sincere in his "homey, just folks" approach to his performance, it was a style that Don Fedderson immediately realized would be perfect for the medium. The manager at television station KLAC, Lucky 13, may or may not have cared about the performer's character; he saw the pianist's skill at manipulating an audience, he knew how television worked, and, unlike the more hidebound network producers, he understood how he could maximize the pianist's impact and translate this talent to a mass audience.

From the beginning of their relationship after he first saw Liberace perform, Fedderson possessed very clear ideas about how to succeed on television and about the entertainer's potential television stardom. At their initial interview after he had performed to the seventeen-member audience at the Del Coronado Hotel, the pianist recalled the station manager instructing him about the nature of the medium:

> Contrary to what everyone believes when you're on television you're not playing to tens of millions of people. Your audience is really small groups; families sitting around in their living rooms, or play rooms or people in beds in hospitals. Maybe it's not a group at all. Your audience may be just one lonely person.
>
> So you see, television is not one huge audience. It is a huge number of small audiences. These are people you are playing to, personally. You are alone with them in their homes. While you are entertaining them, you are their guest. It's a very personal kind of thing, and it's that personal sort of entertainment that you gave us this evening. If you can produce this kind of show on television you'll be holding lightning in a bottle.

To this advice, Fedderson added a class or cultural coda. Prior to his first show, he drove the pianist all over the city, from the wealthiest parts of Beverly Hills to the trailer courts beyond the suburbs. The poor and middle-class districts sprouted the most television antennae, he noted. These people, Fedderson told Liberace, were the ones who had seized the medium "as entertainment the like of which they'd never expected to *see*. It was the seeing that got them, and they were entranced." [36]

The pianist agreed. "That little automobile ride reminded me of what Don said down in Coronado about the little groups of people, possibly lonely people, watching TV," he reflected afterwards. For Liberace, the ride even suggested that the medium had political overtones. "The audience was not the sophisticated, intellectual element that had a kind of snobbish attitude about all popular entertainment anyway, and so had nothing but sneers for TV. It was the solid backbone people of America. The ones who did the work, kept things going and were ready to be friendly to anyone who was friendly to them." [37]

His own ideas, political and aesthetic, meshed nicely with Fedderson's. His act had rotated on this very axis: the breaking down of barriers between the music and the musician, the performer and the audience, upper class and low, highbrow and popular music itself. He wanted and calculated mass appeal. He rewrote the music in performance—popularizing the classics, classicizing pop melodies, improvising one way and then the other. Taking popular requests, inviting individuals to perform with him, and bantering with the audience were only techniques that underlay a larger structure or ideal of his performance art. Achieving this intimacy was nothing to him at this stage of his career, he thought. "It's what I did all the time," he judged. "I tried to set up a one-to-one relationship between me and every individual in the room. . . . The only job I had was how to make it work when I could not get the 'feel of bodies in a room,' and the audience could not, if it felt like it, reach out and touch me." His technique, he related, was to think of the camera itself as a living person. [38]

The pianist insisted that personalizing the camera was his innovation. It was, however, one basis of Klaus Lansberg's successful productions. Lansberg had instructed Korla Pandit to play to the camera, literally, to assume an intimate relationship between himself and the camera, as between guest and friend. It was the same approach that lay behind the pretense of the guest's knock at the hillbillies' door and behind the invitation to sit a spell and join in the pickin' and singin'. With Pandit, as, indeed, with Liberace, the domestic intimacy also suggested sexual intimacy.

Liberace was only capitalizing on or celebrating a technique discovered by others and suggested by the medium itself. He did it better than any of the others, however. And his fame eclipsed theirs immediately, although any viewer could see the relationship between Korla Pandit—the single-instrument performer—and the piano-playing Liberace. If Pandit, indeed, established a precedent, Liberace did him one, two, and three times better. Liberace replaced Pandit's provocative smiles with the winning wink, and, if he used the medium as a perfect stage for his patter, his brother George replaced the Indian's mystical silence with Harpo-comic dumbness. Liberace had his own props, of course; his candelabrum took the place of Pandit's bejeweled turban. He made his own innovations that pushed him into stratospheric popularity. Still, Lee owed his unacknowledged debts to Klaus's Korla.

Through intuition, skill, knowledge—or some intuitive combination of these elements—Lansberg, Fedderson, and Liberace himself were all hitting on something essential relative to the most successful TV. Within a generation of Liberace's first show, scholars were theorizing about the elements that these television pioneers were including in their television performances by 1951. It all begins, one critic insists, with the size of the television set, the dimensions of its screen, and its function as a piece of furniture in a private home. In formulating a "television aesthetic," the critic Horace Newcomb has argued, it is essential

> that the art created for television appears on an object that can be part of one's living room, exist as furniture. It is significant that one can walk around the entire apparatus. Such smallness suits television for intimacy; its presence brings people into the viewer's home to act out dramas. . . . Television is at its best when it offers us faces, reactions, explorations of emotions registered by human beings. The importance is not placed on the action, though that is certainly vital as stimulus. Rather it is on the reaction to the action, to the human response.

One especially thoughtful television cameraman, Jim McMillan, referred to the technique as "shooting for the box"—that is, for the piece of furniture in people's homes.[39]

The logic of television, then, validates intimacy, domesticity, and personality in the programming content. Thus, for example, "the iconography of rooms," the scholar Newcomb continues, "is far more important to television than is that of exterior locations," and faces and personal reactions are more critical than scenes. By this same measure, what happens with individuals or characters takes precedence over large, abstract, or impersonal themes. He might have said political themes, as well—and have contrasted the spectators of Little Ricky's birth with those of Dwight Eisenhower's inauguration. The numerical disparity between those audiences suggests that, when given a choice, folks will opt out of politics and public life altogether for the reaffirmation of what they know at home and hearth. Only, or chiefly, when politics and public life itself becomes domestic and personal does it regain the attention of the viewers.

Dealing with soap operas as a kind of essential expression of this aesthetic, Newcomb argues that such programs "have developed from the time when audiences were made to feel as if they were part of a neighborhood gossiping circle until today, when they are made to feel like probing psychiatrists." The end—concern with individuals—remains essentially unchanged. "Closeness," he insists further, is a natural function of the medium and thus a logical end of television film editing.[40]

As anticipated in the discussion of soap operas as perfect television, the values of closeness, intimacy, and individualism—playing to the box—govern not only the form of television, but its content, too. It all predisposes television toward domesticity and family, the next and most critical ring out from the individual. The role of family, in turn, elicits another stratum of the aesthetic. Family represents the endless repetition and changing configuration of limited or predetermined roles and themes—lover to lover, parent to parent, parent to child, children to parent, sibling to sibling, family to family. This is the stuff of myth and ritual that is both recognizable and familiar and also new and fresh. Through the emphasis on family and family ritual, writes Newcomb, "television manages to entertain vast numbers of viewers with patterns of action and with characters who seem familiar to the cultural consciousness." [41] While enunciated for application to television drama, these concerns pertain with equal power to other forms of programming. Although ritualistic domesticity—and its regular inversion—was essential to both *I Love Lucy* and *The Jack Benny Show,* it applied no less to Liberace's first foray into television. Indeed, almost everything about his show—not least of all its tremendous popularity—confirmed Liberace's appreciation of this television aesthetic long before it was elucidated by scholars.

While no films survive from the live-only productions of the KLAC show, literary evidence confirms that these patterns of intimacy, personalism, family, and ritual characterized both Liberace's first local program and the NBC Dinah Shore replacement program. Indeed, Liberace's show provides virtually a case study for the theory. His performance was ritualistically predictable. The show opened and closed the same way. He used the same equally predictable props, chiefly the candelabrum and fancy clothes. In these regards, his show merely echoed the same characteristics that Klaus Lansberg had imposed on Korla Pandit. Liberace, however, went beyond Lansberg and the Indian organ player to infuse his program with specific and particular domestic values. If his ideal was playing to a happy family circle gathered around the family piano, his intimacy with the camera and with the television audience underlined his familial-like affection for the viewer. It was less vulgar than the hillbillies' domestic circle, but it worked even more effectively. He reified the theme with a close, domestic setting and, still more important, he included real family, his own, in programming. Thus, if he ritualized his performance, he also ritualized family and domesticity into his program. This is what he himself considered the source of his popularity. "When I first started on TV the medium was in its infancy (I came along right after Hopalong Cassidy)," he said. "I discovered at the time that TV viewers were composed essentially of family units. I appealed to and became part of their simple way of life." [42]

Liberace's brother George was a fixture on both programs. His mother was not yet the prop she was to become, but the summer-replacement program anticipated her eventual appearance. He dedicated his first show to her, and later, when he announced she had suffered a heart attack, "the flowers she received filled a room, and the mail could not be squeezed into three big cartons." His mother? She became "Mother" to viewers. He integrated even his absent younger brother, Rudy, into the act. His sibling was serving in Korea during the summer of 1952, and the pianist mentioned on air that the boy was lonely and that Rudy could use some mail. In the first week after the announcement, the agents at NBC who monitored such things reported that the station had received 10,000 inquiries about Rudy Liberace's address. [43]

Liberace persuaded viewers that he was a member of their domestic circle. He also reconstructed a mythical television family around the real-life Liberaces, who, of course, in real life were no more like the projection than the Ricardos were like the chaotic union of Lucille Ball and Desi Arnaz. He made this television family an integral part of his broadcast, but he also beguiled viewers into considering this family their own. He established all this within a context of predictable place and well-ordered home. These elements, combined with his consummate showmanship, made him a hot commodity by the fall of 1952.

If network television, especially after *The Dinah Shore Show,* seemed the logical course to a national audience, the pianist did not go this route. It was his second defeat at the networks' hands. He did not elucidate his failure to win a contract. Circumstances suggest the answer, however. In 1952–53, he was looking for a show at the very time when the coaxial cable was pushing television advertising costs through the roof. Media executives and sponsors had turned aggressively conservative, and they shied from Liberace's unprecedented act. Would the pianist return their investment? His reviews on Dinah Shore's show had been good, but mixed. "He's a good showman, although on the schmaltzy side . . . ," judged *Variety.* "His personality comes across as ingratiating, but a little too saccharine; a more casual, relaxed approach is more suited to tele's intimacy." [44] He remained a tough sell. Networks withheld their endorsement—and their cash. Liberace himself hinted at this years later, when he noted that, "no national sponsor wanted to take a chance on me." [45]

In the absence of anything else, then, he signed not with NBC or one of its competitors for a regular show, but with one of the new, local, independent television filmmakers or syndicators, Guild Films. Newspapers carried the news of the transaction on February 11, 1953. He was contracted for 177 half-hour shorts, each budgeted at thirteen thousand dollars, with financing provided from KLAC-TV and from Guild Films, which was headed by Reuben Kaufman, formerly of Sader Telescriptions.[46]

Kaufman's Guild Films was only one of an extensive series of syndicators in the early years of television, and such companies reveal fundamental issues about not only *The Liberace Show* but also about the context in which it thrived in television's pioneering era.

In the chronological gap between full-time network broadcasting and autonomous local stations, chiefly in the early fifties, syndicators played a critical role. Besides the likes of Kaufman's Guild Films, a series of film companies, like Hal Roach Studios, Screen Gems, Revue, and, most important, Frederick Ziv's operations, cranked out television versions of thirties Hollywood B movies—"screwball comedies, soap opera-ish romances ("women's films"), kiddie Westerns, and pulp adventure sagas." Local stations devoured them.[47]

Other sources encouraged the syndicators. Not only did every station desire to fill the gaps in network programming, but the number of homes with television sets, and the number of stations, grew phenomenally in the period between 1948 and 1954, increasing the demand for shows all the more. In 1948, American families possessed 900,000 sets; by 1949 the number had swelled to 3.5 million. In 1950–51, 107 stations operated in the country; four years later the total had more than tripled to 393. These expansions spelled enormous profits. The networks' revenues offer only one guide to the growth of television's popularity. From $12 million in 1949, their income soared to $127 million three years later, and up to $320 million by 1954.[48] With the networks turning such revenues, local stations did well, too, thereby feeding the need for still more programs.

This was the need that Reuben Kaufman intended to meet. His difficulties in marketing *The Liberace Show* confirmed the networks' general skepticism about taking on the piano player. Don Fedderson had found sponsors for the initial KLAC show after two or three weeks; he had only needed the one bank. Kaufman's task was more complicated. He had to market the program to local stations throughout the country; the local stations then found their own local advertisers. He began on a wing and a prayer. "Scraping together every cent he could get his hands on," Kaufman plunged into production of the first thirteen episodes of the show, which he used to sell the program.

Initially, he had few buyers. "It was a really tough sell, selling the program to conservative advertisers and businessmen," according to Will Lane, a Guild Films executive. "It took the sales genius of Reuben Kaufman (chairman of Guild's executive committee) as much as the talent of Liberace to put it across." No one ever challenged the pianist's appeal to the folks, but it was hard to sell where people didn't know him. Kaufman toured the country with his thirteen films. He signed his first contract with KBTV in Denver.[49] In the first weeks of the series, only fifteen stations had bought in. The next three months brought only twenty more contracts. By September, however, that thirty-five had tripled.[50] The showman was airborne for a thirty-year national and international celebrity ride.

A myriad of factors contributed to the show's national popularity. Liberace applied all the same formulas to the syndicated program that he had to his local show, with comparable effect. It was, indeed, the same act he had perfected in the period between 1947 and 1952, also to comparable effect. But things were different now. The survival of all the kines from *The Liberace Show* allows a closer examination of what was actually going on, what the performer was actually doing. But in understanding the change that was taking place, one must consider more than the performer and his act. The audience, however enthusiastic, was different in content as well as size, and it manifested its enthusiasms in new ways. Liberace was discovering that his victory came at an unexpected price. Now a national celebrity, he ran head on into opinion that he could not charm. For all the adoration of his fans—indeed, as a partial function of their devotion—he encountered animosity he had not experienced since his classmates at Pershing Elementary School and the neighbor children on National Avenue had taunted him and called him "sissy." The present conflict illustrated cleavages in his own persona and his sexual identity, but the animosity—as well as the adoration—also offers a kind of shadowy X-ray picture of American life in these years. He found himself, in part, in the middle of a cultural war between New York and Hollywood—and between New York and Dubuque. And the mythic little old lady from the Iowa town would be a critical soldier in the battle.

*Being a smart piano player as well as a good one,
he has latched onto another 20th Century
phenomenon known as television. A result has
been his emergence in less than a year's time as
TV's first genuine matinee idol . . . It has been
years since the American public has had one of
these animals. It has taken TV to fill the vacuum,
bring back to the public that sense of intimacy
heretofore claimed as the exclusive property
of the stage. His appeal is strictly to women.
The women love him in great droves.*

"Don't Laugh at the Piano Player,"
TV Guide

MUSIC FOR A MAMA'S BOY

Duke Goldstone directed the series. Economy and his own talent informed the production. With a limited budget, he made the most of camerawork and lighting, in particular, to make the show interesting. He used motion-picture spotlighting, he told Bob Thomas, the journalist-biographer, "instead of the flat lighting of most television shows, [which] gave the program clear whites and rich blacks for a sophisticated look." He used two cameras for a split-screen effect so that he could depict the performer playing a duet with himself or make the pianist materialize against a blank curtain. "For 'Danse Macabre,'" he told Thomas, he "employed a skeleton puppet. As an added effect, he reversed the film to negative." A Mother's Day show featured a famed photograph of Frances. The photo sat on the piano and sprang to life at a critical junction: "When Liberace came to the climax of his boogie-woogie, the portrait came to life and Mom shouted, 'Hey!'"[1] Goldstone's camera also resolved the problem of focusing on the pianist-star while also obeying the dictates of the medium itself for movement and visual variety.

The nationally syndicated program was Duke Goldstone's and Don Fedderson's show, but it was, more critically, Liberace's show. They were responding to him as well as to the abstractions of art and the demands of television. The showman knew precisely what he wanted.

Each episode of *The Liberace Show* began the same way, with the heavily backlit performer sitting in darkened profile at a grand piano against an elliptical backdrop of shallow, draped arches. He plays Chopin.

His instrument now is a standard Baldwin, a lucrative contract with that manufacturer having displaced his otherwise beloved Blüthner. A small, electrically lit candelabrum casts obscure light on the left. At the keys, the pianist sits in formal eveningwear. He appears lost in the music as he plays. An unseen orchestra accompanies him. As the lights come up, the camera dollies in for a close-up, and the angle changes. He appears through the open lid of the piano now, over the strings. He looks up as he concludes the piece, shifting his concentration from the music to the camera—to "the box" at home. He smiles, revealing his trademark dimples. He welcomes you to the show in that peculiar voice with odd halts and hesitations, as if he is almost forgetting his cues. Or as if he is not acting at all. He tells you what is coming, and that, of course, varied from show to show in the 177 episodes that Guild Films produced in the two years after 1953.

Some shows had consistent themes. The segment devoted to Stephen Foster is representative. The performer ran through a whole series of the most popular Foster ballads interspersed with film clips of river steamboats and other Southern settings. He also appeared in the high collar and tie of the 1840s and played a boxy, rosewood parlor piano of the period with its frilly Victorian music rack. Periodically, the background drapes parted to reveal illustrative scenes of one kind or another. On one such occasion, as he played and sang "I Dream of Jeannie with the Light Brown Hair," the arch disclosed fields of cotton. A female figure in period costume materializes presently against this agrarian setting, and, as the pianist ended the song, she faded from view—the result of another one of Goldstone's double-image camera tricks.

For the same Stephen Foster program, after a station-advertising break, the pianist appeared again in formal evening clothes and introduced a visitor, whom he announced would sing. In his same cozy manner, he told his visitor—and the audience—that her friend, "Stephen Foster" was in the house and would join them, whereupon Liberace vanished, to return immediately in the 1850s garb of the earlier segment. He devoted another part of the Stephen Foster program to a minstrel show, in which he danced, sang, and faked a banjo version of "Oh, Susannah!" As Mr. Interlocutor, he queried his brother, another minstrel, about one riddle or another, while the ever-silent George answered "I don't know" on his violin.

He developed another show around the theme, "great women." The age of Lillian Russell elicited a piano rendition of "A Bicycle Built for Two," while a Clara Schumann segment was based on the formal music of her husband, Robert. While he played "Dedication," Schumann's musical offering to his bride, the performer, in another camera trick, appeared in a cameo on the upper right of the screen reciting the sentimental tribute Schumann wrote to his wife.

Other installments were more serendipitous, feature numbers having no immediate connection to what preceded or followed. Among these shows, his performance of Schubert's "Ave Maria" is particularly notable. This program included a real-life nun. While the show was filmed, it included a live studio audience, in which the sister had appeared with a group of other habited women. Liberace asked her to participate in the program. She knelt in prayer while he played. Curtains were drawn to reveal a stained-glass image of the Holy Mother, and a choir boy placed the candelabrum on Liberace's piano. It proved a singularly successful production. His recording of the music later became one of his most successful records: his most popular single, "Ave Maria," sold over 300,000 copies. It affirmed the popular conception of his piety. It won the church's favor, too.[2]

In still another production number, the pianist changed from evening-wear to a plain smoking jacket and from the formal studio to a homelike setting to play "Santa Lucia," which he identified with his father. This was one of the only references he made on the program to Salvatore Liberace. He changed costumes many times to fit the music, donning, for example, a "wild number" for "The Beer Barrel Polka" or a military uniform for his dance accompaniment to "Boogie-Woogie Bugle Boy." Sometimes the costume changes illustrated the shifts from classical to popular music. When playing his version of Tchaikovsky's Second Piano Concerto, he wore the traditional white tie and black tails of the concert stage, but when the music segued into "Tonight We Love," the ballad based on Tchaikovsky's theme, he appeared all in white eveningwear—and then went back to black when he returned to the formal composition. Simultaneously, the camera was illustrating the same transformations by depicting the sheet music from the two compositions. Liberace constantly mixed the classics and popular music. Rimsky-Korsakov's "Flight of the Bumblebee" became "The Bumblebee Boogie," while he did an entire segment on Grieg's most singable themes.[3]

Generally, the show began with a major production number followed by the local station's commercial break. The next part of the program opened with the performer chatting intimately with the camera and the audience about some matter of personal or sentimental concern, playing for patients in a veterans hospital, or receiving letters from particular fans. He referred regularly to his mail. This discourse often moved the show into a second production number, which was similar to the first in form.

Thus, the singer determined to send a "musical get-well card" to the shut-ins who had written him, and a lively rendition of "Bye Bye Blues" followed.

While heavy on sentimental productions, Liberace altered the program's pace with Latin rhythms, boogie-woogie, film melodies, and the like, always with costume changes to suit the themes. He was in fact producing a version of the variety show that dominated these years of television. While he entertained actual variety acts—a guest singer here, a guest trumpeter there—he himself provided the chief variety. Unlike the network shows that failed to exploit his particular talents, this time, he was the star. The camera knew it. However he was costumed, however he varied the production, however curious the camera angle, his face seldom left the frame. Judging by its visuals alone, the program hinged on the expressiveness of the performer's face. The one real exception to the face rule was hardly an exception at all: the camera left his face only to concentrate on his hands. If the show, then, was really about personality, and if Liberace's personality resided chiefly in his visage, then his hands became an extension of his face and personality. If hands, of course, lack the distinctiveness of faces, the showman compensated by dramatizing and exaggerating his movements, and, however subtlety and demurely for the time being, by dressing his hands, if only with one discreet pinky ring.

In response to the applause that greeted the conclusion of every number, he expressed extensive appreciation, which again became a kind of trademark. "Thank you. Thank you so very much. Thank you. I thank you very much. Thank you so much. I thank you." In his soft, distinctive, but rather shallow baritone, he closed the half-hour production with what had become his theme song, "I'll Be Seeing You." Sung—performed—directly to folks in their living rooms, the ballad epitomized the performer's ideal of intimacy with his audience.[4]

Especially with its artful lighting and camera work, and its close-in shots of face and hands, the show emphasized the personal and the intimate. The actual personality the star projected underlined these same qualities. His "warm yet almost shy personality," as one reporter called it, came through to viewers unlike anything they had ever seen on the tube before.[5] While his general demeanor embodied the traits, his voice, in particular, did so even more. His peculiar way of speaking was easy to mock and ridicule, as effeminate, for example. Thus one old friend's observation that it was not a voice one would expect to hear at football games. It was not merely that Liberace sounded like a sissy and that sissies did not attend sporting events, although that might have been the point of the observation. More than that, however, the emotional range and even the volume was constricted—in contrast, say, to the noise in a stadium. There was, first of all, the slightly nasal Midwestern whine. Besides that, the voice was soft, hesitant, monochromatic. Perhaps as a reflection of his old speech impediment and the therapy that followed, he tended to breathe in the wrong places. It was not a good speaking voice, no way around it, and yet it served him very well. Once again, he had turned a liability into an asset. His voice made, for example, for an extraordinary—and, one ventures to say, appealing—contrast with the enormous energy, exaggerated emotion, and extended range of his playing. More than "non-threatening," the voice even invited listeners to fill in its blanks, in the way, for example, that one wants to supply the word to a stutterer. Liberace's voice was a source of what was often called his "little boy" appeal. It was as if he could not completely recall lines that he had tried in earnest to memorize, and the audience was encouraging him. One reviewer captured the whole picture nicely: "Liberace talks to his audience with a perpetual smile on his face—the kind of smile a little boy musters to prove to his parents that he's brushed his teeth—and he speaks in the carefully controlled and subdued voice of a kindergarten teacher talking to a nervous child."[6]

He projected a combination of power and vulnerability in other ways as well. Although they were filmed, he insisted that the shoots look "live." He calculated the disarming on-air mistakes and flaws to fit the image he desired. "We made no retakes," he related;

> we filmed the mistakes just as we would have done using electronic cameras with no opportunity to stop and go back and shoot it over. . . . Actually we did use electronic cameras and a live audience, as well as the film cameras. But if I perspired I just mopped away the perspiration with a handkerchief as I do on the stage. Or if I made some kind of a language slip . . . mispronounced a word or committed a grammatical error . . . I just excused myself and corrected what I'd said. It was just the way anything would happen in a family situation. And I came across as a human being, not some sort of a facsimile person, the way some performers do in shows that are filmed and refilmed, and edited and cut and fixed up until they have about as much humanity as a plastic puppet.[7]

The intimacy involved more than his own personality. Even more aggressively than his early forays on the airwaves had, the show played on domestic intimacy. Indeed, the star made no distinctions between personal and domestic intimacy in the program. "I talked to the viewers as if they were my friends, my next door neighbors," he wrote. "We had a kind of over the back-fence relationship. I showed them my pets. I talked about my mother and my sister and my brother. My family became everyone's family, sort of." [8] His blood kin was doubly critical to the show. His brother George was the orchestra director and appeared on camera regularly in that capacity, but he was also as ubiquitous a prop as the ever-present candelabrum; he was another aspect of the program's ritualized production. His mother served the same purpose. Decked out in a huge orchid corsage, she sat in the front row of the studio audience during every program. The sense of family went further. On camera, the performer treated his entire crew as family; off camera, he did the same. Some of his people, like Marilyn Hecht, his harpist, had been with him for so many years that she might have qualified as kin. So had Gordon Robinson, his musical director. Robinson was normally behind the scenes, but, on occasion, Liberace trotted him out as a part of the family, and added to the impact by instructing the musician to "say hello to his mother in Erie, Pennsylvania." The obligatory "Hi, Mom" followed. [9]

There was nothing else like *The Liberace Show,* with its striking juxtaposition of high style and hokeyness, polish and error, urbanity and provincialism, in 1953. It is small wonder that Reuben Kaufman encountered initial difficulties in peddling the show to wary station managers and conservative businessmen in the winter. The turn came in the fall of '53. By September, around a hundred stations had bought in. Four months or so later, the number reached 180. [10] By 1955, the figure peaked at around two hundred. By 1958, when the program was still running in some places, it had more than four hundred advertisers and grossed around $7,500,000 for Guild. [11]

No objective measure exists for ranking how many people really watched *The Liberace Show* between 1953 and 1955, when it was in its prime. There are no clearly tabulated popular ratings, as there would have been for a network program. According to one source, the program was syndicated more widely than any other; more people, according to the same authority, watched *The Liberace Show* than either *Dragnet* or *I Love Lucy,* the two most popular network competitors in this period. In New York, reruns permitted viewers to catch the program ten times a week. [12] Thirty million people, according to other sources, watched the program at any given time that it was shown during its three-year heyday. [13]

The Liberace Show was tapping a huge reservoir of popular desire, but the number of people gathered around television screens across the country offers only one manifestation of the performer's appeal. By 1954, ten thousand fan letters a week flooded his offices. He was inundated with twenty-seven thousand Valentine Day cards that year.[14] Fans mobbed him at every appearance. In New Orleans, he spent two and a half hours signing autographs.[15] He appeared at an autograph party for a local sponsor in his hometown, and even the police could not keep proper order.[16] It was the same story in Miami, where his appearance to publicize the opening of a new bank provoked a riot in which "several women fainted, many were bruised, and a small child was injured."[17]

How popular was the effervescent entertainer? How to measure his attraction? Mob scenes offer one gauge; his recording career offers another. In the great flourish of activity in '47 and '48, he produced about ten discs. In 1949, 1950, and 1951, the record was literally blank. With his KLAC fame, however, his reputation took off. In 1952, Seymour Heller negotiated a contract with Columbia Records for his client. His new label marketed over a score of titles under his name that year alone, chiefly for the Los Angeles market, it would seem. With the national fame of *The Liberace Show* the following year, that number more than doubled. In 1954, he had over sixty-seven separate discs on the market.[18] Liberace recalled this turn of events in his autobiography. He had worked with Mitch Miller, then artist and repertoire man at Columbia Records, he remembered, and his first single in four years, "September Song," had become a smash.[19] According to another source, Paul Weston, "One of our outstanding composer-arranger-conductors" (as Liberace described him) discovered him for Columbia. The two men met at a charity telethon. Weston said he knew the performer only as a TV personality, but his talent as a live performer amazed him. "With nothing but a piano and a smile," Weston related, "Liberace transformed an inattentive audience into enthralled listeners." As West Coast representative for Columbia, Weston immediately urged the company's New York headquarters to sign a contract with the pianist. The company signed the performer and produced three albums, *Liberace by Candlelight, Liberace at the Piano,* and *An Evening with Liberace.* While Liberace had relied on his brother to orchestrate his 1952 records, he recorded with Weston beginning in 1953. Each Weston album placed among the top five best sellers in the country in 1954.[20] By mid-1954, he had sold 400,000 albums, exceeding significantly even the sales of the pop singer Eddie Fisher, then in his own prime.[21]

Over and above the riots and record sales, the popular culture of the period bubbles over with other evidence of Liberace's appeal. He was a mainstay in television beyond his own show. Ed Sullivan invited him to appear on his Sunday night program in the fall of 1955. That most distinguished journalist Edward R. Murrow featured him on his CBS program

Person to Person on January 6, 1956. He cropped up on the screen repeatedly with other notables of the day, like Red Skelton and Jack Benny. While one Jack Benny performance (that also featured Mamie Van Doren) failed to make much of the pianist, another got more comic mileage out of him. Devoid of any pretense whatsoever, and full of great good humor, Liberace satirized and parodied his own persona. In a classic twist on his domestic comedy-cum-variety show, Benny, playing himself, came calling on Liberace to invite him to appear on his show. On a set of Liberace's "home," candelabra occupied every space, and servants were busily lighting the tapers. When the two stars played a duet, a tiny candelabrum even glowed on Benny's violin.[22]

Liberace figured in popular songs of the day. Begging "Mr. Sandman" for a dream lover, the McGuire Sisters crooned about a hero "with a lonely heart like Pagliacci; and lots of wavy hair like Liberace!" He appeared as "Loverboynik" in Al Capp's popular daily cartoon strip, "Li'l Abner." The cartoon episode had its own story. In the fall of 1954, the cartoonist informed the showman that he was creating a character called "Liverachy." Lee was not flattered. His lawyers took up the case. Only then did Capp invent the figure, Loverboynik, a television pianist surrounded by hoards of fans. Capp later informed the press that his character and Liberace could not be one and the same because his character could actually play the piano well and never giggled hysterically.[23]

Major American magazines—*Collier's, Coronet, Life,* and *Time*—profiled Liberace and chronicled his career. He was cover-story and front-page material repeatedly for *TV Guide.* Liberace jokes, meanwhile, circulated everywhere. Next to the price of coffee, remarked one journalist, "the most popular joke on TV is 'I get rich selling dental floss to Liberace.'"[24] He became a household word, according to another critic, "the topic of more jokes than the proverbial mother-in-law."[25] Liberace's candelabrum rose to become "a staple of the airwaves' gagmen, like Benny's miserliness and Bing Crosby's glue-pot horses and Bob Hope's ski-run nose."[26] "Did you ever see such a smile?," joshed Hope himself. "He's got so much ivory in his head, when he takes a bath he and the soap float together. . . . But it isn't his fault, really, you see, he was such a delicate baby that instead of slapping him the doctor patted him with a powder puff, and he's been smiling ever since."[27] Many of the stories played on Liberace's delicacy more directly. Some still circulate after years and years. The comic James Coco repeated one of them as "a Liberace riddle": "What is better than roses on a piano? Tulips on your organ!"[28]

Other measures of his popularity? His escalating revenues and attendance at his performances offer still more evidence of his hold on the popular imagination. He reported earning a very healthy fifty thousand dollars a year before he started doing television; afterwards, his income soared into the millions. Even before his television program was syndicated, his reputation was rippling out from Los Angeles and exciting the provinces. In the summer of 1952, for example, he had filled the fourteen-thousand-seat civic auditorium in Kansas City.[29] In the rush of national fame the following year, he played twenty-four different engagements around the country. These performances grossed over $300,000.[30] This tour broke, according to one observer, "almost every box-office record in every theater, auditorium, field house and stadium he has played." His remuneration reflected the ticket sales. Three sold-out performances in his native Milwaukee netted him over forty-seven thousand dollars; two New Orleans shows added to his income by nearly thirty-eight thousand; one engagement in Sioux City and another in St. Louis brought him twenty-three thousand and over twenty-eight thousand, respectively.[31] New Orleans witnessed the same rush. "In Chicago, the Civic Opera House, sold out four days after his concert was announced, had to schedule two more."[32]

His concerts were unlike anything the country had witnessed. He was the hottest entertainer in the United States. Under the headline, "Liberace to Gross $33,000 Here," his hometown newspaper chronicled one bit of the phenomenon. "Most of the greats that have gone by—Horowitz, Paderewski, John McCormack, Marian Anderson—made one appearance (there were few matinee occasions) in an auditorium confined to half its capacity." In contrast, the hometown boy "will play the piano to a full auditorium and to a full house both nights."[33] The actual concerts, which took place in October 1953, attracted twenty thousand people. If the Metropolitan Opera and the Philadelphia Orchestra could not match these figures, the reviewer noted, neither could such popular entertainers as Bob Hope and Jack Benny.[34]

Seven months later, he repeated the triumph in the city. Richard S. Davis, who had reviewed classical performances for over a decade in Milwaukee, had his own take on the matinee the pianist played on Sunday, May 2. "Man and boy, the present historian has attended a number of impressive musical affairs, but none of them even faintly resembled the triumph under discussion," he reflected. Most of all, he noted the pianist's audience control that never wavered in a staggeringly long performance, "the longest of modern record." Hometown boy, television celebrity, and everything else aside, wrote Davis, "it is still a minor miracle when 6,000 will sit still for nearly four hours on the hard Auditorium chairs, most of the time in ecstasy. The temptation is to be sharp and supercilious about the demonstration, but the impulse must be resisted." He concluded: "The resplendent Liberace clearly has something more than meets the eye."[35]

The pianist was wowing them in Kansas City, knocking them dead in Milwaukee, bringing down the house in New Orleans. Even in New York City he left audiences begging for more. Indeed, his extraordinary New York concerts in 1953 and 1954 provide a model of these others.

Liberace had headlined the great hotels and supper clubs in Manhattan in the 1940s, but he returned in glory and triumph to the city on September 25, 1953, to perform in the venerable Carnegie Hall. He not only filled the house, he could have filled it twice over. Until curtain time, patrons besieged the box office, some, as the *New York Times* reported, "with tears in their eyes," pleading unsuccessfully for tickets.

The performance itself followed a pattern that Liberace seldom varied except in its details. While his brother conducted the twenty-five-piece orchestra, he entered the stage with regal fanfare, resplendent in white tie and tails. He began the show with his usual disarming patter: he squinted into the darkness of the balcony, and crooned, "Oh look, there are people way up there!"

The actual program consisted of a mixture of well-known melodies, classical and otherwise. He played from the standard, classical repertoire, themes from Grieg's Piano Concerto and Debussy's "Clair de Lune"; he also performed somewhat lighter material, more themes, this time from the score "The Warsaw Concerto," and also de Falla's "The Ritual Fire Dance." In addition, he included purely popular material, Latin American music, Italian folk songs, and Broadway show tunes. He also sang, among other numbers, Kurt Weill's "September Song," which was close to being his theme song by this time. Between the musical selections, he interspersed jokes, more patter, and verbal asides.[36] He went through various costume changes, including dressing as a yokel along with his brother, and performing a hillbilly, hayseed, hoedown routine. He ended the performance with his breathy, signature words of appreciation: "Thank you very much, thank you. I thank you, thanks so much." He then plopped himself down on the corner of the stage, dangled his legs over the edge, offered autographs, shook hands, touched the patrons, and accepted embraces.[37] The audience, three-fourths of which consisted of women, loved it all and responded enthusiastically to every number, every joke, and every concluding touch.

The Carnegie Hall performance did not exhaust the interest of the New York audience. Eight months later, Liberace returned to Manhattan in even finer fettle. On the evening of May 26, 1954, he played Madison

Square Garden. Fifteen thousand paying fans turned out. Once more, he filled the hall; only a few of the worst seats went unsold. People wanted to be close to the stage, and they paid for the privilege. No pianist had drawn such an enormous audience since Paderewski had appeared there twenty years before on February 8, 1932. Indeed, this performance won Liberace a place in *The Guinness Book of World Records:* he was paid $138,000 for the performance, the most money a pianist had ever received for one show. He was topping his idol.[38]

The format of his Madison Square Garden performance was almost identical to that of the Carnegie Hall concert. After an overture from Bizet's "L'Arlésienne," he burst onto the stage—dressed completely in white—to a gong's crash, a drum roll, and a harp glissando. He acknowledged the audience itself: "Isn't it great, George? Did you count them?" He instructed the lights to go up, and spots swept the crowded house. More patter: "That makes it even more fabulous. Now I can play."[39]

He offered an exaggerated version of his television performances. One critic described the form, invidiously: "Both his feet are jouncing rhythmically, with vigorous knee action. He flings a hand high into the air after hitting a chord. One instant his fingers are clawing at the keyboard, the next they are caressing or pounding. Often he crosses hands, or lets one hand lie conspicuously at rest on his knee."[40] The program itself also followed the same lines as the Carnegie Hall concert, if perhaps relying rather more heavily on popular tunes. This time, Liberace also sang. Among his vocals he included a number dedicated to his critics, which later became a regular part of his performances: "I Don't Care (As Long As You Care For Me)." He also resorted to much the same pattering asides that had become his trademark: "Have to raise my bench a little more. It's a pretty high-class number," represented the norm. He made small talk about his television sponsors. A tunafish packer, he said, had given him cases of the product. Do any of you mothers in the audience have recipes? Send them along to Mother in California.[41] His mother figured in the performance in other ways. She was seated in a theater box; he introduced her and asked for a round of applause. She got an enthusiastic one. Foreshadowing later days, he also gave up his white tails for a glamorous gold lamé dinner jacket, which was only one among several costume changes. The audience, which was this time estimated to be 80 percent female, ate it up and left wanting more.[42] As one commentator remarked, "The most buzzed about attraction at large in the concert business today does not, of course, in these paradoxical times, give concerts. He gives, instead, himself."[43]

By the mid-fifties, Liberace was earning a million dollars per year from public appearances, with additional income from records, piano-instruction courses, and real-estate investments. His television program made him immensely wealthy: he netted 20 percent of the profits on the first run, and up to 80 percent on fifth runs. His income from his television program amounted to seven million dollars during the show's first two years. He was earning fifty thousand a week. His devotees organized into more than two hundred fan clubs and turned out whenever he appeared.[44]

If all this data represents manifestations of the showman's popularity, its meaning—not to mention its sources—are harder to calculate. What is the significance of popularity? Its sources? How is it calculated? The issue raises a host of problems. In the first place, popularity remains a dubious or even a negative virtue, at least for many analysts. In this view, popular, democratic, or mass taste is debased and debasing by nature. "The popular" is thereby not worthy of thorough study. It is incapable, indeed, of sustaining extended treatment—except as a model of what good art or real art cannot be. One critic put it most succinctly in his discussion of *Gone with the Wind,* perhaps the most persistent icon of twentieth-century popular culture in the United States, not to mention the world: "Great literature can occasionally be popular, and certainly popular literature can occasionally be great. But with a few notable exceptions, such as the Bible but not *Gone with the Wind,* greatness and popularity are more likely to be contradictory than congenial."[45] Second, even when popular culture is considered worthy of examination, some of these negative notions about the masses still come into play, but beyond that, a larger problem looms: How, in short, is popularity measured? Are there nonsubjective standards for calculating the significance of mass appeal, whether of soap operas, McDonald's hamburgers, Danielle Steel's novels—or Liberace? Third, in treating icons of popular culture, how does the critic maintain a balance between the actual object of popular desire and the desiring populace?[46] Other issues arise from these. For example, what is the role of social structures in governing the popular? What of "hype," or advertising, in encouraging or even creating popular appeal? Is popularity foisted on a neutral public?[47] Beyond all this, popularity has its own dynamic and tends to exaggerate itself. This was certainly the case with Liberace between 1953 and 1956. "Liberace" had become a media creation in its own right now, an effigy that critics could do with as they wished. "Under any other circumstances, Wladziu Valentino Liberace would merely be a nice guy, a bit on the naive side, playing the piano for a living," observed one critic in the middle of the pianist's "white heat" years. "Under Hollywood circumstances, he is a Character, a Personality, a Celebrity, and thus fair game for the poison-pen set. They make fun of him, for outwardly he is the perfect patsy for such shenanigans—a perpetually grinning matinee idol, slightly on the pudgy side, who seems for all the world to be an overgrown little boy dependent on his mother." [48]

Behind the effigy, what was there? Beyond the hoopla, extraordinary as it was, Liberace touched something in the American temper. The appeal existed on various levels. His personal and domestic intimacy are important, but they cannot entirely explain the runaway popularity of *The Liberace Show*. If his persona emphasized a " 'homey' quality that quickly made him 'just folks,' " as one reviewer wrote, this was not Klaus Lansberg's *Dixie Showboat* brand of homeyness at all. On the contrary, his formal, after-eight eveningwear, the large, shiny black, very grand piano, and not least, the useless elegance of his candelabra, created a sense of refinement, taste, and class. As with his supper-club performances, this combination, of folksiness on the one hand and style on the other, made for a particularly potent mix and contributes significantly to understanding Liberace's early appeal—and the nature of the American viewing public at midcentury.

Without much if any elegance in their lives, the mass of American folk gathered around their television sets could access culture now in an altogether new way. These people might never dine by candlelight—unless the power failed. They might never own a single piece of silver—much less fancy candelabra. They could boast at best Sunday-going-to-meeting coats, ties, and dresses; few, if any, ever even rented tuxedos and evening gowns, let alone possessed such garments. Some might have owned pianos, but nothing like a costly Baldwin or lustrous Steinway. The differences between Bach, Brahms, and Berlioz might be lost on them. They might not ever know any of this; they might not really want to know it. Nevertheless, the folks, at least in 1953, acknowledged the existence of a world where such things existed, carried import, and were admirable. Liberace played to this sense. He made these elements of High Culture accessible to every home with a television set. In his show, it was not foreign; it was not arcane; it was not hard; its delights were available to anyone. The actual music he simplified, but his presentation of the music — his gentle introductions—made it seem even more natural and easy.

This identification with culture and wealth became a critical part of Liberace's identity after 1953. While it constituted one element of his television program's popularity, he integrated the values associated with money and culture into his personal life so seamlessly that the accoutrements he used to create a high-class ambiance on television became virtually inseparable from the man himself. Off camera as well as on, he calculated his image to fulfill the public longing for wealth, grandeur, and display. He concentrated them all in the new home he built in 1953. He made the place a symbol of his public image; it was a private home yet a public emblem of his achievement. His first "celebrity house" was only on the surface his private domicile; it was, more, one more element in his calculated imagery.

In 1953, he moved from Camellia Street in North Hollywood to Valley Vista Boulevard on the lower northern slopes of the Santa Monica Mountains, still in the San Fernando Valley. Not far from the busy intersection of Sepulveda Boulevard and Ventura Drive in Sherman Oaks, the new home lay about six miles from Camellia Street. This time, however, he wasn't buying a tract house.

Unable to find exactly what he wanted, the showman bought land and hired an architect to execute his dream house. "I contributed my own ideas all the time," he boasted to one visitor. "I made little sketches of the things I wanted. I picked out everything, from hardware to furniture. What you see is what I had in mind. The house has drama, but it also has touches of humor. It's classical, but it's modern, too." The result was "well, pure Liberace," in the summation of this same visitor who reported back to the folks about touring the mansion.

> Candelabras everywhere. The color motif: black and white, like the piano. The living room was huge, necessarily so to house the Baldwin grand piano, which was six inches longer than normal size. A large, glass-topped planter was piano-shaped, and pianos were etched into the bottoms of the lamps. The bookends were shaped like pianos. Shelves displayed a collection of miniature pianos and pictures, each with a printed card of explanation. . . .
>
> The tour continued through the dining room with its music-scrollbacked chairs, and to the bedroom, dominated by an immense bed covered with a satin spread emblazoned with a large script "L" intertwining a piano. More piano lamps, a large oil painting of Liberace on the wall. The large bathroom was done in black and mirrors.

The bathroom, with its sunken tub, delighted Liberace especially. When doing a musical short at RKO, he explained, he had visited a nearby set where the 1952 *Androcles and the Lion* was being shot. "An actor was sitting in billows of suds in one of those Roman baths, and it seemed to me the height of luxury," he later said.[49]

As a young piano player on the make in 1947, had he dreamed of a house with a pool? He got it with a vengeance on Valley Vista Boulevard six years later. It was shaped like a grand-piano top, the shallow end culminating in steps painted an alternating black and white to resemble the eighty-eight keys of a piano. Like the phonograph gimmick, like the Blüthner grand, like "Liber-AH-chee," the pool became a publicity device of extraordinary worth to the entertainer. Photographers couldn't keep away from it. It turned into the representation of the house itself, even as the house emblemized the showman. The dwelling became the "piano pool house," and it acquired virtually legendary proportions in the seven years he owned it. This was the place where Edward R. Murrow interviewed him on *Person to Person* on January 6, 1956. It was his home when he first attained international celebrity; to see it was the object of thousands of tourists driving over from Los Angeles.

If the house fulfilled his own dreams and signaled his arrival, its legendary fame suggests the vicarious fulfillment of the dreams of millions who lived more modestly, those still locked into subdevelopment ticky-tacky, or even still hoping for the suburbs. While the excesses of the Valley Vista house might have appealed to anyone in humble circumstances, it could have been calculated for the men and women of Liberace's own generation. The timing of the Depression and the war had denied them their own excesses; afterwards, the business of raising families and paying bills was hardly conducive to such indulgences. Lee spent for them. Folks delighted in giving him their cash for such splendid vicarious displays. The Valley Vista house had additional significance, however, and introduces other aspects of the piano player's career at this time that suggest, ultimately, added sources of his attraction.

The house memorialized his commercial success, but it did so twice over. It was a sign, of course, of his having arrived at a pinnacle of wealth, but the house itself was a gift of his commercial sponsors. He had built it not with his own funds, but rather through endorsements, through "contributions of various companies for advertising purposes of their own." [50] The house itself, then, was an advertising gimmick. The same held true for his automobile, a white Cadillac limousine with seats done up in the same black-and-white piano motif as his swimming pool. It, too, was the gift of commercial sponsors, even as it also represented the gaudy demonstration of his commercial success. He had no problem accepting the automobile; he had no problems flying to Ohio to assist the donor in selling cars. He liked selling things. He liked advertising. He liked making money. He liked spending money. He promoted himself shamelessly, but he promoted his sponsors with equal commitment. It is not the least interesting component of his celebrity.

From his earliest days on KLAC, he had associated himself with selling, salesmanship, commerce, commercialism, and capitalism. His acceptance speech for the local Emmy awards for Most Outstanding Male Personality of the Year in February 1953 offers an early version of the mode. After crediting his mother, his brother, his managers, and the television station producer, he also thanked his sponsor, "the Citizens National Bank, whose product I admire."[51] In 1953, he had cut a promotional, giveaway record for this same Citizens National Bank.[52] It established a notable pattern for his "white heat" period of fame. As he grew hotter and hotter, he made records for a whole variety of local sponsors of *The Liberace Show.*

Reuben Kaufman had made his first sale to the television station in Denver, Colorado, in 1953, and the showman cut a promotional record for the program's sponsor there, the Denver National Bank, the next year. The 45 rpm record treated depositors to "The Blue Danube Waltz" and "Humoresque." Banks in Cleveland, Ohio; Portland, Maine; New Castle, Delaware; and El Paso, Texas, got their own discs, too.[53] The First Federal Savings and Loan Association of Rochester, New York, was pleased enough with its first recording in 1954 to request a second the following year. The initial one duplicated the program of the Denver bank's disc; the second treated locals to more Chopin: "The Minute Waltz" and "Polonaise Militaire." The First Federal Savings and Loan of Chicago, as befitting the grandest city in the Midwest, offered its patrons a ten-inch, 33 rpm record with eclectic selections that thoroughly typified the performer's mode: "Liebestraum," "Chopsticks," "Tales from the Vienna Woods," "The Dream of Olwen," "I Miss You So," "I Want My Mama," "Maiden's Wish Samba," and his special hit, "September Song." Another sponsor from the early L.A. fame days, Valley National Bank, got this same extended recording in addition to a two-number 45.[54] The salesman cooperated with other sponsors in a similar manner: the insurance company Mutual of Omaha and United of Omaha in 1954; the Union Pacific Railroad the same year; and the otherwise unidentified "Parkview Markets" and "O'Shea's Jewelers," which got "Dark Eyes" and "Lullaby" in 1954, as well.[55]

By the time he had become a national celebrity, Liberace had hundreds of different sponsors for the local broadcasts of his Film Guild show. Besides cutting promotional records, he associated himself with these sponsors in all sorts of other ways. He relished such promotions. He made personal appearances for many, selling cars in Milwaukee and mortgages in Miami, for example. On national television for the first time, he noted his tunafish advertisers, and invited women with recipes to send them in.

Moreover, he made his advertisers a prop as standard as his candelabra, his mother, or his mute brother. "When I appeared in concerts, or in a night club, I did a whole routine about these sponsors," he laughed. These businesses ranged from morticians, bankers, and cookie companies to toilet paper industries—a "well-known manufacturer of paper products," he added slyly.

> As sort of an afterthought I'd say, "Everything but writing
> paper." (Pause) Then I went on, "It was customary for all
> these companies to send me samples of their products." At
> this point some of my audience would begin to anticipate me
> and start to giggle. "Naturally," I told them, "I didn't hear
> from the undertaker—fortunately. Nor the banks—unfortu-
> nately. However I did hear from the biscuit company and the
> paper manufacturer. We had more cookies than the Girl
> Scouts ever dreamed of. And toilet paper to match every
> bathroom in the house. . . . Wallpaper, that is."

He continued: "Just talking about these sponsors in a chatty way enabled me to get hearty laughs from my audience."[56]

A not particularly friendly critic offered a slightly different version of the same sort of performance. The stuff of humor, it was easy for sophisticated New York critics to mock, especially when the showman touted sponsors from the Carnegie Hall and Madison Square Garden stages:

> He enters. Some piano playing ensues, but not much. Comes
> next some talk. One of his sponsors, he explains, is a tuna-fish
> packer who has given him lots of cases of the product. And if
> any of the mothers in the audience have new tuna recipes, he
> hopes they'll send them on to his mother, in the San Fer-
> nando Valley. Another sponsor is a funeral parlor, and he
> happens to have learned there that, in the wills of the de-
> ceased, Debussy's "Clair de Lune" is more often requested as
> the accompaniment to interment than any other number in
> his repertoire. At that the house lights go out, a single spot
> lights up his hands and out pours "Clair de Lune."[57]

Liberace's attitude toward his commercial sponsors reflects a notable manifestation of his character and, ultimately, of his showmanship and audience appeal. It also suggests qualities that permeated his country. Without any pride of art, he identified himself with his sponsors. "If I am selling tuna fish," he said guilelessly, "I believe in tuna fish."[58] This bond, in turn, mirrors a related unity with his audiences. If he and his sponsors were in the act together, the one no better than the other, the same rule held for him and his fans. If he was folksy, humorous, attentive, and sympathetic toward the businesses that bought his program, these same virtues characterize twice over his response to his audiences. The notion that he worked for a funeral parlor delighted his audiences, and he delighted in the humorous incongruity as well. The same held for his witty, double-edged references to his toilet-tissue sponsors.

From the days of the priceless twenty-five-thousand-dollar grand piano, its astronomical moving costs, and insurance fees, money and monetary measures had been an integral part of Liberace's own publicity campaign. It remained a powerful, even compelling, part of his celebrity after 1953: thus the constant references to his unprecedented income, the press releases about the huge revenues from his tours, the repetition of mind-boggling compensation from individual performances. This was "news"; newspaper reporters ate it up. "Liberace to Gross $33,000 Here" was a perfectly appealing headline when he played his hometown. Commercialism, money, and monetary success became so much a part of his persona that he worked it into his act. It became another gimmick or routine that people came to expect—and love. Indeed, the line that won him a place in *Bartlett's Familiar Quotations* represented only the tip of the ledger sheet in his repertoire. It had become legendary—literally—by 1954. One of the earliest references to the quip also established, perhaps inadvertently, the favorable reception of its sentiments. "A particularly scathing review of one of his performances during a Midwest tour drew this letter from the pianist," began the 1954 notice, "'Thank you for your very amusing review. After reading it, in fact, my brother George and I laughed all the way to the bank.' The critics may rake the man over," the reviewer crowed, "but he rakes in the money."[59] If this is the first published reference to the quip, time altered it to the now-standard "crying all the way to the bank." He offered a multitude of similar epigrams based on his joyful commercializing. "I've had so much fun myself that honestly I'm ashamed to take the money—but I will!" "Do you like my outfit? You should; you paid for it!" Over thirty years after he had first purred the lines, they were still evoking guffaws, even when the audience themselves repeated the punch lines with him.

The once-poor kid from West Milwaukee had no complaints about the folks and popular taste, and found nothing objectionable about the desire for making it or getting ahead. Capitalism did not offend him. It was better to be rich than poor. He expressed no guilt about earning a great deal of money or about being wealthy. He relished spending his cash, as well. It was hard earned, too, but he never resented working;

indeed, he lived to work. He had no objections whatsoever to the processes of capitalism. "Everything I do has the hope of making a profit. My career, everything I touch in my scope of entertainment field," he said, was done with money in mind. He expected the same from others. "Nobody works for nothing," he insisted.[60]

Throughout his entire career, he was always casting about for new money-making schemes. While he might have simply squirreled his extra cash away in stocks, bonds, and other securities, this way to wealth failed to attract him. Money and capital in the abstract did not interest him much. He liked investments he could hold and see. With debts to his mother, more than likely, he began and ended his capitalistic endeavors as a petty bourgeois. For a period, he set up shops and sold antiques. He sponsored dieting schemes. He played with a line of men's clothing. There was a plan for music studios. In 1965, he launched Liberace Chateau Inns, a chain of motels that would each boast a mannequin dressed in one of his outfits. Most of all, again with debts to the Zuchowskis, he believed beyond hope of redemption in real property—land, houses, apartments. He bought and sold these investments as passionately as he did the geegaws that filled his mansions.[61] Had his old high school chums remembered him "trying to make a buck all the time"?[62] He never lost the passion.

Capitalistic enterprise was a part of what he considered the rights and privileges of being an American. He was proud to be an American. He was doing what all Americans were doing, should be doing, or would like to be doing. In all these ways, Lee Liberace was a hometown American boy who was speaking to the hopes, desires, and deprivations of all his countrymen. His real audience was the ordinary man in the street. At the same time, his actual appeal was narrower. His man in the street turned out to be a woman. His John Doe was Joanne Doe—better still, Mrs. John Doe, John's harried spouse.

Nothing about Liberace's supper-club act had been oriented, invidiously or otherwise, toward one sex or the other. From his earliest gigs in the forties up to the Dinah Shore summer replacement show of 1952, no reviewers ever mentioned anything about the performer appealing to one category of folks as opposed to another. On the contrary, every notice described him simply as a knock-'em-dead, leave-'em-begging-for-more stand-up piano player and comic. His act was not always sex free—his patter included plenty of sly jokes and double entendre, but his reviews lack any reference to gender. The nature of his audience confirmed the absence of bias. At the elegant supper clubs, he played to couples out on the town, men and women on a fancy date, husbands splurging on their wives. While his audience was generally about half men and half women, if anything, men predominated insofar as males tended to be single and free—footloose service men as the war wore down, or conventioneers and businessmen on the road and staying in good hotels. The latter type describes Clarence Goodwin, for example, who attended the pianist's show three thousand miles away from his Hollywood home when Liberace played Boston's Copley Plaza Hotel just after the war.

Liberace's television show, however, both at KLAC and as syndicated by Guild Films, attracted a different audience. No hard evidence exists to sustain the notion that *The Liberace Show* was a woman's program, but other data support this interpretation. The performer himself gave no evidence whatsoever in the beginning of favoring women above men when he planned and executed the show, but within a year and a half of launching his television career, he recognized the critical source of his new popularity. It could, indeed, hardly be ignored. Of his ten thousand weekly fan letters, the bulk "come from married women between 20 and 60," one journalist noted.[63] His Milwaukee sellouts in October 1953 and May of the following year reflected the same disparities. "The place was thronged with 6,500 worshipful customers," it was reported, "mainly women."[64] Women outnumbered males at both Carnegie Hall and Madison Square Garden. Hundreds of women, too, waited patiently in line to see him in New Orleans; ten thousand females rioted in Miami for a chance to touch his garments.[65] Appalled at his fans, one critic blustered that "He has marshalled these middle-aged mommas and exhorted an intensity of hero-worship that is akin to the earlier demonstrations of their teenage daughters for Sinatra or Johnnie Ray."[66]

Women adored him, and the sources of their affection underline specific elements in American culture in the fifties while suggesting a more profound—even mythic—basis of the entertainer's popularity.

The most potent and obvious source of the performer's appeal to a female audience lay in his definition of the Good Son. Did he calculate this, when he dedicated his first national show, on July 1, 1952, to his mother, or was the dedication a natural outgrowth of his own values? The answer is less important than the fact that his Good Son image provided the basis of his new, national popularity.

Beginning with the KLAC program, the performer had emphasized family. It was a peculiar family configuration he defined, however: it was brother and brother, mother and son. Sisters rarely entered in; fathers more rarely still. In essence, then, he described the central relationship between men and women as that of son and mother. In this way, the ideal man was, by definition, the ideal son. Men were stars, but their purpose was to celebrate women—mothers, rather—not to court or make love to them. Liberace played this role enthusiastically. Women returned the favor. "The women love in him great droves. This figures for Liberace is still tied to a great extent to his own mother's apron strings," analyzed one reviewer. "His habit of introducing her on his tours as 'My Mom' (she's always there) has set critics to gnashing their teeth, but the audience loves it." [67] "You are the man all mothers would like their sons to be," one woman wrote. "Loving and artistic, you take care of your mother. You are nice, warm, gentle, polite, considerate and still have a sense of humor. In other words you might be what most mothers had dreamed their sons would be, but didn't turn out to be." [68] An elderly devotee expressed a variation on the idea. "I have a husband and eighteen grandchildren, but I feel that this boy might have been my very own son." [69] A rather more cynical observer satirized the same identification. Referring to the Liberace "phenomenon" as "musical momism," a writer for *Time* discussed "his quality—which comes out in his bounciness, his sweet smile, his nasal voice, his my-oh-my prose style—of being just a big little boy. And a good boy, too who would never swear or drink or leave his poor old mother." [70]

This was a sex-free relationship, as was proper for the mother-son bond, and yet eroticism roiled just beneath the surface. Liberace's Good Son persona overlapped with that of Model Man, but this icon, in turn, conjured images, willy-nilly, of Ideal Lover. Thus, a vaguely incestuous devotion simmered behind the affection of the mother and grandmother fans. Consciously or unconsciously, the performer played to this effect, insofar as the popular mind associates older women with mothers, younger men with sons. He stirred these waters in the article that appeared under his name in a women's magazine, "Mature Women Are Best." One could even argue that the association between mother and lover existed subliminally in his published narrative of his first sexual encounter with the aforementioned Miss Bea Haven, a much older woman who was also a woman of easy virtue: "She pulled over to the side of the road and took 'advantage' of me. . . . She was twice my age and very experienced but she made me feel grown up and manly at last. After that, being around girls my own age didn't excite me at all. Compared to Miss Bea Haven, they all seemed so adolescent." [71]

In Aeschylus's *Oedipus Rex,* when the king first begins to suspect his sin, he asks his queen (who is his mother, of course) if there is any possibility that a crime of incest has been committed. Jocasta dismisses the concern. Don't worry, she instructs him, you've done nothing, and she reassured him: all men dream of sleeping with their mothers. If, according to Aeschylus, the mother-slut, then, is a standard male fantasy-taboo,

Liberace's story of Miss Bea Haven allows a reading from the opposite side, as well. Here, the older woman is depicted as master; she manipulates and controls the youth for her own ends and satisfactions; of her own authority she provided the agency for turning him into a man, in the process spoiling him for girls his age. Insofar as Liberace's image cultivated these qualities, his appeal underlined female power and matriarchal authority among mothers and "mature women."

"Mature women," however, did not comprise the totality of his audience. Girls, adolescents, and young married women adored him, too. In an early review of his syndicated show, *Variety* defined his sexual appeal to women fans. "Liberace is America's first real television matinee idol—the type that women grow hysterical about." [72] Chicago papers were billing him as "The Greatest Lover Since Valentino." [73] *Time,* observing the hysteria, also remarked upon the propensity of these fans to equate him with the late Italian movie star, an equation that dumbfounded the writer, "since Liberace is pudgy, his curly hair is graying, his brow is broad. And he is not the strong, silent type." [74] Such critics missed, of course, Valentino's own sexual ambiguity or ambivalence—which his harshest contemporary critics had scorned—or his bracelets and flowing robes on the screen; next, critics had warned, he'll be shaving his manly body hair.[75]

After the summer of 1953, Liberace went nowhere without being overwhelmed by masses of adoring females. His erotic appeal to younger women, however, played on some of the same attraction he had to older ones, except that it was inverted. If sexual attraction smoldered behind mothers' affection for the son, the younger women idolized him because he was devoid of overt, physical sexuality. He exerted a unique appeal to them; he was a desirable, attractive man, but one purged of masculine loutishness. "Liberace fills a void in the lives of millions of American housewives whose dull, unromantic husbands," summarized one critic, "can't tell the difference between a rose and a dandelion." [76] "Liberace is the sympathetic type. He looks at you and you feel beautiful. For that alone, I believe in him," one admirer told a reporter. "The main thing about Mr. Liberace, as it hits me," reflected another fan, "is that he is through and through a Continental. When he kisses your hand, you know he isn't going to chew off your arm." A third woman put it even more succinctly. "'What do I see?'" she snorted to the question about Liberace's appeal, "I have a little pleasant relief from what I have to look at every day: Loudmouths! Chest-beaters!" [77] Like the "walkers" of old—homosexual friend/companions usually of older, wealthy women— Liberace reaffirmed the possibility of sophisticated companionship, witty discourse, male strength, and masculine attentiveness without the likelihood of rape or even sex.

Liberace appealed then to two overlapping impressions of masculinity: the eroticized son and the denatured or desexualized lover, which are, of course, flip sides of the same figure.[78] These forms mirror, in turn, comparably paradoxical images of women: the incestuous mother and the lusty virgin. Each role defines an oxymoronic category, suggesting gender bending rather than sexual transgression. These enigmatic relationships are important for all sorts of reasons. In the first place, they suggest hopeless or unthinkable desires projected—or cathected—onto or into art. Just so, they allow a mythic frame in which to appreciate Liberace's popularity: that is, he appealed to deep, pre-historical impulses in human existence, or certainly in Western thought since the ancient Greeks.

In classical mythology, ambivalent male/female, son/mother relations found one striking illustration in the association between Hera, the mother of the gods, and Heracles. He was her beloved—his name means "the glory of Hera"—yet she also hated him, tormented him, and finally drove him to madness.[79] The most popular figure in Greek myth, Heracles—and with him these motives—vanished with Christianity; they reappeared in the Renaissance. Indeed, the Renaissance produced the most vivid and best-known expression of the enigmatic tension between sons and mothers—the eroticized son/denatured lover (and its comparable paradoxes in female imagery) in Michelangelo's *Pietà* in the Vatican. In the sculpture, the god/son is dead and yet, in death, languid in his mother's arms, is sexual and alive. Just so, the sculptor's depiction of Woman, the Holy Mother: she is very young—far too young for a realistic image of a woman with a thirty-three-year-old child. When he is dead, too, she is alive, not only alive but alive with the bloom of young womanhood; she is the eternal woman, even as she contemplates the dead male draped impossibly across her outstretched arms. Michelangelo produced an impossible sculpture in terms of realistic relationships; beyond its specifically religious import, its power arises from mythic truth in the paradoxical relationship between mothers and sons, men and women. It is in the failure of such liaisons to achieve a perfect fit that myth arises. If the profoundest art always echoes, however faintly, mythic truth, one way or another, helter-skelter, Liberace—and his female fans—played the same ancient game about what it means to be a member of a family, what it means to be a woman, what it means to be a mother, what it means to be a son, what, indeed, it means to be a man.[80]

Beyond the possibility of a mythic definition of the performer's appeal, the gender biases of his audience and his personal appeal to women offer specific insights into American culture at midcentury. Thus, one source of women's attraction to the performer lay in the very definitions of culture at this time. There was the sense that "the finer things" were somehow feminine, or that they were the particular domain of women. The days were long past when Thomas Jefferson and George Washington selected fabrics, chose furniture, and pondered the merits of robin's egg versus Wedgwood blue for color schemes at Monticello or Mount Vernon. In this regard, the pretensions of *The Liberace Show* to higher things and culture—the dressy clothes, romantic candlelight, polished grand, debonair manner, fancy costumes, and classical music—suggest gender coding. This was women's stuff, hence Liberace as an idol of females, especially. But this is not all. If culture was feminine, consumerism had heavily female overtones as well: "shopping" was a component of women's culture, not of men's. Liberace's own conspicuous consumption as a critical aspect of his persona offered, then, an additional level of appeal to women. The identity of conspicuousness and culture is almost redundant; so too his offering of consumable culture and art redoubled his gender iconography in the fifties.

A writer for *Time* captured some of this spirit. "Every now and then, as he goes self-importantly about his business, the American male tends to underestimate the power of his women," he began. "He forgets that they helped give him Prohibition and the sunken living room, that they choose his ties and the pictures on his wall, that they make him buy orchid corsages and join the Book-of-the-Month Club. Whenever this male forgetfulness about the real balance of power threatens to become habitual, the women tacitly band together to reassert their authority." So, along with sunken living rooms and orchid corsages, the women now foisted Liberace—one more bit of ephemera, like books, flowers, music, and interior decoration—on the long-suffering male body politic.[81]

If culture feminized—and commercialized—had its origins in the nineteenth century, American values after World War II added to it a new dynamic. The Great Depression and World War II had drawn women out of the home into the work place and the public world—for example, Ma Liberace opening her store and going to work in the cookie factory while Sam failed to provide steady income or much income at all. The postwar period, in contrast, might be seen as a process of restoring the true, gendered order of things. Gender lines sharpened. Family, domesticity, and home represented the clear purview of women; men reclaimed the public sphere for themselves. In the same way, gender attributes applied in a new way to both public and domestic life. In the dark days of the Cold War, men prided themselves on their realism and hard-edged, calculating materialism—in contrast to the hopeful idealizing, sentimentality, and romance associated with women. Catchphrases of the time suggest the gendered biases of the era: Hard-nosed realism was a virtue; being soft—as on communism—was unnatural.

Liberace violated gender boundaries, and, beyond the noisy, aggressive women who pursued him, another category, almost invisible and largely silent, confirmed the transgression. Gay men, gay boys were watching him in awe as well. "Who did I have to relate to as a pubescent homo in Macon, Georgia, for Chrissake!" remembered one old fan. "He was the only role model available." [82] If Liberace was gluing Southern white boys to television screens in Georgia, an Asian-American adolescent in San Francisco had the same rush of recognition. Nineteen fifty-two glowed in his memory after his family moved to Los Angeles and he was catching Lee's KLAC show. "I fell in love with the magic of TV, and I liked Liberace's show best of all. I thought he was very appealing in a low-key way, and when he sang his theme song, 'I'll Be Seeing You,' and winked, I would pretend he was singing it only to me, winking at *me*." "Rick Shaw" connected sexually with a variety of gay men later, including Paul Lynde and Rock Hudson—against type—and longed to meet his piano-playing idol, "but I guess I was never in the right place at the right time. Then I heard that he preferred blonds anyway. . . . That was disappointing but I was still beholden to the man," he concluded.[83]

Still others, like the English lad who would become Elton John, related to the homosexual impulses projected on Liberace's show. "He was what every straight person wants to think gay people are like—so camp, not at all threatening," the pop singer recalled. Liberace was the first gay person Elton John had ever seen on television; he became his hero.[84]

Scattered around the planet, gay boys, transported by Liberace's glamour, generally muted their affection even as they might have hidden their Hollywood scrapbooks and photo clippings of handsome athletes. Conventional masculinity was less reserved and far less enthusiastic. Ordinary fellows saw the same show and drew a different moral based on the same perceptions. Their antipathy, in turn, is just as critical to understanding Liberace's place in American popular culture as is the devotion of women and the admiration of gay boys. Actually, many performers— like Frank Sinatra, Elvis Presley, and later the Beatles—attracted a largely female following. Unlike these men, however, Liberace's appeal was accompanied by a male opposition that has no real counterpart in popular reaction to these other women's idols. As a "woman's man," for one thing—with the full range of meaning in the term—Liberace provoked an extreme reaction among males who identified him with females.[85]

Liberace unsettled other men for the very reason homosexuals admired him. "Men look at Liberace and what they see makes them uneasy," summarized one review of masculine opinion. "They find his dimples too perky, his hair too wavy, and his personality too soft. The phrase 'feminine appeal' is often used to describe him. . . . Many men, after seeing Liberace, have said that their feeling is more like masculine contempt." [86] According to the biographer of Edward R. Murrow, the great newscaster evidenced the same attitude, much more specifically, after he interviewed the performer at the piano-pool house on his network show. According to the biographer's informant, "Murrow looked faintly nauseous" at the interview's conclusion. Murrow had found World War II less offensive to report. " 'In your whole life did you ever see anyone so obnoxious'!" he raged to his associate. He then stalked out of the studio to a nearby bar where " 'He had 3 scotches before he was able to utter another word.' " [87]

A variety of forces contributed to male hostility. Conventional suspicion of the mama's boy or teacher's pet or fairy played its role.[88] So, too, did the practical pendulum swing against the public woman and things feminine after the war, a shift that also echoed the impulses to contain communism abroad and insurgent democracy at home.[89] At least as critical, a theoretical system emerged in these years that gave a powerful shape and form to these values: modernism. Its tenets had been floating around for some time, but they came into their own in the fifties and sixties. This system contrasted violently with the feminine definitions of culture that underlay Liberace's attraction to "the finer things," or of art as sentimental.

With the deepest roots in the Northeast, modernism emphasized materialism, realism, brutality, and prophecy; it scorned fancy, romance, sentiment, and idealism. Power and domination stoked its engines. For a generation, this intensely male-ish, even misogynistic mode dominated formal, artistic values in the United States after World War II. It repudiated the soft, the feminine, the decorative in art, even as the politics of the era spurned political accommodation and international compromise. The conflict over the nature and direction of television and television programming around 1951 hints at some of its values, and if the last half of the twentieth century can be read in terms of the gradual dissemination of modernism through American culture at large, the Northeast spawned and nurtured the system. The women-pleasing, crowd-delighting piano player from Milwaukee became a kind of touchstone of everything modernism eschewed.

The International School of architecture represented one notable expression of the form. The very concept of "international school" suggests some of its bias—the rejection, for example, of provincial, local, or even national modes. With its enormous scale, austere facades, and abstract shapes and designs, the likes of New York's Pan Am Building marched steadily through the center of American cities in the fifties and sixties. In the process, they destroyed many of the greatest monuments of old American architecture, like, for example, the highly decorative, classic-inspired Penn Station, or Grand Central Station, which was obscured by the Pan Am Building. If the literally awesome scale of these new edifices produced a sense of urban pride, the same scale tended to dehumanize the buildings even as cities themselves were becoming increasingly inhospitable and hostile.

The New York School of painting of the forties, fifties, and sixties—abstract expressionism—demonstrated another aspect of the modernist aesthetic. It was as difficult as it was inaccessible. It was not popular art and was never intended for a popular audience. Its perfect home was not private houses but the huge blank walls of the products of International School architecture. The two matched nicely. The absence of popular appeal is no accident, as skepticism and outright opposition to populism and popularity drenched the modernist sensibility. Lonely, rejected men produced art; only the elect understood. Abstract expressionism emphasized technique and painterliness to the complete exclusion of content; indeed, the suggestion of content, narrative, iconography, or tradition set modernist critics frothing. Painting was about abstraction itself. Painting was about painting, nothing else. Thus, for example, the figurative, narrative-inspired painter Andrew Wyeth was a pariah in modernist circles, the son, to make his sins worse, of an "illustrator," N. C. Wyeth. Illustration was only commercial art, and both were double sins among the cognoscenti. If provincials hooted that monkeys could paint as well—and proved it with monkey pictures—this only confirmed the modernists' biases against the folks, popular opinion, and the masses.

Modernism affected music, too. Atonal, arrhythmic music penetrated conservative symphony programs even if it left all but critics and a minority of sophisticates cold. The absence or destruction of lyric line and its debts to international, non-Western music emphasize other elements of the school. Just so, the originators of bebop calculated their jazz to be undanceable as well as unsingable, a nice aural counterpart to abstract expressionism. That only a tiny coterie of aficionados could even tolerate its shrilling pleased its devotees still further. Dancing and singing were for the American hordes.[90] Here as well as elsewhere in the modernist temper, the bourgeoisie and bourgeois taste defined the great enemy. These values even penetrated popular music—if in a traditional melodic line—

as in Pete Seeger's mockery of the suburbs as "little boxes made of ticky-tacky . . . little boxes all the same."

If all of these manifestations of modernist culture tacitly repudiated popular taste, the Beat poets of this same period did so directly. As disdainful of democratic opinion as of commercialism, they completely eschewed beauty and fancy for realism's grime and naturalism's horror; they wore their rejections and failures like badges. If an artist was popular—ran modernism's logic—he had necessarily sold out, surrendered to Moloch, the great enemy. Among modernists, then, popularity itself became a mark of a work's or an artist's failure. By the same measure, insofar as the United States came to be associated with popular democratic tastes, the country itself became Moloch. Allen Ginsberg's "America" summarized the contempt.[91]

Women played little part in modernism. They figured in the system about the way they did in *On the Road:* as servants and as objects of the male world as constructed by Kerouac and Neal Cassady. The presence of a single female, Lee Krasner, among the abstract expressionists was the exception that proved the rule of the male-dominated New York School. After the manner of men, power relationships defined modernist values rather than the softer, communal, and ameliorative ones linked traditionally with women. The system was, perhaps not incidentally, the perfect aesthetic for American Cold Warriors, the hard line against international communism linked indelibly with the pressure for capitalistic expansion abroad. If it contained debilitating paradoxes, such as hatred of the bourgeoisie but dependence on aggressive international capitalism, these faults were less obvious until later in the century.[92]

Liberace's sense of order, aesthetics, and virtue contradicted every aspect of classic modernism. Where the showman believed in the accessibility of art and beauty, modernism held for art's difficulty and inaccessibility. Where Liberace was bright and optimistic, engaging and lavish, romantic and idealistic, modernism was bleak and pessimistic, abstract and sparse, realistic and materialistic. Where Liberace believed in hope and pleasure, modernism issued jeremiads. Modernism lacked tolerance and generosity as much as play and humor—it prophesied, condemned, and called to repentance; Liberace comforted in inclusiveness—he wanted to please, charm, and elevate. Liberace delighted in tradition and sentiment and spoke openly of love. Religious himself, he considered religion an integral part of life and made his act a semi-religious cult. He ritualized family. The modernists considered sentimentality and tradition not only reactionary but the very bane of art, and they sneered at love as only a guise or cover for power and psychological manipulation. Family manifested one more reactionary bourgeois tradition. Modernists were, too, militantly secular, anticlerical, and antisectarian. Liberace loved the local and particular; modernism despised the provincial, preferring the international and the great sweeping forces of history. Modernism loved abstraction and theory—especially Marx and Freud. Liberace lived myth and liked what worked.

The basic tenets of modernism were elitist and insular where Liberace was popular and inclusive; they were leveling and socialistic, however, where was he aristocratic and hierarchical. Thus, if aesthetically Liberace was a practical democrat among these radical antipopulists and anticapitalists, his emphasis on idols and heroes made him elitist where modernism tended toward economic socialism and political egalitarianism. Liberace considered the celebration of stars, demigods, and achievers fundamental to human nature. He worked hard himself, earned his pay, rose in the economic order, and respected others who did the same. Public figures awed him. He had no problem with deference and authority, either economic, cultural, or aesthetic. Little characterizes modernism much more thoroughly than does skepticism about authority and repudiation of the received wisdom of economic, cultural, and aesthetic standards—even if this modernist antiauthoritarianism, paradoxically, became virtually inviolable dogma in its own right.

Whether theoretical, aesthetic, or practical, however, the opposition to Liberace ran deep. With his surrender of the traditional concert stage after 1940, the pianist never again referred to himself as an artist. Specifically repudiating the title, he called himself a performer, an entertainer, and a showman. "I like the word 'performer' a lot better than a stuck-up word like 'artist,'" he protested. "The word artist suggests a self-oriented, inward directed person who creates only what he pleases, for himself, and the public can like it or leave it."[93]

His disclaimers failed to mollify the metropolitan culture's vanguard. "Liberace displays good fingers and prodigious skill at faking 'brilliant' runs up and down the keyboard," judged the *New York Times* critic of his Carnegie Hall concert. "He has two styles of playing—fast, loud and energetic; and slow, with sentimentally exaggerated retards and accelerandos. It is a type of piano-playing that is frequently heard in cocktail lounges, and it is very pleasant to go with cocktails."[94] A later New York performance elicited much the same opinion. The music, wrote Lewis Funke, "must be served with all the available tricks, as loud as possible, as soft as possible, and as sentimental as possible. It's almost all showmanship topped by whipped cream and cherries. Everything is showmanship, including the numerous changes of tuxedos and tails—almost as many changes as Rosalind Russell in 'Auntie Mame.'"[95]

If these critics condemned the book Liberace never wrote, others went on to make him something of a cultural anti-Christ. In the spring of 1954, the *New Yorker* turned its very jaded eyes on the performer, mocking everything about the Madison Square Garden performance.[96] Almost simultaneously, the *New York Times*'s music editor, Howard Taubman, produced a more extended version of the same ridicule in the *Times*'s magazine. The same critic who won some fame later for attacking "a homosexual mafia in the arts," Taubman scorned the pianist himself, but also used the performer in his articles as the perfect representative of a degenerate age, even as he condemned the homosexual "rot at the drama's core" seven years later.[97] Taubman condemned every element of the pianist's performance. Liberace was too easy, too smooth, too faultless, for the critic. He lacked austerity and discipline; he didn't take himself seriously enough; he mocked himself and allowed others to mock him, too. He left nothing to the imagination. The sentiment and sentimentality of the performance offended Taubman profoundly; so, too, did the nostalgia, the demonstrations of piety, the show of reverence. Liberace homogenized everything, Taubman wrote, ignoring the art and intentions of the composers. "Grieg, Chopin, Johann Strauss—they're all easy to reduce to manageable length. Would a mere composer complain if he knew that such a sensitive young musician was bringing his own creative gifts to bear on long, old-fashioned forms?" the critic snarled. "After all, Liberace re-creates—if that is the word—each composition in his own image. When it is too difficult, he simplifies it. When it is too simple, he complicates it. Could anything be more reasonable?" His technique and musicianship provided other sources of the critic's offense: "slackness of rhythms, wrong tempos, distorted phrasing, an excess of prettification and sentimentality, a failure to stick to what the composer has written, . . . a parlor pianist who ought to be kept in someone else's parlor." "So what?" Taubman concluded. "Does Liberace claim to be a Horowitz or Rubinstein? The square will reply then he ought to be a solid jazz player or an honest 'pop' stylist, and he isn't either. His beat doesn't send you. His ideas are not inventive. And he won't let even a sentimental piece speak for itself; he has to make it so maudlin it sticks in your craw." The Jeremiah-critic did not stop here. He issued a moral indictment against the showman from West Allis. "Taste based on denatured music," he declared, "ends in debasement of an art." That was the closing note. Did Liberace's success depend on "the loneliness of old girls and the slushiness of young ones?"

No, not really, Taubman thought. Liberace represented a perfect icon of a decadent era: "He is a product of the superficiality, sentimentality and uneasy nostalgia of our times."[98]

If Taubman only played with the gender biases of Liberace's art, others attacked them head on. Indeed, few national commentators and critics ever failed to note and protest the femaleness of his following. Almost all those who dealt with the issue were male. The notes appeared, almost inevitably, in some more or less overt political context relative to men, women, and their social relationships. In the late spring of 1954, *Time* had produced the article that had spoofed the Liberace phenomenon as "musical momism," taking off on the phrase coined by the violently misogynistic American writer Philip Wylie in his bestselling 1940 book, *Generation of Vipers*. If *Time* writers poked sophisticated fun, other males were baffled and outraged by the performer and his fans. "If women vote for Liberace as a piano player—and I'm sure they do—it raises questions about their competence to vote for anything," wrote the critic of the *New York Herald Tribune* in 1953. "I'm not suggesting we repeal the 19th Amendment, exactly, just that maybe we think about it a little." "Sometimes," he continued, "a man wonders . . . whether the women of this fair land are people or whether some other designation ought to be given them—say, plips—to distinguish them from the rest."[99] The Los Angeles *Mirror* offered another version of the idea. Liberace's popularity, the journalist assayed, "raises speculation over the sanity of the nation's women—particularly those in their middle and late years—who idolize him." He was "the Candelabra Casanova of the Keyboard, the musician-actor who makes millions out of Momism."[100]

As a woman's man, Liberace cut across the "regenderfication" of the social order after the war and violated the new strictures about sexual order. As he was identified with women, misogyny played its role in his condemnation, too. Other elements were also brewing in the social cauldron. Homosexuality was the unnamed eye of newt in this postwar witches brew. If it was perhaps the most critical element in his personal life between 1955 and 1961, it was only one of a series of crises he was navigating in these years as he turned forty.

I began to go from bad to worse until I found myself playing a second-rate club in Indianapolis where I'd made $15,000 in one night. . . . I doubt if that club made that much profit in a whole year.

Liberace

Eight

THE SHOALS OF FAME

When Liberace had signed with Guild Films in the winter of 1953 for a nationally marketed show, he had agreed to perform in 177 separate installments. By 1955, he had fulfilled his obligation. He and Guild Films did not renew the contract. According to one source, Liberace had, in effect, become too expensive, and Reuben Kaufman determined to drop him for a new performer, Florian Zabach, a violinist with an act similar to Liberace's. Why had Guild Films not renewed him? "The cause of death: greed."[1] Other factors played an even greater role. For one thing, with networks extending their broadcasting time, the demand for syndicated films was declining. For another, for a program to last two or three years was not unusual, even for network shows. Just so, Guild's rerun policy had scores and scores of stations from one end of the country to another playing the show over and over. Liberace had given the folks all they wanted, maybe more, in what he had provided them already. Liberace offered his own explanation: he cut back on television because "overexposure" undercut his pulling power in other performances—as if "other performances" were really more important than national exposure on television. The showman might have been reluctant to admit it, but evidence exists that his popularity was already waning by 1955.[2] When the year opened, however, he was rich and busy. The future beckoned.

A second invitation to play the White House early in the new year augured well for 1955. On March 19, he performed for President Dwight Eisenhower. As star studded as his first Presidential performance, this evening in the White House included such guests as George Murphy, Ezio Pinza, Jane Froman, and Danny Kaye. Liberace was front and center of this gathering. The NBC Symphony backed him up, and he played classical works as well as his standard popular music.[3]

Despite the honor it represented, the presidential concert was small potatoes beside the new contract that Seymour Heller had negotiated with the new Riviera Hotel in Las Vegas for the spring of 1955. The gambling town was changing to match new circumstances in the country by the mid-fifties; the showman rode the tide. In the preceding three years, the Strip, the section of Highway 91 west of the city, had boomed with new hotels and casinos. Most of these continued the pattern of the first resorts, like the Last Frontier itself and its immediate predecessor, El Rancho Vegas: they rambled across the desert with bungalow-type lodgings around central dining and gambling facilities. The Riviera broke the pattern. It soared upward, giving the Strip—and the city—a skyline for the first time. The management planned everything about the casino as the biggest, best, fanciest, and, of course, most expensive. Construction cost ran to 10 million dollars, and the hotel touted its continental-style luxury as a clean break with the past. The Riviera wanted an opening act to match its opulence. Liberace was the hottest thing in the country at the time. The management went after him.

By the winter of 1954, Liberace had played Las Vegas twenty-five times over the preceding decade. The Last Frontier was paying him very well: he was earning twenty-five thousand dollars per engagement. He liked the management. He was not eager to leave. He hit on a solution, he wrote later: set a price the new hotel would not match. "Tell the Riviera people I want fifty thousand. They'll never pay it," he instructed Seymour Heller. The Riviera management didn't hesitate. They signed, and the glitzy performer agreed to open the elegant Clover Room on April 20. Fifty thousand dollars was, literally, an epoch-making figure; the fee presaged a future of constantly inflating celebrity salaries in Las Vegas. To that point, Marlene Dietrich, for her 1953 act, had topped out the Vegas salary scale at thirty-five thousand a week. Then, at the height of his glory, Liberace beat her by fifteen thousand. In the same category as the legendary German star! More ambitions fulfilled.[4]

This was not the only triumph Heller was negotiating for his client. In the winter and spring, he was also haggling with Hollywood, and he finally contracted with Warner Brothers. The distinguished German-born director Henry Blanke was charged with reworking an old George Arliss film for the performer. Produced originally in 1922 and then remade ten years later, *The Man Who Played God* chronicles the life of a pianist who is going deaf. He spends his life watching people with binoculars from his apartment. He helps resolve their problems and difficulties, teaching them the way to happiness. Irving Wallace wrote the new screenplay. This version—released as *Sincerely Yours*—plays up the romantic interests. Two women love Anthony Warrin, the protagonist: his socialite fiancée and his secretary. He allows the former to find a new love, while he winds up with his selfless, devoted employee. At the end, Warrin's hearing is restored, he gets the girl who loves him most, he recovers his concert career at Carnegie Hall, and he is surrounded by everyone he has assisted in attaining a better life. It was a completely Liberacean script. Besides the happy ending, the victory of the secretary over the socialite echoed his own social commitment to the little guy.

Shooting began on May 16, 1955, Liberace's thirty-sixth birthday. Gordon Douglas directed. The movie also starred Joanne Dru as the secretary, Dorothy Malone as the socialite, and William Demarest as Liberace's competition for Malone's affections.

In his autobiography, the pianist remembered without much affection this second attempt at a movie career. "It beats starving to death," he replied when asked about being a star. Full of goodwill himself, he disliked the bitter competition of "the Hollywood scene." He complained of the "actors, musicians, writers and directors who occasionally have to work off their aggressions (and their anger at not working)." He singled out an episode with the singer-actor Mario Lanza, of the recently completed *Serenade,* as a particular manifestation of the nastiness. He played Lanza's goat. The singer visited the set daily, offering the novice actor unsolicited advice. Beyond this, Lanza caused still other troubles. In a perfect imitation of Liberace's shy Midwestern twang, he would telephone Blanke every evening, "call him all kinds of names and bawl him out, telling him what he did wrong and what he should have done." The trick strained relations between the director and the star, and while the truth elicited laughs all around, "only Mario thought it was funny," the pianist related.[5]

Moviemaking brought the showman little joy retrospectively. At the time, however, he exulted in his new career. "He was as exuberant as I had ever seen him," reported one newsman who visited him on the set. Liberace drove to the studio in his long white limousine with the piano keys-inspired interior, and he boasted of his oversized dressing room that Judy Garland had used before.[6]

Previewed on October 18, 1955, the movie won early praise. Critics compared it with *Going My Way, Magnificent Obsession,* and *The Jolson*

Story. Early critics and Hollywood insiders considered it, as one headline trumpeted, "Headed for a Bonanza at Box Office." If the film's pervasive sentimentality put off some reviewers, they also noted that its very corniness "is the box-office staff of life." The *Hollywood Reporter*'s notice applauded even the star: "To my utter amazement," wrote Jack Moffitt, "I found him making me gulpy." Similarly, while other reviewers found the sentiment just too much, they could still praise its pianist-hero. If Ruth Waterbury panned the movie, "Nevertheless," she wrote, "the genuine warmth of Liberace's personality radiates from it, and his really superb showmanship frequently rocks you."[7]

The movie had several premieres around the country. It opened in Chicago on October 28 and in Los Angeles at the Pantages Theater on November 22. A month-long publicity tour accompanied these various openings.[8] The film flopped. Jack Warner might have written the preview notices, but another tone governed other reviews. The *New York Times* captured the flavor: "Liberace spends an hour and fifty minutes oozing dimpled sincerity from the screen, frequently skimming the glistening keyboard and bestowing his smile like a kiss. . . . But one can delicately hint that the good fellow is nobody's Barrymore. When he wears his black-sequined jacket, he hits the peak of his acting skill."[9]

The film did no better at the box office. The star was not happy. He grumbled over the critics. He insisted that the movie would redeem itself. "I'm certain we will do well on the picture in the long run. I think some of these newspaper complaints about such unimportant things as my clothes are silly," he fumed. "I feel there is a public which will awaken to the film's theme, which is based on my philosophy of life—to bring happiness to people. It is based on faith, on love of God and your fellow man."[10]

Except for appearing later on television, the movie sank without a ripple. One more time, the pianist had bombed in his attempt to launch a cinematic career. If *Sincerely Yours* busted almost as completely as *South Seas Sinner* had, its failure also generated some of the same resentment on the part of its star as the earlier failure had. Later, he also blamed the film for his decline in popularity. Even so, he had too many irons in the fire to spend time sulking. He still had his forty-week domestic tour, but his American fame had bubbled around the world and had encouraged him to launch international tours.

As early as the mid-forties, he had fantasized about foreign triumphs—tours of Latin America, for example; he had dreamed of being received by kings and queens, of being treated like a head of state himself. His first international engagement—a tour of Cuba in 1956—fulfilled every element of the fantasy. It was a dream trip. In the first place, the tour had been planned by Gaspar Pumarejo, the founder of the "Club del Hogar"—The Housewife Club—which promoted culture and artistic events among Cuban women, chiefly Habaneras: they were Lee's natural constituency. In the second, he played off the extraordinary appeal of the United States and things American in what were actually the last glittery, troubled days of the ancien régime on the island.

Appropriately enough, insofar as Miami, Florida, formed an intimate community with Havana in those days, the Cuban tour actually began in the United States. Pumarejo and Seymour Heller inaugurated the festivities with a press reception for Cuban journalists at the Eden Roc, the flashiest, newest, and most luxurious hotel on Miami Beach, on August 20, 1956. After an interview session in the fourteenth-story penthouse, the promoters treated the entire press corps to an elaborate dinner, during which incredulous journalists noted that the showman had coordinated his own dress with the table dressings.[11] Two days later, the Liberace entourage arrived at José Martí Airport to the most extraordinary welcome. Indeed, the regime treated him like a visiting head of state. All incoming and outgoing traffic ceased. To the distress of some Cuban nationalists, military bands performed both the Cuban and the American national anthems when he appeared. Liberace himself recalled entering the terminal beneath the crossed sabers of Cuban military officers, and the army's salutes with rifles and little cannons.[12] It was, as one somewhat jaded Cuban journalist observed, "an apotheosic reception at the airport—as has never been done in Cuba for any American general, senator, or cabinet member."[13] In keeping with such honors, the president of the republic received Liberace formally at the presidential palace later that day. Batista's lavish style impressed him. He knew nothing about his politics, Liberace protested, "but I admired the way he lived. I guess it was his politics that made such high living possible. Whatever it was," he concluded, "he sure enjoyed it when he had it."[14]

Cheering crowds lined every roadway between Havana and Rancho Boyeros, the airport town. Liberace stayed in the presidential suite at the Hotel Nacional, and throughout his five-day visit, his devotees allowed neither him nor any member of his troupe to pay for anything, anywhere—not in restaurants, not in shops, not even at the gambling tables, he recalled fondly. He was the guest of honor at the Tropicana; he danced with the star performer, Ana Gloria; he attended the dog races, where the ninth race was named for him.[15] And, of course, he performed for turnaway crowds.

The Cuban promoter, Pumarejo, had scheduled three performances chiefly for his Hogareñas at the new, 3,500-seat Blanquita Theater downtown. Within four years, the new dictator would make it a jail for dissidents and rename it after Karl Marx,[16] but in late August of 1956 its only problems were overworked air-conditioning units and a faulty sound system. Although Pumarejo had limited admission to all three performances to dues-paying members of the Club del Hogar, Cuban television broadcast the Sunday evening show to the whole nation. Lee's arrival at José Martí had been one of most-watched events in Cuban TV history, according to reporters; the Sunday night show outdid it twice over. At 8:00 P.M. on August 26, virtually every set in the island was tuned to the Blanquita show.[17] In his memoir, the showman told of how he had delivered monologues in Spanish which he had memorized phonetically, as he did not speak the language. American residents on the island mocked his "muchas grassias," but his efforts won more applause than they did scorn, he wrote.[18]

The Liberace Show had played well on the island, but nothing had prepared the showman for the excitement his tour generated. It possessed "the extraordinary proportions of a national event," observed one not uncritical reporter.[19] It "altered national life," noted another.[20] It influenced both fashion and language; new fabrics named after the performer hit the market, for example.[21] It provided the opportunity, as well, to discourse on the state of national politics. Were patriots offended by the folderol? Liberace only played his role, came the reply. He had not lied or done anything wrong or out of character. The problem lay elsewhere: "If, despite his evident frankness in easily showing us who he is, we Cubans had him parade under flags, to the strains of the national anthem (played by the bands of the navy and the orphanage), and we took him later to the Palace to shake the President's hand, that's our business. . . . In the end, this is not France or England, but rather a laughable little republic in the West Indies [English in the original], where people have to have fun with something."[22]

The showman's lexicon had no space for such jaded, fatalistic sentiments. Nor did he have to bear their consequences. He anticipated only the rosy future. He used the Caribbean excursion as the basis of a new composition and a new record; "Cuba Liberace," he called it.[23] It never made the charts. It didn't matter. He was still off in a thousand directions at once. Most critically, he was calculating a triumphant tour of Europe. He had quit the island on August 27 for Hollywood via New Orleans. He was already fantasizing about greater fame. Europe beckoned. With Cuban cheers still boosting his ego, he sailed for England on September 9.

His European tour in 1956 was not actually his first visit to the continent. He had visited it in 1955 on an expedition arranged by Jack Warner on the last day's shooting of *Sincerely Yours.* The studio wanted European publicity for its van Gogh movie, *Lust for Life,* so Warner was dispatching its star—Kirk Douglas—and his wife on tour. At the last minute, he included Liberace on the junket. Liberace lacked a passport, inoculations, and everything else, but Warner resolved all such details. The musician was still in costume for the film's final Carnegie Hall scene when the studio's photographers snapped his passport photos. The little group landed in Paris the day after Warner had proposed the trip to Liberace.

After a whirlwind of Paris studio parties, the movie stars retired to Jack Warner's home in Cannes. The awestruck pianist described it as "New Year's Eve twenty-four hours of every day." He attended Elsa Maxwell's famous receptions. When he met Grace and Rainier of Monaco, the princess flattered him further with an invitation to perform at a Red Cross benefit gala she was hosting. He played while Danny Kaye was singing and dancing "and doing all the things he does so well." [24] He was awed. "What a show!" he sputtered. He met more famous people than he could remember.

He had never experienced anything like this before. It was too much. He compared himself to "Alice in Wonderland at the Mad Hatter's Tea Party." It prompted most uncharacteristic reflections on who he was—or might have been. He summarized it in the only known reference he ever made to himself in the third person using his christening name: "Young Wladziu was impressed," he mused. "There was nothing like it in West Milwaukee." [25] Cannes was actually a little too far from Kenosha, Sheboygan, and West Allis for his taste. These were not his people. He was Dorothy in Oz. On the whole, he preferred Kansas.

His second trip in the fall of 1956 differed completely from the first. Fastidious planning replaced the grand anarchy of the earlier journey. In place of the hurried airplane flight, he made a leisurely crossing on the greatest of the old liners, the *Queen Mary.* Instead of the famous strangers, Kirk Douglas and his wife, the pianist surrounded himself with home folks and familiar faces—George and his then wife, his mother, and his manager, Heller. [26] Had he felt awkward and provincial in the company of international swells like Princess Grace, Elsa Maxwell, Aly Khan, and scores of others? This time he found popular audiences that loved him as much as his devotees in New York, Milwaukee, Los Angeles, and Miami did. Finally, for the hedonistic pleasures of St. Tropez, he substituted the faith of Rome, and he and his party concluded their trip with a pilgrimage to the Holy City. Filling another ambition of his life, he also won an audience with Pope Pius XII for himself and his whole entourage.[27] The Liberace party spent almost a half hour with him at his summer residence, Castel Gondolfo. The "Ave Maria" episode of *The Liberace Show* accounted for the stroke of fortune. "I discovered that [the pope's] private secretary who was a monsignor had attended a filming of my television show, which included the 'Ave Maria,'" Liberace recalled. "It was because of this Monsignor that we were invited to a private audience with the Holy Father."[28] A fading photograph in the Liberace Museum memorializes the occasion. A group of perhaps thirty darkly clad pilgrims cluster around the white-robed, sepulchral pontiff. Several kneel. Heavily veiled, Frances Zuchowski Liberace, who had been the widow Casadonte for twenty years, stands by her two sons. George's eyes are on the pope; Lee smiles at the camera.

While the trip ended famously, it began well, too. The crossing itself was notable. The entertainer had chosen a sea voyage in part because he was bringing all his most elaborate props with him, like the glass-topped grand piano and his piano-decorated Cadillac. He also took the *Queen Mary* because he loved its luxury and opulence. He anticipated, too, that the world of luxury liners would soon be finished; cheap, speedy, democratic air travel doomed such grandeur. Dining at the captain's table and traveling first class on the *Queen Mary,* he enjoyed the full treatment. He gave, as always, as good as he got. Thus, he had committed himself to a shipboard performance, and he asked the captain that he be allowed to play for the entire passenger list, not merely for those traveling first class. Although the idea might have come to him, he insisted that his fellow passenger, Noël Coward, had put the notion in his head when the two met while strolling the deck. Liberace had recognized the composer (who was also an icon of gay culture); he expressed astonishment that Coward recognized him, knew his work, and even complimented him. "What you do you do very well," he told the entertainer, as he encouraged him to play for the whole ship. The captain had been skeptical, but the scheme worked beautifully. The second- and third-class passengers loved him. "They were my audience," he smiled. "So many of them came that they practically squeezed out the first class passengers. I played to standing room only and when it was over Mr. Coward said, 'Glad you took my advice. Wish I'd thought of doing it myself. Marvelous audience.'"[29]

All of England itself provided an even more "marvelous audience," even if the cheers did not always mask the snarls. Arriving at Southampton on September 25, 1956, the performer's entourage had chartered an entire train, The Liberace Special, to deliver them to London—another one of those publicity ploys the showman delighted in. At Waterloo Station, thousands of women old and young roared greeting to their darling—and virtually prohibited any movement by the Liberace party. The next week, *Time* ran a photo of the pianist crushed against the train by his devotees. The English comic Bob Monkhouse had been on the scene and offered one version of the crush: "I never saw so much female-ness all crowding in one place—all pushing and shoving—to get a look at Lee. Some enterprising tradesman had been outside the station peddling bags of red heart-shaped confetti, and a lot of the ladies brought along rose petals to pelt him with. The stuff lay there on the deck, ankle deep. You never saw such a litter." [30]

Mounted police and bobbies with dogs could not restore order, although they managed to get Liberace to the limousines for the trip to the Savoy. That trip provided another manifestation of the "marvelous audience" of Great Britain. The adoring mobs stripped the car of everything movable for souvenirs, and when the travelers emerged at the hotel, the fans tried to do the same to its occupants. "When we got out they started to grab at our garments, hats, jackets, anything for a souvenir." [31]

Royal Festival Hall had scheduled him for a performance on October 1, Royal Albert Hall for October 15 and 17, and the London Palladium on November 5. Besides these engagements, the showman had scheduled a full tour of Britain; it included television performances and club dates as well as concerts. A week after his arrival in London, he appeared on one of the major television programs in the country, *Sunday Night at the Palladium*. Arriving at the Palladium Theater for the performance at three thirty, he faced another melee. Until police arrived, he could not get out of his car for the crowds. The same mobs prohibited his departure for hours that evening. Finally, fifty bobbies assisted by specially trained German shepherds allowed his departure around ten that night. [32]

London welcomed him in other venues. While the fame of his television show had pushed his old supper-club act far down on his list of priorities, he had lost none of his charm in the smaller and more sophisticated setting, and his England trip proved he could still pack in the patrons. He won kudos at the most famous night spot in England, London's Café de Paris. He won more than kudos: "While he refused to give out the figure he is being paid for his service, he revealed it was '400% more than Marlene Dietrich or Noël Coward had received,'" reported Art Buchwald in the Paris *Herald-Tribune*. [33]

Although headlining such notables as Dietrich, Coward, and Liberace himself, the club's redoubtable manager, Major Neville Willing, won the showman's special commendation for hiring fresh, untested talent, too. Thus, he praised Willing's commitment to the then unknown singer, Shirley Bassey, who later became famous for her James Bond *Goldfinger* music. The showman projected onto Willing his own values: sympathizing with unknown performers, giving new talent a chance, in short, encouraging breaks for little guys. However famous he became, the showman, as he himself admitted, never outgrew West Allis. His affection always lay with the folks.

For all Willing's innovative bills, he also played to the most sophisticated crowds in London. They resembled the swells who had frequented Spivy's Roof a decade before, except more so—"real British blue bloods and international and theatrical celebrities. Night after night they had the classiest crowd I've ever had for an audience," he related, "lords and their ladies, dukes and their duchesses and, sometimes, princes and their . . . friends," he concluded ambiguously. Willing knew how to work even these sophisticates. If no slouch himself at public relations and manipulating an audience, Liberace learned things from the British major. His classy audiences could not get enough of the American piano player. "Long after I'd changed out of my show clothes and into my street clothes the people who had been applauding had come up the stairs and were still pounding my dressing room door," the entertainer recalled. "The major was in full command," he continued. "He opened the door of the dressing room a little bit to give them another glimpse of the man they were applauding. Then he asked them to step back and be patient. He came inside and told me what to do next. And I did it. I put on a white sheared beaver coat and walked out to my waiting Cadillac and drove off into Piccadilly Circus." "Always leave them wanting more," Willing repeated over and over. It was the same advice Hildegard had given him. The results, even in Liberace's hyperbole, were "fantastic." "But for me, *what* a memory," he concluded. "It was the most exciting Club date I ever played." [34]

His triumph at having played the Café de Paris paled beside other English honors. The thought of performing for the British monarchy had fueled his imagination for years. It was like his promise to play the Hollywood Bowl and "crack this town wide open!" back in 1947. In 1953, as his celebrity exploded across the United States, a Milwaukee journalist had written an article focusing on Liberace's ambition and determination. "What's his present goal?" the reporter queried him. " 'To play for Queen Elizabeth,' says Liberace. He'll probably do it too," the writer concluded cheerfully.[35] He got his invitation to play for the Queen, even if events thwarted him, this time at least.

His command performance was scheduled for Guy Fawkes Day, but international fireworks—not domestic bomb plots—forestalled the show.

Since July, an Egyptian crisis had been simmering about the Suez Canal. It blew up soon after he arrived in England—in the middle of his command performance rehearsals, he noted, and the emergency prompted the cancellation of the show. "We at the theater would have liked to pull off a gunpowder plot against the Egyptians and their Suez Canal," he pouted.[36] He got other chances at command performance, and within three years, the queen mother was applauding him as roundly in Manchester as if she'd been a Cockney.

The tour produced mixed results. Adoring fans filled the halls and mashed him in the streets; formal reviews were rather less enthusiastic. He might have smiled over some of them. "Liberace is no more a concert pianist than I am a Zulu princess," shuddered the *London News Chronicle.*[37] Others hit harder. "A cross between a circus turn and a fancy-dress parade," proclaimed one; "a deliberate peacock and a preposterous walking wardrobe" sneered another.[38] The *New York Times* summarized the mix: "Liberace played his first London concert last night and drew squeals of delight from feminine listeners and cries of pain from music critics."[39] *Variety*'s London stringer nailed another paradox in covering the extremely successful performance at the Café de Paris: "That he was able to have his ritzy cafe audience cheering him for minutes on end at the conclusion of his 50-minute cabaret show was positive indication that press and public have powerfully opposing views in their assessment of him."[40]

For the first time, he also encountered still-more active hostility. Angry picketers waved their signs at his arrival at Southampton's docks and Waterloo Station. Nor did they go away. They cropped up all over. "A hostile group, mostly composed of young men" offered their equally hostile opinions outside Royal Festival Hall in London. Marchers carried "We hate Liberace" signs. "Cyprus, Suez, and Now This," read other pickets.[41] At Sheffield, the rowdies actually made it into the hall and disrupted the performance with their chants.[42] In his Midlands performances, some of the audience took to making paper airplanes from the program and sailing them toward to stage to disrupt his act, ran one report. He managed this, mostly. As the paper airplanes floated toward the stage, for example, he began playing "The Daring Young Man on the Flying Trapeze." The wit and verve of it convinced the audience. The disruption ended. It was not all over.[43]

While, back home, Bob Hope joshed about Lee and "powderpuffery," American puritanism tended to inhibit sexual humor; it deflected discussion of homosexuality even more. The British were bawdier. An English comic, Jimmy Thompson, created a ribald skit about Liberace on homosexual themes that he played on a number of different stages. In its television life, Thompson did his impression on a late-night review, *Chelsea at Nine,* but also on the prime-time *Sunday Night at the Palladium.* The skit was salacious enough that one commentator expressed bafflement at how it made it past the censors, according to the profoundly offended American. Thompson also made the performance an integral part of a theatrical review, *For Amusement Only,* which ran for close to two years at London's Apollo Theater. Besides mocking Liberace's sexuality with a wig and other gestures, the skit included a ditty with the refrain:

> My fan mail is really tremendous,
> It's going so fast my head whirls;
> I get more and more,
> They propose by the score—
> And at least one or two are from girls.

Liberace insisted that Thompson grew to regret the characterization, having come to the conclusion that it was defamatory. He tried to apologize with a floral bouquet in the shape of a dove bearing a card on which was written: "To show I had no malice towards you." Liberace sued him. The British comedian settled out of court.[44]

The innuendo and mockery had actually begun very early. The day after Liberace's arrival in the country, the London *Daily Mirror* had published a long article by William Conner—writing under the pen name Cassandra—that Liberace himself took as the source of the scurrility or at least the most vicious manifestation of the temper. "He is the summit of sex—the pinnacle of masculine, feminine, and neuter. Everything that he, she, and it can ever want," snarled the journalist. With English women throwing themselves at this strange male, the scene at the train station, especially, had offended the British writer. "This deadly, winking, sniggering, snuggling, chromium-plated, scent-impregnated, luminous, quivering, giggling, fruit-flavored, mincing, ice-covered heap of mother love has had the biggest reception and impact on London since Charlie Chaplin arrived at the same station, Waterloo, on September 12, 1921," he fumed.[45]

Cassandra outraged the performer. After he left Britain, Liberace's anger grew. Normally, he was thick skinned about criticism, professing that "I Don't Care" as long as he kept his audiences. But the British attacks got to him. Visiting in France for a long weekend around October 11, he complained about the "vulgarity and underlying degenerate tone of 25 percent of the British newspaper stories." "I'm never bitter about things written about me, but I must admit I do become bitter when my love for my mother is described as any kind of ism," he groused, "whether it's Communism, Fascism or momism." "What I don't understand," he said in his interview with reporter Art Buchwald, "is, if I was as degenerate as they claim, and an unmanly man as they indicated, how do they explain the interest all the women have shown in me?"[46]

As time passed, the Cassandra affair agitated him more and more. He consulted his lawyer and decided to sue. On October 22, 1956, the British court entertained his charge of libel against Conner and the *Daily Mirror.* If the Cassandra article had distressed the entertainer, the libel trial entailed its own traumas. The case did not come to trial for three more years, and every year for the next half decade brought the performer additional woes, both personal and professional. Cassandra was only the beginning.

"As Long As You Care for Me," the subtitle of Liberace's composition ran, he "didn't care" what others said or did. By 1955, however, folks had indeed begun caring less. His record sales mark one measure of his decline. In 1953, he had made a total of fifty records, including albums and singles. That figure rose to sixty-seven the next year. In 1955, however, he cut but twenty-three discs, in 1956, ten, in '57, only three. There were thirteen in '58, seven the next year, fifteen in '60, and eight in '61.[47] His drawing power, too, declined as his record production plummeted. In April 1957, he scheduled a four-week run at New York's Palace, where Judy Garland had staged the performance that set her career on fire again. His show closed after two weeks.[48] And there were far more disastrous troubles and signs of trouble. If in 1955 he had dropped the Last Frontier in favor of the Riviera and its offer of a fifty-thousand-dollar salary, the casinos, in turn, dropped him after his 1958 run. For the first time in fourteen years, he was not playing Las Vegas—his oldest, most reliable, and most lucrative gig. He descended to playing clubs that grossed less in a whole year than he had netted in a night in his "white heat" period of 1953–56.

"What happened to Liberace?" popular magazines were demanding by the spring of 1958.[49] By '61, journalists were dubbing him a has-been, identifying him as the "onetime TV idol."[50] His astronomical income dropped with his failing popularity. In April 1956, he testified that he had earned less than $125,000 so far that year.[51] The showman was not poor, not by any means, but $125,000 per quarter was a far cry from the two to three million dollars—or more—he had packed away during each year at the peak of his fame. His manager protested in 1958 that his man "is just as popular now as he has ever been. It's just that the press is no longer writing about him. He's still one of the highest paid performers in show business," he insisted. "During this 'slump' he'll earn between $500,000 and $750,000. In other words, don't feel sorry for him." Seymour Heller added, however, "Time changes some things. That's why Lee's taking this vacation from TV—to give him a chance to think things over and to decide in what direction to move next." [52] The entertainer's once-rosy future had become obscure.

By 1958, the performer himself was referring publicly to a "cooling off" period, which he dated to the failure of *Sincerely Yours* in the winter of 1955–56.[53] By the time of his autobiography, fifteen years later, he was more brutal. He described his career in 1957 as being in "a monster slump."

With his reputation foundering at home, he looked again to his international audience to boost his falling stock. In the late winter of 1958 he launched a tour of Australia. It did nothing he expected. On the contrary, it confirmed, even exaggerated his new liabilities. A legal and public-relations nightmare, it typified the disorder of his career in this period. In his autobiography, he describes it as a disaster piled on top of chaos. The trip began poorly and worsened quickly. He arrived in the country in February, in the middle of an oppressive heat wave. He was competing for headlines with the heat, but also with the queen mother's visit to Sydney. As devoted to the royals as ever, he willingly took second place to the queen, however, when he received an invitation to a reception in her honor. His memoir chronicles his humiliation. On his best behavior and in his most conservative garb, he appeared at the Royal Garden Party only to be charged, first, with being an impostor, and then later with being the real Liberace with a forged invitation. He never met the queen, but he at least left under his own power and in his own time, he consoled himself.[54]

More trouble awaited him. The brouhaha at the garden party threw his schedule off, and he was late, consequently, to a press interview. To make matters worse, several journalists all appeared, each expecting a personal interview. Already fired up by American and British press biases, the reporters then struck the hapless entertainer two additional blows. While Liberace himself noted his ability to captivate even the most hostile critics when he dealt with them in person, his charm did not always work. This was one such occasion. One reporter asked him: "In 1956 when you first went to London, the *Sketch* said, 'Liberace will make thousands of pounds in this. He deserves every penny he gets. Such shameful exhibitionism must be rewarded.' He then looked up and smiled and asked, 'Do these remarks hurt you?'" Liberace's bitterness against the press had been waxing steadily since the Cassandra episode; this affair infuriated him all the more.[55]

These stories appeared the next day, cheek to jowl with reports about the garden party. The headlines read, for example, "LIBERACE CRASHED ROYAL PARTY—THEY WANTED TO THROW HIM OUT." As if this were not enough, he faced another barrage of infuriating press reports the next day, when critics savaged his performance at the Trocadero. "His music is slovenly and sentimental enough to disgrace a mediocre high school student," wrote one. His defenders were hardly better: "Liberace's genius lies not in his ability to play the piano but in his capacity to gauge the taste of his audience with unfailing accuracy. It is quite probable that in the course of his recitals, Liberace heightens the musical appreciation of his audiences by introducing them to music of which otherwise they would be ignorant."[56]

The worst still lay ahead.

As a central part of his act, Liberace offered a medley of tunes from the current Broadway hit, *My Fair Lady*. An Australian corporation, Chappell and Co., which held the rights to the musical "down under," sought and received a legal injunction from the Australian Supreme Court to prevent the performer's use of the score. They refused a ten-thousand-pound gratuity in exchange for allowing Liberace to perform the music. Even the intervention of Lerner and Loewe, the American composers, failed to sway the Australian copyright holders. Finally, the showman broke. Walking onto the stage to traditional fanfare, he read the following pronouncement:

> I, Liberace, an American-born citizen of the United States have been restricted by law from playing any of the compositions from *My Fair Lady,* which constitutes a portion of my program.
>
> Any laws that prevent my democratic right to perform the music of my country are in violation of the doctrines of my government and its people and must be interpreted as Communistic.
>
> Never before in my entire lifetime have I been prevented from expressing myself as an artist, to exercise my democratic freedom of musical speech.
>
> If necessary I will call upon my government of the United States of America to assist my defense.
>
> Until I am once again permitted to perform any and all music of my country without any further restrictions, I am compelled by my American convictions and beliefs to refuse to give any further performances in your country.

After a brief apology, he then walked off the stage.[57]

Although he had served as honorary mayor of Sherman Oaks, California, this statement was as close as the entertainer ever came to enunciating a political theory. The statement is about as complex as his duties as honorary mayor had been. It is, however, perfectly in keeping with his character; it is no less suggestive of values that dominated the American mind and even American foreign policy in the generation after World War II. Liberace was not a thoughtful American, but he was a devoted one. He identified American citizenship with freedom, democracy, and practical rights—especially freedom of speech, freedom to work, and freedom to express oneself artistically. He was uncomprehending of systems and theories that denied what he considered sensible and common-sense prerogatives.[58]Thus, he was as guilelessly anticommunist as he was innocently American. In 1981, on his European tour, he visited the Berlin Wall, and although he lacked any systematic politics, it moved him very deeply, according to Scott Thorson. "Freedom lay on one side—the right to be whatever you dreamed you could be—while a life of severely limited possibilities was on the other. Lee, who had dreamed big and seen those dreams come true, shuddered as he looked through that opening in the wall."[59] Like so many Americans of the Cold War era, he assumed that the world was divided into two antagonistic camps, the Free World and its enemies. If communism represented repression and tyranny, it was, however naïve, hardly exceptional for him to have identified his Australian woes with the Communist Menace.[60]

However sincere and even revealing the American showman's pronouncement may have been, it was highly atypical. He had no interest in politics, and he avoided public conflict at almost any cost. His statement emphasizes the peculiar stress under which he was operating in the spring of 1958. It didn't matter, though. The good people of Sydney would have none of it, under any circumstances.

When he left the stage, all hell broke loose. Loud boos followed a stunned silence in the hall. More banner headlines darkened the papers: "BOOING CROWDS HELD BACK FROM LIBERACE"; "LIBERACE WALKED OUT—THOUSANDS BOOED." There was more to come. Besides his conflict with the Australian legal system and Chappell and Co., he now confronted a legal challenge from the tour's promoter, who threatened legal action if he refused to perform. Chaos reigned. It was a public-relations horror that slopped over into the American press as well. On March 8, 1957, the *New York Times* reviewed the affair and quoted an Australian judge who called Liberace "a petulant child" for refusing to play for the Sydney audience.[61] After paying court fines, making more apologies, and enduring massive ill will, the tour continued, but the affair soured the performer so profoundly that he did not return to Australia for over a decade.

Beyond its implications for the Australian tour, his completely un-characteristic bout of ill temper, his recourse to politics and political dis-course, and, indeed, his overall disposition throughout the affair suggests larger crises in his life as he neared his fortieth birthday. Something was going badly wrong at home and abroad. He found those responsible among his business managers and professional entourage. This led, ulti-mately, to still new trials and woes.

Was his career faltering? He looked for culprits. He blamed Seymour Heller, in part. As early as the spring of 1956, he had determined to re-duce Heller's cut of his income. Their original agreement had stipulated a 10 percent management fee as long as the performer's revenue re-mained above $125,000. In April 1956, that figure kicked in, according to the performer, and the contracting parties reached an oral agreement to drop Heller's share to 5 percent. The relationship deteriorated from here. By late 1958 or '59, Liberace jettisoned Heller altogether. Although Lib-erace devoted considerable space to the breakup in his memoirs, the breach was even more difficult than the entertainer allowed. Thus, for example, the autobiography ignores the lawsuit Heller instituted in 1960 against his old client. Heller charged the showman with concealing in-come when they renegotiated their contract in 1956, and with denying him money that was properly and legally his. Heller wanted $2.3 million dol-lars. Liberace mounted a countersuit, claiming that from the specific date of November 2, 1956, Heller failed to do his job of publicizing the per-former's career.[62]

Was Seymour not earning his keep? The showman had found a new adviser and erstwhile manager. Although John Jacobs eventually came to grief as well, Liberace looked to him as savior in the "monster slump" of the late fifties.

In his memoir, Liberace is not at all clear about when and how he discovered Jacobs. Nor does he reveal the depth of the association. He had engaged Jacobs's services as a lawyer no later than 1950, when news-paper accounts publicized the performer's efforts to change his name.[63] By 1954, however, Jacobs was one of the most important people in the showman's entourage. He seems to have been the force behind Liberace's self-incorporation as International Artists, Ltd., that year. He was cer-tainly one of the three stockholders in the corporation, holding nineteen shares against the fifty-four the entertainer held himself. The rest were allocated to brother George. The corporation was organized chiefly, it seems, as a de facto tax shield, but legally it served "the purpose of producing and promoting concerts featuring LIBERACE as the principal attraction [and] derived its income during the taxable years at issue primarily from sources related to LIBERACE's performance as an entertainer in nightclubs and television appearances and from royalties with respect to the sale of records." [64] The two were business partners and invested in various projects together, among them the apartment building they constructed together in Las Vegas in 1957. [65]

John Jacobs was the contemporary of Sam Liberace—and of Clarence Goodwin, too. The right age to be Liberace's father, this courtly, Virginia-born patrician, in Liberace's memory, looked the part of the ideal patriarch as well. In his crisis, Liberace seems to have given himself over to this parental authority just as he did to Goodwin in earlier times. Beyond this, Jacobs was as aggressive a protector as Seymour Heller had been—or as Goodwin had been, for that matter; as a high-powered downtown Los Angeles attorney, however, he possessed connections and a kind of authority that the more rough-cut, street-smart Heller lacked. In normal times, Jacobs was onto Lee's enemies like a duck on a June bug. He threatened and actually initiated lawsuits against all manner of folk. [66] Crises found him even more aggressively protective. Here, again, the showman found the good father who appeared in troubled times to shield and protect him. Jacobs's growing presence in the showman's life after 1955 suggests the power that this type of character still wielded over him, particularly as his own professional and personal woes increased. Liberace trusted him even when his instincts cautioned him to do otherwise.

It was to Jacobs that Liberace had gone in the Cassandra affair. Jacobs was the one who encouraged the performer to sue the *Daily Mirror;* Jacobs himself handled the details of that suit. On Jacobs's advice, too, the performer had insisted on only an oral contract with Heller after 1955. [67] Also on Jacobs's counsel, Liberace sacked Heller in 1958: "He said that since I wasn't traveling, booking concerts, what did I need a manager for? He said he could do everything a manager did, and at his urging I severed my connection with Seymour." [68] In 1960, when Heller sued Liberace, the former's parallel suit against Jacobs followed naturally. [69]

The circumstances of his life seemed to sap Liberace's genius, and he turned himself over to Jacobs in 1958 to reform his image. Just before his departure for Australia, Liberace anticipated the transformation. "Everybody has seen me," he told a reporter. "They know everything I do. In the future I will display a depth of character that people don't know I possess. I'm not sure exactly what the format will be—but it will be different." [70]

It *was* different. After making the decision to sue William Conner and the London *Daily Mirror,* Liberace defagified himself. At Jacobs's counsel, he determined that charges of homosexuality were responsible for destroying his career. "It hurt me," he said later about the Cassandra affair. "People stayed away from my shows in droves." [71] He read his declining popularity, then, as a function of his identity as a homosexual. He would butch himself up.

At Jacobs's advice, Liberace discarded all his fancy stuff. In the legalese of a tax suit of 1970, attorneys described what happened: "at the urging of his business manager, and prompted by his loss of popularity and reduced income, petitioner discarded the elegant image in favor of a more conservative one. His life style shifted from the spectacular to the conventional." [72] He played it straight, for once in his life. The legendary piano-pool house? In 1961, still under Jacobs's influence, he laughed it off as a cheap trick, "just as the sequined jackets were," he added. "When you're starting out in show business you need these things. Once I was established, I gave up the flamboyant clothes. Actually, I had to do it to find out if the audiences came to see me or all the fancy trappings. It became a matter of personal pride." [73] "To me the image has been something I found amusing in a sense," he told another reporter the same year. "I was caught in a gimmick I really hadn't planned. Then the pattern was established for me as a flamboyant performer. I was a curiosity who had to come up with $50,000 worth of sensation a week." [74]

He altered his act to fit the new image. Playing the 500 Club in Atlantic City in July 1958, he made only one costume change and abandoned the supporting acts of the years before. [75] "Liberace has toned down his spectacular personal habiliments," noted a reviewer of his August run at Los Angeles's Coconut Grove. The new act, the notice continued, "doesn't rely wholly on the ornate glass decor." [76] The performer even repudiated *The Liberace Show*. In 1961, he related how those programs "represented a certain era in TV—an era now long gone. The quality of the shows couldn't match the standards of the 1960s," he insisted. "They were of the low budget category, they were made in a way that would be archaic today—and they certainly were gimmicked. Those old '54 and '55 shows suited the standards of their time, but you'll never see me trying to do the same thing again." [77]

He did not do the same thing again, and when he returned to television, he projected an altogether new image. His show premiered on October 12, 1958. Jacobs had negotiated the new, network show with ABC in the summer. It ran for six months, through April 10, 1959. [78] In a blatant attempt to draw the stay-at-home soap-opera set, the program broadcast in the afternoon. Except in that he calculated the show to appeal to this audience, which was made up almost entirely of women, Liberace presented his butch image when it aired. Engineered by Jacobs, his old television mentor, Don Fedderson, and his agents at MCA, the show rotated around his new, conventional persona. "They cut my hair very short, put me in Brooks Brothers suits and shirts with button-down collars." [79] Everything was different: "No candelabra, no fancy clothes, none of the showmanship, that, it turned out, was responsible for my first big success." [80] *Variety*'s review captured something critical about the show. The star still possessed his powerful personal appeal: "There's still something nice about the man," it judged, but otherwise he "seemed to be under the control of some outside force," for example, by "talking a couple of octaves lower than he is famous for." [81]

The result was disastrous. If his star had been fading before, the new show seemed to obliterate it altogether, he judged later. Fifteen years after the fact, he pronounced it all wrong from the very beginning. First, the new look failed his audience, he insisted. Viewers, he determined, "resented the plain look. Letters began pouring in saying the music was still beautiful, but all the charm, the glamour, the fun was gone out of the show." [82] Nor was the time right. "I am not a daytime performer," he discovered. "Daylight is bright and plain, matter of fact, and very real. . . . Nighttime is different. . . . Everything becomes more glamorous, and that's the way I like it." [83] Third, he resented his problems with advertisers. "I was hardly able to play the piano because my hands were always so full of detergent boxes which I was obliged to hold up and try to sell." [84] He disliked selling certain products. "Nair for briar patch legs!" offended him especially. And he fumed about the inappropriateness of selling a particular product at a particular juncture in the show—Drano, for example, during a Thanksgiving feast. These concerns suggest others, chiefly his lack of authority over anything in the program and his inability to express his own peculiar self. His power as a performer, he determined, lay in his sincerity and believability. He acknowledged that he was not a good actor, that he didn't read lines well, that he couldn't perform effectively if he was doing something he disliked. Here he was, however, violating every tenet of his personal code. Things were very much awry. When he gave himself over to Jacobs and ABC, he surrendered something in himself, and his conflict was not merely external but also internal. He played without conviction. The show failed completely. Afterwards, he considered himself worse off than he had been before. "This show almost put me entirely out of business. When it failed, which was quickly but not soon enough, I not only couldn't get any concert bookings, I couldn't get any TV bookings either," he wrote. [85]

As he approached his fortieth birthday, he reached the nadir of his career. Exaggerated after 1957, his professional woes paralleled difficulties in his personal life after 1955. Indeed, the two intersected and played off each other. The personal problems involved family, his ideals of family, and their contradictions with his homoeroticism. Homoeroticism, in turn, bubbled perpetually to the surface of his career as well. Together, these conflicting elements created the most treacherous crosscurrents he had ever had to deal with in his life.

Liberace talked about family endlessly. He returned to domesticity over and over in his public pronouncements and press releases about his act and career. The subject saturates his autobiography. He himself offers one explanation of the emphasis: it was the source of his audience and his audience appeal, the source, not incidentally, then, of his popularity and economic status. Thus, he insisted, "I have a general family audience appeal, and I don't want to develop only a gay following. It's going to take many, many years for this kind of audience to accept people who are totally gay or come out on Johnny Carson." [86] In this context, one could label his paeans to family as hypocrisy born of necessity. Just so, cynics, aware of his homosexuality, might interpret his piety as a ruse to cover his own deviancy. Neither is altogether foreign to his motives; both fail to capture the whole truth, however. Indeed, his life becomes much more complex, and even emblematic, when one looks at his commitment to family as a sincere one—a credo he believed in even while he himself lived a homosexual life. The dual loyalties informed impossible dilemmas in his biography.

Beyond what he actually said about family and family values, he committed himself practically to the domestic ideal, certainly relative to his own kin. His family was far from perfect; he left evidence, especially late, of actually disliking his kin. None of this affected his loyalty. His involvement of his elder brother in his career reflects the entertainer's insistence on domestic values. Liberace had put George on his payroll right after the war, and had made him his effective manager and an important part of his act. In 1954, when the performer organized his own personal corporation, International Artists, Ltd., he made George one of the three stockholders. By 1955, George and his then wife Jayne had moved to Van Nuys, about a ten-minute drive from his brother's new home on Valley Vista Boulevard, and the two remained close. [87]

His loyalty to his mother was stronger yet. Before all the hoopla about momism came about, he was assuming responsibility for her welfare. In the summer of 1950, while he was filming *South Seas Sinner,* he broke down her insistence on remaining in Wisconsin and moved her to his home on Camellia Street in North Hollywood.[88] By this time, Frances Zuchowski might have been ready to taste the good life. Her life up to that time had not been easy. After separating from Salvatore around 1938 or '39 and divorcing him in '40, she had remarried another local Italian immigrant, Alexander Casadonte, in 1943. Like her first spouse, Casadonte had held his life together as best he could by living with his brother in West Allis and working as everything from a common laborer to a confectioner from 1918 through the Great Depression. According to one report, he and Frances had cohabited before their marriage after Sam moved out of the National Avenue house. He survived for only two years after the actual marriage, leaving his widow, Mrs. Alexander Casadonte, as she was listed officially, to make her own way again.[89] Up to that point, she still resided at the National Avenue house in West Milwaukee with various combinations of her children and their families—Angie and her husband Fred Cole, their two children, sometimes George, and Rudy—in and out of domicile. As she approached sixty, she still worked and maintained her old habits. Despite her son's growing fame and wealth, she rejected most of his proffers of gifts that would improve her life, everything from professional hairdressers to electric ranges and refrigerators.[90]

Nor did much of this change after her move to California. She managed her son's home with the same insistence on domestic economy and petty order that had characterized her residence in West Milwaukee. She was not an easy housemate. Despite the presence of servants, she created "self-imposed tasks for herself" like following her son around tidying up after him, emptying the ashtrays he filled, and turning off the lights that he invariably left burning. As bossy, domineering, and opinionated as ever, she followed the servants around, too, instructing them about how to clean, "adding a touch here and there to achieve her state of perfection," her son noted. She instructed the cooks on how to cook and the gardeners on how to garden, all in no uncertain terms.[91] Scott Thorson, reporting on a later period, related one episode of Mrs. Casadonte's verbal tyranny directed at Liberace's beloved housekeeper/cook, Gladys Luckie: "I can't believe my son is going to have to eat meat loaf when the Blacks in Watts are eating steak!" she had raged at the long-suffering black woman on one occasion.[92] Even her adored son suggested, however guardedly, what it was like to live with her. "She has a green thumb and feels no one but God can make things grow the way she can," he wrote.[93] If she considered herself a co-equal of the divine in terms of her ability to grow things, otherwise she still adhered to her religious faith and practice as narrowly as ever. Not even permissive California could slack the pious devotion and simple Catholic theology of her Polish childhood and young womanhood in Menasha. But here she was, cohabiting with her boy, a lusty young gay man, on Camellia Street after 1950, and on Valley Vista after that.

Not content with involving his brother and mother in his affairs, the performer soon helped relocate his sister, Angie, to California as well. There, after divorcing her first spouse, Fred Cole, she found a new husband, Thomas Farrell, a California contractor. By 1955, she had a house in Sherman Oaks, too, close to her brother in the valley. Like George, Angie also moved onto her brother's payroll. She assumed responsibilities as his private secretary, answering fan mail and the like. At about the same time, the middle brother was in the process of finding a place in California for the handsomest—but least stable and most ill-fated—of the Liberace children, Rudy. After completing his military stint in Korea, Rudy became a neighbor, too. A resident, like George, of nearby Van Nuys, the youngest sibling was employed editing films. Alcoholic and violent, Rudy was the family disaster, and the famous brother rescued him regularly from his self-created scrapes with the law and assisted him with his wife and three young children. It was one more part of family responsibility as Liberace defined it.[94] He hewed to the principle that in regard to family, life defaulted to duty and obligation, not to personal happiness.

His commitments to his family extended into the second generation. He had mothered his niece and nephew, Angie's children Diane and Fred Cole, when he was still in his teens on National Avenue. "I was changing their diapers and, as they got older, dressing them and even making Diane's curls. I loved those kids as if they were my own," he recollected in *The Wonderful, Private World*. "One of the great joys of my later success was that it enabled me to help put Fred through medical school."[95] Diane Cole returned the favor. She and her husband, Don McLaughlin, were faithful to their uncle's last hour.

He matched his affection for his niece and nephew with his fondness of children in general. "I would have loved to have had children," he testified in *The Things I Love*. "I admit that not being surrounded by children sometimes makes me feel quite lonely. I would have been a wonderful father. . . . I would be all right with children," he concluded.[96] His behavior in performance affirms his affection. Regularly, when he spied children in his audience, he brought them on stage and integrated them into his act informally. He also loved kid acts and making them a more formal part of his show. These acts ranged from a youthful troupe of Chinese dancer-singers to single performers like the talented banjo-playing Scottie Plummer. Just so, inspiring youth became an important focus of his life. To this end, he formed the Liberace Talent Club to support young musicians. When he returned to Milwaukee, for example, he visited his old high school to encourage the students. He performed gratis and invited promising young musicians to play with him. One Richard Angeletti, aged seventeen, played duets with him on the stage at West Milwaukee High, but the showman also invited him to participate in his act later at the fancy Empire Room of the high-class Schroeder Hotel. During that same engagement, Liberace requested that four other students, ranging in age from twelve to Angeletti's seventeen, play also.[97] This was standard practice, even as the pianist's wealth and fame increased. Whenever he performed professionally, he also played for high schools, sponsored young talent, and motivated youth's appreciation of music—whether in "The Wildcat Lair" of Las Vegas High School seniors or at Boulder City High School. In 1951, for example, he staged one of his musical talent shows for Las Vegas young people in the Ramona Room of the Last Frontier on a Sunday afternoon, when no one was gambling.[98] When he founded the Liberace Foundation later, its chief purpose was to encourage youthful talent.

He was devoted to domesticity, dedicated to traditional family values, faithful to his own family circle, tender to children, and respectful of youth. Such values drew him toward making a family of his own. Other forces influenced him in the same direction. His own family, especially his mother, encouraged him to settle down with a good woman; the teachings of the church and his own piety glorified marriage while censuring homoerotic coupling. Practically, of course, he acknowledged the power of the heterosexual bond: all social order reinforced the traditional union and penalized the other. Men romancing men was the stuff of comedy and outrage—it merited snickers and pink slips. If sex with women made him anxious, it was not completely alien to his nature, either; from the time of his boyhood, he had labored to cultivate his interest in girls, and he did admit to having had sex with women, even to later homosexual lovers.[99]

If such forces pushed the pianist toward making a traditional family of his own, his fundamental sexual impulses drew him back to his own kind. Men simply interested him more, sexually, than women did. But other issues reinforced his natural impulses and acted as a barrier against his marrying: through the forties, fifties, and even later, his career and schedule were hardly conducive to long-term relationships of any kind. Meanwhile, all the new cities encouraged dabbling in casual homosex as well. On the road, it was all too easy.

Family or not; homosexuality or not: the affair with Joanne Rio fell

16 Local Los Angeles television station KLAC broadcast *The Liberace Show* live for the first time on February 3, 1952. It swept the market. Within a year, the performer had signed on with Guild Films for the nationally syndicated version of the show. With its striking juxtaposition of high style and hokeyness, polish and error, urbanity and provincialism, the production had no counterparts in the industry in 1953. Syndicated to almost two hundred stations around the country, it became the most-watched program in the nation by 1954. *Courtesy of the Liberace Foundation, Las Vegas, NV.*

17 In what he later called his "white heat" period—1953 to 1956—Liberace was one of the two or three most celebrated entertainers in the United States, even the world. Elvis Presley occupied the same category. From their first encounter, the King admired and respected the flashy pianist. On Lee's return to Las Vegas in the fall of 1956, Elvis shared the audience's delight in Liberace's Riviera show. *Courtesy of CORBIS/Bettmann.*

18 (above) In the winter of 1947, the twenty-seven-year-old Midwestern piano player visited the Hollywood Bowl for the first time. Wandering through the empty amphitheater, he promised himself that someday he'd be on the stage and all the seats would be filled. On July 19, 1952, he accomplished his goal. Fabulously attired in custom-made white eveningwear, he set an attendance record with his performance. He was cracking Hollywood wide open, just as he had promised his old teacher Florence Kelly.
Photo: Rothschild Photo, Los Angeles, California. Courtesy of the Liberace Foundation, Las Vegas, NV.

19 (opposite, top) Had Paderewski played Madison Square Garden? Lee determined to exceed his hero's accomplishment. On May 26, 1954, he filled the hall with sixteen thousand rapturous fans, 75 percent of whom were females. A half dozen scowling critics attended, too. The delight of the many was matched only by the rancor of the few. *Courtesy of CORBIS/Bettmann.*

20 (opposite, bottom) With his trademark toothy grin and wavy hair, Liberace was the most recognized man in America in the mid-fifties. He went nowhere without crowds gathering. Every occasion became an opportunity for an almost ritual showing, as here, upon his departure for Europe on the *Queen Mary* in September 1956. *Courtesy of CORBIS/Bettmann.*

21 *(above)* Critics regularly remarked upon the preponderance of
women among Liberace's devotees. Their association of the pianist
and women was seldom flattering either to the showman or to his
followers, but women, indeed, stoked his white-hot popularity in
the fifties. For younger women, as depicted in this 1954 photograph,
he represented a desirable, attractive man, but one purged of
masculine loutishness. "He is through and through a Continental,"
rhapsodized one fan. "When he kisses your hand, you know he isn't
going to chew off your arm." *Courtesy of the Liberace Foundation,
Las Vegas, NV.*

22 *(opposite)* Matrons and grandmothers idolized him, too. They
mobbed him at the New York opening of *Sincerely Yours.* He was
the perfect son-man. One fan described him as "loving and artistic,"
telling him, "You take care of your mother. You are nice, warm,
gentle, polite, considerate and still have a sense of humor. . . .
You might be what most mothers had dreamed their sons would be,
but didn't turn out to be." *Courtesy of CORBIS/Bettmann.*

23 Liberace always argued that staying on top was harder
than getting there. Even at the height of his white-hot
fame, then, he was constantly calculating new moves,
new tricks, new ploys to guarantee public attention.
His spectacular costumes manifested one version of his
ability to seize the popular imagination. No less than
his headline-grabbing clothes, his own family became
an important prop in his publicity campaign as well.
His mother, in particular, played a critical role in his
image-making. The two of them never looked much
better than they do here, at the Hollywood opening of
Sincerely Yours. Courtesy of CORBIS/Bettmann.

24 Liberace's Barnumesque talent for publicity blossomed
extravagantly in fame. It influenced everything he did.
His "piano-pool house," constructed in 1954 in Sherman
Oaks, California, however, captured the essence of his
genius. Here he swims with his little brother, Rudy, that
year. *Courtesy of the Liberace Foundation, Las Vegas, NV.*

25 (above) For all his jazzy public—
even private—shenanigans, Liberace
remained deeply conservative.
Profoundly if unconventionally
Catholic, he never strayed from his
faith. His audience with Pope Pius
XII at the end of his 1956 European
tour marked a high point in his life.
*Courtesy of the Liberace Foundation,
Las Vegas, NV.*

26 (right) Playing a Boston venue in
November 1954, Liberace requested
an audience with Archbishop
Richard Cushing. The honor of meeting the prelate so pleased him that
when a fan turned the photograph
of the occasion into a large painting,
he hung the picture in his otherwise
eroticized bedroom at the Shirley
Street house in Las Vegas. *Courtesy
of AP/Wide World Photos.*

27 (above) No less than his faith, his devotion to family affirmed Liberace's conservativism. Family tradition for the Liberaces centered on cooking and eating. Extending a tradition he associated with both his parents, he boasted his own culinary skills when he was in high school, publicized his talent during the early years of his fame, and published a collection of recipes as his first book. Here, he celebrates a meal with his handsome and ill-fated younger brother, Rudy. Rudy's wife and son appear on the left; between them and Frances stands Seymour Heller, Lee's respected manager and oldest professional associate. George and his then wife, Jayne, (number three) occupy the right. *Courtesy of the Liberace Foundation, Las Vegas, NV.*

28 (left) For all Liberace's primitive devotion to family, the family unit was chiefly mother and sons, rarely mother and daughter, and even more rarely still father and sons. Despite the smiles of the three surviving Liberace men in this 1956 photo, Lee never completely reconciled with his parent after the La Crosse/infidelity crises of 1939. *Courtesy of the Liberace Foundation, Las Vegas, NV.*

29 (above) While he cherished family, even his own flawed kin, he loved children especially. Having none proved a singular regret of his homosexuality. He compensated by including kid acts in his performances, and he founded the Liberace Foundation to assist talented youth. He ad-libbed children into his show at every opportunity, too, as when he interrupted his 1955 performance at San Francisco's Cow Palace to encourage three-year-old Linere Pruitt of Oakland. *Courtesy of AP/Wide World Photos.*

30 (opposite) The afflicted, the marginalized, and the outcast always attracted Lee. When this predilection coincided with his devotion to children, his sympathies knew no bounds. Here, he assists polio-stricken four-year-old Debra Stone in inaugurating the Los Angeles Emergency March of Dimes campaign on August 16, 1954. *Courtesy of CORBIS/Bettmann.*

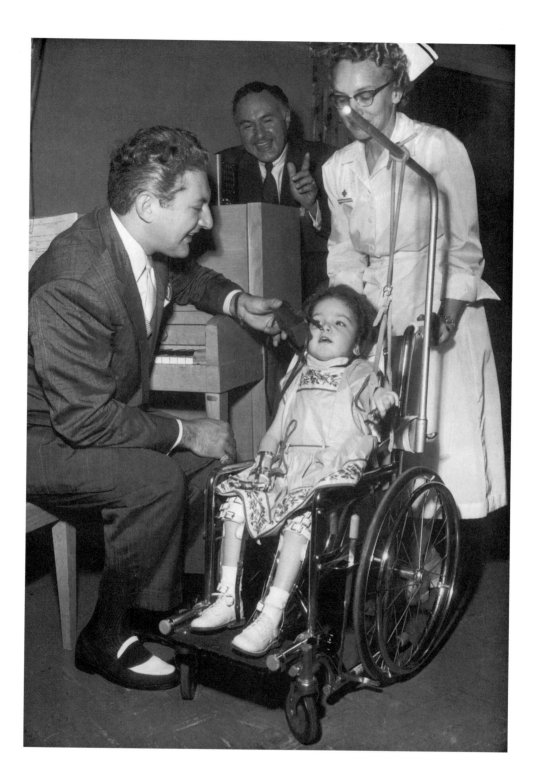

31 (above) Although Lee longed for children of his own, only once does he seem to have genuinely considered marriage. Joanne Rio resembled no other woman he associated with. Eleven years his junior, she danced at Hollywood's Le Moulin Rouge and would double, appropriately enough, for Elizabeth Taylor in films. She had been his neighbor when he lived on Camellia Street between 1947 and 1953. She reappeared in his life only weeks after the first rumors of his homosexual exploits hit the press in the late summer of 1954. *Photo:* TV & Movie Screen Magazine. *Courtesy of the Liberace Foundation, Las Vegas, NV.*

32 (opposite) In the late winter of 1955, after the difficult conclusion of the Rio affair, Lee began dating the wealthy, aging ice-skating queen Sonja Henie. Photographers snapped them together at such classy clubs as El Morocco in Manhattan and L.A.'s Mocambo and Ciro's, where Lee had led the bill a few years before. According to Scott Thorson, Lee claimed a sexual relation with the star, an assertion never made for Rio or any of the other women he dated publicly. He himself compared the relationship to something out of the Gloria Swanson film, *Sunset Boulevard. Courtesy of CORBIS/Bettmann.*

33 (opposite) Liberace's association with Mae West spoke
still more profoundly to his taste in women. He admired her;
they got along famously. Much, much older than he, she was
already an icon in homosexual culture, and no gay man
could have missed the subtext of his connection with the
witty old star who resembled nothing more than a drag
queen. *Courtesy of AP/Wide World Photos.*

34 (above) Like his romantic linkage to Mae West, Liberace's
dating Christine Jorgenson, the famous transsexual of the
age, offered other clues to his sexuality. In July 1956, she
confessed to the scandal rag *Exclusive* that they weren't
really serious. "He's nice," she said, "but a little strange."
Courtesy of AP/Wide World Photos.

35 Personal and professional crises marred Lee's life in the late fifties and early sixties: declining popularity, decreased revenues, the nonrenewal of his Las Vegas contract, homosexual scandals, the "Cassandra" affair and trial, and, not least, the estrangement from his family. Striving to recoup his fortunes, he jettisoned his old managers, altered his image, and sought, for the first time in his life, to make a conventional impression. On June 17, 1959, he could have passed for almost any English gentleman, even if the bobbies and autograph hounds knew his real identity as he departed victorious from the London courtroom after his libel trial against the *Daily Mirror. Courtesy of CORBIS/Bettmann*.

right in the middle of this conflict. In 1948, when he had bought the house on Camellia Street, the Rio family had been his neighbors across the way at 4209. Eddie, the father, headed the L.A. office of the American Guild of Variety Artists. He had been a professional dancer before that. His wife had been a Chicago blues singer who went by the professional name of Mildred LaSalle. Born in 1931, the same year as Rudy Liberace, Joanne, their daughter, was sixteen when Liberace moved in across the street. With dark hair and striking eyes, she was a beautiful young woman who later—and appropriately—doubled for Elizabeth Taylor in movies. Although the new neighbor did not pay much attention to her, she professed to having noticed him both at his home and walking his dog on the street. They also encountered each other at the church where the Liberace and Rio families both attended mass.[100]

In 1953, Liberace won national fame and abandoned his Camellia Street address for Valley Vista Boulevard. The Rios moved the same year. In the fall of the following year, however, the couple met again. Joanne Rio was performing as part of the chorus at the Hollywood nightclub Le Moulin Rouge; Lee was in the audience. She recognized her old neighbor at a front-row table and sent him a note. He invited her over and recognized the now-beautiful woman who had been the girl on his block. The celebrity and the chorus girl began courting. While they attended functions at fancy clubs, most of their dates were low key. After a second performance at the Hollywood Bowl, she related, Liberace had held a reception at his home and had given her a place of honor, next to his mother. The next evening, Rio returned the pianist's hospitality with a dinner party that included not only the Rio family and Liberace but Danny Thomas and his wife, Rosemarie, Virginia Mayo, and Michael O'Shea.[101] Liberace also made a place for the young beauty on the payroll of *The Liberace Show.*[102]

Their association launched a flurry of media speculation about their intentions.[103] By early October, the showman himself was fueling the rumors of marriage. In a news release on the 6th, he disclosed his plans to wed after fulfilling a year's worth of previous engagements and obligations. "Current concert, TV and film commitments would keep him too busy for a happy home life," journalists repeated him. "When I get married I don't want my career to interfere with my marriage like those Hollywood couples such as Marilyn and Joe," Liberace said. "I want to give my marriage the full Catholic treatment. It must be a lasting thing."[104] Religion figured in Rio's responses to her boyfriend, too: "If it's God's will that Lee and I get married, then we will. I'm leaving everything in

God's hands," she told another reporter.[105] Whatever God's will may have been, his family's wishes seem clear, at least in Liberace's mind. "There was a lot of sideline cheering from both our families trying to push things too fast." [106] As he later revealed, the Rios actually opposed the union; the enthusiasm had clearly stemmed from the Liberaces rather than from her people, and "his people" were, chiefly, Frances Z. Casadonte.

Soon after his October 6 press release, the entertainer took off on a five-week concert tour. On October 13, 14, and 15, a series of three articles appeared under Joanne Rio's name in the Los Angeles *Mirror* about her romance with the pianist. Liberace himself knew about these pieces; his sister had contributed to their composition, and Seymour Heller had overseen their creation. Once they were actually in print, however, they offended the pianist. When he returned from his tour, he announced publicly that the essays "embarrassed" him. She replied in kind. "I'm the one who's embarrassed. I just agreed to that article because I thought it would help Lee," she insisted. "Every word of it was okayed by Lee's press agent and if there was anything he didn't like, he should have cut it out then and not waited until it was in print to kick." The romance, she fumed, "was just a lot of publicity, and it looks like I got caught right in the middle of it." [107] The Rio-Liberace romance was history.

Joanne Rio vanished from Liberace's life, but he did mention her in his autobiography two decades later. His references opened the whole affair up again, with Rio, now Mrs. David Barr, suing the entertainer. Her suit, in consequence, elicited still more revelations about their relationship, her old suitor, and how his entourage worked. For one thing, it emphasized Seymour Heller's part in the affair, and his role in managing Liberace's image in general. According to the depositions, Heller had overseen the romance, instructing Rio on how to answer reporter's questions, for example. He had also sanctioned the three-part *Mirror* article. If the entertainer was unhappy with what was printed, he held his agent at least partially culpable. Contemporary newspaper articles limned the showman's irritation. "Seymour, this is all your fault and I'm going to see to it that you are out of this business in six months," one of them quoted him.[108] In a role he would play again, Heller also became the hit man for straightening out the mess.[109]

Joanne Barr's suit also reopened the issue of the performer's sexuality. The *Autobiography* made her hysterical, she warranted; she kept crying to herself, she told her interrogators, "'Why was he degrading me to justify why he never got married? Why was he lying about me?'" Some of her friends and associates, she said, assumed the answers: "'Was he a homosexual? Did you go to bed with him?'"[110] The case also allowed Liberace to give his version of the romance, too, and his testimony played at the edge of the sexual issue, even while suggesting other values that influenced his career.

> As far as I am concerned, Joanne Rio does not exist because this is something that happened twenty years ago. We all agreed it was like a ghost coming out of the past to haunt me. . . . As I remember it, she was a very pretty girl, a very nice girl. I liked her very much. I wanted to marry her, and that's exactly what I said in my book. The reason I didn't marry her was because of these goddamn articles and her father screaming at me and calling me all kinds of names. I suddenly realized I had found out in the nick of time that all was not going to be sunshine and roses.[111]

The record is silent about the sources of Eddie Rio's objections, but one clue to them might lie in what Rio's father was "screaming" about and what kind of "names" he was calling him. Bob Thomas, who interviewed Eddie Rio, reconstructed what transpired in the old hoofer's exchanges with the pianist. Rio was skeptical from the outset about the match and tried to discourage his daughter. His doubts were confirmed later when he received information about "an incident involving Liberace that had the makings of a scandal but had been hushed up." After advising his daughter about the affair, Rio then counseled the pianist. "The marriage wouldn't work," he told him, "and you know in our church there is no divorce." After hearing all this, according to Thomas, Liberace wept softly, accepted Rio's opinion, put marriage out of his mind, and indeed, put the entire affair out of his head until he mentioned it in his autobiography, which conjured these ghosts from the past. Although Liberace considered the suit stupid, it remained alive for almost six years until the showman finally settled out of court for "a substantial amount" of money around 1979.[112]

Was Liberace serious about the romance? Although Rio concluded that the performer was using her as a cover, the affair resembled nothing that happened before or after in Liberace's history. Like other gay Hollywood celebrities, he did find women who provided date material: the queenly old Mae West, the transsexual Christine Jorgenson, or the aging ice-skating queen Sonja Henie. He compared his relationship with Henie to scenes from the Gloria Swanson film, *Sunset Boulevard*—hardly a proper cover story for a normal, lusty man.[113]

Young and fresh, Joanne Rio differed completely from these other women. Perhaps in her case Liberace was indeed flirting with the idea of marriage and family. Beyond such circumstantial evidence of the affair's seriousness, the breakup seemed to have left some psychic residue. Only a few weeks after the exchange with Eddie Rio, the star suffered what his physician described as a heart strain. The doctor prescribed rest and diet change, and the pianist went into a two-month seclusion. Up to now, ever since he recovered from the illnesses of his early childhood, Liberace's health had remained phenomenally good. Until thirty-five years later, when he contracted AIDS and died, this was one of the very few bouts of illness of any kind that he had suffered. Nor had he ever used illness as an excuse or cover for anything before. Even when he was dying, he refused to acknowledge illness. Yet, in this season, he went into a two-month seclusion on the basis of a doctor's recommendation, his brother said. His mother had her own announcement about the break in her son's routine: "He has been giving so many concerts, working and traveling so much without a vacation," she explained. "It has nothing to do with Joanne Rio." [114]

It might have been that Liberace did play with the idea of wedding Joanne Rio, but other evidence sustains Rio's notion that the relationship was indeed another publicity ploy. By the time he was thirty-one, his press agents had already started to become concerned about popular perceptions of his bachelorhood. As early as 1951, they generated publicity releases with headlines like, "Liberace Gives A Few Tips On Wooing Women." [115] Rio's ghostwritten, Heller-checked article in the Los Angeles *Mirror*—not to mention Rio herself—could be seen as a part of a similar campaign; it developed Liberace's image not merely as a romancer but as a certain kind of lover-gentleman; he was "the perfect all-around man any woman would be thrilled to be with," the article ran. "He's so considerate on dates. . . . He never forgets the little things that women love. He brings me orchids. He lights my cigarettes and he opens doors. He makes you feel that when you are with him, well, you really are with him." [116] The publicity played the same angle in an article entitled "Mature Women Are Best: TV's Top Pianist Reveals What Kind of Woman He'd Marry," which appeared in *Coronet,* the popular women's magazine. It appeared, perhaps not coincidentally, right after the Rio affair's conclusion. [117]

Scott Thorson testified flatly that Joanne Rio was nothing more than cover for Liberace's sexual inversion. "The problem was not that he didn't like her, it was that he still loved men," the boyfriend argued. "Lee told me he never planned to walk down the aisle, with JoAnn [*sic*] or anyone else. His engagement served to squelch the rumors about his sexuality—

period!"[118] Thorson's view notwithstanding, neither the "engagement" nor its conclusion ended the gossip at all. On the contrary, the rumors actually grew louder after, and in part because of, the Rio romance. They had been only whispers before Joanne Rio; after he dumped the beautiful young woman from Camellia Street, the hearsay began to filter into the press, and the showman's homosexuality became a furiously guarded open secret that shadowed his career and his public persona in the late fifties. It offered the greatest trials—both literally and figuratively—in the darkest years of his eclipse.

*The pudgy pianist's many faithful fans would
have popped their girdles if they had witnessed
their idol in action last year in an offstage
production that saw old Kittenish on the Keys
play one sour note after another in his clumsy
efforts to make beautiful music with a handsome
but highly reluctant young publicity man.*

"Why Liberace's Theme Song Should Be
'Mad About the Boy,' "
Hollywood Confidential

Nine

YOU CAN BE SURE IF IT'S WESTINGHOUSE

It was perhaps coincidental—and then, again, perhaps it was not—that in the couple of weeks just before the Joanne Rio romance hit the papers, a Hollywood scandal sheet printed the first account of Lee Liberace's homosexuality. The pianist began dating Rio in September 1954. The article in *Rave* had appeared the preceding August. "Don't Call Him Mister" begins with a vicious review of *The Liberace Show,* comparing it to "the Cherry sisters, a vaudeville act which sang behind wire netting to avoid being hit by flying objects thrown by the audience." Dismissing his hobbies of "cooking, sewing, and marcelling his hair," it moves on to more direct homosexual allegations. It implies a bathroom pick-up in the reference to the artist singing "Stranger in Paradise" in a public lavatory— toilets, of course, were famous in gay circles for catching quick, easy sex. Next, it notes that Liberace had given his telephone number to a bodybuilder who appeared on television with him. Finally, it describes "a young Hollywood man refusing to allow cops to investigate a burglary at his home after realizing that the cigarette case taken had the following inscription: 'To my darling, whom the world forbids me to live with, and without whom I cannot live . . . merely exist. L.'"[1] This was only the first such revelation. The next three years witnessed a rash of similar stories in such tell-all gossip sheets as *Inside Story, Private Lives, Uncensored, Whisper, Exclusive, On the QT, Hush-Hush, Top Secret,* and *Hollywood Confidential.*

This was a golden age for gossipmongers. It did not last long. A delicate balance of standards, on the one hand, over against quirky celebrity, on the other, was required to sustain it. If standards and manners were too rigid, as they had been before the Great Depression, gossip couldn't flourish. Nor could it proliferate after the fifties, when everyone became a celebrity and standards and manners lost their power. With the collapse of distinctions between public and private, secrets became either irrelevant—or policy.

In the fifties, high and low alike relished "dishing the dirt." Some scandal sheets catered to the prurience of the masses. Their advertisements spoke volumes to the readership. "I won't be a clerk all my life— I don't *have* to!" blared the notice for the LaSalle Extension University's bookkeeping course. The International Correspondence School advocated "Learning at Home in your spare time to Fix Electrical Appliances" with a drawing of a buff, blond youth, chest out, striking down the road "to success," passing a sniveling, fruity roundhead with a monocle. "How to pass a genius," reads the caption. Along the same lines, another blared: "You can make yourself what you want to be with your hidden brainpower." Or "autoconditioning: The New Way to a Successful Life." Others trumpeted, "i guarantee you new bosom glamour or your money back," and included illustrations. Still another advertised "Swift, simple surgery . . . a cure for frigid wives" or "Now! A Tranquilizing Pill Without a Doctor's Prescription!"[2] If calculated to appeal to the common man—or woman, more likely—such magazines did not have a lock on prurience and gossip. Walter Winchell, Westbrook Pegler, Lee Mortimer, Hedda Hopper, and Louella Parsons represent their appeal to a broader and even more sophisticated audience.[3] Dishing Liberace was more attractive to the former category than to the latter, though. His growing fame after his national syndication exaggerated the potential for scandal.

Within two months after the *Rave* article appeared in August, *Inside Story* took up the same theme, if more indirectly. Instead of referring to hunky weightlifters, it challenged the performer's "feminine appeal" and dwelt on "masculine contempt."[4] The dike broke after this; that is, the avalanche of rumors came after the Joanne Rio affair, not before. In January 1955, *Suppressed* associated Liberace with homoeroticism with the category "Liberace and old lace." It mocked the pianist's effeminacy by repeating a standard joke using two icons of fifties culture—the first transsexual of the new age and an advertising slogan popularized by Betty Furness and television: "The difference between Liberace, Westinghouse and Christine Jorgenson is that you can be *sure* if it's Westinghouse."[5]

"Are Liberace's Romances for Real?" inquired another tabloid in March. "Is he, or is he ain't?" was the burning question America was asking, according to *Private Lives.* "Being queer for the piano is no crime, but the American public expects a little more sweat and a little less lavender-water from their heroes," it postulated.[6] In June, *Whisper* told its readers that "Hollywood snickerers are wondering, in fact, if all the male hormones earmarked for the Liberace boys weren't hogged by George, leaving Lee only with his nimble fingers."[7] George Liberace, by this time, had run through three wives. After this exposé, a standard pattern emerged. Assuming, effectively, Liberace's homosexuality, it asserted that all his dates were "phony romances" and "hoaxes." In this regard, the affair with Joanne Rio became a standard for the conventional wisdom that Liberace fabricated his romances with women.[8]

In September 1956, Liberace was steaming over Cassandra's screed written in Great Britain, but the *Daily Mirror's* tirade only capped this swelling chorus of innuendo in the United States. The entertainer's lawsuit against Conner suggests, then, not merely his quarrel with journalists abroad, but his challenge to the gossip at home. Constantly delayed, however, the suit exaggerated rather than suppressed the erotic scuttlebutt. In May 1957, *Hush-Hush* demanded, "Is Liberace a Man?" "If not, what?" the article inquired further. The headline alone dished most of the dirt, as the article itself is limited to reviewing the circumstances of Liberace's upcoming libel suit against the *Daily Mirror.* It does, however, reprint in toto the Cassandra tirade, and it asserts that the question posed in the article's title had "bothered Americans for years." It was, of course, a subtle way of extending the rumors without saying anything for which the publications could be held liable.[9]

If *Hush-Hush* asked what Liberace really was, that same month, the most radical and notorious of all the scandal sheets provided an answer. *Hollywood Confidential* was the most successful of the expose-all tabloids in the mid-fifties. Its founder, Robert Harrison, had cut his teeth as an office boy at *The Daily GraphiC,* an earlier sensational tabloid.[10] At the conclusion of World War II, he launched his own pornographic enterprise with a series of magazines like *Wink, Titter,* and *Flirt.*[11] With the failure of this business, he cast about for another. He found inspiration in what would seem the unlikeliest place—Tennessee Senator Estes Kefauver's televised crime hearings going on at the time. If audiences' preference for *I Love Lucy* over Eisenhower's inauguration was not a clear enough indication of what the folks were interested in, Senator Kefauver's crime hearings cleared up any remaining doubt on that score. The hearings were politics as salacious television entertainment. Senator Kefauver's success inspired Harrison to launch *Hollywood Confidential*. According to Kenneth Anger, the most famous chronicler of Hollywood sleaze, "Harrison had conceived the idea for the magazine after watching the daily televised Kefauver crime investigations. When he observed that these journalistic reports on vice, crime and prostitution eclipsed all other programs in the ratings, he deduced that the public was hungry for gossip and that a publication that presented such material in a spicy manner and did, in effect, name names, would go over big." [12]

Harrison launched the publication in 1952. Al Govoni, formerly of *True Detective*, edited the magazine. [13] "Tells the Facts and Names the Names," read the masthead. The stories, accompanied by photographs, were short and snappy. In a sardonic style, they mocked indiscretions, chiefly, of Hollywood celebrities. "A born promoter," according to one source, Harrison knew how to sell: "He knew what his customers wanted. He confided to friends: 'Americans like to read about things which they are afraid to do themselves.'" [14] The magazine had an initial press run of 250,000 copies, and by January 1955, more than six times that number were being sold each time it came out. By November of that year, the figure topped four million. The publication had the widest newsstand circulation of any magazine in the country. [15]

The folks loved it. "It appeared in groceries and on newsstands everywhere with catchy headlines about the stars and their sexual/alcoholic/narcotic misadventures," observed one contemporary journalist. Extremely profitable, "it could also support a small army of reporters and private detectives and pay large fees for scandalous information." Cash fueled betrayal. "Hospital nurses, hookers, discharged servants, out-of-work publicists turned informers for *Confidential*. So did legitimate reporters, who risked loss of their jobs to accept a big check for stories they couldn't print." Blackmail was its stock in trade. "In fact, the entire magazine was a quasi-blackmail operation," judged another chronicler. "Like a bargain basement private eye working to 'get the goods' on a spouse in a divorce case, *Confidential* would set about putting together a dossier on a carefully targeted star. Once it was assembled, part of the story might be run—with the rest held back in the hopes of monetary reward." [16] The blackmail did not always involve money. "One gossip columnist was said to have been trapped in a homosexual liaison; in return for *Confidential*'s suppression of the story, he passed along tidbits to the magazines." [17]

Confidential's sales and profits sustained the publisher's lavish style. Chauffeured in his custom-made Cadillac, garbed in white polo coat and white fedora, and sporting an easy woman on his arm, Robert Harrison lived high. The publisher had friends in high places, too. Indeed, he and Walter Winchell established a virtual partnership before 1955.[18] The profits also funded FBI-like investigations. The scandal detectives used regular cameras, as well as infrared and ultra-rapid film, high-powered telephoto lenses, and even sensitive listening devices.[19] In addition, Harrison maintained a stable of lawyers and private detectives to confirm the accuracy of his reports. The novelist James Ellroy used one of these characters as both source and inspiration for his novels *L.A. Confidential* and *Hollywood Nocturnes,* the former of which became an Oscar-winning film in 1997. Before going to work for *Hollywood Confidential,* Fred Otash had been a "leg breaker for the LAPD," said Ellroy. "Freddie was the guy you went to if you wanted a picture of Rock Hudson with a dick in his mouth." "The thing about *Confidential* is, it had the run that it had 'cause everything in *Confidential* was true," Ellroy testified. Otash confirmed it.[20]

Call girls provided a standard source for standard male dalliances, according to the author of *Hollywood Babylon.* Getting the goods on Hollywood homosexuals proved more problematic. The difficulty the scandal sheets had nailing gays illustrates the profound differences between homo- and heteroerotics during Liberace's career.

For one thing, male prostitution did not work the same way female prostitution did. Where were the call boys and male escorts when *Rave* demanded them? They were out there, certainly. As detailed in John Rechy's autobiographical novel, *City of Night,* "rent boys"—to borrow the quaint English term—peddled their wares in standard locations like Times Square in New York, Pershing Park in Los Angeles, or New Orleans's French Quarter. Yet, unlike the Polly Adlers, Heidi Fleisses, and Sidney Barrows of female prostitution, few males came forward to identify their clients. Peculiar elements within heterosexual prostitution actually encouraged such revelations. Within a traditional gender community, a man hires a woman as the "other." He uses her, effectively, for himself. Antagonism and betrayal, revelations and exposés, revenge and retaliation grow naturally out of the opposition. In contrast, homoerotic coupling occurs within an effective community that generally blurs or even transcends such distinctions between the one and the other, the buyer versus the seller. In homosexual transactions, "I" and "you" elide easily to a "we" that becomes "we" versus "they." The sameness of the partners displaces "other"; the opposition is to the world, rather than between the partners, and it is an opposition the world has generally relished and returned in full measure. Sometimes the traditional sort of exchange effects homosexual prostitution, but even there it does so with a twist. John Rechy's protagonist's clients include a high percentage of married men, straights, or "trade." But even when a man bought a boy's services the way he might a woman's, something of this homosexual mutuality still kicked in. While the threat of blackmail hung ominously over such men's heads, a boy who disclosed what had gone on risked disaster for himself as well. In this context, in exposing all, the sellers, as it were, had as much to lose as their customers did.[21] They revealed not only their scores' secrets but their own. They were, in effect, partners in the larger social crime of homosexuality in general. Few rent boys ever came forward with lists of names and dates. When they did, the circumstances seem profoundly different from situations in which women ratted on their johns.

Public prejudice and homoerotic mutuality produced their own effects to resist public inquiry. As David Ehrenstein has written, "Homosexuality has always been viewed . . . as an *ultimate* piece of knowledge. To know *who's gay* is to 'get their number.'"[22] As a consequence, homosex of any kind, commercial or otherwise, has remained profoundly more subterranean, secretive, and unspoken than illicit heterosexuality. Partners swore tacit oaths of secrecy about both the personnel involved in and the specific activity of their couplings. While, in private, the boys and men might trade stories about the celebrities they had done, they tended to circle the wagons against the inevitable straight antagonists. "She's family," ran the gay expression about a fellow who lusted after other males. For all the incoherence within that family, the tribal lines generally held against outsiders.[23] "We had only one security—silence," explained Harry Hays, a founder of homosexual activism in the Mattachine Society. "My security was your silence. That was understood always."[24]

Homosexuality proved otherwise resistant to outside inquiry. Where were the call boys when *Whisper* roared? Who was the call boy and who, indeed, was the caller? The categories blurred. Underlining the overlap between homosexuality in general and homosexual prostitution in particular, the scholar Rictor Norton has argued that much homosexual language originated in the street talk of ordinary prostitutes. The terms "trick" or "tricking," for example, originated among female streetwalkers, but they came into general usage in the gay demimonde to describe a nonpaying date or having sex of any sort.[25]

More specifically, among men the lines between professional and nonprofessional sex were blurred. The "score," or customer, in one context, might be the seller in another. A seller, not uncommonly, too, might not exact a fee when the circumstances were especially pleasant for him. In addition, an ordinary gay man might take to prostitution almost on a lark and then return as easily to his normal life.[26] Along the same lines, any boy or man might turn a cash trick more or less on whim. A man cruises another. They go home together or retreat to some private spot. They have sex. Getting dressed, the one might say something like, "Do you have any cash on you? I need a bus ride home"; Or: "Man, I'm really short right now; could you spot me?" If the partner refuses, the other is no worse off, essentially, for the wear. If the partner is generous, bills change hands, not necessarily with the sense of goods sold but rather in the context of favors traded.

These kinds of transactions were part of Liberace's life. Perhaps the 1954 *Rave* story about Liberace offering his telephone number to the bodybuilder who had appeared on television with him was apocryphal or simply fabricated. Whether or not it was true in its particulars, however, it described a real pattern. A man strikes up a conversation with another. A casual and seemingly innocent invitation to share a drink might follow, or one might say to the other, "We should get together sometime; give me a ring." Telephone numbers are scribbled and swapped. If the other party had no homosexual inclinations, the incident could pass innocently enough. If he did, he could laugh it off if the suitor was not to his taste; otherwise a bodybuilder could find himself a new sexual partner that evening. It might cost the suitor a dinner or a night on the town. If the liaison was particularly pleasant and the pickup partner generous, there might be more nights and more dinners. The cost might rise a bit, say, to the level of an engraved silver cigarette case. No one is selling anything, however.

The randiness of men and the availability of male-male sex constitutes another critical element in understanding the problems of straight culture with the gay world. If the lines between fun and profit were narrow, so were those between sex and society, a contrast that one critic explains as the homosexual versus the homosocial motive.[27] The categories smudged easily. Society threw men together constantly, and randy men were everywhere. Most might have resisted the homoerotic impulse, but many—whether gay, straight, or somewhere in between—did not. Male-male sex was available everywhere, and, not least, it was usually free. Who was the trick? Where did one find "scores"? Tricks and scores could be any man, and men were everywhere. A Brooks Brothered businessman on a crowded morning subway? A bicycle courier between runs? A UPS man delivering packages? A garbage man collecting trash? The rep-tied stockbroker on a lunch break? The fellow admirer of the Velázquez at the museum? The two horny soccer players at the back of the team bus? The bookbagged adolescent on the bus bench? Two drivers caught in a traffic jam? Anywhere. Any man. Everyman. A fellow had only to linger in a public restroom, hang around a bookstore magazine rack, or stroll through a park to find a willing partner whose name he might never even know and who, of course, might never know his name. The courtship could be over in a nanosecond and consisted of the merest glance, grin, or nod; the sexual activity itself might last hardly longer. Sex was free in more ways than one; it was casual, endlessly repeatable, generally forgettable, and completely gratifying after the manner of men.[28]

This form of coupling, which came complete with anonymity and danger, was the sex of choice for many men; its risks and namelessness was an aphrodisiac.[29] However incredible it may seem, the most famous celebrities could and did indulge in such anonymous sex, and more often than not went unrecognized by their equally anonymous partners.[30]

Rock Hudson's career illustrates many of these issues. He became extremely famous after the 1954 premier of *Magnificent Obsession;* he was also intensely sexual, and lived more or less openly with various men even in the fifties. As early as 1953, journalists knew about his sexual anomalies; the water hardly rippled.[31] Although his wife, Phyllis Gates, was steaming, Hudson returned from Europe after *A Farewell to Arms* with a new lover in tow. Problems with this same boyfriend prompted the star to engage the notorious "legbreaker"—and homophobe—Freddie Otash to hasten this fellow's departure back home shortly after. If it was common knowledge among the gossips, no exposés revealed such delicious goings-on.[32]

"The amazing thing is that Rock, as big as he became, was never nailed," mused his friend George Nader. "It made me speculate that Rock had an angel on his shoulder, or that he'd made a pact with the devil, because he seemed under supernatural protection."[33] His homosexuality was an open secret among Hollywood insiders. Robert Harrison was an insider. *Confidential* longed to "tell the facts and name the names" about the megastar's sexual affairs. Harrison knew Hudson's former boyfriends. The sleuths contacted Bob Preble and Jack Navaar, since estranged from the movie star, and offered them big money to tell all. The fraternal conspiracy kicked in. Harrison got nothing out of either man. One story did circulate that the magazine found a Hudson partner willing to confess for cash: the magazine was bought off, however, not to publish. "Every month when *Confidential* came out, our stomachs began to turn. Which of us would be in it?" wrote one of the gay actors in Rock Hudson's set of friends.[34] Few appeared, even so.

The greatest threat to celebrity homosexuals lay not in fraternizing with queers but in crossing over to straight boys who had no vested interest in silence but who, on the contrary, might even relish the opportunity to prove their manhood by fingering a libidinous homosexual star who had come on to them. Perhaps Rock Hudson managed to avoid starring in a *Hollywood Confidential* exposé by virtue of his general discretion, of keeping his appetites within the "family." Liberace had other tastes. If the 1954 *Rave* exposé was true in its particulars, the man with the engraved cigarette case was family and suffered his loss in silence. The bodybuilder might have been different. From the surviving fragmentary evidence of Liberace's sex life and sexual appetites, he would have hit on the body-builder, whether the man were gay or not, without much compunction. "He wasn't discreet, he was daring and rather outrageous about it," a gay television director had recalled the entertainer's escapades in the sixties.[35] Unlike Rock Hudson, Lee was as reckless as he was lusty, and he pre-ferred trade. Scott Thorson affirmed this when the showman was in his sixties. Liberace would hit on almost any man, regardless of the circum-stances. If this much is true according to memoirist's accounts, the *Holly-wood Confidential* exposé sustains it.

The July 1957 issue of *Confidential* had actually hit the drugstores and tobacco shops during the first week of May. Its cover story shrilled, "Exclusive!" "Why Liberace's Theme Song Should Be 'Mad About the Boy'!" In the sardonic mode that typified the magazine's style, the story inside also brimmed with photographs and telling details. Its author, writ-ing under the name of Horton Streete, summarized the scandal at the essay's beginning: "In one of the zaniest plots in theatrical history, this comedy of errors rang up the curtain in Akron, Ohio, played a crazy act two in Los Angeles, and closed in Dallas, Texas, with the wildest finale since 'Hellzapoppin.' The show had everything: unrequited love . . . con-flict . . . mob scenes . . . low comedy. And through it all throbbed the theme song, 'Mad About the Boy.' "[36]

This was the story. A young New York publicity agent had flown in from Manhattan to Akron, Ohio, to promote a Fourth of July celebration that featured the famous pianist. Having organized a huge welcoming ceremony at the airport on July 3, the young man then accompanied the performer back to his hotel suite. According to the story, when he de-clared that, "whatever you want, I'm your boy," it set the entertainer in high mettle. The showman took it as an invitation and made physical moves on the man, who resisted. "Once during the scuffle, the press agent let out a yelp of pain, and no wonder. . . . For Luscious Libby, it was strictly no-holds-barred. Finally with a combination of wristlock and flying mare, the publicity man wrenched loose from his host's embrace and fled from the suite, leaving Liberace sprawled on the floor."

The encounter had two more installments, according to *Confidential*. For legal reasons, the press agent needed to obtain a release from the pianist, and when he flew to Los Angeles to obtain Liberace's signature, round two ensued. Round three occurred when the publicist, still seeking the legal releases, followed the performer to Dallas, where he was performing in *The Great Waltz*. The reporter described the Dallas match as a virtual replay of that in the Akron hotel suite. "The floor show reached its climax when Dimples, by sheer weight, pinned his victim to the mat and mewed in his face: 'Gee, you're cute when you're mad.'" This time, however, the press agent had instructed his associates to check on him, and they leapt to the rescue at a critical moment.[37]

The *Confidential* crisis broke in the middle of Liberace's preparation for a three-week run at the Riviera Hotel in Las Vegas that spring. Almost immediately, on May 7, he announced his intention to sue.[38] He joked about the case to the gamblers, but John Jacobs filed his twenty-million-dollar legal suit on May 14.[39]

Although hardly apparent at the time, the days of *Confidential* and its ilk were numbered. Times were changing, but the stars were fighting back as well. Liberace was not the first. In February, Dorothy Dandridge had sued Harrison's enterprise for two million dollars. A suit filed by Errol Flynn was pending from 1955. Other celebrity lawsuits followed, and the trend produced its own shock waves. In March 1957, the magazine had moved its corporate headquarters to Massachusetts, for example, as an apparent means of avoiding a California venue for these cases. Studio chiefs became involved. They feared that the courts would issue blanket subpoenas and force scores of celebrities to testify about their private doings.[40] The apprehension was justified. "I love it," Robert Harrison gloated. "I've already told my lawyers to be prepared to subpoena every big-name star who ever appeared in the magazine. Can you picture that parade up to the witness stand?"[41] Soon enough, another front opened as well, when grand juries in New Jersey, Illinois, and California began investigating scandal sheets, in general, and *Confidential* in particular. A California state senator had initiated his own inquiry simultaneously. With pressure from Hollywood, the state government won an indictment against *Confidential* for libel and obscenity.[42] From the time of the McCarthy and Kefauver committee hearings, such weighty political inquiries had been the rage, and the scandal-sheet investigations continued the pattern.

The extremely complicated case—or rather cases—wound through the Los Angeles judicial system for a year beginning in August 1957. A grand jury heard evidence for two months on the allegations that the magazine had engaged in libelous, slanderous activity, but it deadlocked for two weeks over Liberace's complaints. A long, second trial threatened. On the defensive, Harrison retreated. On July 2, 1958, papers broadcast the out-of-court settlement with Maureen O'Hara; the next week, *Confidential* settled with Errol Flynn. Finally, on July 16, the magazine reached an agreement with Liberace. He settled for damages of forty thousand dollars. He carried the day on something of a technicality—that he was not in Dallas on the day he supposedly molested the hapless press agent.[43]

The thirty-nine-year-old showman had escaped by the skin of his teeth. He was forty thousand dollars richer, but he could hardly savor the victory. In the summer of 1958, as he walked away from the Los Angeles County Courthouse, his life was a mess, his career a shambles. He was looking forward to launching his television show in the fall, but the disaster of his Australian tour that spring marred that pleasure. Meanwhile, his management crisis was going full tilt, he was turning his image upside down and inside out, and, not least, the queer issue still haunted him. He had hardly put to rest the stories of his homosexuality; indeed, they seemed to fade only with his waning popularity and declining income. All these woes and troubles found a focus in the Cassandra case that had bedeviled him since 1956.

In his memoir, Liberace makes no reference to the *Hollywood Confidential* suit. With the exception of his mention of the grotesquely head-lined "Is Liberace a Man?" he is silent on the tabloids' innuendoes. This is not the case with his suit against the London *Daily Mirror*. The Cassandra case fills the lacunas of these other episodes and happenings. Indeed, the London lawsuit is one of the themes of the memoir. While it crops up throughout the text, Liberace devoted five entire chapters (of twenty-four) to the matter—15 percent of the whole book. His treatment had its function as a public-relations ploy, but his handling suggests that the case had other meanings for him, as well. It absorbed the anxiety generated by the other, unmentionable complications that plagued his life in these years. He treats it, in any case, as a kind of turning point. Even so, it also possesses significance beyond his treatment in his text.

The *Daily Mirror* had run the Cassandra article the day after Liberace's arrival in London on September 26, 1956. With the counsel of his lawyer, John Jacobs, Liberace had decided to sue by the middle of the next month. The trial was scheduled and rescheduled—chiefly because of the showman's performance calendar—until the contending parties finally agreed to a June 1959 date. That spring, the *Queen Mary* carried Liberace to his legal rendezvous. In contrast to his memories of the pleasures of his earlier crossing, however, this time he remembered mostly his distress. His apprehensions multiplied as he arrived in London. He reconstructed his actual emotions with difficulty afterward, he said, but "plain, simple, ordinary fear is what I think I felt," he related. "I had a secret feeling I was about to get clobbered." As he described it, "I find it difficult to put into words how I felt that Monday, June 8, 1959, as I sat in an English courtroom, Queen's Bench Number Four, surrounded by black-robed, white-wigged gentlemen, and prepared to hear myself vilified, as well as defended, and waited to find out whether I'd done the right thing or the wrong one in following the insistence of my conscience and the confirmation of my attorney." [44]

Not coincidental to the case itself, Liberace was in the middle of his hiatus from glitz, and he wore an understated suit, as if to convince the court that he was normal. It brought no comfort. The courtroom also overflowed with curious and loyal fans, mostly women, including Lady Salmon, wife of the presiding judge, Sir Cyril Salmon. This was cold comfort, too. Fans could not sway the proceedings; moreover, the court had impaneled a jury of ten men and only two women. He expected little from the males. Then, too, journalists swarmed like flies to offal. Experience had taught him to hope for nothing good from this quarter. The trial confirmed his suspicions. Newspapers all over Great Britain—and the United States, too, for that matter—tarted up the most sensational elements of the trial. The first days' testimony produced such headlines as "LIBERACE CALLED THE 'SUMMIT OF SEX,'" "NEWSPAPER SUED OVER 'SUMMIT OF SEX,'" and "I'M NOT A SEX APPEAL ARTIST" from the Brits; while even the staid *New York Times* headlined its one version of the trial with "Liberace Denies He Is Homosexual." [45]

Nothing comforted him. His Australian tour had demonstrated his chauvinistic—if innocent—Americanism, and English law and custom unsettled him. He really wanted an American lawyer, and he seemed perplexed at the failure of the British court to allow John Jacobs to defend him. Moreover, the sight of his British attorney, Gilbert Beyfus, recommended by Jacobs, dismayed him. If known in London as "The Fox," Beyfus, at age seventy-six, looked to Liberace like "a toothless old lion," like a Counselor Bumble right out of Dickens. "I watched him fumbling with papers, creating an atmosphere of confusion," the pianist fretted. "He acted like a man who suddenly found himself in a perfectly strange place with grave responsibilities he knew nothing about. My heart sank. I knew then and there that I didn't have a prayer." [46]

He underestimated his counsel. Indeed, the Fox opened well by linking William Conner's diatribe against the American showman to a pattern of smearing Englishmen: his screed had besmirched even the royal family. Conner's slander of Liberace was only the tip of the iceberg that constituted this venal, reckless journalist, Beyfus proclaimed. He called Conner "a literary assassin who dips his pen in vitriol, hired by this sensational newspaper to murder reputations and hand out sensational articles on which its circulation is built."[47] It was the same charge that John Jacobs had used in suing *Hollywood Confidential* two years before. Through Liberace, the English court had the chance to redress all these transgressions. "Here's a piano player," Beyfus declaimed, "giving these people a chance to fight back."[48]

Beyfus began the proceedings proper by reading into the record the entire Cassandra article, titled "Yearn-Strength Five." "'Windstarke Fuenf' is the most deadly concoction of alcohol that the 'Haus Vaterland' can produce," William Conner—alias Cassandra—had begun.

> I have to report that Mr. Liberace, like "Windstarke Fuenf" is about the most that man can take. But he is not a drink. He is Yearning Windstrength Five. He is the summit of sex— Masculine, Feminine and Neuter. Everything that He, She and It can ever want.
>
> I have spoken to sad but kindly men on this newspaper who have met every celebrity arriving from the United States for the past thirty years. They all say that this deadly, winking, sniggering, snuggling, chromium-plated, scent-impregnated, luminous, quivering, giggling, fruit-flavored, mincing, ice-covered heap of mother love has had the biggest reception and impact on London since Charlie Chaplin arrived at the same station, Waterloo, on September 12, 1921.
>
> This appalling man—and I use the word appalling in no other than its true sense of terrifying—has hit this country in a way that is as violent as Churchill receiving the cheers on V-E Day. He reeks with emetic language that can only make grown men long for a quiet corner, an aspidistra, a handkerchief, and the old heave-ho. Without doubt, he is the biggest sentimental vomit of all time.
>
> Slobbering over his mother, winking at his brother, and counting the cash at every second, this superb piece of calculating candy-floss has an answer for every situation. Nobody since Aimee Semple McPherson has purveyed a bigger, richer and more varied slag-heap of lilac covered hokum. Nobody anywhere ever made so much money out of high speed piano playing with the ghost of Chopin gibbering at every note.
>
> There must be something wrong with us that our teen-

agers longing for sex and our middle-aged matrons fed up
with sex alike should fall for such a sugary mountain of jin-
gling claptrap wrapped up in such a preposterous clown. [49]

While the trial took many ducks and turns, one phrase in the article
dominated the proceedings from both sides. This was Conner's identification of the pianist as "the summit of sex—Masculine, Feminine and
Neuter. Everything that He, She and It can ever want." One witness testified that Conner himself assumed that the case would rotate on this axis.
According to the testimony of Dail Betty Ambler, who visited Conner's
home soon after the writ was served in October 1956, the journalist himself had brought up the case and the phrase. "He laughed about it and
said it was going to be a bit of fun," she testified. He continued that "it
was a libel for which Liberace would get a lot of money from the *Daily
Mirror.* She reported that the libel, Conner had said, lay in the 'He, She
or It' phrase." [50] If Conner could smirk about his language, it horrified the
pianist. It named the nightmares from his childhood. "I prayed I'd never
seen that, never heard it and that I'd never hear it again. That was the
passage that decided me to sue. That was the one I was afraid would haunt
me all my life." [51]

The trial did rotate on the phrase. The defendants argued that Conner
had intended it as a statement of the pianist's sex appeal in general. They
calculated all their evidence and witnesses to this end, to prove the "sexi-
ness" of Liberace's act. The plaintiffs countered this strategy by affirming the basis of Liberace's appeal to family and traditional values. They
also leapt onto the phrase's challenge to Liberace's masculinity or maleness. This actually seemed to be what Conner had in mind when he told
his visitor that the libel lay in this usage. If central to Beyfus's general
strategy, however, it was Liberace's own compelling reason for bringing
the suit in the first place. "I had put myself on the block of public opinion
in defense of one of the three most important things in a man's life . . . ,"
he testified, "perhaps all of them. They are Life itself. Manhood. And
Freedom." He elaborated: "Naturally my life, as such, was not at stake.
But the attack on me had threatened my mother's health and so, her life.
And, perhaps the quality of my life had been put in jeopardy. Certainly
my manhood had been seriously attacked and with it my freedom . . .
freedom from harassment, freedom from embarrassment and most importantly, freedom to work at my profession." [52] The issue for the pianist
could be summarized in part in his own, formal testimony when he declared, "This is the most improper article that has ever been written about
me. It has been widely quoted in all parts of the world and has been

reproduced exactly as it appeared in the *Daily Mirror.* One paper had the headline, IS LIBERACE A MAN."[53]

"Is Liberace a Man." He was citing, of course, the headline that had appeared two years before, in May 1957. It was beside the point, of course, that *Hush-Hush* had said that the British were only preparing to answer questions "which have bothered Americans for years." It was true: Americans had been voicing their curiosity about Liberace's sexuality for some time and had been discussing it in print since at least August 1954, two years before Cassandra's harangue appeared, and three years before the publication of the *Hush-Hush* headline. Well before William Conner attacked Liberace's reputation, the American media—scandal sheets and even mainstream press—had described him as a sissy, a mama's boy, and even a homosexual. The salacious article, "'Mad About the Boy,'" makes no reference to the London *Daily Mirror.* It was not necessary. American writers saw the same thing William Conner did, whether or not they knew the Englishman's piece.

Was Liberace a man? Perhaps *Hush-Hush* really got the Cassandra article better than William Conner had, himself. The idea, of course, was that Liberace was homosexual and that homosexuals were not men—not real men, not natural men—not Men. That was the issue for Liberace.

What does it mean to be a man? Was a homosexual not a man, but some "third sex," some subspecies? Did lusting after other men obviate Liberace's manhood? How, indeed, was manhood different from sex or from a man's sexual proclivity for other men? Popular culture had the answers. *Hollywood Confidential* offered the reply in the very edition that had exposed Liberace. The full-page ad for the International Correspondence School had instructed readers in what men were—and weren't. The boy striding cheerfully down the road to job, success, and money (after having completed the course on repairing appliances, of course) caricatures every element of manliness—except the purely sexual. This boy is in the process of overtaking "the genius"—the perfect representation of homosexuality, however ill disguised: the lagger represents the fop, the dandy, the aristocratically pretentious, monocled fruit, the loser posturing on the wayside toward the manly world of work, achievement, and ambition.[54]

Lee Liberace presumed the same connections. Ideologically and culturally, he defaulted to the social definitions of maleness and to the asexual identification of that category with work, achievement, control, public authority. If homosexuals were not men, according to this definition, his commitment to the public definitions of masculinity required his public repudiation of homosexuality.[55] The logic was infallible. Conner's essay, he declared, had "cost me many years of my professional career by implying that I am a homosexual. . . . It has caused untold agonies and embarrassment and has made me the subject of ridicule." [56] Twenty years later, while he had by then loosened the gendered categories, the showman still assumed an inevitable relationship between masculinity, aggression, and livelihood, on the one hand, versus homosexuality, passivity, and ineffectualness on the other. "In 1956, people were destroyed by that accusation. It hurt me. People stayed away from my shows in droves. I went from the top to the bottom in a very short time, and I had to fight for my life." [57]

The showman Liberace was not singular in associating work, competition, and success with masculinity. Nor was he eccentric, singular, or paranoid in acknowledging the threat to livelihood with charges of deviant sexuality. Beyond the aristocratic enclaves of Manhattan's Upper East Side, this was the same motive that drove many if not most gay professionals: homosexual exposure equaled professional, economic ruin. It was what prompted the actor Anthony Perkins into "deep closet maneuvers to hide the fact of his boyfriends and male lovers" even abroad, where no one recognized the *Psycho* star. "'You couldn't be too careful in those days,'" Perkins's manager, gay himself, agreed. [58] "In those days," recalled another member of this demimonde, "if you had sex with a man, that put you in a category from which you could not deviate. You were a fruitcake, and destined to be that all your life." [59] Thus, too, reminisced another gay actor: "We lived in fear of an exposé, or even one small remark, a veiled suggestion that someone was homosexual. Such a remark would have caused an earthquake at the Studio." [60] George Cukor, one of Hollywood's most famous—and barely closeted—gay men, put it another way: "In those days you had to be very virile or they thought you were degenerate." [61] Getting caught out threatened ruin. Rock Hudson's behavior mirrored Perkins's. "He always had two phone lines when he lived with someone, and made sure his roommate never answered his phone. He was careful not to be photographed with a man. On the set, if he met someone, they would exchange phone numbers with the stealth and caution of spies passing nuclear secrets. Rock would wait until one in the morning to make the call. If it was all right, he would drive to the person's house, park two blocks away, look around furtively and then run to the door." [62]

Denying one's homosexuality, then, equaled defending one's manly prerogatives of earning a living. Liberace managed it like George Cukor, Anthony Perkins, and Rock Hudson. In denying his homosexuality, he confirmed his career. Beyond this, he intended the *Daily Mirror* case to resolve the matter permanently once and for all. He had beaten *Confiden-*

tial's claims of his homosexual adventure the year before, but he had done so on a technicality—that in one, only one, of the three encounters with the handsome young press agent, he was not where the scandal sheet said he was. He wanted to kill, now and forever, the claims that he was homosexual. Far away from America, where he had "tricked around," the London courtroom offered a nearly perfect place to make his argument. He phrased it succinctly: "On my word of God, on my mother's health, which is so dear to me, this article only means one thing, that I am a homosexual, and that is why I am in this court." [63] He determined that he would use the *Daily Mirror* case to confound permanently the exposing of his private desires. Thus, it was Beyfus and Liberace who decided to make the trial hinge on homosexuality, per se.

Gerald Gardiner, the *Mirror*'s counselor, actually objected to the plaintiff's introduction of the issue. "There is no suggestion and never has been anything of the kind," Gardiner remonstrated when Beyfus first raised the matter of homosexuality on the trial's first day. Indeed, Gardiner dismissed the issue as a red herring, or worse. The performer, he sniffed, "had a bee in his bonnet" about the issue. The plaintiff insisted on the argument. The pianist himself testified for six hours in two days of testimony, and early on in the questioning Beyfus charged into the breach of his sexual identity and preference, despite the defense's protests. "Are you a homosexual?" Beyfus queried him. "No, sir," the pianist replied simply. He did not leave the issue at that. Beyfus continued the line of questioning. "Have you ever indulged in homosexual practices?" Again, the showman answered simply and directly: "No, sir, never in my life." He did not stop even there. On he plunged. "I am against the practice because it offends convention and it offends society," he finished. [64]

The plaintiff lied. The question remains, however, what to do with his deception. One position holds him completely culpable, and suggests that his lying while giving sworn testimony, is, effectively, a mark of the larger and more profound hoaxes of his life and career. This argument, perhaps paradoxically, finds its most aggressive proponents among late-twentieth-century gay progressives. It condemns Liberace himself more eagerly than does the specific lie he told. Thus, argues David Ehrenstein, "to anyone familiar with Liberace, Cassandra's remarks would appear to be perfectly fair comment." He continues:

> Liberace's act centered on a display of blatantly "effeminate" mannerisms that stood in polar opposition to the (equally ostentatious) "masculinity" of a John Wayne. Liberace knew exactly what he was doing: just how far to go. His every word

and gesture was crafted to raise the question of his sexual
identity in the minds of his adoring fans, only to stave off
their actually bringing it up in earnest at the last minute. . . .
His only "offense" would pertain to taste—which was in fact
the heart of the "Cassandra" broadside.

To imply that Liberace might be anything other than heterosexual, it was argued, was damaging on its face—notwithstanding the fact that Liberace's entire performing persona
ceaselessly exploited the notion that he might be other than
heterosexual.[65]

This position does not exhaust the explanations of the lie. Thus, another argument holds that the very structuring of homosexuality within a
heterosexual world distorts or reforms the very nature of truth for gays.
Marcel Proust introduces the idea. "The lie, the perfect lie, about people
we know, about the relations we have had with them, about our motives
for some action, formulated in totally different terms, the lie as to what
we are, whom we love, what we feel with regard to people who love us . . .
—that lie is one of the few things in the world that can open windows for
us on to what is new and unknown, that can awaken in us sleeping senses
for the contemplation of universes that otherwise we should never have
known."[66] Michel Foucault describes something of the same idea, with
greater passion. "To call homosexuals liars is equivalent to calling the re-
sistors under a military occupation liars," he said. "It's like calling Jews
'money lenders,' when it was the only profession they were allowed to
practice."[67] If a philosophical or epistemological issue in this treatment, it
has a practical side as well: the world's prejudice against homosexuality
costs money. Liberace himself believed that the allegations about his homosexuality produced the decline in his popularity, status, and income.In
this circumstance, then, he lied the way gay men have most often prevari-
cated to defend themselves.

There is still a third way of understanding his deception. Liberace
lied. He lied outright. But, paradoxically, he told the truth as well, if not
exactly as Proust, much less Foucault, might have predicted he would.
While he lied about having sex with other men, he did respect convention,
and he did honor social mores. If cavaliers and peasants might have frol-
icked with other men for hundreds of years, bourgeois morality, from the
nineteenth century especially, coupled with powerful Christian biases, put
men and boys like Walter Liberace in a very tight spot. How might one
respect convention and traditional mores on the one hand, and, on the
other, honor one's own sexual instincts and affectional preferences as a

gay male? What happened when those very proclivities violated semi-sacred social norms? Another way of framing the question: Is it possible for a man to believe in traditional social norms and conventional sexuality—as Liberace testified that he did—and still have sex with other men? The easiest answers might be the best. Perhaps the solution is either to share Foucault's notion that "compulsory heterosexuality" forces dishonesty among gay men, or to concede that Liberace indulged in practical, predictable, self-defense and self-serving hypocrisy, whether justified or not. There is another solution to the conundrum, however, though it is rather more complicated.

What would it mean to believe genuinely in conventional mores on the one hand and to practice homosexual activity on the other? Phrased a little differently, what would it mean to be a public conservative and a private radical? To be so suggests, most critically, a profound separation between public and private. The former, defined by law, is literally legitimate and thereby real, even as logic necessitates definitions of illegitimacy and the ephemeral for the latter. By this measure, sex unrecognized by law is insubstantial and transient—in short, unreal. Insofar as the law—customary, legal, and religious—defines sexuality as a function of public life in the production and maintenance of families, and families with the actual and social reproduction of itself, any sex outside of this structure is ephemeral, without public consequence. Thus, a "bastard," strictly speaking is illegitimate spawn, an illegitimate child, one who does not exist in law insofar as it is unacknowledged by the father. Sexual relations outside legally sanctified marriage work the same way: not existing in the law, they lack substance and, in short, reality of themselves. The rule applies, theoretically at least, to extramarital—extralegal—sexual coupling, whether of a man with a not-wife woman or a not-wife man. The meaning? In this context, only marital, legally sanctioned sex is real. Beyond the law, other forms and expressions of sex lack formal authenticity; they lack, just the same, formal public vocabulary even for discussion. By this definition, a gay man—Liberace—might frolic with other men privately and secretly, precisely because such activity lacks social sanction.

Given the judicial presumption of the state to intervene in the bedchambers of gay men, where it would not presume to invade the sanctity of the bedrooms of traditional families, this position is not without gravest difficulty for homosexuals.[68] Beyond this, other problems plague the stance. For one thing, such conservative values, otherwise defined, run completely counter to the modern temper. Since the eighteenth century, Western thought has celebrated the idea that reality resides not in the social, legal, or conventional order but rather in the individual unit of society. One manifestation of this value appears in the American Declaration of Independence, with its proudly unsubstantiated assertion—the "self-evident truths"—that "all men are created equal and endowed by their Creator with certain unalienable rights." According to this notion, rights do not come not from law, society, religion, family, or other social institutions, but they rather adhere within our very existence. It makes the individual atoms of the social order the source and repository of all virtue. Thomas Jefferson, no less than John Locke or Adam Smith, judged that if left to their own devices, these virtuous individuals make a naturally harmonious order; they assumed, just so, that the public sphere—politics—is a logical, progressive expression of this harmony. Jefferson and Locke, perhaps drawing on the political capital of previous times, supposed that mankind defaulted to order and reason rather than to sexuality, desire, and passion. Insofar as appetites, sexual appetites, and plain old ordinary lust drive personal ambition, Jefferson and the theorists misjudged the man. Thus, while the author of the Declaration of Independence himself rejected any discussion of his private sexual life as an unnatural deviation from rational, political discourse, it is altogether natural, fitting even, that the twentieth century trumps his political engagement with an illicit sexual liaison with a slave woman, his African-American sister-in-law, Sally Hemmings. In effect, the sexualization of both the ends and the means of politics follows naturally from Jeffersonian assumptions.

This shift to the personal possesses the most powerful political implications. The politicization of the personal and domestic, for example, alters the very definitions of the public and political. Thus, if the Declaration of Independence gets it one way, Jean-Jacques Rousseau gets it another, when in his *Confessions* he advertises his need to be beaten before he could be aroused sexually. His private sexuality, otherwise defined, becomes a notable part of his individualism, his natural rights, effectively. His individualism, in turn, is public and political of its nature. Publicizing personal sexuality, Rousseau legitimized the discussion of sexuality, which almost by definition becomes whimsical or deviant sexuality. Thus, the subject of public discourse changes even as the same process foreshadows the alteration in the process of discourse as well: the means growing as overheated as the end.[69] As Western society has redefined public life, however, it has made corresponding alterations in private life. As the distinctions collapse between what is ostensibly public and private, the defenses of the more purely personal disintegrates, too. In short, no activities can be rightly termed completely private any more, if indeed they ever were.

Like issues of sex and gender roles, questions of public and private help define public debate as the twenty-first century opens. The gay community itself mirrors the contradictions and paradoxes of the discourse. In the argument that the state has no purview over personal, sexual activity, one category upholds old distinctions between public and private. Another insists on the artificiality of this polarity itself as an invention of a powerful, manipulative state or social order, and deflects to the destruction of the state and traditional laws.[70]

Although capable of a consistent aesthetic and a coherent social and psychological world view, Liberace himself made no pretense to being a thinker, systematic or otherwise. Philosophical discussions of gender, political treatises on privacy, and historical analyses of power would have baffled him. If he had never read a single political tract in his life, however, he possessed a clear sense of what virtue entailed. For all his giddy public shenanigans and private indulgences, he was intensely conservative, even reactionary. This provides, then, a context for understanding his denial of his own homosexual activity. Such activity was simply not real. He preferred 1750 to 1950, and for all his innumerable debts to modernity—for his very fame, indeed, celebrity itself—public disclosure of an inner life was incomprehensible to him. So, in an odd way, he told the truth even as he lied as he issued his testimony in a British courtroom in the late spring of 1959.[71]

The jury of ten men and two women found in his favor on June 18. He won twenty-two thousand dollars, and the defendants were required to pay court costs as well. This constituted the largest settlement of any libel case in British history. It was the very verdict that Oscar Wilde had sought two generations before, and on similar grounds. Wilde had lied as flagrantly as Liberace, of course, but Wilde lost. The American entertainer redeemed that judgment. And, the showman determined, his name was cleared. Publicly and officially, he could proceed with his life. He won more than the specific verdict, too. The case proved that he would go to very great lengths indeed to fight charges of sexual deviancy. His will was obdurate and his pockets deep, as his contentious ex-lover would discover twenty-five years later.

While his willingness to resort to litigation chilled discussion of his sexuality, the American press, almost inadvertently, joined the campaign as well. David Ehrenstein has chronicled journalists' complicity in a conspiracy of silence about homosexuality before the seventies, even after. If homosexuality did not know what to call itself, the straight world hardly knew what to call it, beyond epithets, either. Namelessness actually protected gay men on the prowl in Liberace's time. The discussion of sex, and especially of illicit sex, was the stuff of scandalmongers, but Ehrenstein has also allowed as how even the scandal rags hardly knew what to do with the topic. The exposé that outed Liberace in 1957 was anomalous. "In fact, for all their supposed sophistication," wrote Ehrenstein, "the 'scandal' rags were painfully naïve when it came to same-sex matters, running such decidedly unshocking stuff as 'Whoops! Why Those Gay Boys Just Love Bette, Joan, Tallulah and Judy!' in the July 1964 issue of *Inside Story*." [72] Mainstream media demonstrated some of the same obscurity in regard to the Cassandra trial. While some papers, notably the *New York Times,* headlined the plaintiff's formal assertion—"Liberace denies he is homosexual," [73]—most avoided the specific terminology. The majority of broadcasters rejected the term in describing the case. Critics noted that two New York City stations employed the word "homosexual," but that most newsmen resorted to euphemisms. [74]

Publicly and officially, Liberace was not a homosexual. Privately, he continued the pattern that had characterized his life for close to twenty years. That pattern, however, like his testimony to the British court, was full of contradictions and impossibilities. He was a man who indulged in homosexual activity. He had lied. He had taken part in sex with men. He had, in truth, enjoyed a great deal of sex with a great many men.

Evidence for sexual activity is hard to come by, especially in the case of a man like Liberace who fetished concealment, devalued gay culture, and who—rightly—considered his "deviancy" a Damoclean sword over his career. Just so, gay fraternal oaths of silence prove more obdurate than the secret codes of Masons. The paucity of data has led some to confirm the performer's own denials of homosexuality. His first biographer interviewed a number of men who knew him well from his early television days, and they offered no evidence of his sexual inversion. "Duke Goldstone, who directed Liberace for long hours daily and traveled across the country with him, saw nothing. Nor did Paul Weston, who worked intimately with Liberace on record albums. There were no willowy young men in his entourage, nothing like that. Everyone simply thought he was a mama's boy." In the absence of "willowy young men"—sissies, flits, and queens, otherwise defined—in his entourage, Bob Thomas concludes that Liberace was merely "confused about his sexual identity" and that he "suppressed the homosexual side of his nature." [75] He misjudged.

The Federal Bureau of Investigation knew better. Thus, the agency kept a file on the showman entitled "compromise and extortion of homosexuals." [76] Scott Thorson knew better, too. Liberace's companion of five years, Thorson memorialized the performer's own recollections of his early sexuality, and *Behind the Candelabra* offers a logical starting place for reconstructing the showman's earliest homosexual history. Underlining his sense of privacy or secrecy even with his lover is the fact that Liberace disliked speaking of the past and even hushed those who did so in the younger man's presence. He did repeat the story, however, of his first lover, the remarkable episode with the Green Bay Packers lineman. The showman also revealed that even while dating Joanne Rio publicly, "he continued to have secret dates with young men." [77] If mostly without reference to specifics, Liberace also revealed how he lived before his fame. In the early days, he told Thorson, "no one had ever questioned his sexual preference. It had never been an issue as long as he didn't flaunt his lifestyle," remembered the young lover. He wasn't scaring horses. "He'd been able to quietly patronize known homosexual bars and clubs without attracting undue attention. In the gay vernacular, he'd 'tricked around' with a series of lovers, many of them struggling performers, too. After ten years on the circuit, he was familiar with gay hangouts in every city where he appeared—and he had frequented them all." [78] Fame altered this pattern, constricted his freedom, and forced new arrangements on the performer.

According to Thorson, again, Liberace now indulged his sexual appetites through an extensive network of gay friends, several of whom worked on his staff. These men assisted in the performer's assignations. Liberace arranged these encounters, in Thorson's telling, in a North Hollywood apartment near the Valley Vista house. "Lee's closest associates were gay men who worked for him. When Lee needed companionship or a sexual encounter he called men he knew and trusted. In turn they'd call a friend, or a friend of a friend, until they found someone who could deliver the kind of kid that appealed to Lee. Then a meeting would be arranged. For Lee, it was as easy as snapping his fingers, and almost as risk free." [79]

While this essentially describes the way Thorson himself found his way into the master bedroom, one even earlier account confirms the norm. As a young street hustler, the writer John Rechy encountered the showman under identical circumstances. It was the late fifties; Lee still made his home at the piano-pool house in the valley. Rechy knew a couple of Liberace's former boyfriends. They invited him to dinner with the performer. "I didn't realize," Rechy related, "that I was being offered to him by my hosts." [80]

There were other men, and many other ways of getting them. While his patron spoke reluctantly, if at all, about his old loves, Thorson had gotten wind of some of them. Thus, for example, he treats the rumor of the romance between his boyfriend and that other most famous closeted gay star, Rock Hudson. He dismisses it. Rock wasn't Lee's type, he sniffs. They were too much alike, he insists.

> Most important, they both had giant egos; they were stars and the rest of the world (friends, lovers, family) damn well better not forget it. That alone would have negated any possibility of those two having a relationship. Men like that cannot tolerate equals. Had Lee and Rock actually met, I think they would have disliked each other on sight. They were much too much alike to fulfill each other's needs and too egocentric to want to try. Such an encounter would have been more the clash of rutting stags than the true meeting of minds. In the years we were together, Lee never mentioned knowing Rock. . . . The two men moved in completely different circles, socially and professionally.[81]

Thorson's incredulity notwithstanding, such an affair did occur, by Rock Hudson's own admission. Hudson, along with John Rechy and Thorson himself, was an exception to the generally rigorous homosexual rule of kiss, don't tell.

Hudson had revealed the circumstances of the affair to Boze Hadleigh, a Hollywood writer and the author of *Conversations with My Elders,* interviews with six gay or bisexual men in the film industry, of which Hudson was one. Hadleigh omitted the Liberace revelation from his text because he refused to "out" anyone against their will. Liberace died on February 4, 1987; two days later, newspapers carried the news of the sexual liaison between the two celebrities.[82] In a second book on homosexuality in Hollywood in 1996, *Hollywood Gays,* Hadleigh returned to the Hudson affair, this time discussing it at greater length.[83] Interviewing the movie star, Hadleigh related how Hudson had first alluded to the affair. Incredulous, the writer asked for details. Hudson described the liaison. "It was just a few weeks—a fling, fun while it lasted," said Hudson. "Lee was very patronizing. A kind man, generous, and we shared an interest in classical music. His piano-playing knocked me out. But he was quite patronizing even then, and he treated everybody like his protégé."[84]

What Hudson told Hadleigh offers a new take on both men, even as it illuminates obscure corners of homosexual culture in the fifties. Protesting rumors of the affair, Scott Thorson had objected that Hudson was not Lee's type, nor vice versa. Hudson liked "handsome younger hunks. Preferably blond ones."[85] Thorson defines something of the same type, if younger perhaps, for Lee. Liberace and Hudson, then, were each very far from the other's supposed ideal. What of that? One closeted Hollywood publicist considered the "type problem" minor. For Hudson, he judged, the default was not to type but to power. Rock, he insisted, "was something of a groupie. He'd go to bed with big names, or try to. Especially when he first arrived in Hollywood and was chasing after his idols Jon Hall and Errol Flynn."[86] There is another answer to the problem, too: typing is not particularly relevant to pickup or casual sex. Fragmentary evidence suggests that this was a form of sex, too, that fit Liberace's taste, in particular. According to the recollections of "Rick Shaw," who idolized Liberace but went to bed with Hudson, the tall, dark movie star was not rigid on this issue, either.

Thorson also speculated that the two could not have been lovers because of their mutually vaulting egos. "They were much too much alike to fulfill each other's needs and too egocentric to want to try," Thorson insisted. Hadleigh's evidence suggests, however, that the two men's needs were rather more primitive than intellectual or spiritual communion. At the same time, Thorson did come close to something in discussing the two men's egos. If ego did not keep the two apart, it hastened, by Hudson's own reckoning, their separation. Twice in his short recollection, Hudson referred to the pianist as patronizing—one manifestation of the ego Thorson noted. At the time of their affair, in the very early fifties, Hudson remained only a contract actor, playing roles like that of *Taza, Son of Cochise* and spouting such deathless lines as "Taza will build Una's wikiup." He was not yet the star of *Magnificent Obsession,* much less the megastar of *Giant* (1956) and *Pillow Talk* (1959). If his ambition was no less vaulting in 1953 than it would be in '56 or '59—and, one might add, no less grandiose than Liberace's at any time—he had little basis for boasting earlier. He was not, in effect, the piano player's equal when they trysted, probably in 1952 or 1953. They may or may not have met like stags in heat, but, clearly, Thorson's notions of Liberace's ego corresponds to Hudson's description of the showman as "patronizing."[87]

This raises another point. Liberace left no evidence of preferring equals as sexual partners. Hudson, for example, wound up with Tom Clark, a professional man roughly his own age, and his other companions often had comparable claims to professional or at least middle-class status. No one like this appears among Liberace's old paramours. On the contrary, the stories are of cruising Mexican boys on Sunset Boulevard, picking up weightlifters, or taking on young people out of a chorus line, or in the case of Thorson himself and his successor, Cary James, latching onto unsteady teenagers. Liberace preferred inequality. This was not, incidentally, unusual. Serial flings with handsome young men more or less of the lower orders also characterized George Cukor's sexual habits. John Rechy chronicled a couple of such men in *City of Night,* and elaborated on the picture in other writings and interviews.[88] Not coincidentally, either, Cukor auditioned potential boyfriends much in the same way Liberace did.[89] Beyond the definition of the showman's ego and his sexual tastes—and the fact that Liberace had sex with Rock Hudson—what do these revelations demonstrate? They suggest something about the nature of sexual affairs between men in general, for one thing, and about Liberace's affections, in particular: that neither the showman nor, for that matter, Rock Hudson, stuck to types; that "a meeting of minds" is not critical when two randy men turn each other on. Indeed, the absence of natural compatibility can even encourage and intensify a relationship, even as it dooms it, too. The image of stags in heat takes on a new light in this context.

The Hadleigh interview coupled with Thorson's recollection suggests still other things about Liberace's private life. Even though Thorson affirms repeatedly his lover's instinct toward concealment and dissembling, he still insists that he would have known of the liaison had it actually occurred. Liberace's faithful servant Gladys Luckie used the same justification for rejecting the tale. The showman could not have been that closed, they assume, that secretive. Evidence suggests their error. In effect, then, for all the length and intimacy of the Thorson-Liberace relationship and for all Thorson's awareness of Liberace's character, the younger man still underestimated the showman's secrecy. As a young, handsome man who matured after Stonewall, perhaps Scott Thorson was incapable of conversing with his elders—and vice versa, of course—about the strictures and standards of homosexuality when Rock Hudson and Liberace were young. He lived in a different social order. A later generation of young gays had less desire or need for camouflage and concealment. That was simply not the case before the Stonewall riot. In this regard, Hadleigh's interview reveals still another side of the generational demand for masks and pretense. Thus, when Hadleigh asked Hudson about his relation with the piano player after their affair, he replied: "We're on good terms but not friends. For instance, if I went to one of his concerts or he came to see me in a play I'm doing, people might talk. Certainly it would be noticed."[90] Feed no new rumors. Bar the closet door. These defined the assumptions of the Hollywood gay world.It was just as Rechy described Cukor, "Beyond that circle of friends, Cukor was incredibly closeted. Of course everybody *knew.* But that was another kind of closetry, because he kept the two worlds so separate."[91] It was the open secret.

And other significance of the Hudson-Liberace liaison? If other evidence were necessary, finally, Boze Hadleigh's interview with Rock Hudson affirms that Liberace indulged in sex with other men. Other fragmentary evidence confirms the fact as well.

One critical fragment comes from the Liberace family itself. It relates not only to homosexuality, but to the complex of difficulties the entertainer experienced in the mid-fifties. It begins with the violent separation of the two elder Liberace brothers. Their conflict underlines the depth of the piano player's crises as the fifties wore down, and the way his career crises intertwined with family, personal, and even legal crises.

On December 3, 1957, the *Las Vegas Review-Journal* printed an obscure notice stating that the two brothers had split.[92] With benign references to their desire to pursue their own career goals, the notice resembled the innocuous explanations for the disruption of celebrity marriages. As in those cases, the blandness of the announcement masked the depth of the major players' animosity. Thus, missing from the public announcement was the showman's expulsion of his brother from his business enterprise. In 1954, when Liberace had incorporated himself as International Artists, Ltd., he had made George one of the three stockholders, and had given him twenty-seven of the one hundred shares issued. In 1957, he redeemed all these, simultaneously eliminating his brother from his inner circle and cutting him off financially.[93]

They stopped speaking. Telltale references in the press in the next year bear testament to the ill will that characterized their separation. On his television show, which had begun that fall, the showman had made an offhand remark about his brother going into the pizza business. His sibling had gone into the business and was trading on the Liberace name with his restaurant, "Liberace's by George."[94] George bristled: "Everybody knows that I am no longer with my brother. But let it not be said I make my living selling pizza pies. Music is my life and shall always be." From his new residence in Palm Springs, the showman patronized his older brother right back. "George left me of his own volition. I wish him all the success in the world and I am happy he is doing so well. I am sorry about the pizzas," he added, "but I thought George was still in that business. By the way, I ate some and they were good." Even their mother was drawn into the maelstrom. The rumor circulated that she had locked her son out of his own house on Valley Vista. She denied it. She did volunteer, however, that she was boycotting his shows and refused even to watch his daytime television program. "I love both my boys," she told a reporter. "They have both been wonderful to me. But I cannot watch either until they are back together again."[95] Contributing to the family's disorder, also, was the death of Rudy, the youngest, most beautiful, and most ill fated of the Liberace sons who had literally drunk himself to death in a sleazy motel on April 30, 1957. He was only twenty-six.[96]

The split was extraordinary. In the first place, professionally, George Liberace had been his brother's strong right arm since they had exchanged clothes and performed together at Sam Pick's Club Madrid in Milwaukee almost twenty-five years before. Second, it violated the entertainer's deepest commitments to family and domestic harmony; such values had been a constant in his life. Third, it reflected a revolution in his professional career, as his brother and mother had been a critical component of his public image. Was he scorning the candelabra? The piano-shaped swimming pool? The gold lamé jackets, sheared beaver coats, and sequins? He also jettisoned his family props. He sacked his brother. He eliminated him in the same way he had eliminated his father and other unpleasantness from his life. Although the entertainer dwelt at considerable length on the rupture of his relations with Heller—including his eating crow and taking his old manager back by 1961—his memoirs ignore completely the break with George. At that writing, in 1973, the two remained unreconciled. Only later in the decade did they make peace and establish an unsteady truce. As late as 1977, without any knowledge of the earlier feud, Scott Thorson chronicled the distance that still separated the two men. While Lee groused about his brother taking advantage of him, otherwise, "the brothers treated each other with a distant, uncomfortable politeness."[97]

The breach was as private as it was wide. The memoirs' silences suggest its involvement with literally "unspeakable" things. Mrs. Casadonte herself suggested what things. The source loops back to "Mad About the Boy."

On October 23, 1958, when Frances Liberace Casadonte had gone public with her family's domestic dissension, she had noted that her showman son no longer made his home with her on Valley Vista. He only visited at the Sherman Oaks house. She explained: "Lee lives in Palm Springs most of the time surrounded by a gang of what I call hillbillies and freeloaders." She did not identify these rowdies, but she insisted that they were mostly responsible for the breakup with George. "Lee is too trusting. He doesn't know who his true friends are," she concluded.[98] Lee had found new associates. Palm Springs was where he felt free to entertain them. It had become his retreat from work, from family, and from traditional sexual mores, too. "Hillbillies and freeloaders"? They were the saucy young men and the trade of Lee's cruising, the "hooligans" of Quentin Crisp's comparably named British ideal.

By 1950, Liberace had moved his mother to Camellia Street to live with him. He was just thirty-one. Her scruples—not to mention his own—prohibited his bringing dates home with her there. While casual "public" sex might have solved a part of the problem, he found another solution, he told Scott Thorson, in maintaining the separate apartment in North Hollywood. His mother never suspected, he said. "Although he tried to keep his homosexuality completely hidden from her, other members of the family told me he used the apartment a lot," recollected Thorson.[99]

With the exaggeration of his fame after 1952 and the move to the piano-pool house in 1953, the complications of his personal life multiplied. The presence of his mother, all his siblings, and all his siblings' children in the neighborhood cramped his freedom, too. The apartment solution to his private desires seemed less tenable even as he discovered Palm Springs.

Palm Springs lies about 120 miles east of Los Angeles. Although still served by rail in the fifties, the automobile trip was already becoming standard. While only two or three hours separated the desert resort from bustling downtown Los Angeles, the barren desert that lay between them made the distance seem more than geographical or chronological. Everything about the place suggested a different world. The origins of the town lay in the water that separated it from the surrounding badlands, and the oasis previewed itself to drivers on the highway in the tall, spiky, lollipop-like Washingtonian palms that became visible down the road. Otherwise, the town sprang from nowhere in the wasteland. Dead flat, the desert floor beyond the springs sprouted inhospitable mountain ranges more forbidding than the desert itself, yet their red-brown hues against the painful blue of the moistureless sky were awesome, too. With all these contrasts, the place, no chiaroscuro, was strikingly theatrical, stunningly dramatic. It was a Liberacean setting.

It was an oasis, but it offered more than geographical sanctuary to its denizens.[100] Controlled by the rich and powerful and catering to celebrities desiring to obscure their celebrity for a time, the town provided a respite from stardom and the vigilance of the public media. A contemporary refugee here, the old superstar Loretta Young summarized the motive that has characterized the residents for almost three quarters of a century. It is a "personal little haven," she reflected. "You can do whatever you want to do, if you want to do it. Or you don't have to do it if you don't want to do it. And they really don't squash you the way they do in Beverly Hills." [101] It was the perfect asylum for indulgence. "Palm Springs is the most boring place on the face of the earth. There is *nothing* to do except to live comfortably and to seek your own pleasure," observed a modern resident of the community. Others were explicit about the nature of that pleasure: "What did people come out here to do? They came out here to drink, to lie in the sun and fuck each other crazy. It was all about hedonism." [102]

It was—and is—also a happy homo-hunting ground. Angelenos of a certain persuasion "would go to Big Bear or Laguna or Lake Tahoe, or Palm Springs," according to Harry Hays, to look for men. "They were all 'getaways' for a time, but some of them—like Palm Springs—became too obvious." [103] Very little was too obvious for the fancy pianist. Palm Springs looked different. It felt different. It both encouraged and ignored difference. The showman loved it on first encounter.

Duke Goldstone, the director of *The Liberace Show*, had introduced the performer to the Springs probably in the summer of 1953. [104] He related that the owner of the Lone Palm Hotel had closed his lodgings for the summer, given the keys to Goldstone, and invited him to use the place at his leisure. Goldstone and his wife had then driven the performer to the desert and put up in the empty hotel in the almost-deserted town, which enchanted the star. Immediately, he determined to have a residence there. [105]

He bought first the house at 1441 North Kaweah Road. [106] As was his wont, he decorated and remodeled, so that one visitor, years later, could refer to it as "a little jewel." [107] He restyled the place after a French Country house, with some major modifications. Thus, while the place boasted a Louis XIV room and another in French Provincial style, it also contained an Olympic-sized swimming pool connected to the living room, in whose center burbled a fountain. [108] In another pattern that characterized his later life, he also began buying up nearby houses, making a kind of compound. By the mid-sixties, he owned almost a neighborhood of four or five dwellings.

As the decade turned, he determined to change the site of his Palm Springs compound. Not far from the Kaweah house, he discovered an abandoned inn that delighted him. "The Cloisters," he explained, "was an exclusive, small hotel, built almost like a monastery with high walls and lovely sequestered gardens surrounding it." Built in "Spanish-Mexican" style, the place in the mid-sixties sat on a large, palm-filled tract of gardens, with patios and a pool. It had been intended as a hideaway for Hollywood celebrities, but had attracted none and had been effectively

abandoned. It was desolate when Liberace decided to buy around 1967.[109]
The owners asked $210,000, but they took $25,000 less; "he considered it
too cheap to pass up," one friend remarked. He then spent $136,000 to fix
it up. He celebrated New Year's Eve there for the first time in 1968 with a
coterie of gay friends and coworkers, according to one of them, his old
associate Jamie James.[110]

The bougainvillea-crowned, head-high walls of the Cloisters provided
the privacy the piano-playing entertainer needed to live the life he chose,
protected from publicity by the town itself, with its own conspiracies of
silence, and from his family by distance and the desert. He loved the
place. In the most paradoxical ways, it embodied his own conflicting views
of life and virtue. Although the house lay just across an open lot from Our
Lady of Solitude—where his sister and mother attended mass when in
residence—he clung to the place as much as anything because of the
chapel and shrine he created within the Cloisters. Yet, even so, he used
and intended the house as a homosexual retreat, and furnished the place
accordingly.

The Cloisters was Casa Liberace. It is where he chose to die. He did
his share of living here as well, and he lived as intensely as he performed,
even if only echoes of that life survive. Silence persists almost fifty years
after Liberace first moved to the Palms, and over a decade after his death
in the huge master bedroom at the back of the house. However faint,
those echoes suggest the meaning of Casa Liberace for the performer,
and, before he bought it, of Palm Springs in the fifties and sixties.

The present owner of the mansion has maintained Liberace's touches
after a decade. The archaic Greek-inspired wallpaper depicting amorous
men survives; so does the shower curtain, with its humorous takeoff on
that icon of gay culture, Michelangelo's monumental sculpture of David.
In this version, the image is doubled, so as to create the illusion of two
identical figures holding hands. It is not a straight man's bathroom.

The voices of the rowdy times sound elsewhere. Liberace gave great
parties even at the Kaweah house. One young man had driven in from San
Francisco in the mid-sixties with friends—men the likes of which Frances
Casadonte dismissed as "freeloaders and hillbillies." The entertainer was
treating the crowd to a sumptuous brunch when the very handsome young
man from San Francisco caught his eye. The visitor was not a hillbilly but
a cultivated Swede on his way to making an American fortune. "Although
I understood he liked younger men, at the time I could have passed for an
adolescent; I looked ten years younger than I was," the man recollected.
The entertainer invited him to stay, they spent the weekend together, the
young man returned home, and that was that. After the homoerotic fash-

ion, they indulged in decent talk, had friendly sex, parted amicably, and never saw each other again.[111]

Other sources confirm the patterns of Liberace's homoerotic life in Palm Springs. In *Sexual Outlaw,* John Rechy describes being picked up by "a famous star," and receiving an invitation to a Palm Springs "white party," in exchange for agreeing to go to bed with the celebrity. He identifies this "star" elsewhere as Liberace himself.[112] He had not wanted to stay, but "what the hell," he mused. The invitation to the Palm Springs party was soon forthcoming. He attended and left a striking record of the party that followed at Liberace's Kaweah Street compound.

> I wear a white-bloused, see-through open Cavalier shirt, white boots, and pants with two rows of buttons in front.
>
> A greenhouse with exotic flowers. Listen to the delicate water spray, like kisses. Oh, a brook! And alcoves. Look! a large swaying hammock. And minstrels in white, playing flutes.
>
> Men and boys in white jockstraps wander along the multi-leveled gardens. A man turns up in tennis drag. Men sit along the tiered ledges watching the parade.
>
> A few women idle about, ignored. There's a sultan in see-through pants. There's a man in white ballet tights, genitals exposed. A dazed-looking young man with a very bad complexion and wearing nothing but crossed belts on his skinny body wanders aimlessly.
>
> I think suddenly of a dull, white purgatory.
>
> Over a hundred guests in white.
>
> A producer arrives with harnessed "slaves." There's appreciative applause from the tiers.
>
> "It's lovely. Lovely. So innocent," says a man standing benignly on a balcony like a voyeuristic high priest.[113]

Decades later, as the showman himself lay dying, another man recalled similar affairs and more. "He once held great parties in his home, and regularly frequented a popular gay bar in Palm Springs. He would often make a grand entrance late in the evening, surrounded by a group of male friends and looking splendid in extravagant outfits and heavy makeup and an incredible array of jewelry."[114]

Jamie James, Lee's longtime publicist, also sounded other memories of these days. A consultant for one of the television movies made about the showman after his death, he was responsible for some of the homoerotic scenes in the film, the reality of which he had shared. There were the gay spas in the Springs, like "the famous Chi Chi Club (which Jamie James remembers Liberace once had the wild impulse to buy as a lark, as a place for him and his boys to frolic and 'play for free')." The pretty boys came and went up Palm Canyon Drive. They caroused at Ruby's Dunes, "even in the produce aisles of the local supermarkets." [115]

Such goings on might have prompted some eyes to roll, but more conventional citizens had their own secrets; they cultivated privacy for their own reasons. The oasis village had nothing to gain by outing him. Thus, even traditional folk participated in the conspiracy of silence of the gay fraternity. He thrived in Palm Springs. The community gave him time and space to do what he wanted in a way he had not been able to before. It was this that put him at odds with his brother. George seems to have counseled him about the inappropriateness of this behavior at the very moment that Liberace was making public claims against his homosexuality. [116] George got it wrong. George got expelled. The star determined he would have it both ways. He lived the life he chose, he fought the gossips, he sued his detractors, he jettisoned his brother. Not least, he fought to regain his popularity with the folks. He would have it all.

His skill at steaming up an audience, slowing it down and sending it jumping again is surer than it was years ago. He simply holds them in the hollow of his dexterous hands and knows it. He obviously likes to play for them, clown for them and dress up in outlandish formal ensembles for them.

Variety

Ten

GETTING BACK

Jack Paar was the first of the great late-evening television talk-show hosts, and he set a high standard for his successors like Johnny Carson and David Letterman to maintain. His broadcast on the evening of November 23, 1963, typified the wit and variety of his programming. That evening he was interviewing Liberace. It was not really an interview, of course, but bantering between two men: Paar in his conservative suit and tie, Lee in his spangly dinner jacket, which he described as "Hart, Shaeffner, and Cartier." The buttons spelled out his name in diamonds. One of Paar's favorite guests, the showman had appeared numerous times on *The Tonight Show*. This evening, the television host suggested why he liked Liberace: it was because of the entertainer's rapid-fire repartee. "I won't ad lib with you," Paar laughed. "You're too fast!"

For over twenty years, the showman had been squelching hecklers, converting skeptics, and re-delighting old fans with his wit, and people came to hear his banter as much as his music. He was perhaps even better at the former than the latter. He was very funny, and this appearance with Paar demonstrated the pianist's mastery. Indeed, Paar was hardly more than a straight man to Liberace's comic that night. "When you are out and people recognize you, do you get much reaction?" inquired the talk-show host. And, in a voice best described as purring, the entertainer smiled coyly and replied: "Oh yes, it takes courage to come up to me, and they will say, 'Are you . . . or aren't you . . . ?'" With his calculated pauses and fey manner, the performer had his host and the audience in stitches with the sly humor, double entendre, and self-mocking mode of phrasing the question "Are you . . . [Liberace/gay]?" Just so, he could make comparable jokes about Judy Garland, the greatest icon—then and later—of gay culture in America.

While his jokes with Paar bordered on the cute, his irony and self-mocking tone generally saved them from being precious. And, even when he verged on the saccharine, he projected such warmth, sincerity, and affection that he managed to carry off the performance. Although he succeeded with the sophisticated, urbane Jack Paar, he could perform equally well with other types entirely. With Zsa Zsa Gabor, he repeated his routine—perfected and practiced for over two decades of club work—of giving piano lessons. He used the exact same jokes: "Closer," he told her, and when she squeezed nearer to him, he replied, "No, your hands." One more time, in the thousands upon thousands of repetitions, Gabor and Paar cracked up, and the audience guffawed.

The same evening on which Paar challenged him with being too fast for comfort, the talk-show host also interviewed the young and audacious world heavyweight boxing champion Cassius Clay. The two performers—both of them brimming with old-style American optimism, innocence, and vim, in those days before Vietnam, Muhammad Ali, tanks in downtown Detroit, and political assassinations—made a delicious twosome. Both born poor, both self-made, the two performers were perfect American lads made good by their own energy and daring, and they gave a splendid performance, Lee and Cassius. Instructing the boxer on just where to stand in front of the camera—and the piano—so as to place both of them at good angles, Lee then improvised music for Cassius's recitation of his poetry. It was as charming as it was funny—these two men, otherwise antithetical, having a splendid time while entertaining the nation.

It was all terribly poignant too, for this perfect little vignette of American culture had been filmed earlier in the week, just before the murder of President John Kennedy on the streets of Dallas, Texas, on November 22. The show was broadcast the next evening, as the world mourned. The program went on as originally filmed, but Paar had created a post-assassination preface to it based on that terrible event. It was a moving statement about the tragedy that cast a ghastly pall over the show's smiles.[1]

The Kennedy assassination was a watershed in American intellectual life. November 22, 1963, held special implications for Liberace, too, for personal reasons. His own desperate encounter with death occurred at this time, as well. Although he made the two events coterminus in his memoir, his ordeal actually took place the day following the assassination. The evening after Americans had watched Jack Paar ad-libbing with the piano player and Liberace playing games with Cassius Clay, physicians rushed the performer to St. Francis Hospital in Pittsburgh, Pennsylvania, with renal failure.[2] Unlike the American president, he survived, and the ordeal came to be both a capstone to his recovery of his career and a harbinger of how he would live his later life.

On Saturday, November 23, the performer was playing a club called the Holiday in Pittsburgh. A blizzard outside had restricted his movements, and he had also taken the opportunity to clean some of his own costumes when the hotel staff protested their inability to finish the job by showtime. He had ordered a gallon of cleaning fluid so he could work on his clothes. After finishing, he lay down on the bed—in his unventilated room—and drifted off to sleep. After an interruption from his wardrobe man, who criticized him for cleaning his own clothes, he slept again, rousing himself reluctantly to do the show, which he really had expected the management to cancel because of the assassination. He did not make it through the performance. At the hospital, doctors diagnosed him with kidney failure caused by carbon tetrachloride poisoning. He had been poisoned by the cleaning fluid he had been breathing all day in a closed room.

When his kidneys failed to kick in, the doctors informed him that he was dying. "Put your house in order," the physician instructed. "It's a bewildering piece of news to be given," he reflected later. "First you feel a terrible shock. Then a benign sense of inevitability and sadness at the thought of all the people you love whom you will see no more. It's strange. You mourn for your friends before they get a chance to mourn for you." In a typical gesture, then, he decided to honor old associates and family members by giving away whatever money existed in his estate after the obligations of his will were met. He ordered his house by going on a binge of generosity. "I had charge accounts opened at Cartier's, Tiffany's, Saks Fifth Avenue and all the other good stores, and the nursing sisters at the hospital each day would phone in what I wanted ordered and where to ship it." The benefices multiplied. "The gifts ranged from a house in Beverly Hills for my sister to a mink coat, pearls and jewels for my Mother, and a boat for a member of my staff which numbered twenty-eight people. The men got everything from cars and motorcycles to gold jewelry, the women, diamonds and furs."[3]

Miraculously, amid this frenzy of giving, he began to recover. "Don't ask for any scientific explanation but you're going to make it," the physicians told him. After a month in the hospital, he flew back to Los Angeles and celebrated Christmas 1963 at home. He did not ask for a scientific explanation. On the contrary, he welcomed the chance to justify his recovery with religion and faith. One day, he related, "a nun I'd never seen before came into my room and sat next to my bed and said softly, 'St. Anthony has performed many miracles. Pray to him.' Then she touched my arm softly and left the room." He did pray to St. Anthony; he did recover. If that were not miracle enough for him, he determined, after a studied search failed to turn up any sister of this description, that the nun herself was a part of the miracle.[4]

Liberace had always fulfilled every ambition he had ever established for himself. As a sixteen-year-old, he had predicted he would play the Pabst Theater. Four years later he did so, fifteen years ahead of his own schedule. He had vowed to play Carnegie Hall and the Hollywood Bowl. He achieved both ambitions. A mansion in Hollywood? Performing for the Queen of England? Untold wealth? He set the goals; he fulfilled them. He achieved his purpose through relentless drive and unflagging will. Now, however, he could credit his fortune to Providence. God, or at least St. Anthony, was on his side. Had he escaped the clutches of *Hollywood Confidential* and veronicaed Cassandra's horns? Had his health been miraculously restored? The nameless nun's hand was there. The restoration of his career, in shambles between 1956 and 1962, now appeared providential too. Given the state of his fortunes after the Cassandra trial, he might well have credited his salvation, in retrospect, to St. Anthony—or better, to St. Jude, the patron of impossible causes.

From the lowest ebb in his career in 1959, he had pulled himself back to being virtually an institution in the American entertainment industry by 1963. The process of recouping his fortunes is a remarkable part of show-business history. He got back, in part, exactly the way he made it in the first place: he worked as relentlessly as he ever had as a hopeful, hungry, ambition-driven youth. At the depths of his eclipse, neither his stamina nor his will ever wavered. Years later, when he was well into his sixties, the same motives still drove him. "This is a funny business," he told a reporter. "The longer you stay in it, you always think that just around the corner is some new thing, some new triumph. Take Jack Benny. He works like a dog. . . . He doesn't have to. But I'm sure it would almost crucify him to become a has been. And I think that's the biggest fear that anyone in show business has. They want to die famous. No one ever wants to give up."[5] If in success he drove himself, how much more driven he was when his fortunes waned! Still eclipsed in 1961, he described an agenda that was part whistling in the dark, but all ambition, too. "What I'm going to do in the next few years, God willing, will make people say, 'Sure he played Madison Square Garden and got $50,000 a week at Las Vegas and all those things but that's nothing compared to what he is doing today.'"[6]

In his obscurity, as the decade turned, the entertainer recouped his fortunes by returning to the folks. If films scorned him after 1955, if Las Vegas had dropped him after 1958, if television had failed and then forgotten him after 1959, his faith in the folks and in his ability to delight them never wavered. He loved the hinterland; the hinterland still loved him. He started again here. He hit the local scene with as much energy, enthusiasm, and expectation as he had as a young man playing the supper-club circuit in 1943. While he disappeared from the national media in this period, local papers chronicled his climb back to fame.[7] He puffed himself up to a reporter from the Milwaukee *Sentinel* in 1961. "His present tour, Liberace explained, is built around supper and night club shows, an attempt to extend his appeal beyond 'the legend and my loyal following.'" He was playing a club called the Holiday House at the time.[8] The same year, his hometown newspaper detailed his activity "on the vast club-concert circuit that stretches from Yakima, Wash., to Bell Vernon, Pa. and overseas points."[9] Yakima, Washington? Bell Vernon, Pennsylvania? No town seemed too small.

He returned to the places that echoed his teenage musical tour in the late thirties: Madison, Eau Claire, Appleton, and, yes, even Wausau. He was playing the burg of Jackson, Minnesota, in September 24, 1961, when he offered a telephone interview to prime still another Milwaukee gig that fall. He was preparing a run, this time, at Milwaukee's Oriental Theater. In contrast to his interview six months previously, he now told the journalist, "I'm doing more theater work and less in night clubs."[10] He was doing whatever he could, wherever he could, for whoever was willing to pay him.

He was relentless. No longer booked at Madison Square Garden and San Francisco's Cow Palace, he was still in demand elsewhere. "There is hardly an open date in his 1961 itinerary. And he still commands an impressive salary in the nation's foremost nightclubs and theaters," observed another reporter. "His engagements this year have or will take him to such places as the Flamboyan Club in San Juan, Puerto Rico; the Chase Hotel in St. Louis; Blinsturb's in Boston; the Miami Beach Auditorium; Harrah's Club in Lake Tahoe, Nevada; the Meadowbrook in Cedar

Grove, NJ; the Royal Poinciana Playhouse in Palm Beach, Florida, and the Palmer House in Chicago."[11]

He returned to the community concert circuit that he had abandoned in 1940. Most of these appearances are lost to the record. They crop up almost at random. How many performances did he play like the one in 1960 or 1961 in the provincial mill town, Greenville, South Carolina, population 100,000, suspended about halfway between Charlotte, North Carolina, and Atlanta, Georgia? That community concert series had also included the celebrity pianist, Van Cliburn, and at least one young Greenvillian, while glad to hear the Texas classical performer, attended the Liberace show almost under duress. "I was a young sophisticate and budding intellectual in 1961, I guess it was, when I got tickets to a Community Concert starring Liberace," the one-time concertgoer recalled. "I thought Van Cliburn was fine, but I took the Liberace tickets because I had to. I didn't really want to go, but I have never seen anything like it. I don't remember anything about Van Cliburn, his playing or anything else, but Liberace's act is as vivid right now, over thirty years later as it was then. I have never seen a performer who gave so much, so memorably, so long. I hated to leave; it was so much fun. Everybody wanted more."[12] Thus, the showman pleased his old fans and wowed new ones everywhere he played in this uncongenial time.

The audiences were smaller, and so were the venues, but he generated the same reaction in the darkest days of his eclipse. Even the skeptical recorded his extraordinary ability to work an audience. Besides his concertizing, wrote the reviewer of his March 1957 Miami Beach engagement, "his ya-ta-ta is intriguing in a comically odd sense, but he works out the monologs with all the aplomb and assurance of a vet performer who knows he's got it made."[13] As typified in his return engagement at Chicago's Palmer House in 1959, he joked about the most awful episodes in his career, turning sows ears into funny silk purses: "Liberace makes of his 75 minutes or so an attractive exhibition of self-kidding cunningly compounded of coyness and candor."[14] He simply dominated audiences: "There can be no denying the showmanship of Liberace. . . . He oozes geniality and friendship all the way, and leaves the customers in a happier frame of mind than when they entered."[15]

He pulled the same trick in New York, returning to Manhattan for the first time in five years. And if neither Carnegie Hall nor Madison Square Garden, the famous Latin Quarter was no small potatoes. He played four weeks. Although *Variety*'s reporter gibed at "the chorus of aaahs from the geriatric set," the showman packed in the folks, senile or not.[16] As another reported observed, "He is playing to turn away audiences at a time when nightclubs are dying all over the country." [17]

Besides his almost incredible will, energy, and drive, the showman's successes had an external source as well, at least according to Liberace himself. He altered his management team again. In 1961, he returned to Seymour Heller. That took some doing, too, for things had gone from bad to worse in regard to his old adviser. At John Jacobs's prompting, the showman had sacked Heller back in the summer of 1958. In February 1960, Heller and his publicity firm initiated multimillion-dollar suits against the entertainer and his attorney, Jacobs. Lee countersued. With endless rounds of depositions and hearings, the affair twisted its way through the courts until September 16, 1961, when the parties resolved their official difficulties. [18] With the legal issues settled, Liberace determined to reestablish their relationship. He called. "I asked him if he'd meet with John Jacobs, the lawyer who had talked me into getting rid of him, and work out a new management deal." Predictably, Jacobs failed to negotiate anything acceptable. "So I, personally, took over the arrangements," wrote the showman. "Almost immediately he turned my career around, got it on the right track . . . ," allowed the performer. [19]

Facilitated by his own hard work and assisted by St. Anthony, St. Jude, and now good old Seymour, Liberace was flying high again by 1962. He reestablished his name; once more he had become a desirable commodity. Other entertainers loved him in any case and were delighted to encourage—and to tap—his restored popularity. His guest spot on *The Tonight Show* on November 23, 1963, was actually only one of numerous appearances he made on the show when Paar was hosting it. Indeed, on his final show on June 6, 1965—a recap of his most notable programs—Paar used film of the quick-witted piano player in a featured spot with his other favorite guests: Jonathan Winters, Richard Nixon, Barry Goldwater, Billy Graham, Richard Burton, Bette Davis, Oscar Levant, "Nicols and May," and Bea Lillie. [20] Johnny Carson liked Liberace almost as much as Paar did, judging by the performer's many appearances on the new *Tonight Show*. He even hosted one segment of the program. Still later, David Letterman rediscovered what Paar and Carson had known all along: Liberace was surefire company.

Not to underestimate the significance of *The Tonight Show* appearances, his return to *The Ed Sullivan Show* in 1962 had put another important imprimatur on the showman's recovery. Broadcast to millions of homes every Sunday night, this program both introduced new acts and guaranteed legitimacy to the old. It was classic hodgepodge vaudeville.

The program on the night of Liberace's appearance on December 16, 1962, was typical: besides Lee at the piano, Sullivan also presented Xavier Cugat's band accompanying Aby Lane; the singing Clancy Brothers had come from Ireland; and Victor Julien appeared with his trained dogs. In addition, viewers that evening could catch a ventriloquist, a dance troupe, a group of circus tumblers, a comic, and, not least, the fresh young singer, Barbra Streisand, in her initial appearance on the tube. It was, incidentally, neither her first nor her last encounter with the master showman.

The pianist had appeared on the show only once before, on November 16, 1955, when he had performed the novelty song, "Putti, Putti, Cement Mixer," in accompaniment to the great opera diva, Risë Stevens.[21] Seven years later, Sullivan effectively welcomed the showman back to celebrity, when, in a voice as distinctive as Liberace's, he instructed his television viewers on December 16, 1962, "And now back to our stage after much too long an absence—Liberace!" Dressed in black dinnerwear with spangled cuffs, the showman wore a reasonably discreet outfit, although his candelabrum was now oversized. The show was typical Lee, except the tunes were contemporary now. He offered "Moon River" in standard form, but produced "Mack the Knife" as Kurt Weill wrote it, then as a waltz with some "Blue Danube" thrown in, in bossa nova style, and then in ragtime. After his breathy, signature thank yous, an off-stage voice yelled, "Hey Libby, let's do the twist!" whereupon the performer launched, tails flying, into a shameless Chubby Checker dance routine.[22]

Half in fun, always for the publicity and cash, Liberace institutionalized himself once again in television from this time on. He appeared in all sorts of shows, from sequences of *Batman* to *The Muppet Show* and *Saturday Night Live*. The mid-sixties saw his face on the big screen again as the wonderfully, oleaginously American casket salesman in Tony Richardson's *The Loved One*. Like the Auntie Mame phenomenon, this film was a nearly perfect evocation of pre-Stonewall queer culture packaged wittily for the straight world.[23] Most of the movie's participants were bent. Thus, the gay Christopher Isherwood, who had turned the fey Evelyn Waugh's novel into a script, had remarked about the production: "I think most of us on both sides of the camera, this time around, are gay or bisexual." [24] It exuded campiness, and Liberace's cameo performance was perfect as a caricature of a caricature—of a caricature.

He was a name again. His production of records after 1962, and increasing album sales, affirms his new status.[25] All this reflected in his earning power. His earnings climbed back where they had been in the fifties.

From a low of $300,000 in 1959, they were back to a million dollars a year by the mid-sixties.[26]

He was a name again, and the final verification of his re-arrival was a new contract to play Las Vegas in 1963. He had been away five years. Providence guided his career. Like his brush with death that same year, the return to the casinos marked a milestone in his life. It sealed, just so, a return to the glamorous style that had distinguished his first fame. Glitz and glamour even became contractual obligations in his Las Vegas performances; he was required to outdo himself. By this means, the return to Las Vegas symbolizes less his return to elegance than to his campy commitment to the spectacular that became his indelible hallmark after 1963. From this period on, in fact, he dubbed himself "Mr. Showmanship," a sobriquet that quickly became inseparable from his public identity.[27]

Style and elegance had, of course, been his stock in trade from his schooldays. As he acquired a career and reputation in the forties, he practiced a fairly conventional form of elegance—tuxedos, tails, and, of course, the candelabra after 1945. By the early fifties, however, he began pushing the limits of convention. At his Hollywood Bowl performance in 1952, for example, he had exchanged the standard white tie and black tails for an all-white version of formal eveningwear. The outfit grabbed headlines. He was "the new Cab Calloway . . . the hidey-ho man of the Hollywood Bowl." [28] The "snowy sheared beaver dress suit" he wore to the premiere of *Forever Yours* in 1955, or his Christian Dior-designed gold lamé jacket of his Las Vegas performance of the same year, represented more play with fashion. Under the direction of John Jacobs, he gave all this up after 1957. He went straight and plain, sans glamour, for almost five years.

As he regained fame and celebrity after 1961, he also reclaimed glamour. While his reassertion of real flamboyance did not take place until 1962, he had begun establishing the new style earlier, privately and domestically. Indeed, it was in his home that he first began the really radical development of what might be termed fashion as spectacle. This, too, bears a direct relationship to his career.

As he had retreated to a more conservative public image after the *Confidential* and Cassandra trials, his homes and houses had absorbed more of his creative ambitions, even as they anticipated the fancy of his Las Vegas style after 1963. Perhaps again because of career problems and his longing for something new, he had become disenchanted with the Sherman Oaks house on Valley Vista by 1958, at the very time, too, that his relations with his family became attenuated. The Sherman Oaks house had other problems. It lacked privacy, sitting as it did directly on the street without hedge, fence, or walls. Tourists haunted the premises. It was easily and often vandalized, with unwelcome guests damaging or making off with the piano decorations on the mailbox, the lights, and other ornaments. In the summer of 1957, in the midst of the *Confidential* crises, it had also been the scene of a mysterious attack against his mother, when strangers lay in wait and beat her. Afterwards, the showman felt the necessity of maintaining twenty-four-hour security guards. Beyond the dwelling's physical liabilities, it bored him. He spent little time there; moreover, he wanted something bigger, finer, grander. In March 1959, he put the piano-pool house on the market.[29] He found his third Hollywood "dream house" in the Hollywood Hills.

Kings Way snakes up the southern side of the mountains just off Sunset Boulevard, and Harold Way branches off from it a short distance up the road and twists across and up the flank of the hillside. Eighty-four thirty-three occupies a huge lot on the north side at a major elbow in the narrow, winding lane. It lies on a major elevation just above the valley floor looking down on Sunset Strip. Indeed, Lee could almost throw a stone to Ciro's, the club that had helped guarantee his West Coast reputation in the late forties. The mansion at 8433 Harold Way provided a spectacular panorama of the L.A. basin. "I've always been fascinated by the carpet of lights that is the international trademark of the sprawling City of Los Angeles," Liberace related, and at night the view was glorious. But he wanted more, and more he got. "I wasn't about to buy just any house with a view and enough rooms to accommodate my worldly goods," he insisted. "I wanted a house with some history, some color, some background."[30] The mansion also provided other amenities. While the pianist was silent on the subject, it lay in an area so notoriously gay that cognoscenti called it "the Swish Alps." Down on the Strip, West Hollywood boasted one of the most sophisticated gay scenes in the entire United States.

He got history, color, and background all at once. The house had been built in the 1920s in a development called Hacienda Estates. The movie stars Rudy Vallee and later Anne Harding had owned it at one time. Unoccupied for years, however, it had deteriorated badly. "The kids in the neighborhood said it was haunted. It sure looked like it," he judged. "It was just a tumbled-down mess."[31] Its physical state proved not to be a problem: he had the cash to make repairs and bring it up to par. The deterioration actually pleased him; he loved redeeming the unlikely, mending the broken, reclaiming the forgotten, recovering the abandoned.

He had demonstrated the characteristics back in West Milwaukee when he and Angie decorated the pounds of cookie fragments his mother brought home from work, or when he fastidiously repaired the Christmas toys his baby brother smashed. This personality trait became more pronounced with time, especially after this period. It governed his interest in the Cloisters at Palm Springs. It also influenced his affection for people. In the case of the Harold Way house, the fix-up cost $250,000—over two and a half times the original purchase price of $95,000. The repairs took over six months from the purchase date in December 1960.[32] He moved in on Bastille Day, 1961.

The house was grand enough to meet even the showman's exacting standards of grandiosity. He called it his Hollywood Hills home. "My family," he related, "calls it 'the palace.'" His family was closer to the mark.[33] With three stories and twenty-eight rooms, by legal definition, it was palatial. Alone comprising fifteen hundred square feet, a studio and living room dominated the ground floor; the latter also boasted a twelve- by fifteen-foot stage. The first floor also held the kitchen and a dining room. The second floor contained another dining room; another living room— "the most prominent and exquisitely furnished in the house," with an even larger twelve- by twenty-one-foot stage; a bar/lounge; three sitting rooms; and a bedroom. On the third floor were three more sitting rooms, two more bedrooms, and a huge dressing room; these were his personal quarters. In addition, the house plan revealed eight baths and twenty-five storage areas, among other miscellaneous rooms. The property itself enclosed an Olympic-sized heated swimming pool, a large cabana, and statue-endowed gardens—where the showman also installed outdoor heaters to ward off the chill of Hollywood winter evenings.[34]

Visitors entered the mansion through a gold-leafed door that led into a golden foyer with a grand stairway curving to the third floor. The main living room lay to the right; it was done in French blue and more gold. Here is the pianist's description: "It is furnished in tapestries and pieces from the sixteenth, seventeenth and eighteenth centuries, upholstered in ivory and the palest of yellow satins and velvet. The chandelier, suspended from a gilded mirror is 18-karat gold and Baccarat crystal. The piano, on a dais, was once owned by Chopin. To the left of this is a small art gallery with some of my treasures."[35]

Off the second-floor living room, the organ room boasted a gold-leaf-encrusted theater organ capable of reproducing bird calls, drums, tambourines, and chimes, in addition to making more ordinary organ sounds. On the lowest level, the studio was decorated in a contemporary style, all black and white, with mirrored walls and a ceiling spangled with twinkling stars.[36] Here he auditioned, formulated, and rehearsed his shows.

Liberace himself did not actually own the house; rather, it had been bought and was maintained by his corporation, International Artists, from whom he leased his private quarters on the third floor. The showman—under the advice of John Jacobs—made this arrangement for tax purposes. In 1968, the IRS challenged the scheme, and Liberace now locked horns with the Feds in still another major lawsuit.[37] While the court failed to sustain International Artists completely, it did allow a tax deduction of 50 percent of the expenses connected with the house.[38] In the process of the ruling, the judges also affirmed the business/publicity motives behind the acquisition and maintenance of the spectacular house. The court conceded the petitioner's chief claim that International Artists was providing "a home for Liberace which would enhance his image in the eyes of the public." "The purchase of Harold Way in 1960 was clearly undertaken, to a significant degree, for business reasons," the court declared. If, indeed, it was the corporate headquarters for International Artists, "in appearance, however, the home was simply the spectacular personal residence of Liberace." Beyond this, the court chronicled the ways the Harold Way mansion served as a publicity and advertising function of the corporation:

> The home was extensively photographed. Brochures customarily distributed at Liberace performances emphasized by photograph and reference the 'palatial home' of Liberace. The appearance of the home was commonly imitated on stage, including in one instance the reproduction of the circular staircase found at Harold Way. Magazine and newspaper photographers were invited and encouraged to visit the premises for publicity purposes. Press parties attended by members of the press and celebrities, calculated to generate publicity for Liberace, were sometimes, though not frequently, held at Harold Way.
>
> As a result of the promotional efforts of International Artists, various news media often carried articles or references about Liberace. His unusual home was invariably mentioned in these articles, with description and photographs of the home figuring prominently in some instances.[39]

Even more than with the Sherman Oaks house, Liberace was capitalizing, literally, on his domestic arrangements. And what held true for the

Harold Way house followed, of course, from his larger creed: "Everything I do has the hope of making a profit. My career, everything I touch in my scope of entertainment field," he said, had monetary motives.[40] He had rediscovered that glamour was not only profitable but highly profitable after 1961. Folks craved it. He was delighted to satisfy their longing. Not least, he enjoyed the spectacle. Show had been his metier since high school, but the conservative eclipse had proven to him, finally, that this was where his future lay. He gave over to glitz like never before in his career. His spectacle now outstripped anything he had ever tried before and, indeed, what anyone had done before.

By 1961, when he moved into the new house, Liberace was slowly emerging from his monster slump, but his real apotheosis still awaited his return to Las Vegas not quite two years later. At that time, the palace on Harold Way became one more piece of evidence, not only of the new Liberace but also of the Las Vegas style that the performer came to embody and that became his hallmark for the remaining twenty-five years of his life. He was destined for Vegas, but Vegas was destined for him.

Back to Vegas. This was the great tribute he had paid to Seymour Heller. He "got me back in Vegas" after the desperate five-year hiatus.[41] Lee had always loved the place, from the time of his first engagement there back in 1944. Going back was going home. No entertainer would have longer or more comprehensive associations with the gambling resort. In many ways, his career matches the city's history, and together the two represent one of the extraordinary, daffy, and striking phenomena of the second half of twentieth-century American history.

Despite its contemporary fame, Las Vegas was slow getting invented. Although the Nevada State legislature had legalized gambling in the state in 1931, the act had little immediate impact. Gambling was, in effect, a local matter that especially in the thirties played on the boomtown, single-man mentality that accompanied the construction of the Boulder Dam during the Depression. As the thirties closed, however, various circumstances combined to make the city a regional and then a national entertainment center.

In 1938, reformers in Los Angeles inaugurated a campaign against prostitution and gambling in Southern California. Their crusade pushed the gamblers across the state line to betting-friendly southern Nevada. At the same time, while the completion of the Boulder Dam dried up the pool of high-rolling construction workers at the gaming tables, the flood of tourists to that spectacular construction site offered a new source of bettors. Las Vegas provided a convenient stopping place for tourists from

Los Angeles, and the possibility of betting offered those passing through extra inducement to stop over in the town.[42] Simultaneously, the outbreak of the European war and the American military buildup resulted in the general area being awash with money and increased domestic spending. There was cash for tourism, cash for gambling. All this laid the groundwork for the Las Vegas that emerged later in the decade.

Changes in the town's demography reflected these other patterns at work after 1939. In the thirties, the betting "industry" had focused on downtown, or "Glitter Gulch," as the ad men called it. In 1940–41, however, gaming moved west, beyond the city limits, to what would be known as the Strip. Highway 91, the new improved motor artery to Los Angeles, proved the inspiration. In 1941, a West Coast hotelier, Thomas Hull, opened a new-style hotel resort three miles west of the city's center just outside the town limits. One of a chain of El Rancho hotels, mostly in California, El Rancho Vegas catered to drive-in, drive-through guests to whom Hull offered lodgings mostly in its sixty-three bungalow-type rooms. Located on a huge thirty-five-acre tract out in the desert, its stables, mission-style structures, and other outbuildings sprawled across a fifth of this plot. It was an extraordinary innovation, and Las Vegas's first tourist facility that combined hotel, casinos, resort amenities, and a luxurious environment, all of which was easily accessed by automobile. With an eye to publicity and catching motorists' attention, Hull crowned the entrance with a trademark windmill with neon-lit blades. In another flashy public-relations ploy, he opened the facility on April 3, 1941, with a bevy of young Hollywood stars and starlets.[43]

El Rancho Vegas soon inspired other investors. Buying land a mile farther west out Highway 91, a Texas theater-chain owner, R. E. Griffith, constructed a still more elaborate, in effect grander version of Hull's resort hotel the next year. He christened it the Last Frontier. It was intended to be bigger, catchier, and more spectacular in every respect than El Rancho. The complex included horseback and stagecoach rides, pack trips, and, a little later, "The Last Frontier Village," a reconstructed pioneer community filled with artifacts from olden times. For all the primitive accoutrements, Griffith hyped his establishment as "The Early West in Modern Splendor." The amenities confirmed the slogan with the personalized chambers, Zuni-decorated passages, and, not least, the main banqueting hall that more than doubled the entertainment space at El Rancho.[44]

Opening in October 1942, the Last Frontier also planned entertainment to exceed anything its competitor offered. Maxine Lewis was one of the Hollywood starlets who had participated in El Rancho's inauguration ceremonies eighteen months before. The management of the Last Frontier hired her as entertainment director; she was good. By the end of 1943, she hit on the scheme of contracting with big-name entertainers and celebrity performers to headline the Last Frontier's shows. The practice distinguished the new hotel twice over: the names pulled in the customers, and a headline-blackening salary attracted attention in its own right. Lewis inaugurated this program in January 1944 by offering six thousand dollars a week to Sophie Tucker, "the rough, tough star of Broadway, nightclubs, radio, and screen," to headline the show at the Ramona Room. After the sixty-year-old star had arrived to cheering crowds at the train station downtown, the hotel, in keeping with its larger strategy, arranged for her to travel the four miles to the resort on a fire truck, to play on her image of "The Last of the Red-Hot Mamas." Just so, sirens broke the desert calm at her performance, while searchlights swept the sky during her two-week engagement. In the lusty, robust style she had made her trademark, she belted out her signature tunes, such as "Pistol-Packin' Mama," costumed in a "cowgirl" outfit to fit her own image as well as that of the Last Frontier.[45]

When Sophie Tucker was barnstorming in the Nevada desert's fancy motel, Walter Liberace was tickling the ivories and pattering with tuxedoed gentlemen and their gowned ladies at the Normandie Roof in Montreal's elegant Mont Royal Hotel. During his Canadian engagement, he had mailed Maxine Lewis one of his advertising cards, which asked, "Have you heard of Liberace?" Lewis called him back. Yes, she had heard of Liberace, she told him. He professed ignorance of her and the Last Frontier, and he knew little more about Las Vegas itself. At the time, of course, the desert resort had almost no reputation outside the Nevada-L.A. corridor, and the pianist had never been much west of Dubuque or south of Fort Lee. As a hungry and ambitious performer, however, Liberace had jumped when Lewis offered to match his income at the Normandie Roof. He was earning $350 a week, but he said he was making $700. Lewis agreed to this figure and offered him a six-week run. He began his engagement on Thanksgiving weekend, 1944.[46]

Liberace—and perhaps Maxine Lewis as well—touted his engagement at the Last Frontier in the context of the "superstar" Sophie Tucker. You'll be following her, Liberace quoted Lewis as saying. He used the information to reflect on his own circumstances: "Knowing the stature (no pun intended) of Miss Tucker at that time, this should have told me immediately that I'd asked too little or that they planned to make up on me what they overpaid her. But none of that ever crossed my mind. I was elated at the thought of playing Vegas." [47]

The reality was different.

Tucker was long gone from Las Vegas by the time Liberace showed up. She had played the Last Frontier almost a year before. Stars, super or otherwise, were nowhere near when Liberace opened at the Last Frontier in November 1944. Indeed, "Walter Liberace" was only one element in a nightclub "review." He neither led the bill nor opened the show. He shared the stage with Rolf Passer, "the world's mental wizard," Ray Smith's puppet show, Lola and Andre Dancers "In costumed Splendor of SOUTH AMERICA," and "Lester Cole and His Debs," a singing group notable for filling popular requests—"Hit Show Tunes, Irish Ballads, Popular Novelties, Old Favorites." Lester Cole's act actually won top billing in the Last Frontier's initial newspaper advertisement for the show.[48] But, regardless of whether or not, in his own mind, Liberace was competing with Sophie Tucker rather than the mind-reader Rolf Passer, he presented a show worthy of Broadway. His combination of energy and ambition, talent and art paid off. According to his memoir, Maxine Lewis appeared in his dressing room after the first night's show and volunteered to up his already inflated salary. "After that show you gave tonight," he quoted her, "I feel guilty about paying you seven hundred and fifty dollars." She doubled his compensation then and there to fifteen hundred a week, he related. It was a personal landmark. He had broken through a three-figure weekly salary for the first time, he remembered.[49] For his six-week Thanksgiving-to-Christmas run, Maxine Lewis paid him nine thousand dollars.[50]

Did it really happen the way Liberace tells it? The local newspaper, the *Las Vegas Review-Journal,* offers some confirmation of his account. The day after the opening, the paper described him as "the big hit of the show." And after his initial performance, the Last Frontier boosted him to top billing in the newspaper advertisements.[51]

While, inexplicably, he missed Las Vegas in '45, the showman returned in September '46 to play a second engagement to the same enthusiastic audiences in the Ramona Room. He was back again six months later, receiving still livelier reviews and generating more impressive advertising copy.[52] Maxine Lewis had a winner. She almost lost him. The gangster Bugsy Siegel wanted him, too. In 1946, the mob had broken into the Las Vegas with the Flamingo Hotel, the Strip's third casino. The hotel opened in the '46 Christmas season, but financial difficulties closed it soon after. Siegel planned a reinauguration in March.[53] In the interval, he discovered the Ramona Room star. He intended to have him for his new show. The mobster's assassination in early '47 saved Liberace for Maxine Lewis.[54]

With no regrets about missing out on playing the Flamingo, the pianist delighted in repeated lucrative contracts from the Last Frontier for almost another decade. Indeed, while the Flamingo foundered, the Last Frontier thrived, and, with it, its star piano-playing artist. In 1948, he led the prestigious New Year's Eve show, and he returned again that September. Long before his television fame, Las Vegas accepted him as simply a fixture in the town's entertainment scene but also as one of the most popular entertainers of the gambling town's history. Thus, typically, one *Review-Journal* critic began his article with the words "Liberace is back," followed by the observation, "We might stop right there and make this the shortest show review on record and sufficient to send droves of people crowding into the Ramona Room to hear this master young piano virtuoso," so popular and appealing was the entertainer.[55]

In 1954, Liberace had played the Last Frontier twenty-five times. His ten-year contract with the hotel was expiring. At the same time, the resort was encountering financial problems because of growing competition on the Strip. Other hotels had taken their cue from the Frontier's efforts to beat El Rancho, and the competition had destabilized profits and management.[56] Indeed, the newest of the challengers planned a facility that would eclipse anything Las Vegas had seen before and that would remake the Strip completely. For over a decade after the Last Frontier had opened, the Strip's hotels had accumulated at a steady pace: after the Flamingo's completion in 1946–47 came the Thunderbird in '48, the Desert Inn in '50, the Sahara and the Sands, both in '52, and the Desert Showboat Motor Inn in 1954. Despite different decorative modes, all resembled in profile the earliest resorts on Highway 91. None rose more than three stories above the desert floor. The Riviera broke the pattern. Towering more than ten stories above the street, it gave the town a profile. It changed the way Las Vegas looked; it escalated the pattern of more, better, different—and costly—to a new level.[57] Its main entertainment facility encapsulated the changes. The Clover Room's ten-thousand-square-foot space could accommodate twelve hundred diners—double the number that the thirteen-year-old Ramona Room could hold. Each patron possessed an unobstructed view of the huge stage, which measured eighty by forty feet. With four turntables and the most sophisticated lighting available, it could handle a full Broadway musical. And, in contrast to the old-fashioned, rustic elegance of the Last Frontier, the Riviera's management had customized the Clover Room with a "Tiffany setting of classical design." It was "draped in swathes of platinum gray velour, faced with Empire green, hanging from huge brass rings beneath a jet black ceiling illuminated by huge spheres of starlight constellations," as a local reporter described it.[58]

Searching for an act to inaugurate these spectacular arrangements, the management turned to Liberace, much as the Last Frontier had hired Sophie Tucker years before. The fifty-thousand-dollar salary persuaded him to leave the Last Frontier, and the Riviera got one of the hottest names in American entertaining to head its opening bill. The hotel, too, benefited from all the publicity, not only of Liberace but of that astronomical fee, as well.

Liberace's opening show in the Clover Room on April 20, 1955, matched the opulence of the space. It consisted of three "gigantic production numbers": "The Riviera Story," "The Liberace Story," and "The Magnificent Candelabra Ballet."[59] Beyond all this, the pianist added his own glittering personal touch. Ever eager to give his patrons and employers their money's worth, for this opening show, the showman created the first of the spectacular costume changes for which he would become known. He opened the performance in a white silk lamé tuxedo he had commissioned from Christian Dior. His second-act costume topped it: a hand-stitched tuxedo jacket with nearly a million and a half shimmering sequins, according to giddy press reports.[60]

The Riviera was the place to be. And so it was for a few years, too. Liberace was there, but so were a crowd of other notables, including the hottest pop singer around, the teenage heartthrob who was changing the face of American popular music, Elvis Presley. The King had not quite acquired his dominion, however, at least not in Las Vegas, where he made his first appearance in 1956. After Liberace jumped ship to the Riviera, the Last Frontier had scrambled to recoup its declining fortunes, and this effort included modernization, a name change to Hotel New Frontier, and a new entertainment bill. The revamped hotel opened in April 1955, the same month as the Riviera, and the new management offered to the Mississippi rocker a contract to headline its show in 1956. Liberace was playing the Riviera for his second season when the New Frontier engaged the pop singer. Presley had just made his celebrated "waist-up" appearance on the Ed Sullivan Show, but the twenty-one-year-old singer's New Frontier act went nowhere. Not until he returned in 1969—taking a leaf from Liberace's notebook—did the King conquer Las Vegas.[61] Much earlier, during his aborted 1956 engagement, the glittery pianist had counseled the younger performer along these very lines—to adopt more glitz, in effect, to show off. From the outset, Elvis's New Frontier act failed to work. His manager, at least according to Liberace's recollection, appealed to the showman appearing across the strip at the Riviera. "Elvis's manager, Colonel Parker, came to see me. He said, 'My Boy'—as he used to call Elvis—'is appearing across the street. He's havin' some problems.' He told me what was happening and then added, 'He admires you so much. If I could bring him over for a picture, he'd really appreciate it.'"[62] The two performers did get together for a photo session; the camera reveals the rock and roller as awkward and rather ill at ease. That fall, Elvis attended Lee's Riviera show after the conclusion of the pianist's European tour. In showy white tails, Lee serenaded the rocker, who was seated immediately stageside. A famous publicity episode followed. Lee's geniality helped Elvis relax, and these two icons of the entertainment world exchanged instruments and clothes: Elvis in the gold lamé jacket, Lee in Elvis's broad-striped sportcoat. While Elvis banged away at the piano, Lee strummed a guitar, and they dueted for nearly a half hour, to the delight of photographers—and, of course, of their publicity agents. "Elvis and I may be characters—me with my gold jackets and him with his sideburns—but we can afford to be," Lee had burbled to the reporters.[63] Presley never forgot Liberace's generosity. Every time Lee opened a new Las Vegas show thereafter, Elvis sent him a guitar made of flowers. It was not pro forma. "'I only send them to the people I love,'" Presley told him.[64]

Elvis's act, with or without the pianist's advice, had bombed. Liberace would soon face the same fate. He still had two more years, however, to play the scene. In 1957, the year after his Presley session, he cashed in on the current reincarnation craze, calling his show, "Liberace Takes a Bridey," for the reincarnation story of "Bridey Murphy," as described in the bestseller, *The Search for Bridey Murphy*. He hired the doddering Bela Lugosi to play a mesmerist who would hypnotize the pianist so that the latter could explore his previous lives. He described what followed: "I sing, dance, do comedy, ballet, have ten changes and work in everything from tails to tights."[65] The magic wasn't working. With the Riviera in financial trouble, too, the showman played Las Vegas one more time in 1958. His white-heat fame had cooled. With Cassandra looming over his life, maybe the gay chickens were coming home to roost as well, as he himself believed. His contract was not renewed in 1959 or for the three years following. His four-year absence from the gambling casinos epitomized the collapse of his career and reputation.

When he returned to Las Vegas on July 2, 1963, for a five-week engagement at the Riviera, it was a victory, then, indeed.[66] It marks, most critically, the redemption of his reputation as a performer and a crowd pleaser. His career never flagged again. The return signals, too, his turn to the splendid excess that would become synonymous with his name, synonymous with a new identity and still another new name he chosef for himself, "Mr. Showmanship." Even to the point of moving his legal residence to the gambling town, Liberace chose henceforth to associate himself ever more closely with Las Vegas, and, by the same token, he became a model of what Las Vegas represented in American life from this time on.

As early as 1955, when the Riviera opened, Las Vegas was changing, and its changes mirrored critical transformations in the nation itself. Before the Riviera, Las Vegas remained bound essentially to Los Angeles, the West, and regional culture. Afterwards, the pattern altered. Las Vegas became a national rather than a regional entertainment center. The expansion of air travel and the creation of interstate highways helped fuel the shift. But other elements, like the huge growth of domestic wealth and disposable income during the period, contributed to the change as well. A demographic revolution undermined people's affection for the local and stimulated their desire for travel—which, of course, new highways, cheap cars, cheap fuel, leisure time, and the new wealth all exaggerated. Most appropriately, 1956 saw the construction of the first stretch of the interstate highway system. Television played an essential role in the nationalization of culture, too. All these elements together further enhanced the image of Las Vegas as a national center. There emerged, then, something like a national village, in which Las Vegas became a sacred or semi-sacred spot.

Disneyland was another such place, and the role of Las Vegas in American popular culture corresponds nicely in both time and content to the Disney enterprise; indeed, Las Vegas could be aptly labeled Disneyland for Adults.[67] Disneyland was being built at exactly the time when the new Las Vegas was taking off, and both enterprises, as well as Disney World, which was built in Florida a little later, were founded in spectacle, and not just spectacle, but, in effect, in vulgar spectacle, in the sense of popular appeal. No subtlety here! Haul in dream spinners! Everybody wins! These new cultural centers came to symbolize, then, not only the nationalization of taste and culture but its radical democratization as well. As Robert Venturi noted in *Learning from Las Vegas,* the vulgar celebration of spectacle might indicate the cheapening of taste, but it was also wildly exuberant and visually splendid, as exciting and dramatic as it was brassy and tawdry.

Las Vegas became a microcosm of the new America anticipated by suburban wealth. The exuberant search for tourists and gamblers—and almost unlimited capital—led Las Vegas entrepreneurs to exceed what they or their competitors had done yesterday or might do tomorrow. They engaged in a war to outdo each other in creating a Fantastic Kingdom in the desert. Changing yearly, or more frequently, Las Vegas was a fabricated world that was part county fair, part *Alice in Wonderland,* part hyperventilated bazaar, and all-American in its totality. The motives that created this phenomenon were the same ones that drove the engines of the American social, cultural, and economic order after the war. They inspired the Milwaukee-born piano player no less. This was an America where streets were carpeted with gold lamé. As one chronicler of the gambling city wrote, "Liberace epitomized what he called the 'ever better, onward and upward attitude' of Las Vegas. Each stage performance surpassed the previous one for gorgeous—often outrageous—outfits that glittered in cunningly conceived stage sets and skillfully executing lighting."[68] This was what he called "topping" or "topping himself"—to exceed himself, to go where no man had gone before and go there gaudier. Another reviewer summarized the issue concisely. "His audience is mostly old. Too bad—young people should turn out in large numbers and learn about show business. Besides Ringling Bros. and Disneyland, they have little opportunity to see what production really is."[69]

Liberace knew who he was, he knew Las Vegas, he knew the country, and he knew precisely what he was doing all along. He knew, not least, production. He was a consummate performer. The most sensible critics knew the same thing. His act "is a display of elegance and opulence so extreme it practically mocks the American dream of wealth and status."[70]

After 1963, Liberace played the greatest venues in Las Vegas. Besides his long-term contract with the Riviera, he also starred at the Sahara, Caesar's Palace, and MGM Grand. Had his association with Las Vegas and the Las Vegas temper ever been in question, his partnership with the Hilton International Hotel guaranteed it. In 1971, the Hilton chain bought out the International Hotel. The management commissioned Liberace as the lead opener and extended him a long-term contract with the mind-numbing salary of $300,000 a week. He earned his pay; he gave his bosses their money's worth. Indeed, his show in the Internationale Room in 1972 set a standard for both him and Las Vegas. This was the largest room he had ever played, and he took advantage of the size with a particularly striking opening. He had always liked grand entrances. His earliest reviews remarked on his dramatic flair—darkened lights and sudden spots, for example, at the Plaza or the Terrace Room. Later, he used drum rolls, brass fanfares, or harp glissandos to mark his appearance on the stage.[71] He was chauffeured onto the stage in a custom-designed Phantom V Landau Rolls-Royce, only one of seven—in Blüethner grand/Liberace/Las Vegas hype—ever produced. John Lennon owned one of them, Queen Elizabeth another. To match the car, he appeared in a calf-length ermine coat trimmed with diamonds over a gold lamé jumpsuit, the same outfit he had worn for his most recent command performance for Queen Elizabeth. He also closed the act with an another automobile entrance: this time, he wore jeweled red knickers and appeared on stage in a fire-engine red Model A roadster. Other acts, other performances showcased similarly outrageous outfits, similarly incredible cars.[72]

Topping himself may have been written into his contracts, but he didn't do it just out of legal obligation. He loved it. He delighted in doing something new or offering a new twist on old themes. He supported a small industry of costume makers. First Ray Acuna and afterwards Michael Travis elaborated on and executed his designs, or offered proposals of their own. Period costumes, or variations thereof, especially delighted him. History was a costume drama for him. Hollywood presented history the way he liked it. The Chopin movie, *A Song to Remember,* had given him his candelabra. He loved the Hollywood costumes of *Beau Brummell,* the 1954 film starring Stewart Granger and Elizabeth Taylor and based on the life of the Regency dandy. A junk-store photograph of George V in coronation robes inspired another costume. Different fabrics and textures, fur included, enchanted him. For his Internationale Room show, in addition to the ermine outfit he had worn, he had also donned a mink-trimmed one. In 1973, he appeared on stage in a $35,000 coat made of one hundred Danish mink pelts. In 1982, when he returned to the Riviera to headline its show, he inaugurated his performance in a cape of virgin fox for which he had paid $300,000. "How do I know they're virgin?" he winked to the audience. "It takes one to know one."[73] Less costly than outlandish, his costume for his Caesar's Palace show in May 1971 consisted of a red, white, and blue hot-pants outfit with a streamered, starred, bespangled jacket. Las Vegas News Bureau photographer John Cook captured him in this getup in mid-act, and the resulting photograph made history: it was the most widely run wire-service transmission ever dispatched from Las Vegas.[74] Perfect.

The entertainer pulled still other tricks out of his sleeve. There were always new cars—and frequently handsome new chauffeurs, as well. He devised other sorts of "topping" techniques. For his 1975 Internationale Room show, he rigged himself up with wires, à la Peter Pan, to fly off and on the stage, trailing a cape of white ostrich feathers. On another occasion, he wired himself, literally, so that his costume blossomed into a thousand twinkling lights when the theater cut the spots. He appeared with monkeys, elephants, chimpanzees, and Russian wolfhounds in performance and for publicity—the two were hardly separate categories by the seventies. In 1967, outside the Sahara, he was lowered by block and tackle to a giant cake on his forty-eighth birthday, and he rode a hot-air balloon to another opening.

While it seemed that there was nothing he wouldn't do to capture popular attention—whether it involved mink coats, rhinestones, leather hot pants, hot-air balloons, or custom-made cars—his shows were structurally very conservative. He practiced a general form of production that changed little in his lifetime and that drew, still further, on old vaudeville variety shows from a half-century before. It was, of course, the same stuff that early television capitalized on in such programs as *The Ed Sullivan Show, The Kate Smith Show, Cavalcade of Stars,* and *The Texaco Star Theater.* Liberace stuck to the pattern throughout his career, and even his last Las Vegas shows resembled his first appearance at the Last Frontier. Maxine Lewis had programmed the finger-synching pianist along with a hypnotist, a puppet show, costumed dancers, and an all-girls chorus specializing in popular requests. The pianist orchestrated almost identical shows for himself later, with jugglers, puppets, juvenile performers, and other novelty acts, otherwise defined, even as he himself always occupied the center ring with his glitter and amusing patter.

These were the shows he took on the road, too, after reestablishing himself in Las Vegas. One bill included "a grinning magician ('Mr. Electric') and a fine boy banjoist ('my protegee, Scotty Plummer')," according to one press report.[75] "Dieto, a European hat juggler and fledgling pop singer" also traveled with Liberace for a time.[76] In 1969, appearing in New York City, the pianist employed a Trinidad steel band "which played everything so well," according to one report, "that Ethel Merman sang out 'They're like a symphony'!"[77] His touring show in 1977 featured "the internationally famed Dancing Waters, a backdrop of superbly programmed water fountains that turned their fluid patterns and lights into a ballet to accompany Liberace's playing of Johann Strauss waltzes." It also showcased Barclay Shaw, "an incredible puppeteer" and a less critically acclaimed British trio of two Scotsmen and a Welsh girl. Then, too, there was the subtle piano playing of "the talented Vince Cardell," described as "Liberace's handsome protege." [78] Cardell had been a part of the act for three years, according to a second notice in 1978. Before he began playing solos and duets with his boss, he had been his chauffeur. It was not, incidentally, Cardell's only appearance in the Liberace saga.

Liberace loved singers and discovering new talent, too. The hefty, big-voiced Fay McKay performed regularly with him, and so did the Metropolitan opera singer, Jean Fenn. The showman also introduced Barbra Streisand to Las Vegas through his act. The New York singer was on the make. Critics had raved about her part as Miss Marmelstein in the Broadway production, *I Can Get It for You Wholesale.* She had also produced record albums, and she was singing in a Greenwich Village club when the pianist first caught her act. They had performed together on the same Ed Sullivan show in 1962.[79] She wowed the showman. He wanted her in his act. She made his 1963 show at the Riviera, but initially, at least, she impressed neither audiences nor critics, both of whom complained about her makeup and grooming as well as her voice. Others viewed her more favorably, including the producer Ray Stark and lyricist Jule Styne, who were collaborating just then on a new musical, *Funny Girl.* Streisand, of course, got the part that catapulted her to fame.[80]

Liberace searched constantly for new talent and novelty acts to include in his show, just as he pushed the limits with his own outfits and his own behavior. Yet, within a larger frame, nothing at all changed about his performance. Indeed, the constancy of his act was another manifestation of his ultimate conservatism. His show was almost ritually predictable. The audience's wonder and delight came not from what was going to happen but from how the familiar would appear this time. While many critics, especially in the East, complained about the lack of real innovation on the one hand and the insubstantial novelty on the other, this complaint, reversed, offers another clue to Liberace's audience appeal. The showbusiness trade journal got it just about right in reviewing his opening at the Riviera in the summer of '63: "Liberace is back at the Riviera with the same glittering corn which established him as one of the phenomenal novelties of the biz. The singer-88er's warmly extroverted showmanship, complete with three spectacular costume changes, is an unchanging type which made him a legend."[81] The next year, his Americana Hotel show in New York won a similar notice. "He's a hard pro, able to charm the oldies, overcome the resistance of the young with an easy and familiar pattern of music. . . . He trods [*sic*] no new musical paths . . . the audience is comfortable with his style of music. . . . He has that air of surefire professional skill." [82]

It was the jazzy repetition of the familiar. The allure of his show was not dissimilar to the appeal of the Catholic mass. Indeed, Liberace himself spoke constantly about the analogies between religion, theater, performing, and show business. Drawing deeply on his Catholicism, he worked out a coherent aesthetic theory and a practical approach to theater and performance. His almost unprecedented half century of success suggests the power of his perceptions.

I don't give concerts, I put on a show.

LIBERACE

TROMPE L'OEIL

The song was already popular when Hildegard, Liberace's fellow Milwaukeean, first recorded it and made it central to her act at fancy nightspots around the country during the war. It is not exactly clear when Liberace adopted it. It has a graceful melody and lovely lyrics. At the same time, the verses have special meaning for Liberace's life and values. "I'll Be Seeing You" reaffirms the showman's sense of an audience, his aesthetics, and his underlying notions of art itself. It hints, too, at the sexual elements of his show.

> I'll be seeing you in all the old familiar places
> That this heart of mine embraces all day through;
> In that small café, the park across the way,
> The children's carousel, the chestnut trees, the wishing well.
>
> I'll be seeing you in every lovely summer's day,
> In everything that's light and gay,
> I'll always think of you that way.
>
> I'll find you in the morning sun
> And when the night is new,
> I'll be looking at the moon, but I'll be seeing you.

On the most fundamental level, the song is a simple, romantic, and sentimental evocation of a lost love, friends parting, or companions separated by time or space. It is a song of promises and commitment. It possesses other meanings, however.

First, Liberace himself sang it with specific intent. Using it to close every performance, it honored his audiences and marked his own devotion to his fans. A song of his own composition, "I Don't Care" did the same thing, as indicated by its subtitle, "As Long as You Care for Me." He loved performing; he loved his audiences; he thrived on their applause: the song expresses his gratitude. When he closed his shows with the number, he demonstrated his warmth and attachment; he was giving back a portion of what his admirers had given him. "When the performance is over, I will still be thinking of you," runs the sentiment. It reaffirms, then, his oldest motives in performing, from the time of the "Three Little Fishies" concert: the ambition to redefine the relationship between the artist and the audience in terms of personal affection.

There are still other ways of interpreting the lyrics. These illuminate Liberace's ideas of art even as they suggest latent sexual motifs in his performance.

Most critically, of course, the song is about seeing and sight. Just so, it is about enumerating physical objects within a line of vision—the café, the park, trees, a carousel, a wishing well, the moon. This emphasizes the significance of actual, physiological seeing for Liberace. Visual apprehension played a completely critical role in his performance. But the lyrics also suggest another kind of seeing that is equally important in his aesthetics. It is not mere seeing or these mere objects of sight that the lyrics chronicle. Their poetry involves illusion, optical illusion, or even self-conscious delusion; the song is about looking at one thing and seeing something else. It introduces, then, the mind's eye or an inner vision. It is about the conjuring of the absent or the unseen, about the restructuring of the natural world, the refiguring of the scene to include objects of fancy or the imagination. The lyrics celebrate, then, not mere things but images of things, and imagination itself. It chronicles the mental reconstruction of the world.

Issues of this inner vision or imagination complicate the ballad's meaning. To whom exactly are the lyrics addressed? The "you" is ambiguous. The object of affection may or may not be present. Is the poetry directed toward a lover who is to depart and will soon be recalled affectionately? Is the song, in contrast, not a dialogue but a monologue, a reflection about a lover already departed, about love already gone? There is still another option: the love is not only reconstructed in the imagination, but the lover is altogether imaginary. If "you" is there even when unseen, the love is then essentially an object of fancy or a creation of the imagination. By this means, the lyrics suggest some of the fundamental motives in art and artistic creativity.

The imagined "you" of the song functions like the artist's muse, like Dante's Beatrice, for example: the poet did glimpse in passing a real girl in Florence by this name, but she is nothing in comparison with his vision of her, a vision that inspired, in turn, his poetry. The real Beatrice, the physical presence, is restructured into something else in the imagination. The "something else" is beyond the reach of time. It is like art. It begins with seeing or a sight and turns into a vision, something that exists on its own. This reordering of the natural world into something transcendent is what art, at least traditionally defined, is all about.

Finally, the lyrics also underline connections between sex and seeing in the creative process. Insofar as art involves the visionary recreation of the natural world, that vision itself classically begins with a look, a glimpse, a glance, a visual attraction transfigured into poetry. It was Dante and Beatrice, again, or Petrarch and Laura, or, in more modern times, William Faulkner and the little girl "with muddy drawers"—the vision that inspired and focused in his novel *The Sound and the Fury*. In this context, it is critical to note that this sort of seeing is a sex-linked activity generally associated with males. Just so, men's imaginative looking suggests not only sexuality, but forbidden sexuality as well. Tradition and myth confirm the linkage. The Jewish elders did not physically rape Susannah; they merely saw her at the bath. The hunter Actaeon did not even mean to spy on the naked goddess Artemis. Both stories, however, equate seeing with sexuality, indeed, with a sexual violation of the woman. To have a woman visually was to have her physically. Seeing equals seizing. It was within this primitive context, too, that Southern white men lynched scores of black males for looking wrong at a woman or for merely looking at a white woman. The crime of rape, in this context, had nothing to do with the physical penetration of a woman's body, but rather with possessing her with the eye and imagination.[1]

Associated with both art and sex in general, seeing/looking possesses more discrete associations with homosexuality. Just so, it underlines an alignment between homosexual impulses and the creative process. These ideas lurk beneath the surface of Liberace's theme song, too.

"I'll Be Seeing You" possesses both general and specific homosexual import. The references to "seeing you in everything that's light and gay" is only the most obvious element. Beyond this, the lyrics suggest both specific and general elements within homoeroticism. On the simplest, more immediate level, looking, a particular function of males, is doubled, effectively, for homosexual males. Both within and without the gay underground, the glance, the look, appearance define the essence of sexual identification and desire. With what a future generation would call "gaydar" (as in homosexual radar), Walter Liberace himself first experienced the recognition process when he was a twenty-year-old playing the Wunderbar in Wausau, Wisconsin. Long before and well after, this visual understanding has made the homosexual world go 'round. In *Cities of the Plain,* Marcel Proust described this ocular recognition, according to Leo Bersani's summary, as the basis of "a universal freemasonry of inversion."[2] The homosexual lodgemen "recognize one another immediately by natural or conventional, involuntary or deliberate signs," writes Proust. If obscure to others, these visible signs mark, in turn, the most diverse members of the fraternity to each other. Thus, they

> indicate one of his kind to the beggar in the person of the nobleman whose carriage door he is shutting, to the father in the person of his daughter's suitor, to the man who has sought healing, absolution or legal defence in the doctor, the priest or the barrister to whom he has had recourse; all of them obliged to protect their own secret but sharing with the others a secret which the rest of humanity does not suspect and which means that to them the most wildly improbable tales of adventure seem true, for in this life of anachronistic fiction, the ambassador is a bosom friend of the felon, the prince with a certain insolent aplomb . . . , on leaving the duchess's party goes off to confer in private with the ruffian; a reprobate section of the human collectivity, but an important one, suspected where it does not exist, flaunting itself, insolent and immune, where its existence is never guessed; numbering among its adherents everywhere, among the people, in the army, in the church, in prison, or on the throne; living, in short, at least to a great extent, in an affectionate and perilous intimacy with the men of the other race, provoking them, playing with them by speaking of the vice as of something alien to it—a game that is rendered easy by the blindness or duplicity of the others.[3]

Using his examination of Proust as a basis, Bersani describes homosexual visuality more grandly: "The world is nothing but a massive enlargement of the image in the invert's eye."[4]

Looking and homosexuality possess still other ducks and turns, as suggested by Liberace's theme song's lyrics. Looking at one thing and seeing something else has it one way; not looking at something and seeing anyway—the ungaze—has it another, another phenomenon of the homoerotic subculture. As a young, mostly latent gay man, the writer Walter

Clemmons first noted the homosexual unlook. "Queers had funny eyes," he observed. "And I only gradually worked out what it was. It's the cautious homosexuals that looked at you without moving their face. In order not to be caught looking, you're suddenly aware that you're being looked at by a face that's frankly not looking at you at all. So the eyes look very peculiar. It's a kind of snake-eyed look."[5]

Critical in homosexual culture, the glance or look produces recognition; it is generally preliminary to sex as well. The sentiments behind the theme song's lyrics, however, suggest something both less and more than physical activity or community. In his biography of the French writer Jean Genet, Edmund White relates the story of Genet's first "crush," or first discovery of homoerotic desire. Genet saw—and this is critical in the story—he *spied* another boy, he related, and, in effect, "fancied" him. His desire manifested itself in the wish not to do something to the boy but rather to be the boy. This is, of course, an impossible longing; it is fulfillable only in fancy, in the imagination, or in some inner vision. The optical image of a real boy, then, triggers something else: the pre-adolescent homosexual voyeur reworked the image to produce a mystical coupling and transformation of reality, otherwise defined. Liberace's theme song suggests the same sensibility.[6]

With the ambiguity of the object, the song suggests an imaginary love, unconsummated, indeed, unconsummatable in the transformation of the physical world to a world of imagination or ideas. From Plato to Walt Whitman, Thomas Mann, and Jean Genet, such idealizing of desire has figured centrally, even critically, in homoerotics. It involves very much the same process in heterosexuality—as in Dante's Beatrice, Petrarch's Laura, or Faulkner's Caddy, although the male-male form tends to multiply the effect. In ancient Athens, a man spied the beautiful boy, the *kalos*, in full knowledge that the boy would thicken, coarsen, age, and die. This beloved—the *eremenos*—is then frozen in a vision of youth in the imagination of the lover, the *erastes*: the boy becomes both the source and object of art and imagination—the Boy. This defines the most fundamental component of Socratic or Platonic love: the idealization of love, love that cannot, indeed, that must not be consummated. The language Leo Bersani uses to dissect Proust's relation with Albertine confirms the homosexual reading of "I'll Be Seeing You" in this visually idealized regard: "Albertine was always within Marcel; but he becomes aware of her presence only when she disappears from his field of vision as a desired object and desiring subject."[7]

High-flown language of perception, treatises on epistemology, and academic discourses on reality and aesthetics were equally foreign to the piano player from Milwaukee. He left no evidence that any such theoretical understanding contributed to his favoring the graceful lyrics of "I'll Be Seeing You." He betrayed even less evidence of having any theoretical conceptions of homosexuality. Even so, Liberace's act suggests a clear, well-formed aesthetic. Still further, his autobiography offers a practical theory of aesthetics that mirrors what he actually did in performance. Both sources confirm the artistic themes embedded in his song about vision, seeing, and sight. Not least, some of this touches on themes of homosexuality, as well.

First of all, everything about Liberace's career emphasizes the centrality of seeing, light, and vision in performance. Was his theme song about "seeing"? So was his act. Throughout his career, he often repeated the admonition that performers should always remember the importance of the "show" of show business. As he wrote in 1972, "Too many young performers have forgotten that the most important part of show business is not the second word, it's the first. Without the show there's no business."[8] This notion lies at the heart of his appeal. Seeing and showing, however, existed on several levels in his career.

On the most primitive level, show relates to seeing, to giving spectators something to look at: providing an "audience"—hearers—something to see. As a pianist, of course, Liberace's primary appeal was not to sight at all but to hearing, yet he believed people needed a visual object in a performance. As a pianist at a large, static piano, his impulse toward the visual posed a critical problem. He solved the problem in a variety of ways in the course of his career, ultimately making his instrument only one element in what amounted to pure spectacle. From the beginning, however, he was critically concerned with visuals, visuality, sight lines, light, and color as essential elements of entertainment and the art process.

When he was still a supper-club performer, he made lighting a vital part of his act. Repeatedly, critics singled out this aspect of his performance for special praise; it indicated his professionalism and fastidiousness, they all agreed. He was his own lighting director, and it was in the process of calculating this part of his act that he joked about mistaking millionaire Howard Hughes for a lighting flunky during his first engagement at Las Vegas's Last Frontier in 1944.[9] As he cast about for new avenues to celebrity after 1948, he tested and repudiated radio. The absence of the visual element played its part in eliciting his skepticism. When he moved to television, the problems of performance changed, but his emphasis on visuals did not. The medium demanded new techniques for being seen. He required that the camera focus on him, but he knew his static instrument offered little to show. He resolved the problem variously: by exaggerating his hand movements, offering visual surprises in the form of costume changes, using two cameras for split images, and the like. The dramatic black silhouette that always opened the show indicated another aspect of his concern. In this regard, lighting and dramatic lighting were virtually synonymous to him.

When he changed the venue to public concerts for thousands, he came up with still new resolutions for problems of visuals. By the time of his Hollywood Bowl performances in 1952 and 1954, he had developed an articulate theory of performance as a chiefly visual activity—a show. When he first went to California in the late forties, he had tromped through the great outdoor amphitheater and had stood on the stage imagining what it would be like to play there. He made two commitments: One, he promised himself "that someday I'd be on that stage again, but playing the piano with all the seats occupied." Two, he determined that he would be seen. Being seen, in turn, involved all sorts of corollary issues and problems that illuminate his practical aesthetics.

The Hollywood Bowl sat over twenty thousand people, and Liberace's first visual problem was that of how to be seen at all from the upper ranks of seats. As he surveyed the amphitheater before the performance, the most distant audience members were almost indistinguishable as individuals. It worked the other way, too: "It was perfectly clear to everybody that if I sat there, wearing the conventional black tails of the concert circuit, with a whole orchestra behind me in black tuxedos, I'd just blend into the 'background' and lose my identity." He did not lose his identity. He had his tailor make him the famous white evening clothes, and he appeared in them on that sellout evening. Everybody saw him.[10] While to those poor patrons on the highest benches of the Hollywood Bowl Liberace might have been only a white speck on the stage on July 19, 1952, he was still visually apparent. Photographs from the farthest reaches of the Bowl reveal that he was indeed visible. In his second appearance on September 4, two years later, he implemented still other innovations in his visual presentation. As the *Los Angeles Times* put it: "A Liberace show puts a great strain on electrical equipment. . . . The lights go up and down and change color so often." And, the critic added, the showman used "enough spotlights to forestall an air raid."[11] By 1954, the lighting itself had become a part of the spectacle; it was no longer the means of being seen but an end in itself.

The initial Bowl performance also introduced the other, imaginative kinds of seeing foreshadowed in the visionary "you" of his theme song. Liberace not only made sure that he would be seen physically, but he contrived to inspire the imagination with a discrete image or persona. His costume that evening triggered this other sort of vision. It excited the mind's eye. Liberace knew the power of apparition was far more potent than mere physiological seeing. His fancy costume at the Bowl allowed him to be seen practically or physically, but, more critically, it gave him an "identity"—as he himself called it—that lived in the fancy of his fans. He created, in effect, a powerful impression by making or remaking a visual persona for himself that his devotees could conjure even in the absence of actual vision. As in the lyrics of "I'll Be Seeing You," this image in the mind is alive, even when the actual object has vanished, or, from the point of view of the spectators in the upper reaches of the Hollywood Bowl, is mostly a white speck.

Appreciation of the overlap between these two kinds of seeing made up the basis of Liberace's act: the real seeing and the vision or mental image he inspired. "I didn't get dressed like this to go unnoticed" was one of his standard lines repeated over and over to countless audiences over the years. Just so, he always instructed his fans "to look me over." It never failed to draw knowing and familiar laughter. He calculated appearance to produce in the audience the effect of Beatrice on Dante; his image triggered the audiences' fantasy, and the adoring fans then wrote their own plots and drew their own pictures in their imaginations.

Liberace knew what he was doing in all this. "Liberace is a creation," he himself insisted, using, appropriately, the third person. "Little by little he was created by me and by the public who accepted him. He's a combination of music and personality and a certain amount of shock value. It's a fantasy. I'm a one-man Disneyland. It all sort of developed gradually [but] none of it is accidental. I'm always trying to see how far I can go." [12] Critics acknowledged the truth. "Liberace is primarily a visual showman," wrote one.[13] "Liberace was a visual rather than an acoustic phenomenon," confirmed another.[14] "For Liberace, it's what you *see* that counts," echoed a third.[15] "Liberace has entrenched himself in the minds of his public as 'the' pop keyboard artist through masterful application of a simple formula: Wrap a variety of music in visuals," elaborated still another. "His slick well-paced special must have satisfied his fans' expectations. He epitomized his own 'Mr. Showmanship' sobriquet." [16]

Other elements of sight, seeing, light, and show were critical to the entertainer's career. Thus, he identified show and show business in part as "showing off." He interpreted showmanship as caricature. He employed the same techniques of exaggeration as did eighteenth-century Italian comic opera, with its pot bellies, putty noses, and overblown gestures. It was himself, however, that he caricatured. The idea was not only the visuals of performance, but bold-stroke visuals. Liberace developed this aspect of his act into a very refined art, however unsubtle the final product may have been. Long before he turned to showy costumes, he was using movement to capture people's visual attention and to make—literally—an impression.

As a matter of actually playing the piano, his grand gestures—like his exuberantly lifted hands at a piece's conclusion, or his racy, signature arpeggios—were hardly necessary musically; they were, however, thoroughly appropriate both as a means of adding a visual component to the music, and, no less, as a way of "showing off" and caricaturing piano playing. They turned an auditory experience, otherwise defined, into a visual act or performance. His bejeweled fingers served the same purpose of concentrating eyes upon his hands and focusing visual energy on his playing.

For all his emphasis upon visuals, Liberace actually possessed a more elaborate idea of sensual perception, of which sight was only the queen element. "It's not easy to be glamorous, the image that I always strive for, when nobody can really see you," he wrote. "To enjoy the clothes I wear the audience must be close enough so that their eyes can almost feel the texture of the fabric." [17] To touch with the eyes, with a combination of the senses: the notion constitutes another critical basis of Liberace's ideal of both performance and success.

His basic idea of performance, then, was appealing not only to sight as well as hearing, but exciting the senses in general. He wanted, in short, to give a sensuous performance. Sight was the easiest sense to access. Although his dancing acolytes failed to swing incense burners in his act, smell was the only sensory perception the performer did not exploit. Ritualized touching, for example, constituted an important element of all his performances. "People like to touch a performer," he wrote. "In fact, touching has become a sort of cult among some people." He always invited people onto the stage to feel his clothes, handle his jewelry, and touch his hands. At the end of his performances, too, he allowed kisses, hugs, handshakes, and caresses. He especially liked playing in the round because of its physical access to the audience. "I've been doing it almost since in-the-round theater was revived," he said. "I found the round stage made it easier for me to make contact with my audience. . . . I find it much easier to bridge the gap between performer and audience when there are no foot lights, no orchestra pit to divide us. And it can be done without losing any of the excitement I love." [18]

His ideas about the senses and about sensuousness dominated his act. They also help account for his otherwise curious inclusion of a discussion of the deaf and the blind in his autobiography. While the entertainer was kind, compassionate, and sympathetic, especially to the young, his inclusion of references to the problems of the deaf, blind, and mute suggests his larger appreciation of the role of sensory understanding as a part of his life—and act. "Can you imagine what it must be like deprived of those three senses, isolated in a dark, silent world, unable to say what you think, ask for what you want? The thought makes me shudder." [19] These handicaps, however, precipitated a call to those who had them to use their senses fully. The world overflows with things of wonder, he testified, "and it is almost sacrilegious not to enjoy them to the fullest. No one in the world has any right, ever, to be bored, because it's true that the best things in life *are* free: Sight, sound and everything those senses open to us." [20]

Most critically of all, behind his glorification of the senses lay a coherent theory of beauty and aesthetics. He expressed it in part, at least, through his discussion of royalty. The nobility galvanized his imagination. Russian czars and French kings fascinated him. He made trophies of imperial possessions, like the elaborate ormolu-mounted desk that had belonged to Nicholas II, and he numbered among the great triumphs of his life his command performances in Britain, and actually meeting the queen and the queen mother. "I love pomp and ceremony . . . heads of state . . . Presidents, Kings, Queens, Princes. I've played for three of our Presidents, Truman, Eisenhower and Nixon," he boasted in 1973. "I've entertained for Queen Juliana and Prince Bernhard of the Netherlands and for everyone in the British Royal Family. These are the kind of people I respect most deeply. I admire what they represent and admire the way they go about representing it. . . . For they inject beauty and pageantry into the lives of those who yearn for something better . . . those who can only dream. It's showmanship of a very high order. The changing of the guard, the Beefeaters' old uniforms, the velvet, fur-trimmed robes of state, the impractical but luxurious quality of everything . . . the gold." [21]

Much closer to home, literally, religion, at least Roman Catholic religious practices, filled the same function. Indeed, he followed his celebration of royalty and royal pomp immediately with a paean to Catholicism, religious ceremony, and visual splendor as the basis of the church's institutional power and influence. It was all about beauty and awe, he wrote. Catholicism's appeal lay in "the mystery of flickering candles, the glory of statuary and art," the spectacle of the Sistine Chapel. As with royalty, he insisted, the church's power arose from the knowledge that people need "escape into another kind of world." [22]

The simple nave of West Milwaukee's St. Florian's was hardly grand; still, this was no chaste Presbyterian chamber or ascetic Methodist hall. Nor did the officiators at the mass resemble the ministers of these other faiths in their black robes or business suits—not to mention the parishioner-priests of the Society of Friends who wore everyday street clothes each First Day. The ceremonies at the neighbor parish church in West Milwaukee offered something profoundly different. Tinkling bells echoed against St. Florian's stone and marble to herald the miracle of the Eucharist. Attended by acolytes, priests in brilliant vestments swung fragrant censers and chanted ancient liturgies by the mystical light of tapers and votive candles. Liberace had it right. This was show and brilliant spectacle indeed, even in its provincial manifestations.

Liberace was profoundly Catholic in his world view, profoundly Roman Catholic. His ideas of religion set him at odds with the theological precepts and ritual practices of Protestantism. His Catholicism provided, just so, an additional source of the WASPy skepticism of his act. While disquieting to the American Judeo-Protestant mind, his views opened him to a much broader understanding of both religious impulses and human nature than were available to the ascetic, rationalized puritanism of the American establishment. He assumed the mythic validity of the ritualization, ceremony, visual splendor, and hierarchy of the mass. His own act provided something of a secular version of the Catholic festival.

His act echoed other elements of traditional religion in its ritualistic repetition, for example. For all the novelties of his performance, he also offered what amounted to a ceremonial show, complete with ritualized jokes. As a function of the ritual, he appeared; he showed himself, old but ever fresh. As much as the eucharistic celebration, the performance was an unnatural act that broke completely with the routines of daily life. This secular communion was as real as the mass, and Liberace himself was the Eucharist. As *Look* magazine observed as early as 1954, "In these paradoxical times, he doesn't give concerts. He gives, instead, himself." [23]

The eucharistic image fits. In 1981, the writer Michael Segell wrote a caustic essay in *Rolling Stone* about Liberace and religion. With passing references to "the Church of Liberace," Segell sneered that the performer "founded a fey sort of evangelism that celebrates schmaltz, glitter, and vanity." The writer mocked the star's declaration of religion "as a form of show business," and show business, in turn, as a manifestation of the religious impulse. The showman had instructed Segell that people need "to worship whether it's religion, an entertainer, or a movie star." [24] Another writer for the equally skeptical *Village Voice* made similar connections a little later. "We entered the Temple of the Holy Most, longing for a vision of excess," he began his review of the showman's last appearance at Radio City Music Hall in the fall of 1986.

> Liberace's act makes of commodity fetishism a quasi-religious
> experience. He gives emptiness form—specifically, a crust of
> rhinestones and fluff. He just can't overdo his overdoing, since
> a stage can't hold the surfeit we long for. Liberace understands
> this. That's why he began the evening with a film—sort of a

'Lifestyles of the Glutted and Flaunting It" let loose in his Las Vegas home—so we could see the ceiling of the Sistine Chapel re-created over his bed, the piano keyboards woven into rugs and bedsheets and painting along the pool, the mirror-lined rooms choked with a veritable Versailles of gilded gewgaws. Embarrassment of riches? Ain't no such thing.

In fact, sharing it with us is the key to Liberace's success. . . .

The ritual ended with Liberace blessing us with his microphone like a priest dispensing holy water. The subtext to these rites, though, was the exhibitionist/voyeur relationship between performer and audience exploited to the max for pleasure on both sides. I could feel the electricity of audience desire with each new flash of sequins and fur, like "baby, just let me feel it." Twice, he let us. A few shameless ones down front got to come forward and stroke. . . .

These fetishized fashions are the ultimate consumer goods—really unnecessary, virtually unusable, and completely awe-inspiring. They transport us to the heaven we heard so much about in Sunday School—all dazzling light, jewels and harmonies. No wonder the show ended with a quasi-hymn, folks around me breaking into "Let Me Call You Sweetheart" during the finale. Liberace smiled, said he knew we wanted to sing. And he promised to keep wearing his outfits just as long as we wanted him to. Liberace is really the essence of celebrity, a job in which one makes a spectacle of oneself. And makes no waves doing it.[25]

As demonstrated in these articles in *Rolling Stone* and the *Village Voice,* the association of show biz and faith lends itself to ridicule. However invidious the essays, they capture, nevertheless, something essential in Liberace's show. His show, in turn, mirrors not only fundamental elements in the mass, but even older, more primitive notions of the relationship between religion on the one hand, and showing, performance, and art on the other. Did Mr. Showmanship know about the Mysteries of Eleusis, the cult of Demeter in ancient Greece? It is unlikely. Yet his notions of show mirror one of the first great shows of Western life. The Eleusinian Mysteries, in turn, underline still other sources of Liberace's mystical, even mythic appeal to audiences.

One of the holiest spots in the ancient world, Eleusis, on the Saronic Gulf not far from Athens, marked the legendary site of Hades' abduction of Persephone, the daughter of Demeter, the goddess of earth and plenty. With her daughter gone, Demeter fell into deep mourning. Without her attention, the earth went barren. The goddess of life and plenty became, then, in effect, the divinity of death and desolation. Heeding mankind's pleas, however, Zeus intervened to restore the child to the mother, so earth flowered again in spring and summer; as a part of the bargain, however, Persephone returned to Hades half the year, hence fall and winter.

Far more than a cultic explanation of the seasons, the Mysteries at Eleusis touches upon fundamental, elemental mysteries of human existence: life, death, birth, rebirth, sex, generation, and regeneration. As significant, these mysteries came to be demonstrated or acted out in formal, ritualized ceremonies of the Eleusinian Mysteries. For nearly two and a half millennia, people came from all over the Mediterranean world to be inducted into the rites. Show, showing, and light constituted the main elements of these initiation ceremonies. The induction actually formalized showing in two ways. In the first place, the ceremony involved a visual reenactment of Hades' rape of Persephone—a dramatic caricature, in effect, of that electric scene. Late at night after a day's fast, the initiates made their way through the sacred precinct. Suddenly, without warning, blazing torches illuminated the brilliant specter of Hades stealing the terrified girl away from her mother. The show stunned the initiates' senses. There was a second showing, too. Demeter had left sacred objects with her devotees, and the culmination of the initiation involved the hierophant's ceremonial revelation of these objects to the congregants. This was show business of the highest and most profound form. It involved pomp, ceremony, mystery, seeing, and revelation at their most elemental. It engaged all the senses, and did so in an explicitly sexual context of rape and mother love and procreation. Thus the sacred objects, for example, seem to have been phalluses.

The holy show at Eleusis involved life and death, potency and impotence, men and women, and it celebrated the mysterious, mystifying margins where these primal elements intersected. That these elements lent—and lend—themselves to comedy and caricature as much as to tragedy and awe goes without saying. The late-fifth-century military and political genius Alcibiades lost his country in his comic—camp—reenactment of these very rites. The insouciant, incorrigible student of Socrates had it right. Indeed, the intersection of comedy and tragedy is itself another manifestation of art's mystery. In *The Bacchants,* Euripides prompts the audience to smile when the devilish Dionysos persuades King Pentheus to cross dress, yet foreknowledge of the protagonist's grisly end deflects the humor. This is the way art works. It plays with margins, boundaries, and limits of human, even biological order. It transgresses even as it affirms. It violates; it flirts with pain and punishment; it speaks the unspeakable, sees the unseen. Its power matches its dangers. Liberace called his performances "calculated outrage," and from very early in his career, he recognized the power "in daring to do something different, in challenging the conventional. I realized...I had lightning in a bottle...or, at least, in one of the pockets."[26]

As his remark attests, Liberace knew that to place oneself on the margin—of life, death, sex, gender—is to participate in magic and power. Explicitly and implicitly, too, he and his act acknowledged the close intersection between comedy and tragedy, delight and horror, vulgarity and transcendence. "It isn't all spectacle and laughter; it's a combination with tears and pathos," he admonished.[27] "To do a good show," he said elsewhere, "you must run the gamut of emotions and have the audience laugh, cry, excite them, calm them, give them nostalgia, give them modern sounds—bring the audience from wild cheers to a silence so total you can hear them breathe. Make them glad they came."[28]

The greatest showman of the twentieth century might have never heard of Eleusis, Demeter, and Persephone, yet he intuited a critical kinship between sacred and profane performance. Like the show at Eleusis, Liberace cut across boundaries that limit, confine, and curtail normal existence. He transcended boundaries in other ways, too. If the ultimate end of art is to make the congregant live a new life through the performance and to transcend himself, he assumed that show business served a similar end. Make audiences forget their woes, forget time even: "Make them glad they came." He wanted to offer them a new life, at least temporarily, to lift folks out of themselves. That is what religion does, classically. It's why Marx condemned it as an opiate, and why Mr. Showmanship remained faithfully Catholic.

Building on his sense of how both royalty and religion operated, Liberace worked out a still more elaborate aesthetic, even if he presented it in hokey, practical terms. Most critically, he assumed that art—like religion—was essentially escapist. He insisted over and over that art was mysterious and exotic in and of its very nature. It denied daily routines, it transformed normal existence. It involved the alteration, deformation or distortion of reality. It is, as the song lyrics suggest, looking at one thing, a children's carousel, and seeing something else, one's beloved. People neither want nor need realism or reality in their shows, Liberace insisted. They want illusion. "Now, the public demands a certain amount of escapism and fantasy from performers," he explained. "The ones who dare to give it are the ones who skyrocket, like Michael Jackson and Prince. Even at rock concerts, the Madonnas and Boy Georges are the sellouts."[29]

Insofar as art denies reality, illusion and optical illusion assumed a critical place in Liberace's thinking. They illuminated his aesthetics again. As he did in his allusion to votive lights before an altar in a darkened church, Liberace associated beauty with night or darkness, but, better, with half light, stage light, moonlight, and starlight; he associated it with mystery, imagination, and fancy. "I'll find you in the morning sun," his lyrics ran, "And when the night is new, I'll be looking at the moon, but I'll be seeing you." Associated with reality, the sun did nothing for art. Nighttime was another matter. "The stars twinkle, the moon casts a mysterious white light, the shadows take on beautiful shapes, everything becomes more glamorous and that's the way I like it. The clothes I wear when I'm working are not daytime clothes, they're nighttime clothes because the night is when people like to dress up. There's a little bit of make believe in every night and it's reflected in the gowns the women wear and the more imaginative clothes the men wear. The night is full of mystery and vibrations. It's show business. And to pretend that it's not is like putting Marlene Dietrich in a Mother Hubbard." [30]

The reference to the German movie star prompts further discourse on the nature of beauty. Royalty and Catholicism got the show just right; so did celebrities like Marlene Dietrich. In her seventies, Dietrich had played Las Vegas, but not like "The Last of the Red-Hot Mamas," Sophie Tucker, however memorable that earlier performance may have been. In a spectacular see-through outfit, the siren of *The Blue Angel* was still fabulous and sexy, still playing effectively to her image. Half-light helped; still, she played the goddess, and people should worship at her altar, Liberace insisted. He did. Star beauty, celebrity beauty, glamour beauty—like the pageantry of royalty and the visual splendor of the mass—exists for itself and demands submission. "I don't care if she's a grandmother, a 'Hausfrau' in her spare time," he wrote about his idol. "To me she's a star. And what's wonderful about it is that *she* never lets me forget it. She lives up to her talent. You never see Joan Crawford 'schlepping' around in a mumu. She, too, knows the meaning of glamour and its importance to the people who—without any themselves—love to look at it in others." [31]

He applied the same glamour/star theory to politicians and other public figures. He used the example of the then notorious New York politician representative Adam Clayton Powell to illustrate his point. Was the dashing, extremely handsome, womanizing minister of the Abyssinian Baptist Church in Harlem abusing his trust? The question was irrelevant, the pianist implied. Powell was behaving like a star. He was giving his people/his constituents what they wanted. "At least one of them was making it. They admired Powell's daring," he insisted. "It was his very outrageousness that they, themselves, could not indulge in, that they looked up to in Powell. Through him they defied the power structure that was trying to submerge them. Through him they lived a vicarious life of luxury and maybe sin. He had fun and they loved him for it." [32]

Precisely the same motive governed his own act. "When I ride onto the stage in a Rolls-Royce there's something of the same association. Who wouldn't want to do that?" he demanded. "Or if he didn't actually do it, be able to afford to do it." [33] It was the same motive behind the gold lamé, the sheared beaver coats, the mink capes, the jewels, "the palace" on Harold Way, his other mansions scattered around the country, and indeed, his whole outrageous ostentation. He hypostatized Everyman's fantasy.

Show and showing, sight and illusion figured in still other ways in Liberace's ideas of artistic virtue. In this regard, how he looked and how he dressed assumed a critical place in his aesthetic notions.

Costume actually figured variously in the showman's career. Practically, rather than aesthetically, Liberace saw dress as one more gimmick to attract attention and secure an audience. He was a master of self-publicity. It worked the same way his candelabrum did. It was a hallmark, a signature, a calling card. Why did he wear a white mink coat in 1972 for a command performance for the queen and the queen mother? "I didn't come here to go unnoticed," he repeated for the umpteenth time. And he continued: "That was not a silly remark on my part. I knew what I was saying. I knew it would be quoted. It's part of the showmanship that I rely on. The clothes attract attention. They get me newspaper headlines and interviews. They get me audiences." [34]

On a rather higher level, however, Liberace also recognized how dress provides identity or even self. At his 1952 Hollywood Bowl performance, he dressed to be seen on the stage from the most distant seats, but he dressed for other reasons, too. He did not want "to lose his identity," he said. On the contrary, his peculiar costume that evening allowed him to gain an identity, to make a persona, to create a presence. Clothing made the man. He re-created a character called "Liberace" that night. He put on white tails, "and all kinds of wonderful things began to happen."

Liberace professed no faith in the romantic concept of "natural beauty." We are what we wear, he proposed. We are indistinguishable from one another naked. Nakedness is democratic; adornment makes us individuals. Costume and dress disguise our sameness and allow the lustrous hierarchies of personality, glamour, and beauty to emerge. That his costumes grew increasingly outré was no accident, either. Costume was not supposed to be natural any more than celebrity was natural. Art and beauty are about outrageousness, he asserted, about bending and distorting reality. Celebrities are not supposed to dress like normal people. Stars should be recognized as such. "I truly hate to dress up when I'm not appearing before the public," he confessed. "When I *am,* I want to look like their image of me." [35]

He gave audiences what they wanted when he danced onto the stage.

> Liberace like to tell his audiences to stand by "while I go slip into something more spectacular." For 35 years that was the best part of watching him perform—waiting in delicious suspense to see in what outrageous guise he might appear next. A Norwegian blue shadow fox cape with a 16-foot train? A 24-karat gold-braided Russian czar's outfit? Why not? Liberace was SHOW BUSINESS stripped down to its gaudy heart and then blown up much bigger than life, and when he stepped through the curtains, no costume was too fantastic, no production number too elaborate, no entrance too grand. He never disappointed an audience. [36]

The cultural critic Camille Paglia has asserted that when women dress as men, they are laying claim to traditional male power; when men cross dress, they claim divinity. Liberace never cross dressed, but he did something almost comparable by pushing the outer limits of the acceptable in his attire. He did it consciously and calculated the outrage. On tour in Australia, he appeared in a long gold embroidered coat over a pair of lace pantaloons and patent leather boots, the only costume, he figured, less notable than that of his second-act opening. A critic described it: "The glamorous and talented Liberace pranced onto the stage in a patriotic red-white-and-blue hot pants suit complete with baton. For anybody else, it would have been a poor attempt at drag humor. But the crowd loved it and the star loved it even more." [37] "Mr. Showmanship is Mr. Everyman doing what Everyman dreams he could do if only he had a chance. And everyone can't get enough of him." [38]

Dress also provided answers to other, subtler questions in the performer's life. The "naked civil servant," Quentin Crisp, offered insights into this deeper, even paradoxical significance of the costumes. "He radiated a childlike glee at being popular," observed the Englishman. "I think it is very unlikely that his gaudiness was just any old way of increasing his income. I think it was much more probable that, as his capacity for dealing with—or rather, winning—his audience increased, his self-assurance grew, and he became more like the bejeweled icon that he always longed to be. As he grew more artificial, he became more genuine." [39] In 1984, still somewhat skeptical about the performer's transgressions, *Time* called

Liberace, a "Peacock Androgyne."[40] Given the nature of androgyny, "peacock" is probably redundant.

Behind his notions of art, beauty, performance, costume, and even peacock androgyny, Liberace possessed a clear and distinctive understanding of human nature. His huge popularity, again, suggests that he got it right. He applied the same rules to himself in caricature as he did to royalty, the church, Adam Clayton Powell, Marlene Dietrich, and Joan Crawford. People wanted to see his outrage. It satisfied their deepest longings. People live humdrum lives, the showman believed. By and large they accept their fate. Not much changes. They will not get wealth or fame, much less power and glory or celebrity. Still, they appreciate these qualities. They admire, moreover, those who achieve or represent these virtues. They look up to them, they stargaze. They worship movie stars. They revere royalty. They idolize celebrities. They deify even politicians. Popular taste is itself, then, hierarchical and submissive to the power of beauty and glamour, which, by extension, folks recognize on sight. This suggests still another element of both art and human nature. In describing the breach between art and reality or between stars and common people, Liberace emphasized the hierarchical nature of beauty. Beauty presupposes deference. It demands submission. It mocks equality. It makes us servile worshipers, he suggested. Beauty, glamour, and stars turn us into children; they make us "do childish things," as he testified about himself.

Fantasy and make believe fill the breach between the gazer and the star, and beauty lends itself—indeed, demands—not only fancy and fantasy, but mythology, myth making, legend, romance, dream, and dreaming. This was his essential art, and it addressed fundamental issues of the human condition. Nothing will change, but, through art, one can experience change, transformation, transcendence. This is another aspect of the inner vision adumbrated in the lyrics of "I'll Be Seeing You." In the half-light of the moon, the flickering illumination of candles, the glow of footlights, and the glitter of stars, illusion becomes a new reality. People need, demand fantasy, he insisted. "I try to help them do this for a little while, to help them forget work and problems and enjoy, vicariously, a folderol of fun, good music and fancy dress. I give them a little recess from the humdrum."[41] "That's why we have entertainment," he repeated toward the end of his life, "to make people forget all the troubles of the world."[42]

While emphasizing hierarchy, celebrity, and stars, however, Liberace also gave the theory a twist that was all his own. It was a unique contribution. He played Megastar for Everyman, but he never abandoned the Everyman in himself. To interpret the issue slightly differently, he added an Everyman component to his star persona or, alternatively, created a second persona that stood outside his own stardom. He celebrated himself as a hierophant of art and beauty, on the one hand, a simple Joe on the other. This curious combination produced all manner of effects in his career.

Even in megastardom, Liberace insisted on this humbler identity. He bragged about shopping at K-Mart and drinking André Cold Duck, for example. Just so, he never took his own fame for granted nor ever lost his awe at beauty, glamour, and the people who represented it. He could identify with the humblest member of his audience. "If I live to be 100, I'll be in awe of celebrities. I really don't consider myself one," he said.[43] "I am a star-gazer from way back in the days when I was much younger and very new in the world of glamorous entertainment," he wrote. "But I've never lost the fascination that success holds for me. I don't think that if I live to be a hundred I'll lose the excitement of meeting someone I admire, a celebrity . . . someone who has written a great book, painted a great picture, written a great play or made a great movie. When I see one of these people, I sometimes do childlike things."[44]

His little-boy innocence provided a critical source of his charm as a man and a performer. Friends and associates emphasized over and over how decent, fun, generous, and sincere he was. "He was exactly the same off stage as on, but funnier," reminisced Julie Budd, who had begun touring with him as a teenage prodigy in 1975. "There was an ease about him . . . he was the most genuine, caring, sincere guy who ever was."[45] The generosity he evidenced in the hospital room in Pittsburgh in 1963 pervaded his life. It took the most striking turns. Invited to the White House by Ronald and Nancy Reagan, for example, he asked his housekeeper at the Cloisters, Dorothy McMahon, to accompany him. To quiet her anxiety, he bought her appropriate clothes. When she fretted about her teeth, he paid for them to be capped.[46] His personal bounty equaled his material largess. Almost every friend or associate noted it. He was like the croupier who sympathized so completely with the players that he could hardly resist letting them win.

The same qualities permeated his act. "That little boy image, that warm sincerity you see onstage, it really is him—backstage, in his leisure time," testified Terry Clarkston, his friend and wardrobe manager. "He just wants everything and everyone in life to be happy."[47] "Few entertainers ever gave themselves over to their audiences so fully, and with such obvious affection," noted a critic. "To criticize him for excess was like complaining that Dolly Parton wasn't Joni Mitchell."[48] A fellow performer, and no slouch himself at controlling an audience, Milton Berle called him "one of the warmest . . . gentlemen I ever met, and I believe that the feeling flowed over the footlights and embraced the audience."[49] A hometown journalist captured the same quality near the end of the show-man's life. After summarizing the technical qualities of his April 1986 per-formance, the critic continued to the heart of Liberace's appeal: "Mr. Showmanship has another more potent, drawing power to his show: the warm and wonderful way he works his audience. Surprisingly enough, be-hind all the glitzy glitter, the corny false modesty and the shy smile, Libe-race exudes a love that is returned to him a thousandfold." [50]

A Las Vegas writer described the same characteristic: "He has that magic quality that makes him a star. It's called LIKABILITY." He contin-ued: "People LIKE Liberace. It doesn't matter that at times, he's outra-geous. Looking at the faces of the SRO audiences in the Hilton show-room, and that of the entertainer, you know they like each other. And, as friends are wont to do, they try to please each other. He in his perfor-mance, they in their applause. A magic formula that works." [51] "His act was based on excess. But the man himself was without pretense," ob-served another critic. "Underneath the feathers and the finery and trains fit for a coronation, he remained an eternal child, as dazzled by the won-derland he inhabited as the tourist who regularly paraded before his many houses, hoping to catch a glimpse of him." [52] "Liberace's sincerity is be-yond reproach," observed still another. "His joyful flamboyance is rooted in a child's wonderment. He's still the child with his nose pressed against the shop window. Only the window is Tiffany's." [53]

As an additional source of his appeal, this modest, flip side of celeb-rity also allowed him to objectify and even mock his own megastar cre-ation with all its excesses. Half of his jokes hinged on making fun of him-self and his various woes, otherwise defined. Was he "Mad About the Boy"? He was making light of the *Confidential* case even as his lawyers mounted their big guns against Robert Harrison. Was he terrified of being caught out in homosexual activity? That was subject for his stage humor too. "His gift was an infectious mixture of self-mockery, indefatigable en-ergy, and an almost childlike desire to please," one observer noted. [54] "He exaggerated the very elements of his persona and performance that had earned him his early notoriety," wrote another astute observer, so that "finally, it was impossible to make fun of Liberace because he was having too much fun making fun of himself. He was in on the joke; he may have created it." [55] He showed off his wealth, but he did so as if it belonged to someone else—while he remained the simple boy from Wisconsin. "In his show, he'd look at the audience, then at his dazzling apparel and say with a laugh, 'You know, sometimes I can't believe this myself,'" his old friend Jamie James chuckled long after. [56] "His self-deprecating humor and 'Gee whiz, aren't I lucky' attitude towards his wealth prevent him from alienating people when he flaunts those riches," wrote a *Los Angeles Times* reviewer. "He supplies fantasy fulfillment for everyone who yearns to revel in affluence."[57] "The piano was merely accompaniment to the good-humored vulgarity that was the real focus of his performances. . . . And he invited his audience to join him in giggling at the sheer silliness of it all," remarked one more reviewer.[58] His hometown newspaper got his performance on the money: "It would have all been difficult to endure if he had given the slightest indication of taking it seriously. That's clearly one secret of Liberace's success: He is fully aware that he's something of a joke, and he's very much in on the joke."[59]

The performer had it both ways. He compelled his audiences with his sincere pleasure and childlike delight in making them smile, even as he celebrated splendid stardom. The little-boy humanity, however, even multiplied the wonder of the accoutrements. The stage was his own escape from who he was, and he led his audiences from their own humdrum lives with the special enthusiasm of one who knew whereof they spoke. He was escaping into art and beauty on the very stage before the audience's very eyes. He transformed himself in every performance. And the stage and art transformed him, even as his own transformation changed and transported the audience. Every performance reenacted—like the mass—the miraculous transformation of the audience, and of the little boy himself.

Here, then, was the core of his performance, the basis of his act, and the aesthetics of his show. It was apparent from the beginning, back in La Crosse. He executed it modestly at first, in the supper clubs and fancy nightspots, with his elegant white tie and tails, the fancy candelabra. He continued the same expression in his television shows. He expanded the usage in his Las Vegas shows in the mid-fifties with his gold lamé and white sheared beaver. While he backed away from this aesthetic during the crises after 1957, in the last twenty-five years of his career he returned to radical visuals, stylistic extremism, and all the other elements of his practical definitions of art and beauty. Classically, in this regard, he reduced—or expanded—the solidest objects to sensory manifestations of light and splendor. He turned his piano itself into light and movement. Playing Caesar's Palace in 1985, he performed on a rhinestone-covered piano, "and when he launches into the finale, it starts to revolve, a merry-go-round shooting off splinters of light like a glitter ball on prom night."[60]

By 1962, then, the entertainer had not only reverted to his primary notions of show, he had moved into a new realm of showiness that made all his earlier costumes and performances look almost flat and colorless. By his own design and plan, his exaggerations accelerated yearly. While his devotees still loved him, the sixties and seventies were not generally congenial to his act. Although the entertainer hit on key themes in tradi-tional definitions of art and myth, he still contradicted other important elements and tenets of American culture. If his astonishing popularity reflects the degree to which he played on fundamental elements in show-manship, opposition persisted and found a new voice after 1963. Estab-lishment culture remained almost as skeptical as it had been in the fifties; what was increasingly called "the counterculture," however, had even less affinity for his art. As does the male vexation that characterized the fifties, countercultural opposition reveals essential elements in that culture itself.

In the sixties and seventies, the umpires of culture, centering in the Northeast, dealt with the Liberace phenomenon basically by ignoring him. The *New York Times,* that ultimate arbiter of the acceptable in estab-lishment culture, mentioned his name in print only four times between 1959 and 1980. In this very period, however, while his popularity was swelling in the heartland, even New Yorkers were mobbing him. In 1962, he performed at Manhattan's famed Latin Quarter where he played "to turn-away audiences." [61] Eight years later, he opened "so spectacularly," according to one report at the Waldorf-Astoria's Empire Room, "that he helped reawaken New York's long sleeping night life." [62] All this was be-neath the *Times*'s notice. In this regard, Liberace was something like Las Vegas itself in these years, a kind of national embarrassment. While Robert Venturi's study, *Learning from Las Vegas,* helped spark an intel-lectual interest in the gambling resort in 1977 as an important phenome-non of American culture, Liberace had to wait until the eighties for the cultural elites to pay him any mind.

When the high-toned critics took the time in these years to notice him, they dismissed him even more profoundly than they had in the fifties. Back in his hometown, even, one reviewer led his notice with the obser-vation that "there is one thing you have to give Milwaukee's Liberace—he violates everything including himself. What he has done to his God given talent is unforgivable. What he does to the music of Chopin is un-mentionable." He continued: "No man with any sense of self-respect would present himself on stage in a sequined gold jacket. Liberace does. No pianist worth his keep would make the mish-mash Liberace does of the lovely Chopin airs and polonaise themes. In the last analysis, no one would hold up one's relatives to such ridicule as this person does."

Was the showman playing a high school benefit concert to raise funds for a new piano? The critic conceded nothing. "The cause is commend-able. The performance was inexcusable." New York had penetrated even the Midwest heartland, and the critic actually paraphrased a line first of-fered by the ferociously condescending critic at the *New York Times* in conjunction with Liberace's 1953 Carnegie Hall performance.[63] "Given a certain number of cocktails in an agreeable lounge, you might enjoy his music. With luck, you might not even hear it."[64]

The Milwaukee reviewer made these observations in 1962. In 1975, another hometown critic echoed the same opinion. Besides dismissing the pianist's "hokey" monologues, he wondered "if all the vulgarity that convulses his middle aged and older audience is really necessary." There was something pitiful, too, he added, "about Liberace's pudgy little boy smile." Unlike the other reviewer, however, he conceded the pianist's musical talent. "All the kitsch may be integral to Liberace's act and success. But his pianistic skill and serious musicianship make the act bearable." What he gave he immediately retracted, however, with the invidious reference to the performer's commercialism: "Liberace will repeat his money making act for another sold out house at 8 p.m. Thursday."[65]

His commercial success, his popularity, and pandering, as it was called, to his audience still left high-toned critics apoplectic. The *New York Times* and its devotees in the provinces represented "culture" as it was formally defined in the United States, but its alternative—the counterculture—found even less to admire in the boy from West Allis. Liberace, in turn, found the sixties revolutionaries as objectionable as he had his old critics, maybe even more so. Tenets of the counterculture actually resembled many establishment values apparent in the 1950s debates over early television. The radicalism of the sixties exaggerated some of these and added others, all of which ran completely against Liberace's ideas of life, art, and performance.

In form, at least, rebellion and rejection dominated the values of the generation maturing in the sixties. It was literally reactionary—it was *counter*culture before it was anything else, even when its antagonism assumed a positive, if countervailing epistemology. Radically egalitarian and individualistic, it mocked authority and challenged any order outside a subjective sense of things. The bumper-sticker slogan, "Challenge Authority" fit nicely. Naturalistic and realistic, it assumed power and power relationships as the most fundamental elements of natural order. Politics, in this frame of reference, was nothing more than the gross or subtle manipulation of power, and politics became, thus, the essence of everything. It assumed the politicization of art, for example, in painting and protest songs, but no less in sex and racial issues. It spawned feminism, gay rights, and Black separatism. Its forays into fantasy were drug-induced, but even drug use was justified as a political activity. In a supreme oxymoron of the age, dropping out became a political act. As objects of scorn, all traditional institutions came under attack, not to mention tradition, itself, of course: family, religion, the state, universities—the formal institutions, as well as masculinity, femininity, capitalism—the informal ones.

The counterculture challenged everything Liberace cherished, and if the piano player from Milwaukee was not important enough to be bombed in his Palm Springs or Las Vegas digs, he recognized the threat and took occasion to criticize the movement in most of its particulars. His criticisms underscore his own aesthetic but also his profound, deep-dyed conservatism.

Liberace had no interest in politics, and certainly not in radical politics. He joked about his two terms as honorary mayor of Sherman Oaks: "I didn't like it," he asserted. "So enough of politics. It's not my cup of confusion." [66] If he voted at all, his values lay with Midwestern, conservative Republicanism. He believed in the importance of individual responsibility, for example. Social evil? No, he answered, "Much of the sorrow that exists is brought about by the individuals themselves." Whether "a pianist or a bricklayer or a senator," he continued, "as long as you do your work with sincerity and dedication, as well as a happy outlook on life, you can avoid many unhappy burdens." [67]

Liberace's idea of the polity resembled that of his fellow Midwesterners Ronald Reagan and Rock Hudson, who had also gone West to make their fortunes in Hollywood. He disliked "big government" and taxes, for example. He grieved over the loss of wealth and aristocratic grandeur to federal taxing policy, in particular. His own long, drawn out run-in with the IRS exacerbated his antagonism. "Not many people realize that I have a partner," he complained in *The Things I Love.* "Whenever I make a dollar, fifty cents of it goes to taxes. There was a time when if you made a million dollars, you had made a million dollars. You didn't have to say, "Well, only half of it belongs to me; the other half belongs to Uncle Sam." He concluded: "How America is changing!" [68]

Liberace's dislike of unions was another manifestation of his personal conservatism. In a world that favored individual enterprise, he saw no need for collective bargaining; on the contrary, unions ran completely against this ideological grain. He would have known of leftist strikers and communist sympathizers from their campaigns at the Allis-Chalmers plant in his hometown in the thirties and forties, and perhaps they exaggerated his natural antipathy. Union opposition had made him abandon the phonograph part of his old act in 1947. He considered the objections frivolous. Just so, he took no cognizance whatsoever of a musicians' strike when he was playing the Sahara Tahoe in the late seventies. Scott Thorson repeated that after a most unlikely dinner with Bella Abzug and Shirley

MacLaine, Liberace expressed astonishment "when Bella refused to be his guest at our show because she didn't want to cross a picket line. Bella and her concerns were totally alien to him, a part of the wider world that Lee chose to ignore," Thorson claimed.[69] Liberace had immediately followed his objection to the welfare state with a criticism of unions and unionization. They represented, he mused, one more manifestation of changing times and American decline.[70]

The leftist politics of the sixties and after left the entertainer completely cold. On that memorable evening they spent with MacLaine and Abzug, Thorson related, his lover nearly passed out as the conversation grew more and more political. While the two women waxed increasingly passionate, the pianist "got quieter and quieter until his eyes began to glaze. I remember that Shirley and Bella were quite agitated about a recent incident involving police brutality, but by then," Thorson remembered, "I was so afraid that Lee might actually fall asleep at the table that I don't recall where or when the police brutality was supposed to have taken place."[71]

The showman grew more heated, however, over stars—like Jane Fonda and Ed Asner—who used stardom to advance a leftist agenda.[72] Over and over he returned to the theme: "An entertainer's function is to entertain, not to preach." He concluded, "So I'm very apolitical; I do not want to get involved in politics at all. An entertainer should stay out of it."[73] "I never go on the stage to preach," he repeated. "I do my thing, and I do it sincerely. I want the audience to love me; and the only way to do that is to let them know that I care about them and love them. I sometimes wonder what would happen if I planted a different seed (which I have seen other performers do), a seed wherein you incite riot and disorder. If only you could get an audience all thinking one way, and thus create a feeling of congeniality, you could dispel many of the world's problems."[74]

He played the White House for Truman, Eisenhower, and Nixon; he was a special White House guest of Ronald and Nancy Reagan. Each of these politicians mirrored the mainstream American values that dominated Liberace's life. He did not perform for John and Jacqueline Kennedy. Nor did he dance to the tune of social activism and political engagement announced in Kennedy's thousand days and delivered in Lyndon Johnson's Great Society. His autobiographical treatment of racial issues clearly limns his larger commitments—and his alienation from the activism of the era. In discussing a command performance before the queen of England in 1960, he related, incidentally, how Nat King Cole and Sammy Davis Jr. had occupied the same bill. Without any specific reference to race, he described how Davis was catching flak from the press because he was married to a Swedish woman, May Britt. Liberace's outrage had nothing to do with race. "Those yellow tabloids in London, in those days," he grieved, "lived on picking the bones of personalities. I felt very sorry for Sammy because I knew what he was going through."[75] Along the same lines, he respected Lena Horne beyond almost any other performer, but as with Sammy Davis, without any specific racial referent. He honored her for the same reasons he admired Davis—for her courage, persistence, and determination to triumph over the odds of making it. "She's been through so much adversity and prejudice—and triumphed over it all that every time I see her up on stage wowing an audience, I get goose bumps!" he told Scott Thorson.[76] In this context, racial prejudice was only one adversity, and his celebration was analogous to praising blind deaf-mutes who learn to speak: a manifestation of will and energy over debilities and handicaps.

He addressed racial politics more directly when discussing a tour of South Africa in the seventies. He related how, while on his way to Johannesburg, he was quizzed by reporters on his Heathrow layover. When one reporter asked him, "Why are you going to South Africa?" he knew the trouble that was brewing. He used the issue to reflect on race, politics, and art. "Anybody who knows my personal life knows that the color of a man's skin means nothing to me. I think segregation is indecent and inhuman and I loathe the idea of it. But I don't think that it's the place of an American piano player to try to change the quality of life in the Republic of South Africa." "I do not intend to get involved in internal problems," he told the reporter. "I'm going there to bring entertainment and, I hope, happiness to people. Their way of life is something they have to work out for themselves." He concluded: "I guess I just can't see the sense of mixing politics and show business the way some of my friends do." Within a counterculture context of politics, of course, the only thing worse than playing a South African venue would have been the very justification he offered in separating politics from performance. By asserting that art is apolitical, he violated one of the fundamental tenets of a generational prejudice.[77]

He elaborated on his notions of art and politics elsewhere. The Kennedy family prompted another discussion. He had bought a monogrammed dinner service that had belonged to the Kennedys. His guests' opinions on his use of the china varied. "Some of my friends who are more politically minded than I am sometimes question my use of the Kennedy plates. Some feel they're too sacred to eat from, others act as if they thought the plates were poison. Personally, I think both reactions are inexcusable," he mused. "I hate to think that things of great beauty created by master craftsmen must have a political connotation. I feel the same way about music and books of certain countries being banned. I don't think genuine works of art, music and literature are capable of doing harm. I don't think beauty and politics mix. The former depends on dreams, the latter on realities." [78]

If he resented the counterculture's politicization of art, the radicals' anticommercialism, anticapitalism, and repudiation of the work ethic puzzled him no less. He liked to work, and he worked hard. He liked making money. He assumed his audiences did so as well. He made a lot of money, and he spent a lot of money. At the same time, he also refused to take getting and spending completely seriously, either. It was the stuff of jokes and humor. As for monetary compensation, he always insisted on giving every audience its money's worth, too. And more. This was a part of the American way as he perceived it: the United States was a kind of racetrack that encouraged its citizens to run as far and as fast as their energy and natural talents allowed them; it rewarded their swiftness. He liked this American way and loved his fellow countrymen, the ordinary folk. Just so, in respecting his countrymen, he honored the United States in a time when patriotic values were declining and national pride fell to new lows.

His ideas about the rewards for running the American race also contradicted the pop wisdom of the counterculture. In one of the key aphorisms of the era, Andy Warhol claimed that everyone got fifteen minutes of fame. This democratization of celebrity offended the showman's deepest values. He dismissed the "Johnny-come-lately performers, who cut a record in a garage and find they have a hit on their hands. . . . They make a fast buck but they shorten their careers," he said. "Of course, there are some to whom one freak hit *is* their career," he added. [79] Celebrity and fame, he insisted over and over, were neither democratic nor leveling. They were hard to achieve and harder still to keep. And, of course, the object was to get and then to keep one's status. Fifteen-minute fame made no sense to him. Celebrity was based, instead—if variously—on merit, virtue, hierarchy, style, or calculation. It was aristocratic, not egalitarian, of its nature. Stars, royalty, presidents, and popes earned the deference of common folk who would not, could not ever claim status, not for fifteen minutes, not ever. He believed stars should dress and behave like stars. "It worries me when I'm on a plane and someone with me says, 'You know who's on this plane?' Then they mention some name that I may have read about. 'He's just made his third gold record.' That means he's sold over 3,000,000 records. I think that's exciting," he wrote. "I look around and there's not a star in sight." [80]

The age's infatuation with chemical-induced fantasy also horrified him. "It is such a shame these days to see bright and talented performers ruin their careers and their lives with drugs and alcohol," he moaned.[81] This pronouncement resonates with a consistent line he took against drugs in any form, even cigarettes. Thus, while he was a heavy smoker, he did not like being photographed with a cigarette. Scott Thorson maintained in his memoir that his lover was actually a heavy drinker as well as a smoker, and criticizes him, in effect, for hypocrisy. The charge rings true. "Do everything in moderation," the entertainer pontificated in his memoir. "Drinking, smoking, sex . . . all in moderation. They joy of that is that you get to do everything longer, particularly sex."[82] This admonition runs counter to his own glorification of excess; even so, it offers evidence of the entertainer's sharp differentiation between public and private or between image and reality that was essential to his life and aesthetics.

Style and dress also put him at odds with the younger generation. He was a hierarch and a dandy. Raised up on the glamour and savoir faire of Fred Astaire, Cary Grant, Cole Porter, Joan Crawford, Claudette Colbert, Bette Davis, and the Hollywood idols of the thirties, he was baffled—despite his aesthetic and personal tolerance—by the stylelessness of the period, by wailing folk singers in ragged clothes with acoustic guitars.

He loathed "the dirty, hippie look," and condemned the values that produced them: " 'hippie' is such a distorted image; some hippies are just not to be admired," he instructed one reporter.[83] Why did Barbra Streisand, who had one of the most fabulous voices he had ever heard, dress like a hobo, he wondered. "The first time I saw Barbra down in the Village," he recalled, "it looked as if she'd just been to a rummage sale and was wearing it. Standing next to Emmett Kelley, the clown, she would have made him look like a well-dressed man." "Kooky clothing was sort of an obsession," with her, he mused; the one thing "she hadn't discovered about show business was the value of glamour. It almost seemed as if she'd never even heard the word." He was relieved, however, that finally "this, too, got through to her."[84] His discussion of Streisand's discovery of glamour reveals another aspect of his viewpoint. "Soon, inspired by the sort of clothes she obviously liked to wear because in some odd way their oddness suited her, the big couturiers began designing things especially for Barbra, and she has become a leader in the fashion world."[85] He was open to the way counterculture stylelessness could become style in itself. It was, however, a major, conscious transformation.

Rejecting the age's insistence on naturalness and stylelessness, he also repudiated "kookiness," as he used the word in reference to Streisand. He included in this category a kind of self-conscious mockery of fashion and style. "The only person who I think outrages would be Elton John," he reflected in 1977, "but he goes for laughs." Thus, he dismissed the British singer's outfits as "bizarre." "His costumes are not meant to be attractive. They're meant to be amazing, bizarre." [86] He did not like to see high style ridiculed any more than he appreciated its being repudiated. While he might have used the word "outrage" to define his own style, he always modified it with the term "calculated." He did not want to outrage the public but rather to push the limits of the acceptable, or to play, literally, with design and fashion. Whether he crossed the line or not, however, this seemed his intent in distancing himself from John's violation of the public order.

He found other clothing innovations of the era equally objectionable. Nudity, for example, did not interest him at all. It was, in effect, too democratic. "Nudity doesn't show anything that everybody hasn't got," he objected. "We dress to improve our natural endowments." [87] He objected, particularly, to women's tendency to wearing fewer and fewer articles of clothing in the sixties. "Their scheme doesn't seem to be working. The law of diminishing returns has set in. The more they show the less attention they get." [88]

If nakedness nullified style—and with it glamour, celebrity, distinction, and the like, not to mention accepted conventional notions of public decency—Liberace had other reasons to dread baring all. He defined a natural calculus, in this regard. "When business began to fall off in the film houses and theaters because people were becoming disenchanted with what they were seeing, producers began to throw in a little nudity," he wrote. "But pretty soon a little nudity became dull and they had to throw in a little more nudity until there was nothing very interesting about it." The inevitable "topping" process led to other excesses, he related. Jaded with nakedness, he continued, "The need seems to be for nudity, pornographic explicitness and violence." [89] The entertainer disdained nakedness also because it led, he believed, inevitably toward the brutalization of the human spirit. A little nakedness, he thought, led to more nakedness; more nakedness led to overt sex; sex led just as inevitably to violence and brutality. He disdained naturalism, realism, and animal instincts for slaughter and rapine. Art as fantasy, make believe, and escape provided an outlet or alternative to this tendency inscribed, as the entertainer would have it, in human nature itself. From personal experience, too, he recognized the human disposition toward the pornographic. In separating art from nature, he also tried to manage the conflicting aspects of his own nature. He did so fitfully, and, in the end, his own animal instincts helped destroy him.

I considered at the time that we were lovers at the time. He stated often—one time I reminded him of his kid brother Rudy. Another time he told me he always wanted children, but he couldn't have them. He thought—it is so hard to explain.

SCOTT THORSON

Twelve

AN IMAGE IN THE WATER

"The queens are rioting! The queens are rioting!" the man kept repeating to his associate. When asked for an explanation, the man related that "the queens" were the drag queens, their admirers, and other patrons at a local gay bar on Christopher Street in lower Manhattan not far from the Greenwich Village restaurant where they had dined a little earlier. "They're fighting the cops!" he jabbered.[1] It was June 28, 1969. The New York City police were raiding the Stonewall Inn. In the heady days that gave the world Black Power, Woman Power, Chicano Power, Student Power, and animal rights, among other novelties, homosexual revolutionaries were coming up on Concord Bridge. With the Stonewall Inn raid, sang the hyperbolic prose of the New York *Daily News,* "Queen power reared its bleached-blond head in revolution."[2]

As early as 1964 or 1965, gay radicals and activists were already developing strategies, tactics, and an ideology that corresponded to the other power movements of the era, but the summer of '69 formalized early efforts and plans. "Stonewall" became the rallying cry for freedom and liberation, autonomy and integrity, legitimacy and public authority for American homosexuality after 1969. "Pre-" and "post-Stonewall" became categories for understanding attitudes both about and within homosexual culture. The latter connoted both public and private acceptance, political legitimacy, honor, and authenticity—one of the especially favored virtues of the age. The other signified antithetical values: victimization, shame, deviance, and crime. Post-Stonewall assumed a break with the past and a new era. As homosexuality moved out of the darkness into public life, so, too, individual men abandoned secrecy for Gay Pride. They demanded accommodation in the public arena. New values emerged; so did new enemies. "Closet Queen" became analogous to "Uncle Tom" as the categories of the Black Power movement slopped over into the politicization of homosexuality. And there were other parallels between what was happening within the black community and the gay one. Indeed, in various ways, the radical politicization of both the Black Power and the Gay Power movements reflected similar forces at work.

In the cases of both black and homosexual politics, a new ideology overlapped with and reinforced generational antagonisms. Conservative or moderate homosexual men, like conservative or moderate blacks, lost standing, even legitimacy, among their fellows. This worked two ways, both from within and from without. From within, young radicals seized the initiative, attacking not only the failures of the American system but, effectively, the failures of their accommodationist predecessors as well. Their puritanical, very American disposition to see the world in absolute categories of right and wrong exaggerated the evils of oppression for them and cut the ground from under moderates—even as it elevated their own standing as the vanguard of justice and righteousness. Just so, their demands for unity privileged their own position and their own leadership.[3] From outside, the dominant culture reinforced their position. It did so through a certain cultural ideology; it did so practically as well. Insofar as blacks and gays remained the Other in the mainstream order, the institutions of that order tended to lump all together into undifferentiated categories: a black was a black; a homosexual a homosexual. Even so, a peculiar fascination with otherness tended to exaggerate the mainstream's interest in the most extreme and bizarre manifestations of the Other. More practically, outré made good newspaper copy and television coverage. The most outspoken, then, were accepted as the norm, effectively, for both subgroups. Their public fame, in turn, boosted their standing within the gay and black movements.[4]

The sixties witnessed the radicalization of the world and the fragmentation of the social, political order. If the factionalization of the political order into competing power blocks could be seen in the classic political context of Madison's *Federalist Number 10*, real life was not so simple as the theory. It baffled the celebrity piano player from Wisconsin.

The Stonewall Riot had erupted in the very early morning hours of June 28. Seven weeks before, on May 16, Lee Liberace had turned fifty. By this time, he had long before worked out his own compromises with his sexuality and with American life. He had settled in. Nothing in his background had prepared him to abandon these adjustments. The alterations in the public scene were so profound, however, that as a gay man he could not have avoided them entirely, even had he chosen to do so. He did not, and he paid heavy penalties for liberation. For Liberace, the Stonewall revolution was as much a millstone as a milestone.

For homosexual culture as well as for Liberace himself, the Stonewall rebellion had various, even contradictory effects. One was to normalize male randiness. From the forties and fifties, homosexual memoirists have chronicled the frequency and variety of their sexual partners. "The *thousands* of people I went to bed with!" Ned Rorem had exclaimed, characteristically, of the war years.[5] Just so, the elegant, handsome and well-born Otis Bigelow kept a journal of his tricks that fascinated Alfred Kinsey, not least for the numbers. "That's what one did in those days—you'd have four or five in an hour, if you were attractive and had some nerve."[6] Stonewall registered subtle and not-so-subtle shifts in attitudes about promiscuity. If homosexuality were unexceptional, ran the logic, the extremest manifestations of the activity were, perforce, normal too. Indeed, after the sixties, homosexual promiscuity came to be claimed as a kind of right. Institutions of promiscuity—bars, clubs, the baths—thrived. Effectively, society and the law confirmed these trends, with the waning of police raids and government surveillance, for example. Baths and bathhouse sex, of course, had existed earlier—as in Gore Vidal's account, but they and the kind of sex they fostered did not constitute the norm, even in homosexual havens like New York, San Francisco, or Los Angeles. Such institutions made sex easy, even acceptable, where it had been difficult, even objectionable before. Where the Otis Bigelow of one generation had scorned clubs and "dark cruising," Edmund White, of another, celebrated such activities as the very essence of homosexual life. When Bigelow recorded having multiple sexual partners within a single hour, he was not referring to anal sex, either. The baths and back rooms of clubs of White's generation, in contrast, facilitated and even encouraged such activity. Much more critical, such institutionalized randiness proliferated over the whole country. Baths, clubs, and bars, once mostly isolated and rare even in the great cities, now sprouted everywhere.

The liberation of the homosexual libido, however, was only one effect of the Stonewall movement. Another one moved in a different direction. If homosexuality were normal, then normal monogamy should apply to homosexuals as well. The appeal for male-male marriage, marital benefits for homosexual unions, and the like came after the rawer sexual liberation, but it flowed logically from the normalizing movement. As the twentieth century winds down, thirty years after the Christopher Street raid, the two tendencies still figure in debates within the homosexual community, with the more radical, libertarian types attacking the more conservative types, who advocate discipline and monogamy. Both camps arose, however, from the same source: the normalization of the homosexual impulse. The difficulty lay in determining the proper outlet for that desire.

In the sixties and early seventies, these issues hardly affected Liberace's life. According to Scott Thorson, most of Liberace's closest professional associates were gay. They fell mostly within his own age cohort. This was his informal, subterranean cosmos. He separated it from the rest of his life. Even when the two worlds overlapped, he failed or refused to acknowledge the tangent. He hewed, practically, to the line that homosexuality was an activity, not an ideology. In his memoir of their life together, for example, Scott Thorson makes regular if incidental references to his mentor's failing or refusing to identify himself sexually at all. "Although the family never discussed Lee's sexual identity, they had to know he was gay," Thorson postulated. "His mother may have known too. But she undoubtedly thought there was nothing wrong with her son that the right woman couldn't cure. . . . Frances seemed utterly unconcerned by my presence in her son's life. She knew we lived together, went everywhere together; she may even have suspected that we shared a bed. But, like Lee she had an extraordinary ability to close her mind to anything that might have been unpleasant. She always greeted me warmly, with the same welcoming embrace she gave her son."[7]

Liberace's family's failure to acknowledge his homosexuality outlived the showman. After his death, his sister repeated flatly that her brother had not died of AIDS; he had not been gay either, she testified. "He was just unique. He was special because he was born with a caul," she said.[8] She had not seen what she had seen. Homosex was everywhere, but it was nowhere, too.

Sexually, the fifties foreshadowed the outline of the last three decades of Liberace's life. He seems to have indulged in mostly pickup sex or short-term affairs. The sexual encounter with the young actor Rock Hudson around 1952 or '53 suggests the pattern. Beyond Hudson, John Rechy has been the most famous of Liberace's pickups to reveal the steps of the showman's sexual minuet. The two former Liberace protégé-employees had arranged a dinner, and Rechy described his first encounter with the showman during their meal. "He put his hand on my crotch right under the table. This was rude. You don't want to say anything, because it's a dinner. So when he left, he wanted me to go with him, and there was this big fuss because his bodyguard was with him and saw what was going on. Later he called back. He was crying 'Please come, I'm so lonesome. Please, please come!'" This was the same line he would feed Scott Thorson twenty years later, and, like the blond teenager, the light-eyed, dark-haired young hustler was actually moved. He accepted the invitation to visit the house on Valley Vista Boulevard. "I thought I was being humane. But I was being naive, too," he mused. "So I went into that incredible black-and-white house he had in Los Angeles. He had these poodles that were black and white. They were running all over, and suddenly *I* was running all over because he was actually quite aggressive. He was an incredibly, incredibly aggressive man. He was just *determined* to get sex. He offered to show me the house, and every time we turned around it was another bedroom. Finally there was his big one. I had to run out."[9]

Ever horny, he put the make on almost anyone. There was, for example, the handsome young Swedish luncheon visitor from the pre-Cloisters Palm Springs days. The Miami-based theatrical manager of the Danish piano comic Victor Borge told a story of another such encounter. "Whenever Lee came to Florida, he'd call me up and I'd drive up to see him in Palm Beach. On one of these visits, it must have been in the late sixties, I took a young friend with me," the impresario related. "Frank must have still been in his teens. Liberace insisted we go to dinner with him. We hadn't dressed so he provided some clothes for us for eating out—they were really garish with ruffles and piano-shaped cuff links. Really vulgar stuff. He was also taken with Frank. I came home alone that night. I didn't hear hide nor hair from that boy, and I was worried about what his parents would say. But after his 'night of bliss,' he made it home safe and sound that Sunday evening."[10] The young man was tall, slender, with dark Italian good looks. Thirty years later, the former teenager still guarded the confidences of his evening with the celebrity. "He was a very aggressive gentleman is all I will say," the man recalled.[11]

There are other such stories of still more casual encounters. "I lived really close to his house on Valley Vista Boulevard. His mother and mine were friends. I was just a teenager and not his type at all—I'm Indian! He liked blonds! We didn't do anything serious, but we just messed around and made out," reported a trim, swarthily handsome real-estate salesman of his sexual adventure with the showman in the late fifties or early sixties. The same man, before his marriage, also made similar alliances with Rock Hudson and a raft of other L.A. types.[12]

Cruisy encounters and boy pickups became a part of the Liberace underground lore. A gay Hollywood insider reported similar episodes. "In the '60s, you could often see Liberace cruising the Akron store on Sunset Boulevard with his little doggie in hand, dressed all in white—Lee

I mean—trying to pick up Mexicans in the store's parking lot," the television producer chuckled. "He wasn't discreet, he was daring and rather outrageous about it. He'd stand in the lot and try and pick up young men parking their cars. Most didn't recognize him!"[13] None of this is very different from the gossip sheets' earliest stories in 1954 about Liberace picking up strangers in bathrooms and hitting on weightlifters. Nor, of course, does it fail to fit with the particulars of the episode chronicled by *Hollywood Confidential* in the spring of 1957.

What was the nature of these affairs when they actually panned out? An afternoon or evening tryst might have stretched into a weekend liaison or even—as the one with Rock Hudson did—to a couple of weeks; some extended even longer. In the absence of hard empirical evidence, to say exactly how much longer is problematical, as is determining the number of men the showman took in after 1970. Lucille Cunningham, the performer's longtime accountant, was in charge of disbursing cash, including paying Lee's companions' bills. By the time Scott Thorson came along in 1977, she was pressing seventy-five years old. She had been around; she had seen plenty of Lee's tricks. They came, they went; she stayed. She had little patience any more. Thorson, who was only a teenager then, dropped by Cunningham's desk one day to instruct her about paying some charges. His vanity offended the septuagenarian bookkeeper. To put the boy in his place, she attacked him with a list of his predecessors. "'You really think you are something,'" she hissed. "Well let me tell you, Mr. High and Mighty, Lee's had a string of boys like you. Has he told you about Bobby or Hans or the male stripper who used to live with him? We called that one 'the country boy' because he was such an ignorant hick! I've seen them come and I've seen them go. You won't be any different. One of these days Lee with tell Seymour Heller to get rid of you and then you'll be out on your ear too!"[14]

Scott Thorson had come into the showman's life in 1977. He was eighteen. Before him, according to the bookkeeper's account, there had also been "Bobby," "Hans," and "the country boy." Thorson left no information about them other than their names. John Rechy knew others, but he assigned them no names. His tryst with the showman in the late fifties turns up the presence of the jealous, nameless "bodyguard-lover" who interrupted the star's vulgar groping at Rechy's audition dinner.[15]

Others crop up here and there. While being deposed in his palimony suit against the showman, Thorson mentioned in passing some of his predecessors in Liberace's bed. He did not describe the duration of the relationship, but he mentioned that Lee had tricked around with one man, Chris Cox, years before on the East Coast. They remained friends afterwards when the old lover operated the Odyssey, a gay club in Los Angeles. Indeed, Cox himself came to figure in the palimony suit as one of Lee's allies against Thorson.[16] This suggests still another aspect of Lee's relationship with his sexual partners. His liaisons might have been as short as they were numerous, but he split without rancor and took care of his companions afterwards. His loyalty to the "underworld-type" figure Chris Cox, as Thorson described him, repeated itself with others. "Liberace was tougher than people imagine. I saw how he worked," reported John Rechy. "I saw the bodyguards he had to protect him. But he did take care of people who stopped being his main boyfriend. He would hire them to work for him." Pondering the showman's character further, he concluded: "He was a *nice* man."[17]

Who were Liberace's boyfriends? What were they like? What do their mostly ephemeral forms reveal about the showman's desires and needs? What was the nature of his relationships with these men? Lucille Cunningham's description of "the country boy" as an ignorant and uncultivated male stripper offers a clue to the showman's taste. So does the presence of the hustler Rechy in the entertainer's retinue—insofar as the budding writer-intellectual studiously proletarianized himself and artfully disguised his intelligence and creativity.[18] So, too, of course, does the showman's cruising the Mexican parking-lot attendants off Sunset Boulevard.

A pattern emerges from this fragmentary data of the entertainer's sexual proclivities: tricks, tricking around, one-night or weekend stands, temporary or transient relationships, an attraction to younger men, a devotion to inferiors. This pattern implies other sexual elements: libidinousness, aggressiveness, and promiscuousness. Other data, already mentioned, supports the conclusion. "He was an incredibly, incredibly aggressive man," repeated John Rechy. Another old associate put the showman's aggressiveness in clearer focus still: "Oh, Lee was a top! He liked to fuck."[19]

Scott Thorson had access to none of this information. Indeed, consciously or unconsciously, Liberace tried to keep all of it from him. Thorson, however, confirmed and elaborated on these accounts through his own observations of the entertainer, with whom he lived for almost five years.

Upon their first meeting, the showman put the make on the teenager almost immediately—echoing the style John Rechy had described. Not incidentally, the approach also resembled *Confidential*'s 1956 reconstruction of the pianist's encounter with the "handsome young press agent." According to Thorson, Liberace possessed "an insatiable sex drive." Reflecting on his early career, Liberace told Thorson about "spending more time thinking about sex during those years than he spent thinking about his act." Nor had his appetites diminished with time and age. They were "at an all-time high," his boyfriend repeated of his sixty-year-old patron. With Thorson, "he wanted sexual encounters a couple of times a day." [20]

In the popular parlance, Lee was "oversexed." Besides admitting that he thought about sex all the time, he satisfied his craving with pornography, again according to Thorson. "He used pornography to become aroused and ready for sex," Thorson wrote. "Each time Lee viewed one of his tapes he'd want to have sex." [21] In a somewhat different context, however, Thorson related that Liberace loved the material for itself. He described his mentor's pornographic films as a "consuming interest." "His collection was extensive and well used," he said. "Before my arrival he'd watched hard-core pornography as a steady diet." Although he apparently stopped doing this upon Thorson's arrival, the young man also declared that Liberace used to share his films "at all-male parties." Particular sex scenes turned him on. "The variety of sexual acts he saw in the screen fascinated him. Nothing made him hotter than watching a three-way." [22] Liberace relished live pornography where it was available. In 1981, on international tour, Lee took his young companion sightseeing through the European sexual underground. "We'd been told that Hamburg had the most outrageous night life—porno palaces—and Lee was determined to see them for himself." The city fulfilled his patron's expectations with nightclubs "where the entertainment consisted of a variety of sex acts performed on stage. . . . He sat, riveted by the action, as a series of acts—homosexual and heterosexual unfolded in front of us." While Thorson found it distasteful, he said, the show transfixed his lover. [23]

Stateside, the showman satisfied his desires, again according to Thorson, with visits to porno emporiums and "adult book stores." These functioned not only as merchandising outlets for pornographic material, but as assignation spots as well. Indeed, visiting them was a kind of sexual experience in itself. Lee's young friend described a trip to one of these places in Ft. Lauderdale, Florida, in 1981. Since 1980, because of U.S. Supreme Court rulings, pornography has become a legitimate industry, and supermarketlike emporia with names like Pleasure Palace II sprout their meters-high pink neon signs across freeways in all major cities. Nevertheless, the old form, as described by Thorson, persists in small-town America still. In "one of Lauderdale's sleazier neighborhoods," the porno market "presented a blank, windowless face from the street," he related.

> Inside, racks loaded with pornographic books and magazines
> lined the front of the store, while shelves of merchandise—

whips, chains, other objects used in sadomasochistic sex acts, even dildos and other things . . . were near the back. . . .

There was a series of viewing machines, like old-fashioned nickelodeons, where you could watch sex flicks to your heart's content—heterosexual, homosexual, sex acts featuring animals or children; they had it all. . . . The bookstore also had private cubicles in the back with what are known in the gay world as "glory holes." For a small fee a man could rent one of the cubicles, put his penis through the "glory hole," and wait for a response.

The scene, the younger man insisted, transfigured his mentor. "Lee's eyes gleamed as he took it all in," Thorson remembered. He "was soon going from viewer to viewer, grinning all over the place." [24]

Scott Thorson insisted he had accompanied his lover here under duress. Moreover, he considered it dangerous for his patron to have visited the shop. The next morning, he hectored him about the transgression. "About last night," he admonished. "You're a well-known star and you're out of your fucking mind to go in a place like that! What the hell would you have done if someone, a reporter, had seen you in there? How would you explain that to all the little old ladies?" [25]

For all Thorson's outrage, Liberace's visit to the Ft. Lauderdale porn shop is perfectly consonant with his cruising boys on Sunset Boulevard in broad daylight in full Liberacean regalia. They sprang from the same preoccupations. If a part of Liberace's indulgence arose from egomania and out of a disregard for getting caught—as suggested by Thorson—he may also have been driven by the opposite motive: the excitement of the illicit. In snappy gay parlance, "Danger Queens" flirt with risk and peril as a source of sexual arousal. Along the same lines, the forbidden-fruit aphorism applies. In this regard, sexual expression that is generally unaccepted offers a double dip of the forbidden—since homosex is illicit of its nature, participation in illicit homosexual activity makes for an extra rush. Even so, the illicitness—the source of danger—also provided limits. Those limits were the social sanctions against such forms of sexuality. Every decade after Stonewall brought a reduction of those social constraints. Whether Liberace liked it or not, whether he approved or not, the gay scene—political and social—was developing aggressively through the mid-sixties. The self-consciousness increased afterwards. After Stonewall, it acquired more legitimacy with each passing year. Liberace participated in this new world, in part, as an extension of his old values. Were gay clubs more numerous and more open, for example? He visited them. As one associate from the Springs recalled, he would sweep in, bedecked in his extravagant outfits, covered with glittering jewelry and heavy makeup, and surrounded by beefcake. Although he steadfastly refused to make a statement about his sexual preferences, he did loosen up a bit publicly. By the mid-seventies, he had gone from an absolute denial of his homosexuality to a professed lack of interest in the topic. "I hate it when people whisper things and think they're giving me a juicy bit," he grumbled, "Like, 'I just heard something about someone you know. It's so-and-so. He sucks cock.' I say, 'Great! Fantastic!' It's all a lot of shit. Who cares?" He no longer cared, he insisted; nobody cared. The Cassandra trial, he ruminated in 1975? "Now people couldn't care less about that sort of thing. I kid about it on stage in my shows, talk about my balls and all that kind of thing. People love it. They couldn't care less how I swing." [26] While he never owned up to the specific nature of his relationships, he was playing around the edges of admission by the mid-seventies, when he introduced his chauffeur(/lover) on the stage as "my friend and companion." By 1982, he was acknowledging "the gay drift of his show and speaking sympathetically of all sexual preferences" even while admitting that his own audiences would never "accept people who are totally gay or come out on Johnny Carson. . . . But with a name like Liberace, which stands for freedom," he added, "anything that has the letters L-I-B in it I'm for, and that includes gay lib." [27]

If Gay Liberation encouraged his openness, Stonewall affected him in other ways. Perhaps especially because of his age—he was plunging into his mid-fifties—he evidenced notions of regularizing his unspoken relationships. Aspects of his own character pulled him in this direction, too. He loved family. He treasured domesticity. If this is very clear from his relationship with Scott Thorson and with Thorson's successor, Cary James, his relationship with Vince Cardell foreshadows some of it as well, even as it draws more on the zippier old tradition.

Unlike the mostly faceless names and nameless liaisons of Liberace's romantic attachments before 1975, Vince Cardell has a name, a face, and even a history. He figures in Scott Thorson's memoir under the name "Jerry O'Rourke," but he crops up in Thorson's later palimony depositions, too. Beyond this, he earned a small public reputation of his own. The dates of his coming and going are obscure, but he probably appeared in Liberace's life in late 1974. [28] Memorialized by photojournalists, he was a fixture in the entourage by March 1975, by which time he was helping his partner open his first museum. A part of the showman's troupe, on stage and off, he was hardly a memory by '79.

According to the earliest published source on Vince Cardell, the young man was performing as a lounge pianist at a Ramada Inn club in New Jersey in 1975. Liberace was doing a big show ten minutes away. "I was hoping he would come in for dinner one night," Cardell told the interviewer. Eventually, the showman did appear. Alas, it was the player's night off. A friend called. Cardell rushed back to the dining room. He introduced himself. The star responded appropriately. "He invited me over to see his show, and while I was standing backstage watching, the guy that normally drove the cars onstage got a message that his father had just died. He had to go home and take care of his mother, so he asked me if I was interested in the job, and that's how it all got started." [29]

Liberace had used fancy automobiles in his act for the first time in 1972. Chauffeured onto the stage in a Rolls-Royce limousine or a Mercedes Excalibur, he added various cars to his routine over time, including a VW Beetle done up special as a private vehicle for his fancy fur capes and coats. He made his chauffeurs a part of the act. It was a means, too, of integrating his lovers and companions into his stage show. This was how Cardell broke into the routine.[30] Liberace named Cardell's predecessor as Bob Fisher, the man apparently released at his father's death.[31] Most curiously, Cardell insisted that Liberace did not even know he made his living playing the piano. According to Scott Thorson, Cardell was actually not making much of a living off the piano and drove a truck for a diaper service during the day to support himself. The "trade" element would have added a special appeal for the showman.[32]

Was Cardell waiting for Liberace? The star was ready to be ambushed. The young lounge entertainer was around twenty-five when they met. He was very handsome, dark, and sultry, with a distinctive dimple in his chin. He wore his hair fashionably long and sported thick sideburns.[33] He was big, over six feet, although short of Thorson's six foot three. Thorson, ten years his junior, found Cardell's scowling looks and "mature, powerfully muscled body" more than a little intimidating.[34] Did he look like a truck driver, too? This would also have counted in his favor with Mr. Showmanship. Did the pianist prefer blondes? No matter.

What was the exact nature of Cardell's relationship with the showman? In his published memoir, Thorson is coy regarding this matter. He insists that he will not call Cardell by his real name, for one thing, although two editorial slips reveal "O'Rouke's" true identity.[35] He calls Cardell "Lee's former companion," while he quotes his mentor referring to Cardell as "my protege."[36] Without being specific in his memoir, however, he leaves little doubt about the nature of the affair. When he first saw Cardell performing with Liberace, he describes the two of them "dressed in identical silver outfits, wearing the same jewelry. Their hair had been teased into identical, high pompadours and sprinkled with sequins. To me they looked like a matched pair of queens. Whether it was true or not, they appeared to me to be lovers."[37] The young man was bolder in his palimony deposition. Describing his initial meeting with Liberace, he noted that he had greeted him "in his dressing room with his present lover Vince Cardell."[38] The younger pianist certainly lived with Lee at the Shirley Street house. Cardell himself asserted that he had shared space for "six years" in the Liberace mansion.[39] He continued to reside there after Thorson moved in. Liberace himself introduced Cardell to his Las Vegas audiences as "my friend and companion."

As he did with other protégés and lovers, Liberace also supported Cardell's career. Not without talent, Cardell became a minor celebrity under Liberace's aegis. He played major hotels in Las Vegas, performed at the Waldorf-Astoria in New York, and appeared with his mentor on *The Tonight Show* with Johnny Carson. His patron cut a disc with him in 1975, *Liberace Presents Vince Cardell,* and a second in 1976, *Piano Gems.*[40] Liberace also sponsored Cardell's solo album, *Vince.*[41] Cardell toured extensively with the showman. In Milwaukee, in August 1977, a reviewer referred to Cardell as "Liberace's handsome protege."[42] The following year, the good-looking young lounge pianist accompanied the performer on his extended European tour that included a performance at the London Palladium from April 23 through May 7, 1978.[43] As late as August 1978, the two were performing on the same stage. The Milwaukee *Sentinel* affirmed the protégé's presence at that time, even as it compared him invidiously to his patron. "Less effective was the star's associate and protege, Vince Cardell," began the this notice. "Once Liberace's chauffeur, Cardell has developed a pleasant enough musical personality and sounded okay during a 'Slaughter on 10th Ave.' duet with his boss. But his solo rendition of 'Ebb Tide' was so overblown, that, lacking a gimmick, Cardell's career potential seemed modest in comparison with Liberace's."[44]

Perhaps the performer's inadequacy at Milwaukee's Alpine Music Theater in August of 1978 arose from his difficulties at home with his boss/companion. Scott Thorson had been Liberace's "main boyfriend," as Rechy termed it, for a year by this time. When Thorson had first come to Las Vegas in 1977, Liberace had complained that he could not get rid of Cardell because of a contractual obligation.[45] That contract seems to have been expiring by midsummer 1978. After August, playbills no longer carried Cardell's name. Long before this time, difficulties had corroded the relationship. Scott Thorson offers both first- and secondhand accounts of the problems. For one thing, Liberace had a competitor for Cardell's affection: Thorson reported that Cardell was married with children, and the wife did not surrender her man without a struggle. She "came West to try to save her marriage," reported Thorson. By Thorson's lights, "Lee, still smarting years later from what he perceived as a rejection, was outraged because Jerry actually had the *nerve* to sleep with his wife."[46] The patron found still greater cause for alarm in Cardell's personal behavior, according to Thorson. Taking his mentor's objections at face value, Thorson related that Cardell was "drinking heavily, getting in fights." One night he had driven off in an expensive Mercedes that belonged to John Ascuaga, the owner of the Nugget Casino in Tahoe. Pursued by police, Cardell had wrecked the vehicle and wound up in jail, to his patron's complete horror. "Lee, afraid the press might find out what had happened and ambush him as he walked into the jail, had fearfully gone to bail Jerry out. Lee told me," Thorson repeated, "it had taken all his influence to keep the incident out of the courts and out of the papers."[47]

In the summer of 1977, the air was thick with tension between the two even before Thorson appeared. Meeting Liberace for the first time with Cardell, the new boy smelled sulfur. Every time Thorson encountered them together, he sensed that he had just interrupted another argument. In retrospective analysis, he played his own history with Liberace back to Cardell: the showman was trying to get rid of this "monster" of ingratitude who no longer understood or cared about his needs but wanted only to take advantage of his bounty. "I'm surrounded by takers," he wept to the boy about Cardell. "Do you know what it feels like to have no one you can trust? They've all got their hands out. Gimme, gimme, *gimme*! Everybody wants a piece of my action!" he protested to the eighteen-year-old.[48]

Thorson's joining Liberace's entourage did nothing to relieve the difficulties. In his innocence, he expressed surprise that his presence might actually have exacerbated the tension between the two feuding males. "When we arrived at the house Jerry was there, looking upset. I'd been hoping he'd be gone before I arrived. The incredibly awkward situation I'd gotten myself into finally hit me. I'd be sharing the house with Lee's former companion, a man who saw me as his replacement and had every reason to hate me."[49] This arrangement persisted for months. The circumstances became more chaotic when Cardell himself took to sharing *his* bed with *his* companion, his valet, according to Thorson. With the two other men shouldering him aside and taking "delight in intimidating me," Thorson described the Shirley Street house as a hotbed of intrigue and hostility—all of which, according to Thorson, the master blithely ignored until Thorson himself forced his patron's hand.

Behind the Candelabra describes the denouement with the glowering young piano player: "Tears, anger, coldness, had no effect on him. Saying he had no place to go, Jerry simply stayed on in the Vegas house on Shirley Street. So Lee did what he always did when he needed someone to play the heavy. He called in Seymour Heller. . . . According to Lee, they agreed that Jerry must be made to understand the jeopardy of his position. Lee didn't want to risk rejecting Jerry and having him take his revenge by telling the world that Lee was a homosexual. In the past Lee had gone to great lengths to protect his name and his reputation, to keep the secrets of his homosexuality from the world. He was prepared to do so again—and he wanted to be sure Jerry knew it." Lee and his hovering houseboy, identified as "Carlucci," then found a house for the hapless former protégé and made a secret deposit. "Then Carlucci, acting under Lee's orders, packed Jerry's belongings. Jerry came home one afternoon to find his bag and baggage neatly stacked outside by the front door." Carlucci instructed him to leave quietly or be removed physically. He vanished from Shirley Street forever, according to Thorson.[50]

What were the personal dynamics of the relationship between the two piano players? How different was this affair from the ones that preceded it? How different was it from the two that followed? Cardell himself is silent. Before his death in 1997, Liberace's last lover, Cary James, left fragmentary evidence of his five-year relationship with the showman. These shards offer clues about Liberace's love life, his sexual relations, and the values that inspired his biography. Scott Thorson's memoir offers a much fuller picture.

Behind the Candelabra is no more the whole truth than what Liberace himself spun out as autobiography, but the former illuminates vast areas of Liberace's furiously guarded person and persona. Indeed, it is the richest source of answers to questions that Liberace himself, or even Thorson, hardly contemplated. What do you call a lover? What is the nature of homoerotic desire? What is homoerotic bonding? What is the source of order in homosexual unions? How is it maintained? How do men love each other? What is life like between two men? What is family for gay men? Who, in short, does what, and when? The performer was silent about his love affairs, but they can be reconstructed, if partially, from his lover's account. Beyond all this, especially in conjunction with James's recollections and other still more fragmentary data, Thorson's book offers essential material for understanding such questions as they apply to the Liberace.

Where does the homosexual bond fit within modern life? Throughout the twentieth century, as individual desire has taken increasing primacy over social obligations and institutional restraint, issues of authority and governance have bedeviled even the most traditional family order in Western society. Liberace himself suffered from the disjunction between the individual and social order as applied to normal relations, otherwise defined, between men and women, husbands and wives, parents and children. Was the traditional male function first to spawn, then to defend and provide for his family, while the woman bore children, nurtured them, and ordered the hearth in deference to the husband's defense of the sill? If so, Liberace's parents were both disasters. Salvatore Liberace was inconstant as a provider or even as a presence in the household, while his wife bore the burden both of mothering and of providing income, even if she did neither particularly well. She lacked appreciation for her spouse and harped on his failures; he, meanwhile, responded in kind and added physical force to his rebuttals. Adding insult to injury, he then philandered, abandoned his own brood when his youngest was still in grade school, and left Walter, his second son, still in his teens, to act as the "man of the family." This chaos followed the Liberaces into the next generation. Just as Liberace's own parents divorced and remarried, his brother George wed five times, his sister Angie twice. Rudy's life was a disaster from beginning to alcoholic end. The problems extended even into the third generation, when kinky, underground "'zines" gossiped about Rudy's daughter Ina subjecting the television star Kristy McNichol to a palimony suit.[51]

While such chaos could disrupt even the more socially acceptable heterosexual union, what was to be made of homosexual transaction, beyond mere physical act or activity? Exterior to the laws of the state and religion, beyond the sanctions of custom and tradition, and, most critically of all, unrelated to bearing and raising children, the homosexual bond was still more vulnerable, fluid, and arbitrary, more subject to whim and fancy. Although mostly after Liberace's time, some social critics and reformers have addressed the issue by advocating the legalization of homosexual marriage. Proposed at the very time when the formal sanctions for traditional marriage and family are disintegrating, such efforts seem almost quaint. The appeal, however, speaks to problems of stability and order within homoerotic desire.[52]

If homoeroticism is a love that dares not speak its name, naming defines other difficulties within it. What to call men who couple with other men, men who *prefer* other men sexually, has always been something of a problem in discussing such activity. Indeed, the same problem applies to the activity itself. Gender studies in the last third of the twentieth century have multiplied these difficulties by emphasizing theory, language, or semantics over actual activity. By this measure, Michel Foucault and his deconstructing followers maintain that only with a name does an activity acquire meaning. According to this logic, there was no such thing as "homosexuality" before the term was invented in the late 1860s. Hence follows the raft of titles around the theme: *Inventing Homosexuality, Inventing Heterosexuality,* and even *Before Sexuality,* where intellectual manipulation of words supersedes, say, the physical manipulation of a penis. Leo Bersani offers a nice critique of what he calls these "*desexualizing* discourses": "You would never know from most of [these] works . . . that gay men, for all their diversity, share a strong sexual interest in other human beings anatomically identifiable as male."[53] The academic preoccupation with categories of language has obscured not only anatomy but also the consistency of homoerotic desire over time. Every age—not to mention every culture—has had its own terms for same-sex sex and those who participate in it; these change about as often as clothing styles: pederast, pederasty, sodomite, sodomy, catamite, bugger, sissy, molly, fairy, fruit, faggot, queer, libertine, and "the fashionable vice," as described by the Duchesse d'Orleans, the wife of the stableboy-loving brother of Louis XIV.[54] "Gay" has come to be more or less standard usage, yet it, too, possesses liabilities for many: in the first place, it is so loose and vernacular as to lack exactitude, and is applicable to men as well as women, for example; at the same time (as with its cross-gender meaning), it is so closely associated with a political phenomenon and a cultural movement as to compromise its larger homoerotic and even sexual significance, even as many actually prefer it for these very reasons.[55] Does any reality lurk beneath the changing language? The historian Rictor Norton, for one, argues yes. For all the variety of semantic usages, he argues, whatever the fellow calls himself or is called by society, the end—and even the form and process—of homoerotics changes little; the mincing Agathon in Aristophanes' fifth-century *Thesmophoriazusae,* in this view, is still recognizable in any modern queer enclave from San Francisco to Berlin to Tokyo.[56]

Difficulties in naming the activity or phenomenon of homoeroticism have still other manifestations. How does a man identify the object of his homoerotic affection? While Gay Pride has stressed the legitimacy of introducing a mate as one's "lover," doing so does not come without its problems, as it emphasizes the emotional or passionate elements in a relationship rather than the social bonds. "Boyfriend" has some of the same liabilities and is also somewhat precious. "Partner" or merely "friend" possess powerful currency and work especially well in a particular context. "Companion" has its usage, even as it suggests more formal relations missing from "friend," much less from "lover." "Longtime companion" or "life companion" is the stuff of obituaries, but the terms get at something of the permanence lacking in "friend." "Spouse" works, but it has little currency; "significant other" has a high descriptive quality even as it suggests a kind of jocular sociology. "Mate" works like "spouse," and a mate, especially in the absence of that mate, is often referred to only half in jest as a "husband" or a "wife." All of these naming problems—with their deeper implications for human relations and human bonding—thread through the lives and sexual affairs of men who love men, and they appear throughout Liberace's sex and social life.

The showman worked out his own solutions to such problems. For one thing, his sexual engagements generally seem to have been fleeting, at least prior to the 1970s. He solved the conundrum of homosexual bonding by failing to bond. He solved the problem of naming by not identifying sexual partners at all. The homosexual transaction became, then, essentially a "physical act or activity." He made sex itself the end of a relationship, which, almost by definition, became transient, temporary, impermanent, and—in its own way—as unreal as it was illicit.

"Tricking around," as Thorson called it, did not require either names or commitment; even so, it also introduces another element in Liberace's sexual character. It is important for itself. He was the aggressor; he called the shots; he determined the length and duration of the act. His sissy persona notwithstanding, he was the pursuer, the hunter, the initiator—the "man," as traditionally defined—in relationships. Indeed, there is actually something of a rule, here, suggested in the maxim of the gay underground, "butch on the streets; queen in the sheets." If this suggests one truth, the inversion also applies: the more feminine appearing a man, the more likely he is to be a "top." Homosexual relations are not so rigid as to preclude playing off one role against another, so the character of the "butch bottom" emerges, an aggressive partner who demands to be serviced sexually. Especially post-Stonewall, all sexual categories within the gay community became more fluid, and while these shifting models might have affected Liberace's sexual attitudes and practices, his impulse to control a relationship never altered.

With his relentless ambition, driving will, and furious pace, elements of his own character suggest his predisposition toward domination well before his celebrity. Fame exaggerated the trait. He was only thirty-four in 1953 when he had his fling with the fledgling actor Rock Hudson, who was just six years his junior. According to the actor, however, "Lee was very patronizing . . . and he treated everybody like his protege." Over three decades later, his last lover, Cary James, could still have offered the same generalizations about Liberace's manner, although James voiced no objections to being patronized.

In reflecting on the love affair between himself and Liberace, Scott Thorson assumed that the homosexual convention is founded in equality and in "the true meeting of minds." Thorson, however, offers only one example of the things that link men; elsewhere, even in his own memoir, he gives vivid evidence of inequality as the essential, defining component of Liberace's love for him, not to mention his own love of Liberace. Liberace himself never betrayed any evidence that "a meeting of minds" was a part of his own romantic calculus. On the contrary, he did not want equals in bed with him and expressed no longing for a "meeting of minds." Indeed, he did not particularly like dealing with his own mind, much less with the minds of others. As a very function of his ego, not to mention the peculiarities of homosexual affection, Liberace's greater impulse was to chose partners not despite but because of their inferiority.

Equality and give-and-take relations with peers, sexual or otherwise, played little role in Liberace's life. Despite his own celebrity, he called himself a stargazer who worshipped the famous. Just so, in his social or business relations, he liked men like Clarence Goodwin, John Jacobs, or even Seymour Heller, who were older or authoritative or both. Growing older, he replayed this role of patron/protector to a host of young performers. Although he certainly did not have sex with all the theatrical upstarts in his act over the years, his making of Vince Cardell's career after 1975 offers a case in point to illustrate Liberace's adopting the ordinary and making it special. The motive informed his romantic affairs as well.

Seeing the world in relentless terms of superiors and inferiors satisfied various needs in Liberace's sexual as well as his social life. They echo the debilities of his youth, even as they anticipate his difficulties in establishing loving relations with others.[57] When he was younger, he told Scott Thorson, he preferred older men as sexual partners. As he matured, he reversed the order. He needed to play one role or the other. In addition, he always loved the shoddy, the secondhand, the raw, the unpolished, the unfinished. He preferred things the world rejected—run-down houses, broken furniture, stray dogs, and, not least, human flotsam. One reporter captured the quality. " 'I've always liked to take something that is ready to be destroyed, decadent almost, and prove that it can have another life by restoring it,' " he told the journalist. " 'Some of my furniture that people admire most was wrapped in rope when I found it. It had to be glued back together. It's much more of a satisfaction for me, if it's really broken down.' He has saved houses, pianos, vintage automobiles, old movie props. He has saved a pound's worth of canines. . . . If, you find yourself thinking, he's had his occasional troubles with people, it's probably because he's wanted to save them, too."[58]

Was the Harold Way house an abandoned wreck when he bought it? Did he made it sparkle? He did the same with people. Was Vince Cardell driving a diaper truck to supply food for his wife and babies, leaving no time for him to cultivate his career? Lee would save him and make him shine, too. The model applied best of all to Scott Thorson.

Speaking to crucial needs in Liberace's life, the protégé-as-lover model also entailed a self-defeating logic. What happens when the protégé outgrows his status, tires of dependence, and wants to stand alone or to acquire equality? This transformation suggests some of the problem that Liberace eventually had with Vince Cardell. The performer needed neediness; he did not need success, even if he himself had cultivated Cardell's budding celebrity. Liberace possessed no obvious ability for making the jump to a new understanding. There were, meanwhile, always new boys to nurture, even as his loathing of conflict and confrontation predisposed him against dealing directly with a mate's growth and need for independence. This was certainly the pattern he followed in his relationship with Scott Thorson; as Thorson described it, it also corresponded to Liberace's relationship with other lovers and protégés. Men make poor protégés; youths make good ones.

Issues of equality versus inequality, superiority versus inferiority, or refinement versus roughness influenced Liberace's sexual bonding in still other ways and also helped make up for the gaps in the language of homoerotics. He was his companions' patron; he was also their boss and their employer, even if he had to invent jobs for them to perform.

As suggested in his inclusion of virtually his entire family on his payroll at one time or another, economics represented a means by which the showman both bonded with but also formalized, objectified, and, effectively, distanced and controlled his loved ones—whether they were siblings or bedmates. By virtue of the exchange of cash and the semiformal and sometimes formal contractual basis of his affairs, Liberace, willy-nilly, affirms a Lockean principle that permeates American cultural history, that all human relations, however intimate, are, ultimately, based on the reasonable exchange of goods and services. That exchange is a means of rationalizing and organizing, of limiting and controlling—even denying— the mindless vagaries of love and passion.

While the seventeenth-century English philosopher developed his theory of human understanding to apply to all traditional institutions— from government to family, he might well have balked at the application

of contractual values to homoerotic exchanges. At the same time, the fluidity of those associations implies a comparably greater demand or need
for order. Liberace's effort to formalize his love affairs through contracts
and money, then, reveals his own attempts to regularize the affair as well
as to dominate his lovers. It offers resolution to fundamental problems
within homoerotic relations and returns to the issue of what to call a lover.

"I'd like you all to meet my friend and companion, Scott Thorson,"
the showman purred to his audiences during the time of this chauffeur's
tenure.[59] What to call a lover? "During my years with him I was variously
described as a chauffeur, bodyguard, and secretary/companion," wrote
Scott Thorson. "My predecessors had been called valets, proteges, yard-
boys, or houseboys, depending on their individual talents. Some, like
me, wound up in the act."[60] When they split in 1982, Liberace dismissed
Thorson publicly as "a disgruntled employee." Lover and employee: what
defines the relationship?

"He always thought love was about buying."[61]

From the beginning of their affair, Liberace worked to pin down his
relationship with Thorson through a cash or commercial nexus. "How
would you like to go to work for me?" beamed the showman. "You could
be my secretary." When Thorson protested that he had no typing skills,
the patron-to-be ran through a list of things the boy could do. "Hell, Scott,
I can pay people to type. But I need a companion, a bodyguard, someone
to keep Vince off my back, someone I can talk to the way I've talked to
you tonight."[62] For such general duties of providing companionship, Lee
promised him three hundred dollars a week, plus expenses. The boy
agreed. Almost immediately, the older man took advantage of the situation. "One minute we were talking, and the next he grabbed me. . . . Lee
wanted sex then and there!"[63]

Thorson had no secretarial skills, nor could he have been a bodyguard
in any but the loosest, most inexact construction of the word. Others had
filled this bill. John Rechy provided the evidence. When Rechy had first
met the showman, Liberace's "bodyguard-lover" had caught his boss red-
handed at Rechy's zipper.

> Alerted by other similar times, he stands abruptly behind the
> star and looks down. The star withdraws his stumbling
> fingers.
> "I knew it," says the bodyguard-lover.
> "Piss," says the star.[64]

Scott Thorson was no secretary or bodyguard; he was, however, a chauffeur, if only a fake one. He drove Liberace on and off the stage in the

various "prop-mobiles" of the showman's performances. He also sold programs and concessions, later on, at concerts. What was true for Thorson
applied to Liberace's other companions before and after the big blond
boy became a member of the pianist's entourage. Liberace employed his
last lover, Cary James, as a private secretary. Like Thorson, James was also
the performer's stage chauffeur. Vince Cardell began his tenure in the
entourage as chauffeur as well, before he graduated to playing duets on
stage with his boss.[65]

"Protégé" was another term that suggested both a homosexual bond
and a protector-employer connection, although it meant neither, necessarily. The first meaning applies to the young people Liberace encouraged
in his act through theatrical employment, but the expression is also used,
ambiguously, to suggest a sexual or quasi-sexual relationship in other
contexts. Thus, while Liberace applied the word without sexual overtones
to a variety of young performers in his act, for example, to the banjo-
plunking Scottie Plummer, it conveys something else when applied to
Vince Cardell, Thorson, and Cary James.

And then there was the term "houseboy." The word connoted some
erotic bonding sublimated in an employee-employer relationship, too.
Liberace kept a series of these men in his entourage. Who was Gregory
Scortenu? In *The Things I Love,* Liberace identified his houseman of the
Cloisters as Gregory and Rumanian.[66] He made the news scene, too. Papers described him as Liberace's houseboy in 1975. This information
made the press because Liberace was spending the night at the houseboy's
$100,000 Bel Air home when thieves broke in and lifted an expensive
necklace. What was their relationship? What was a houseboy doing in
such expensive digs? What was he doing with expensive jewelry? What
was Liberace doing there? The newspaper article's superficial objectivity
hinted at answers, even as it failed to ask the questions.[67] Lee had a whole
gaggle of such men. They came. They went. Liberace's numerous houses
each required management. There was always a good-looking man to do
the job. With his heavy French accent and sexy looks, George Llinares
ran the house in Palm Springs from the late 1970s to the early eighties.
When Liberace sacked him, he raged "that God would get him and,
worse, that he would tell all to the *National Enquirer.*" He did not get his
revenge until after his patron died.[68] Depositions in Thorson's palimony
suit revealed that the "houseman" at Las Vegas was named Flynn.[69] Was
this the same clucking, intrusive Las Vegas houseboy that Thorson identified as "Carlucci" in *Behind the Candelabra?* Whether or not Flynn
equals Carlucci; whether or not Liberace had sexual relations with the
one, the two, or none, the majordomo at the Las Vegas establishment, as

described by Thorson, still fulfilled the general role as defined in homo-erotic culture. The houseboys and house managers, for one thing, were all exotics. A string of them appeared after Liberace's death to testify at court hearings about his will, and the reporter for the *Los Angeles Times* recorded his amused wonder at the flashy assembly and unnatural behavior: "There was an uncommon amount of weeping on the stand, an uncommon number of male witnesses who arrived with shirts unbuttoned far down their chest, an uncommon seasoning of invective." [70] Thus he described the bitchy, weeping homos on parade for the delectation of the newspaper-reading Los Angelenos.

Although gay himself, young Scott Thorson had not experienced anything like this before moving into Shirley Street, and he memorialized his own astonishment at the types and forms. Carlucci, insisted the boy from the provinces, resembled no servant he had ever imagined. "He wore conspicuously tight jeans, a shirt open to the navel, and a thick gold chain around his neck. He had a narrow face, a beaked nose, dark olive skin, and eyes that darted about with lively curiosity. I later learned that he'd been a maitre d' before being discovered by Lee and becoming a member of Lee's household." [71]

Carlucci failed to act like any servant the teenager had ever heard of either, although the pattern of bossy, patronizing, and fey valets, butlers, and other such characters appears elsewhere in homosexual culture, for example, in Rock Hudson's entourage. [72] According to Thorson's description, Carlucci the houseboy played the gender-inverted role of good wife or solicitous mother in the Liberace household. He behaved like a protective former lover. At meals, he hovered like "a mother hen," clucking at the diners to eat more of this, less of that. [73] "Carlucci seemed to be in charge of every phase of his master's private life," Thorson mused. "He monitored Lee's spending, his intake of food and drink. He laid out his clothes in the morning, ran his bath, and even tucked him into bed at night, oblivious of my being in the bed too. . . . Acting as if I wasn't there, he fussed with the bedcovers, making sure Lee was comfortable and had everything he needed." [74] Carlucci also oversaw Vince Cardell's removal from the Shirley Street house in Las Vegas. Just so, Thorson engineered Carlucci's own removal from the household only a little later. The housefolk came, the housefolk went. Boys and men arrived; they vanished soon enough. Lovers came; they disappeared as inevitably, just as Lucille Cunningham had predicted. With access to the patron's power, however, the favorite exercised imperium, as in late Rome. [75]

Employer, boss, teacher, mentor, and patron all defined Liberace's role within his homoerotic relationships. The solution worked on a day-to-day basis. He got what he wanted and needed out of such men. Like the slippery stuff of naming, contractual obligations satisfied the most immediate obligations of his desire. Long term, however, they failed to fill the bill. Again, perhaps as a function of his age or of the legitimizing of homoerotic affection after Stonewall, after the sixties, such liaisons no longer fully satisfied the piano player's longings. There's the rub. What was the nature of his desire? What is the meaning of one man loving another? What does the nature of Liberace's attraction suggest about homoeroticism in general, and about men loving each other in contrast to loving women? Who or what was the lover to the beloved, the beloved to the lover? Names, again, this time informal nicknames, offer clues to what was going on. If Liberace's lovers might have been "protégé," "chauffeur," "houseboy," "secretary," or "bodyguard," they were something else, too, and he assigned them names to match. These hint at the deepest longings in his character.

His last lover, Cary James, describing his relationship with the showman, told a reporter, "'I called him Lee. His pet name for me was "Boo," a name he just pulled out of thin air.'"[76] Unbeknownst to the eighteen-year-old dancer in 1982, or even twelve years later, when the young man broke his devotion-imposed silence, the air was not actually so thin. The nickname had its own history. The showman had used a variation of the term for Thorson, calling him "Boober" or "Boober-loober." More interesting still, Thorson and Liberace shared the nickname: they were both Boober and Boober-loober to each other.[77] But the name is freighted with deeper meaning from Walter Liberace's childhood. As a toddler, he himself had been "Boo," or "Boo-Loo." Sam Liberace had bestowed the nickname. In discussing its origins in his memoir, Liberace repeated what Cary James had said when asked about the name by which Liberace referred to him: "That was dad's nickname for me," the showman said. "Why he called me that even he couldn't remember." He had just picked it out of the blue.[78]

Besides the fact that it alluded to mysterious intimacies between fathers and sons, the name possessed other significance. Liberace associated it with his first memory, when he was two or three years old—a memory he also linked with both his father and with the abandonment of or separation from his father. He also associated it with a triumphant discovery of his own identity. He repeated the sequence in his memoir. Sam, significantly enough, had reversed gender roles, and he was playing mother or first caregiver to the toddler. "But there were times when conditions were such that Dad couldn't take 'Boo-Loo' with him," he continued, notably writing in the third person. Abandoned by this father/mother to another's care, the child wandered off to discover the Wisconsin State Fairgrounds, where the police then discovered him. Who are you? they quizzed the child. He was just the generic "kid" to his mother, he said; to his father, he was Boo-Loo. He is explicit: as the father's son and with his father's signifier, he had discovered the world. With this Boo-Loo identity, too, he did not merely discover the glittering world of the fairgrounds, but he won the attention of the world as well—in the police motorcycle ride home. Still further, once home, he dominated his family's life, even as his mother, finally, moved back into the picture. He had triumphed on every front as his father's Boo.[79] And this was the variant of the name he applied to both of his last two lovers.

What did the entertainer have in mind? Names and naming were extremely important to him. This name was especially critical. It defined his earliest identity. In choosing it for his two adolescent lovers, he replicated his father's role for him, so that he became, effectively, father to these later sons. Just so, as namer, he could become Salvatore himself—literally, savior. As Salvatore, in turn, he could be father to himself; he could father— make—himself. The name suggests even more complex issues. In some labyrinthine, narcissistic way, he was still his own father's Boober to these men, so that they could play his father. If evoking fathers and sons, however, the name also tends to collapse the very distinctions it affirms. As simultaneously father, son, brother, and lover, Boo/Boober/Boober-loober denotes undifferentiated maleness.[80]

While this sort of imaginative reconstruction of the other or of lover-as-self permeated Liberace's attitude toward Scott Thorson, Cary James, and perhaps his other companion-love objects, it figured most literally in his relations with Thorson. Who was lover to the beloved? Who was Scott Thorson to Liberace, Liberace to Thorson? And, by extension, who was Liberace to himself? Beyond the naming evidence, a particularly revealing, even grotesque episode affirms the complexity of their bond. When Thorson and Liberace had lived together for about a year, Liberace determined to undergo a round of cosmetic surgery. On this occasion, however, he did not submit alone; Thorson underwent the surgical procedure as well. It was certainly not to make him look more youthful, as he was only nineteen or twenty at the time. It was, instead, to reshape his face to resemble his patron/lover's. Thorson describes the incident in his book. In a session with the plastic surgeon, the showman had exclaimed, "I want to talk to you about doing some surgery on Scott." When the physician quizzed him, according to Thorson, "Lee jumped up and ran into another room returning with a large oil portrait of himself. 'I want you to make Scott look like this,' he said, propping the painting up in front of the

doctor. . . . It was a full-face portrait of Lee and one of his favorite paintings of himself, clearly showing his prominent cheekbones, slightly arched
nose, and pointy chin the most flattering way.[81]

This was exactly the look the physician imposed in a two-step operation. He first used silicone implants, Thorson recounted, "to reshape my
round face into a reasonable facsimile of Lee's heart-shaped one." Five
days later, the doctor lengthened and narrowed his nose to the same end.
The result? "I looked like a younger, Nordic version of Liberace." He
could hardly recognize himself, he insisted, "I remember taking time to
stop and stare in fascination at the Liberace look-alike I'd become."[82]
Thorson's palimony suit summarized the event, too. "You went along with
it?" the lawyer queried with some incredulity. "Are you happy you did
it?" he pressed. "Yes," Thorson concluded, "because I thought I was making him happy."[83] He elaborated on the incident in his memoir. "The truth
is it never occurred to me to oppose Lee. My future was completely in his
hands, as it had been from the day I accepted his offer of employment,"
Thorson related. "Lee was much more than my lover, from the beginning.
If he wanted me to spend the rest of my life with a new face, one that
looked like his, that's exactly what I would do."[84]

Embedded within the silliness of a pet name and the physical trauma
of restructuring bone and skin, the complex, multilayered relationship of
the homosexual bond between Thorson and Liberace manifested itself in
still other ways. Just as likely, it influenced Lee's affair with Cary James as
well, the other recipient of the nickname if not the knife.

In his memoir, Thorson related that after his surgery, people often
asked if he were Liberace's son. "Lee was thrilled every time someone
suggested a blood kinship between us," Thorson said. "Over the years, I'd
changed from being his lover or companion to become a perfect reflection
of Lee himself—flamboyant, a little crazy. Lee had often talked about how
much he would have liked to have a son. Even before my surgery it wasn't
unusual for him to say that in many ways I'd become a son to him. We
felt psychically connected to each other in ways that had nothing to do
with sex."[85]

Behind the Candelabra offers additional explanations of this other
level of bonding. "He spoke of his love of children and how saddened
he was at never having his own. 'I want to be everything to you,' Lee
said, 'father, brother, lover, best friend.'"[86] The feeling was mutual and
reciprocal.

> Lee had a deep desire to pass his name on to someone else,
> while I wanted us to be legally bound so that Lee would al-

ways be part of my life. More than my lover, he was my mentor—the rock on which I'd built my entire existence. I was wet behind the ears when we met, untutored and unsophisticated, and I'd grown up under his guidance. My view of the world had been shaped by his interests, my opinions formed by things he'd told me. I shared his love of animals, of cooking, of decorating. Mentally—and physically, following the plastic surgery—I was Lee's creature. He'd been my Pygmalion. Although it sounds crazy now, I'd begun to think of myself as an extension of Liberace, a part of him rather than a full-fledged individual. Even now, looking back, I sometimes feel that my life began the day Lee and I met and ended the day we parted. [87]

"Lee exercised complete control over my life," Thorson related. "He told me what to wear, where to go, who to see once I got there. There were times when he acted more like a father than a lover." [88] After the disruption of their union, Thorson could still talk about the complex bonds that linked them: "He had been my lover, my father, my confidant, and my best friend while I grew to manhood. He'd meant more to me than anyone in the world." [89]

For both of them, then, the perfect resolution of this bonding seemed to reside in formalizing and institutionalizing their union. Liberace would find a name for his companion; he would legitimize his affection. He would confirm the underlying sources of his longing in the process. Thorson summed it up: "Adoption sounded like the logical culmination of everything we'd been to each other." When they had first began living together, the older man had often spoken of adoption, but after the plastic surgery, the option became still more attractive. "When we had established our relationship Lee had talked about adopting me, but we'd never taken the trouble to find out what it would take legally. Now the constant comments about how much I looked like Lee made him seriously consider the idea. 'You know, Scott,' he said, 'no one's ever been closer to me than you. I want to make sure that you're cared for forever, no matter what happens to me.'" [90]

In a different context, Thorson offered another version of the bonding. His lawsuit against his old lover revealed some of the facts of the case, even as the lawyers tugged at the mysterious threads of the homoerotic bond. Just as the transcript preserves his lack of polish and his incorrect use of language, his deposition also reveals his uncertainty about what was going on between him and the showman. The attorney pushed relentlessly.

"He wanted me to think of him as a father-type image," Thorson muttered, when questioned by the lawyer.

"Are you telling me that the sexual relation with Liberace stopped at a point in time?"

"It never stopped," Thorson replied. "It wasn't as often as it was in the beginning."

Lee's attorneys ran with the lure: "Is what you are telling me, then, that you contemplated having sex with your father? You contemplated a sexual relation with an adopted father relation didn't you, as a part of this oral agreement?"

"I still don't know how to answer that. I am sorry."

Mr. Showmanship's lawyers were not paid excellent money to be sympathetic to their client's enemies. Son? Brother? Father? Sex? they queried. "When you put those together you have incest, don't you?"[91]

Scott Thorson was not trained in the intricacies of the law nor in the beauties of language. He wasn't trained in much of anything. His only half-articulate answers, however, come closer to the enigmas of his old affection than does the lawyers' logic. Employer, boss, teacher, mentor, patron: Liberace's response to his lovers played on all of these, but underneath the labels and superimposed on them were other images in the world of men and of homoerotic desire—brothers, lovers, fathers, sons, and self; a shadow in a mirror—rippled reflections on water.

Between 1978 and 1982 we had a loving and intimate relationship. We shared fully on and off the stage. Liberace was to me, like a father and lover in one. We had great times together and enjoyed each other's company very much.

SCOTT THORSON

THE GARDEN OF EARTHLY PLEASURES

"You look like an Adonis," Lee told him. "My own blond Adonis."[1] Actually, Scott Thorson looked more like a Viking prince than a Greek demigod. He was classic Nordic. He stood just under six foot three and weighed a rather soft 190 pounds in 1977. He brushed a longish shock of yellow-blond hair away from his clear blue eyes and pale, round face. His skin ruddied quickly in the sun—or under tanning lamps. He was striking.

Scott Thorson's looks were his chief asset. He had little education, and less culture and polish. He had weathered more than his share of difficulties by the time he graduated from Walt Whitman High School in the spring of 1977. He had been born eighteen years before, on January 23, 1959, in Liberace's old stomping ground in the upper Midwest, indeed, in the city that changed the pianist's life—La Crosse. The boy's Wisconsin years were disastrous, his family life chaotic. He had seven brothers and sisters. His mother's first marriage to Nordel Johansen produced four children: Wayne, Sharon, Gary, and LaDon. Upon leaving her first husband, she wed another Scandinavian, Dean Thorson, who gave her four more kids: Annette, Carla, Scott, and Jimmy. She had brought two of the children from her first marriage into her second. The two she abandoned were the lucky ones. Highly unstable, even psychotic, according to Scott, "she'd disappear for days, leaving us to fend for ourselves. Once when we'd been left with nothing to eat, I begged our landlady for food. She gave us peanut butter and jelly sandwiches and called the authorities." When the mother was institutionalized for a year, the state put the children in orphanages. After her release, she reclaimed her brood of blond kids and headed for California, where the pattern repeated itself: erratic behavior, disappearances, hospitalization for her, orphanages and foster homes for the kids. Thorson described it, perhaps in understatement, as a "hard, loveless life."[2]

The six children were shuttled between a variety of foster homes and state-run public facilities. Scott Thorson did not even recall them all. He loved Rose and Joe Carracappa, but his mother reclaimed him shortly after he moved in with them. Marie and David Brummet stood out, too. They took in him as well as his pets on their Marin County ranch. When doctors diagnosed David Brummet with cancer a year and a half later, however, the idyll ended. Now going on sixteen, Thorson once again faced the possibility of returning to a public facility for homeless children. Desperate, he worked out an arrangement to live with his much older half brother Wayne Johansen, one of "the lucky ones" who had remained with his father. Johansen lived in San Francisco.[3] It was 1975, Stonewall plus six. The teenager was headed for San Francisco, Stonewall Nirvana.

Scott Thorson does not claim that his brother was homosexual, but as a bartender in heavily gay San Francisco, Thorson related, Wayne Johansen knew the scene and "had wide acquaintance with California's gay community." Thorson professed not to particularly like living with his brother, in part because his sibling's friends put the make on him. Nor, he claimed later, did he particularly care for Johansen himself, who was fifteen years his senior.[4] The bad blood grew worse. When the Thorson-Liberace feud went furiously public in the fall of 1982, Wayne Johansen allied himself effectively with the Liberace team against his kin. Later, he assumed an even larger role in the affair, when he claimed that his sibling had been a boy prostitute in his teen years and had carried on a sexual relationship with one of his foster fathers, David Brummet.[5] Thorson denied the allegations, but he did admit to having his first homosexual experience while living at his brother's apartment. He was around sixteen.[6]

Although Thorson described himself as being bisexual in his teens, girls figure nowhere in his memoir. By his own account, his adolescence was exclusively homosexual. From this time, his personal life, he wrote, revolved "around a few gay friends I'd made while living in northern California."[7] His legal deposition in the palimony suit elaborates upon this picture somewhat. During high school, he related, he had lived with another gay man, Louis Barraza, but they had never had sex. Indeed, he insisted that he had little sexual experience at all before the fall of 1977. How many men? "Less than 10? Less than 5?" the lawyers queried. Yes, he finally agreed, less than five.[8] One of these men was Robert Street, as

Thorson identified him in his deposition, or Bob Black, as he named him in his memoir. He had met Street through his Northern California circle of friends. A choreographer-dancer, Street was pressing forty when they met, but Thorson described him as "extremely good-looking in a blond, Nordic way, nicely dressed, well-spoken, and easy to talk to."[9]

Deposed in the palimony case, Thorson left testimony that not only suggests elements of his relationship with Street but also offers insights into male-male sexual relations in general. Had you and Street been lovers? the deposing attorneys inquired. Thorson said no. They rephrased the question: Had you had a sexual relation? they asked. Now he said yes. The lawyers seemed incredulous. This is not being lovers? they demanded. "What does 'being lovers' mean to you?" they pressed. "When you want to be lovers? In other words, a permanent, exclusive relationship?" "Yes," he said. "Without anybody else on the side?" "Right." "That is being lovers to you?" "Well," Thorson mulled the question over, "there's many different terms of being lovers. I wouldn't know." Others? they demanded. "Living together and committing themselves to each other and no one else," Thorson concluded.[10]

If the older, well-established Street was a model of stability in the gay teenager's chaotic life, he was otherwise important in the Liberace story, too. Street drove a flashy Mercedes sports coupe, and after a few months' acquaintance, in July 1977, he invited the boy to make a road trip with him. Their destination: Glitter Gulch in the Mojave Desert.[11] Thorson liked the car. He liked Bob Street. He had never visited the showy gambling casinos. Hobnobbing with Street's star acquaintances excited him. A greater excitement, of course, awaited him.

Once in Las Vegas, the two men attended a variety of shows, including Liberace's. The younger man had never heard of the entertainer, he admitted, until a couple of weeks before. From what he knew, he expected to dislike the show. He didn't. "I was spell-bound," he conceded. "The man seemed to be having such a good time that I couldn't help being caught up by the fun. His humor sounded so fresh and spontaneous and he did such a terrific job of poking fun at himself that I got the impression he was ad-libbing all the way. . . . It was pure camp and great fun."[12]

As a dancer, Bob Street had a variety of connections, not least with Ray Arnett, Lee's stage manager, who had broken into the Liberace show as a young hoofer over twenty years before. According to Thorson, Arnett figured centrally in the showman's gay inner circle. This connection got the visitors great seats at the show; it won them a backstage interview as well. An invitation to have brunch with the showman the next day followed. That invitation prompted another exchange. "Here's my unlisted telephone number," burbled the showman, as he passed the young Viking a piece of paper.[13]

Two weeks later, back home, Thorson retrieved the scrap of paper from his pants pocket. He called the number. The showman issued another invitation, to return to Vegas. The boy accepted. And then, once Thorson returned, came Liberace's proposal that he join the entourage, be a secretary, "a companion, a bodyguard, someone to keep Vince off my back." The boy agreed. Thorson's "okay" unleashed the showman's libido. They spent the night together for the first time. It was late July or perhaps early August. The showman now had a new bodyguard, companion, chauffeur, protégé—and lover. Did the blond Wisconsin boy know what he had? He knew he had a diamond ring straight off the maestro's finger, and he knew he had three crisp hundred-dollar bills in his pocket. Beyond that, the big teenager professed to having had only inklings of the shape of his future.

After a trip back to L.A. to gather his small collection of goods, Thorson moved into the Shirley Street mansion in Las Vegas, and into Liberace's bed as well. The exotic intricacies of the household distressed him, he related. Cardell's jealousy, the former boyfriend's relationship with his own valet, and Carlucci's hovering made him crazy, he insisted. After only a few weeks in Las Vegas, he threatened to leave. His warning provoked a histrionic confession from his patron. He had been smitten from the first time he'd seen him backstage with Bob Street all those weeks before, the showman cried. "I couldn't take my eyes off you. I felt something grabbing my guts, something that said this kid is one in a million. It killed me, those two weeks hoping and praying you'd call. And when you did, I can't tell you how happy it made me. You see, Scott, I love you."

Lee had certainly felt Cupid's sting before. The showman fell in love easily. He had made plenty of attachments like this during his career. There was the young hustler John Rechy; there were Hans and Bobby and Chris and Vince and the buffed-up country boy. Maybe, in his own way, he was in love with each of them. But did he see something else when he looked at the strapping boy who, a generation earlier, could have been a farmhand on his grandfather Zuchowski's place? Was he looking at Scott Thorson and seeing the moon? One in a million, he had told Thorson. Maybe it was so.

Scott Thorson might have been created to fit Liberace's special qualifications. Did the showman adore the shoddy? Love the abandoned and obscure? Celebrate the neglected and unwanted? Thorson had been even more untended and uncared for as a child than Lee had been, more disregarded than any pup the pianist had ever brought in off the street.

36 When Lee renounced his conservative phase after 1961, he did so with a vengeance. His homes became an inseparable part of this new, outrageous public persona. He made his bathrooms, tubs, and even toilets objects of public glamour. Although he had posed in bubble baths as early as the Valley Vista days, the marble and gold of the Las Vegas house provided an even more exotic setting for publicity shots. Bejeweled and bewigged for the cameras, he bathed like a king or a Roman emperor—or at least the way he imagined such a scene. While demonstrating his own fantasies, such publicity also touched on another American fascination: bathrooms and cleanliness as well as over-the-top luxury. *Courtesy of CORBIS/Bettmann.*

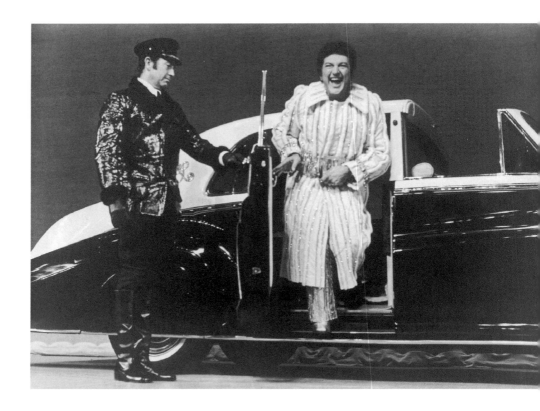

37 (above) Liberace's triumphant return to the Las Vegas casinos in 1963 sealed his commitment to "calculated outrage." Indeed, what he called "topping himself" became a contractual obligation after 1963. Every year brought some new trick. At the opening of his June run at the Las Vegas Hilton in 1972, he drove onto the stage in a fancy custom car, a gimmick he was to repeat many times thereafter. The innovation underlined the old American obsession with the automobile and the new. He was living Everyman's fantasy pushed to its limits with the cars, the jewels, and the furs, and he was having so much obvious fun that folks encouraged the profligacy. *Courtesy of the Liberace Foundation, Las Vegas, NV.*

38 (opposite) Two years after he first drove onto the stage, he came up with an even more spectacular exit—flying off. He loved the trick; so did audiences, even when they knew what was coming, and even when the wires showed all too clearly. *Photo: Las Vegas News Bureau. Courtesy of the Liberace Foundation, Las Vegas, NV.*

39 Always looking to exceed his own fabulousness, Liberace supported a cottage industry of furriers, sequin makers, and designers. Mostly inspired by picture-book or moving-picture history, his outfits—like his life—occasionally echoed his personal dramas. His "heaviest costume," for example, which weighed in at forty-three pounds and was electrified with four thousand miniature light bulbs, produced a spectacular effect, but it also parodied, intentionally or not, the Sousa-type band uniforms his own father wore even into his dotage. *Photo: Las Vegas News Bureau. Courtesy of the Liberace Foundation, Las Vegas, NV.*

40 (left) Royalty delighted in Liberace's spectacle as much as the folks did. In 1953, he predicted he would play for the queen of England. Within three years, he was scheduling his first command performance. Over the next twenty years he played over and over for royalty, from the queen mother and Elizabeth herself to the other crowned heads and heads of state around the world. *Courtesy of the Liberace Foundation, Las Vegas, NV.*

41 (below) Liberace played for American royalty, too. Indeed, his invitations to the Reagan White House were particularly appropriate. The president and the performer were both conservative Midwesterners who had captured the American dream from a base in Hollywood. They both played style and performance. With their dual promise of tradition and prosperity, the Reagan years were made to order for the gaudy showman. *Courtesy of the Liberace Foundation, Las Vegas, NV.*

42 While dining with kings and heads of state in public, in private Lee kept his own company. Described by Scott Thorson as Lee's old lover, Vince Cardell was around twenty-five when he first appeared in the showman's life in the mid-seventies. As was the showman's wont when he took a shine to a young man, he offered the darkly handsome lounge pianist a job at their first meeting. Cardell graduated from chauffeur to playing the piano in the act, and moved into the showman's house soon after. *Courtesy of the Liberace Foundation, Las Vegas, NV.*

43 Despite Cardell's continued residence at the Shirley Street mansion, eighteen-year-old Scott Thorson moved into the house—and into Liberace's bed—in the summer of 1977. The young man had various sources of affinity with the showman, like his love of dogs, affection for cars, and desire for the limelight. By 1979, Lee spoke of adopting his new companion, and at the showman's insistence, Thorson underwent cosmetic surgery to make him resemble his patron. Here, recovered from the cosmetic operation, Thorson appears with Lee and Michael Jackson indulging in one of their common passions—shopping. *Courtesy of the Liberace Foundation, Las Vegas, NV.*

44 Although the showman called him "my blond Adonis," Thorson's neediness attracted Liberace as much as his beauty. The two remained together almost five years, but the elements that brought them together drove them apart as well. Thorson's cocaine addiction and crack habit, and Lee's roving eye, doomed the relationship. They were on the skids when this photograph was made in Boston in 1981. *Courtesy of AP/Wide World Photos.*

45 Cary James was nineteen, Lee sixty-four, and brother George, on the right, seventy-two when this picture was snapped only months prior to the elder Liberace's death. It was about a year after James took Thorson's place in the showman's life. James lacked Thorson's mania, and the performer might have anticipated a peaceful conclusion to his randy, hectic life. AIDS ruined the idyll by 1985. *Courtesy of the Liberace Foundation, Las Vegas, NV.*

46 Lee bought his first house in Palm Springs around 1953. Fifteen years later he purchased the Cloisters, his favorite residence. The house was semi-sacred to him, in part because it contained his shrine to St. Anthony, whom he credited with saving his life in the fall of 1963. In devotional appreciation he transformed the old concession area of the Cloisters into a shrine to his patron. It was a Liberacean mishmash of religious brick-a-brack, modern church windows, and late-Renaissance statuary. He resorted to the shrine increasingly after 1984, as the virus destroyed his immune system. *Photo:* Twin Circle Magazine *(12/31/78).Courtesy of the Liberace Foundation, Las Vegas, NV.*

47 (right) By 1980, playing Radio City
Music Hall had become Liberace's oldest
unmet ambition. He finally achieved it
when he played there three times in 1984,
'85, and '86, setting records that remain
unmatched. He was mortally ill with only
three months to live during the last
engagement. Emaciated and sucking
oxygen at every break, he demonstrated
anew the will that had driven him all his
life, offering a performance that would
have exhausted a much younger, healthy
man. He allowed no photographs. The
strain caused by the virus showed even in
1985, when he was sixty-six. *Courtesy of
AP/Wide World Photos.*

48 (below) From the earliest days of his
act, Liberace had touched his audiences.
Later, he made physical touching a part of
his performing ritual. But there were other
forms of touching. To the last of his days,
he could make even skeptics misty-eyed
with his nostalgic versions of old songs
and new. Even death did not completely
vanquish that power. *Courtesy of the
Liberace Foundation, Las Vegas, NV.*

Thorson had been one of eight struggling for an afflicted parent's affection. While his father played no apparent role in his life, Thorson failed even to give his mother a name in his memoir. He had lived a hardscrabble life since he was born; in his youth, economic deprivation had coincided with psychological poverty. He was perfect human material for a patron, guide, protector. That he shared the showman's love of dogs and animals added to the attraction.

Circumstances fueled Thorson's appeal for the showman too. Devoid of stability in his life, the young man needed security even more than Lee did. His affection for Bob Street suggested his attraction to older, established men, as well. If bedding a sixty-year-old man—complete with makeup and heavy jewelry—gave the adolescent pause, Liberace also made up for more than the economic deficiencies of his life. Lee's declaration of love? "That was the first time in my entire life that someone had said, 'I love you,'" he related. "When I was little I used to imagine my mother taking me in her arms, hugging and kissing me, and saying she loved me. But it had never happened. Not with her and not with anyone else." [14]

They went hand in glove, these two. But one in a million? There was more.

Liberace believed in numerology, fate, and fortune, and the fact that he had met Thorson was actually a minor marvel in itself. [15] He adhered strictly to a rule, for example, against receiving visitors between his first and second shows. But he had broken it this once; meeting Thorson resulted. "I've often wondered why he permitted two strangers like [Street] and myself to come backstage," reflected Thorson. "Was he hoping that someone like me would come along?" [16] Here appeared, then, miraculously, a needy boy, just as Liberace was feeling needy himself. This was not, however, just any needy boy. This one hailed from his neck of the woods, indeed, was a native of La Crosse, where the showman had experienced his epiphany. Here Liberace had discovered his own voice—or hands; it became clear to him that his future lay in his being an entertainer rather than a concert pianist. La Crosse represented much more to him, however. This was where he broke with his father. Here he declared both financial and aesthetic independence from his parent. Indeed, in La Crosse, he dismissed Sam Liberace as an active element in his life forever. And just as the boy from La Crosse, Wisconsin, appeared in his life in 1977, Sam left it. Salvatore Liberace, in his ninety-third year, had joined the symphonic orchestra in the sky on April 26. Walter had never made peace with him. He had never resolved the breach that separated them. Despite eliminating his father from his life, he had nursed resentment against his parent for years. If his bitterness, even, was love gone bad, the appearance of this boy, in some weird way, gave him the chance to do it right again, to take it from the top, to start from tow—from La Crosse again. He could play the good father to this son, but through the new boy from Wisconsin, he could also relive his own youth and redress his own old hurts. Scott was Boober to his dad's old Boo.

One in a million. Despite hyperbole and gush, perhaps his declaration of affection got it right after all.

"I hate my life," Liberace had unburdened himself to the eighteen-year-old. "He looked shrunken, vulnerable, and very alone," Thorson recalled of their first intimate conversation. "I couldn't help feeling sorry for him. Here he was, the biggest star in Vegas, and yet, when the curtain went down, I would see he was completely alone. Logic told me that if had any *real* friends, anyone he could trust, he'd have confessed his problems to that person rather than to a comparative stranger." [17] Liberace had lain the identical spiel on John Rechy. "Please come, I'm so lonesome. Please, please come!," he had cried. His plea had persuaded even the streetwise young hustler in 1957.[18] Twenty years later, it still worked. It was more than just a line.

Liberace's needs never waned. They remained a driving motivation throughout his five-year union with Thorson. Indeed, they dominated his relations with Thorson's successor, Cary James, as well. "He demanded my constant companionship," Thorson observed.[19] "He hungered for companionship. He couldn't stand to be alone and needed to know someone would always be there for him," Thorson observed.[20] "The longer Lee and I were together," he wrote elsewhere, "the more I understood his sense of isolation, his need to have a confidant and full-time companion."[21] In keeping with this opinion, Thorson insisted that they parted company under almost no circumstances. His successor, Cary James, echoed this observation.[22]

For three years, maybe four, it worked. According to Thorson's published record, they were excellent together, at least early on. If their mutual needs and neediness drew them together, they helped keep them together, too. As for the forty-year difference in their ages, Thorson seldom returned to it after he described the initial shock of bedding an old man. This appears curious on the surface. While Liberace's age would seem a striking liability, one of the most astute observers of homoerotic bonding has argued that such radical differences actually make for durability in homosexual unions. "Many successful gay relationships are based on a difference in the partners—a difference in age, race, social status, or personality," writes Richard Isay. "Complementation is not so important to heterosexual relationships, because of the gender difference."[23]

Given the norm of "long-term" homosexual relationships, the Liberace-Thorson union not only worked, it worked well.[24] Scott and Lee had a good life. It remained peculiar, however. If not unique in the gay world, it was notable because the two were strangers when they joined company. They had known each other a total of about an hour and a half when Lee invited Scott to live with him. Other curiosities distinguished their union.

Besides Liberace's personal eccentricities, his work dictated the shape of their life together. The showman still toured for over half the year. He, his lover, and his entourage lived out of suitcases and hotel rooms for much of this time. During the Thorson years, Liberace not only toured the United States but also played two major European engagements, in the spring of 1978 and 1981. Thorson's memoir makes almost no reference to being on the road.[25] Indeed, it reveals very little sense of place or locale, and its reflection of time or chronology is just as weak. Thorson's life with Liberace, as the young man reconstructed it, lacked physiological or chronological milestones. For the adolescent companion, one place simply melded into another, one day into another, and indeed, day into night. When he was performing, Liberace's day did not begin until the afternoon; his main meal was, effectively, a dawn "breakfast" that he consumed as he wound down from his show after 2:00 or 3:00 A.M. He slept until mid- or late afternoon, when he began preparations for the next performance.

The showman's inversion of the standard workday determined the same inversion for his lover. Their life was like swimming in mineral oil. "We usually got home between two or three in the morning," Thorson remembered. "It might have been the crack of dawn to most people but for Lee the workday had just ended. We'd have a snack, watch movies, play with the dogs, or sit in the Jacuzzi smoking and having drinks until he unwound enough to go to sleep, usually about seven in the morning. The outline had been established long before I arrived on the scene and, although I often felt isolated and missed having other people around, Lee refused to alter his restrictive and reclusive life-style."[26]

The collapse of the distinctions between night and day represented—and guaranteed—the pair's isolation from all normal patterns and associations and from conventional behavior. Normal markers lacked point in this world. If work separated the showman from conventional time, his people protected him from other normal constraints: "His loyal staff protected him from having to deal with the real world. In fact, Lee lived a sheltered existence, free from almost every worry," Thorson observed.[27]

Liberace himself professed to dread the alienation this isolation produced—hence his demand for a constant, ever-present companion, who would be like a window on the world. While Thorson chronicled the crystal bubble-like isolation of their lives, he notes, paradoxically, that his patron also actually disliked company. While photographs in *Behind the Candelabra* memorialize Scott and Lee socializing with a variety of folk, from Frank Sinatra to strippers and stagehands, Thorson insisted that Lee distrusted sharing either him or their world with others. He entertained visitors after his show, according to Thorson, but seldom otherwise. "To describe him as an intensely private man doesn't seem adequate. Once he left the theater he didn't want anyone around him other than his lover. A 'cross at your own risk' line divided his public from his private life."[28] These strictures applied to everyone, including kin. "He didn't really like to have his family or mine around much. He was very strange that way—he liked the two of us to be alone."[29] Thorson observed that his lover's "need for privacy bordered on paranoia. Even members of his inner circle, old and trusted friends like Ray Arnett, were restricted to a limited number of invitations to Lee's home each year," Thorson said. "After Lee's performances ended and we went home, the world narrowed down to just Lee and me." "When we went home after a show Lee locked himself away from the outside world."[30]

Thorson described their private life as being as sedentary and uneventful as it was solitary. They almost never entertained. Nothing like the exotic "white party" of Rechy's memory occurs in Thorson's memoir. "Lee preferred living like a hermit," Thorson insisted. "Our socializing consisted of talking to salespeople in the various stores we frequented. When Lee wasn't working he hated getting dressed and often spent the entire day unshaven, lounging around the house in an old terry-cloth robe so worn it was full of holes."[31] They seldom went out, never partied. They had no hobbies or interests outside of the house—and the ever-present pack of dogs. The dogs, actually, occupied a critical place in their lives together. A poodle had first gotten them together. Thorson was working in a veterinary office when he met the showman, and he offered advice about the ancient, ailing Baby Boy, Lee's favorite pet. The animals remained a crucial source of their mutual pleasure, and they figured notably in their legal parting. They fought over the animals as a married couple might over children. While Thorson loved the pets, however, Liberace virtually obsessed over them. He always had, and his affection marks another curious episode in his biography.

As early as 1947, as the surviving press kit from that year indicates, the pianist had touted his love for dogs—cocker spaniels in that particular instance. Soon came poodles—a white toy named Suzette who participated in the Joanne Rio affair, and a black standard, Jo-jo. The checkerboard pair together figured in John Rechy's memory of his assignation at the Valley Vista house. While the showman never recovered from his poodle mania, he wound up with shar-peis and simply innumerable mutts and strays from the pound and off the streets. He preferred those with disabilities of one kind or another: "They were mixed breeds, or the runts of the litter, or had delicate health. Nobody else wanted them. I guess my first reaction is always to reach out to the underdog."[32]

He indulged the animals completely. He set places for them at dinners and fed them off the table to the amusement, horror, or disgust of his company. When he dined alone, his housekeeper set places for them. He slept with them nestled between him and his various bedmates. They had the run of all of his homes. His costliest carpets emitted the fragrance of a kennel, while the incessant yapping was music to his ears. His heart remained with the pack when he was on the road. "When I travel, I carry framed pictures of them to place around the hotel suites," he related. "I call home long distance just to speak to them. When they hear the sound of my voice on the phone, they literally go 'crazy,'" he rhapsodized.[33] They even accompanied him on his cruising, pickup missions on Sunset Boulevard.

While lovers came and went, the dogs, collectively at least, remained forever. He even provided for them in his will. He weathered his mother's death without a tear; he wept for days over blind, deaf, Baby Boy's demise, according to Thorson. He was the pianist's "most favorite dog, because he needed me the most."[34] Over and over, he described his dogs as his only real, true family. The animals' brute loyalty filled some void. "My dogs make me feel wanted," he insisted.[35] The intensity of his devotion speaks to the magnitude of that lack. "I won't say I spoil them; it's more the other way around. They spoil me with endless loyalty, love and fascination."[36] He was loyal, free, and uncalculating toward the animals in a way that he could not be toward human beings. The pets provided the impossible, ego-free family ideal he demanded of others and could never fulfill himself.[37]

Thorson's love of animals, then, provided an important affinity, even as the dogs helped focus their lives in the absence of other activities. They had little else. Except for the singular reference to Thorson's swimming laps at the Cloister's Olympic-sized pool, there was no exercise or sports. Except for watching soap operas in the afternoons—which Liberace adored, Thorson and his companion left no record even of the impact of television on their lives. There were no outings to films or theaters, although they watched old movies on video. They read no books or newspapers, and the only magazines that appeared seemed to be tabloids like

National Enquirer, Globe, Star, and the like. Their only pastime was shopping. This hobby, however, compensated for the absence of all others. Lee lived to shop.

Thorson suggested that buying came close to an addiction for his patron. "He transformed shopping into a quasi-religious experience," Thorson said. "He reveled in spending, gloried in it, devoted a large part of his waking time and energy to it." [38] "Lee craved shopping the way an addict craves a fix. He felt the day was incomplete if he didn't purchase something. Buying his own groceries and browsing in supermarkets would do if nothing more seductive and costly loomed on the horizon. He could wax ecstatic over imported cheese, fresh vegetables, prime beef. 'Oooh, fabulous!' he'd say in his benevolent whine when something pleased him." [39] The pattern continued after Thorson left. One of the showman's later servants, Yvonne Dandurand, recalled that Lucille Cunningham, the old bookkeeper, allotted her boss ten thousand dollars a month in spending money, all of which he dispersed. "Expensive crystal, clothes, pants, and fresh-cut flowers," he'd buy anything, related Dandurand. "One day it took us an hour and half to unload his car after he'd been out buying towels, bedspreads, cookware sets, coffeepots and baking dishes. He insisted on showing us everything he'd bought, like a child with a new toy!" [40] Sometimes he bought more than geegaws and kitchenware. Interviewed at the time of his former lover's passing, Thorson related how the two of them might "wake up in the middle of the day and go out and buy houses on a whim." [41]

Beyond shopping, however, for Liberace there was only work, home, and lover; for the lover, only Liberace and home. Home shaped their lives as much as work did. Always concerned with domesticity, the showman focused attention on his houses almost obsessively after the mid-seventies. The place of the lovers' sequestration, Liberace's multiple houses excited many of his shopping frenzies, too.

During his years with Thorson, Liberace maintained various residences. Casa Liberace—the Cloisters—in Palm Springs was perhaps his favorite. Scott liked it best, too. The showman still owned the palace on Harold Way, but he had already determined to sell, and he turned a huge profit on its transfer in 1979. The year before, he had purchased a major office building on Beverly Boulevard in Los Angeles, using profits from selling a block of commercial buildings on nearby La Cienega, near Santa Monica Boulevard, where he had sold antiques for a period after 1968. Liberace and his sidekick spent close to half a million dollars in a four-week frenzy to "fix up" the Beverly Boulevard building. The makeover included transforming its fifth floor into a typically gaudy, spectacular showplace of a penthouse apartment. They stayed there when visiting L.A.[42] There was an oceanfront house in Malibu they visited occasionally, a condominium at Lake Tahoe they used hardly at all, and the place where they spent most of their time, the quite remarkable compound on Shirley Street in Las Vegas, where Thorson first slept with the entertainer.[43]

This was Liberace's main house after he moved his legal residence to income tax-free Nevada in the mid-seventies. Besides enabling him to take advantage of the state's tax benefits, maintaining a Vegas residence was otherwise convenient, as he spent over half of his thirty-two working weeks each year performing at the casinos there.[44] This house was pure Vegas. It was essential Liberace.

The Shirley Street community lay on the extreme southern side of Las Vegas, very near McCurran International Airport and conveniently close to Interstate 15. The development lacked any distinction, except that its mostly moderate-sized dwellings sometimes gave way to very modest houses, its well-kept lawns to junky yards and residents that might have stretched the definition of middle class. Its other streets bore names comparable to Shirley. There was Monika Street, Lulu Street, Merle Street, Carol, Jane, and Sara Lee Streets. The variants were male versions of these commonplace monikers—like Wilbur Street. Liberace first bought here in 1976, purchasing one of the larger, but still modest, dwellings in the neighborhood. He soon acquired the house in back, actually on Wilbur Street, and began an extraordinary remodeling campaign to link and glorify the two. The showman finally wound up with twenty rooms spread over 10,500 square feet of space. A wrought-iron fence, made up of elaborately scrolled and gilded "L's," went up around the compound. A new roofline was created in a classic seventies mode of shingles laid on in an abbreviated mansard style. The hodgepodge outside concealed nothing short of grotesque splendor inside. Knocking out the back walls of both houses, the showman had created a huge crystal passageway to join the dwellings. Interior walls came down to open up vast living spaces, although the failure to raise the ceiling heights made these enormous areas vaguely oppressive. Marble, prisms, mirrors, gold, glass, and crystal shone and sparkled everywhere. Thorson left only one description of the place. "The huge entry hall, much bigger than the living room in my current foster home, was guaranteed to make a first-time visitor gasp. Marble floors, mirrored walls, a curved stairway with clear Lucite banisters that looked as if it had been suspended in midair, and gushing fountains vied for the viewer's attention. Millions of dollars' worth of antique furniture, crystal, priceless china, objets d'art, fresh flowers, paintings, crowded every available surface."

This was only the entrance. There was also the expansive main salon, "huge and even more ornately decorated than the entry," the awed Thorson related. In the summer of 1977, Liberace had toured Bob Street and his young, blond friend through the fancy dining area and another chamber called the Moroccan Room. This latter, Thorson said, "featured a peacock-blue tiled floor covered with Persian rugs, mirrored and tiled walls, a soaring glass roof, and more Lucite furniture. The decor combined potted plants in wicker baskets, assorted candelabras, and antiques. Matched sculptures of pantalooned harem boys, each carrying an electrified candelabra on his head, flanked a mirrored bar. A breakfast table had been set with priceless oriental porcelain, as though Lee were expecting a second group of brunch guests. The room's pièce de résistance was a stuffed peacock on a mirrored stand above the bar."[45]

Finally, there was the master bedroom. This is where the two of them had bedded down for the first time, surrounded by the yapping dogs. This was the most outrageous room in the house, according to Thorson. Larger than most people's houses, he said, it "could have held a football scrimmage." Beside the huge canopied bed with its ermine spread, sofas, cocktail tables, a secretary, bureaus, chests of drawers, mirrors, chairs, the ever-present candelabra, and the like, the room also boasted a ceiling painted after the fashion of the Sistine Chapel, complete with its languid Adam in the center. The image of Liberace himself flitted among the sibyls and cherubs. It was not the only way in which the room's decor hinted at the church: one wall held a large painting of the kneeling entertainer kissing the ring of (then Archbishop) Richard Cardinal Cushing of Boston—whom Thorson identified as the pope. It had been painted by a loyal fan. The painting did not hinder the homoerotic devotions that occurred regularly in the huge bed across the room.

The master bath returned to pagan influences. From his first full flush of fame, the showman had had a thing for bathing grandeur. A Roman movie set had inspired the Valley Vista bath. He had posed repeatedly in that sunken tub for publicity stills. The Las Vegas bathroom was more of the same. "A gigantic oval tub circled by marble pillars stood in the center of the room. Hot and cold water came from gold fixtures in the shape of swans. There was enough marble on the ceiling and floor to restore a Roman bath," Scott Thorson wrote.[46] The showman scrubbed here cheerily for flashing cameramen; the lovers never appeared inside the frame.

For all the excesses of the Shirley Street and other residences, it was still a narrow life for Scott and Lee. "We might as well have been stranded on another planet instead of living just blocks from the glittering, twenty-four-hour-a-day world that is Vegas," mused Thorson.[47]

Domesticity defined their lives completely. Insulated from the world, Liberace liked playing house. He and Scott both loved cooking, for example, "and when we had time," Thorson recalled, they "dismissed the chef so we could prepare our own meals."[48]

The Shirley Street mansion provided only one locus of their domestic reclusion. After they had been together a year, around Christmas 1978, according to Thorson, Liberace bought still another house, this one for Thorson himself, five blocks south of the Shirley Street complex, at 933 Laramore.[49] It became their special secret hideaway, insisted the younger man. Its fourteen hundred square feet cost $58,000, but the showman poured over $100,000 into the little house, including $40,000 for furnishings that one of Thorson's later lawyers dismissed ungenerously as "early Levitz."[50] After the last show at the Hilton, they fled here together in a complete escape from the world. No one knew of their whereabouts, and only the faithful Gladys Luckie even had the telephone number, according to Thorson. "Lee loved that house more than any of his mansions and took more satisfaction in it," Thorson insisted. Here, according to Thorson, Lee lived out his domestic fantasies. "In my house, he played at being a hausfrau. He cooked and cleaned and fussed over me like a bride. My best, happiest memories of him come from the time we spent there. Pushing a vacuum, dusting furniture, fixing lasagna, Lee and I pretended to be equals."[51] The star derived pleasure from playing equal to Thorson, but likewise from Thorson's playing his superior. He had "a corny sense of humor [and] loved to be teased, to have me make fun of his superior status. At night when he prepared for his performance, I joked that he was better dressed than Queen Elizabeth. 'But I am an old queen,' he quipped back."[52]

From 1977 to 1979, the two delighted each other. Liberace told Thorson he never wanted another lover, "I saved the best til last," he said.[53] They planned wills that would include each other as beneficiaries. They discussed the adoption issue at this time. As the capstone of their bonding, in 1979, Liberace dreamed up the notion of plastic surgery for his young lover. He was twenty, Lee sixty. That was 1979, 1980. Trouble was already brewing in paradise.

For one thing, Thorson rankled under the isolation and control Liberace imposed. "In those days," Thorson wrote, "Lee didn't like me to have large blocks of free time. He wanted to know where I was and who I was with every minute."[54] If Thorson grumbled at the isolation of their lives, there were always presents to compensate. The "happy-happies," as the celebrity called them, ranged from dogs to diamonds, unlimited clothing to Rolls-Royces. Thorson's closet held many of these gifts: besides fur coats, he counted 200 shirts, a couple of hundred pairs of slacks, 50, 60, or 75 sports jackets, 15 to 20 pairs of leather pants, leather jackets, and 200 pairs of shoes.[55]

When the presents failed, Lee nagged about his young companion's "kvetching." If he was ravenous for the very bonding Liberace also needed, Thorson was only a teenager when they met, and presents, however costly, could not compensate him for his lack of contact with the outside world. Conversely, the showman himself resented his protégé's longing for a larger society than Shirley or Laramore Streets, or the Cloisters.

Sequestration and power were only two complaints that marred their union. Did Thorson joke about inverting their status? How much he did so is difficult to calculate, as it seems that he himself was only half aware of the problem, but the young man was arrogant, possessive, and demanding in his own right. If, in his memoir, he returns repeatedly to his patron's authority, his offense came in part from the same tendency in his own character. Neither modesty nor humility numbered among his virtues. "I was probably the only person in the world who didn't treat him like a star twenty-four hours a day, kissing his behind at every opportunity," he boasted.[56] If he joked with his patron, he also scolded him, for example, about visiting porn shops. Did the millionaire put his family up in hotels when they visited? "For God's sake Lee," Thorson stormed, "they're your *family*. How can you ask them to stay in a hotel when we have so much room?"[57] Angie stayed with them from then on.

"I've been told I was the only one of Lee's lovers to insist on playing more than a passive role in his life," Thorson reflected.[58] He recounted how he altered Lee's staff—getting this houseboy sacked or transferring another one he liked. While he engineered Carlucci's removal, he oversaw Gladys Luckie's transfer from Hollywood to Las Vegas, for example. He demanded salary changes among the staff. His aggressiveness set others' teeth on edge. "Evidently I intimidated some and made others jealous," he said.[59] Lucille Cunningham's explosion about all the boys who had preceded him confirms his judgment. Innocently enough, he himself offered other evidence of agitating the Liberace faithful. Looking for proof of his mentor's willfulness, he produced evidence of his own. After six months with Lee, he mentioned, incidentally, that he was "still having trouble with some of the staff." His complaint prompted a meeting in which the star declared: "The most important person in my life is Scott! His job is to make me smile and keep me happy."[60] If the Liberace people snapped to at their boss's veiled threat, it was not the kind of pronouncement calculated to curb Thorson's vanity.

The boy's arrogance offended others beyond the staff. Thorson glowed over Debbie Reynolds's visit to Shirley Street, insisting she was more like a peer than a famous star.[61] Reynolds herself, however, found her friend's companion irritating, obtrusive, and thickheaded: "Why do you keep interrupting?" she exploded to Thorson on one occasion. "I came here to talk to Lee, not you. Why don't you go walk the dogs?" After the boy left, Liberace thanked her. "He doesn't understand when he should just listen." She then admonished the showman about having such people in his entourage. "I know, I know, but you know how lonely it is on the road," he offered.[62] If Thorson's aggressiveness appealed to one part of Liberace's character, it offended another. The showman's hatred of confrontation—as indicated by the Reynolds story—suggests another difficulty that plagued the relationship. It would have its own consequences later.

If Thorson was hardly sensitive to the way his own ego aggravated the showman, he did describe other problems more clearly. Sex was not the least of them. While the difficulties increased with time, Thorson zeroed in on two problems at the outset, his patron's effeminacy—"queeniness"—on the one hand, and his sexual appetites on the other.

The first is important in Thorson's memoir, although it is not the most critical problem he discusses. He himself showed up at one of his legal depositions wearing makeup, but he describes his initial offense at the showman's mascaraed eyes when he memorialized his first visit to the Shirley Street mansion.[63] "Liberace not only *looks* like a queen, he *lives* like one," he protested.[64] Just so, his patron's full makeup revolted him at first, he said. "I was unaccustomed to a 58—or whatever—year old, 59 year old man seducing me with a full face of make-up on, to go bed with hands full of diamonds, wearing his make-up."[65]

However calculated or even hypocritical his objections, Thorson's skepticism about a feminized gay style reflects one standard opinion within homoerotic discourse, particularly among men of his generation. While the Stonewall riot actually began with a revolt of drag queens, men in female attire, what quickly followed was a shift in homosexual sensibility, which favored the "macho," "butch," or even a caricature of traditional masculinity. Cowboys, cops, leathermen, and stevedores came to represent the visual norm, what was termed the "clone look" at the time. "When I was a boy, gay men were always mooning over straight GIs; now we lust after each other. Perhaps that's the origin of the Clone," wrote the critic Edmund White of the phenomenon: "We've become what we always wanted."[66] The gay musical combo of the times, the Village People, with their macho costumes and "Macho Macho Man" lyrics, got it just about right. If the peroxided queen never disappeared completely, she was subtly displaced by old images of "trade," or, better still, "rough trade"—straight men of the working classes who periodically favored sex with men. The celebration of this form of masculinity dominated the gay world Thorson considered standard. Being gay was no big deal to him, he insisted. Thorson protested that "I'd grown up thinking being a homosexual was neither good nor bad, but simply a fact of life." Liking men or liking men as well as women was no big deal: it "didn't seem like much of an issue. I accepted it the way I accepted being blond and blue-eyed, as part of the package called Scott Thorson." [67] The only difference between gay and straight men was that the former desired men, not women. "Fagginess," effeminacy, and queeniness embarrassed Thorson, he insisted. Men should be men; they should look and act like men regardless of their sexual orientation.

By this logic, if gay men should look like normal fellows, their culture should also resemble that of traditional men. Thus, Thorson expressed appreciation for homosexual unions that replicated those of heterosexuals. "Two of Lee's oldest and dearest friends served as a role model for the relationship I hoped he and I would share," he related. "They'd been together two and a half decades." He encouraged Lee to bring them out West. "I hoped their obvious stability, so different from most of the gay behavior that we saw day in and out, would rub off on us. Most of all, I hoped that Lee and I would have a long-lasting relationship like theirs." [68]

Thorson's preference for manliness and his desire for a heterosexualized gay culture, however, was only part of his problem with his new patron. A second category related: Thorson disliked his mentor's sexual style. Lee's randiness created various tensions between the two men, according to Thorson.

For one thing, his mentor's desire for constant sex irritated him. "I'd completely underestimated Lee's sex drive," Thorson grumbled. [69] Had the star attempted, to Thorson's dismay, to bring him off during their first private encounter? He would put the make on his companion almost anywhere. "I was scared to death the staff would catch us," Thorson reflected. "Lee didn't share my concern. His sex drive was at an all-time high and it made him reckless." [70] He was "the world's happiest most amorous drunk," Thorson insisted. Fellow airline passengers got a Liberace Special when the entertainer had downed a couple of drinks. "I often found myself having to fend off his advances on the plane," Thorson reflected. "We'd made a pact that I would treat him like a superstar in public but that was a little hard to do when he got high and started patting my leg and calling me 'Boober' in front of some wide-eyed stewardess. It was embarrassing and humiliating. I'm not ashamed of being gay, but I hated being groped in public. At the same time, I couldn't help laughing. We must have been quite a sight."[71]

Liberace's insatiable sex drive created secondary issues that came between them. For one thing, his body failed to keep up with his desire. Suffering a problem of impotence, he underwent surgery for "a silicone implant that made him semierect all the time." It did not always help. "Although his interest in sex was at an all-time high, his ability to achieve satisfaction had greatly decreased. Despite the silicone implant he had difficulty achieving full arousal." If he had sex-related problems, his additional attempts at solutions, according to Thorson, caused more difficulties. Amyl nitrite—"poppers" in gay parlance—snorted during sex radically intensifies orgasmic sensations; according to Thorson, Liberace used the drug to heighten or achieve orgasm, and this offended his boyfriend, who refused to share the contents of the little vials.[72]

Thorson identified a second and still more intense source of conflict between them in Liberace's affection for pornography. In Thorson's mind, the predilection related to Liberace's demanding sex to begin with. "I hated those films, hated the fact that Lee like them so much and wanted me to watch them with him. They aroused him, while they turned me off. Each time Lee viewed one of these tapes he'd want to have sex," he fumed. But he also disliked the films because he associated them with another of his preconceptions. He considered them "sad" or "boring," but he also complained "that homosexual pornography seemed embarrassingly *faggy*. . . . Lee's porn films often starred men who in the vernacular would be called 'flaming fags.' There are guys like that out there but they're not representative of the homosexual population as a whole," he reiterated.[73]

Thorson named still other sex-related issues between them. For his patron, Thorson objected, sex was essentially kinky sex. Sexual experimentation turned him on, "the kinkier the better."[74] If Lee's eyes had glowed at the dildos and other sexual paraphernalia in the Ft. Lauderdale porno shop, Thorson insisted it all left him cold. Although anal sex was a standard form of homosexual intercourse, the young man also considered it "kinky," unfortunate, or even sick—a manifestation of the post-Stonewall gay licentiousness he eschewed. Although Liberace himself was reputed to be a top man who favored this particular mode of sexual expression, he and Thorson lived together for five years, without, according to Thorson's memoir, indulging in the activity. If Thorson found the mere desire for the act unsettling, Liberace, conversely, found in his companion's refusal to indulge him a source of complaint as well. The conflict increased with time. "If you loved me you'd do what I want," the patron insisted. Anal sex was not low on his list of desires. "If you really cared about me you wouldn't ask me to do things I hate," the adolescent shot back. Anal sex? "I hated even the thought," fumed the protégé.[75]

As another manifestation of his kinkiness, Lee, insisted his lover, "preferred to have a *variety* act—on stage and behind closed doors."[76] Liberace liked a lot of sex from his lover, but he was used to a lot of sex from a lot of men, as well. The entertainer was always on the prowl. His eye roved constantly. Although Thorson believed that his companion had been sexually faithful up to the very end of their relationship, the show-man flirted outrageously. "He'd always been flirtations towards other at-tractive young men, but now his flirting became so obvious that it embar-rassed me. When he had a few drinks he'd come on to teenage boys as though I wasn't even there."[77] Thorson professed his hatred of promis-cuity and his devotion to monogamy. By his own reckoning, he was in-tensely jealous. Early in their relationship, they accepted an invitation to attend a dinner with the comic Dom DeLuise. While the host seated Thorson next to him, he put the guest of honor next to a strikingly hand-some fellow, and Thorson steamed throughout the meal, fretting about whether his lover "was attracted to his handsome companion."[78]

Both miserable, they reached an impasse in 1981. They agreed to try an "open relationship," Thorson said. While providing the showman with the opportunity to indulge in the sexual experimentation he craved, ac-cording to Thorson, it allowed the younger partner, in turn, to keep a home of his own. "We would continue to live together as friends and companions. . . . We'd just be sharing a part of ourselves with other people." The experiment foundered because of mutual jealousy, and their romance became even more sour. They stopped having sex at all, which fueled Thorson's suspicions that Liberace was seeing someone else. "I knew Lee too well to think he'd gotten hooked on celibacy."[79]

These sociosexual problems did not define the extent of the couple's difficulties. Indeed, perhaps the greatest difficulty of all lay in the young boyfriend's accelerating drug use after 1979. Thorson himself discusses his growing drug habit as a descent into hell. He tends, however, to justify his drug use as an effect of his difficulties at home. Thorson relates that by 1980, his patron was simply tiring of him, searching for occasion to drop the "aging" twenty-one-year-old for a new, younger boy. He was "a Dra-cula who never wearied of the taste and touch of youth."[80] Drugs soothed Thorson's jealous pain, he explains. This response does full justice neither to his patron's motives nor to his own addiction.

If Liberace preferred young men to old, a source of this preference lay in his desire for control and order. In this regard, he might have experienced less anxiety about Thorson's being long in the tooth by 1981 than about his being out of his mind on drugs. Thorson's own summary of Liberace's breakup with Vince Cardell confirms this assessment. In the first place, Cardell was not an adolescent but a twenty-five-year-old man when he moved in with the showman in the mid-seventies. He neither looked nor acted boyish. It was not his age that strained the relationship, according even to Thorson himself; it was rather Cardell's drinking and fighting that put the boss off. If Cardell's behavior distressed the showman, Thorson's was much worse.

After 1981, Thorson lurched toward disaster. He possessed a virtually unlimited amount of money and no constraints: a disastrous combination for almost any adolescent male, especially one who had been undisciplined by family, church, or social institution. His excesses were becoming public, too. It was reported that he came to shows drunk; the Las Vegas Hilton management objected to Thorson driving onto the stage any more.[81] If his drinking was escalating, his drug habits were worse still. Thorson himself blamed his habit on the plastic surgeon, Dr. Jack Startz, who had first prescribed him diet pills and painkillers in 1979. Thorson insisted that he kept his cocaine habit at "a manageable level for two years," but he also suggests that his addiction absorbed all of his enormous allowance—and more. Thus, he related how he bought jewelry on a credit card "and then turned the jewelry over to the doctor in return for prescription bottles full of pills."[82] Quaaludes, amphetamines, and pharmaceutical cocaine soon turned to regulation cocaine. According to later testimony, his use of coke had become habitual by late 1980.[83] He was still far from the lowest rung of hell, however. Soon enough, snorting became freebasing. He became a crack addict.[84]

He was out of control. Nothing Cardell had done could match his capriciousness. His memoirs record a measure of his irresponsibility; even fragmentary data in legal depositions hint at more. Liberace himself left evidence of his lover's state of chaos. One evening, in January 1982, he said, Thorson disappeared. The showman and a friend discovered him at 933 Laramore. They could see him through the window. His stupor was so profound, they could not determine if he was still breathing. The showman was frantic, but publicity, always his nemesis, lurked in the background. "If you break a window (and he's alive) he can accuse you of breaking and entering and you'll get in the newspapers and it will be bad publicity," insisted the friend, Fred Favorite. Therefore, they resorted to the Las Vegas fire rescue squad.[85]

By Christmas 1981, things had been going on like this for months. Thorson had new masters. He had plunged himself into an underworld of sex and drugs, corruption and exploitation, excess and illegality. The scene evokes the fictional cosmos of the 1997 movie *Boogie Nights,* which chronicles the world of pornographic film, illicit sex, uncountable cash, unlimited drugs, violent crime, corrupted norms, and, not least, incalculable hubris. Indeed, the film was specifically inspired by the very drug-addled hell into which Thorson had descended.

Of its nature, this world is murky, its actors obscure. Thorson's deposition named some of its chief protagonists. Chris Cox ran the Odyssey—"a homosexual night club," and Odyssey Restaurant. Cox was also Lee's former lover, Thorson said. Liberace had introduced them.[86] Nick—a.k.a. Anthony—Papadakis managed the Odyssey; he became Thorson's sometime lover or sexual partner. Still more critical was Eddie Nash, legally Adel Nasrallah, who "owned a chain of strip joints and punk-oriented nightclubs in LA." Nash dealt drugs: "Eddie was Scott's cocaine connection," pronounced the *Los Angeles Times.*[87] Just as Thorson was beginning his legal wrangle with Liberace, in April 1982, Nash was being convicted of drug trafficking; authorities suspected him of still more violent crimes. These people and their circle had become Thorson's closest associates as 1981 closed. They supplied him with drugs, friendship, sex, and other connections—like the lawyers he would use to attack his old patron after their split.

If his deposition and news reports offer one window on this world, his memoir left another, although he veiled the characters with pseudonyms. Chief among these underworld figures was "Mr. Y, someone I met through Lee." This character generally corresponds to Chris Cox of the depositions. Thorson detailed the relationship in his book. "Y was an easterner from the Boston area. He and Lee went way back; they'd tricked around when Lee was scrounging a living playing small East Coast Clubs. Mr. Y was one of the more unsavory characters in Lee's life. He ran a gay nightclub in Hollywood and openly boasted of his underworld connections. At one time, after a publicized gangland-style killing Y even hid out in one of Lee's properties."

A man he called "Joe" in the text, "one of Mr. Y's close friends," was equally disreputable. This character appears to represent the real-life Eddie Nash. "Joe" had been charged with "equally serious crimes" to those committed by "Mr. Y."[88] The two "must have thought of me as the perfect mark, a guy with a drug problem and, through Lee, the means to support it," he averred. "For the next year Y, while pretending to be my friend, served as my supplier. He and Joe systematically stripped me of my savings and some of my cars, and Y introduced me to freebasing, the most dangerous form of cocaine addiction."[89]

If he considered Nash the source of his problem before 1982, Thorson had changed his mind by the time he published *Behind the Candelabra.* He named Ed Nash in his preface and thanked him for his "personal support and understanding." This corresponds to his tribute to "Joe," who "in a totally ironic twist of fate," he wrote, "has become a sort of mentor to me, and has more than made up for things that happened in the past." [90] History and the courts proved the shallowness of Thorson's devotion to Adel Nasrallah.

As *Behind the Candelabra* was going to press, complete with its commendation of Nasrallah, Thorson was preparing to reveal Eddie Nash's sins and crimes, even as he exposed the involutions of the whole Odyssey drug/sex scene. By this time, Thorson was mired even deeper in his addiction. By 1987, he found himself in desperate straits. An initial settlement with Liberace from 1982, which included various automobiles, was long gone. Ed Nash had gotten the Rolls, Chris Cox the others. It was a trade for which Thorson never saw any cash. [91] Money from a second settlement of January 1987 vanished just as quickly. He still had his habit. He turned to theft. In 1988, he was in jail awaiting sentencing "for a drug-related armed robbery in which he pleaded guilty." To reduce his time, he snitched on his old sometime mentor, Eddie Nash. [92] His revelation re-created the insidious world of 1981 in which he had lived for a year or more. It hinged on coke, sex, and murder.

In 1981, four people had been bludgeoned to death in a home in Laurel Canyon. Police fingered the Odyssey group. They did not get exactly what they wanted. They settled for John Holmes instead. Like the Mark Wahlberg character, Dirk Diggler, in *Boogie Nights,* Holmes had founded his huge pornographic reputation on an equally huge sexual organ. A colossus, as it were, of the 1970s pornographic scene, Holmes had moved in the same circle as Cox, Nash, and Thorson. He, like the protagonists of the film, also succumbed to drugs, sex, and violence. He died in March of 1988 of HIV-related infections. In 1982, the state charged him with the Laurel Canyon murders. The jury acquitted him. Later, police insisted that they had known all along who had actually committed the crime but lacked evidence for an arrest. In his own trial, Holmes had fingered the Odyssey characters. "The porn actor," according to news reports, "told police that he had led killers to a home in the Laurel Canyon area of Los Angeles at the behest of a revenge-crazed Nash, who two days earlier had been robbed of cocaine and $10,000 by two of the murder victims." [93]

During the time of the Holmes trial, Chris Cox had told Thorson that the wilds of Laurel Canyon could absorb more victims. Whereupon, Thorson retorted, "Chris, if you were smart you would pull my teeth"—

in reference to dental identification.[94] If Thorson could make morbid jokes about such things, he also professed to know what was going on. Had the cops gotten the wrong man in Holmes? Thorson now set them right. In September 1988, the *Los Angeles Times* carried the headline, "Scott Thorson Testifies against Convicted Cocaine Trafficker Adel (Eddie Nash) Nasrallah and Gregory D. Diles at Their Pretrial Hearing for the Drug-Related 1981 Murders of Four People."[95] The boy from La Crosse, not yet thirty, had seen the last of fame and notoriety. His name and face vanished from the news. His old patron was two years in the grave. He hadn't been a prisoner in paradise for seven years when he confronted incarceration someplace rather short of the pearly gates in 1988.

The idyll was long gone. The relationship had become something very different well before the two broke up. As 1981 came to a close, Thorson said, "we had terrible fights, instigated by me when I caught Lee paying attention to a younger man, or by Lee when he thought I was stoned. We'd wind up in a shouting match that always ended with Lee calling me a 'monster.'"[96] Notwithstanding his conflicted protests of love and affection in his memoir, depositions in the palimony suit confirm that Thorson was thinking about splitting in January or February—splitting and getting his due, as well. At that time, he consulted a lawyer about confirming the agreements he had reached with his old mentor.[97]

The confrontations between the two men turned nastier still. Thorson towered over his mentor by perhaps half a foot, and if cocaine encourages mania, Thorson, clean and sober, was also capable of violence and destructiveness. Hyped by cocaine, his jealousy careened toward violence. While he professed shock that his lover might fear him, he described himself smashing everything in sight when he discovered the older man's infidelity. His patron's anxieties were well founded. This state of affairs continued for perhaps six months. It ended—and with it the relationship—more or less officially around the first day of spring, 1982.

Out of town for the funeral of one of his favorite foster mothers, Rose Carracappa, he said, Thorson returned to Lake Tahoe to discover that his fantasies about his lover's faithlessness had finally materialized. As he described it in his memoir, he confirmed that in his absence Lee had bedded Cary James, a tall, blond, eighteen-year-old member of the Young Americans, a singing-dancing troupe in the Liberace show. Thorson went ballistic. With the showman cowering downstairs, he destroyed the Tahoe condominium bedroom. Still raging, he flew back to Los Angeles, where he holed up in the penthouse apartment at the Beverly Boulevard building. "Mr. Y" visited him the first night. He brought coke. They snorted; Thorson ranted.[98] Papadakis, from the Odyssey, appeared too. He brought himself. They had sex.[99] After a couple of days of this, Thorson said, he flipped again when he received news from the Cloisters that Lee had appeared in Palm Springs and " 'had two French kids here with him in bed.' " "The anger I'd felt in Tahoe," Thorson responded, "was child's play compared to the rage that shook me after learning that Lee had been tricking around as he'd done before we met." He called the Cloisters. "How dare you? How dare you do that to me?" he ranted to his old lover. "I could kill you!"[100] "He shouted all sorts of obscenities at me," Liberace himself confirmed under oath. "He threatened to kill me. 'I will kill you,' " he repeated. He was very disturbed about the French houseguests, the showman explained demurely.[101]

This impossible state of affairs ended on March 25. That very day, the pianist was scheduled to play for the fifty-fourth annual Academy Awards ceremony. He planned to stay at Beverly Boulevard. The apartment was, of course, occupied. He instructed Heller to resolve the matter. With an entourage that included Wayne Johansen, the half-brother; Tracy Schnelker of Tracy International, a private detective agency; and three of Schnelker's employees, Heller appeared to evict the deposed favorite. In a wild melee that ensued in the penthouse, Thorson managed to get a call through to Mr. Y, who sent over four men "led by the manager of his gay nightclub." Heller accused Thorson of threatening blackmail. Thorson shouted about the agreements he and Lee had made. Heller replied, according to Thorson, "that there was never no contract of some sort."[102] The disorder became either comic, surreal, or both when Thorson's real-estate agent showed up in the middle of the fracas with papers for Thorson to sign for a condominium in Los Angeles.

Still in his nightclothes, and clutching his jewelry box, Thorson finally left the free-for-all in the parking lot and headed home with Papadakis, the Odyssey manager. Using Lee's credit card, the two of them soon took off on a two-week excursion to Hawaii. Back by April 10, Thorson initiated a legal confrontation with his old lover. Within half a year, their private affections and domestic hatreds had been splashed across newspapers around the world, but Thorson was exiting history even as he was entering it. As for his lover of nearly five years, Liberace, at sixty-three, faced, one more time, the nightmare of having his sexual life scrutinized by the public. His handling of this horror during the last five years remaining him suggests both how little and how much his life had changed after Stonewall.

He's so unlike the rest of us. He doesn't much
care for the real world, you know.

ANGIE LIBERACE

 *Fourteen*

PETER PAN

Liberace was not a reader. He left no evidence at all of devotion to the written word. In the numerous photographs of his homes, books appear nowhere. In his nearly seventy years, he mentioned only one book by name. This one, however, he considered a semi-sacred text, and Claude M. Bristol's *The Magic of Believing* offers a nice guide to the entertainer's values, not least in the distracted last five years of his life. It does more. It illuminates significant aspects of popular culture in the United States; just so, it offers additional insights into the sources of Liberace's extraordinary appeal in the American heartland.

Born around the turn of the century, Bristol formulated a theory of success in the interwar years. It might have been based on F. D. Roosevelt's first inaugural maxim, "we have nothing to fear but fear itself." The guiding principle was that nothing was real except what we willed to be so; this was true of both success and failure. By this measure, we willed fear; the anxiety itself produced the Great Depression—or as Bristol himself consistently referred to it, "the so-called depression." The usage suggests much. He eschewed any negative expression whatsoever. "Fear"? The mere use of the term actualized the anxiety and hence exacerbated the problems of economic recession.

With an evangelical's faith, Bristol testified about how he proselytized as a public speaker at social and business meetings. He promulgated his ideas in brochures or pamphlets, too. *The Magic of Believing,* first published in 1948, summarized his system. A hugely popular volume, by the time Liberace discovered the book in the mid-fifties, it had gone through seventeen editions in less than four years. It appeared with a whole raft of related volumes after the war. Between 1946 and 1954, the *New York Times* bestseller lists had included Ayn Rand's *The Fountainhead,* Liebman's *Peace of Mind,* Dale Carnegie's *How to Stop Worrying and Start Living, A Guide to Confident Living,* and *How I Raised Myself from Failure to Success in Selling.* Most notably, Norman Vincent Peale's *The Power of Positive Thinking* remained on the *Times* bestseller list for over four years between 1952 and 1956.[1] If less polished and sophisticated than any of these, even, Bristol's volume still fits the pattern. Indeed, its very vulgarity virtually caricatures American values in these years.

The book's fundamental premise assumes the power of the mind to shape all reality. By this measure, the external, physical world (Bristol never mentions "nature") is completely plastic and malleable. In outlining one of the more extreme versions of the idea, he cites "a distinguished British scientist" for proof. Dr. Alexander Cannon, he says, had declared "that while a man today cannot grow a new leg (as a crab can grow a new claw), he could if the mind of man hadn't rejected the possibility. . . . I know that such a statement may sound absurd or at least incredible," Bristol avers, "but how do we know that it will not be done some day?"[2]

According to Bristol, we get what we imagine or crave. The problem, he continues, is that most folks do not want much. Rather, a man simply accepts the social, institutional, or traditional definition of what he should desire. Failing to exercise self-conscious will, most people are governed by their unconscious. Their unconscious minds determine, in the most haphazard fashion, what is true or what they derive from life. *Magic* proposes a way to change this. It proposes that individuals can seize the potential of mind power and lay claim to the authority inherent in the mental process to shape the material world.

Bristol presents all this as science, literally. Thus, he insists that the brain generates magnetic waves that govern the external world. He offers other kinds of proof of the power of positive thinking. His evidence is mostly commonplace and traditional. All religion, for example, arises out of the power of belief to shape reality, he proclaims. He identifies faith healers and miracles at Lourdes as self-evident proof of his argument. More frequently still, he cites authority. The number of authorities he draws on is virtually incalculable. He marshals "psychic researchers" like Thomson Jay Hudson and Richard Maurice Bucke, authors of such tomes as *Law of Psychic Phenomena* and *Cosmic Consciousness,* to prove his point. Physicians, engineers, and academics dance across his pages—the likes of Thomas Alva Edison, "Dr. Frederick Kalz, noted Canadian authority," "the late Charles P. Steinmetz, famous engineer of the General Electric Company," Sir Arthur Eddington, "the famous English physicist" and "the late Sir James Jeans, who was equally famous in the same field." The actress Marie Dressler dashes on and off the book's pages; so do novelists like Marie Corelli and Louis Bromfield. Paracelsus, the medieval alchemist, appears. So does Pythagoras, also "Hermes Trismegistus and the ancient Hermetic philosophers." In one of the best examples of Bristol's proofs, he refers to Cato the Elder. The Roman statesman ended every speech with the phrase, "Carthage must be destroyed!" and sure enough, by golly, Carthage *was* destroyed!

For all these notables, Bristol's personal and anecdotal data play an even greater part in his argument. Indeed, he herds even the "noted authorities" into this net of the personal and commonplace. By this measure, his own life and biography become the essential element of his proof of mind power. This is critical to his system. His "authorities" are, then, essentially window dressing to his own personal testimony, which remains the primary evidence. He tells his story; he shares his revelation with the enthusiasm of the camp-meeting convert. As a young man, he had experienced an epiphany. He was a penniless, despairing soldier in World War I when he heard his own voice, not God's, speaking to him in a secular version of Paul's Damascus Road experience. The voice instructed even as it predicted, "when I returned to civilian life, 'I would have a lot of money,'" He discovered his fate and future, and with this assertion, he insisted, "The whole pattern of my life was altered at that moment."[3] This transformation of his life is what he extended to his readers.

His science is, then, much more of a highly personal, even idiosyncratic "witness" in a traditional Christian, Protestant manifestation or confessional of proof: this happened to me; the revelation changed my life; it led me to discover it happened to all these other people; it can happen to you. At the same time, he also worked out what he calls a scientific method by which readers could replicate his own control of mind—and, of course, his worldly success as well. This involved lecturing to oneself in mirrors, posting signs around the house, carrying note cards on one's person, and ritually repeating one's goals. Naming these goals, however, preceded all this. In this regard, Bristol distinguishes, first, between needs and desires as proper purposes. It is desire, not need, that drives the engine, he asserts. He insists that individuals must both define and cultivate desire, the more beyond need the better. Desire, not need, changes everything. "It is desire for something new, something different, something that is going to change your life, that causes you to make an extra effort," he proclaims, "and it is the *power of believing* that alone sets in motion those inner forces by which you add what I call *plus-values* to your life."[4]

While Bristol allows for nonmaterial aspirations, practically, his book focuses attention on things and matter—on material goals and concrete purposes. He allows for the materialization of a desire from thin air—as when he wished himself a particular type of cheese on a trans-Pacific cruise; by and large, however, he assumes that we must first gain money to fulfill our wishes. In short, his book describes how to get rich in order to buy things that we have previously cultivated the desire for. Paradoxically, then, while he celebrates the mind and mental processes, that mentality lacks all spiritual, elevated, lofty, or even intellectual ends, and only circles back to material purpose.

In Bristol's essentially material world, only individuals possess power and authority. His cosmos is shaped exclusively by individuals' will, by personal aims and goals. Community, society, politics, law, the common good, and social institutions—family, church, the state, history, and tradition, for example—lack all form and substance in his scheme. When they appear at all, they exist as either negative powers or as objects to be effected by the self-willing, self-activating man.[5] Self-help is the *only* help. Bristol describes, effectively, a society held together exclusively by will and choice, by common adherence to the purposes of individual volition. This is the only politics of the text. He assumes the state—or at least the American republic—to be simply the aggregate of its self-willing individuals. Once, however, he actually articulates the notion. He does so under duress, sensing that his most cherished system is being threatened. Although his insight is circumscribed by his general optimism and by his unwillingness to concede anything negative or evil, he speaks as an American of the heartland when he hints at powers of darkness that threaten the collective folk of free will in the United States with the Cold War going full tilt:

> I am cognizant of the fact that there are powerful forces at
> work in this country that would dominate us, substituting a
> kind of regimentation for the competitive system which has
> made America great among nations. They would attempt to
> destroy individual thinking and initiative, cherished ever
> since our Pilgrim Fathers established this country in defiance
> of Old World tyranny. I believe we must continue to retain
> the wealth of spirit of our forefathers, for if we don't we shall
> find ourselves dominated in everything we do by a mighty

few and shall become serfs in fact if not in name. Thus, this
work is written also to help develop individual thinking and
doing.[6]

In a stroke, he vanquishes Nazism, fascism, communism, socialism, unionism, and even corporate capitalism and Catholicism, among other "isms"
and ideologies, for the American way of unfettered liberty, the free-
market system, practical reality, and common sense.[7] As the Cold War
dawned in 1948, Claude Bristol offered the perfect embodiment of Americanism, but his ideology had much deeper American roots.

Complete with its vulgarity, a considerable portion of which Bristol
himself genially acknowledges, *The Magic of Believing* is a quintessentially
American text. Besides its skepticism about history, tradition, culture, and
institutions, it possesses still other characteristic American biases. Ami-
able, optimistic, materialistic, untheoretical, nondogmatic, and personalistic, it is a hodgepodge of sources, impressions, and sentiment with the
same degree of consistency as Whitman's *Leaves of Grass*. Nor, on the
most mundane level, is it far from Ralph Waldo Emerson's pronouncements about the nature of things. Indeed, with its notable nod to New
England and "our Pilgrim Fathers," it identifies its distinctive philosophy with the particular forms of Protestant Christianity of the Yankee
mind. Truth as personal witness or revelation is not the least of these.
Indeed, all manner of classic New England, Calvinistic elements percolate
through the text. It has been said that a social or theological system's
heresies and taboos arise as hedges against the most profound, latent tendencies of that very system itself. In this regard, the Yankee proscriptions
of antinomianism—radical individualism otherwise defined—and Armin-
ianism—salvation through works—illustrate the mode completely: with
God leached from the system, the grossest heresies of colonial New England became the norm for a New Englandized America—radical individualism and a self-driven work ethic.

Bristol lived in the same ideological world as Whitman and Emerson, Mary Baker Eddy, and P. T. Barnum, and hardly less in that of William James and Abraham Lincoln. If far less artful than they were, he
described the American creed that motivated their careers, as well. Here,
anyone can get ahead. Here, one can do anything one desires. Here, indeed, desire is limitless, and the perpetual impulse is to create and re-create
desire itself, over and over. Where problems arise, they are resolvable by
hard work and energy activated by ambition and will. Its sin is the failure
of desire and imagination, of pep and spunk. It is a world of impossible
dreams, where men can fly and Ponce de León's springs of eternal youth

well up in shopping malls and suburban housing developments. It is a magic kingdom of queens for a day and fame by sortition. It brims with wonder and marvels.

Liberace loved the American promise even as he admired Claude Bristol's artless rendering of the American way. It possessed special power for him, too, as he seems to have discovered the book at a critical juncture—the mid-fifties—when he was losing his grip on his career and even on his life. Thus, he wrote a preface to the 1955 edition, and in 1958 he wrote and then recorded a song with the title, and on the theme, of "The Magic of Believing." He cut one disc for public sale; the other constituted his last promotional record, made, apparently, in conjunction with Bristol to sell his book.[8]

Thirty years after first reading *The Magic of Believing,* he had made his life a testament to Bristol's homilies. In 1984, at sixty-five years old, when he flew, literally, across the stage at Radio Center Music Hall, he gave form to Bristol's admonitions about daring, desire, and executing the impossible. Just so, as his Tinkerbell/Peter Pan excursion through the air hypostatized his own fantasies, so his flight personalized his countrymen's impossible dreams as well. The dream of audience and actor united; his wingless flight—if Oz-like fantasy—became a metaphor of that old American trick of pulling off the impossible. "The difficult we do immediately," boasted World War II Seabees; "the impossible takes a little longer." Liberace lived by the same maxim. "My attitude is that nothing is impossible, it just takes a little longer."

Long before he discovered Bristol's book, Lee was living the dream *The Magic of Believing* celebrated. The poor little Polish boy with courage and ambition that surpassed even his talent could have been a model of Bristol's ideal type. Think positively. Avoid woe. Don't kvetch. Look ahead. Work hard. Sell yourself. Believe! While he left no evidence of actually writing down these maxims and posting them on his shaving mirror as Bristol recommended, they were written on his heart and psyche long before he first opened Bristol's *Magic.* He actually did memorize some of the great motivator's epigrams, however:

> To experience *happiness,* one must express happiness.
> To find *love,* one must give love.
> To possess *wealth,* one must value wealth.
> To acquire *health,* one must live health.
> To attain *success,* one must positively think success.[9]

Claude Bristol never distinguished between self-fulfillment and the desire for gain, on the one hand, and, on the other, the common good.

Indeed, he effectively collapsed the categories. This tendency runs deep in American social thought. Liberace did the same thing. Serving his own ends and turning his talent to profit, he served and delighted the commonwealth as well. This viewpoint permeated his career. He wanted to give people what they wanted; he wanted to reify their fantasies as well as his own. His performances did so perfectly. So did his lavish consumerism. The museum he founded and the memoirs he wrote did so precisely. While turning handsome profits and securing his image, these enterprises also delighted the folks. They represent the genial boosterism of the American spirit quite as much as does anything found in Claude Bristol's prescription for positive living. At the same time, these autobiographical and memorial enterprises represented still other facets of Liberace's life and American values.

Liberace had conceived of a museum in the early seventies. He launched the enterprise in February 1975, when he opened the mansion on Harold Way to paying visitors, at six dollars a pop.[10] He noted that when he appeared on Cher's television program, he had touted the enterprise, and, as a result, seventeen thousand fans requested reservations. The pathlike road that wound up the Hollywood Hills to the mansion-museum was hardly conducive to tourists and tour buses, however. Nor were locals happy about having a commercial enterprise among their fancy homes overlooking Sunset Boulevard. The neighbors sued to end the operation.[11] He quit Hollywood Hills. He did not give up.

He next scouted his hometown for a museum site. A great Victorian mansion on Milwaukee Avenue in the suburb of Wauwatosa seemed perfect. Neighbor anxiety helped eliminate that site, too. So did the threat of a lawsuit by the property's former owner and present tenant. The showman dropped his bid for the property.[12]

None of these difficulties applied to Las Vegas. Here, anything could fly. It was here that Mr. Showmanship himself had first actually taken to the air on invisible wires as a part of his act in 1975. Las Vegas was a natural for the museum. Various issues propelled him toward the Nevada gambling center. Since the mid-seventies, this had been his official home, as he had moved his legal residence here for both work and tax reasons. However much he loved the Cloisters, the Shirley Street house had not only become his primary residence but had rapidly come to embody his very person. He loved Vegas. Its delicious vulgarity might have been made to order for the museum.

By October 1978, he had settled on a specific site in the gambling resort, a shopping center that he purchased for three million dollars. It was a few minutes' drive from the Strip. Abetted by his new young companion, Scott Thorson, Liberace turned museum making into a full-time enterprise that fall and winter. There were, first, the costumes and the replicas of his jewelry to put on display. Among his automobiles, he gave up the piano-key stationwagon, the red, white, and blue Rolls-Royce, the Auburn, his first limousine, and his '57 Thunderbird. Not least, there was the furniture and the objets d'art that had been his passion for twenty-five years. "We stayed up three nights straight just going through the Vegas house, and the task had to be repeated in all the other homes," Thorson reminisced.[13]

The Liberace Museum opened for visitors on Easter Sunday, 1979. Some tourists had waited in line as long as three hours when Mr. Showmanship showed up in person to greet the first visitors. Decked out in a "pink, blue and yellow checkered sports jacket with matching yellow shirt and slacks, he wore a huge gold cross around his neck and sported six diamond-studded gold rings, each the size of an enormous peach pit," a reporter noted. Photographs had memorialized that his then companion Vince Cardell had helped him inaugurate the Hollywood Hills museum in 1975. The guard had changed in two years, as recorded by journalists. "During the opening he was joined by his 23-year old [sic] companion/road manager/onstage chauffeur named Scott Thorenson [sic], who wore almost as much diamond-studded gold as the maestro," the journalist reported further. Thorson gave his own interview. " 'I did wear a lot of jewelry before I met Lee,' said the deeply tanned Thorenson. 'But as you're with Lee, you gotta keep the image. And it's fun. It's become a company thing, a trademark for all his employees.' "[14]

What did the institution mean for the entertainer? In retrospect, Scott Thorson treated the enterprise cynically. He considered it mere ego stroking, a way to get rid of things without selling them, an opportunity to buy new things to "fill the gaping holes" created by the moving vans, and not least, a "tax shelter to end all tax shelters." Controlled by a tax-exempt foundation, the museum became so profitable that, according to Thorson, the showman even tried to rearrange the management so as to tap this new source of revenue.[15]

Thorson missed other motives. Liberace himself offered a different take on the enterprise: "When you have something beautiful, it's a shame not to share it."[16] As with all his ventures, the showman saw no contradiction in charging people to share his treasures. As always, he drew no distinctions between personal profit for himself and providing the folks with what they wanted. He knew what people liked; he liked pleasing them; he gave them what they wanted; they paid for the privilege; he turned a profit: everyone was happy. As with his performances, so with the museum.

The skeptical *Rolling Stone* writer mocked the museum as the "Church of Liberace" and the Liberace cult as "a fey sort of evangelism." Minus the cynical language, Liberace himself agreed with the general outline of these sentiments. He always had a sense of the semi-sacred, quasi-religious dynamic of art, beauty, and show business. He acknowledged the totemic response of folks to glamour and specific objects of glamour. The museum institutionalized these values, even as it represented one more manifestation of his cultivation—and capitalization, literally—of his image and his fancied self.

There were other, subtler things at work in Liberace's founding of the museum, too. Scott Thorson missed them. So did *Rolling Stone*. The piano player wanted to be remembered. The museum memorialized his life.

The showman himself conducted the first tours, and when asked to indicate his favorite display, he passed the Chopin and Liszt pianos, his numerous commendations and awards, the jewels and other treasures. He pointed to an unassuming cabinet that contained an ancient French horn. His father had died exactly two years before. Despite the fact that he'd had virtually nothing to do with his parent since 1941, his father's old instrument still touched him.[17] He was remembering his father, and, without children of his own, he did not want to be forgotten, himself. "I would like to be remembered as a kind and gentle soul, and as someone who made the world a little better place to live in because I had lived in it. "Obviously," he continued, "I would like to think that my music will be remembered. But I hope also that some of the beautiful things I have collected in my homes will be preserved. In fact, I have formed a trust so that my personal belongings and my homes will be shared by the world long after I have gone." [18]

His trust—the Liberace Foundation—like the museum it sponsored, served various purposes, both magnanimous and venal. As Thorson implied, it did provide a major tax shelter, as indeed any such foundation does. No less, it reaffirmed and institutionalized some of the oldest, most generous impulses in the pianist's character. If he had always loved children, and if he missed having his own, the foundation helped compensate. If he had always made a place in his performance for young and fresh talent, the foundation continued the tradition. If he longed to live after he was dead and to have future generations remember him fondly, again, his foundation addressed the longing. The trust operated the museum and generated fresh revenues, but the showman defined its chief purpose as that of assisting young musicians and struggling popular performers, in particular. In his lifetime, it sponsored contests for young artists and funded scholarships for these same folks. Long after his death, it still does.

The museum and the Liberace Foundation would memorialize him "after he was gone." His books fulfilled the same objectives. He produced four: an autobiographical cookbook and three autobiographies.

His books honor Claude Bristol's creed, but they fit just as nicely into a still broader spectrum of American thought that had originated in the time of Benjamin Franklin. The Philadelphia founding father supposedly composed the bit of doggerel that ran:

> If you would not be forgotten,
> After you are dead and rotten,
> Write something worth the reading
> Or do something worth the writing.

The patriot's life confirms the notion that if one gains monetary compensation in addition to immortality from the written word and public acts, that is all the better. Franklin's *Autobiography* bears an even more direct relationship to the showman's memoirs. It chronicles Franklin's self-creation, even as it played a major part in his actualization of himself. Franklin wrote an autobiographical success story about his triumph over adversity and his rise from poverty to—literally—dining with kings. He intended it, too, as a model or instruction manual for those who followed him. Claude Bristol's vulgar interpretation of the same ideas draws on the same principles. So do Liberace's autobiographies, right down to the bits about meeting kings and queens.

Published in 1970, *Liberace Cooks! Recipes from His Seven Dining Rooms,* is so personal as to be virtually autobiographical. He had joked that he preferred the title *Mother! I'd Rather Do It Myself!,* a takeoff on one of the hugely popular advertising slogans of the day, and the book brims with all manner of personal material. It was founded in the personal as well. Food was important to Liberace. He had loved the kitchen since before his high school days, when he encouraged the establishment of a home-ec class for boys. His press kit of 1947 includes pieces on cooking and eating, and even recipes. Cooking was one of the few things that both his parents had enjoyed and done well, and most of the dishes he included in his cookbook hark back to his childhood, or even further, to his parents' pasts in Poland and Italy. While his love of eating evoked the primitive passions of his immigrant parents, eating was another manifestation of his American consumerism, literally, as well. Scott Thorson wrote of how the star made trips to the market a shopping adventure when nothing else was available to amuse him. And if, as Thorson also insisted, his patron had difficulty showing love, cooking relieved this problem, too. He and Thorson delighted in the kitchen together. Consuming the product of their efforts resulted in the young man having to loosen his belt by several notches, while his successor, Cary James, added sixty-five pounds to his slender frame after moving in with the cookbook author. Liberace simply gorged his protégés, not only with gifts but also with food. As a final auto-biographical element, *Liberace Cooks!* also offers readers a variety of glossy color photographs of the showman in the process of preparing food and dining in the crystal glamour of his various homes.[19]

For all the personalistic elements of *Liberace Cooks!* the showman also wrote more purely autobiographical books that, in both form and content, are even more important for gaining an understanding of his life.

At least from the sixties, Liberace had begun producing biographical-type writings, which he had printed in large format booklets, like the twenty-four-page *Liberace Legend,* which he sold at concerts. Heavily pic-torial, *Legend* includes a couple of pages each on "Liberace at Home," "His Palm Springs 'Hideaway,'" "A Second Career" (selling antiques and objets d'art), and the like. Such booklets were doubly or triply commer-cial. While they were printed to sell at a profit, they also contained actual advertisements. One page carried the showman's endorsement of Bald-win Pianos, another touted his latest albums for Dot Records. "Your Own Command Performance!" sang the headline. They were commercial in still other ways, too. More than anything, they advertised Liberace him-self. They shaped and marketed an image of the performer.[20]

These were only the performer's initial forays into biography. While maintaining many of the motives and impressions of the biographical bro-chures, Liberace's memoirs, written between 1973 and 1985, formalized and regularized his impression for a larger audience.

The showman published his first life story in 1973. He left a contradic-tory record of its creation. One version survives in legal documents. The book's references to his old girlfriends had prompted Joanne Rio Barr to sue. Liberace's depositions in the suit emphasize his own role in the text's creation. Around 1972, he had contacted William Targ of G. P. Putnam's Sons, he testified, about publishing his memoirs. Targ came out from Manhattan to meet the performer at the Westbury Music Fair on Long Island. "I had written six chapters of the book, which I was anxious for Mr. Targ to read, and while I was performing on stage," testified the show-man, "he read the six chapters, and then after the performance ended, I cleared everyone out of my dressing room, and he sat down to tell me about his reaction to the six chapters that I had written." Targ liked the project; he offered a contract. Soon after, Liberace hired his own research assistant, Carroll Carroll, who went on Putnam's payroll. "He researched a lot of things for me," Lee stated. "I can remember—like I said, I have great recall, but I have difficulty remembering dates. I think he was able to go through old scrapbooks and magazines and newspaper files and libraries and he was able to come up with a lot of chronology that I needed for the book."

"Did Mr. Carroll contribute to the actual writing of the book as opposed to editing?" the lawyers queried. "No," the showman replied flatly. "All the words in my book are my very own, and he did help me with punctuation and spelling and things like that, and dates. I had the wrong dates about some shows that I had seen. Things like that."[21] A contemporary interview confirms some of this: a journalist reported that Liberace wrote the book over a fourteen-month period after and between professional engagements.[22]

While it might have served his purposes in these legal proceedings to emphasize Carroll's role in the book's production, he did not. At the same time, he left evidence that Carroll might have played a larger role in the volume's production after all; thus his dedication of the book to his researcher "for his editorial assistance." Thirteen years later, he contradicted his earlier sworn testimony with the suggestion that none of his autobiographical writing was "the real thing" but was "written in collaboration with somebody else. The trade term was 'as told to.'"[23] Along these lines, some of the book seems a transcription of tapes, with Wausau, Wisconsin, being rendered as "Warsaw," and his high school friend Del Krause's German-pronounced name appearing phonetically as "Krausy," for example.

Regardless of how the book was put together, it bears Liberace's indelible imprimatur. Its chatty, discursive flavor comes with everything but his nasal, Milwaukee whine. If his act always flirted with being precious, the off-setting self-mockery works less well in print, and the tone is often saccharine. It is, however, his own. The book also possesses no particular structure; one story triggers another; it lacks chronological order altogether. In this regard, it operates very much like Liberace's performances—which never had a set program—or like his pattering asides, which possessed no more order than does any conversation between friends. The same sort of idiosyncrasy also characterized *The Magic of Believing*. Both were founded in the essentially American value of the primacy of an individual's feeling or sentiment rather than in formal rules and order.

The book's relentlessly sunny tone is also quintessential Liberace.

The text tends to gloss over or ignore unpleasantness—such as the *Hollywood Reporter* allegations, for example—or to consider problems—like the Cassandra trial—merely as obstacles to overcome. In this regard, the book demonstrates classic American cheerfulness and optimism, the expectation that the future possesses limitless opportunities that also pervades Bristol's work. Such cheeriness is a quality that, for example, makes tragedy a contradiction in American culture. Does one fall or fail? It's no loss. In the language of popular tunes, one moves another rubber tree or picks oneself up, brushes oneself off, and starts all over again. Good vanquishes evil, and victors have only to work hard and keep their eyes on the goal to achieve their aims. One has only to trust oneself to conquer.

If, as Alexis de Toqueville noted in his *Democracy in America,* this individualistic imperative undercuts the social good and social responsibility, this philosophy offers its own antidote to anarchy. R. W. Emerson framed one answer: by internalizing order, the American system channels and controls even more effectively than do external constraints of law and guards. Then, too, by framing social values exclusively in material and economic terms, it puts everyone on the same track of production and consumption. Even so, it eliminates or reduces class identity by holding out the promise of material benefits to everyone who works diligently. Last, but hardly least, the victors in the competition possess their own social obligations to inspire others to fulfill their own potential. Inspirational or self-help literature, then, is inseparable from these values. Benjamin Franklin's autobiography could be placed in the category, and self help is the informing motive of Claude Bristol's manual. Liberace's memoir is equally evangelical, however "schmaltzy, glittering, or vain" it might be. Indeed, the showman introduces the volume with a tribute to courage, overcoming fear, transcending inner conflicts, and trusting "the validity of [one's] instincts." Even more appropriately, it opens with a tribute to Claude Bristol himself. Quoting the preface he wrote for *The Magic of Believing,* Liberace makes his own book an accolade to self-reliance.[24] He closes his introduction with a ringing appeal to his readers: "So never let yourself lose your belief in yourself. With that you can be the greatest salesman in the world, selling the most important product in the world . . . YOU!"[25]

Liberace's *Liberace: An Autobiography* affirms classic elements of the American creed and falls into place among many other memoirs of its type. It provides, effectively, a motivational model summarized along the lines of: trust oneself, show no fear, work hard. These convictions are easy to satirize. They are the stuff of skits on *Saturday Night Live.* They are very much the point of the *Rolling Stone* review in relating Liberace to a "fey sort of evangelism," too. Detecting the same qualities in the book, one critic called it "a conspirational collection of anecdotes . . . that reveals [the author] to be as shrewd as a cat stalking a fly while he exhorts us readers to pull ourselves up by our bootstraps." [26]

The book sold self-confidence even as it sold Liberace himself. He wrote it to sell, as well. Did you plan on making a profit, the deposing attorneys in the Barr case inquired? "Everything I do has the hope of making a profit," he replied guilelessly. "My career, everything I touch in my scope of entertainment field and that would include the publication of a book, yes." "Nobody works for nothing," he added elsewhere, as if to drive the nail home.[27] Did he write it to sell? The folks, one more time, did not disappoint him. First hyped with excerpts in the *National Enquirer* on November 18, 1973, *Liberace* sold furiously. By the time it had been out three weeks, 250,000 people had snatched up copies. In England, it was the second- or third-best-selling book during the same time period.[28] Who bought and read it? The serialization in the *National Enquirer* helps define the audience.

The 1973 volume was the most important of Liberace's autobiographical writings. His second and third books contain elements of the first. *The Things I Love,* written with Tony Palmer, appeared in 1976. This volume adds little to the personal elements revealed in the autobiography, but it does record a shift in his life after the early seventies. While he had always loved things, celebrating his objects is the chief purpose of this volume. His last book does the same thing with even greater determination. Contracted in 1985 by Harper and Row and published the following year, *The Wonderful, Private World of Liberace* is excessive and fantastic — even by the showman's standards.

Lee's "wonderful world" possesses no homosexuals, much less homosexual lawsuits. Scott Thorson's name comes up nowhere, although his face seems to appear in the photograph of a receiving line for Great Britain's Princess Anne: cropping would have eliminated the very flattering image of his patron standing next to him.[29] Although Cary James's photograph appears, the caption lumps him indiscriminately with the singer Kenny Rogers merely as "my friends." [30] References to age are as conspicuously missing. Completely bald except for a fringe around the back of his head, Liberace protests that his toupee is his natural hair. Just so, he denies having had cosmetic surgery, although his face reveals the transformation, which was not necessarily to his benefit. Dr. Startz had reduced his previously large eyes to slits, while the deep skin peel turned his complexion into the shiny, peachy parchment of a fresh scar. Banishing both faggotry and age, so too he eliminated sickness from his private world.

Although he was both HIV positive and symptomatic when he signed the publishing contract with Harper and Row in 1985, *The Wonderful, Private World* fails to hint at any of this. On the contrary, the showman covers his illness with a preposterous story of a "watermelon diet," which, he related, "robbed my system of essential nutrients, which was causing me to experience a letdown in my normal high energy level. . . . As a result," he continued, "false rumors started to circulate about my health. According to the gossips, you name it, and I had it. Let me assure you," he concluded, "I've never felt better in my life!"

There was no homosexuality, no illness, and no conflict in Liberace's literary Neverland. Evil for the showman simply did not exist, insofar as he monitored his own thoughts. His depositions in Joanne Rio Barr's suit in the mid-seventies offer one manifestation of the characteristic. He saw "nothing in my book that was damaging or derogatory about Miss Rio," he insisted, but this was hardly the sum of his response. He was incredulous about her suit. "As far as I am concerned, Joanne Rio does not exist because this is something that happened 20 years ago," he testified. "It was like a ghost coming out of the past to haunt me." [31] He didn't like it? It wasn't good? It did not exist. His father was another such phantom. Banished to the netherworld of yesteryear, Salvatore hardly existed after 1941. Liberace's brother George fell into much the same category after the two fought in 1957. Recording the affair with Vince Cardell, Scott Thorson noted the specific ways his patron eliminated unpleasantness and bad memories. Cardell's hostility filled the air when Thorson moved into the Shirley Street house, but Lee simply ignored it once he took a new lover. Then, when Thorson forced the issue, Liberace turned the ejection over to his houseboy, Carlucci, and Heller, his manager. Once Cardell had been physically banished, Lee then eliminated every piece of evidence of Cardell ever having been part of in his life, according to Thorson. "When [Cardell] finally departed it happened so quickly and completely that I felt as if someone had waved a magic wand. Once he'd gone Lee went about systematically removing all traces of the life he and [Vince] had shared. He stripped [his] bedroom and bath down to bare walls, disposing of the furniture and repainting and papering. He went through the house, gathering every item they'd bought together so Carlucci could get rid of them. Clearly, Lee wanted no reminder of [Vince] in the home we now shared." [32]

As Scott Thorson's rendering depicts the affair with Vince Cardell, the Bristolian admonitions to think only positive thoughts dominated Liberace's career, his writing, his life, and, not least, his sense of himself and others. It played a critical role in his affair with Scott Thorson and, to a large extent, shaped much of his response to the horrors of his bout with AIDS.

Dealing with Thorson was perhaps the greatest crisis of Liberace's life. Liberace may or may not have stripped the walls bare in the rooms the two had shared, but otherwise, when the pair split in the spring of 1982, the showman stripped the young man from his life. Locks on every joint residence were changed within forty-eight hours after Heller had ejected Thorson from Beverly Boulevard. Lee instructed his devoted Shirley Street housekeeper, Gladys Luckie, to pack up everything of Thorson's at both Las Vegas dwellings. That was finished within two or three days, too. Probably to Lucille Cunningham's relief, Thorson was formally eliminated from the payroll within hours. In the hubbub, everyone forgot the joint credit cards. Thorson took advantage of the oversight and ran up a bill in excess of three thousand dollars to cover his and his friend/lover Papadakis's junket to Hawaii at end of March and beginning of April. If not soon enough, the entertainer caught the mistake within two weeks.[33] The young man himself was not canceled as easily as a MasterCard.

Between 1982 and 1987, the rejected lover refused to disappear. Thorson wanted to fight. On his return from Honolulu in April after the Beverly Boulevard affair in March, the young man began looking for a lawyer. He found one through his old drug connection, Eddie Nash, and the owner of the Odyssey, Chris Cox. His counselor did not encourage him. David Schmerin advised him that Liberace was a tough adversary who "would litigate this thing all the way and he had a very deep pocket and would hire the best counsel."[34] Indeed, by the time Schmerin was offering this advice, the showman had already turned the case over to Joel Strote, the forty-three-year-old attorney who had replaced the venerable John Jacobs as Liberace's chief counsel in 1971.

Strote and Schmerin began conferring in mid-April. The palimony issue figured significantly in their conversations. Ever since Michelle Triola Marvin had sued her companion, actor Lee Marvin, for financial support in the late seventies, the press had hyped the concept of alimony for live-in lovers. Journalists had dramatized the issue by quoting one judge, who averred that " 'Marvin' would do for women's rights what Miranda did for criminal law and what Brown did for school integration." Shortly afterwards, Marilyn Barnett's suit against her lover, tennis star Billie Jean King, lent additional currency to the furor while adding homosexual titillation to the concept.[35] Palimony was in the air, in any event, long before the Liberace-Thorson breach. Indeed, when they were still comfortable together, Thorson and his mentor had even joked about the latter case. "Billie Jean—what a guy!" Liberace laughed; "You're next," joshed Thorson.[36]

While ultimately nothing came of all this legal media excitement, it seemed critical at the time, and Thorson had pressed his lawyer to take up the matter. Schmerin discouraged him.[37] Indeed, Schmerin instructed him that a court of law would not uphold the legality of a contract between two homosexual men to guarantee their affair.[38] Schmerin had little confidence in the case; he had less in Thorson himself. His doubts grew with time. They had met through Thorson's old drug connection. They first deliberated in Ed Nash's living room, and Thorson was snorting cocaine during their interviews, according to press reports. Schmerin thought Thorson "edgy and goofy" and figured he was "bound to get caught in his lies" if the case went to court and he had to testify.[39] If skeptical of his own client, he admired his legal antagonists. In sworn testimony, he related how he and Strote had "talked about how kind and generous and benevolent and—I can't think of other adjectives to describe Mr. Liberace's treatment towards Mr. Thorson." [40]

Thorson's later advocates insisted that Schmerin gave poor counsel. In any case, Schmerin did advise Thorson against going to court. He also counseled him to sign the settlement he had worked out with Strote. "He suggested that I could go on and lead a normal life and I should just sign it and get it over with," Thorson himself testified. "He just felt that I should just sign the release and mutual agreement and that I could go on in life, a completely normal life, I wouldn't have threats." [41]

On April 22, 1982, Thorson did sign the agreement. The document stipulated that he forfeit the title to three of his six cars and surrender the Laramore Street house in Las Vegas and all its contents. He also waived any other claims against his former patron. Even more critical, he promised never to reveal the nature of his relationship with the performer. In return, Liberace pledged him his three remaining cars, three of their dogs, and seventy-five thousand dollars—although the showman tried to get the three thousand Thorson had spent on the Hawaii trip deducted from the total. The agreement also stipulated that as soon as practical after the signing, Thorson could collect "all the clothes and personal belongings now in the possession or control of Liberace." [42]

Liberace had won. Not least, the commitment of silence confirmed the entertainer's credo to speak no evil. He had won, but the fuse still smoldered. Thorson was bitter. The cars and cash vanished almost immediately in the maw of his drug dependency and his debts to Cox and Nash. By summer, he possessed little but vengefulness and spleen. Time increased his rancor. He fired his lawyer. Schmerin was glad to go. He engaged new counsel. Michael Rosenthal sympathized with him. To-gether, Rosenthal and Thorson plotted a new strategy as summer waxed. They detonated the powder keg in early fall.

On October 14, 1982, Thorson filed a twelve-point formal complaint with the Los Angeles Superior Court against his former lover and a host of co-defendants. These included, among others, Seymour Heller, Joel Strote, and Tracy Schnelker, the private detective from the penthouse raid. Rosenthal had advised waging a two-front war, and Thorson initiated a publicity campaign to coincide with the legal proceedings. With news having been leaked to the press, the two men entered the courthouse to the light of flashing cameras and television spotlights as an army of jour-nalists and reporters thrust microphones into their faces. Had the show-man sworn Thorson to speak no evil? The October 14 show marked only the beginning of Thorson's violation of the April 22 agreement's silence clause.

Along with directing the media blitz at the L.A. County courthouse, Rosenthal had been negotiating an exposé in the *National Enquirer.* Less than three weeks later, that journal headlined the story, "Boyfriend Tells All about Their 6-Year Romance." [43] A week later, the second installment ran: "Superstar's Boyfriend of 6 Years Reveals Liberace's Secret Life." [44]

The war had just begun.

David Schmerin had warned Thorson about the depth of his adver-sary's pockets; he anticipated Liberace's willingness to litigate. He might just as easily have advised against the publicity campaign Thorson and Rosenthal had mounted. However deeply Liberace might have dreaded public exposés, he was, as has already been shown, a public-relations genius, and he was willing to fight on this second front as hard as he would in the courts. The showman's entourage limbered up their cannons immediately.

If the *Enquirer* had effectively taken Thorson's side, the Liberace camp got its publicity licks in through the competing tabloid, the *Globe.* "GAYS OUT TO ASSASSINATE ME, SAYS LIBERACE," blared the banner head on November 2. "This is not the first time Liberace has been the victim of slander at the hands of the gays," a spokesman told the journal. "It's a battle he has had to fight throughout his career. Every time it's happened before, we've fought it and won. And we'll win this time—and every other time—too." The article described Thorson as "a former dis-gruntled employee" who "was fired because of excessive use of drugs and alcohol, and because he carried firearms." The article concluded with the revelation that the showman had hired a hypnotist to help him heal a bro-ken heart. The quotation rings completely true. "When negative people are around me, I say to them, kvetch, kvetch, kvetch—and they usually snap out of it. If they don't I avoid them in the future and keep them out of my life."[45]

As one manifestation of his hatred of "kvetching" and "negative people," Liberace exerted every effort to distance himself from the affair entirely. He left the struggle to his minions. "He was a pussycat," Thorson judged about their breakup. "He doesn't like to handle messy situations, and I think it was arranged by someone else."[46] Thorson indicated Seymour Heller. Heller had managed the Joanne Rio affair; along with Joel Strote, he had done the same with Thorson. The "disgruntled employee" fingered Heller as the source of the antigay references in the November 2 *Globe* story. Although the episode is especially murky, Thorson also identified Heller with the second installment of the tabloid wars in December, when once more, with feeling, the *Globe* weighed in on the Liberace side. "Wicked Past of Gay Suing Liberace" ran the headline. This piece contained Wayne Johansen's revelations about his half brother's turning tricks for pay as an adolescent and his carrying on with a foster father. From the time of the Beverly Boulevard raid, the Liberace camp had counted Johansen as an ally. The other revelations came from a shadier source but one who also had connections to the entourage, Dirk Summers, who had supported the allegations that Thorson had once been a boy prostitute.[47]

Beginning with the original court case of October 14, 1982, and accelerating with the tabloid wars, the litigation spread like a cancer, producing an almost endless sequence of court cases. Thorson sued the *Globe* over the "Wicked Past" article. David Brummet's widow, Marie, took up legal cudgels as well. Liberace's attorney, Joel Strote, brought his own case against Thorson and his attorney, Rosenthal. Rosenthal, in turn, formally charged Strote with slander. Meanwhile, Tracy Schnelker, who helped evict Thorson from the penthouse apartment, got in the action with a case against Liberace, while Liberace sued Dirk Summers, the éminence grise behind the second, "Wicked Past," *Globe* article. This was not the end.

The threats and actual suits proliferated into 1984. On December 15, 1983, Lee appeared on *Good Morning America.* The showman's answer to one of host David Hartman's questions about the case set more legal millstones grinding. Hartman's January 26 on-air apology satisfied the Thorson camp; no formal suit was filed. The scorned lover sought formal damages, however, following a similar episode that took place later that year. On May 7, *Newsweek* had interviewed the showman about the case. "I could have stopped the whole thing before it started by paying off," the star protested, "but that would have been blackmail, and blackmail never ends." The statement defined more Liberacean fantasy, for he had, of course, already paid Thorson off, and Thorson was, indeed, greedy for more. In any case, Thorson filed an additional multimillion dollar lawsuit against Liberace and an altogether new suit against *Newsweek*. It was October 1984. The legal wrangling had been going on two years.[48]

In the middle of the fight, other difficulties struck. For one thing, Liberace's elder brother died on October 16, 1983. This left only Lee and Angie. Rudy had virtually killed himself almost thirty years before. They had buried their father, at ninety-one, in 1977; he had left the world a senile old man in an old folks home in Sacramento. Their mother fought to the last and survived to 1981, when she died at age eighty-seven. Lee had supported them all, but their passing did not seem to grieve him. Indeed, Thorson remember his lover's relief on hearing of Frances's death rattle. He appeared dry eyed at George's memorial, too. His brother was seventy-two. While they had never completely reconciled after the rupture in 1957, the showman had demonstrated his old family loyalty by appointing George as the director of the museum in 1977, when the older brother had little else. Whether Liberace liked his brother or not, George's funeral marked a milestone. Liberace was next in line. He delayed his deposition in the Thorson suit to attend to his brother's last affairs.

That case, meanwhile, continued to twist its way through the legal system. Earlier in '84, the showman had won a significant victory when the courts rejected the palimony clause in the lover's suit.[49] The clause was as hollow as it was predictable. Indeed, Thorson's first lawyer, Schmerin, had anticipated this result early on. So had Thorson's most recent counsel, Ernst Lipschutz. Engaged in 1983, Lipschutz had actually recommended dropping the ninth clause of the original twelve-point suit before the court had a chance to reject it. This was the heart of the case: it was founded on Liberace's commitment to adopt and take care of Thorson financially. Lipschutz, like Schmerin, had instructed him that such an agreement was an extralegal and therefore unenforceable contract for sexual services. The basis for two lovers' understanding? No, it was an agreement for prostitution. Thorson rejected the advice. His personal, private motives superseded the legal objectives: "Exposing Lee to public ridicule, holding him up to the world as a liar was more important," he related. "I wanted to punish Lee and the best way to do that was to go right on reminding the public, through the palimony portion of the case, that Lee was gay."[50]

After this, the questions remained purely legal and traditional, dealing with issues of assault and battery, extortion, conversion, and the like, and having nothing formally to do with love, rejected love, homo-eroticism, or extralegal unions.[51] Eroticism, however, still framed the case like a lurid mandala. The love that dare not speak its name remained unspeakable; so, too, did the passion that replaced it. Five years after the first suit was filed, innumerable legal hours later, countless depositions later, one heart attack later, one death later, and more ill will than could ever be calculated later, at least one of these cases still festered in the courts. If the legal wrangling went on for almost five years, now it played as a dumb show for the hard motives and reckless passion that inspired the action back in 1982 and 1983. "I'd never anticipated that so much time, energy, and talent would be consumed by what had started out to be nothing more than a lover's quarrel," wrote Thorson.[52]

The suit consumed Thorson himself. Besides wanting revenge, he also stuck with the case for the money, as his drug debts were soaring, along with his financial obligations to his lawyers. But other forces beyond either Thorson or Liberace drove them on, too. "As Lee said in one of his depositions," Thorson recalled, "he was caught in a 'war he never made.' There were times when I too wished I could forget the whole thing. But we'd long since passed the point of no return. The suit had developed a life of its own. By then our attorneys had an interest in winning that was so consuming that at times it seemed as if they were the injured parties."[53]

This legal malignancy reflected the temper of the times. Vince Cardell had not litigated against his mentor, but the world had shifted in the interval since 1977, and, ten years Cardell's junior, Scott Thorson belonged to a different generation. His America reflected the erosion of deference and discretion. It also represented Bristolian democratic extremism multiplied twice over. The era's radical egalitarianism encouraged every individual to celebrate his—or her—own privileges and prerogatives and to assume that any restraints or limits violated some intrinsic right. This opened the way for the most private, personal, and domestic issues—otherwise defined—to become the subject of political, public, or legal action. With the concurrence of the courts and judicial system, there followed the further disintegration of distinctions between public and private, which even fastidiously worded congressional legislation failed to restore. Indeed, the Right to Privacy Act actually multiplied causes for litigation. With the collapse of public-private distinctions, legal rights merged subtly with assumptions about human rights; human rights, in turn, became simply another element in human interest. Human interest, in due and necessary measure, merged with the public's desire—now defined as rights—to know anything and everything about anyone it chose, the more intimate the data, the better. Lines between news, gossip, and entertainment disintegrated. By this means, body-bag journalists and paparazzi reporters became essential or critical arbiters of social value, even as this very form of human-interest information became equated with the intrinsic concept of news itself.

Within this frame of reference, it was perfectly appropriate for Scott Thorson to have used the legal system—as he himself confessed to doing—for purely personal, psychological reasons. He sued, he insisted, "because it was the only way I could continue to be a part of [Liberace's] life, the only way I could ensure that he wouldn't forget me. . . . I didn't care if the suit made Lee hate me, just so long as he didn't forget me. Anyone who has ever been rejected by someone they still love will understand my motivation." [54] Within the same value system, it was equally logical and appropriate that he and his attorneys would use the press and broadcast journalism to make his case, as well. As Socrates anticipated 2,500 years ago, the court of public opinion is as potent as, if not more potent than, the actual law itself in radical democracies.

If Thorson's case represents all the vagaries of his particular era as the twentieth century wound down, it also reaffirms other deeper themes having to do, once again, with names and relations and the fundamental difficulties of these issues in homosexual liaisons. If exaggerated by contemporary social order, the chaos of Thorson's case also underlines other, more profound questions in homoerotics: What is the nature of homosexual love? How do men love each other? What is the responsibility or relationship of the lover to the beloved, the beloved to the lover? What, in sum, does a companion call his lover?

Through all the proceedings of Scott Thorson's case against his old benefactor, Liberace himself, in the parlance of the day, stonewalled it. He never altered his line. He admitted nothing about homosexuality. He was not Thorson's lover. Thorson was a disaffected associate. He vowed to fight to the finish. He had his minions, too, to carry out the struggle when he himself would not see evil, nor hear it, much less speak it. Meanwhile, despite his obstinacy, the showman continued to live with his new lover, Thorson's replacement, Cary James, to be seen with him in public, and even to be photographed with him and other homosexual men in gay settings. This was the dichotomy that had initiated George Liberace's admonitions back in 1957—and that won his dismissal from his brother's inner circle. Lee had won that match. He determined to win this one in the same way—on his own terms: he'd do it his way. He would carry on as normal, despite the abnormality of his circumstances after 1981. More abnormalities loomed as well. The disparities increased almost yearly. He acknowledged none of them. Will, work, and energy had always resolved his difficulties. Will, work, and energy would provide a solution one more time to the contradictions of his life.

On the very day of the Thorson donnybrook at the Beverly Boulevard penthouse, Liberace drove up from the Cloisters for an engagement that satisfied him profoundly. He had been invited to perform a very elaborate production number for the fifty-fourth annual Academy Awards presentations in Los Angeles that evening. Diffident, standoffish, and a little ill at ease among most of his showbusiness peers, he still craved their recognition, and the invitation to play all the musical nominations for the ceremonies in 1982 was an affirmation that he had "arrived" in a way that his millions of fans and millions of dollars could not have proved, exactly.

With four Godzilla-sized candelabra as a backdrop for his Lucite-topped Baldwin, he appeared in poofy hair, heavy makeup, and spangled tails to recap all the musical nominations of the year, the themes from *Chariots of Fire, On Golden Pond, Dragonslayer, Ragtime,* and *Raiders of the Lost Ark.* Introduced by the master of ceremonies, his old fan from the *Tonight Show,* Johnny Carson, Lee offered a little speech off the Tele-PrompTer that was virtually normal, if a little wooden and grotesque in the context of the upheaval in his life over the preceding weeks that had culminated in the horrors of that very day only miles away from the Dorothy Chandler Pavilion downtown.

As at the Academy Awards, in the rest of his life, work and performance equaled salvation. There was no help but self-help. The Thorson affair did not affect Liberace's work schedule or public life at all. He played as if nothing disastrous whatsoever were happening in his private life. Actually, he played enthusiastically to even more and broader audiences. His reputation grew during this time. His performance in Chandler Pavilion on the evening of March 25 signaled a new departure in his work. Even as he danced on the cusp of his dotage, he was coming into his own in a way even he might hardly have imagined ten or even five years before. As *Time* writer William Henry judged with some astonishment, "He survived the 1960s as a cheery anachronism, and during the last three decades averaged a gross income of $5 million a year."[55] If he had wept his way to the bank for a quarter century, he shed still bigger tears on the trip in the Reagan years. The world of the 1980s, folks and critics alike, was more ready than ever before to take the showman to its gaudy heart.

After the astringency of the Nixon era and the self-conscious de-stylization of Jimmy Carter's years, the United States was catching its breath and letting go by the time Ronald Reagan was elected president in 1980. With his Midwestern Americanism and Hollywood glamour, Reagan represented a version of Liberace's own career and values. They were of the same generation, too, these two Hollywood stars and heartland celebrities. The first lady's elegance and polish—so different from any of her predecessors', even Jacqueline Kennedy's—established a standard for style and stylishness that Lee could only admire as well. Nancy Reagan, no less than Liberace, celebrated wealth, beauty, and celebrity. The couple practiced Hollywood in Washington without apologies for eight years. Government policy echoed and occasioned analogous influences in the national economy and social life. Easy money fueled a soaring GNP and ever-accelerating consumer spending. Consumer spending, in turn, tended to channel into luxury expenditures. Liberace's life might have been the model for the kind of opulent surfeit that Tom Wolfe mocked and celebrated in that great satire of the era, *The Bonfire of the Vanities.*[56] This age of cheerful excess honored profligacy in all its manifestations, not least, of course, in sexual extravagance. If the devil leered just off-stage, it was still Morning in America, and Liberace was the decade's Sun King, or Sun Queen—the distinction being almost irrelevant in the decade's theatrical liberation of the American libido and economy.

On these very grounds, of course, the showman had never lost his appeal in the heartland and the hinterland. The folks had always loved his self-mocking opulence, his exuberant consumerism, his sunny excess. As one critic judged appropriately, Liberace appreciated "that in the heartland where he found his audiences, less remained less and only more was more."[57] In this regard, he continued to play the provinces as successfully as he ever had. The Las Vegas engagements continued. So too did the performances at Lake Tahoe and Reno. He kept up his furiously popular national tours in the wake of the Thorson affair. He was packing folks in and making millions off his provincial gigs. Even though he had reduced his touring to only fourteen weeks in 1985, he still grossed 3.5 million dollars that year alone. His Caesar's Palace contract by itself netted him $400,000.[58] The performances back in Milwaukee stand in for the rest. In the summer of '82, he played to nine thousand fans at Milwaukee's Summerfest.[59] Two years later, he was back again for a five-day stand at Uihlein Hall of the Performing Arts Center, where he played to maximum-capacity audiences. Between the March and August 1986 runs at Caesar's Palace, he filled the Riverside Theater in his hometown.[60]

All these appearances now drew the same sort of appreciative reviews. Even when the journalists arrived skeptical, they generally departed incredulous at their own pleasure. After reviewing the performer's chronicle of his personal acquisitions and achievements, one reporter noted that "under normal circumstances, all his boasting might have been wearisome. But Liberace plays the role of peacock to such an extreme that he practically parodies himself. He is also able to laugh at himself by cracking winning, if corny jokes with that sly grin ever in place." "Some may call him the king of schlock," the reporter concluded, "but Liberace does what he does so well that one can only relax and marvel as he turns excess into a thoroughly entertaining extravaganza."[61] Similarly, two years later, another reviewer expressed the same combination of horror and delight at Liberace's excesses. It was "hideously flamboyant but thoroughly enjoyable," he declared.[62] Wrote another: "Everything Liberace did was calculated, tested, and sure-fire. He commands an audience."[63]

His appeal now radiated far beyond the provinces, too. He played the great venues in the East. The national capital celebrated his excesses. The reviewer for the *Washington Post* waxed as enthusiastic as the old Midwestern critics. Scott Thorson? Palimony? Homosexuality? HIV and AIDS? It was all invisible. "At 66, the pianist who was once the butt of more jokes than Brooklyn is again the height of fashion and popularity and he's lapping it up like cream from a solid-gold saucer," observed the critic. "In a land that honors conspicuous consumption, he has become His Lord High Excellency of Glitz, the spiritual granddaddy to a generation of rock stars who wear sequined gloves and gleefully turn our notions of gender inside out."[64] The *Post* article assumed his legitimacy in American culture, his arrival, in the same way his performance at the Academy Awards ceremony in 1982 did. He was, indeed, a tremendous hit in Washington, visiting the Reagan White House, and collecting a whole series of articles in the *Washington Post* called "The Liberace Watch" that chronicled his comings and goings like a public-relations agent's dream. He was, in short, News.

At sixty-five years old, he was crackling. In 1984, he offered a major performance in Los Angeles for the first time in fifteen years. It was a remarkable show. The reviewer for the *Los Angeles Times* mixed about equal parts horror, delight, and respect in writing up the show. "The Sultan of Schmaltz also reconfirmed that he may be the sharpest showman since P. T. Barnum," he judged. "To the cynical, Liberace may bring to mind Mencken's adage, 'No one ever went broke underestimating the taste of the American public.' But the key to Liberace's success is that his fans never depart wanting for more. . . . The 65 year-old Liberace knows how to charm an audience."[65]

He was winning important notices not only in L.A. and Washington, D.C., but in New York City. He had arrived among the arbiters of elite culture in the country. Indeed, what marked his altered status in the eighties was his acceptance—however tenuous—by the cultural establishment in Manhattan. This actually suggests some of the problems with that decade, not to mention with the culture of the age. Although Liberace took his act seriously, he had made wit, parody, and self-mockery an essential, inseparable part of the act itself. He burlesqued—even as he honored— American values. To be taken seriously when he was spoofing suggests a dimension of the difficulty. He was, however, taken seriously by the cultural umpires of American taste in the era. However he did it, he made it in New York. He won almost unanimous praise for the first time since he had wowed audiences in the Persian Room in 1947.

If succeeding in New York is the goal of all great entertainers, success is not an absolute commodity. When Walter Liberace first played the Plaza back in 1945, audiences adored him. So did critics. In 1953, he had performed at Carnegie Hall and the next year at Madison Square Garden, but the enthusiasm of the audience was matched by the disdain, this time, of critics. Condemning every aspect of his performance itself, they also attacked the piano player in moral terms even, as representative of "the superficiality, sentimentality and uneasy nostalgia of our times." That sentiment won out over the popular devotion. For the next thirty years, the showman was virtually a nonperson in Gotham. The world had changed by 1984. If he suffered from the change in the litigiousness of the social order, for example, he profited from it in other ways.

Radio City Music Hall was a national institution. Like Carnegie Hall, Madison Square Garden, or the Hollywood Bowl, it occupied an iconographic place in the American mind, especially for members of Liberace's generation.[66] The showman had honored the legend by including the Rockettes in his Las Vegas review by 1980. As a part of that decision, he had negotiated with the management and toured the Rockefeller Center facilities in 1979. "It fired his imagination," wrote Thorson, who had accompanied him. Play Radio City? "'It would be totally outrageous,' he said, giving the place the highest praise he could imagine."[67] As early as 1941, the twenty-two-year-old pianist had determined he would play this venue. It was one of his last unaccomplished goals. His advisers discouraged him. They feared the old prejudices that had dominated the establishment opinions since the reviewing debacle after Carnegie Hall in 1953. "Play Long Island. That's like New York. And you won't be taking any chances," they said.

"Do you realize there are six thousand seats in that place? What if you do only half a house? It'll hurt you career-wise."

"Stay in the hinterlands. Stay out of the big cities."

"You know the New York press. If they don't like you, they'll murder you." [68]

Seymour Heller might have huffed and puffed against the venture, but Scott Sanders, on the theater's management staff, shared the showman's enthusiasm about an engagement.[69] Overcoming the advisers' qualms, Liberace agreed to a spring date in '84. Sanders wanted him on with the theater's traditional "Glory of Easter Pageant." The performer demurred. "Either you can have the resurrection or you can have Liberace," he supposedly exclaimed, "But you can't have both." [70] The resurrection lost out.

The *New York Times,* the organ of establishment opinion, had little use for upcoming news of the performance, even as it had ignored the performer for the preceding twenty-five years. The paper, however, had miscalculated the news; the *Times,* the times. David Letterman had not. If the Letterman show, and David Letterman himself, offered another representation of the eighties' vulgarity and excess, Liberace was completely at home on the late-night program. His first appearance, at Christmas 1983, delighted everyone concerned. It was the first of many. His appearances on another television phenomenon of the era, *Saturday Night Live,* taught the same lesson. This later generation of TV people were discovering what Jack Paar and Johnny Carson had acknowledged years before, what Abel Green had articulated in *Variety* as early as 1945: Liberace knew how to work an audience. Liberace equaled "box office boff." By the time the show actually opened on April 4, 1985, even the staid *Times* was catching on. "There was a front-page story in the *New York Times,* headlined 'Liberace Is Here, with His Glitter Undimmed.' It was absolutely precedent shattering," he gloated. "About the only way an entertainer makes the front page of the *Times* is with a little box in the corner that announces you can read about him on the obituary page." [71]

Even before the *New York Times* carried the formal announcement of the Rockefeller Center show, the theater had already sold a phenomenal 65 percent of all the available seats for the scheduled performances. With dollar signs clinking, the management wrangled an additional four shows to be added to the slated ten. Few reporters remained from thirty years before. Then, Manhattan critics had ridiculed the teary patrons begging tickets for the Madison Square Garden performance of 1954, when the showman had counted his money and wept over his deposit slips. But it was the exact same story in 1984. The music hall could have sold more tickets, had seats been available. Even with the augmented schedule, every performance was completely sold out, an unprecedented occurrence at the Rockefeller Center Theater. It was the same story in 1985 and again in the fall of 1986, the date of his last performance.

As astounding as the rush for tickets—at least on the surface—was what the patrons crowded the theater to see. In form, the show virtually duplicated the flashy performance that had opened the Riviera in 1955, with its completely self-referential act, "The Liberace Story" and "The Candelabra Ballet." Selling himself, being himself, performing himself—parodying himself—remained the very core of Liberace's act. He entered wearing an impossible white fur cape. He played Chopin to accompany the color-coded "dancing waters." He showed a film of what it was like to be a ring on his finger. He kicked with the Rockettes. He changed costumes. He played more. He took popular requests. All this he sandwiched between jokes, chit-chat, and patter. After the performance's hyperactive two and a half hours, he stood on the edge of the stage and received the audience that was reluctant to leave the hall.

The Easter show of 1985 repeated in its general form the 1984 performance, although Liberace added a spectacular entrance, appearing on the stage for the first time in one hundred pounds of feathers as he emerged from a Fabergé-type Easter egg. While he missed the Easter engagement in 1986, he appeared in the fall for another extensive run. He flew onto the stage this time, and this show also included two films, one a grandiose vision of his ring collection, another a tour of the Shirley Street mansion.

Again, nothing changed but details. The show's request segment, for example, followed the same pattern he had hit upon in La Crosse in 1939. The dress-up had always been there, too. The cars had figured predictably in the act since 1972. So too had all the jokes and pattering lines: "Well, look me over, I don't dress like this to go unnoticed!" and "I'm having so much fun, I'm almost ashamed to take the money. But I will." Crying to the bank made its appearance, and his rings elicited another thirty-year-old gag: "I'm glad you want to see them because—let's face it—you bought them." He still joked about raising his piano bench—"as this is a very high class number." And audiences knew by heart, too, the answer to his question, "How do I play with all these rings?"—"Very well, thank you."

Nothing fundamental about his act had changed, but critics had. They alone offered a new story. Granted, there were some holdouts. The *Village Voice* still hawked the old line, virtually unchanged from the opinion of 1953. He was "a celebrity whose only portfolio is sheer excess," carped the hardliners at that publication. The New York *Daily News* and the *Post* were generous, but even the *Wall Street Journal* gave him his due:

"Liberace has transcended ordinary everyday life to such a stupefying degree that he occupies his own special rhinestone-studded niche in the American Dream." [72]

Most critically of all, however, the *Times* capitulated. In 1984, it cited the commendation of the composer John Corigliano and the praise of the classy jazz pianists George Shearing and Earl Wild—"I think Liberace is a fabulous entertainer," had testified the latter. [73] Recording the show's hokey finale, during which fans surged down the aisle to touch the hem of his garment, the reviewer had gotten into the feel of such demonstrations. "'I feel like the pope,' joshed Liberace in mid-encore," Neal Karlen wrote, adding without invidiousness, "his ageless smile serving to reassure the assembled that some things, gratefully, will never change." [74]

The 1985 *Times* notices were more effusive still. For one thing, the paper got on board the Liberace hyperbole wagon before the show. If not quite so breathless as "The Liberace Watch" of the *Washington Post,* the great "newspaper of record" had caught the drift that Lee was news. The *Times*'s William Geist of "About New York" had remarked upon the variety of Liberace's special guests—from Diana Vreeland, Glenda Jackson, and Walter Cronkite to the entire cast of *Saturday Night Live* and Chuck Zito, head of the Hell's Angels. Not unlike "The Liberace Watch" had, Geist also chronicled the variety of the performer's activities in Manhattan. "Since arriving a few days ago," he wrote, "Liberace has been seen here, there and everywhere appearing on almost every known talk show, showing up on 'Saturday Night Live,' dancing with some Rockettes at a professional wrestling match, stopping in at the Rolls-Royce dealer to talk valve jobs and mink carpeting." The wrestling focused Geist's attention. What was he doing on the wrestling circuit, the reporter inquired? "Because the fans were found to be one and the same," the showman replied. But he spun out more of the deadpan joke: My mother loved wrestling, he told the reporter; she was thrilled when she met Gorgeous George: "She said they used the same lavender rinse on their hair." The reporter himself got into the spirit of the joke, moreover, as he interviewed "the rock promoter backstage at the wrestling spectacular, which featured appearances by Liberace, Muhammad Ali, Billy Martin and Mr. T., [who] spoke reverently of Liberace as the 'sage of the glitter age.'" [75]

The *Times*'s actual review of the performance in '85 was as generous as it was appreciative. Stephen Holden began with the showman's classically self-parodying first appearance. "It was as grand and amusing an entrance as any performer has made on a stage famous for its grand entrances," he began. He offered a straightforward analysis of Liberace's playing and pianism as well as of his showmanship, however, recognizing the pianist's profound musical debts to late romantics. "If his fondness for ostentation has influenced two generations of pop-music showmen, the iconography of his presentations is 19th century romantic. His forerunners are Chopin and Liszt. . . . The blending of Hollywood, Las Vegas and 19th-century romantic mysticism," he judged, "informs Liberace's musical style as much as it does the decor." "Liberace," he intoned, "has arrived at a style that is not classical, jazz or pop but an ornamental genre unto itself." The showman is "a one-of-a-kind musical monument," he concluded, "in whom romanticism and conscious self-parody merge into a complex, endearing caricature."[76]

The folks had detected as much all along. The New York crowds reaffirmed the truth. They roared their approval as enthusiastically as the Las Vegas and Milwaukee crowds had. They clapped as hard as the good folk of Kansas City, Tulsa, and Pittsburgh. They went home no less happy, it seems, than had the concertgoers in La Crosse, Wisconsin, almost fifty years before. At least as late as 1985, the magic had not dimmed by a single glittering sequin. Margaret Thompson Drewel, an anthropologist at Northwestern University, left a compelling reminder of the performer's power. A specialist in Yoruba performance rites, Drewel had attended the Radio City Music Hall show in 1985 as a scholarly obligation. A determined critic of "corporate capitalism" and a scornful judge of the showman's subservience to the economic engines of American life, Drewel also chronicled her own reluctant surrender to his charm. The rhinestone-spangled upright rolled in. Lee was taking requests. It was La Crosse all over again.

> When he broke into "Let Me Call You Sweetheart," the entire audience began to sing. The acoustics in the theatre created a warm, sonorous sound so that I too was finally drawn into the spectacle. I found myself singing and feeling misty-eyed. . . . And then Liberace played "You Made Me Love You," and the audience, including myself, continued to sing. At that moment the spectacle worked even on me, even as I was analyzing and taking notes. It engendered a *communitas* and broke down the bicameral roles of the performer and spectator, making the spectators part of the spectacle.[77]

Playing to fans and converting the hardest skeptics, he was doing the same thing he had been doing for almost half a century. Entertainment professionals—from fellow performers and stagehands to showbusiness journalists—had long conceded his talents. The writers at *Variety*, for example, freely and repeatedly acknowledged his performing skills from their first notice in 1945 to those at his death four decades later.[78] As even ideological opponents sometimes admitted, he possessed an extraordinary ability to manipulate an audience. No small measure of this talent lay in his ability to appear spontaneous, natural, and sincere even when he was most calculating, artificial, and contrived. It was no accident or audience fluke, for example, that produced the old standby, "Let Me Call You Sweetheart" in the "request period." He managed to hear the title repeatedly in New York as well as in his Washington, D.C., performances, and he turned the exact same trick everywhere, reducing even foes to tears and cheers, while the devotees had hardly left his palm since his first appearance on the stage.[79]

He had done it one more time. Liberace's Radio City Music Hall engagement set a record that has not yet been matched, years after his death. Seventy thousand seats, every single potential space, were occupied for his fourteen performances in 1984. Since the theater's inauguration in 1933, this had never happened. It was exactly the same story the next year, when he played the same Easter venue. He repeated the whole phenomenon, selling out all seats for the now expanded seventeen-performance run. A twenty-one-performance run in October 1986 produced the same results. Had earlier critics consistently reviled his audience as blue-haired women from the provinces? The thousands of people jostling one another for tickets and applauding enthusiastically represented a decent cross section of age, sex, and status: young people rubbed elbows with the aged; men competed with women for good seats; blue jeans were as well represented as furs. It was the same at other venues. The Washington reviewer summarized the scene: "Contrary to popular mythology, the Kennedy Center last night was not awash in ladies with blue hair; the audience was a broad cross-section of Middle America, clad in everything from black tie to T-shirts and sandals, covering a spectrum of age and economic status that was limited only by the steep ticket prices."[80]

All these people knew what they were going to get, and it was what they wanted: corny jokes, gaudy furs, glittering jewels, embellished arpeggios, and, not least, "Let Me Call You Sweetheart," which was guaranteed to be comfortingly familiar, even if not everyone in the audience knew the words. The performer was still flying around the stage on invisible wires, too. Taking to the air had been a central part of his act since 1974. "Mary Poppins, eat your heart out!" he had cried to delighted audiences on first sweeping across the stage. "People who keep coming back to see me deserve something different each time," he had explained the innovation, and *People Weekly* captured some of the excitement of the trick: "Liberace's bejeweled 185 pound bulk dramatically arpeggios 20 feet above his see-through Steinway into a breath-stopping final exit," the writer exclaimed. "The old cocktail tinkler is, at 56, still the hottest two-armed bandit on the casino circuit. Right up there with Sinatra and Presley, he commands $125,000 a week."[81] Audiences soon came to expect the aerodynamics as much as they did the costumes, sly patter, and musical drama.

After more than a decade, the trick still never failed to elicit the crowd's gasps. Liberace generally saved it for his grand exits. In 1986, however, he altered the act to open airborne. Actually, he gave this part of the performance a special twist by opening not by flying in first himself, but by sending his empty capes and gowns sweeping gloriously across the stage, alone. The furs had lives and personalities of their own. They had their own cars and their own chauffeurs; now they had their own airborne choreography. Horrified and disdainful, the *Village Voice* described the scene. Liberace, observed the critic, "got rich showing off, for knowing things like How To Make An Entrance. This time he flew. First, of course, he had an orchestra rise out of a pit and roll to the back of the stage and then a couple of his outfits flew through on wires—all praise to them— and then Mr. Showmanship himself sailed in like Peter Pan."[82]

He made soaring across the stage look easy and natural, like he really did belong not on earth but in the air. It was like his costumes. For all their outrageousness and impossibilities, he made them seem somehow plausible. And even though audiences now came expecting to see him airborne, the trick always provoked gasps and wonder. Here was Oz at the end of the yellow brick road. It was all humbug, but here, too, was the willing suspension of disbelief. It was humbug and genuine magic mixed indiscriminately. The magic came with a mythic penumbra, too, of course, of Peter Pan and Tinkerbell and pirates and lost children and Neverland. The magic of flying, just so, came with deeper mysteries, just as James M. Barrie's original play flirted with the margins of gender, sexual identity, and transvestism, and explored the paradox of boys who never grew up.[83] Flying in was perfect for the American boy from West Allis, who himself at sixty-seven retained his own boyish wonder of the world. Here was the magic of believing in action. I am flying! he demonstrated to his audiences. Soar with me! Inside the theater, it was Neverland. Peter Pan appeals to the audience: Clap, clap! Stay death! Tinkerbell doesn't have to die! It's Neverland!

Tinkerbell and Peter Pan worked gloriously at Radio City Music Hall. They were less successful beyond the footlights. By the mid-eighties, Liberace was failing to distinguish Neverland from the mundane world. He had become the ever-youthful creature of his own imagination. And as parasites and germs—not to mention normal aging—made that creature resemble the real man less and less, he would see this through an increasingly fantastic lens of magic and believing. The man of flesh and bone, by this reasoning, became ever more subordinated to the cliché. "I've retained my entertainer image, because it was created by the public. If I destroyed it, I would no longer be me," he had declared early in career.[84] The pronouncement took on ominous overtones as he aged and sickened.

The great showman had always scanted his interior life. He read no books, he cultivated little art beyond his own music making, he possessed no mind for the larger issues of the world. For all his personal genius, he expressed no appreciation for the profound psychological motives of his life. His neglect of the spirit was perfectly consonant with the Bristolian dream of material success and of reforming the world to his own image. Indeed, as he had always focused his ferocious energies on image, performing, and performance, he had little left over for an inner life at all. In his *Wonderful, Private World,* he promised to chronicle his private life. He didn't; there wasn't any. This defined his great strength, his awful weakness: the two combined almost inseparably throughout his career. With no interior life, he had no alternative but to press on, and then on more. He had just turned sixty-three when he compared being a "has been" to crucifixion. He was congenitally unable to do anything but continue and keep up pretenses. Offstage, the ruse seemed increasingly shallow.

In 1985, Duke Goldstone, Lee's old friend from *The Liberace Show* days, visited him for the first time in years. Despite the pall of his own mortality, the entertainer gushed as much as ever. "My God, how he has changed!" Goldstone reflected afterwards. "He really believes his own publicity!"[85] This is the same sense that the filmmaker John Waters detected in *The Wonderful, Private World of Liberace.* Liberace's fantasy reached such extremes that it astonished even this celebrant of American banality, the cinematic author of *Pink Flamingos* and the creator of its transvestite heroine, Divine. Liberace's book painted a world with no apparent attachment to anything real. It was the purest version he had encountered of essential American qualities, he thought. "I'm convinced he's so all American that he's gone over the edge," judged the filmmaker.[86]

He was Peter Pan in Neverland in the theater. He was young forever. The world was not Neverland. The performer resisted the world. The world would not be permanently denied.

*He died at just the right moment: he was old
enough to know that there was nothing more
that he could achieve and young enough to avoid
having been long forgotten.*

QUENTIN CRISP

ET LUX PERPETUA

In 1982, with the manic Thorson out of his life, Lee Liberace expected to restore normality to his existence, or at least what passed for normality for a randy, reclusive, hyperactive, aging homosexual superstar. If he fretted over Scott Thorson, he never let on in public. Audiences, in turn, did not seem to care very much about Thorson's charges or about the whole legal donnybrook going on under their noses. They continued to pay to laugh at the showman's antics; he continued to maintain the arduous work schedule he had been following for the preceding forty years. If nothing changed at all on the public front, on the domestic front, calm returned straightaway. Liberace had moved almost immediately from old lover to new, and after the excitement of the Thorson relationship, he might well have breathed easier with his malleable new boyfriend, Cary James.

Like Thorson, Cary James was tall and blond. He was only eighteen years old when the sixty-two-year-old performer plucked him from the chorus line in the spring of 1982. If he lacked Thorson's presence, he possessed his own charms. According to one source, "He had a beautiful body, a dancer's body that he let run all to fat after Lee died." [1] With his moon face, deep dimples, and pink complexion, he looked even younger than Thorson had five years before. His very fashionable, short mustache hardly obscured his boyishness. Everything about him radiated guilelessness. Indeed, he had met the showman while singing with the troupe the Young Americans, which had made youthful enthusiasm and simplicity its stock in trade. His innocence was sexual too: He had never had a lover before, he insisted. "Liberace was the first true love I'd had," he related.[2]

In the early winter of 1981–82, James began appearing backstage with the performer with some regularity. "James hung out around our dressing room all the time, and Lee often favored him with a private chat. Catching the two of them with their heads together, having what looked like an intimate conversation drove me to a fury," Thorson related. The aging showman began gracing the teenager with small gifts. Thorson heard the rumor of the presents and went berserk. He forced a confrontation, Cary James disappeared, and the Liberace-Thorson household returned to its normal state of chaos.[3]

Matters stood here in March when Thorson left for the funeral of one of his foster parents, Rose Carracappa. Returning to Tahoe, Thorson discovered through his sister Annette's husband, Don Day, that Lee, in Thorson's absence, had bedded the blond teenager from Florida. The discovery, of course, precipitated the series of events that began with Thorson smashing the Tahoe condominium and flying back to L.A. It peaked in the Beverly Boulevard raid and culminated in the legal wrangles of the years that followed. After March 1982, Thorson saw his old lover only once or twice, except through stacks of legal pads. He was out; James was in.

In Cary James, Lee found a pliable companion in contrast to the mercurial Thorson; otherwise, their life together repeated the pattern Thorson described. "For five years," James said later, "I lived the life of a superstar."[4] Liberace's old munificence toward Thorson now directed itself toward James. Photographs of the new boy in the furs and jewels that once bedecked his predecessor bear out Liberace's generosity. "I want you with me all the time, onstage and off," Liberace had told Thorson. His life with James mirrored the same ambition. "Everything that Liberace did, I did," recollected the new lover. "I traveled with him, shopped and dined with him and shared every facet of his life."[5] In the later legal suit over the showman's will, James testified that they were together "seven days a week, 24 hours a day" from April 1982 until Lee's death.[6]

If Lee took James into his life and heart as quickly as he had Thorson, their liaison did not prevent his eyeing other pretty boys and handsome men. He did more than ogle. While Lee had spent one night with James in Thorson's absence, within the week he had picked up two other young men who stayed over with him at the Cloisters, where he had fled after the Tahoe fracas. Indeed, the two French youths' night with the performer had outraged Thorson even more than had his lover's coupling with James. Perhaps Lee continued such extramarital carryings on after the spring of 1982. Thorson's memoir affirms the lover's libidinousness, delight in group sex, and affinity for promiscuity. Extremely stubborn and willful himself, Thorson curbed these tendencies during their relationship. James might have shared his predecessor's biases against such goings on, but he left no evidence that he had any of Thorson's determination to force the issue.

James, indeed, left no evidence of much ego at all. As a Florida-born Southern boy, his reticence may have reflected the Yes Ma'am deference of the region. Thorson had possessed a vivid, even egotistical sense of self; not James. Thus, Thorson angled his own interviews long before the palimony suits were underway; he relished going public with his claims against his patron afterwards. In contrast, James kept the lowest profile. Completely silent in the five years he lived with Liberace, he spoke out only once in the decade after his lover's death.

While he left virtually no record of his time as Liberace's lover, photographs suggest his character. They contrast vividly with Thorson's images. Cameras lit Thorson's fuse. Almost invariably, snapshots reveal him clowning, kicking up his heels, and mugging for the lens. He flashes a broad, toothy grin. He glitters even more than his mentor. James's pictures reveal nothing of the sort. He inhabits the background. He stands behind his patron. He never mugs or clowns. Thorson's images reveal high spirits, even if they were alcohol or drug induced. Not James's; they suggest, actually, Thorson's sedentary antithesis. Liberace stuffed both his lovers, but Thorson's increased bulk made his presence more impressive. In addition, the photographs reveal Thorson's effort to keep weight off, even if with amphetamines, while James appears rounder and rounder, softer and softer, as time passes.[7]

The two men's characters elicited different responses from their patron. Thorson's force won a modicum of trust he withheld from the more passive James. His attitude about his baldness hints at the disparity. The showman was almost neurotic about his hair and hairpieces, according to Thorson's record. It was as sensitive an issue to him as homosexuality was, and in an odd way was even more so. Thus, while he played publicly around the edges of his homosexuality and was frank about it within his inner circle, he lied relentlessly about having hair, even privately. Thorson related how the showman almost refused to undergo his facelift when the surgeon, Dr. Startz, said he would not operate unless Liberace removed his wig. In his final illness, he actually rejected medical services when doctors made the same demands. He argued the line of his "natural hair" so completely that even after his death, the otherwise levelheaded reporter for the *Washington Post* could claim the charges of toupees a dastardly canard. In the five years that James and Lee cohabited, the young man never saw him unwigged; he knew the truth only because of gossip. "I knew from his hairdresser Piny that Lee was totally bald, except for a small fringe of hair around his ears. He wore his wig to bed and even in the summer. It's stifling hot in Las Vegas," he continued, "and I know he must have suffered enormously." [8] If he failed to refer to his most intimate secret to James, he not only revealed himself as bald to Thorson, but, more telling, he made his lover from La Crosse the keeper of his hairpieces.

Cary James was not created to be a reality check on his patron's physical or sexual fantasies. He evidenced none of the strength necessary to limit Liberace's randiness, even had he so chosen. These elements of the last lover's character are triply important. They point up Liberace's own character: his domineering will, his impulses toward control, his secretiveness even with his intimates. They suggest that his relationship with Scott Thorson was unique, that James's predecessor was, in truth, "one in a million." Not least, they offer clues to the showman's morbidity and death.

How did Lee contract the AIDS virus?

Cary James left no record of his and Liberace's sex life. That information comes from Thorson. James and Lee had slept together at Lake Tahoe in March 1982, he says. Within days, however, the showman was apparently tricking with the two French boys who stayed with him at the Cloisters and accompanied him to the Academy Awards ceremonies. Did he have sex with others? Did he contract the virus from them? Was he already positive when he lived with Thorson?

Despite scientific advances, HIV remains a strange ailment twenty years after its first appearance. Its agent is actually delicate, hard to transfer, and survives ill outside most peculiar environments. It is passed from person to person in blood-to-blood transfers or semen-to-blood exchanges. In the natural course of things, the human organism resists the infection, unlike, for example, during past epidemics such as the Black Death, the Bubonic Plague, the mass mortality chronicled by Thucydides in Periclean Athens of 430 B.C., and the influenza epidemic of 1917, which hit everyone in the general population. The ailment is otherwise curious. While medical researchers as of 1999 still lack absolute certitude about the illness's course, they have determined that the virus seems to operate chiefly by killing the white blood cells that defend the organism from the infinite germs, parasites, and other infections that lurk everywhere in the environment. Once lodged, even, the ailment still follows an unusual, curious pattern. Some people infected note an immediate reaction on contracting the virus—seroconversion; others do not. Even those revealing immediate symptoms, however, virtually never move immediately into what is termed "full-blown AIDS," that is, continued symptoms of secondary infections. Rather, the virus normally produces no outward signs of its presence. This defines its insidious nature. Without testing viral counts, one might have no notion of having contracted the malignancy, and might show no outward sign of having done so, yet otherwise healthy and completely asymptomatic men and women can pass on the virus as readily as can those whose white-blood count can be figured on one's toes and fingers.[9]

More mysteries characterize the illness. The virus destroys the white cells rapidly in some people, in others hardly at all. A couple infected simultaneously might react diametrically, one partner failing rapidly, the other showing no declining T-cell count at all. In the eighties, before accurate testing, convention had it that the disease possessed "an incubation period" of five years. With no symptoms after this time, one could breathe free. This is not the case. For reasons not at all clear, cases are recorded of people being HIV positive for fifteen years or perhaps more without experiencing any infections whatsoever. The writer Edmund White, for example, testifies to being positive for this length of time; he has buried numerous acquaintances, friends, and lovers, yet he himself remained symptom free in his second decade of infection. The disease manifests other anomalies, too. While one man's viral load might register nil, his white-blood count might remain unaccountably low as well, thus opening the way to secondary infections.

Still another notable aspect of the disease is the way it has affected peculiar communities. Early on, it was associated with Haitians, among whom the incidence was extremely high. It affects intravenous drug users. Not least, of course, it has ravaged the homosexual community. In the eighties, few had any clear idea about the source of the disease's penetration of the gay world. HIV was associated with promiscuity or with drug use, for example. Whatever the origins, however, the infection rate stood so high among gay men that the ailment came to be considered, among conventional folk, a homosexual disease. This identity, in turn, effected the public stance of the radically activated gay political movement that had found its own powerful voice in the fifteen years after the Stonewall Inn riot.

Defending gay men's social, economic, and political interests, homosexual activists on the left engaged in increasingly sharp and rancorous debate over the virus, with antagonists on the right ready to associate the disease not only with homosexuality but also with divine retribution for violating the Torah's prohibitions in Leviticus, Protestant morality determined in Paul's Epistle to the Romans, and St. Thomas Aquinas's strictures for Catholics. Besides religious morality, the conventional right in the United States was also responding to growing alarm over the disintegration of traditional norms of every sort after the 1960s, but the corrosion of the conventional family focused its attention in particular. If feminism and the liberated woman might have been the right's real enemy, gays offered a still more attractive target. In many ways, the gay man became a symbol of their concern—the individual standing outside family discipline offered a critical source of anxiety: the rogue, literally, honored none of the laws of the tribe, by definition. The gay man who actually corrupted the family—by seducing sons, for example—offered a kind of mythic expression of this primal fear. Even so, the advocacy of gay marriage or the social legitimizing of homosexual union or homosexuality in general suggested the radical redefinition of family, the very object conservatives most opposed. In practice if not necessarily in theory, then, such gay initiatives—of their nature—undercut the conventional family.[10] Along with the advocacy of homosexual interests as rights and privileges, all these elements of the gay agenda prompted a profound reaction among traditionalists and within conventional opinion in the United States. For these folk, homosexuality—even if natural—lay outside the protection of both religion and the law. Traditionalists rankled increasingly, then, over what they considered privilege seeking by a small and unrepresentative category of deviants. The AIDS epidemic focused their anxiety and ire.

The growing reaction on the right, in turn, helped shape the position of homosexual activists who already had allied with the American left after Stonewall in radical defense of individual privilege against authority of virtually any kind. In order to accelerate funding for AIDS research, for example, it was logical to desexualize and also dehomosexualize the disease. Thus, the issue of heterosexual infection achieved a prominent or even critical place in the discussion of HIV. Out of all proportion to the actual numbers infected in the United States, babies with AIDS, women with AIDS, and hemophiliacs with AIDS, for example, became poster folk in the campaign. Along the same lines of normalizing AIDS came the tendency to conventionalize homosexual activity, homosexual union, and homosexuality. A new orthodoxy emerged, which was increasingly dominant in mainstream American opinion as represented, for example, in the *New York Times* and weekly newsmagazines.[11] AIDS then was just another disease, and gay men were no different from straight men or straight women, even. This position produced it own consequences among gays themselves. While obscuring the association of HIV with homosexuality, more critically, it also masked the association of HIV with particular homosexual activity. There were indeed norms for the transmission of the virus. If God cursed folks with this disease, it was not homosexuality, per se, He damned but unprotected receptive anal intercourse. And if the divinity can be credited with caring about such minutia, He grew particularly plaguey over the practice of *promiscuous* unprotected receptive anal intercourse.[12]

Whether God wished it or not, the delicate membranes of the rectum have to suffer very little trauma before blood vessels break and open to HIV-laden seminal fluids. If this process virtually guarantees transmission of the virus from a single individual man to another individual man, changing social, sexual customs within the subculture after Stonewall offered predictable results within the community at large. Truly, social customs and changing norms within the gay community did make HIV a social disease.

As liberation became the catchword of a generation, sexual restraint declined as a virtue. Monogamy may or may not be a natural state; promiscuity may or may not reflect a physical tendency of men. While scholars might discuss these matters dispassionately, the times clearly discouraged the former and encouraged the later, even as "the pill" and the law itself—no-fault divorce, for example—abetted a kind of "just do it" attitude toward sex in general. The times associated restraint with reactionaries, misguided or oppressive authority, and the like. While "closeted" or "closet queen" represented terms of opprobrium, "out"—"out of the closet"—represented their opposite, toward which the movement tended. While this usage represented a political position, it also represents a model for sexual activity, the legitimizing of gay sex for itself. Although the incidence of homosexual activity rose after Stonewall, the legitimation of homosexuality as merely one more "lifestyle choice"—to use sixties terminology—blunted the debilities of being gay or of practicing homosex, as well.

Other social issues played a role in making the disease an epidemic among gay men.

Even if promiscuity was common before Stonewall, homosexual sex usually took the form of incidental sexual encounters with straight men. This involved the normalization of sex outside the cultural unit. When promiscuity came to center within the cultural unit itself—the gay sub culture—it opened the tribe to the accelerating transmission of all sorts of diseases. It did so, too, just as that community was expanding quantitatively.

Effectively, society and the law encouraged these tendencies, with the waning of police raids and government surveillance, for example. More critical still, the development of institutions for homosexual pleasure-taking followed naturally from these other trends. This development made it easier for men to have sexual relations with each other.

Up to the sixties, homosexual meeting places had been careful secrets. They were the particular phenomena of large cities, too. In contrast, the seventies and eighties witnessed the rank proliferation of clubs, bars with back rooms, and, most notably, public baths, virtually all over the country. One might now have sexual intercourse several times a night with a variety of men, and one might go out and do the same thing again four or five times in a week. Hundreds of sexual partners for every variety of sexual activity in a single year was not uncommon. The lines between receptive and insertive sexual partners mostly collapsed as well. In this context, even the most occasional forays into this hothouse by otherwise essentially monogamous men—gay or straight—had awesome consequences. If the writer Paul Monette is to be believed, he and his partner were completely faithful to each other from the early seventies—with one exception. In one isolated episode, Monette's partner tricked with a stranger in Boston after the couple had had a spat. Infected without his knowledge, he then passed on the virus to his lover. If infected themselves, Monette and his boyfriend, afterward completely monogamous, infected no one else. That was not the norm for the Stonewall generation.

The great urban centers of American culture—New York, San Francisco, Miami, New Orleans, Atlanta, Boston—multiplied the possibilities of this life-threatening activity, but even the most provincial way stations in the Southern Bible Belt—like Montgomery, Alabama; Augusta, Georgia; and Asheville, North Carolina—spawned their own homosexual institutions that provided opportunities for local men to satisfy their craving for other men. Moreover, the increasing self-consciousness and nationalization, in effect, of homosexual culture—or plain old homosexual activity—increased the potential of even more exchanges of diseased bodily fluids, from the great centers to such remote outposts in the American provinces. The completely asexual institutions of American society of the age—like the interstate highway system—assisted the flow. One could drive from New York or Washington to, say, Johnson City, Tennessee, in a matter of hours, a long day's trip, but makeable. "Hotlanta," as the Georgia capital was called among gays, was closer still to such over-grown villages. The sexiest clubs, the hottest baths, the most beautiful men, by this measure, lay within touching distance of the most provincial bergs with the hokiest homosexual rendezvous, like the Connection; the poorest inner-city motels—the Mid-Town Inn; and the most forbidden hometown cruise spot—Rotary Park, all in Johnson City—Nowhere-ville—Tennessee. The disease was only a day away. By the eighties, this very Tennessee community harbored literally scores of the infected. And so HIV spread even to hillbilly hollows and, from there, to moun-tain-cove mobile homes, as far as one could possibly imagine from Man-hattan's ritzy clubs and Midtown Atlanta's sportin' life.[13] There is, dread-fully, no evidence that Johnson City, Tennessee, was in any way exceptional; it was only better reported than other, similar towns. The result? In 1982, the gay world was an uncovered Petri dish waiting to cul-tivate debility and death.

How did the virus get into Liberace's system? Perhaps he contracted it orally. However rarely, the infection has been passed this way. A cut in the mouth or a bleeding gum might have provided lodgment for the virus during oral sex. While evidence exists for this form of transfer, it is not the standard process by which the disease is spread.[14] If this sort of transmission might be rare, problems also arise in ascribing the stan-dard transfer of the virus to Liberace. For one thing, the entertainer possessed a street reputation as an insertive rather than a receptive sexual partner. Even so, various elements might have accounted for his playing the other role. Thorson testified to Lee's passion for variety, for one thing. Softening lines of homosexual roles encouraged such experi-mentation, too. Finally, Thorson also described his old lover as suffering from impotence, which might have prompted his trying other forms of sexuality.

What are the details of his infection? Perhaps Liberace carried the disease before 1982. It is not implausible that he did. He did not, how-ever, infect Thorson who tested negative after their breakup. For all the showman's propensity for being the active, aggressive partner in sexual intercourse, Thorson insisted they never indulged in anal sex; this would have kept him relatively safe even if Lee already harbored the virus. While it is not impossible that Liberace was infected prior to his involve-ment with Thorson, it seems rather more plausible that the infection fol-lowed the disruption of his union with the youth from La Crosse. Among gay men, a riotous period of liberation frequently follows the disruption of a long-term relationship. That Liberace would have followed in this pattern makes particular sense given the peculiarities of the Liberace-Thorson affair, especially Thorson's sexual prohibitions. Thorson himself toyed with the idea that the two French boys were the source of his old lover's infection. In addition, 1982 was perhaps the most dangerous time for playing the sexual field in homosexual America. Sexual liberation remained at a peak, and the disease was spreading insidiously through the gay community, but no one knew what was happening, or how. Few were taking precautions of any sort. One way or another, Lee fell into the trap.

The first news of a "gay cancer" and of curious occurrences of a rare form of pneumonia among homosexual men were circulating in both professional and popular journals in the last half of 1981. From '82 on, with ominous frequency, friends and lovers were checking out under the most mysterious—and horrible—circumstances. The lucky ones got pneumonia and died quickly. Others simply shit themselves to death as a result of uncontrolled intestinal parasites. Disfiguring Karposi cancer destroyed men's beauty before it killed them. Brain lesions corrupted the minds of even the brightest before they too died. By the summer of 1983, scientists had isolated the white blood cell-killing virus that led to such physiological catastrophes. How was the virus contracted? Nobody knew. Each year brought more deaths, more anxiety. Lee Liberace shared the fears. Almost overnight, being gay had become a scary health prospect. Queers had always had social and political debilities, but World War II had brought penicillin for syphilis and clap, the most dreaded venereal diseases. Something worse was in the air.

In 1985, things were out of whack at Shirley Street. In February, Liberace had hired a new housekeeper, Yvonne Dandurand, who worked for him for six months. She determined that he was ill. "He kept losing weight and slept most of the day," she said.[15] By November, newspapers carried reports of his signing into the hospital under an assumed name, "Lee Michaels," suffering from back pain and blood in his urine.[16] Other reports of the illness's progress differ. Another account has him detecting a worrisome swelling in his groin in the late summer or early fall. It was probably nothing, it couldn't be much, but he scheduled a doctor's appointment. By one report, he entered Valley Hospital in Las Vegas for doctors to investigate in late September. He demanded an AIDS test. It came back positive.[17] Cary James offered another version of the nightmare that lurked in every gay man's mind. "It was August 1985," he mused. "Lee had gotten his annual physical at Dr. Elias Ghanem's office, and two days later his secretary phoned and asked me to come by for an 'anemia test.'

A week later Lee returned to the doctor's office. Then an hour later I went in—and the doctor told me Lee and I both tested positive for the HIV virus."[18]

This shattering news was delivered in an especially devastating context. On July 25, newspapers had blared the information that Rock Hudson was deathly ill with HIV-related infections. Since *Magnificent Obsession,* over thirty years before, Hudson had been Hollywood's biggest, secret homosexual star. Like Liberace, two impulses had fueled his life: his career and homoeroticism. He had rigidly separated the two, the publicity of one matching the secrecy of the other. As a conservative Midwesterner whose sympathies lay much more with Barry Goldwater-Ronald Reagan Republicans than with Michael Dukakis-Jimmy Carter Democrats, Hudson shared still other similarities with the piano player from Wisconsin. As they did with Lee, Hudson's social and political ideology reinforced the logic of his separating public and private life, celebrity and homosexuality. In his last decade, however, Hudson began chaffing at the bifurcation. This explains, for example, his discussions of homosexuality with the journalist Boze Hadleigh, who interviewed him on several occasions between the mid-seventies and 1982. His revelations included, of course, a description of his early fling with Liberace.[19] If he was becoming more open about his sexuality in this period, Hudson still resisted public alliance with the gay movement. The reluctance persisted after he was infected with the AIDS virus, too. Circumstances dictated another course in the summer of 1985.

In Paris for treatment, Hudson found himself trapped between his own silences and French medical procedures. The cat leapt yowling from the bag on July 25. The information triggered an explosion. With the oldest gossip now public fact, Hudson made necessity something of a virtue as his publicists scrambled to redeem his reputation. Uncloseted even as he was exiting the house altogether, he even authorized a biography to publicize his secret life.[20]

Hudson barely survived the trip from Paris back to Los Angeles. He died less than ten weeks later, on October 2. The funeral notice failed to stifle the furor. The media had been rioting over the news for weeks. Hudson's death exaggerated the uproar. The frenzy affected Liberace profoundly. And right in the middle of the uproar, he discovered that he, too, was HIV positive. If he had ever doubted his Claude Bristolian commitment to blind faith and positive thinking, the Hudson affair steeled his resolve. It was a horrible time.

At first, he took time off from touring. In September, he announced that he was canceling performances. The self-imposed retirement did not last long. He took to the stage again in March of '86. He could not resist performing; it was life itself to him. Audiences inspired him. The infection did not hear the bravos. By August 1986, only a year after his initial diagnosis, the virus was eating up his white blood cells at a furious pace, and a variety of secondary infections attacked his body. Doctors informed him that he was suffering from AIDS proper. He could not keep weight on. His body wasted, but his will did not. The stage still galvanized his energy. His physical condition notwithstanding, then, he honored his commitment for a third string of performances at Radio City Music Hall in the fall of 1986, thereby performing one of the extraordinary feats of entertainment history. Its heroism has few parallels.

Unlike the 1984 and 1985 shows, reviewers were not so enthusiastic as before. "The thrill is gone," intoned *Variety*. "Maybe not for some of his adoring fans, but certainly for the less-than-committed and apparently for the performer himself."[21] Stephen Holden, the *Times* critic who had celebrated him as "a musical monument" two years before was less happy still. "His heavy-miked pianism is at once metallic sounding, exaggeratedly florid in ornamentation and unbendingly rigid in tone and phrasing." It wasn't fresh anymore.[22]

Holden detected the problem, not its source. The showman was running on pure will. That will remained astonishing. He had lost perhaps fifty pounds, yet still he hoofed with the Rockettes in his old hot-pants outfit. The physical feat of flying onto the stage would have taxed the stamina of a young, healthy actor. At sixty-seven, Liberace was not young. He was definitely not healthy; he had only three months to live. The wonder is not that his performance was wooden and contrived, but that he was on the stage at all.

Despite the energy, hype, and hoopla, people had begun to notice. Robin Leach of television fame visited the performer backstage at Radio City Music Hall. The star's condition horrified him. "What alarmed me most was that every time he left the stage, he would take massive gulps from an oxygen tank kept in the wings," he wrote. Still, he noted, at a distance everything looked normal; that was the wonder. "From the audience, you could not even tell he was sick—it was like watching a different person clumping around the stage in those incredible costumes, and flying in on a trapeze. That's why his nickname is Mr. Showmanship. I think that the most startling thing was having just seen him perform brilliantly for two and a half hours, then going backstage and seeing how frail he was."[23]

He was both Tinkerbell and Peter Pan, imploring applause and then reviving to the cheers. The applause did not banish the virus. Tinkerbell's light was dimming; Peter Pan could hardly move his feet.

Leach had also interviewed the showman before the New York show. He had suspected that something was wrong even then. Liberace's energy had always amazed him, Leach professed, "But this time I was disturbed and upset at how gray he looked. As if to disguise how frail and thin he had become, Liberace wore a caftan that covered him to the neck, but it could not quite conceal how much weight he had lost." He was speaking to a very sick man, he thought. "The spirit was still there, and the friendship and the warmth, but I was looking at a man who was not well, even if he refused to admit it." He did indeed refuse to discuss any illness; at the same time, he spent much of his interview time discussing death. Liberace devoted half the conversation to reflecting on his own mortality—even if his ruminations were couched in his recollecting his near-death experience in 1963, when his kidneys had shut down for two weeks. At the time, Leach had considered the interviewee's preoccupation with that event odd. Only later, the interviewer insisted, did he put two and two together to make sense of the affair.[24]

About the same time that Leach interviewed him, the showman made another television appearance for Merv Griffin to celebrate Phyllis Diller's thirty years in show business. He loved and admired Diller the same way he respected Debbie Reynolds. Diller had the distinction, too, of being another devotee of Claude Bristol. He would not have turned down the invitation for anything. His appearance dismayed the comedienne. Even beside the octogenarian Bob Hope, he looked dreadful. It was her revelation: "Dear God, he has AIDS!"[25]

The Wonderful, Private World of Liberace had appeared in the autumn, and he toured with the book as a part of his contractual obligations after the New York show closed on November 3. "He was signing at the national booksellers convention in New Orleans that fall," one publicist recalled. "He looked awful."[26] He would not quit. A friend from Palm Springs encountered him in November and "scarcely recognized him," by one account. "'He had lost about 75 pounds,' she says. 'I had never seen an upright human that thin before.'"[27]

The cadaver tried to keep up appearances. Over Seymour Heller's objections, Lee honored his commitment to appear on *The Oprah Winfrey Christmas Show,* which was to be prerecorded around Thanksgiving. And, once again, as he had with Robin Leach, he turned the subject to his own mortality, discussing his brush with death in Pittsburgh twenty-five years before.

He was dying. Sometimes he admitted it; mostly not. Indeed, he still talked of cures and miracles, better still, miraculous cures. This was one context for his repeated references in these days to the miracle of his restored health in November 1963. The Bristolian wish would father the man; the prayers of the righteous would avail much.

The Magic of Believing suggests that people might be like crabs and restore their missing claws if only they wished to do so deeply enough. Claude Bristol had insisted that prayer and religion arose in the same self-help, Christian Science sort of logic. Indeed, he offered religious miracle cures as primary evidence of "mind power." The Midwestern self-reliance of West Allis, Wisconsin, had inculcated such mainstream American principles in Wally Liberace long before he opened *The Magic of Believing* for the first time. But still more primal forces encouraged him to put his faith in miracles: he believed in saints and wonders, as of old. Wladziu Valentino Liberace had been baptized in churchly miracles and supernatural intervention. Catholic mysticism, religious faith, and the simple piety of Italian and Polish immigrants provided a still more potent source of his holy confidence. Faith had saved him once; faith might save him once again.

On the surface, Lee Liberace was no orthodox Catholic. Not least, his sexual proclivities put him at odds with religious dogma. From another perspective, however, his life derives its meaning from his deepest commitment to Catholicism. Even his unorthodoxy makes certain sense within the Church tradition. If institutional, ritual orthodoxy of Polish Catholicism—daily mass, confession, and the like—might have led him in one direction, the mystical piety of that same tradition led him in another. His Italian heritage had made anticlericalism and even opposition to ritual performance another potent element in his religious life, but, even so, Neapolitan and Sicilian religious practices celebrated the world of supernatural appearances and metaphysical phenomena, the world of magic and marvels, superstition and wonders.

Completely aside from Bristolian admonitions to wish himself well, then, Liberace, in full confidence, believed a miracle had occurred in December 1963 when he did not die when he was dying. Indeed, in specific contrast to Claude Bristol's admonitions, he had actually surrendered to death, settling his estate and making his peace with the world. Just then, he had experienced an apparition. He often repeated the miraculous story of the unidentifiable nun who had appeared in his hospital room and told him to pray to St. Anthony, which he had done. Cary James got one version. "A priest had given him the last rites," James repeated.

"But he bounced back, and had always attributed his recovery to his faith in God."[28]

His life changed afterwards. "I think the experience of finding I was going to live after expecting to die was inspirational to a degree. My first reaction when I was told I was going to make it was that I must have done something right in my life, because I was being spared and given another chance. That's the way I looked at my new life—and it absolutely was a new life."[29] As a believer, the crisis helped convince him that God had chosen him for a special purpose, that he had been singled out from among all the faithful for favor. Not least, even if he never admitted it, it seemed to have eased his conscience to some degree, if not completely, about his homosexuality. If the divine had chosen to redeem him, lusting after men and all, he could not be completely wrong, and even church dogma could not be completely right on this matter. He seemed to see no contradiction in displaying the large portrait of him kissing Cardinal Cushing's ring in the very bedroom on Shirley Street where he romped with his lovers. The nun episode also confirmed other manifestations of his unorthodoxy, otherwise defined. He rarely attended mass after that incident, and he avoided, in general, institutional faith, even as his personal piety, if anything, grew. His death sentence in 1985 brought out all the old devotion.

He needed double miracles now, too. Guilt as well as HIV gnawed his vitals: he had infected his young companion. On returning from the physician with his own news of infection, James had found his patron sobbing in the lavatory. "As I held him and comforted him, Lee said over and over: 'Boo, I'm sorry. I'm so sorry. How could I have done this to you?'"[30] Where was the little nun in the hour of extremity? Not in Las Vegas, Lee determined. Palm Springs seemed a more likely place to find her. The couple moved there in the fall. The Cloisters seemed more conducive of miracles.

When he had bought the Cloisters, Liberace had created his own private chapel. Had the angel in disguise admonished him to pray to St. Anthony? The chapel became a shrine to his new patron, complete with a rare, three-hundred-year-old polychromed wood representation of the saint. The chapel and the presence of St. Anthony comforted him. "Liberace's a very religious man," Scott Thorson told an interviewer in these days. "That's why he is dying in his own home, because in Palm Springs he has his own private shrine, his own private chapel that the bishop blessed. Palm Springs is his sacred house. It's a very sacred home to him. The chapel is right off the master bedroom."[31] Thorson's successor confirmed the same characteristics. "Lee was an old fashioned, very religious man," Cary James noted, who "prayed regularly at a chapel he had built at his Palm Springs, Calif., home." If he had frequented the chamber often before, from 1985 on it became a special refuge. "Everyday Lee kept believing a miracle would once again pull him from the jaws of death," James remembered. "He still faithfully believed that a miracle would save him." [32]

In addition to praying to St. Anthony, the showman looked to home remedies to quell the virus. He and James began a regimen of health foods and megavitamins. [33] "'He's taking multitudes of vitamins, sleeping 10 to 14 hours a day, and flushing his system with fruit juices, mineral water and health foods,'" reported one source. Saints and vitamins, not physicians, medicine, and conventional practice, would save him. [34] Indeed, he conceded nothing to convention in his distress. He refused the doctors. When he finally allowed himself to be admitted to the hospital in January, it was only at his sister's insistence. He had told her nothing. She had heard rumors of AIDS. As the silences and rumors increased, however, "she called demanding that I immediately take him to the Eisenhower Medical Center in Rancho Mirage, California," Cary James reported. [35] She appeared soon after. If less skeptical than her brother about medical science, Angelina also kept up the family faith. She offered prayers for her brother, according to the source, "in a small room of the Palm Springs estate that contains religious artifacts blessed by a Roman Catholic priest." [36]

In Liberace's mind, silence was as critical as self-help and prayer. Denial imposed its own regimen. He spoke of his illness to almost no one, not to doctors and not even to Angie, except in extremis. Indeed, on the day he was diagnosed as being HIV positive, he swore his twenty-one-year-old companion to silence. "That night Lee and I made a pact never to tell another soul about our AIDS. His worst fear was that his fans would find out he was gay." [37] "'I don't want to lose my fans' respect,'" he told another friend. "'I don't want them ever to know.' He felt that a public admission of homosexuality would destroy his fans." He was "devastated over his plight, a source close to Liberace revealed," according to one reporter. "'But his worst fear is that he will be remembered not as a great entertainer but as a homosexual,' the source said." The nightmare of Rock Hudson's illness and death loomed perpetually in his mind. "Liberace fears that public reaction to his illness will be similar to the fire storm that surrounded Rock Hudson," one friend reported. "Liberace is tortured by the thought that his genius will be forgotten and his name sullied forever," revealed the associate. "When Rock Hudson died,

Liberace was very distressed and told me: 'The only thing people will remember Rock for is the fact that he was gay and died of AIDS.'" "I'll never go public with the revelation that I have AIDS," he wept to another friend. "I'll take my secret with me to the grave."[38]

Was his oath of silence to protect his fans? Other skeletons rattled in his closet. Robin Leach quoted another associate's observation about the showman's religious anxieties that the miracle of 1963 had not absolved completely: "According to a friend, Liberace's religious fervor was behind his denials that he was gay and was dying of AIDS. 'The Church looks upon homosexuals the way it does on divorce,' says the friend. 'And Liberace always had a great fear of being excommunicated and falling out of grace.'"[39]

The silences coupled with his rapidly deteriorating physical condition led to a predictable conclusion: he became a complete recluse. In 1986, for the first time in anybody's memory, he ignored Christmas. He had always turned the season into an orgy of decorating, spending, gift giving, and celebrating. The festival lasted for days. It cost a fortune. Scott Thorson had said that for Christmas of 1977, which was not atypical, they had spent twenty-five thousand dollars on decorations alone. It involved "eighteen huge Christmas trees, more than 350 red and white poinsettias, table decorations, greenery, wreaths—enough candles, lights and tinsel to stock a department store."[40] No more. Nineteen eighty-five witnessed no celebrations. There was no joy. There was, effectively, no Lee. He barely communicated with even his closest associates. At Shirley Street, Gladys Luckie, his faithful retainer for almost forty years, got only a printed card. It was the same story for Jamie James, his old publicist, and Ray Arnett, who had been with him twenty-five years. Both were charter members, according to Thorson, of Liberace's homosexual inner circle. He saw almost no one now but Dorothy McMahon, his Cloisters housekeeper; Cary James; and two of his oldest friends and nearest neighbors, Vince Fronza and Ken Fosler, a gay couple who had been together for decades.

He tried in his own way to make his peace with the world. For one thing, he called Scott Thorson. Early in 1986, completely out of the blue insofar as the scorned lover was concerned, his old patron rang him up. After the most conventional pleasantries, he continued: "And your health, how's your health?" Rumors were already circulating about Liberace's own condition. Thorson had heard them; he had rejected them. The conversation altered his perception. "He wanted to do the right thing," Thorson judged, "to warn me he had AIDS. Then, despite his good intentions, he couldn't go through with it. So he'd concentrated on making sure I wasn't sick, knowing I'd put two and two together and go see my own doctor." A few months later, in June, the two ran into one another at the Beverly Center in Beverly Hills. The showman had dropped thirty or forty pounds, Thorson said, and "under his makeup he looked pale, sick, and old." That was not all. "He asked about my health again and then again, staring at me almost as hard as he had the night we first met. The message was plain," thought Thorson, "if I had the guts to deal with what he *meant* rather than what he said. I didn't need to hear a doctor's diagnosis to know what ailed Lee." [41]

In 1986, the two men had been locked in legal combat for four years. In September, Liberace declared peace. He appointed a new attorney who immediately began negotiating a settlement with Thorson's people. The four-year-old donnybrook ended in mid-December. Although the Liberace entourage still demanded silence, the press gained the information, and on December 20, the *Los Angeles Times* published the details. One more time, Lee's camp rumbled about lawsuits. None followed. It was not quite over, however. Liberace had more peace to make. Some time after Christmas, he called Thorson one more time. He requested that Scott visit him at the Cloisters. Thorson drove to Palm Springs a little later. "Lee was in a deep depression," Thorson related. "He was very scared. He never mentioned the word AIDS, but he kept asking 'Why me? Why me? I didn't do anything wrong.'" [42] His conversation rambled, Thorson said. "It took him a while to get to the point. But he finally looked at me and said, 'I'm not going to make it." He wept. He gave Thorson small presents as of old, some jewelry—"to remember me by" and a giant panda. He told him, too, that he was still "a boy in a million," according to Thorson. "You made me the happiest," Thorson quoted him. And one more time, he swore Thorson to silence about their meeting. [43]

Despite the oaths of secrecy, the silence had begun to roar by the time of Thorson's visit. The rumors grew irresistible. On January 14, Hank Greenspun, publisher of the *Las Vegas Sun,* wrote an editorial on the paper's front page directed at the ailing recluse, who, for the time being, remained anonymous. An Orwellian combination of sympathy, concern, and morbid curiosity, the article condemned Liberace's silences on the grounds that he should be seeking professional medical attention. "In lonely desperation one of entertainment's brightest stars has sealed himself from the rest of the world because he cannot or will not face the fact that he might be dying of AIDS," the publisher intoned. "We urge the victim to face reality with courage and determination to lick the disease if there is a way." [44] Ten days later, the *Sun* dropped the sympathetic pose—

and with it the anonymity. "World-renown pianist Liberace, a longtime show-stopper on the Las Vegas Strip, is terminally ill with AIDS and has been diagnosed as having less than a year to live," the paper told its readers—and the world.[45] The vultures were circling.

Only hours before the story broke, the showman had been wheeled into the Eisenhower Medical Center for a blood transfusion to bring up his dangerously low hemoglobin count.[46] He refused further diagnostic evaluations. "He told the doctors that he had AIDS, and that further tests are useless," one source told journalists.[47] He wanted to die at home. By the 26th, he was in his own bed at the Cloisters again.

The *Las Vegas Sun* article prompted a chain reaction in the Liberace camp. Although the showman was already moribund, it set Lee's bulldog snarling one more time. Seymour Heller had been doing the same thing for nearly forty years. He reacted automatically. "The *Las Vegas Sun* has printed a story based on gossip and false information stating that Liberace has AIDS," he growled. "We are categorically denying that Liberace has AIDS. We are demanding a retraction and if this is not done, we intend to immediately file a libel suit."[48] He repeated the fiction contrived much earlier that his client was suffering from anemia brought on by a watermelon diet.[49] Later, by way of apology, Heller related that Lee had insisted to him that he did not suffer from the disease. By that time, however, Heller was out of the loop. Even his entry into Lee's sick room had been prohibited.[50] The emperor was dying, and new voices interpreted his desires.

Despite Heller's formulaic denunciations of the *Sun*'s disclosures, the next day, other Liberace sources issued a formal statement confirming the showman's state, without reference to its cause. Under instructions from Palm Springs, Lee's publicist in New York issued the following, unelaborated statement carried by the papers on January 26: "It is my great regret to inform you that Liberace is gravely ill with pernicious anemia, complicated by advanced emphysema and heart disease." Heller still rumbled in the background.[51] The same day, news flashed across the papers and television screens about the showman's just-ended hospital stay. Heller still stuck to the watermelon-diet story.[52]

The hall was darkening. On January 22, Joel Strote, who had been Lee's attorney for seventeen years, presented him a new one-hundred-page will to sign. Most critically, the new document made Strote the chief guardian and director of the Liberace estate, estimated to be worth fifteen to twenty million dollars; by the same token, it eliminated Heller from any management position after Lee's death. The dying man scrawled his distinctive signature at the bottom. The next year, the courts ruled that he had been fully cognizant of what he was doing.

Whether he was in control of his faculties or not, he did not have long left to live. His loyal housekeeper at the Cloisters, Dorothy McMahon, described his enfeeblement. He was depressed, she related, "shuffled instead of walked because he couldn't bend his knees, had difficulty holding his head up when he sat on a couch and spoke very little. 'He wasn't talking in normal sentences,' she said. 'The most he would usually say was "Ok." Sometimes he didn't talk. He just smiled.' " [53] "He was a dying man, he needed a lot of tender loving care," his nurse Norma Gerber insisted. "He was so childlike—like he didn't know what he was saying." [54]

On Sunday, February 1, his dear friend and neighbor, Vince Fronza, came over from next door. "Angie and I are going to mass. Wanna come along?" he asked. No, the invalid smiled. He was still sentient. [55] In the bedroom, while the television played videos of *The Golden Girls,* he lapsed in and out of consciousness. On Tuesday, Jamie James, who had been his L.A. publicist for decades, appeared. "He was lying there, his eyes open. His nurse told us to talk to him. She said, 'Maybe he can hear you.' " Recalling the Pittsburgh miracle that Lee had repeated so often, James continued, "I found myself looking down at him and thinking, 'God, I wish that little nun would come in and solve his problem again.' " [56] No nun appeared.

Later, someone called a priest. He administered the rites of extreme unction. "Through the holy anointing, may the Lord in his love of mercy help you with the grace of the Holy Spirit, Amen," he recited. "May the Lord who frees you from sin, save you, and raise you, Amen." Another priest in Pittsburgh had given him the church's last rites almost twenty-five years before. Liberace had survived the anointing. It was not to be this time. [57] He was already comatose.

On Wednesday, the morning of the third, his nurse recognized the death rattle. Joel Strote held a press conference in the driveway at the Cloisters. "Mr. Liberace's condition has worsened. He is very pale. He is obviously resting comfortably and is not in any pain. He is comatose. He has a low pulse and rapid breathing. Death is imminent." [58]

He was dying. His intimates had been gathering, although records of the visitors conflict. His sister and Dora, George's widow, took turns staying with him in the room, along with Angie's daughter and son-in-law, Diane and Don McLaughlin. Seymour Heller and Jamie James came and went. Gladys Luckie and Dorothy McMahon stood by with Tido Minor, Don Fedderson's former wife, whom Liberace had known for thirty-five years. She had been nursing him for days. His oldest friends Vince Fronza and Ken Fosler grieved nearby. The favorite of his "children"—his sharpei, Wrinkles—was in the room. His lover of five years, the twenty-three-year-old Cary James, said he lay in the same bed with the older man.[59] Someone, probably his sister, wrapped a rosary around his right hand, according to Jamie James. "There was no jewelry. The rosary beads were his jewelry."[60] His pulse stopped at 11:31 on the morning of Wednesday, February 4.

A dreadful little ceremony followed. Just after he drew his last breath, the nurse replaced his toupee, which he had not worn in his last days. She wanted "to give the man a little dignity," said an anonymous source. She combed the hairpiece, washed his shrunken body, and tied a hospital gown around the emaciated form. The attending physician arrived three hours later and signed the death certificate. He listed cause of death as "cardiac arrest and congestive heart failure brought on by subacute encephalopathy (degenerative disease of the brain)." Angie's son-in-law, Don McLaughlin, announced the death at 2:50. A half hour later, the Forest Lawn hearse arrived.[61]

When Joel Strote had announced his client's imminent passing, he had also called the assembled company to which he spoke "a circus." Bedlam defined the scene better. So it had been for a fortnight. The Cloisters and Our Lady of Solitude Church around the corner fronted a large, vacant lot. For the past two weeks, hundreds of people had been swarming there like flies to road kill. This space and the surrounding streets were now thronged with trucks, cars, and electric generators—reporters and paparazzi doing their duty. Security guards caught one reporter scaling the wall. Cops arrested him.[62] They charged a *National Enquirer* photographer with trespassing, too.[63] Scores of people milled about, and every time they detected movement at house, the mob rushed the door. The melee ruined the flowerbeds.[64] Gawkers and drive-bys increased the tumult. Occasionally the whop-whop-whop-whop of helicopters broke the desert air. There were still other monstrosities. In the evening, each new car approaching the security guards at the gate set off the mechanical roar of the engines that powered klieg-like lights that drowned the stars and shattered the darkness.[65] Between these explosions of noise and light, the bored journalists found solace in interviewing fans and gawkers, who themselves had their own moment of fame. Some sounded more sincere than others. "'He loved us. We loved him,' said Sara Hempling, who had taken a week's vacation from her job in Seal Beach to join the crowd. 'He'd want friends around.'"[66]

It was the very disaster Liberace had dreaded. More followed, the likes of which he would have refused to imagine.

The hearse carrying Liberace's body had sped away from the Cloisters at 3:20 on February 4 toward the peace of Forest Lawn, but even a police escort did not deter the reporters and photographers weaving in and out of traffic behind the vehicle, much less the TV-station helicopter breaking the smoggy air in hot pursuit. As an additional indignity, traffic jams made the trip last three hours. The circus continued. Had the showman over and over sworn family, friends, and lovers to the oaths of silence? The tradition persisted, but facts were clogging up his system. His death certificate made no reference to AIDS and his contagion. It violated the law. The state of California intervened. The media fury over AIDS prompted Raymond Carrillo, the Riverside County coroner, to investigate. He subpoenaed hospital records. He challenged the death certificate. He demanded an autopsy. Soon the showman's pitiful remains were speeding back east to Palm Springs on the interstate. Already embalmed, the body resisted the probe. Finally, though, science won. On February 10, Carrillo published the results to media flashbulbs: death had resulted from cytomegalovirus pneumonia—"AIDS pneumonia"—which had indeed resulted from an HIV-related infection.[67]

At the very time the coroner was sectioning the showman's withered flesh, mourners were gathering at Our Lady of Solitude for the first of the memorial services. The little church overflowed. Among the grieving, Scott Thorson found a pew and heard Vince Fronza deliver the eulogy. Thorson had once said that the relationship between Fronza and Ken Fosler, his companion of decades, was exactly what he had wanted for himself and Liberace. The officiating priest, Father William Erstad, reminded the congregation of God's benevolence not least "to those who used his gifts as generously as Liberace did."[68] He read a telegram from the president and the first lady: "Lee was a gifted musician, a man who truly earned the title 'superstar' and a caring individual who time and again responded generously when called upon to benefit those in need. . . . He will be remembered in many ways, but most importantly as a kind man who lived his life with great joy. We are grateful that he has left us such a rich legacy of memories, and they will be our joy."[69]

Six days later, Las Vegas had its chance to remember the showman one last time. A thousand gathered at St. Anne's Church to celebrate his life. Perhaps they found solace in the priest's admonitions about Lee standing naked before God and "all of the accolades, all of the tributes in a lifetime of entertaining . . . all of these things [paling] and [fading] in the presence of truth and justice." [70] Father John McVeigh offered rather Irish, puritan consolation. If theologically true, the homily would have rung flat for the Christian primitive who had loved pungent incense and silky chasubles, who fantasized about flickering votive lights and raptured saints, who believed in miracles and apparitions, and who knew the transforming power of both piety and art.

I don't want to be remembered as an old queen
who died of AIDS.

Liberace

Epilogue

Between the first memorial service in Palm Springs and the second in Las Vegas, Lee's body itself finally won its long-deferred entombment. He was laid to rest alongside his brother George and their mother at the Liberace mausoleum in a very small, very brief service on February 7. He left other memorials besides the elaborate, inscribed marble tombstone at Forest Lawn. He could not have predicted everything his legacy would be.

The showman had always wanted to control everything. He planned every gesture, calculated every move. If he wanted mastery even beyond the grave, it did not work out exactly as he'd figured it would. The medical autopsy and religious memorials resolved the issues of Liberace's flesh and soul, but the social and legal beasts his death released were only just stretching their thick limbs at the beginning of February 1987. The fracas outside the Cloisters barely introduced the disorder.

The clamor over the showman's HIV infection had grown steadily louder since the *Las Vegas Sun*'s revelations of January 16 and January 24. The rumors inspired a carnival of speculation. Official notice on February 10 that Liberace had indeed died of AIDS-related infections did nothing to calm the ruckus. On the contrary, the coroner's report set off more shock waves, even as it created a new media hero for a few days, Riverside County Coroner Raymond Carrillo. Journalists achieved new heights of investigative journalism. They faithfully reported Carrillo's warnings to Dr. Ronald Daniels, who had signed the death certificate. The latter would be reported to the California Board of Medical Quality Assurance, the corner insisted. The papers publicized Carrillo's threats to sanction even the venerable institution of Forest Lawn Hollywood Hills Cemetery.[1]

Liberace's death now provided every pundit in print and broadcast journalism the opportunity to issue pronouncements about the most arcane social topics and difficult legal questions. "AIDS: How Wide the Coverup?" pontificated *US News and World Report* after the showman's death.[2] Talking heads bobbed now, not merely about medical confidentiality but about rights to privacy in general, to homosexual confidentiality in particular. In heroic seriousness, Ted Koppel and his *Nightline* guests pondered the depths of "why Liberace did not reveal his gay lifestyle."[3] Politicians lumbered onto the scene. Representative Henry Waxman of California, chairman of a House health subcommittee, furrowed his brow dramatically for an audience of millions on *Good Morning America* about the same issue. "It was very sad that Liberace in his final days felt that he had to hide his illness from the public . . . when he could have taken the role that Rock Hudson had taken and been a great benefit to educating the public," he intoned.[4] The other side weighed in as well. "Did Anyone Really Gain from Disclosures about Liberace?" queried E. H. Duncan Donovan, "a civil liberties activist," in the *Los Angeles Times.*[5] The commonfolk might have had little tolerance for such formal categories of debate, but they had their own opinions—which also found voice in the national press in the wake of all this fury. By the lights of the *Globe,* the *National Enquirer,* and the *Star,* the disclosures set many a tooth on edge. Without necessarily any affection for the American Civil Liberties Union, the folks tended to share the biases that Liberace's illness was nobody's business but his own. "I think they should just leave him alone. That was his personal life. He hurt nobody," complained one fan. "It just made me sick when I heard all this digging up dirt," echoed another. "I resent anyone going into anyone's private life." Wept another: "They should let the man rest in peace. I don't care what he had. That's his private business."[6]

In the middle of this uproar, newspapers around the country broadcast the titillating news of the showman's sexual alliance with Rock Hudson. The author of the story, Boze Hadleigh, had committed himself not to out any of his subjects against their will—at least as long as they were living. The entertainer's passing freed the journalist from his oath of silence.[7] The revelation provoked a frenzy. The information qualified as legitimate news at many newspapers, but the tabloids and talk shows reveled in the story. The television personality Larry King featured a show on "the late, flamboyant, and controversial Liberace," for example, with Hadleigh as a special guest, and for weeks, the *National Enquirer* and the *Star* offered their readers new tidbits, pro and con, about the affair, which merged with the pandemonium over AIDS.[8]

Autopsies? AIDS? Homosexuality? Gay rights versus gay responsibilities? Individual rights to privacy? Public rights to know? Freedom of the press? It was hunting season. The dead showman was weapon as well as target. His death had created a media free-fire zone. So it continued for years. Liberace was not there to charm and reassure the audience. He was not there to protest and to threaten litigation. He was not there to sic Seymour on the enemy. Indeed, Heller himself slogged into the fray, this time not against Lee's enemies but against his friends, otherwise defined. The deathbed will proved the issue of contention—and more cause of media attention. A little over a year after Liberace's entombment, a clutch of his intimates sued to reduce or eliminate Joel Strote's power over the estate. The plaintiffs included Cary James, Angie Farrell, Gladys Luckie, and Dorothy McMahon, and, of course, Seymour Heller, whom Strote's management cut out more completely than he had any of the others. They filed suit on April 18, 1988; the case did not conclude until August.

The suit shredded Lee's well-constructed order still further. For months, the litigants' acrimony reverberated through the Clark County Courthouse in downtown Las Vegas. The charges and countercharges recognized few limits. Cary James claimed Strote insisted that the body must be cremated immediately, without waiting for the funeral—even while the family stood in the same room in which the showman was still breathing.[9] McMahon attacked Strote with the revelation that he offered naked midnight swims as his client lay expiring nearby. She also insisted that the lawyer hoodwinked the debilitated Liberace because her boss was too far gone to have any idea what he was signing on January 22. "Mr. Strote was saying 'He looks fine, he looks good.' I was thinking, 'This guy's nuts.'"[10] Insisting she was penniless, Angie claimed Strote was bilking her by charging illegitimate items against her trust fund—like her brother's Palm Spring funeral the year before.[11] Meanwhile, in all apparent sincerity, she insisted that she had pursued the suit against Strote at the direct instruction of her dead brother from beyond the grave.[12]

While Strote's counsel kept more to the issue of proving good management, the defendant fought as he was fought. Thus the defense introduced George Llinares, the former domestic manager, who reviled the whole household of plaintiffs, excepting only the kindly Gladys Luckie. Without saying the word "homosexual," he discussed Scott Thorson's and Cary James's relationships with his boss, characterizing them as being "of a sleazy nature."[13] There were other strategies. "They have made their living off of Liberace," Strote's people railed. They "have attempted to sensationalize [the evidence] in order to continue to bask in the glory of Liberace." [14]

The judge ruled for the defendant in August. Was the estate settled? The trial failed to solve other problems of Liberace's legacy. Odd silences still permeated the proceedings. Despite the occasional allusions to "sleazy relationships," the terms "homosexuality," "gay," and, more curious still, "AIDS" appeared nowhere in the court proceedings. As the *Los Angeles Times* writer covering the trial noted, "for all the graphic intimacies they volunteered, the plaintiffs always balked when the subject was AIDS." He continued: "Liberace, they said outside court, had known he had the disease for more than a year, but never came fully to terms with impending death. Denial was a practice in the house of Liberace, and it continued into the court." [15] The denial went far beyond the court.

Scott Thorson had wondered about Lee's failure to identify him as his lover to his family. They must have known; they had to have known, he concluded. Not necessarily. There is knowing and there is knowing. For all the time she spent with him, for all the companions that she had seen come and go, for example, Angelina Liberace Farrell, for one, denied her brother's homosexuality to the end of her own life. Not long before she died, she was visiting with Lee's dear old friend Vince Fronza and Stefan Hemming, who had bought the Cloisters around 1990. In Hemming's recollection, she explained everything to the two, including her brother's peculiarities. They did not include homosexuality. "Angie couldn't accept her brother was gay. She absolutely derided the idea. She sat right there with her crew cut (she had been taking chemotherapy) talking to me and Vince and explained to us, 'He was just unique. He was special because he was born with a caul. He wasn't that way.' She also insisted that 'He did not die of AIDS; the doctors killed him.'" [16] Although Angie hated Dora, her sister-in-law who had gone over to the enemy, Strote, George's widow seemed to have shared the same opinion. "He did not have AIDS," a docent at the Liberace Museum confided to one visitor after the musician had been dead for over a decade. "Dora told me so," she whispered. [17]

What was true; what was false? Reality grew even messier after Lee's passing than it had been during his life, when at least he had dominated the fictions. Thus, two years after his death, the peculiar memoir, *I'll Be Seeing You: The Young Liberace* appeared, in which its author claims to have borne Liberace's love child in 1943. The author also protests that her Lee contracted the HIV virus not from homosex but from tainted blood after a facelift. [18]

Whatever the reality of his life, Liberace continues to fascinate the public long after his death. Publishing offers one measure of his continued hold on the American imagination. Besides the most eccentric revelations of his supposed mistress, various books trafficked in his fame. Although *The Wonderful, Private World of Liberace* had lost Harper and Row a bundle in 1986, St. Martin's Press capitalized on the furor over the showman's passing and released a biography when Liberace was hardly cold in his crypt. Its author, Bob Thomas, had already cranked out a score of books and journalistic biographies on the likes of Ethel Merman, Bing Crosby, Ricardo Montalban, and William Holden. He had known Liberace for thirty-five years or so. He had produced interviews with him from the Valley Vista days even as he had helped fuel the media hype over Liberace's romance with Joanne Rio in 1954. He also worked in tabloid journalism and had generated articles about the showman there after Liberace's death. He was a natural. *Liberace: The True Story* appeared within months of the performer's death.[19] Very shortly after Thomas's biography went on sale, E. P. Dutton published Scott Thorson's memoir, written with Alex Thorliefson, *Behind the Candelabra: My Life with Liberace*. Both books circulated widely. In 1994, Ray Mungo published another, short biography in the series edited by the historian Martin Duberman, Lives of Notable Gay Men and Lesbians, created for young adults. It approaches its subject less as an authentic character for himself than as a model for how society distorted—or distorts—homosexual men.

Other books featured the glitzy showman. Although the Hollywood writer Boze Hadleigh refuses to disguise his contempt for the performer, *Hollywood Gays,* as well as its successor, *Sing Out! Gays and Lesbians in the Music World,* continue to trade on the showman's name and reputation.[20]

Nineteen-ninety four marked the beginning of what passes for methodical, systematic work on the musician, with Karl B. Johnson's *Liberace: A Collecting Guide to the Récordings of Liberace, and His Brother George.* If not widely available and if intended chiefly for collectors and not for scholars, it nevertheless registers by year, label, and content almost seven hundred records, albums, and titles produced by the showman or associated with him in some other way.[21] The following year, Greenwood Press added an important research volume about Liberace, written by Jocelyn Faris, to its Bio-Bibliography Series in the Performing Arts.

Books, however, mark only one measure of Liberace's place in the popular imagination. Perhaps more important, he still sells. As of 1994, thirty-one new editions of his records had been issued since his death seven years before.[22] Just so, attendance levels at the Liberace Museum remain high in the second decade after his death, with over one hundred thousand visitors a year arriving to admire all the performer's stuff. The museum is one of Nevada's top three tourist attractions. The Liberace Foundation, which controls the museum, also sponsors a regular newsletter for fans and patrons of the institution. Generating more publicity, the foundation funds scholarships in the showman's name. While the newsletter draws attention to Liberace imitators, the showman's impersonators have a life of their own, if they are not so notorious as those of Lee's friend Elvis.

Liberace still fascinates. Early on, television cashed in on his appeal. In the late spring of 1988, not one but two television networks announced upcoming television movies on the superstar.[23] ABC sponsored one, called, simply, *Liberace,* while CBS did the other, *Liberace: Behind the Music.* Had Judge Wendell in Las Vegas settled the legal conflict of the estate in August? These television productions continued the war by other means. Joel Strote signed on with the ABC production as executive producer; Liberace entouragers Terry Clarkston and Jamie James joined him. Predictably enough, Seymour Heller advised the CBS crews. Both camps made their pitches for their own people. Heller, for example, is invisible in the one, Jamie James in the other. The two productions, also perhaps predictably, precipitated new legal suits and countersuits.

Although two sets of television executives believed that gold hid in Liberace's glitter, their interpretations of the market varied significantly. Stephen Farber, the *New York Times* journalist who reported the productions, chronicled these justifications—even as he betrayed some of the fundamental New York biases against the showman. He seemed incredulous that even one studio would do Liberace: "Why is there such tremendous interest in telling the life story of an entertainer who was regarded by many as a minor camp figure?" he inquired half rhetorically. Gavin Lambert, the CBS screenwriter, shared some of the same bias. "It's the AIDS connection," he replied. "If he had not died of AIDS, I don't think there would have been a biography within a few months of his death or two competing television movies." Allen Sabinson at ABC offered a different take: "Liberace was an American original. He is still regarded with great affection by a large audience of fans. And there are many other people who weren't his fans who are curious about him. They want to know, 'Who was this odd, flamboyant duck?'" If ABC's movie was aiming for this more general audience, it specifically played down the homosexual angle. Just so, the Lambert script at CBS counted on both AIDS and homosexuality to sell.[24]

The Strote-ABC production did soft-pedal homosexuality. Jamie

James had delighted in the Liberacean homoerotics of Palm Springs, and his influence can be detected in the bevy of boys who cruise the movie's Palm Canyon Drive, but this is a minor part of the film. Joel Strote got the gist of it: "We show Liberace as the wonderful, magnanimous, caring, sensitive, kind human being he was. We don't say he was patently homosexual," the lawyer said. "That would be gross." He added, "I hear. CBS is taking a more negative approach."[25] Whether or not homosexuality was gross and negative, the ABC film actually takes a very similar line to the one the showman himself had assumed publicly. It concludes with the palimony suit and a female journalist posing the question, "Do you still claim you're not a homosexual?" Played by Andrew Robinson, who bore an uncanny resemblance to the showman, the actor repeats a Liberace line almost verbatim: "I'm not claiming anything. I just don't happen to believe that entertainers should publicly air their sexual or political tastes. . . . I've always admitted that my act borders on drag but I'm not a female impersonator. I have a general family audience appeal and I don't want to develop a gay following."[26]

The ABC, estate-authorized film aired on October 2. Exactly a week later, the CBS production premiered. As promised by its hype, it does place greater emphasis upon the musician's inner life and sexual impulses. It stresses the tension between his parents and between him and his father. It makes rather more of his affair with Scott Thorson than does the first movie. It compromises his homosexuality, even so. Lifting a page directly from Bob Thomas's biography, it assumes a conversion to homosexuality in the mid-fifties. At the same time, as summarized by the *New York Times* critic John J. O'Connor, even the CBS film is "insistently discreet. If anything, Liberace emerges as something of an asexual Teddy bear, always looking vaguely puzzled when dealing with the advances of either men or women."[27] The film, then, tends to confirm rather than alter the showman's own public denial and ambiguity about his sexuality. The CBS Liberace wonders aloud, for example, when hearing of Rock Hudson's infection, "Why would he tell everyone?" and the movie ends with the showman contemplating—and rejecting—a public declaration of his homosexuality as he himself expires. Thus, for all the hype, CBS's production actually diverges very little from ABC's. "It's a little dispiriting to think that two TV movies, separately developed and presumably antagonistic, should come out so interchangeable," continued the writer for the *Hollywood Reporter.* "[It is] an indication of how slavishly they both conform to the rules of televised biography."[28]

After a decade, both movies, however shallow, still show regularly on the tube, keeping the showman's name and image alive and kicking.

In these same years, production companies have created two different documentary-type biographies on the showman for television audiences. These telecast regularly as well. If nobody much seems to care about *South Seas Sinner, Sincerely Yours* plays periodically on late-night television; it still makes at least some folks "gulpy," as previewers predicted it would. Fans can purchase a whole series of Liberace videos, too. These range from excerpts of *The Liberace Show* to films of his Las Vegas performances. In short, the Liberace industry still thrives.

Despite the incredulity of many, like the *Times*'s writer Stephen Farber in 1988, this "minor camp figure" remains a name to reckon with. Attendance records at his performances are still unmatched in books of world records. *Bartlett's Familiar Quotations* has institutionalized him by including his witticism about crying all the way to the bank. A decade after his entombment, the cartoonist Gary Larson elicited more chuckles, probably, with his visual jokes about the performer, than Al Capp did forty years before with his character Liverachy. The showman's name and character have become a part of the fabric of American culture. Thus, when a major American newspaper described the glitzy old Miami Beach hotel, the Eden Roc, in reference to "a Liberace style," no elaboration was necessary. A Liberace joke in the 1997 film comedy, *Austin Powers,* drew familiar laughter from audiences who were not even teenagers at his death. After the manner of the folk, Liberace is honored in the most various and even peculiar ways. Milwaukeeans have seen an opera based on his life and loves staged in their city. Poets ponder Liberace's appeal in various works and even title collections on the theme: *Why My Mother Likes Liberace: A Musical Selection.*[29] An English recording group, the Bomb Party, produced an album called *Liberace Rising* in 1987. Five years later, the Pontiac Brothers recorded their tune "Liberace's Dead" on a Frontier Records album, *Fuzzy Little Pieces of the World.*[30] In 1999, the "shock jock" radio personality, Howard Stern, touts a wacky rap performer, Niggerace, who plays off the showman's cognomen.

While the late entertainer is a part of popular discourse in America, the specific meaning of his life or his place in American culture remains as controversial and contested as his legal estate. He won his reputation as a musician, but where does he fit in music history?

Liberace has attracted almost no formal examination among musicologists and historians of music, but two general positions seem obvious: one treats him as a classical pianist, a second as a popular entertainer. While these two are not completely exclusive, a third opinion tends to combine these categories into something different yet.

Even among the classicists, at least two positions appear. The first condemns him as a failed artist who degraded good music. Howard Taubman's *New York Times Magazine* article of March 14, 1954, offers the clearest, early manifestation of the complaint. Without taste or discrimination, Taubman insisted, Liberace simply debased his art and corrupted music, even popular music or jazz. He produced neither one thing nor the other. He was a fake. This jeremiad conceded nothing.[31] Forty years later, the academic critic Kevin Kopelson confirmed this opinion in the chapter on Liberace in his study, *Beethoven's Kiss.* Although a pianist himself, Kopelson is more concerned with Liberace as a queer phenomenon than as an artist. And as a phenomenon, "the man simply haunts—and taunts—my imagination. Liberace baffles me," he declares. The source of his bafflement lies, in part it seems, in the contrast between the showman's huge appeal, especially for straight women, and the inadequacies of his talent. In this regard, Kopelson accepts uncritically the most negative reviews, especially of the mid-fifties, of the showman's performances, including even Cassandra's, though Cassandra never even attended a performance. Kopelson dismisses Liberace, then, as a "bad pianist" with "technical disabilities" and middlebrow sensibility who "belittles and bastardizes" classical music.[32]

Also a pianist, Samuel Lipman offers a third and more studied, if less widely circulated version of this "debased art" view.[33] First, unlike either Taubman or Kopelson, Lipman grants Liberace's real, pianistic skill. "He displayed at all times a large, accurate, and brilliant technique," he writes, "even indulging himself from time to time in impressive displays of octaves, scales, and complicated passage work." He concludes: "All in all his playing purled and glittered just the way an accomplished pianist's should." His talent, if anything, made Liberace's offense all the more damning. Like Taubman and Kopelson, Lipman argues that Liberace debased music by appealing to people who did not know anything about art—in specific contrast to disciplined musicians and "sophisticated audiences" who possessed such knowledge. Liberace profaned the sacred by pandering to the untutored. Beyond this general sin, Lipman also argues Liberace's specific role in the degradation of classical music by relating him to the careers of other performers, like operatic tenor Luciano Pavarotti and, most critically, the Texas pianist Van Cliburn. Liberace and Cliburn specialized in the same kind of late romantic music—Tchaikovsky and Rachmaninoff, for example—already marked as decadent by its vulgarity and bombast, in effect. Such scores were "hugely appealing to an enormous public" that had little other interest in serious music. More specifically, the Milwaukeean actually broke the ground for the Texan in legitimizing a kind of heartland America approach to performance, argues Lipman. Cliburn's manner "seemed not just authentically American but, like Liberace's, authentically non–New York American." While "Liberace's great commercial success from 1956 on—using as it did television and hyped personal appearance to sell a debased version of classical music"—prepared the way for Cliburn's triumphs after 1958, the Texan, in turn, bore his own burden in the degradation of classical music. His career confirmed "contest mania among young performers all over the world." This mania led to the proliferation of contests, competitions, and winning and to "a dearth of interesting performers growing up at their own pace." He considers the reputation of both musicians "great but ephemeral" and concludes that each "provided spectacularly inapplicable models for the careers of serious musicians."

Where Taubman is polemical and Kopelson coy, Lipman is ironic and resigned. Thus emerges his final observation that Liberace and his Texas heir represent the culmination—and collapse—of a splendid 140-year epoch during which music in general and the piano in particular defined Western cultural aspirations. "The piano in the living room, like the candelabrum . . . in the dining room, became an emblem of cultural advancement and participation. It was this touching aspiration which made possible [these] two huge successes. . . . Whatever the future holds in store for music in general, the piano will probably never again enjoy such popularity and prestige."

Taubman, Kopelson, and Lipman speak for the degraded art-school approach to Liberace's performance; another opinion diverges significantly. It considers the Milwaukeean more generally—and generously—within a musical genealogy of flamboyant, romantic performers from the early nineteenth century: From Liszt and Paderewski—to Liberace. Thus, Edward Rothstein, music critic of the *New York Times* and later of the *New Republic,* evaluated the Wisconsin pianist most specifically in the context of that other great showman Franz Liszt, who proclaimed, "Le concert, c'est moi!" and boasted of "affecting the Louis XIV style."[34] "Both then and now, in both Liszt and Liberace," Rothstein continues, "the insistence upon regal mythic powers in the midst of ordinariness— all this is not extraneous to the figure of the virtuoso, but part of his substance, the signs to an audience of the meaning in this nineteenth-century music or its contemporary popular musical descendants. It is not only pure sound that is at work, but an entire world of associations; what is dreamed of in the music is made real on the stage; what is heard is also seen."

Rothstein allows the difference between the virtuosi; the contrasts, he argues, reflect in part the difference in two ages. He concedes that Liberace transformed the Lisztian nineteenth-century bourgeois desire for transcendence into nostalgia, "as frequently happens when Romanticism begins to decay. The result," he offers, "is kitsch, warm and beloved." Yet kitsch, he argues, permeates the modern age. And even kitsch touches the ultimate object of art, he insists. How does he compare to the modern virtuoso, Vladimir Horowitz? "Liberace is more representative of our time," he cautions. "He is simply an exaggeration of the character of our musical life, which itself is a distorted, peculiar transformation of nineteenth-century musical culture, thriving on invoked images, ritualistic signs, and commercial energies." What he takes with one hand, however, he returns with the other. Thus, while he judges that Liberace's performance was built on nostalgia and double layers of artifice, he also describes the pianist's genuine power to move his audience—à la Liszt. As remarkable as the general audience's response to the 1984 Radio City Music Hall show is Rothstein's own reaction to the performance, which, as he describes it, "left even a hard-nosed critic admiring." As of old, the virtuoso took requests from the hall. The showman improvised an impossible medley of "New York, New York," "Let Me Call You Sweetheart," and "Chopsticks." "And what happens is a shock," the critic writes, "a surprise that again echoes images of the virtuoso's past. For the music is so genuinely sweet, so sensitively lyrical, that it becomes *moving*." [35]

Respectful of his performance—like Rothstein—or not—like Taubman and Lipman—the classicists dominate the critical judgments of Liberace's place in music history. If far less articulate, however, another position holds that his real significance lies not in high art at all: it proposes that he is most appropriately studied within a context of popular music and popular performance. It would consider him in the context of the later Elvis Presley, Michael Jackson, Glam Rock, and perhaps most critically of all, Elton John or Madonna. Advanced mostly as a kind of common-sense position among journalist/critics, this argument has yet to find a coherent exegesis among musicologists or music historians even of American popular culture, who mostly ignore the Milwaukee piano player.

A third assessment is hardly more developed than the one that would establish him within the history of American popular music. It rather assumes the collapse of distinctions between high art and low and makes Liberace something like a classic "American original." A *New York Times* review of his 1985 Music Hall performance adumbrates this position. It begins, ironically enough, with the same assumption that Howard Taubman made exactly thirty years before—that Liberace is neither fish nor fowl. In contrast to "the square's" horror in 1954 at the jumble, Stephen

Holden finds it the source of the showman's genius. Liberace, he judged, "has arrived at a style that is not classical, jazz or pop but an ornamental genre unto itself" with its blend of Hollywood, Las Vegas, and "19th-century romantic mysticism." [36]

So where does Liberace really fit in music history? Musicologists can't agree. Controversy characterizes other aspects of his legacy as well. Indeed, nothing, not even his musical significance, has attracted as much contention as has his sexual import. From his first heady days of national fame in 1953, he functioned as a lightning rod of sexual controversy. He was, first, a woman's man, and few critics ignored conclusions based on the preponderance of women, especially middle-aged ones, among his devotees. Fewer still were neutral. Given the gender bias toward males among reviewers, the judgments ranged from bewilderment or amusement to outrage. Misogyny, latent or overt, permeated most critical opinion. Behind the misogyny, and not altogether separate from it, lay the fear and distrust of homosexuality. In the 1950s, Liberace found his bitterest antagonists among straight men. The revulsion of the American newscaster Edward R. Murrow and the contempt of British journalist William Conner represent the view.

While straight male mockery of "blue-haired ladies" and ridicule of "gentlemen of a certain persuasion" penetrated many reviews to the very end of Liberace's career and after, most critics eased off on these biases in the seventies or ignored them altogether by the eighties. Ironically or paradoxically, the post-Stonewall era has witnessed the most profound opposition to Liberace within the gay movement itself. In a peculiar turn of events, some of the showman's particularly vehement antagonists number themselves among the outspoken proponents of Gay Liberation.

As already noted, the gay academic critic Kevin Kopelson is more concerned with Liberace's homosexuality than with his music, per se, and hardly disagrees even with Cassandra's 1956 diatribe, which he quotes in its entirety. "I find this quite as appalling as it claims to find Liberace. I also find it rather appealing," he confesses, "to the residual snob in me, if not to the residual homophobe." He continues, however, to conflate his snobbery and latent homophobia: "It can be hard to separate the two—as 'Cassandra' himself . . . should have realized." [37] David Ehrenstein, another gay writer, expresses even more impatience with the showman in his *Open Secret*. While approving Michel Foucault's assertion about the impossibility of honesty for homosexuals, for example, Ehrenstein then denies the application of that rule to Liberace. The rich and powerful, he would claim—if only for the gaudy showman—have no right or privilege to remain closeted. "There is an enormous difference between a person

of average ways and means lying about his or her same-sex affinity in order to keep a job, a residence, or family peace, and the lie of a highly paid
and well-connected showbusiness figure who had successfully promoted
modest pianistic ability into a career in nightclubs, concert halls, film and
television. Moreover, an overt appeal to the sexual sensibilities of his audience was very much a part of Liberace's act." [38]

Boze Hadleigh, a more famous chronicler of gay Hollywood, offers
the clearest manifestation of post-Stonewall homosexual biases against
the Milwaukee performer. [39] In his treatment, Liberace becomes a model
for everything gay men should not be—a selfish, self-loathing, hypocritical, closeted, conservative Republican, stereotypical sissy. He associates
him, just so, with a whole phalanx of unsavory elements: "bigots," "red-
necks," hicks, the religious right, "powerful men in politics and pulpits,"
and "the Polident generation." [40]

Hadleigh condemns the showman, not least, for failing in his responsibility to act as a positive "role model" for young gay boys. Beyond this,
he burdened the performer—at least by association—with the still-graver
error of actually perverting and polluting the youth of America. After
noting that Liberace "occasionally 'stepped out' on his steady with an escort or call boy or even a runaway," Hadleigh proceeds through a trail of
sin that sounds something like a homosexual inversion of *The Music
Man*'s "Trouble in River City." Thus, "runaway" triggers the following
sequence: a "shocking percentage" of runaways are gay kids rejected by
homophobic parents, mostly dads; these lads turn to prostitution as a necessary evil; and, finally then, "AIDS is not an uncommon end to the sur-
vivalist lifestyle forced on these youngsters by their unloving and unthink-
ing parents who believe their sexuality is a 'sin' and/or changeable." [41]

Paradoxically, perhaps—and not unlike Kevin Kopelson—Hadleigh
can't get very far away from Liberace, despite his distaste. The showman
crops up often in his other interviews, even when Hadleigh refuses the
pianist any honor. The journalist himself brought up the late entertainer
in conjunction with Cesar Romero, for example. While Romero shared
Hadleigh's laughter over the flashy queen, the aging star also expressed
sympathy for the indignities of Liberace's end. "I felt sad for him," mused
the old actor. The young interviewer would have none of it. "Dignity begins at home," he snapped. [42]

All these activists actually apprehend critical elements of the career
and personality of the piano player from West Allis, Wisconsin. Except
for Hadleigh's claim that Liberace perverted American youth, they see
little, in fact, that most of Liberace's most devoted fans did not also detect.
One category of critic praises these elements of the performer's character

and work; the other sees only the liabilities. Liberace's life and career did violate virtually every element of the new gay orthodoxy after Stonewall. Despite his own homosexuality, his long-term relationship with Thorson and then with Cary James, and the homosexuality of his professional inner circle, he scanted gay culture and gay liberation. Indeed, in the Thorson affair, he had actually attacked, at least indirectly, homosexuals and homosexuality when headlines quoted him saying "Gays Out to Assassinate Me," and when his spokesman condemned this "slander at the hand of the gays." Over a forty-year period after 1940, he had worked out his own compromises with his homoeroticism that involved the public disavowal of his affections. He was, in the parlance of the day, very deeply closeted, and thus, according to the same criteria, just as deeply hypocritical.

If a poor model for political activists, however, Liberace's life, even closeted, possesses its own power and significance for the gay experience. In reviewing the two made-for-television movies of the showman's life, David Kipen of the *Hollywood Reporter* observed that "Liberace's life was one of colossal denial, not only of his sexuality but of his prodigious and under appreciated musicianship. It would have made a fascinating movie, but instead, posthumously, the denial continues." [43] Perhaps Kipen was onto something about the dramatic power of denial itself. The literary critic Eve Sedgwick suggests as much when she affirms that the most fascinating of all narratives is the coming out story that doesn't come out. [44]

Liberace's career, denial and all, has perhaps even more immediate reference to gay men's lives. Indeed, even as the millennium turns, it may be more defining of the norm among homosexual men in America than radicals might allow. For whatever reasons, then, however much activists scorn the closet queen, the old showman continues to hold the imagination of the rank and file of ordinary gay men. The affection emerges in odd ways and places. In the Gay Olympics in New York, for example, the American press gave full coverage to the diver Greg Louganis's public declaration of his affectional preference for other men. In the course of this celebration of one athlete's coming out, the papers also turned, willy-nilly, it would seem, back to Liberace, of all people. "Now we can have someone besides Liberace as a role model," one overheated fellow at the games declared. Perhaps the journalist was actually poking fun in citing the anonymous source—not unlike the stifled snickers of the *Los Angeles Times* reporter at the parade of gaudy men on the witness stand during the legal contest over Liberace's will. Perhaps the interviewee himself intended mockery. And then again, perhaps not. Whether he was a role model or not, gay men continue to honor his memory. On February 4,

1997, diners in a posh New York restaurant noted a table across the room set with candelabrum and burning tapers. Shortly, two distinguished-looking men appeared, garbed in the fanciest eveningwear. The maitre d' ushered them to the table. Only later did at least one other set of diners appreciate the connection between the two men and the memory of the showman. The dinner had taken place on the tenth anniversary of Liberace's death.[45] Still more poignant evocations of the man appear. No one has more patches, all glittery and spangled, in the AIDS quilt than he. There are worse fates, even in the gay community, than to be remembered as an aging queen who died of AIDS: the old sister is a brother, too. Somehow or the other, then, for all the well-placed, well-ordered, politically useful opposition to Liberace and the life he led, his career still touches the lives of other gay men.

Such small tokens of affection—like patches on the AIDS quilt—also suggest the larger potential of his life to ordinary men and women as the second decade since his death rolls by. Did he deny his homosexuality? Denial works two ways. He understood that affirming his homosexuality would have entailed denying a raft of other forces and influences in his life. These, in turn, occupied as critical a place in his conception of himself and his relations to others as did sexual preference. There was honor on both sides. In this regard, the paradoxes of his life become less sexual hypocrisy than, in their own way, a recasting of the normal circumstances of most people's lives: coveting youth when age sags jowls; the desire to be free amid obligations and responsibility; the craving for beauty when faced with dirty dishes and clogged drains; the apprehension of transcendence before the commonplace and routine; the longing for immortality in a mortal world. In this regard, his homosexuality in a heterosexual world allowed him a handle on larger paradoxes in human nature, and in the American spirit, too. Did he pander to the lowest common denominator of popular culture? If so, he also captured something essential in human longing. He was Mr. Everyman. He was Peter Pan, the boy who never grew up, the lad who flew. He lived in Neverland, but he never left West Allis. He was born and died an American boy.

NOTES

ONE

1. The curious circumstances of the showman's birth are discussed in various sources. Bob Thomas's *Liberace: The True Story* (New York: St. Martin's, 1987), 1, offers one description; Liberace's old lover provides another in Scott Thorson with Alex Thorleifson, *Behind the Candelabra: My Life with Liberace* (New York: E. P. Dutton, 1988), 6. A third comes from his sister Angelina, or Angie. Around 1990, Stefan Hemming had purchased "Casa Liberace" in Palm Springs. He knew Angie Liberace Farrell. To him, she repeated the story of her brother being born with a caul, which he heard and repeated as "tail." She explained to him that the circumstance of the birth anticipated and accounted for her brother's genius and peculiarities. Stefan Hemming, interview with the author.

Bob Thomas garbles the story of being born "under the veil." He identifies the phenomenon with the dead sibling and ill portents. This is not the case at all. Angie Farrell's version gets it right. For other versions of the mysterious gifts of the caul-born child, see Tina McElroy Ansa's novel, *The Baby of the Family*. Ansa's definition of genius is clearly what Angie Farrell had in mind rather than the fatal notions Thomas suggests. For other lore about birth cauls, I am indebted to my friend Elena Maubrey, who was also born with one, in Havana.

2. Stephen Meyer, *"Stalin over Wisconsin": The Making and Unmaking of Militant Unionism, 1900–1950.* (New Brunswick, N.J.: Rutgers University Press, 1992).

3. "Liberace Out-Glitzed Hometown," Milwaukee *Sentinel,* July 23, 1982. The Milwaukee Public Library, Milwaukee, Wisconsin, has kept a clipping collection on the hometown entertainer. While the material it contains is also available on microfiche, this collection provides the easiest access to it. This is File #71 of that collection. Hereafter, this material will be cited as Liberace File, Milwaukee Public Library, with the appropriate number of the file, the date, and the title, where they are apparent.

4. "Liberace Out-Glitzed Hometown," July 23, 1982, Liberace File #71, Milwaukee Public Library.

5. Meyer, *"Stalin over Wisconsin,"* passim. Although Meyer chronicles the history of the union movement here, not the social history of the community, his study offers useful insights into Liberace's social environment.

6. Liberace, *Liberace: An Autobiography* (New York: G. P. Putnam's Sons, 1973), 48, 53–54.

7. Ibid., 49.

8. The idea of economic deprivation permeates Liberace's reconstruction of his childhood, especially but not exclusively in his memoirs. The idea, then, of his father as a poor provider—a "failure"—fits this larger pattern. The sense of deprivation, however, fits an even larger, general pattern in his assessment of his childhood and his own career: the notion that nothing was ever quite good enough. As he repeated stories of his earlier life to Scott Thorson, who became his lover, what stood out, for Thorson at least, was a rancorous, even bitter tone. This tone characterizes Liberace's description of various episodes, according to Thorson: playing private parties in New York, including those hosted by oilman Paul Getty, in the early forties, and Liberace's discounting of his performance with the Chicago Symphony Orchestra as a young man. Both of these topics are treated below. Occasionally, the tone penetrates even his public record. See the following, also treated below: the bad memories of making *Sincerely Yours,* his barely veiled sarcasm in his treatment of supper-club performing, and his suggestion that he was doing something akin to charity work when he played such great clubs as Mocambo and Ciro's in Hollywood in the late forties and early fifties. Liberace's dissatisfied tone is important in itself. It distorts the Liberacean record in various ways. While it has the effect of diminishing his achievements under some circumstances, it led, almost paradoxically, to the exaggeration of achievements in other; it forced, effectively, the image to live up to his own ambitions. This is particularly but not exclusively true relative to money matters. Under all circumstances, the inclination complicates the difficulties of the biographer trying to describe the life beyond the images Liberace projected. How poor was he during the Great Depression, for example? By the memoirist's standards, his poverty was indescribable. To cite one example: in 1982 he granted an interview in which he testified that, "I spent 17 years of my life in the nearest thing to poverty you can imagine, and I hated it with a bitter passion. And I vowed I would never be poor, nor my family." ("Reviewing His Life over the Years," July 23, 1982, Liberace File #37, Milwaukee Public Library.) From a more objective vantage point, if judged only by his family's both owning and maintaining real property throughout these years, their circumstance was not so horrible after all. What is going on? Initially, Liberace's disquiet provides an important glimpse of the almost manic ambition, or sources of ambition, that drove him relentlessly throughout his life. He was always looking for something better, newer, grander, richer. Whatever the manifestations, of course, this discontent echoes to the depth of his psyche, even as it offers the first example of how he could turn a deformity into a virtue, leveraging self-loathing, for example, to achieve enormous success. In whatever guise, the trait appears throughout the showman's life; it is an important part of his biography and a critical element in my assessment of his career in this study.

9. Liberace, *Liberace: An Autobiography,* 48–50, 54.

10. See photographs in the Liberace Museum, Las Vegas.

11. For Salvatore Liberace, see Milwaukee City Directory 1911, 1912, and West Allis City Directory 1918. For the Casadontes, see West Allis City Directory 1918, 1929, 1931.

12. Liberace, *Liberace: An Autobiography,* 68.

13. Although Liberace dates his parent's union to 1909 and places it in Me-

nasha, legal documents establish the September 1910 date and the Milwaukee place. See the Liberaces' divorce, Case No. 173-705, Aug. 8, 1941, Circuit Court, Milwaukee County, Milwaukee County Courthouse, Milwaukee, Wisconsin.

14. For the physical description, see Salvatore Liberace's naturalization papers at the Liberace Museum, Las Vegas, and also photographs of both him and Frances in that collection, reproduced in this text.

15. See, for example, her photograph at the Liberace Museum.

16. Thorson, *Behind the Candelabra,* 7.

17. Liberace, *Liberace: An Autobiography,* 53.

18. Thomas, *Liberace,* 6.

19. Liberace, *Liberace: An Autobiography,* 273.

20. Ibid.

21. Ibid.

22. Ibid., 59.

23. Ibid., 54. Despite Liberace's testimony about the site of his brother's birth, George's obituary in the *Los Angeles Times,* Oct. 17, 1983, lists his birthplace as Menasha, Wisconsin; see also the bibliographical data on George Liberace in Karl B. Johnson, *Liberace: A Collecting Guide to the Recordings of Liberace, and His Brother George* (Tucson, Ariz.: John Carlson Press, 1994), 16.

24. For Valentino as a Liberace family name, see the photographic portrait of Salvatore Liberace's father at the Liberace Museum.

25. Liberace, *Liberace: An Autobiography,* 53.

26. Ibid., 47, 54. See also Liberace, *The Wonderful, Private World of Liberace* (New York: Harper and Row, 1986), 34, for an illustration of Frances "behind the counter at her (Nina's) Fruit Shoppe which she expanded into a grocery and deli through her hard work."

27. Liberace, *Liberace: An Autobiography,* 47, 54.

28. See West Allis Directory, (published every other year) 1918, 1921, 1923, and 1925.

29. "He Dusts Off Stories after Death of 'Lee,'" Feb. 8, 1987, Liberace File #70, Milwaukee Public Library.

30. Liberace, *Liberace: An Autobiography,* 63, 64.

31. Liberace, *The Things I Love,* ed. Tony Palmer (New York: Grosset and Dunlap, 1976), 82.

32. Liberace, *Liberace: An Autobiography,* 160.

33. Ibid., 48.

34. Ibid.

35. Ibid., 54–55.

36. Liberace, *The Things I Love,* 51.

37. Liberace, *Liberace: An Autobiography,* 59.

38. Ibid.

39. Ibid., 55, also 54.

40. Ibid., 55.

41. Ibid., 56.

42. Ibid., 56–58.

43. Thorson, *Behind the Candelabra,* 169; 8–9; 7; 9–10.

44. Liberace, *Liberace: An Autobiography,* 59.

45. Thorson, *Behind the Candelabra,* 10, 34, and 174.
46. "Band Leader, Speech Expert Helped Liberace," Feb. 7, 1987, Liberace File #60, Milwaukee Public Library.
47. Ibid.
48. Thorson, *Behind the Candelabra,* 10–11.

TWO

1. The photograph was reprinted in the Milwaukee *Journal-Sentinel* on February 2, 1987. See copy in the Liberace File, Milwaukee Public Library.
2. Liberace, *Liberace: An Autobiography,* 62, 71, 63.
3. "Liberace Out-Glitzed Hometown," Feb. 7, 1987, Liberace File #71, Milwaukee Public Library.
4. Liberace, *Liberace: An Autobiography,* 51.
5. See photographs in the Liberace Museum.
6. Robin Leach, "Liberace in His Own Words," *Star,* Feb. 17, 1987.
7. See photographs in the Liberace Museum, Las Vegas.
8. Liberace, *Liberace: An Autobiography,* 52. Why his grandmother should have been speaking in some Germanic rather than in a Polish dialect is interesting in itself. Liberace elsewhere affirms a German connection. While the pianist knew or spoke little of his genealogy, he does relate that his mother's mother had lived in Berlin, and had supposedly worked there with the Polish virtuoso Paderewski when both were young.
9. Liberace, *Liberace: An Autobiography,* 51, 52.
10. Ibid., 68.
11. N.t., n.d., Liberace File #7, Milwaukee Public Library.
12. Liberace, *Liberace: An Autobiography,* 68.
13. Liberace, *Wonderful, Private World,* 36.
14. Liberace, *Liberace: An Autobiography,* 68.
15. Thorson, *Behind the Candelabra,* 8.
16. Liberace, *Liberace: An Autobiography,* 69; for other evidence of their employment, see the Milwaukee city directories between 1931 and 1937.
17. "Liberace: The One and Only," July 23, 1982, Liberace File #36, Milwaukee Public Library. The end of this article states that when the showman repeated this story to a Milwaukee audience long after, the local supervisor of social services for Milwaukee County checked out the matter and discovered that the family had received formal government assistance in the amount of $100.
18. Liberace, *Liberace: An Autobiography,* 161, 259.
19. In addition to the city directories for this period, see also Liberace, *Wonderful, Private World,* 39.
20. This information is drawn from the city directories of this period, and also from "Elder Liberace Dead," Apr. 28, 1977, Liberace File #28, Milwaukee Public Library.
21. Thorson, *Behind the Candelabra,* 8.
22. "Band Leader, Speech Expert Helped Liberace," Feb. 5, 1987, Liberace File #60, Milwaukee Public Library.
23. "He Dusts Off Stories," Feb. 6, 1987, Liberace File #70, Milwaukee Public Library.
24. See the divorce proceedings, Milwaukee County Court.

25. Liberace, *Liberace: An Autobiography*, 271, 272.

26. Ibid.

27. Ibid., 275, 271, 272.

28. Ibid., 272. As noted above, here is another manifestation of Liberace's sense of deprivation. The reality is harder to calculate, most specifically with respect to his little brother. One of the younger sibling's friends, John Romanos, remembered Rudy's great model-railroad layout. "He had Lionels and American Flyers. The attic was all set up with trains." "Liberace Out-Glitzed Hometown," July 23, 1982, Liberace File #71, Milwaukee Public Library.

29. Liberace, *Liberace: An Autobiography*, 75. See also the Angie interview, in "Liberace: The One And Only," July 23, 1982, Liberace File #36, Milwaukee Public Library.

30. "Band Leader Helped Liberace," Feb. 5, 1987, Liberace File #60, Milwaukee Public Library.

31. Liberace, *Liberace: An Autobiography*, 72, 286. See also Thomas, *Liberace*, 7–8.

32. Liberace, *Liberace: An Autobiography*, 71.

33. Thorson, *Behind the Candelabra*, 10.

34. N.t., n.d., Liberace File #7, Milwaukee Public Library.

35. Thorson, *Behind the Candelabra*, 10.

36. See the Parish records among the files of the Church of the Latter Day Saints in Greenfield, Wisconsin.

37. Liberace, *Liberace: An Autobiography*, 156. In differentiating between the "aesthetic" and the "theological" attractions of the church, I have profited enormously from discussions with my son-in-law, Alex Martinez.

38. Liberace, *Liberace: An Autobiography*, 53.

39. Eve Kosofsky Sedgwick, *Epistemology of the Closet* (Berkeley and Los Angeles: University of California Press, 1990), 140.

40. John Rechy, *The Sexual Outlaw: A Documentary* (New York: Grove Press 1984; originally published 1977), 66–67.

41. Thorson, *Behind the Candelabra*, 14, 10.

42. N.t., n.d, Liberace File #7, Milwaukee Public Library.

43. Liberace, *Liberace: An Autobiography* 54–55.

44. N.t., n.d., Liberace File #7, Milwaukee Public Library.

45. Ibid.

46. Liberace, *Liberace: An Autobiography*, 55, 67.

47. Ibid., 62.

48. Ibid., 63.

49. Adam Zamoyski, *Paderewski* (New York: Athenaeum, 1982).

50. Ibid.

51. "Liberace Coming Home for Show; Will Make His Third Movie Soon," Mar. 29, 1951, Liberace File #2, Milwaukee Public Library.

52. Liberace, *Liberace: An Autobiography*, 66.

53. Ibid.

54. Ibid.

55. Ibid., 67.

56. *Wisconsin College of Music Bulletin, Season of 1930–1*. Milwaukee Public Library. She is also listed in the bulletin for 1932, but for no other years before or

after. See also n.t., n.d., Liberace File #17, Milwaukee Public Library; "Band Leader Helped Liberace," Feb. 5, 1987, Liberace File #60, Milwaukee Public Library.

57. Kevin Kopelson's treatment of Bettray-Kelly deserves attention. His discussion of Liberace's background ignores the exigencies of the time—like the necessity to work and eat: thus, he identifies Bettray-Kelly "as somewhat middlebrow herself," offering the proof that "after all, they both played popular music on the same Milwaukee radio station, and at more or less the same time." Kopelson, *Beethoven's Kiss: Pianism, Perversion, and the Mastery of Desire* (Stanford, Calif.: Stanford University Press, 1996), 160.

58. "Band Leader Helped Liberace," Feb. 5, 1987, Liberace File #60, Milwaukee Public Library.

59. If he scants the social reality of the Great Depression as they affected these characters, Kopelson is much better on the psychological meaning of Florence Kelly in her student's life. He calls her "another mother figure" but adds, immediately, "or father figure." He extends the trope a little later: "Liszt and Chopin, father and *mother*, are one woman to Liberace—Bettray-Kelly." Kopelson, *Beethoven's Kiss,* 160.

60. N.t., n.d., Liberace File #17, Milwaukee Public Library.

61. N.t., n.d., Liberace File #7, Milwaukee Public Library.

62. N.t., n.d., Liberace File #17, Milwaukee Public Library.

63. Ibid.

64. Liberace, *Liberace: An Autobiography,* 76.

65. N.t., n.d., Liberace File #7, Milwaukee Public Library.

66. Although Kelly remembered the date as 1931, a dated photograph in the Liberace Museum places the year as 1930.

67. N.t., n.d., Liberace File #17, Milwaukee Public Library.

68. Ibid.

69. N.t., n.d., Liberace File #10, Milwaukee Public Library.

70. Ibid.

71. Liberace, *Liberace: An Autobiography,* 79.

72. N.t., n.d., Liberace File #17, Milwaukee Public Library.

73. Ibid.

74. N.t., n.d., Liberace File #10, Milwaukee Public Library.

THREE

1. "Liberace Coming Home," Mar. 29, 1951, Liberace File #2, Milwaukee Public Library.

2. "He Dusts Off Stories," Feb. 6, 1987, Liberace File #70, Milwaukee Public Library.

3. Liberace, *Liberace: An Autobiography,* 75, 73.

4. Ibid., 75.

5. N.t., n.d., Liberace File #7, Milwaukee Public Library; "Liberace Coming Home," Mar. 29, 1951, Liberace File #2, Milwaukee Public Library, confirms Angie Liberace's version of events, placing the "Fanchon and Marco revue" at the Wisconsin Theater and making the boy's age thirteen, not ten.

6. Liberace, *Liberace: An Autobiography,* 75.

7. "Class of '37 Remembers Liberace," Feb. 10, 1987, Liberace File #77, Milwaukee Public Library.

8. Liberace, *Liberace: An Autobiography,* 75, 72; Del Krause, interview with the author.

9. Ibid.

10. Ibid.

11. "Play It Again, Wally," Apr. 25, 1987, Liberace File #51, Milwaukee Public Library.

12. Ibid.

13. Del Krause interview.

14. Thorson, *Behind the Candelabra,* 11.

15. "Play It Again, Wally," Apr, 25, 1987, Liberace File #51, Milwaukee Public Library.

16. Del Krause interview.

17. "Class of '37 Remembers," Liberace File #77, Milwaukee Public Library. Liberace himself deals with this period on page 77 of his autobiography. He refers only to the Mixers. He also dates his association to 1937 or 1938. External evidence in newspaper interviews confirms his errors in this regard. He conflated the Mixers and the Rhythm Makers, and perhaps other groups, too, and he remembered their personnel wrong, as well.

18. Liberace, *Wonderful, Private World,* 39.

19. Liberace, *Liberace: An Autobiography,* 78.

20. "No Place for Liberace in His High School Band," *Detroit News,* Feb. 5, 1987, cited in Jocelyn Faris, *Liberace: A Bio-Bibliography* (Westport, Conn.: Greenwood Press), 235.

21. Liberace, *Liberace: An Autobiography,* 73–75.

22. "He Dusts Off Stories," Feb. 6, 1987, Liberace File #70, Milwaukee Public Library.

23. "Play It Again, Wally," Apr 25, 1987, Liberace File #51, Milwaukee Public Library.

24. Del Krause interview.

25. Ibid.

26. Thorson, *Behind the Candelabra,* 20, 11.

27. "Band Leader Helped Liberace," Feb. 5, 1987, Liberace File #60. Milwaukee Public Library.

28. Del Krause interview.

29. "Class of '37 Remembers," Feb. 10, 1987, Liberace File #77, Milwaukee Public Library.

30. Ibid.

31. N.t., n.d., Liberace File #7, Milwaukee Public Library.

32. "Class of '37 Remembers," Feb. 10, 1987, Liberace File #77, Milwaukee Public Library.

33. N.t., n.d., Liberace File #7, Milwaukee Public Library.

34. Liberace, *Liberace: An Autobiography,* 71.

35. "Class of '37 Remembers," Feb. 10, 1987, Liberace File #77, Milwaukee Public Library.

36. N.t., n.d., Liberace File #7, Milwaukee Public Library.

37. "Liberace Whips Up Music, Muffins at His Old School," n.d., Liberace File #3, Milwaukee Public Library.

38. "Class of '37 Remembers," Feb. 10, 1987, Liberace File #77, Milwaukee Public Library.

39. Del Krause interview.

40. "Class of '37 Remembers," Feb. 10, 1987, Liberace File #77, Milwaukee Public Library.

41. N.t., n.d., Liberace File #7, Milwaukee Public Library.

42. Susan Sontag's seminal essay, "Notes on Camp," republished in *Against Interpretation* (New York: Dell, 1967), introduces a casual connection between camp and homosexuality. Later critics have reasserted the relationship in the strongest terms. While Sontag, with some ambivalence, discusses camp as an un-political or apolitical strategy in "Notes," later critics, in the wake of political activism after Stonewall, have tended to make camp, even drag (which is camp at its height) a political activity that asserts Gay Power, challenges the social order, and attacks what is referred to as the Heterosexual Dictatorship, or Compulsory Heterosexuality. Others, however—especially radical feminists—attack the gay/camp connection—and drag, in particular—from a political perspective, on the grounds that it represents a collusion with the patriarchal order and an affirmation rather than a criticism of dominant cultural values. Against all this, Lypsinka protests that a girl just wants to have fun. For a full discussion of these ideas, see, in particular, Moe Meyer, ed,, *The Politics and Poetics of Camp* (New York: Routledge, 1994), and David Bergman, ed., *Camp Grounds: Style and Homosexuality* (Amherst: University of Massachusetts Press), 1993, especially Meyer's own essay, "Under the Sign of Wilde," in the former.

43. For a particularly compelling treatment of popular antipathy to homosexuality, see Guy Hocquenghem, *Homosexual Desire,* (Durham N.C.: Duke University Press, 1993; originally published 1972), 55–61, especially. Hocquenghem takes standard Freudian definitions of homosexual paranoia and inverts them as a means of explaining societal opposition: "So it is society as a whole that defends itself against the sexualisation of its investments," he writes, "and struggles with all its might against homosexual desublimation" (60).

44. This response recalls the popular reaction to black troops in battle in the Civil War. After virtually every battle, sympathetic white officers protested that now no one could attack the sable troops for their want of courage or valor. The very protests tended to affirm that the normal expectation was of cowardice. Two generations after Walter Liberace pranced through the halls at West Milwaukee High School, this response remains an interesting benchmark of the community's latent skepticism about sexual deviance, particularly among the self-consciously tolerant, who seemed to think that acceptance of a homosexual or of homosexuality requires justification.

45. Thorson, *Behind the Candelabra,* 16, 14.

46. Ibid., 14.

47. Experimentation, play, and fluidity—including the ultimate play of camp—come very close to defining essentials within the homosexual experience. In truth, in the practice or even the physics of homosexuality, it raises innumerable problems and secondary issues within and without the gay community among both adherents and detractors. Is anything normal for homosexuality? Is anything, everything up

for grabs? What does this mean? Is, thus, this characteristic (or style) a manifestation of individuals' arrested development and irresponsibility, or does it offer a positive, open model for an otherwise constricted, hidebound social order? There are other issues and problems. "Homosexual sensibility" touches upon the very nature of homosexuality itself and raises still thornier problems of the sources of gender deviancy and, by extension, of the sources and meaning of sexuality in general. Are queers born or made? Is homoeroticism a social construction? Is sexuality itself equally artificial? The academic tomes on the theme proliferate. Theorists might answer such questions one way; more often than not, even the most abstract back and fill when it comes to dealing with practical immediate concerns. These issues tangle almost every contemporary discussion of gender and gender deviation. To cite one example, Michael Bronski generally hews to a constructivist position yet has made significant forays into defining a gay sensibility: See his *Culture Clash: The Making of a Gay Sensibility* (Boston, Mass.: South End Press, 1984).

48. "Class of '37 Remembers," Feb. 10, 1987, Liberace File #77, Milwaukee Public Library.

49. Thorson, *Behind the Candelabra,* 13.

50. N.t., n.d., Liberace File #7, Milwaukee Public Library.

51. "Mr. Showmanship's Stage Fashions Hard to Beat," n.d., Liberace File #68, Milwaukee Public Library.

52. Liberace, *Liberace: An Autobiography,* 79.

53. See photograph in the collection of the Liberace Museum.

54. The poster and the publicity shots are preserved at the Liberace Museum.

55. "Liberace Coming Home," Mar. 29, 1951, Liberace File #2, Milwaukee Public Library.

56. "Our Liberace is Going Strong after 25 Years of Candlelight," Liberace File #14, July 21, 1965, Milwaukee Public Library.

57. Liberace, *Liberace: An Autobiography,* 81.

58. Liberace, *The Things I Love,* 86.

59. Liberace, *Liberace: An Autobiography,* 82–83.

60. N.t., n.d., Liberace File #17; and "Walter Busterkeys Played at Old Plankton Arcade," Feb. 5, 1987, Liberace File #59, Milwaukee Public Library.

61. See Walter Liberace to Max Pollack, letter, Jan. 30, 1940, Liberace Museum, Las Vegas.

62. Don Asher, *Notes from a Battered Grand: A Memoir* (New York: Harcourt, Brace, Jovanovich, 1992), 90, 91–92.

63. See Walter Liberace to Max Pollack, letter.

64. N.t., n.d., Liberace File #17; and "Walter Busterkeys Played at Old Plankton Arcade," Feb. 5, 1987, Liberace File #59, Milwaukee Public Library.

65. Ibid.

66. "Play It Again, Wally," Apr 25, 1987, Liberace File #51, Milwaukee Public Library.

67. "Old Friends Knew Liberace Would Hit the Big Time," Feb. 5, 1987, Liberace File #62, Milwaukee Public Library.

68. N.t., n.d., Liberace File #9, Milwaukee Public Library; Liberace, *Liberace: An Autobiography,* 79–80.

69. Liberace, *Liberace: An Autobiography,* 80; Thorson, *Behind the Candelabra,* 20.

70. Liberace, *Liberace: An Autobiography,* 80. He offers a somewhat different version of the conflict with his father in *The Things I Love,* 58, in which he credits his performance with the Chicago Symphony with softening Salvatore's objections to his playing popular music.

71. Karl Fleming and Anne Taylor Fleming, *The First Time* (New York, Berkeley Publishing Corporation, 1975), 148.

72. See Cal York, "Remember You Read It First in *Photoplay,*" Jan. 1976, cited in Faris, *Bio-Bibliography,* 257.

73. Fleming and Fleming, *First Time,* 148.

74. Ibid.

75. Liberace, *Liberace: An Autobiography,* 48.

76. "He Dusts Off Stories," Feb. 8, 1987, Liberace File #70, Milwaukee Public Library.

77. Thorson, *Behind the Candelabra,* 8.

78. Segell, quoted by Michelle Green, "Liberace the Gilded Showman," *People Weekly,* Feb. 16, 1987, 31.

79. Liberace, *Liberace: An Autobiography,* 74.

80. Fleming and Fleming, *First Time,* 146, 147.

81. Liberace, *Wonderful Private World,* 40.

82. Thorson, *Behind the Candelabra,* 16.

83. Ibid., 17.

FOUR

1. N.t., n.d., Liberace File #10, Milwaukee Public Library.

2. Ibid.

3. Ibid.

4. Ibid.

5. "Local Man Entertains," n.d., Liberace File #1, Milwaukee Public Library.

6. N.t., n.d., Liberace File #10, Milwaukee Public Library.

7. "Local Man Entertains," n.d., Liberace File #1, Milwaukee Public Library.

8. Liberace, *Liberace: An Autobiography,* 80.

9. Thorson, *Behind the Candelabra,* 19.

10. N.t., n.d., Liberace File #10, Milwaukee Public Library.

11. *Bohemia,* Aug. 26, 1956. My thanks to Kevin Taracido for the translation from Spanish.

12. Quoted in "Liberace: Musical Showman Dies at age 67 in Palm Springs," *Los Angeles Times,* Feb. 5, 1987.

13. Liberace, *The Things I Love,* 47.

14. N.t., n.d., Liberace File #10, Milwaukee Public Library.

15. Liberace, *The Things I Love,* 61.

16. Ibid., 20.

17. See the Times Square photograph at the Liberace Museum, Las Vegas. The apartment photograph appears as plate 10 in this text.

18. Thorson, *Behind the Candelabra,* 22.

19. N.t., n.d., Liberace File #9, Milwaukee Public Library.

20. Liberace, *Liberace: An Autobiography,* 89–90.

21. Thorson, *Behind the Candelabra,* 23.

22. "Our Liberace Is Going Strong," July 21, 1965, File #14, Milwaukee Pub-

lic Library. Although Liberace allowed that "he was still in his teens," he offers no evidence that he did other work that would put him in a league with Morgan until this later period.

23. Liberace's autobiography regularly skews time and dates, in this period, particularly. Thus, for example, after discussing his engagements at fancy clubs around Fifty-second Street, he refers to returning to the Plaza Hotel "seven years later" in 1945. Perhaps taking a cue from Lee's memoir, Thorson also gets dates wrong. Bob Thomas is worse still in this regard. Liberace's 1947–48 press kit lists the Ruban Bleu engagement in 1945, and Liberace himself associated that gig with Spivy's Roof and with playing ritzy Upper East Side parties. By 1945, his reputation was certainly taking to the air, but it seems less likely that he would have been able to pick up such elegant and sophisticated venues during the earlier period. See below. For these reasons, I treat the performances that I think more likely to have taken place later not here but when I discuss the period after his return to Manhattan.

24. Liberace, *The Things I Love,* 61. Bob Thomas relates a much more involved version of the West Orange story on page 30 of his book. He writes that Jay Mills had disbanded his orchestra, moved East, and invited his pianist to join him. This, he argues, prompted Liberace's decision to go to New York. If the narrative might contain seeds of truth, it is, like much of Thomas's work, highly suspect, as he regularly spins a line or two from some secondary source into a full-fledged episode. The story is fanciful, with "tearful farewells to Mom" and good-byes to the Mixers—who had long since parted ways with their much younger colleague. Besides the fictionalization, one additional problem with Thomas's New York story is the way it downplays how much the performer's own initiative and spunk contributed to his taking off on his own for Manhattan. In this regard, Thorson's version of the story seems more in keeping with the patterns in the pianist's life. Otherwise, his less-elaborate version seems closer to fact, as well.

25. "Piano Virtuoso Is Big Hit of New Show at Hotel Last Frontier," *Las Vegas Review-Journal,* Nov. 25, 1944.

26. Untitled, undated review from the Liberace press kit, Las Vegas Public Library. This press kit, which dates from around 1947, is the single most important source for the period covered in this chapter. It is also an important document in itself in illustrating the performer's publicity genius. Hereafter, I refer to it simply as "press kit."

27. Thorson, *Behind the Candelabra,* 23.

28. N.t., n.d., Liberace File #10, Milwaukee Public Library.

29. Liberace, *Liberace: An Autobiography,* 84–85.

30. Ibid., 85.

31. Ibid., 87.

32. Press kit.

33. Ibid.

34. Ibid.

35. Ibid.

36. Ibid.

37. Ibid.

38. Liberace, *Liberace: An Autobiography,* 174; also press kit.

39. Liberace, *Liberace: An Autobiography,* 123.

40. "Hildegard Recalls Memories of Liberace," Feb. 10, 1987, Liberace File #76, Milwaukee Public Library.

41. Liberace, *Liberace: An Autobiography,* 87.

42. "All Time High Is Reached in Frontier Show," *Las Vegas Review-Journal,* Sept. 16, 1946.

43. Press kit.

44. Ibid.

45. Liberace, *Liberace: An Autobiography,* 88.

46. Ibid., 87. *The Things I Love,* 62, offers a very different version of playing for Getty: Liberace performed at Getty's upstate New York estate and missed the public conveyance back to the city.

47. Thorson, *Behind the Candelabra,* 22. This chronology, which is perhaps based on Liberace's own mixed-up dates, is off as well. Beyond the matter of dates, the treatment illustrates the showman's retrospective hostility, as noted in chapter 1.

48. Press kit.

49. Ibid.

50. Ibid.

51. Ibid.

52. Liberace, *The Things I Love,* 63.

53. Liberace, *Liberace: An Autobiography,* 171.

54. Ibid., 90.

55. Ibid., 81.

56. Press kit.

57. "Liberace Coming Home," Mar. 29, 1951, Liberace File #2, Milwaukee Public Library.

58. Liberace, *The Things I Love,* 86.

59. Thorson, *Behind the Candelabra,* 35.

60. Ibid., 24.

61. N.t., n.d., Liberace File #10, Milwaukee Public Library; and press kit.

62. N.t., n.d., Liberace File #10, Milwaukee Public Library.

63. Thorson, *Behind the Candelabra,* 23.

64. George Chauncey, *Gay New York: Gender, Urban Culture, and the Making of the Gay World, 1890–1940* (New York: Basic Books, 1994), 349.

65. Charles Kaiser, *The Gay Metropolis, 1940–1996* (New York: Houghton Mifflin, 1997), 8.

66. Chauncey, *Gay New York,* 349–50.

67. Ibid., 350.

68. Ibid., 131.

69. Kaiser, *Gay Metropolis,* 7.

70. Ibid., 12.

71. Ibid., 16.

72. Ibid., 39, 40.

73. Ibid., 39.

74. Gore Vidal, *Palimpsest: A Memoir* (New York: Random House, 1995), 101–2.

75. Chauncey, *Gay New York,* 350.

76. Ibid., 350–51.

77. William Henry Harbaugh, letter to the author.

78. Vidal, *Palimpsest,* 101–2.

79. Kaiser, *Gay Metropolis,* 8.

80. Vidal, *Palimpsest,* 101.

81. Ibid.; Chauncey, *Gay New York,* 216.

82. Chauncey, *Gay New York,* 349.

83. For a 1930s version of what went on in such circumstances, and how, see the account left by the sometime homosexual Whittaker Chambers as recorded by his biographer, Sam Tanenhaus. Sam Tanenhaus, *Whittaker Chambers: A Biography* (New York: The Modern Library, 1998), 344–55.

84. Vidal, *Palimpsest,* 101.

FIVE

1. Press kit.

2. The timing of Liberace's move to California is uncertain. While he himself admitted his chronological confusion, he often solves the problem, as here in his biography, by failing to date things at all. Bob Thomas and Jocelyn Faris compound the chronological confusion. Thomas, for example, puts Liberace in Long Beach during the war itself. No evidence exists for this assertion. Liberace's press kit offers clues to his postwar relocation in the West. He played Las Vegas for the first time in 1944, and then did not do so again until 1946, after which the gigs became regular. The kit makes no reference to California until the late winter/ spring and summer of 1947, the time of the San Diego and Long Beach jobs. His autobiography tends to support the idea that he made his shift West during the postwar period, too. Thus, when he discusses the Goodwin family, he makes reference to two young, but grown, unmarried sons. If the autobiography can be trusted here, he must surely have stayed with the Goodwins after the war, as it is highly unlikely that both of the Goodwin sons would have escaped service. For the initial encounters with Mr. Goodwin, see Liberace, *Liberace: An Autobiography,* 144–45.

3. Ibid., 145–46.

4. Ibid., 123.

5. Press kit.

6. Liberace, *Liberace: An Autobiography,* 146.

7. Press kit.

8. Liberace, *Liberace: An Autobiography,* 309–10.

9. Ibid., 288.

10. John Rechy, *City of Night* (New York: Grove Press, 1984; originally published 1963), 212. Santa Monica also figures notably in Rechy's *Sexual Outlaw.*

11. Rechy, *City of Night,* 177.

12. See also E. Michael Gorman, "The Pursuit of the Wish: An Anthropological Perspective on Gay Male Subculture in Los Angeles," in Gilbert Herdt, ed., *Gay Male Culture in America: Essays from the Field* (Boston, Mass.: Beacon Press, 1992). Also David Ehrenstein, *Open Secret: Gay Hollywood, 1928–1998* (New York: William Morrow, 1998), especially, 33–42.

13. "Milwaukee Entertainer Wows 'Em With His Big 'Priceless' Piano," Liberace File #1, 1947, Milwaukee Public Library.

14. Liberace, *Liberace: An Autobiography,* 85.

15. "Milwaukee Entertainer," n.d., Liberace File #1, Milwaukee Public Library; press kit.

16. "When It Comes to Glamour, Liberace Rates an A Plush," June 30, 1969, Liberace File #19, Milwaukee Public Library. Also press kit, and "Milwaukee Entertainer," n.d., Liberace File #1, Milwaukee Public Library.

17. Liberace, *The Things I Love,* 80.

18. "A Master Showman, but Liberace Also Valued His Privacy," Feb. 5, 1987, Liberace File #64C, Milwaukee Public Library.

19. Press kit.

20. Besides the story ideas, the press kit also contains actual reviews. These newspaper articles reveal their debts to the press kit itself.

21. "Liberace Coming Home," Mar. 29, 1951, Liberace File #2, Milwaukee Public Library.

22. Liberace, *Wonderful, Private World,* 16.

23. See photograph credits in the Liberace Museum.

24. Jack Cortez, "That's for Sure,"*Las Vegas Review-Journal,* Sept. 23, 1951.

25. See advertisements in the *Las Vegas Review-Journal,* May 21, 1948; Dec. 31, 1948; Feb. 22, 1949; Sept. 22, 1949.

26. N.t., n.d., Liberace File #2, Milwaukee Public Library.

27. See the dated photograph in the Liberace Museum. Also, "Liberace in Hollywood," n.d., Liberace File #1, Milwaukee Public Library, which also dates the White House performance to March. Bob Thomas takes this date and moves it back to 1949.

28. David Richards, "Liberace, Laughing Last," *Washington Post,* July 19, 1985.

29. Liberace, *Liberace: An Autobiography,* 83, 84. Lest this all be taken as Liberacean hyperbole and self-justification, one might also consult the hilarious memoirs of another, slightly younger supper-club/café performer, Asher, *Notes from a Battered Grand,* passim.

30. Thorson, *Behind the Candelabra,* 20.

31. Ibid., 22–23.

32. Johnson, *Liberace: A Collecting Guide,* 22, 31.

33. Ibid., 95, 18, 91.

34. Ibid., 18, 49, 90, 95, 91.

35. Press kit; also Liberace, *Liberace: An Autobiography,* 64.

36. Cortez, "That's For Sure."

37. Liberace, *Liberace: An Autobiography,* 110.

38. Paul Monette, *Becoming a Man: Half a Life Story* (New York: Harper Collins, 1992).

39. Although she does not deal with the gay affinity for Hollywood, Marjorie Garber, in *Vested Interests: Cross-Dressing and Cultural Anxiety* (New York: Routledge, Chapman, Hall, 1992), has increased my own understanding of the illusionary aspects of dressing, "gender coding," and related issues of sex and sexuality in American culture.

40. Thorson, *Behind the Candelabra,* 30.

41. "Piano Virtuoso Is Big Hit," *Las Vegas Review-Journal,* Nov. 25, 1944.

42. "All-Time High Is Reached in Frontier Show," *Las Vegas Review-Journal,* Sept. 16, 1946.

43. "Liberace in Hollywood," n.d., Liberace File #1, Milwaukee Public Library.

44. "Liberace in Hollywood," n.d., Liberace File #1, Milwaukee Public Library. This articles seems the source for Bob Thomas's rather more fanciful and elaborate tale in *Liberace,* 51–52.

45. Liberace, *Liberace: An Autobiography,* 110–13.

46. "Liberace in Hollywood," n.d., Liberace File #1, Milwaukee Public Library.

47. Liberace, *Liberace: An Autobiography,* 114.

48. Ibid., 44–45.

49. Ibid., 45.

50. "Liberace Coming Home," Mar. 29, 1951, Liberace File #2, Milwaukee Public Library.

51. "Liberace: Musical Showman Dies," *Los Angeles Times,* Feb. 5, 1987.

52. Liberace, *Liberace: An Autobiography,* 146.

53. Ibid., 45.

54. Thomas, *Liberace,* 60; Liberace, *Liberace: An Autobiography,* 46.

55. Thomas, *Liberace,* 60–61.

56. All of these quotations are taken from *Joanne Rio Barr v Liberace,* Los Angeles Superior Court.

57. Thorson, *Behind the Candelabra,* 75, 76. See also "A Day in the Life of Seymour Heller: Veteran Personal Manager for Liberace and the Treniers Lives Musical Life," *Billboard,* May 6, 1969.

58. See the depositions in Barr's case against Liberace, in which both Barr and Liberace testify to the degree to which Heller managed everything relating to the publicity of their relationship. Also, the Scott Thorson case that was tried ten years later affirms that Heller was the aggressive manager carrying through on Liberace's determination to get Thorson out of his life.

59. Thorson, *Behind the Candelabra,* 89.

SIX

1. "Liberace Coming Home," Mar. 29, 1951, Liberace File #2, Milwaukee Public Library; Cortez, "That's For Sure"; press kit; and "Liberace in Hollywood," n.d., Liberace File #1, Milwaukee Public Library.

2. N.t., n.d., Liberace File #9, Milwaukee Public Library.

3. Ibid.

4. N.t., n.d., Liberace File #4, Milwaukee Public Library.

5. Harry Castleman and Walter J. Podrazik, *Watching TV: Four Decades of American Television* (New York: McGraw Hill, 1982), 63.

6. Tim Brooks and Earle Marsh, *The Complete Directory to Prime Time Network TV Shows. 1946—Present,* 4th ed. (New York: Ballantine Books, 1988), 963.

7. For the Benny show, see Castleman and Podrazik, *Watching TV,* 81.

8. Ibid., 75.

9. Ibid., 63.

10. Ibid., 75.

11. Ibid., 78.

12. Ibid.

13. Andrew Ross, in *No Respect: Intellectuals & Popular Culture* (New York:

Routledge, 1989), ignores movies and television, but he introduces some of these problems by focusing on music, literature, and intellectual culture in general.

14. N.t., n.d, Liberace File #3, Milwaukee Public Library.

15. This information on early Los Angeles television is drawn from two sources: "KTLA at 45" (1992) and "Happy Birthday LATV" (1977). Museum of Broadcast History, New York.

16. "What Happened to Liberace?" *TV Guide,* May 3, 1958.

17. Thomas, *Liberace,* 63.

18. Liberace, *Liberace: An Autobiography,* 94–96.

19. Ibid., 96, relates to Liberace's signing on with Heller. At least one document confirms that Heller did not sign on as agent until 1952: see the letter of Dec. 31, 1952, from Liberace to Heller in the official records of proceedings in *Richard Gabbe, Sam Lutz, Seymour Heller, William Loeb v Liberace, International Artists, John Jacobs, et al.,* Los Angeles Superior Court, July 15, 1960. This confirms that there was a contract beginning on January 1, 1953, to run for two years. Perhaps another letter existed from two years earlier; conversely, perhaps there was no letter at all: elsewhere, the legal proceedings affirm that John Jacobs instructed his client against a written agreement. Evidence from the Scott Thorson palimony case also confuses the dates.

20. N.t., n.d., Liberace File #4, Milwaukee Public Library.

21. A search of the television listings of the *Los Angeles Times* confirms that the show appeared for the first time on February 3, 1952, at 7:30 P.M.; the same source confirms these other programs. Thomas and Faris list other dates, perhaps on evidence from Milwaukee, which asserts other information. Thus, the drama critic of the Milwaukee *Sentinel* wrote on January 17, 1952, that "Liberace has decided to take some time off from supper club appearances and give TV a try. On Tuesday in Hollywood, he began his own weekly half hour show."

22. N.t., n.d., Liberace File #10, Milwaukee Public Library.

23. N.t., n.d., Liberace File #4, Milwaukee Public Library.

24. N.t., n.d., Liberace File #10, Milwaukee Public Library.

25. Richard Donnovan, "Nobody Loves Me but the People," *Collier's* 134 (Sept. 17, 1954), 74.

26. Thomas, *Liberace,* 67.

27. Marjorie Dent Candee, ed. *Current Biography: Who's News and Why* (New York: W. H. Wilson, 1954), 408–9.

28. See for example, "Popular Piano," *Time,* Oct. 5, 1953.

29. *Current Biography,* 408–9.

30. Liberace, *Liberace: An Autobiography,* 158.

31. N.t., n.d., Liberace File #9, Milwaukee Public Library.

32. Thomas, *Liberace,* 69.

33. N.t., n.d., Liberace File #3, Milwaukee Public Library.

34. *Los Angeles Times,* Feb. 6, 1953.

35. "Fishing for an Idea," n.d., Liberace File #9, Milwaukee Public Library.

36. Liberace, *Liberace: An Autobiography,* 96–98.

37. Ibid., 96, 97–98.

38. Ibid., 9.

39. Horace Newcomb, "Towards a Television Aesthetic," in Horace New-

comb, ed., *Television: The Critical View* (New York: Oxford University Press), 1982), 480–81.

40. Ibid., 481, 483.

41. Ibid., 489, 490–93.

42. "What Happened to Liberace?"

43. "Mail Call for Brother Rudy," n.d., Liberace File #4, Milwaukee Public Library.

44. *Variety,* July 16, 1953, quoted in Faris, *Bio-Bibliography,* 110.

45. Quoted in "Liberace: Musical Showman Dies."

46. "Liberace Signs Huge TV Deal," *Down Beat,* Feb. 11, 1953.

47. Castleman and Podrazik, *Watching TV,* 75.

48. Frank Sturcken, *Live Television* (Jefferson, N.C.: McFarland, 1990), 24, 42.

49. "What Happened to Liberace?"

50. N.t., n.d., Liberace File #9, Milwaukee Public Library.

SEVEN

1. Thomas, *Liberace,* 76.

2. Liberace, *Liberace: An Autobiography,* 214.

3. The data above is drawn from videos of *The Liberace Show* and also from *Liberace: The Golden Age of Television,* vol. 1 (compact disc), #D2-74516, Curb Records (Burbank, Calif.).

4. For a full discussion of the theme song, see below.

5. Keith Monroe, "Liberace and His Piano," *Coronet,* May 1954, 121.

6. Harvey Taylor, *Detroit Times,* quoted in "Liberace—Virtuoso or Ham?" *TV Guide,* Aug. 28–Sept. 3, 1954.

7. Liberace, *Liberace: An Autobiography,* 99, 100.

8. Ibid., 99.

9. See, again, videos of *The Liberace Show,* and also *Liberace: The Golden Age of Television,* vol. 1.

10. N.t., n.d., Liberace File #9, Milwaukee Public Library.

11. "What happened to Liberace?"

12. *Current Biography,* 408–9.

13. Liberace (as told to Edythe Witt), "Mature Women Are Best: TV's Top Pianist Reveals What Kind of Woman He'd Marry," *Coronet,* Oct. 1954.

14. "Goose Pimples for All," *Time,* June 7, 1954.

15. "Popular Piano."

16. "Liberace Warms Crowd with a Smile and 'Hello,' " n.d., Liberace File #5, Milwaukee Public Library.

17. N.t., n.d., Liberace File #8, Milwaukee Public Library.

18. Johnson, *Liberace: A Collecting Guide,* passim.

19. Liberace, *Liberace: An Autobiography,* 64–65.

20. Howard Taubman, "A Square Looks at a Hotshot: An Ivory-tickling TV Virtuoso like Liberace Really Drags this Music Critic by His Long Hair," *New York Times Magazine,* Mar. 14, 1954; see also Johnson, *Liberace: A Collecting Guide,* passim, and Thomas, *Liberace,* 83–84.

21. *Current Biography,* 408–9.

22. Thomas, *Liberace,* 89–90.

23. *Time,* Oct. 1, 1954, quoted in Faris, *Bio-Bibliography,* 251.

24. "Fishing for an Idea," n.d., Liberace File #9, Milwaukee Public Library.

25. N.t., n.d., Liberace File #9, Milwaukee Public Library.

26. Taubman, "A Square Looks at a Hotshot."

27. Thomas, *Liberace,* 89.

28. Boze Hadleigh, *Hollywood Gays* (New York: Barricade Books, 1996), 113. Ten years after Liberace's death, some of these jokes were still making the rounds: When Liberace died and appeared at the pearly gates, St. Peter told him he had sinned and could not enter. "What have I done wrong?" Liberace asked. "You fucked a parrot," replied St. Peter. Liberace thought for a while, brightened and replied, "I never fucked a parrot—I only sucked a cockatoo."

29. Thomas, *Liberace,* 69.

30. Taubman, "A Square Looks at a Hotshot."

31. Donnovan, "Nobody Loves Me," 28.

32. "Popular Piano."

33. N.t., n.d., Liberace File #4, Milwaukee Public Library.

34. "Key to Whole Thing Is More than Keyes," n.d., Liberace File #6, Milwaukee Public Library.

35. "Not Rain or Popcorn Can Deter Liberace," May 2, 1954, Liberace File #6, Milwaukee Public Library.

36. "Liberace Plays; Tells Jokes, Too: Capacity Crowd at Carnegie Hall 'Delighted' by Recital—Pianist Gets Fanfare," *New York Times,* Sept. 26, 1953.

37. "Popular Piano."

38. Thomas, *Liberace,* 89.

39. "Liberace Charms 15,000 at Garden," *New York Times,* May 27, 1954.

40. Monroe, "Liberace and His Piano," 119.

41. "Music by Horowitz, Motions by Liberace" *Newsweek,* June 7, 1954.

42. "Goose Pimples"; "Liberace Charms 15,000."

43. "Why Women Idolize Liberace," *Look* 18 (Oct. 19, 1954), 1014.

44. Thomas, *Liberace,* 133.

45. Floyd C. Watkins, "*Gone with the Wind* as Vulgar Literature," in Richard Harwell, ed., *"Gone with the Wind" as Book and Film* (Columbia: University of South Carolina Press, 1983), 210.

46. In his unpublished essay, "The Academic Elvis," Simon Firth treats these difficulties especially well. His essay has illuminated and enhanced my own understanding not only of Elvis Presley—that most unlikely competitor of Liberace's—but of popular culture in general.

47. See also Ross, *No Respect,* for a more general treatment of the same problems. Sharply ideological, his study is also elliptical in both prose and content, but *No Respect* makes brilliant work of the American popular culture that also informs this biographical study.

48. "When Will Liberace Marry?" *TV Guide,* Sept. 18, 1954.

49. Thomas, *Liberace,* 86–87.

50. *International Artists, Ltd. v Commissioner of Internal Revenue, Respondent Walter V. Liberace, Petitioner, v Commissioner of Internal Revenue, Respondent.* Docket Nos. 1569-68, 1570-68, United States Tax Court, Oct. 22, 1970.

51. Thomas, *Liberace*, 67.

52. Johnson, *Liberace: A Collecting Guide*, 95.

53. Ibid., 42, 95, 31, 84.

54. Ibid. 42, 84; 70, 42.

55. Ibid., 31, 42, 41.

56. Liberace, *Liberace: An Autobiography*, 167.

57. "The 'Great' Liberace," *Look* 18 (June 29, 1954), 62.

58. Donnovan, "Nobody Loves Me," 74.

59. "Don't Laugh," *TV Guide* Feb. 26–Mar. 4, 1954.

60. *Barr v Liberace,* Los Angeles Superior Court.

61. For the specific reference to the motel chain, see Faris, *Bio-Bibliography,* 243. Otherwise, the pages of this reference book contain almost innumerable references to Liberace's moneymaking schemes.

62. "Class of '37 Remembers," Feb. 10, 1987, Liberace File #77, Milwaukee Public Library.

63. N.t., n.d., Liberace File #8, Milwaukee Public Library.

64. "Key to Whole Thing," n.d., Liberace File #6, Milwaukee Public Library.

65. N.t., n.d., Liberace File #8, Milwaukee Public Library.

66. Les Perrin, "Liberace-Purveyor of Musical Pop-corn," *Melody Maker,* Aug. 11, 1956, quoted in Faris, *Bio-Bibliography,* 241.

67. "Don't Laugh."

68. "Why Women Idolize Liberace," 1014.

69. Donnovan, "Nobody Loves Me," 30.

70. "Goose Pimples."

71. Liberace, *Wonderful, Private World,* 40.

72. N.t., n.d., Liberace File #9, Milwaukee Public Library.

73. "Liberace Bares Teeth in Chi Sheets," *Billboard,* Mar. 13, 1954, quoted in Faris, *Bio-Bibliography,* 204.

74. "Popular Piano."

75. Incredible to the *Time* writer, this linking of Valentino and Liberace makes perfect sense to Garber in *Vested Interests*. She cites the male reviewer's rebuke of Valentino's femininity on pages 361–62. As suggested by his lesbian wife and his own homoerotic tastes, of course, Valentino's sexual ambiguity went beyond mere perception of the old girls at matinees, too. Although apparently unaware of the Liberace-Valentino connection in the popular mind, Garber makes Liberace one of a trilogy with *The Sheik* star and Elvis Presley in her study of dressing.

76. Jackie Freers, *Indianapolis News,* quoted in "Liberace—Virtuoso or Ham?"

77. Donnovan, "Nobody Loves Me," 73.

78. Although Kevin Kopelson focuses exclusively on the homosexual aspects of Liberace's fascination for women, his analysis otherwise parallels my own: "It's also possible they liked the fact that he was gay. It meant they had a man they could talk to, if only in their dreams—an intimate associate who engaged in conversations their husbands weren't keen on, but who wouldn't prove to be a sexual 'threat.' For homophilic female fans, then, Liberace was a nonsexual lover, whereas for homophobic fans he was a presexual, or infantile one—one they, too, could mother." *Beethoven's Kiss,* 143–44.

79. For an early, sociological rendering of such relationships, see Philip E. Slater, *The Glory of Hera: Greek Mythology and the Greek Family* (Boston: Beacon Press, 1968).

80. Here I have drawn specifically on Camille Paglia, *Sexual Personae: Art and Decadence from Nefertiti to Emily Dickinson* (New Haven, Conn.: Yale University Press, 1991), but, in a more general way, Paglia's work has been important to informing my own understanding of Liberace's life and the significance of his career. It was *Sex, Art, and American Culture: Essays* (New York: Vintage, 1992) and then *Sexual Personae* that finally convinced me in the fall of 1992 to undertake this biography.

81. "Goose Pimples."

82. J. Wayne Taylor, interview with the author.

83. Quoted in Hadleigh, *Hollywood Gays,* 148.

84. Quoted in the *Miami Herald,* July 10, 1997; original reference in *Rolling Stone.*

85. Perhaps the antagonism of males to females' idols is actually an unexplored reality. In her *Vested Interests,* Marjorie Garber has chronicled some of this masculine hostility to Rudolph Valentino; see above, this chapter. Just so, it crops up in contemporary notions of the pop singer Johnnie Ray (who also had homosexual connections) and even of Elvis Presley, who possessed a certain early reputation as a sissy.

86. "What Do Men Think of Liberace?" *Inside Story* (Oct. 1954), quoted in Faris, *Bio-Bibliography,* 254.

87. Joseph E. Persico, *ERM: An American Original* (New York: McGraw Hill, 1988), 350.

88. Exploring the sources of societal antagonism toward homosexuality has offered a particularly interesting sidestreet in gender studies as our century winds down. Hocquenghem's insights in *Homosexual Desire,* cited earlier, are especially useful, not least in that they illustrate why male-ordered society, for example, focuses its most intense skepticism on male-male sexuality rather than on lesbianism. Male sexuality, liberated from the family, threatens social order altogether in this paradigm. In proof of the contention, Hocquenghem cites the work of André Morali-Daninos: "Were homosexuality to receive, even in theory, a show of approval, were it allowed to break away even partially from the framework of pathology, we would soon arrive at the abolition of the heterosexual couple and of the family, which are the foundations of the Western society in which we live" (Hocquenghem, 60).

If the French scholar uses such references as proof of societal "paranoia," some gay critics begin, effectively, with similar insights to argue for the ways homosexual subculture can guide and instruct a postmodern world in which family (not to mention Western Civilization) has already disintegrated: See Morris B. Kaplan, *Sexual Justice: Democratic Citizenship and the Politics of Desire* (New York and London: Routledge, 1997), and Bronski, *The Pleasure Principle: Sex, Backlash, and the Struggle for Gay Freedom,* (New York: St. Martin's Press, 1998). Edmund White's essays tend to confirm the same view.

89. See Ross, *No Respect,* for a persuasive argument linking the two kinds of containment during the Cold War.

90. See Ross, *No Respect,* for an excellent treatment of how bebop and its aficionados fit this pattern.

91. Again, see Ross, *No Respect,* for the degree to which such biases still permeate scholarly discourse. My seminar on twentieth-century American culture at my university in 1999 enriched my own understanding of these movements. Alex Ayala, a student in the seminar, offered me special insights into Ginsberg in particular and also into the other Beats and their relationship with national culture.

92. Ross, *No Respect,* draws brilliant conclusions about the relationship between intellectual culture in the United States in these years and American foreign policy.

93. Liberace, *Liberace: An Autobiography,* 21.

94. "Liberace Plays, Tells Jokes, Too."

95. Lewis Funke, "The Theatre: Liberace," *New York Times,* Apr. 22, 1957. While no one developed this Liberace-"Auntie Mame" connection, only Camille Paglia has paid much attention to the potential importance of the "Mame" phenomenon, which has enormous potential for gender studies, homosexual culture and values, and popular culture. Charles Kaiser in *Gay Metropolis* illuminates potential sources of the connection in his interview with "Stephen Reynolds," who identifies Mame's author, Patrick Dennis, with the "Taffeta Twelve" of the American Field Service that served with the British in North Africa during World War II. "He got married to a very nice girl and then he ran off with a Mexican boy," Kaiser quotes his source on page 35.

96. "Liberace," *New Yorker,* June 5, 1954.

97. See Kaiser, *Gay Metropolis,* 165.

98. Taubman, "A Square Looks at a Hotshot," 195.

99. Thomas, *Liberace,* 80.

100. Ibid., 82.

EIGHT

1. Thomas, *Liberace,* 116.

2. If record sales are an indicator, he was in a recessionary state by 1955. See below.

3. Thomas, *Liberace,* 79; also photographic evidence in the Liberace Museum.

4. Thomas, *Liberace,* 106–7.

5. Liberace, *Liberace: An Autobiography,* 116–17. Here is another manifestation of Liberace's retrospective tendency toward sour grapes and self-justification. At the same time, this affair underlines the performer's alienation, internal as much as external. Although he was doing what he wanted for decades—making a Hollywood career—he felt uneasy among the stars and celebrities. The dual tendencies, here and elsewhere, constantly threw him slightly off stride, as is particularly evident in his reconstruction of such episodes.

6. Thomas, *Liberace,* 111.

7. Ibid., 112–13.

8. See Faris, *Bio-Bibliography,* 96.

9. *New York Times,* Nov. 3, 1955, quoted in Faris, *Bio-Bibliography,* 14.

10. "Liberace Sees Silver Lining to His WB Pic's Present Cloud at B.O.," *Hollywood Reporter,* Dec. 12, 1956, quoted in Faris, *Bio-Bibliography,* 215, also 96.

11. *Havana Post,* August 25, 1956, and *Bohemia* [Havana, Cuba], August 26, 1956. For this and the other translations of Spanish from *Bohemia* and *Dario de la Marina* I am indebted to my friend and former student Kevin Taracido.

12. Liberace, *Liberace: An Autobiography,* 128.

13. *Bohemia,* Aug. 26, 1956.

14. Liberace, *Liberace: An Autobiography,* 128.

15. Ibid., 129; *Bohemia,* Sept. 2, 1956; *Havana Post,* Aug. 25, 1956.

16. I thank Kevin Taracido and his grandmother, Guillermina Rubio de Taracido, who attended this concert, for this information.

17. *Bohemia,* Sept. 2, 1956; *Dario de la Marina,* Aug. 26, 1956.

18. Liberace, *Liberace: An Autobiography,* 130.

19. *Bohemia,* Aug. 26, 1956.

20. Ibid., September 2, 1956.

21. Personal interview with Carmen Regalado, who, after four decades and a country change, still glowed in recalling the events of August 1956.

22. *Bohemia,* Aug. 26, 1956.

23. Johnson, *Liberace: A Collecting Guide,* 41.

24. Perhaps he had a fling with the comic, too. This red-haired, vivacious, sometime lover of Laurence Olivier had some sort of special relation with the piano player, as a singular photograph of the two of them preserved at the Liberace Museum suggests. As with his veiled remarks about the "gay" New York club, Spivy's Roof, his singling out Kaye at all and remarking about his "doing all the things he does so well" hints that their association may have been more than just professional.

25. Liberace, *Liberace: An Autobiography,* 119–21.

26. Ibid., 22.

27. "Liberace with Brother Received by Pope," *New York Times,* Nov. 3, 1956.

28. Liberace, *Liberace: An Autobiography,* 214.

29. Ibid., 24.

30. Ibid., 25, 224.

31. Ibid., 26; also 25.

32. Ibid., 225.

33. Art Buchwald, "Liberace Abroad," *Los Angeles Times,* Oct. 12, 1956.

34. Liberace, *Liberace: An Autobiography,* 30–32.

35. "Open House for Fans," n.d., Liberace File #9, Milwaukee Public Library.

36. Liberace, *Liberace: An Autobiography,* 29.

37. Quoted in Faris, *Bio-Bibliography,* 57.

38. Ibid., 56.

39. *New York Times,* Oct. 3, 1956, quoted in Faris, *Bio-Bibliography,* 57.

40. Quoted in Faris, *Bio-Bibliography,* 57.

41. Ibid.

42. Liberace, *Liberace: An Autobiography,* 209.

43. Ibid., 32–33.

44. Ibid., 222, 224, 226, 234.

45. Quoted in Thomas, *Liberace,* 121–22.

46. Buchwald, "Liberace Abroad."

47. Johnson, *Liberace: A Collecting Guide,* passim.

48. Thomas, *Liberace,* 153.

49. "What Happened to Liberace?"

50. William Leonard, "Liberace Will Rise Again!" *Chicago Sunday Tribune Magazine,* June 25, 1961, quoted in Faris, *Bio-Bibliography,* 200.

51. *Gabbe, Lutz, Heller and Loeb v Liberace.*

52. "What happened to Liberace?"

53. Ibid.

54. Liberace, *Liberace: An Autobiography,* 185–89.

55. Ibid., 189, 190.

56. Ibid., 188, 190.

57. Ibid., 192, 193.

58. See below, chapter 14, for Liberace's connection to the self-help book, *The Magic of Believing,* and the connection of its author, Claude Bristol, to these very currents in American popular thought. Perhaps not incidentally, Liberace seems to have discovered Bristol about this time. He wrote an introduction to the 1955 edition, and in 1958, the same year as the Australian tour, released a promotional record—on the same disc as "Cuba Liberace"—named after the title of Bristol's book. See Johnson, *Liberace: A Collecting Guide,* 41.

59. Thorson, *Behind the Candelabra,* 162.

60. The film *Truth or Dare* memorializes an almost identical defense offered by the performer Madonna when the Italian government censored her show as pornographic. The church, in this case, was the villain. Her defense of her "constitutional rights"—on the Via Appia—echoes every element of Liberace's argument in Sydney. It is worth noting here, that of the various performers who have been most often been compared to Liberace—Madonna, Boy George, Michael Jackson, and, most critically, Elton John—Madonna actually comes closest to Liberace's full genius, which hinged on promotion as much as on talent. As much as he, she has mastered the art of imagery and audience appeal. Her play with sexual roles, too, and her integration of gender and sexuality into the fabric of her persona and performance, match Liberace's, so too does her self-conscious projection and use of glamour. Her energy and ambition are as indefatigable as his. Their common immigrant Italian backgrounds offer still another basis of comparison.

61. "Liberace in Court," *New York Times,* Mar. 8, 1957. See also *New York Times,* Mar. 8, 9, 14, 1958.

62. *Gabbe, Lutz, Heller and Loeb v Liberace.*

63. See Faris, *Bio-Bibliography,* 241.

64. *International Artists v Commissioner of Internal Revenue.*

65. "Liberace and George 'Dig' Local Ground Breaking Ceremonies," *Las Vegas Review-Journal,* June 23, 1957.

66. See, for example, Thomas, *Liberace,* 82–83; 92; 108–9.

67. *Gabbe, Lutz, Heller and Loeb v Liberace.*

68. Liberace, *Liberace: An Autobiography,* 104.

69. See *Gabbe, Lutz, Heller and Loeb v Liberace.*

70. "What happened to Liberace?"

71. Fleming and Fleming, *First Time,* 143.

72. *International Artists v Commissioner of Internal Revenue.*

73. "When It Comes to Glamour," June 30, 1969, Liberace File #19, Milwaukee Public Library.

74. "Liberace Puts Punchline First," n.d., Liberace File #16, Milwaukee Public Library.

75. *Variety*, July 16, 1958, quoted in Faris, *Bio-Bibliography*, 65.

76. *Variety*, Aug. 13, 1958, quoted in Faris, *Bio-Bibliography*, 65.

77. Leonard, "Liberace Will Rise Again!" quoted in Faris, *Bio-Bibliography*, 200.

78. *The Complete Encyclopedia*, 562.

79. Liberace, *Liberace: An Autobiography*, 104–5.

80. Ibid., 153.

81. *Variety*, Oct. 15, 1958, quoted in Faris, *Bio-Bibliography*. 17.

82. Liberace, *Liberace: An Autobiography*, 153.

83. Ibid., 155.

84. Ibid., 104–5.

85. Ibid., 105.

86. James R. Gaines, "Liberace," *People*, Oct. 1, 1982.

87. "Silent George Comes to Town and Gives All of the Latest Facts on the Liberaces," June 7, 1955, Liberace File #18, Milwaukee Public Library.

88. "Liberace Coming Home," Mar. 29, 1951, Liberace File #2, Milwaukee Public Library.

89. Thomas, *Liberace*, 29. also, Milwaukee City Directories, *passim*. 1918–49. Scott Thorson also quotes information he gleaned from the *Globe* that alleges that "Frances began sharing her home with Casadonte shortly after Salvatore moved out," which is possible, and that "she lived as Casadonte's common-law wife for sixteen years," which is impossible: *Behind the Candelabra*, 9.

90. Liberace, *Liberace: An Autobiography*, 272–73.

91. Ibid., 274.

92. Thorson, *Behind the Candelabra*, 170.

93. Liberace, *Liberace: An Autobiography*, 274.

94. "Silent George," Liberace File #18, June 7, 1955, Milwaukee Public Library.

95. Liberace, *Wonderful, Private World*, 44.

96. Liberace, *The Things I Love*, 181.

97. "Liberace Whips Up Music, Muffins at His Old School," n.d., and "Liberace Chooses 5 Young Pianists," n.d., both Liberace File #3, Milwaukee Public Library.

98. "Wildcat Lair Star," *Las Vegas Review-Journal*, Nov. 8, 1951, and "Thanks Liberace!" *Las Vegas Review-Journal* Nov. 11, 1951; also "Lessons from Expert," *Las Vegas Review-Journal*, Oct. 8, 1952; "Wins Contest," *Las Vegas Review-Journal*, n.d.; "Young People's Piano Contest Set by Liberace," *Las Vegas Review-Journal*, Apr. 30, 1953. See also press kit: "Pianist Makes First Appearance for Purely Teen-Age Audience" (Minneapolis).

99. Thorson, *Behind the Candelabra*, 38.

100. Thomas, *Liberace*, 96.

101. Ibid., 97.

102. See the depositions in the files, also newspaper clippings that focus on Heller: *Barr v Liberace*.

103. See for example, "Meet Liberace's Favorite Date," *TV Guide,* Nov. 13, 1954, with Rio and Liberace on the cover.

104. "Liberace Tells Marriage Plans," *Las Vegas Review-Journal,* Oct. 6, 1954.

105. Thomas, *Liberace,* 99.

106. Liberace, *Liberace: An Autobiography,* 310.

107. "Liberace Love Affair Declared 'Just Publicity,'" *Las Vegas Review-Journal,* Nov. 25, 1954.

108. See clipping in the case files, *Barr v Liberace.*

109. See the depositions in the files, also newspaper clippings that focus on Heller: *Barr v Liberace.*

110. Thomas, *Liberace,* 104.

111. Ibid.

112. Ibid., 101.

113. Liberace, *Liberace: An Autobiography,* 311–12; Liberace told his boyfriend that he actually carried on a sexual affair with the skating star, who was seven years his senior. Thorson, *Behind the Candelabra,* 42.

114. Quoted in Thomas, *Liberace,* 102.

115. *Las Vegas Review-Journal,* Oct, 6, 1950.

116. Thomas, *Liberace,* 98.

117. Liberace, (as told to Edythe Witt), "Mature Women Are Best."

118. Thorson, *Behind the Candelabra,* 38.

NINE

1. Cited in Faris, *Bio-Bibliography,* 206.

2. I have lifted these more or less at random from the July 1957 edition of the most notable of these magazines, *Hollywood Confidential,* which features the exposé of Liberace.

3. See Neal Gabler on the most notorious of the gossips: *Winchell: Gossip, Power and the Culture of Celebrity* (New York: Alfred A. Knopf, 1994).

4. "What Do Men Think of Liberace?" cited in Faris, *Bio-Bibliography,* 254.

5. Michael David, "Why is Liberace on the Pan?" *Suppressed,* Jan. 1955, cited in Faris, *Bio-Bibliography,* 186.

6. "Are Liberace's Romances for Real?" *Private Lives,* Mar. 1955. Cited in Faris, *Bio-Bibliography,* 176, 12.

7. Edna Carpenter, "Liberace Did Her Wrong!" *Whisper,* June 1955, cited in Faris, *Bio-Bibliography,* 182, 12.

8. See "Whose Torch Melted the Ice Queen?," *Rave,* Aug. 1955; Sylvia Tremaine, "This Month's Candidate for the Pit . . . Liberace: The Ham That Was Overdone," *Whisper,* June 1956; also John Cullen's much less direct "Mama's Boy in Curls," *On the QT,* Sept. 1956, and Harry Willis, "The Men in Liberace's Life," *Uncensored,* Mar. 1955. All cited in Faris, *Bio-Bibliography,* 254, 251, 185, 255.

9. Jay Collins, "Is Liberace a Man?" *Hush-Hush,* May 1957, cited in Faris, *Bio-Bibliography,* 183.

10. Kenneth Anger, *Hollywood Babylon* (New York: Dell, 1981; originally published 1975), 374. For other data about *Hollywood Confidential,* see also Ehrenstein, *Open Secret, passim.*

11. Gabler, *Winchell,* 468.

12. Anger, *Babylon*, 374.

13. Ehrenstein, *Open Secret*, 99.

14. Anger, *Babylon*, 375.

15. The circulation figures are from Anger, 375, and from *Liberace v Hollywood Confidential et al.*, Los Angeles Superior Court, May 14, 1957.

16. Ehrenstein, *Open Secret*, 99.

17. Thomas, *Liberace*, 126–27.

18. Gabler, *Winchell*, 468, 503–5.

19. Anger, *Babylon*, 377, 379–80.

20. Ehrenstein, *Open Secret*, 102–3, 104.

21. Homosexual blackmail forms a separate category of pre-Stonewall gay history. It certainly constitutes one of the threads of discourse in that era. Circumstantial data suggest the fear was as critical as actual blackmail. Even so evidence also implies that blackmailing is a semiofficial function of government and the social order in these decades.

22. Ehrenstein, *Open Secret*, 20.

23. This value persists. It is not unlikely that Liberace had hundreds of sexual partners, some of whom passed more than a night with him. Of these, no more than two have come forward to publish their revelations. In the process of researching this book, I have turned up, almost incidentally, a few more men who admitted to having gone to bed with the showman. When pressed, one refused to speak for the record with a name; the other insisted that the veil of silence had to fall across what actually transpired between the two.

24. Ehrenstein, *Open Secret*, 50–51.

25. Rictor Norton, *The Myth of the Modern Homosexual: Queer History and the Search for Cultural Unity* (London: Cassell, 1997), passim.

26. Edmund White's autobiographical novel, *The Beautiful Room Is Empty*, depicts the protagonist, otherwise described as a middle-class professional, taking a turn at prostitution virtually for the hell of it. Just so, my friend Howard Kaminsky has described an academic associate, not unknown in his field, who spent at least part of his sabbatical taking money for sex in San Francisco in the late sixties or early seventies.

27. See Sedgwick, *Epistemology of the Closet.*

28. This form of sexual activity also suggests peculiarities of male-male desire. If the object of male heterosexuality is the penile penetration of a vagina, satisfaction in homoerotic activity is much more varied. While anal intercourse remains a standard conclusion, it is very far from a universal norm. Indeed, anecdotal evidence suggests the great majority of *actual* homosexual acts centers on mutual masturbation or even on one partner gratifying himself, without achieving his own orgasm, by bringing off his mate or by watching his comrade get off. In this regard, homosexuality offers a model of full equal partners rather than one in which there is an antagonistic polarity and "otherness," as is the case with heterosexual coupling.

29. For an old and somewhat ideological but still useful account of public sex, see Laud Humphreys, *Tearoom Trade: Impersonal Sex in Public Places* (Chicago: Aldine, 1975; originally published 1970). This manifestation of homosexuality has engendered considerable debate even within the gay community in the late twentieth century. One category advocates public sex as a manifestation of true Gay

Liberation, asserting that it is an almost essential form of male sexuality. Another group disdains it as a perversion foisted on homosexual men by a repressive social order. Still another tends to dismiss the practice altogether as a fabrication of a "homophobic" mainstream; normal gay men, this position maintains, do not indulge in this form of sexuality, and where it exists at all it is practiced by maladjusted, closeted men locked into unsatisfying marriages. A fourth category, which is less political and less ideological than the others, appears in such works of art as Edmund White's autobiographical novels, *A Boy's Own Story* and *The Beautiful Room,* where anonymous public sex is practiced as a kind of natural, thoughtless, and even reflexive norm.

30. Only his arrest a few years ago in a Virginia Key park in Miami elicited one man's identity as one of the most important dramatists in America. When I began working on this book, the American airwaves crackled with stories of the British pop singer George Michael being arrested for "indecent exposure" in a park loo in Beverly Hills. Taking their cues from this episode, numerous talk shows and newspapers have run exposés on public homosex since then. It seems abundantly clear that this sort of sex is hardly an aberration.

31. See the journalist Earl Wilson's thinly veiled references to the movie star in the summer of 1953, quoted in Ehrenstein, *Open Secret,* 13–14; Ehrenstein's treatment of Hudson is otherwise useful, too, in understanding the circumstances of gay celebrities.

32. Ehrenstein, *Open Secret,* 104.

33. Rock Hudson and Sara Davidson, *Rock Hudson: His Story* (New York: William Morrow, 1986), 49.

34. Hudson and Davidson, *Rock Hudson,* 49. David Ehrenstein (*Open Secret,* 100) believes that "a formal blackmail payment would be the only logical explanation for [*Confidential*] holding back on Hudson."

35. Carl David, quoted in Hadleigh, *Hollywood Gays,* 149.

36. *Hollywood Confidential* 5, no. 3 (July 1957). This copy exists in *Liberace v Hollywood Confidential et al.,* Los Angeles Superior Court, May 14, 1957.

37. Thomas, *Liberace,* 127–28.

38. See Faris, *Bio-Bibliography,* 61; "Liberace to Sue Magazine for 20 Million," *Los Angeles Times,* May 8, 1957.

39. *Liberace v Hollywood Confidential, et al.*

40. Anger, *Babylon,* 380.

41. Quoted in Gabler, *Winchell,* 504.

42. Gabler, *Winchell,* 504.

43. Anger, *Babylon,* 381–83; *New York Times,* "M O'Hara drops '57 $1-million libel suit," July 2, 1958; "E Flynn '55 suit settled," July 9, 1958; "Liberace settles libel suit against Confidential for $40,000," July 16, 1958. Also Thomas, *Liberace,* 129.

44. Liberace, *Liberace: An Autobiography,* 201, 202.

45. Ibid., 204, 213; *New York Times,* June 9, 1959.

46. Liberace, *Liberace: An Autobiography,* 202.

47. Thomas, *Liberace,* 131.

48. Liberace, *Liberace: An Autobiography,* 203.

49. Ibid., 204–5.

50. Ibid., 228.

51. Ibid., 216.

52. Ibid., 201.

53. Ibid., 217.

54. For the association of homosexuality and aristocratic foppery in contrast to masculinity and bourgeois energy, see Thomas A. King, "Performing 'Akimbo': Queer Pride and Epistemological Prejudice," in Meyer, ed., *The Politics and Poetics of Camp.* In keeping with this linkage, "ineffectual" provided a kind of code word for "homosexual" well into the twentieth century. "Effete" served as exactly the same code word.

55. The sexual over against the social definitions of maleness (or for that matter, femaleness) in particular, and gender in general, constitutes perhaps the central issue of the debate over gender roles in contemporary society, but especially in academic controversies. Inspired formally by such scholars as Michel Foucault, the dominant school of thought collapses hard, natural distinctions between male and female, gay and straight, public and private; nature requires no social roles or formal behavior, it maintains. Thus the right to work, to demand public authority, and to expect subordination is no manly right at all. It is no masculine prerogative, in the first place, but might apply to women as well as to men. In the second, and more fundamental place, it is hardly the right of any person to make such natural claims over another in this system of thought: far from a right, it is actually a wrong. See, for example, the writing of the academic philosopher Judith Butler, the literary critic Eve Kosofsky Sedgwick, the classicist David Halperin, the political philosopher Morris Kaplan, and the historian Jonathan Ned Katz for manifestations of such values in a variety of scholarly disciplines. This approach does not go unchallenged. Criticism against Judith Butler, for example, summarizes objections from a Marxist, materialist, or more formal political left position to this entire system: see, for example, Martha C. Nussbaum, "Professor of Parody: The Hip Defeatism of Judith Butler," *The New Republic,* Feb. 22, 1999, 37–45. Nussbaum develops her argument against the latent nihilism that obviates progress and political activism or even morality within the Foucaultian matrix. This left-oriented criticism is developed still more generally in Paul R. Gross and Norman Levitt, *Higher Superstition: The Academic Left and Its Quarrels with Science* (Baltimore, Md.: Johns Hopkins University Press, 1994).

If without much academic legitimacy, a third position challenges the premise of both others in maintaining the legitimacy or naturalness of sexual roles and gender-linked social behavior. Rictor Norton offers the most aggressive defense of this position—and the most aggressive attack against the constructionists—in his recently published *Myth of the Modern Homosexual.* This position is not without its difficulties. As with the more problematical version of the stance in the work of Frank Browning, especially his *Culture of Desire,* it supposes a kind of tribal, anthropological identity among gays and lesbians; as with Norton's text, it makes historical continuity the source of cultural authenticity and integrity. Its politics, most broadly defined, suggest simply the normalization of homosexuality, as, indeed, something like a third sex, a tactic assumed by the earliest mid-nineteenth-century sexual reformers, for example. A variation on this position appears with later sexual reformers, among them Harry Hay, one of the founders of the Mattachine Society, a 1950s organization that advanced this agenda politically by advocating the decriminalization of homosexual activity.

Each of these positions has its own liabilities and inconsistencies. Liberace's position possessed still greater drawbacks; nevertheless, they are not without their instructional quality. By taking the most aggressive attitude of identifying masculinity with the public performance of males in the workplace, he radically circumscribed his own sexual freedom. He resolved this problem, at least practically, by falling back on the rigid distinctions between public and private: see above.

56. Thomas, *Liberace,* 139.

57. Fleming and Fleming, *First Time,* 142. Although I had read this passage a score of times, it took student inquiries in my colleague Mitchell Hart's graduate seminar in autobiography to point out the double meaning of top/bottom in this revelation. The usage is interesting. In effect, Liberace defends his economic manhood in terms of being a top or on top. He was a man, he was ambitious and hard working; he was not a woman, he was not passive, he was not a bottom. This usage also raises other issues in homosexuality and gender relations, notably the old assumption that only receptive partners in male-male sex are the deviants, because they play a "passive" or a "woman's role."

58. Hadleigh, *Hollywood Gays,* 201.

59. Hudson and Davidson, *Rock Hudson,* 42.

60. Ibid., 49.

61. Gavin Lambert, *On Cukor* (New York: G. P. Putnam's Sons, 1972), quoted in Ehrenstein, *Open Secret,* 15.

62. Hudson and Davidson, *Rock Hudson,* 33.

63. "The Liberace Show," *Time,* June 22, 1959, quoted in Faris, *Bio-Bibliography,* 217.

64. Liberace, *Liberace: An Autobiography,* 233.

65. Ehrenstein, *Open Secret,* 118–19, 120. Kevin Kopelson's *Beethoven's Kiss* confirms the same position, even to the point of assenting, as Ehrenstein does, to "Cassandra's" polemic, too. Where Kopelson, however, admits to a potential connection between his distaste for the performer, snobbery, and even his own latent homophobia (see the epilogue of this book), Ehrenstein argues from assumptions of the objective truth of his position. His position is otherwise clear, however, in his references to Liberace's "modest pianistic ability," "turning performances of classical music into a form of parlor trick," and reaping a "publicity bonanza" from the trial.

As should be apparent from the text, my own understanding of the Cassandra affair and trial is rather more complicated. During the early stages of this study, more than once, I could have echoed Kevin Kopelson's expressions of ambiguity on reading Cassandra's diatribe. The piece was profoundly discomforting from both a sexual as well as cultural position. Here was the question: Was Cassandra merely dealing with matters of taste, as Ehrenstein insists, or was William Conner's diatribe governed by homophobia? It is more involved yet. What is the nature of homophobia itself? Was it homosexuality that offended, or rather the performer's queeniness? The issue still reverberates through even contemporary discussions of homosexuality: What is homosexuality's error? Is it indulging in same sex practices, or bending social definitions of gender? Is a queer Jack Armstrong passable, a flitty—and chaste?—Richard Simmons not? If such matters are not complicated enough in themselves, class issues tangle the question more. As George Chauncey and Rictor Norton have argued, the "fairy" or swishing queen appears usually from a lower- or working-class background (one might add the aristocracy as well), while the bourgeoisie, both gay and straight, has tended to repudiate this form of sexuality or gender play for a stricter definition of masculinity. Nor do the complications stop here. Insofar as the United States is the bourgeois nation par excellence, being "American" or a "good American" affects— and even confounds—these sexual issues. Are the working-class Italian boys looking for tricks in Bryant Park, with their plucked eyebrows and swishy mannerisms—as Chauncey describes them, good Americans?

Such issues as these have, at least in part, inspired this book. In contrast to the dismissal of Liberace characteristic of fifties critics like Howard Taubman and William Conner or modern ones like David Ehrenstein and Boze Hadleigh, this examination approaches its subject as mediating and negotiating various and mostly conflicting loyalties and obligations in one man's life.

66. From *The Captive,* as quoted by Sedgwick, *Epistemology of the Closet,* 67.

67. Michel Foucault, "Sexual Choice, Sexual Act," interview conducted by James O'Higgins, *Salamagundi,* fall/winter 1982–83; reprinted in *Foucault Live, Semiotext(e),* Foreign Agents series, 1989, quoted in Ehrenstein, *Open Secret,* 118. In treating this episode, while giving with one hand, David Ehrenstein takes back with the other. Offering the Foucault quotation, he immediately judges that it applies only to the lowly or talented, not to "a highly paid and well-connected showbusiness figure . . . [of] modest pianistic ability. . . ." Thus, he also exempts George Cukor and other gay actors from the condemnation of leading double lives, if not actually lying under oath about their affection for other men.

68. See Kaplan, *Sexual Justice.* Additional problems with male-male sex arise given the peculiar circumstances of homosexual activity. As described by much of the literature, much of gay sex transpires *outside* the traditionally defined privacy of the home, in "public," in effect. While some sexual reformers argue for the anomalousness of such "violation" of public space as a function of heterosexual oppression that would deny "home" and "domesticity" to gays, others see it as a natural outgrowth of normal male libidinousness, and especially of homosexual male lustiness. By this measure, the state's effort to police such sexuality is just as oppressive as law officers' entry into private homes. Contradictions pervade both positions.

69. The modern tendency to sexualize public discourse has a paradoxical antithesis as well. Thus, the leading proponents of radical academic discourse on sexuality have virtually eliminated sensuality, passion, sexuality, or even feeling from their writing. Sexuality in most of their treatises is so abstract, that, as Leo Bersani, one of their critics, has noted, it is difficult to imagine that a core of gay identity might actually reside in one man's delight in another man's penis: Leo Bersani, *Homos* (Cambridge, Mass.: Harvard University Press, 1995). Rictor Norton's criticism of the deconstructionists and other adherents of Foucault resembles Bersani's.

70. See Kaplan, *Sexual Justice.* Kaplan, a scholar-activist, defends the latter position and advocates the radical restructuring of social, economic, and sexual order in contemporary society, but he also offers a clear and important analysis/overview of the categories of the discussion, with particular relevance to homosexuality.

71. In still another manifestation of the peculiarities of public and private, Liberace himself trumpeted over and over, especially in his last book, *The Wonderful, Private World of Liberace,* that he was indeed revealing the most private parts of his biography. If he took readers into his bath and sleeping chambers, however, he created, one more time, a public fiction called Privacy. The paradox borders on the grotesque. While not ideologically driven, it is, as John Waters has indicated, more than mere hypocrisy as well—even though that motive is hardly absent from *The Wonderful, Private World.* Waters calls this last book "over the top Americanism," a fabrication so fabulous it becomes credible.

72. Ehrenstein, *Open Secret,* 101.

73. *New York Times,* June 9, 1959.

74. "Networks Shadowboxed with 'Homo' in Reporting Liberace's Libel Action," *Variety,* June 24, 1959.

75. Thomas, *Liberace,* 95.

76. "FBI's Files Offer Quirky Treasures," *Chicago Tribune,* Nov. 24, 1984, quoted in Faris, *Bio-Bibliography,* 190.

77. Thorson, *Behind the Candelabra,* 38.

78. Ibid., 33.

79. Ibid., 33, 39.

80. Ehrenstein, *Open Secret,* 122; for an earlier, published version of the encounter without names, see Rechy, *Sexual Outlaw,* 87–88.

81. Thorson, *Behind the Candelabra,* 38–39.

82. Chuck Conconi, "Personalities," *The Washington Post,* Feb. 6, 1987.

83. Hadleigh, *Hollywood Gays,* 146–47.

84. Ibid., 146.

85. Quoted in Hadleigh, *Hollywood Gays,* 147. See also Hudson and Davidson, *Rock Hudson,* passim; and the quotations from Marc Christian, Hudson's former lover, in Alan Brabam Smith, "Storm over Author's Claim Linking Liberace & Rock Hudson," *National Enquirer,* Mar. 4, 1987.

86. Quoted in Hadleigh, *Hollywood Gays,* 147. See also Hudson and Davidson, *Rock Hudson,* passim.

87. See, generally, Davidson and Hudson, *Rock Hudson.*

88. Rechy, *Sexual Outlaw,* 87. See also the Rechy interview in Ehrenstein, *Open Secret,* 73.

89. Ibid.

90. Hadleigh, *Hollywood Gays,* 146.

91. Ehrenstein, *Open Secret,* 73.

92. "Liberace and George Split," *Las Vegas Review-Journal,* Dec. 3, 1957.

93. *International Artists v Commissioner of Internal Revenue.*

94. Johnson, *Liberace: A Collecting Guide,* 16.

95. "Liberace Family Unity Broken by Dissention," *Hollywood Citizen-News,* Oct. 23, 1958.

96. Faris, *Bio-Bibliography,* 10.

97. Thorson, *Behind the Candelabra,* 78.

98. "Liberace Family Unity."

99. Thorson, *Behind the Candelabra,* 32, 33.

100. Ray Mungo's *Palm Springs Babylon: Sizzling Stories from the Desert*

Playground of Stars (New York: St. Martin's, 1993) promises more than it delivers. Although devoting a chapter to Liberace, it adds little to Thorson's account, upon which it seems chiefly based.

101. Bob Colacello, "Palm Springs Weekend," *Vanity Fair,* June 1999, 211.

102. Ibid., 192.

103. Ehrenstein, *Open Secret,* 53.

104. Here again, the dates are unclear. Mungo offers 1952 as the year the showman first appeared here; if Goldstone indeed introduced him to the Springs, however, it was probably not before their association, which began in the early winter of 1953.

105. Thomas, *Liberace,* 150.

106. See information in Liberace Museum.

107. Stefan Hemming, interview with the author.

108. See *The Liberace Legend,* n.d., n.p. (ca. 1968), the program brochure of Liberace's concerts.

109. Liberace, *Liberace: An Autobiography,* 267.

110. Mungo, *Palm Springs Babylon,* 120.

111. Stefan Hemming interview.

112. See the same episode in *Sexual Outlaw,* 87, with names attached in Ehrenstein, *Open Secret,* 122.

113. Rechy, *Sexual Outlaw,* 89.

114. "Liberace's Desperate Battle with AIDS," *National Enquirer,* Feb. 10, 1987.

115. James Robert Parish, *Gays and Lesbians in Mainstream Cinema: Plots, Critiques, Casts and Credits for 272 Theatrical and Made-for-Television Hollywood Releases* (Jefferson, N.C.: McFarland, 1992), 123.

116. Thomas, *Liberace,* 151, allows this same interpretation of events, but he fictionalizes the affair and fabricates a conversation between the two brothers, including George's criticism of Lee "hanging out in The Springs with a bunch of faggots."

TEN

1. *The Jack Paar Show,* New York. T82:0144, Museum of Broadcast History.

2. "Liberace Condition Good," n.d., Liberace File #12, Milwaukee Public Library.

3. Liberace, *Liberace: An Autobiography,* 304, 305, 306.

4. Ibid., 306.

5. "Reviewing His Life over the Years," July 23, 1982, Liberace File #37, Milwaukee Public Library.

6. "Liberace Puts Punchline First," n.d., Liberace File #16, Milwaukee Public Library.

7. The *New York Times*—and its index, of course—offers a neat gauge of status in the United States insofar as having a name in New York is tantamount to being a national figure. After the Cassandra trial, then, Liberace virtually vanishes from the pages of the great "newspaper of record." Between 1959 and 1982, he appears only four times. As another judge of his changing status afterward, his name becomes a regular item after 1981.

8. "But Where's Rock and Roll?" n.d., Liberace File #11, Milwaukee Public Library.

9. Liberace Puts Punchline First," n.d., Liberace File #16, Milwaukee Public Library.

10. "Liberace Candles Light Up Big Season," Sept. 24, 1961, Liberace File #12, Milwaukee Public Library.

11. "Liberace Concert Slated on Sept. 27 at Oriental," n.d., Liberace File #12, Milwaukee Public Library.

12. Jane Heylmun Roberson, interview with author.

13. *Variety,* Mar. 20, 1957, quoted in Faris, *Bio-Bibliography,* 60.

14. *Variety,* Sept. 9, 1959, quoted in Faris, *Bio-Bibliography,* 72.

15. *Variety,* June 29, 1960, quoted in Faris, *Bio-Bibliography,* 69.

16. *Variety,* Mar. 21, 1962, quoted in Faris, *Bio-Bibliography,* 72.

17. N.t., n.d., Liberace File #16, Milwaukee Public Library.

18. *Heller v Liberace,* Los Angeles Superior Court.

19. Liberace, *Liberace: An Autobiography,* 105.

20. *The Jack Paar Show,* "The Final Program," T80:0074, Museum of Broadcast History.

21. Faris, *Bio-Bibliography,* 112. Although he offers no substantiation, in *Liberace,* Bob Thomas maintains that Liberace offended the TV host, who vowed he would not invite him back.

22. *The Ed Sullivan Show,* Dec. 16, 1962, Museum of Television and Radio, Los Angeles, California.

23. In his autobiography, Liberace himself does not seem exactly clear about what to make of the movie or his part in it. Unable to acknowledge its campy queerness, the source of the movie's endearing charm (and of his own part), he apologizes for its "raunchiness"—which he also concedes wasn't very raunchy. Oddly, he uses the movie to defend artistic integrity against censors and to criticize "nudity, pornographic explicitness, and violence" in contemporary films as one explanation of why he doesn't make movies. His treatment offers a fairly typical version of his sincerity, playing to his audience, and self-serving explanations that often characterize the "morals" of his narratives. The explanation caters to his audiences even as it provides evidence of the showman's propensity for providing self-serving justifications of his career. See *Liberace: An Autobiography,* 117–19.

24. Quoted in Hadleigh, *Hollywood Gays,* 142. Liberace sets Hadleigh frothing. He introduces the showman with the movie, and develops on the first page the objections that dominate his treatment: the showman as a sissy, contradictory liar.

25. Johnson, Liberace: A *Collecting Guide,* passim.

26. *International Artists v Commissioner of Internal Revenue.*

27. He released his first album, *Mr. Showmanship,* using the name in 1963 on the Dot Label, and subsequent albums and tapes followed regularly for almost twenty years. He institutionalized the identity. While its invention is interesting for itself, even more extraordinary—and suggestive, too—was Liberace's power to impose its usage on critics, commentators, and reviewers. Whether they loved him or loathed him, journalists, almost to a person, quickly fell into rank. This

offers another manifestation of what that earliest of Milwaukee newspapermen referred to as Liberace's public-relations genius.

28. Liberace, *Liberace: An Autobiography*, 159.

29. See Faris, *Bio-Bibliography*, 243.

30. Liberace, *Liberace: An Autobiography*, 261.

31. Ibid.

32. *International Artists v Commissioner of Internal Revenue.*

33. Liberace, *Liberace: An Autobiography*, 261.

34. *International Artists v Commissioner of Internal Revenue;* also Liberace, *Liberace: An Autobiography*, 261.

35. Liberace, *Liberace: An Autobiography*, 262.

36. Ibid., 262, 263.

37. See "Disputes IRS in US Tax Court," *New York Times,* Apr. 16, 1968. Also, *International Artists v Commissioner of Internal Revenue.*

38. See "Court Allows Him Tax Deduction," *New York Times,* Nov. 1, 1970.

39. *International Artists v Commissioner of Internal Revenue.*

40. *Barr v Liberace.*

41. Liberace, *Liberace: An Autobiography*, 105.

42. Eugene Moehring, *Resort City in the Sunbelt: Las Vegas, 1930–1970.* (Reno: University of Nevada Press, 1989), 42.

43. Moehring, *Resort City,* 43–44, and Donn Knepp, *Las Vegas: The Entertainment Capital* (Menlo Park, Calif.: Lane, 1987), 34–35.

44. Moehring, *Resort City,* 45–46; Knepp, *Las Vegas,* 38–39.

45. Knepp, *Las Vegas,* 35, 43.

46. Liberace, *Liberace: An Autobiography*, 172–73; also *Las Vegas Review-Journal,* Nov. 23, and 27, 1944; and "Piano Virtuoso Is Big Hit," *Las Vegas Review-Journal,* Nov. 25, 1944.

47. Liberace, *Liberace: An Autobiography*, 173. Here, again, the performer simultaneously overplays and underplays his achievements. He was nowhere near the category of Sophie Tucker at this time, despite the references that would tend to put him there. If this reflects his vanity and ambition, his statement about being underpaid, even at $700 a week, suggests that he often felt that he was not being adequately compensated. Thus, while he identifies himself with superstars on the one hand, he downplays his compensation on the other. The response permeated his sense of himself, and even entered into his act: he was Mr. Everyman boasting of his riches; Mr. Showmanship mocking his own celebrity.

48. For the bill, see the casino's advertisements in the *Las Vegas Review-Journal,* Nov. 23, 1944.

49. Liberace, *Liberace: An Autobiography*, 174–75.

50. In 1944, this was an enormous amount of money, and the sum is all the more impressive, considering that this was only one gig of many. It is not unlikely, of course, that Liberace parlayed this figure to up his salary for other engagements, as well, just as he had done in that notable letter he wrote to Max Pollack of Milwaukee's Plankton Arcade Red Room. It is worth noting that in his autobiography, however, he was still poor-mouthing his economic status, despite the fact that his yearly income had reached perhaps fifteen thousand dollars, which

probably put him in the top 10 percent of all American households in terms of earnings.

51. "Piano Virtuoso Is Big Hit," *Las Vegas Review-Journal,* Nov. 25, 1944. For the shift in advertising, see the local newspaper for Nov. 25, 1944, and Nov. 27, 1944, when he assumed top billing.

52. "All Time High Is Reached in Frontier Show"; also "Classical Pianist Heads New Show," Mar. 28, 1947, and "Piano Artist Delights All At Frontier," Mar. 31, 1947.

53. Knepp, *Las Vegas,* 44–45, also Moehring, *Resort City,* 49.

54. Liberace, *Liberace: An Autobiography,* 175–76.

55. "Piano Artist Delights All At Frontier."

56. Moehring, *Resort City,* 46–47.

57. Ibid., 78.

58. "Riviera's Premiere Stars Liberace," *Las Vegas Review-Journal,* Apr. 21, 1955.

59. Ibid.

60. Thomas, *Liberace,* 106–7; see also Liberace, *Liberace: An Autobiography,* 177.

61. Moehring, *Resort City,* 47; Knepp, *Las Vegas,* 112–13, 176–77.

62. "Fresh Flowers from Friend Elvis," n.d., Liberace File #83, Milwaukee Public Library.

63. Knepp, *Las Vegas,* 66; Thomas, *Liberace,* 117.

64. "Fresh Flowers from Friend Elvis," n.d., Liberace File #83, Milwaukee Public Library.

65. Thomas, *Liberace,* 116.

66. See Faris, *Bio-Bibliography,* 73.

67. I am indebted to my friend Alberto Bueno for this insight. The mob's loss of control of Las Vegas, coupled with sociological changes within America after the early eighties, has changed the meaning of the gambling center for American culture in yet other ways. Las Vegas has shifted its focus to families and even children in the last twenty years, so that the relationship between Disneyland and Las Vegas has become closer still.

68. Knepp, *Las Vegas,* 132.

69. *Variety,* Nov. 11, 1977, quoted in Faris, *Bio-Bibliography,* 79.

70. *Variety,* Nov. 11, 1978, quoted in Faris, *Bio-Bibliography,* 80.

71. See chapter 4, for example.

72. Liberace, *Liberace: An Autobiography,* 182, 289–90.

73. Thomas, *Liberace,* 212–14; "Sequin Expert Keeps Liberace in Stitches," July 3, 1977, Liberace File #28, Milwaukee Public Library.

74. Knepp, *Las Vegas,* 132.

75. "Pianist's Garb Dazzles Fans," July 3, 1975, Liberace File #26, Milwaukee Public Library.

76. "Still Some Skill Behind the Glitter," Aug. 2, 1978, Liberace File #34, Milwaukee Public Library.

77. N.t. ,n.d., Liberace File #21, Milwaukee Public Library.

78. "Whatever It Was, It Was All Liberace," Aug. 9, 1977, Liberace File #30, Milwaukee Public Library.

79. Liberace, *Liberace: An Autobiography,* 178–79; 179–81.

80. Ibid., 178–79; 180. Thomas, *Liberace,* 162–64.

81. *Variety,* July 10, 1963, quoted in Faris, *Bio-Bibliography,* 73.

82. *Variety,* June 27, 1964, quoted in Faris, *Bio-Bibliography,* 74.

ELEVEN

1. Paglia, *Sexual Personae,* offers a thorough discussion of visual perception, sensuality, art, aesthetics, and beauty. I am indebted to her insights.

2. Bersani, *Homos,* emphasizes the centrality of seeing in homoerotic culture throughout his work.

3. Marcel Proust, *Cities of the Plain,* in *Remembrance of Things Past,* tr. C. K. Scott-Moncrieff and Terence Kilmartin, 3 vols., (New York: Vintage, 1982), 2: 638–39.

4. Bersani, *Homos,* 134.

5. Kaiser, *Gay Metropolis,* 119.

6. Besides White's *Genet,* see also Sedgwick, *Epistemology of the Closet,* especially 212–51, for an important if sometimes obscure description of homosexual visuality; see also 131–81.

7. Bersani, *Homos,* 141.

8. Liberace, *Liberace: An Autobiography,* 157.

9. Ibid., 174.

10. Ibid., 158–59; also Thomas, *Liberace,* 78.

11. "Strain Put on Fuses at Liberace Concert," *Los Angeles Times,* Sept. 6, 1954; for quotation, see Faris, *Bio-Bibliography,* 54.

12. Quoted in Larry Kart, "Liberace, 67, Pianist Turned 'One-man Musical Circus,'" *Chicago Tribune,* Feb. 5, 1987, cited in Faris, *Bio-Bibliography,* 30.

13. *Dance Magazine,* July 1984, quoted in Faris, *Bio-Bibliography,* 85.

14. William A. Henry III, "A Synonym for Glorious Excess," *Time,* Feb. 16, 1987.

15. Randy Lewis, "From Liberace, More and More and More," *Los Angeles Times,* June 21, 1984.

16. *Billboard,* Feb. 18, 1978, quoted in Faris, *Bio-Bibliography,* 117.

17. Liberace, *Liberace: An Autobiography,* 160.

18. Ibid., 166.

19. His sympathy for blind deaf-mutes has another potential source, too, in the circumstance of the homosexual unable to speak or describe his passions to a heterosexual audience.

20. Liberace, *Liberace: An Autobiography,* 116.

21. Ibid., 156.

22. Ibid.

23. "The 'Great' Liberace."

24. Michael Segell, "It's All Wunnerful for Liberace: An Extraordinary Visit with the Gilded Cherub of American Camp," *Rolling Stone* (Oct. 1, 1981). Quoted in Faris, *Bio-Bibliography,* 247.

25. C. Carr, "Astonish Me," *Village Voice,* Oct. 28, 1986. Both Carr and Segell write out of certain horrified incredulity. With rather less horror, not to mention incredulity, and employing remarkably detached prose, the West Indian writer

V. S. Naipal has come up with a very comparable cultic analysis of the devotees of Elvis Presley. See his *A Turn South.*

26. Liberace, *Liberace: An Autobiography,* 159.

27. Leslie Bennetts, "Liberace Out to 'Top Himself' at Music Hall Show," *New York Times,* Apr. 13, 1984.

28. Patricia E. Davis, "Liberace Riding New Wave of Popularity," *Hollywood Citizen-News,* Apr. 16, 1970, quoted in Faris, *Bio-Bibliography,* 186.

29. N.t., n.d., Liberace File #68, Milwaukee Public Library.

30. Liberace, *Liberace: An Autobiography,* 155.

31. Ibid.

32. Ibid., 156–57.

33. Ibid., 157.

34. Ibid., 17.

35. Ibid., 119.

36. Bill Barol, "Wladziu Liberace, 1919–1987," *Newsweek,* Feb. 16, 1987.

37. Liberace, *Liberace: An Autobiography,* 195.

38. Jay Joslyn, "Liberace Thrills Crowd as Usual," Apr. 30, 1986, Liberace File #54, Milwaukee Public Library.

39. Hadleigh, *Hollywood Gays,* 154–55.

40. Henry, "Synonym for Glorious Excess."

41. Liberace, *Liberace: An Autobiography,* 156.

42. Bennetts, "Liberace Out to 'Top Himself.'"

43. "Liberace: His Lord High Excellency of Glitz," (reprinted from the *Washington Post*), July 24, 1985, Liberace File #47, Milwaukee Public Library.

44. Liberace, *Liberace: An Autobiography,* 155.

45. Both quotations from Green, "Liberace the Gilded Showman."

46. See Liberace, *Wonderful, Private World,* 95–105.

47. "Liberace: His Lord High Excellency," July 24, 1985, Liberace File #47, Milwaukee Public Library.

48. "Liberace's Appeal Went beyond Musicianship," Feb. 5, 1987, Liberace File #58, Milwaukee Public Library.

49. "Gifted and Glitzy, Showman Dazzled the Common Man," *Detroit News,* Feb. 5, 1987.

50. Joslyn, "Liberace Thrills Crowd," Apr. 30, 1986, Liberace File #54, Milwaukee Public Library.

51. "Musical Talent, Likeability, Make Liberace a STAR," *Las Vegas Sun,* May 27, 1979.

52. David Richards, "The Sparkling Showman," *Washington Post,* Feb. 2, 1987.

53. "Liberace: His Lord High Excellency," July 24, 1985, Liberace File #47, Milwaukee Public Library.

54. "Liberace's Appeal Went beyond Musicianship," Feb. 5, 1987, Liberace File #58, Milwaukee Public Library.

56. Richard Corliss, "The Evangelist of Kitsch," *Time* 128 (Nov. 3, 1986): 96.

55. Quoted in Ruth Ryon, "Liberace Called Tune in His Many Real Estate Ventures," *Los Angeles Times,* Nov. 29, 1987.

57. Randy Lewis, "From Liberace, More and More and More."

58. "King of Keyboard Fashion," *Maclean's,* Feb. 2, 1987.

59. *Billboard,* Apr. 27, 1985, quoted in Faris, *Bio-Bibliography,* 87.

60. "Liberace: His Lord High Excellency," Liberace File #47, Milwaukee Public Library.

61. N.t., n.d., Liberace File #32, Milwaukee Public Library.

62. N.t., n.d., Liberace File #21, Milwaukee Public Library.

63. "Liberace Plays; Tells Jokes, Too." See above, chapter 7.

64. "Critic Deplores Liberace's Musicianship," Oct. 1, 1962, Liberace File #13, Milwaukee Public Library.

65. "Liberace Glistens for Devoted Fans," Apr. 3, 1975, Liberace File #26, Milwaukee Public Library.

66. Liberace, *Liberace: An Autobiography,* 249–50.

67. Liberace, *The Things I Love,* 148.

68. Ibid., 218.

69. Thorson, *Behind the Candelabra,* 128.

70. Liberace, *The Things I Love,* 218.

71. Thorson, *Behind the Candelabra,* 128.

72. Ibid., 7.

73. Liberace, *The Things I Love,* 220.

74. Ibid., 151.

75. Liberace, *Liberace: An Autobiography,* 247.

76. Thorson, *Behind the Candelabra,* 129.

77. Liberace, *Liberace: An Autobiography,* 249.

78. Ibid., 285.

79. Ibid., 160.

80. Ibid., 157.

81. "Liberace Heading for Home," July 6, 1984, Liberace File #42, Milwaukee Public Library.

82. Liberace, *Liberace: An Autobiography,* 163.

83. "Nobody Can Hold a Candelabra to Liberace in the Mod Music Mood," Mar. 26, 1970, Liberace File #11, Milwaukee Public Library.

84. Liberace, *Liberace: An Autobiography,* 180–81.

85. Ibid., 181.

86. "Milwaukee's Liberace Still Sets Eyes Popping with His Colorful Act," Feb. 4, 1977, Liberace File #27, Milwaukee Public Library.

87. Liberace, *Liberace: An Autobiography,* 164.

88. Ibid., 11–12.

89. Ibid., 163, 119.

TWELVE

1. William Dreyer, interview with the author.

2. Jerry Lisker, New York *Daily News,* July 6, 1969.

3. Kaiser, *Gay Metropolis,* offers a good example of this process. Under the pseudonym of Donald Webster Cory, Edward Sagarin had published *The Homosexual in America: A Subjective Approach* in 1951, which Kaiser calls "the first essential document of gay liberation in the United States" (125). By the mid-sixties, gay activism was repudiating Sagarin, even as he returned the favor. Although hardly a youth in 1964, the forty-year-old Frank Kameny represented the full tilt of Judeo-Calvinist righteousness that was delegitimizing moderates as well

as conservatives. Kameny led the charge both within and without the community. Organizing public demonstrations at Independence Hall in 1965, he also relegated Sagarin to the realm of queer outer darkness: "You have fallen by the wayside," he instructed him. "You have become no longer the rigorous Father of the Homophile movement, to be revered, respected and listened to, but the senile Grandfather of the Homophile Movement, to be humored and tolerated at best; to be ignored and disregarded usually; and to be ridiculed, at worst." (Kaiser, *Gay Metropolis,* 142).

4. Only within the 1990s have these identities been seriously challenged. Among African Americans, Clarence Thomas, Thomas Sowell, and Ward Connolly defy both the internal and external hegemony of the left, while individuals like Andrew Sullivan and groups like the Log Cabin Republicans dispute the hegemony of the straight order on the one hand, and radicals' domination of homosexual politics on the other. The cartoonist Garry Trudeau captures both the post-Stonewall legitimizing of homosexuality and the contemporary—and ambivalent—relegitimizing of homosexual conservatism in one series of "Doonesbury" comic strips. Outing his character Mark, he couples this former radical leftie with a caricature of a button-downed, overweight, WASPy stockbroker type. In one strip, the lover is holding forth to Mark's father. "The way I see it, Phil," he says, "being gay is a private matter, not a political rationale for offensive public behavior. In my view, the flaunting of homosexuality is all part of a larger breakdown of an orderly society, of common decency, of civil virtue!" Dumbfounded, Phil then inquires of his son, "Is he just sucking up to me here?" Whereupon Mark responds, "No, no—He really IS a fellow Nazi!" The fictional Mark's affectionate tolerance of his boyfriend's conservatism, however, hardly characterizes the general response. Indeed, both black and homosexual challengers of the post-sixties radical orthodoxy continue to elicit the most rancorous antagonism.

5. Quoted in Kaiser, *Gay Metropolis,* 54.

6. Ibid. The issue of promiscuity in male-male sex remains an intensely debated and even political issue. In the first place, how characteristic is it of the gay community? Second, even accepting the tendency of homosexuals to have more sex than heterosexuals do, problems still remain. Thus, does the tendency represent something pathological or something natural? Can an activity be both pathological and natural? Gay Power's friends and foes alike wind up on both sides of the debate.

7. Thorson, *Behind the Candelabra,* 40, 169.

8. Hemming interview.

9. Ehrenstein, *Open Secret,* 122. For another version of the encounter, see Rechy, *Sexual Outlaw,* 87–89.

10. George Campbell, interview with the author.

11. "Frank," interview with the author. The interviewee requested anonymity.

12. "Raji," interview with the author. The interviewee requested anonymity.

13. Carl David, quoted in Hadleigh, *Hollywood Gays,* 149.

14. Thorson, *Behind the Candelabra,* 85.

15. Rechy, *Sexual Outlaw,* 88. See also Rechy's interview in Ehrenstein, *Open Secret,* 122.

16. See Thorson deposition, in *Thorson v Liberace,* Los Angeles Superior Court.

17. Ehrenstein, *Open Secret,* 122.

18. See his *City of Night* for Rechy's discussion of his conscious effort to disguise himself and the odd consequences when the mask slipped.

19. Campbell interview.

20. Thorson, *Behind the Candelabra,* 39, 40, 79, 180, 73.

21. Ibid., 180, 176.

22. Ibid.

23. Ibid., 162–63.

24. Ibid., 179.

25. Ibid.

26. Fleming and Fleming, *First Time,* 143.

27. James R. Gaines, "Liberace," *People,* Oct. 1, 1982.

28. Dates, as always, remain a problem when one attempts to reconstruct Liberace's life. Scott Thorson's chronology is often confused. Thorson met the celebrity in 1977, and he maintained that Liberace had discovered Cardell "four years earlier"—or in 1973. After Liberace's death, Cardell himself told a reporter for the *Las Vegas Review-Journal* (Feb. 6, 1987) that he had lived with Liberace for six years. That would put his initial encounter with the entertainer at around 1972. The earliest published references to the Cardell-Liberace relationship is also a little vague. Its general chronological order suggests late 1974 or early 1975 for the first meeting: See Bob Doerschuk, "Vince Cardell: Liberace's Piano Protégé,"*Contemporary Keyboard,* Jan. 1978. As Cardell had cut a record with the showman by 1975, it would seem more plausible that their relationship began around this date or perhaps a little earlier.

29. Doerschuk, "Vince Cardell: Liberace's Piano Protégé."

30. The story of the grieving chauffeur is a little odd on its own terms, but it is more curious still in that Scott Thorson, Cardell's successor as driver, was called home for his foster mother's death in 1982, and Liberace plugged Cary James into the old driver spot almost at once, even as he substituted James for Thorson in his bed.

31. Liberace deposition, *Thorson v Liberace.*

32. Thorson, *Behind the Candelabra,* 70.

33. See "Leapin' Lizards, It's Liberace!" (video LFV 2001), copyright 1978, Liberace Foundation for the Performing Arts.

34. Thorson, *Behind the Candelabra,* 69, 70.

35. Ibid., 51. "Midway through the act Lee introduced his protegee," Thorson says, "a man I will call Jerry O'Rourke." See pages 66 and 209 for the slips.

36. Ibid., 69, 64.

37. Ibid., 51.

38. See *Thorson v Liberace.*

39. See the Cardell interview after Liberace's death, *Las Vegas Review-Journal,* Feb. 6, 1987, in which he is quoted as referring to Liberace as "the inspiration for my career since childhood." The reporter also asserts that Cardell appeared with Liberace for more than five years. "I got to live in his fabulous Las Vegas house for six years. To work with him was an honor, but to have him as a friend was something I never imagined." The dates and chronology here, again, are very loose.

40. Johnson, *Liberace: A Collecting Guide,* 111. While Johnson does not cata-
logue the second album, Faris, *Bio-Bibliography,* names it on page 147.

41. Doerschuk, "Vince Cardell: Liberace's Piano Protégé."

42. "Whatever It Was, It Was All Liberace," Aug. 9, 1977, Liberace File #30,
Milwaukee Public Library.

43. See Faris, *Bio-Bibliography,* 79.

44. "Still Some Skill behind the Glitter," Aug. 2, 1978, Liberace File #34, Milwaukee Public Library.

45. Thorson speaks specifically of a "six-month" obligation, but this does not
make sense given the fact that Thorson met Liberace in August 1977. Cardell
performed with Liberace for exactly a year, not six months, after this.

46. Thorson, *Behind the Candelabra,* 69, 70.

47. Ibid., 65.

48. Ibid., 66.

49. Ibid., 69.

50. Ibid., 81–82. Inexplicably, Thorson fails to note that Cardell continued to
participate in Lee's act at least through his European tour of the spring of 1978
and on to the summer of that year.

51. See Matias Viegener, "Kinky Escapades, Bedroom Techniques, Unbridled
Passion, and Secret Sex Codes," in Bergman, ed., *Camp Grounds.*

52. The issue of homosexual marriage touches some of the deepest chords
and profoundest disagreements in homosexual and mainstream culture. Andrew
Sullivan has offered one defense for formalizing homoerotic unions in *Virtually
Normal: An Argument about Homosexuality* (New York: Knopf, 1995). He bases
his argument in human sympathy, Christian charity, and the natural and, effectively, legitimate affection between same-sex partners. Morris Kaplan's much
more formalistic, legalistic treatise, *Sexual Justice,* arrives at the same conclusion—in the process repudiating Sullivan—from the philosophical deconstruction
of the social, political order. If one is a journalist and the other an academic, their
disparities also reflect in part the differences between the Catholic Christian and
the Jewish intellectual traditions. Thus, the more traditional and churchgoing Sullivan longs, in effect, to integrate homosexuality within the larger loving family of
Christians, while Kaplan sounds the prophetic voice for a radical restructuring
of the entire social order. The redefinition of family, however, is critical for both.
One part of both arguments revolves around a tacit understanding, for example,
that childbearing and childrearing no longer drive the family. Both are tone deaf
to the significance of children in a marital or family unit. Insofar as male same-sex
couplings have nothing at all to do with children, their arguments make an effective case for homosexual unions as the model for the new marriage, the new family. While much less concerned with formalizing marriage and family, Michael
Bronski, in *The Pleasure Principle*, extends this notion of homosexual love providing the basis of a new, improved social order. He wants no institutionalization of
homoeroticism, but advocates the extension of homoerotic plasticity to all human
relations. Plastic and fluid of its nature, homoeroticism, for Bronski, provides the
perfect model for love and human relations in a plastic and fluid world.

53. Bersani, *Homos,* 5–6.

54. The king's sister-in-law herself actually referred to homosexuality as a

"horrible depravity." She noted the other term in quoting one of the court ladies who had mentioned the French noblewomen with loose morals: "When people tell Madam Cornuel what a shameless life these ladies from the Faubourge Saint-Germain lead, she says, 'Good Heavens, you mustn't blame them. They have undertaken a mission to reclaim the young men from the fashionable vice'!"

55. The issue of naming the activity or divining the relationship between names and actions initiates virtually all contemporary discussion of sex and gender. Besides Halperin, *One Hundred Years of Homosexuality* (New York: Routledge, 1989), see also, among others, Katz, *Invention of Heterosexuality* (New York: Plume, 1996); also Sedgwick, *Epistemology of the Closet*. John Boswell offers the richest history of the word "gay" in his *Christianity, Social Tolerance, and Homosexuality: Gay People in Western Europe from the Beginning of the Christian Era to the Fourteenth Century* (Chicago: University of Chicago Press, 1980); Rictor Norton's *Myth of the Modern Homosexual* is equally good. If many, like Bersani, object to the desexualization of the term "gay," Edmund White considers it a source of the term's virtue: see his collection of essays, *The Burning Library*, David Bergman, ed. (New York: Vintage International, 1995).

56. Norton, *Myth of the Modern Homosexual*. This historian takes a very hard line, not only in repudiating the abstraction and theorization of homosexuality by modern academics, chiefly, but also in insisting on the essential qualities of being queer. Thus, in this regard, he repudiates bisexuality as a category as "a fig leaf" for being gay. He does the same with "the libertine's" sexual free for all, which is only homosexuality by another name, according to him.

57. Liberace could serve as a model of a homosexual type as analyzed in Richard A. Isay, *Being Homosexual: Gay Men and Their Development* (New York: Farrar, Straus, and Giroux, 1989). His discussion of men with insatiable sexual appetites, numerous partners, and problems with peers—like Liberace, also entails his analysis of family structures that mirror, almost uncannily, the circumstances of Wally Liberace's household in West Milwaukee and West Allis. Isay repudiates the antihomosexual biases of contemporary Freudian analysis and defends homosexuality against charges of pathology and deviance. He insists that the homosexual is born, not made. At the same time, he suggests that certain homosexual practices are pathological. In this regard, he shifts his grounds somewhat to argue that homosexual promiscuity itself is not natural but is a product of social pressure rather than itself being another manifestation of natural impulses. Just so, he offers an example of health and a resolution of pathologies in long-term, "good marriage"-like homoerotic unions. Beyond this, Isay's arguments about homosexual boys and their relations with their fathers, who serve as the central icons in the sons' lives, confirms my own reading of Liberace's biography.

58. Richards, "Liberace, Laughing Last."

59. Thorson, *Behind the Candelabra*, 90.

60. Ibid., 74–75.

61. Green, "Liberace the Gilded Showman."

62. Thorson, *Behind the Candelabra*, 66. This also marks the first place in which Thorson slips, revealing that Vince Cardell is the fictitious Jerry O'Rouke.

63. Ibid., 67.

64. Rechy, *Sexual Outlaw*, 88.

65. "Still Some Skill behind the Glitter," Aug. 2, 1978, Liberace File #34, Milwaukee Public Library; also Doerschuk, "Vince Cardell: Liberace's Piano Protégé."

66. Liberace, *The Things I Love,* 184.

67. "Liberace Again Theft Victim," Apr. 24, 1975; and "Liberace Loses Gems to Burglars," Apr. 24, 1975: both Liberace File #26, Milwaukee Public Library. Also, "Liberace's $28,000 Necklace, $5,000 in Other Gems Stolen," *Los Angeles Times,* Nov. 30, 1975.

68. Peter H. King, "Liberace's Last Agony," *Los Angeles Times,* Aug. 19, 1988.

69. *Thorson v Liberace.*

70. King, "Liberace's Last Agony."

71. Thorson, *Behind the Candelabra,* 56. Also, 62, 69.

72. See Hudson and Davidson, *Rock Hudson,* passim.

73. Thorson, *Behind the Candelabra,* 62.

74. Ibid., 70.

75. Hudson and Davidson, *Rock Hudson,* is also good on the intrigue that dominated these households.

76. Patricia Towle, "Liberace Died in My Arms," *National Enquirer,* Nov. 1, 1994.

77. Calling one another by the same nickname was not unique to Thorson and Liberace. Edmund White offers fictional accounts of the same phenomenon taking place between two of his friends, first in his collection of stories, *Skinned Alive,* and then again in his novel, *The Farewell Symphony* (New York: Knopf, 1997).

78. Liberace, *Liberace: An Autobiography,* 57.

79. Ibid., 57–58. While the episode is important enough in that it introduces Liberace's relation with his father and his lovers, it also establishes in almost caricatured Freudian language what men do: play horn in the hole.

80. Beginning with a Freudian definition of character formation, Richard Isay, in *Being Homosexual,* innovates the model by arguing that a homosexual boy will attach to his father as his first love object. This new model offers peculiar insights into the traditional definition of the "distant" father among many homosexual memories. It offers the most useful model of all in understanding Liberace's troubled attachment to his own father and his sense of fatherhood as the model of lover. Edmund White's autobiographical fictions illuminate the same eroticized tension of the boy for the father.

81. Thorson, *Behind the Candelabra,* 143.

82. Ibid., 151, 153.

83. Some disparity exists between his legal testimony and Thorson's published memories of this affair. Thus for example, he insisted that he wanted a dimple in his chin, despite the absence of this feature in his mentor. It was a demonstration of his own will: "At the last minute, in a brief rebellious moment, I asserted myself enough to ask Startz [the physician] to give me a dimple in my chin—even though Lee didn't have one. After all, it was my face!" (Thorson, *Behind the Candelabra,* 152). In his deposition, he insisted, "Liberace instructed his plastic surgeon to put that in there as a—he wanted me to have a cleft in my chin." The showman instructed the surgeon, he continued, "to put a cleft in my

chin along with an insert in my chin and along with silicon injections to make my cheekbones more outstanding. Facial structure, bone structure come out more. . . ." (Thomas, *Liberace,* 229–30).

84. Thorson, *Behind the Candelabra,* 144.

85. Ibid., 154.

86. Ibid., 77.

87. Ibid., 154–55.

88. Ibid., 108.

89. Ibid., 196.

90. Ibid., 154–55.

91. See deposition, *Thorson v Liberace.* Thomas, *Liberace,* 228–29, also offers a slightly altered version of this original testimony.

THIRTEEN

1. Thorson, *Behind the Candelabra,* 90.

2. Ibid., 47–48.

3. Ibid., 48–49. In his deposition, Thorson offers a rather different chronology of his foster homes. He says he lived with his brother Wayne, then with Marie Brummet, after her with Tammy Cranwell, and finally with Rose and Joe Carracappa, before moving in with Liberace.

4. Ibid., 49.

5. Mike Snow with Wayne Johnson, "Wicked Past of the Gay Suing Liberace," *Globe,* Dec. 7, 1982.

6. Thorson, *Behind the Candelabra,* 49.

7. Ibid.

8. Thorson deposition, *Thorson v Liberace.*

9. Thorson, *Behind the Candelabra,* 49–50.

10. Thorson deposition, *Thorson v Liberace.*

11. Thorson, *Behind the Candelabra,* 50–51.

12. Ibid., 51.

13. Ibid., 59.

14. Ibid., 72.

15. See, for example, ibid., 162; also Liberace, *Liberace: An Autobiography.* passim.

16. Thorson, *Behind the Candelabra,* 88.

17. Ibid., 65.

18. Ehrenstein, *Open Secret,* 122.

19. Thorson, *Behind the Candelabra,* 77, 123.

20. Ibid., 176.

21. Ibid., 108.

22. Towle, "Liberace Died"; also King, "Liberace's Last Agony."

23. Isay, *Being Homosexual,* 89.

24. While Richard Isay, for example, is completely sympathetic to the homosexual condition, supportive of stable, long-term homosexual unions, and defensive about gay promiscuity, he also considers any homosexual union "a long-term relationship" if it lasts even a year. For all those couples that last ten, twenty, even thirty years or more, the average length of what might be inexactly termed "really long-term relations" is probably closer to five years. One observer of the gay scene

described this tendency with the witticism: "One gay year is equal to seven straight ones."

25. While he mentions the 1981 tour of the continent, with various shows in different countries, he ignores the earlier tour altogether. That is strange for various reasons, not least because his "rival," Vince Cardell, was still a part of Liberace's act at this time. Just so, Thorson ignores the domestic tours in 1978, for example, the trip to Milwaukee, where Cardell also figured centrally in the Liberace show as much as one year after Thorson became a part of Liberace's domestic ensemble.

26. Thorson, *Behind the Candelabra,* 89.

27. Ibid., 98.

28. Ibid., 88.

29. Green, "Liberace the Gilded Showman."

30. Thorson, *Behind the Candelabra,* 98–99.

31. Ibid., 123.

32. Liberace, *Wonderful, Private World,* 77–78.

33. Ibid., 73.

34. Liberace, *The Things I Love,* 184

35. Ibid., 187.

36. Liberace, *Wonderful, Private World,* 73.

37. Other men and women have shared this attitude toward animals. The Southern writer Ellen Glasgow offers another illustration of a devotion to dogs that transcends eccentricity: see Susan Goodman, *Ellen Glasgow: A Biography,* (Baltimore, Md.: Johns Hopkins University Press), 1998.

38. Thorson, *Behind the Candelabra,* 99.

39. Ibid., 88.

40. "Maid Tells What It Was REALLY Like in Private Life," *National Enquirer,* Feb. 24, 1987.

41. Green, "Liberace the Gilded Showman."

42. Thorson, *Behind the Candelabra,* 106–7.

43. Ryon, "Liberace Called Tune."

44. Ibid.

45. Thorson, *Behind the Candelabra,* 55, 57–58.

46. Ibid., 58–59. See also photographic illustrations of the house in Liberace, *Wonderful, Private World.*

47. Thorson, *Behind the Candelabra,* 123.

48. Ibid., 77.

49. *Thorson v Liberace.* Thorson consistently spelled the street name wrong, as "Larrimore" instead of "Laramore."

50. Thorson, *Behind the Candelabra,* 107. For David Schmerin's remarks, see *Thorson v Liberace.* "If you are asking me what I would have paid for them, I wouldn't have given you a thousand dollars for everything," he concluded.

51. Thorson, *Behind the Candelabra,* 107.

52. Ibid., 76.

53. Ibid., 79.

54. Ibid., 146.

55. Thorson deposition, *Thorson v Liberace.*

56. Thorson, *Behind the Candelabra,* 177.

57. Ibid., 148.

58. Ibid., 80.

59. Ibid., 85.

60. Ibid., 97.

61. Ibid., 126.

62. Quoted in Thomas, *Liberace,* 223.

63. *Thorson v Liberace.*

64. Thorson, *Behind the Candelabra,* 55.

65. *Thorson v Liberace.*

66. White, *The Burning Library,* 149.

67. Thorson, *Behind the Candelabra,* 114, 50.

68. Ibid., 183. Thorson does not identify the couple, but his general description suggests that he is referring to Vince Fronza and Ken Fosler in Palm Springs.

69. Thorson, *Candelabra,* 73.

70. Ibid., 79.

71. Ibid., 122.

72. Ibid., 79, 180, 73.

73. Ibid., 176.

74. Ibid., 163.

75. Ibid., 178.

76. Ibid., 39–40.

77. Ibid., 144, 177. He was not, of course, the first of the celebrity's lovers to suffer thus. The 1950s "lover-bodyguard" of John Rechy's memory steamed in public over his patron's flirting, too.

78. Ibid., 124.

79. Ibid., 181.

80. Ibid., 38.

81. *Thorson v Liberace.*

82. Thorson, *Behind the Candelabra,* 156, 157.

83. *Thorson v Liberace.*

84. Thorson, *Behind the Candelabra,* 147.

85. *Thorson v Liberace.*

86. Thorson deposition, *Thorson v Liberace.*

87. "Liberace Lover Is Key in Crime Probe," Milwaukee *Sentinel,* Sept. 16, 1988.

88. Thorson, *Behind the Candelabra,* 157.

89. Ibid., 157, 158.

90. Ibid., 157.

91. Thorson deposition, *Thorson v Liberace.*

92. "Liberace Lover"; "New Testimony Linking Drug Trafficker Adel (Eddie Nash) Nasrallah and Ex-employee Gregory De Witt Diles to 1981 Beating Murders in Laurel Canyon Reportedly Comes from Deceased Pianist Liberace's Then-Lover Scott Thorson," *Los Angeles Times,* Sept. 16, 1988; and "Scott Thorson Testifies against Convicted Cocaine Trafficker Adel (Eddie Nash) Nasrallah and Gregory D. Diles at Their Pretrial Hearing for the Drug-Related 1981 Murders of Four People," *Los Angeles Times,* Jan. 11, 1989.

93. "Liberace Lover."

94. *Thorson v Liberace.*

95. "New Testimony" and "Scott Thorson Testifies."

96. Thorson, *Behind the Candelabra,* 183.

97. *Thorson v Liberace.*

98. Thorson, *Behind the Candelabra,* 186.

99. *Thorson v Liberace.*

100. Thorson, *Behind the Candelabra,* 187.

101. Liberace deposition, *Thorson v Liberace.*

102. Ibid.

FOURTEEN

1. I am indebted to my student Carlos Reyes for this information, which comes from his essay, "Postwar America: Visible Trends in Literature and Society."

2. Claude M. Bristol, *The Magic of Believing* (New York: Prentice-Hall, 1955; originally published 1948), 15.

3. Bristol, *Magic,* 8.

4. Ibid., 36.

5. It is critical to note here that Bristol himself uses gender-specific language but that he opens all this self-actualization, traditionally associated with Western masculinity, to women. He devotes an entire chapter, "Women and the Science of Belief," to the subject.

6. Bristol, *Magic,* 3.

7. Liberace did not need Bristol to inform his politics, but this sense of foreboding about becoming "serfs" is just the sort of stuff that influenced the performer's pronouncements about the Communist menace when he was on his Australian tour in 1958.

8. Johnson, *Liberace: A Collecting Guide,* 41.

9. Liberace, preface to Bristol, *Magic,* viii.

10. "StarLine Sightseeing Tours, Inc.: Visit Liberace's Hollywood Museum," *Los Angeles Herald-Examiner,* Feb. 24, 1975; "Liberace's Lair, at $5.90 per Person," *Los Angeles Times,* Mar. 30, 1975; and "People," *Time,* May 24, 1975.

11. "Come Fly with Lee: It's Not Lucy but Liberace in the Sky with Diamonds," *People Weekly,* July 28, 1975; also "Liberace's Home Museum Proposal Sparks Neighbors' Promise of Suit," *Hollywood Reporter,* Oct. 21, 1976. Cited in Faris, *Bio-Bibliography,* 217.

12. "Liberace May Buy Mansion in Tosa," July 2, 1977, File #31; "Lawsuit Threatens Liberace Museum," Aug. 2, 1978, File #33; "Liberace Planning Tour of Mansion," July 30, 1978, File #32; all Milwaukee Public Library.

13. Thorson, *Behind the Candelabra,* 111.

14. "A Grand Opening for the Liberace Museum," *Los Angeles Times,* Apr. 17, 1979.

15. Thorson, *Behind the Candelabra,* 111–13.

16. "Glitter Museum," *Look,* June 11, 1979.

17. Liberace Opens Museum," June 27, 1979, File #35, Milwaukee Public Library.

18. Liberace, *The Things I Love.*

19. Liberace, as told to Carol Truax, *Liberace Cooks! Recipes from His Seven Dining Rooms* (Doubleday: Garden City, N.Y.: 1970).

20. Brochure in the possession of the author.

21. Liberace deposition, *Barr v Liberace.*

22. "Currently One of the Biggest Hits in the History of the Las Vegas Hilton," *Las Vegas Sun,* Mar. 8, 1974.

23. Liberace, *Wonderful, Private World,* 7. While this statement seems a clear and forthright reversal of his legal testimony, it is no less suspect, because he might have judged that the pronouncement would sell more copies of *Wonderful, Private World,* which he declared to be newer and better than the earlier volumes.

24. Liberace, *Liberace: An Autobiography,* 9–10.

25. Ibid., 10.

26. "By the Light of the Silvery Candelabra," *Chicago Tribune,* Nov. 25, 1973, quoted in Faris, *Bio-Bibliography,* 234.

27. Liberace deposition, *Barr v Liberace.*

28. "Currently One of the Biggest Hits."

29. Liberace, *Wonderful, Private World,* 148.

30. Ibid., 128.

31. Liberace deposition, *Barr v Liberace.*

32. Thorson, *Behind the Candelabra,* 82.

33. *Thorson v Liberace.*

34. David Schmerin deposition, *Thorson v Liberace.*

35. "Palimony Proves Elusive Pot of Gold," *Los Angeles Times,* Jan. 30, 1986.

36. Thorson, *Behind the Candelabra,* 198.

37. Schmerin deposition, *Thorson v Liberace.*

38. Thorson deposition, *Thorson v Liberace.*

39. See references in *Thorson v Liberace.*

40. Schmerin deposition, *Thorson v Liberace.*

41. Thorson deposition, *Thorson v Liberace.*

42. Thorson, *Behind the Candelabra,* 184–87, 190–95, 202.

43. *National Enquirer,* Nov. 2, 1982.

44. Ibid., Nov. 9, 1982.

45. Quoted in Thorson, *Behind the Candelabra,* 208–9.

46. Green, "Liberace the Gilded Showman."

47. *Globe,* Dec. 2, 1982. See also *Thorson v Liberace* for Summers's connection to Heller; also Thorson, *Behind the Candelabra,* 210–11.

48. "Liberace Facing Lawsuit for Libel, *Las Vegas Sun,* Oct. 31, 1984, quoted in Faris, *Bio-Bibliography,* 207–8.

49. "Palimony Claims against Liberace Tossed Out," *Los Angeles Times,* Mar. 1, 1984. In discussing this action, Thorson gets his year wrong, listing it as 1983.

50. Thorson, *Behind the Candelabra,* 214–15.

51. Ibid.

52. Ibid., 222.

53. Ibid., 222–23.

54. Ibid., 206.

55. Henry, "Synonym for Glorious Excess."

56. Sedgwick, *Epistemology of the Closet,* offers fresh insights on consumerism, commercialism, and homosexual culture, too. See 131–81.

57. Henry, "Synonym for Glorious Excess."

58. Thomas, *Liberace,* 253.

59. "Charm, Poise at Center Stage as Liberace Plays Entertainer," July 30, 1982, and "All That Glitters . . . ," July 30, 1982, both Liberace File #39, Milwaukee Public Library.

60. "Liberace Heading for Home, July 6, 1984, and "Liberace's Concert Glitter is Pure Fun," July 12, 1984, both Liberace File #42, Milwaukee Public Library; "Liberace Still Dazzles Fans after 40 Years," July 12, 1984, Liberace File #43, Milwaukee Public Library.

61. "All That Glitters . . . ," July 30, 1982, Liberace File #39, Milwaukee Public Library.

62. "Liberace's Concert Glitter," July 12, 1984, Liberace File #42, Milwaukee Public Library.

63. "Liberace Still Dazzles Fans after 40 Years," July 12, 1984, Liberace File #43, Milwaukee Public Library.

64. "Liberace: His Lord High Excellency," July 24, 1985, File #47, Milwaukee Public Library.

65. Lewis, "More and More."

66. See, for example, Margaret Thompson Drewel's discussion of the hall's history in "The Camp Trace in Corporate America: Liberace and the Rockettes at Radio City Music Hall," in Meyer, ed., *The Politics and Poetics of Camp.*

67. Thorson, *Behind the Candelabra,* 164–65.

68. Liberace, *Wonderful, Private World,* 21.

69. See Thorson, *Behind the Candelabra,* 165; and Thomas, *Liberace,* 235–36.

70. Liberace, *Wonderful, Private World,* 22.

71. Ibid., 22–23.

72. Quoted in Faris, *Bio-Bibliography,* 86.

73. Leslie Bennetts, "Liberace Out to 'Top Himself' at Music Hall Show," *New York Times,* Apr. 13, 1984.

74. Neal Karlen, "Liberace: Still a Hot Ticket," *Newsweek,* May 7, 1984.

75. William E. Geist, "About New York," *New York Times,* Apr. 3, 1985.

76. Stephen Holden, "Pop: Liberace, a Piano, Rockettes and Rolls," *New York Times,* Apr. 7, 1985.

77. Drewel, "The Camp Trace," in Meyer, ed., *The Politics and Poetics of Camp,* 160. See also Carr, "Astonish Me," for a similar response to this almost irresistible appeal as treated above, in chapter 9.

78. For a survey and summary of *Variety*'s notices, see Faris, *Bio-Bibliography,* passim. That its reviewers changed over time and that the notices were not uniformly flattering makes the general consensus about his genius even more compelling. Ray Mungo, *Liberace* (New York: Chelsea House Publishers, 1994), in this volume of the series of "lives of notable gay men and lesbians," errs significantly, then, in maintaining that Liberace received few good reviews.

79. For an another version of the conversion of the hardnosed critic at this same juncture in the performance, see Edward Rothstein's *New Republic* review, as treated below in the epilogue.

80. "All That Glitters . . .," July 30, 1982, File #39, Milwaukee Public Library.

81. "Come Fly with Lee."

82. Carr, "Astonish Me."

83. See Garber, *Vested Interests,* 165–85, for the complexities of Barrie's work.

84. William Glover, "Liberace Puts Punchline First," n.d., Liberace File #16, Milwaukee Public Library.

85. Quoted in Thomas, *Liberace,* 247.

86. John Waters, "Why I Love Liberace," *Vogue,* Nov. 1986, 270.

FIFTEEN

1. Hemming Interview.

2. Towle, "Liberace Died."

3. Thorson, *Behind the Candelabra,* 184.

4. Towle, "Liberace Died."

5. Ibid.

6. George McCabe, "Friends Claim Liberace Upset with Attorney," *Las Vegas Sun,* May 4, 1988, quoted in Faris, *Bio-Bibliography,* 227.

7. For the photographs, see Thorson, *Behind the Candelabra,* Thomas, *Liberace,* and Towle, "Liberace Died."

8. Towle, "Liberace Died."

9. The image comes from my dear friend John, comic to the last, in our last conversation in the spring of 1991, three months before his death. His T-cell count had fallen so low that he had named the cells remaining, he insisted.

10. Again, for the social anxiety relative to *any* legitimizing of homosexuality, see the reference in Hocquenghem, *Homosexual Desire,* 60, quoted above.

11. Kaiser, in *Gay Metropolis,* charts the conversion of the *Times,* for example, from a decidedly antigay position to this new, receptive orthodoxy. While Kaiser himself offers the justification, in effect, of new enlightened editors and managers simply seeing what was true and right, in contrast to the bad old days in which the homophobic Stanley Kauffmann, Howard Taubman, and A. M. Rosenthal reigned, the same evidence from a different political viewpoint demonstrates the degree to which the newspaper simply changed its biases and politics to favor a gay agenda.

12. In one of the wittier exchanges on this subject, a hospice nurse, my friend Marguerite Geer, was lecturing on AIDS in rural Kentucky to a group of local nurses. A hand rose cautiously in the rear, and a timid voice asked about AIDS being divine retribution. "If AIDS is God's curse, lesbians are God's chosen people," came the response.

13. See Abraham Verghese, *My Own Country: A Doctor's Story of a Town and Its People in the Age of AIDS* (New York: Simon and Schuster, 1994), for a elegant rendering of the disease's actual course from New York, Washington, and Atlanta to this provincial city in East Tennessee.

14. Evidence for oral infection is hard to come by, but the writer Andrew Sullivan, for example, affirms he contracted the disease orally, as he never had unprotected anal intercourse.

15. "Maid Tells What It Was REALLY Like in Private Life."

16. "Liberace Released after Tests," *Las Vegas Sun,* Nov. 7, 1985.

17. "Liberace's Desperate Battle with AIDS," *National Enquirer,* Feb. 10, 1987.

18. Towle, "Liberace Died."

19. Hadleigh, *Conversations.*

20. See Hudson and Davidson, *Rock Hudson.*

21. Quoted in Thomas, *Liberace,* 257.

22. Stephen Holden, "Concert: Liberace and the Rockettes," *New York Times,* Oct. 19, 1986.

23. Robin Leach, "Liberace's Own Story: A Stunning Interview by Robin Leach," *Star,* Feb. 17, 1987.

24. Ibid.

25. Quoted in Thomas, *Liberace,* 257.

26. Jane Pasenen, interview with the author.

27. Green, "Liberace the Gilded Showman."

28. Towle, "Liberace Died."

29. Leach, "Liberace's Own Story."

30. Towle, "Liberace Died."

31. Leach, "Liberace's Own Story."

32. Towle, "Liberace Died."

33. Ibid.

34. Quoted from the *Las Vegas Sun* in "Liberace's Desperate Battle with AIDS."

35. Towle, "Liberace Died."

36. Leach, "Liberace's Own Story."

37. Towle, "Liberace Died."

38. "Liberace's Desperate Battle with AIDS."

39. Leach, "Liberace's Own Story."

40. Thorson, *Behind the Candelabra,* 100–102.

41. Ibid., 223, 225, 227.

42. "Liberace's Last Words: 'I'll Be with You Soon, Mother," *National Enquirer,* Feb. 24, 1987.

43. Thorson, *Behind the Candelabra,* 235; also "Liberace's Last Words."

44. Quoted in "Liberace's Desperate Battle with AIDS."

45. "Liberace Victim of Deadly AIDS," *Las Vegas Sun,* Jan. 24, 1987.

46. "Nurse Recalls Liberace's Condition," *Las Vegas Sun,* Apr. 28, 1988, cited in Faris, *Bio-Bibliography,* 178.

47. "Liberace's Desperate Battle with AIDS."

48. "Liberace Manager Says *Sun* AIDS Story Untrue," *Las Vegas Sun,* Jan. 25, 1987, quoted in Faris, *Bio-Bibliography,* 212.

49. "Liberace's Manager Threatens Libel Suit over AIDS Report," *Variety,* Jan. 28, 1987.

50. "Liberace Told Manager He Did Not Have AIDS," *Las Vegas Sun,* May 3, 1988, quoted in Faris, *Bio-Bibliography,* 228.

51. "Liberace Called Gravely Ill, but Publicist Denies AIDS Report," *The Detroit News,* Jan. 28, 1987, quoted in Faris, *Bio-Bibliography,* 205.

52. "Liberace Hospitalized with Watermelon-Induced Anemia," *Los Angeles Times,* Jan. 26, 1987.

53. "Liberace's Mental State Questioned," *Las Vegas Sun,* Aug. 9, 1998.

54. "Nurse Recalls Liberace's Condition," *Las Vegas Sun,* Apr. 28, 1988, quoted in Faris, *Bio-Bibliography,* 178.

55. Thomas, *Liberace,* 269.

56. "Public Services for Liberace to Be Next Week in Las Vegas," Feb. 5, 1987, Liberace File #58, Milwaukee Public Library.

57. Leach, "Liberace's Own Story."

58. "Liberace Lapses into Coma," *Las Vegas Sun,* Feb. 4, 1987, quoted in Faris, *Bio-Bibliography,* 234.

59. For the various accounts of the deathwatch, see Green, "Liberace the Gilded Showman"; Towle, "Liberace Died"; "Liberace's Last Words"; and Thomas, *Liberace,* 270.

60. "AIDS test ordered for liberace," *Las Vegas Review-Journal,* Feb. 5, 1987.

61. "Liberace's Last Words."

62. "Liberace Friends Maintain Vigil," Feb. 3, 1987, Liberace File #57, Milwaukee Public Library.

63. "Liberace in Coma; Priest Called," Feb. 4, 1987, Liberace File #57, Milwaukee Public Library.

64. "Liberace: Musical Showman Dies," *Los Angeles Times,* Feb. 5, 1987.

65. Green, "Liberace the Gilded Showman."

66. "Liberace: Musical Showman Dies."

67. Dean Murphey and David Haldane, "Liberace Entombed: Autopsy Tests for AIDS Are Incomplete," *Los Angeles Times,* Feb. 8, 1987; "Coroner Cites AIDS in Liberace Death," *New York Times,* Feb.10, 1987.

68. "Family, Friends Gather to Remember Liberace," Feb. 7, 1987, File #72, Milwaukee Public Library.

69. Quoted in Faris, *Bio-Bibliography,* 25.

70. Quoted in Faris, *Bio-Bibliography,* 19.

EPILOGUE

1. "Coroner Ties Liberace Death to AIDS," *Chicago Tribune,* Feb. 10, 1987, cited in Faris, *Bio-Bibliography,* 184–85.

2. *US News and World Report,* Feb. 2, 1987.

3. Brian Greenspun, interviewed on *Nightline,* quoted in *Las Vegas Sun,* Feb. 6, 1987, and cited in Faris, *Bio-Bibliography,* 181.

4. "Liberace AIDS Story Debated," *Las Vegas Review-Journal,* Feb. 11, 1987, quoted in Faris, *Bio-Bibliography,* 203.

5. *Los Angeles Times,* Mar. 13, 1987.

6. "Liberace's Grieving Fans Distressed by Autopsy," Feb. 9, 1987, File #74, Milwaukee Public Library.

7. Conconi, "Personalities."

8. Hadleigh, *Hollywood Gays,* 146–47; Smith, "Storm over Author's Claim; and Eva Fellows, "Liberace's Secret Affair with Rock Hudson," *Star,* Mar. 3, 1987.

9. Pauline Bell, "Attorney Strote Refused Funeral for Dying Liberace, *Las Vegas Sun,* May 6, 1988, cited in Faris, *Bio-Bibliography,* 178.

10. "Liberace's Mental State Questioned," *Las Vegas Sun,* Aug. 9, 1988.

11. "Liberace's Sister Says She's Penniless," *Las Vegas Sun,* Aug. 11, 1988, cited in Faris, *Bio-Bibliography,* 220.

12. King, "Liberace's Last Agony."

13. Robert Maxy, "Attorneys Introduce Sleaze," *Las Vegas Review-Journal,* Aug. 11, 1988, cited in Faris, *Bio-Bibliography,* 225.

14. "Liberace Kin Says Executor Robbing the Grave," *Las Vegas Sun,* Apr. 19, 1988, cited in Faris, *Bio-Bibliography,* 227.

15. King, "Liberace's Last Agony."

16. Hemming Interview.

17. Personal recollection of the author.

18. Harriet Miller, *I'll Be Seeing You* (Las Vegas, Nev.: Leesson, 1989). The book lacks any sort of documentation about the relationship, but the assertion that both Miller and Liberace had moved to California by Feb. 1943, when their child was born, is not borne out by data. All evidence confirms that the showman did not move to California—or even visit there—until 1946. See above, chapter 5.

19. Some of Thomas's sources are evident from standard newspaper articles, notably the collection of Liberace clippings at the Milwaukee Public Library. He also credits a variety of personal interviews. The book documents nothing. In the complete absence of any formal sources, one uses this biography with caution.

20. Boze Hadleigh, *Sing Out! Gays and Lesbians in the Music World* (New York: Barricade Books, 1997).

21. Johnson, *Liberace: A Collecting Guide.*

22. Ibid., 16.

23. See Faris, *Bio-Bibliography,* 226.

24. Stephen Farber, "2 Networks Vying on Liberace Films," *New York Times,* Sept. 13, 1988.

25. "Rival TV Treatment," *People Weekly,* Sept. 19, 1988.

26. Quoted in *Gays and Lesbians in Films,* 223.

27. John J. O'Connor, "Second Look at the Liberace Legend," *New York Times,* Oct. 2, 1988.

28. Quoted in *Gays and Lesbians in Films,* 225, 220.

29. Diane Wakoski, *Why My Mother Likes Liberace* (Tucson, Ariz.: SUN/gemini, 1985), and *Emerald Ice: Selected Poems 1962–1987* (Santa Rosa, Calif: Black Sparrow Press, 1988). Kopelson treats these at some length in his *Beethoven's Kiss.*

30. Johnson, *A Collecting Guide,* 121.

31. Taubman, "A Square Looks at a Hotshot." For a fuller rendering of this essay, see above, chapter 7.

32. Kopelson, *Beethoven's Kiss,* 148–49, 150.

33. Samuel Lipman, "Success without Respect," July 19, 1987, Liberace File #90, Milwaukee Public Library.

34. Edward Rothstein, "The Franz Liszt of Las Vegas. Liberace, The King of Kitsch," *New Republic,* July 2, 1984, 25–29.

35. Rothstein was not alone among "hard-nosed critics" whom the pianist charmed and convinced even against their will: See Margaret Thompson Drewel's account of the same performance, in "The Camp Trace," in Meyer, ed., *The Politics and Poetics of Camp,* 160, as treated above in chapter 14.

36. Holden, "Pop."

37. Kopelson, *Beethoven's Kiss,* 151.

38. Ehrenstein, *Open Secret,* 118.

39. One source of Hadleigh's otherwise-disputed credibility about the Hudson-Liberace sexual coupling lies in his own incredulity that someone he admired, like Hudson, would deign to mate with Liberace, whom he loathed.

40. Although he allows the possibility that the contemporary sin of "ageism"—prejudice against the old—might influence opinion, his reference to "the Polident generation" rather obviates the insight. His reference, just so, to Liberace as an inspiration to one young gay man in the 1950s, the pseudonymous "Rick Shaw," is more anomalous. His judgments about Liberace and the young also tend to cancel out this testimony.

41. Hadleigh, *Hollywood Gays,* 155–56.

42. Ibid., 47, 57.

43. Quoted in *Gays and Lesbians in Films,* 225, 220.

44. *Epistemology of the Closet,* 248.

45. Jorge and Elizabeth Reynardus, interview with author.

INDEX

Numbers in italic refer to the photographs

JUN 29 2000

2 8 AUG 2000

BASEMENT